AESTHETICS: PROBLEMS IN THE PHILOSOPHY OF CRITICISM

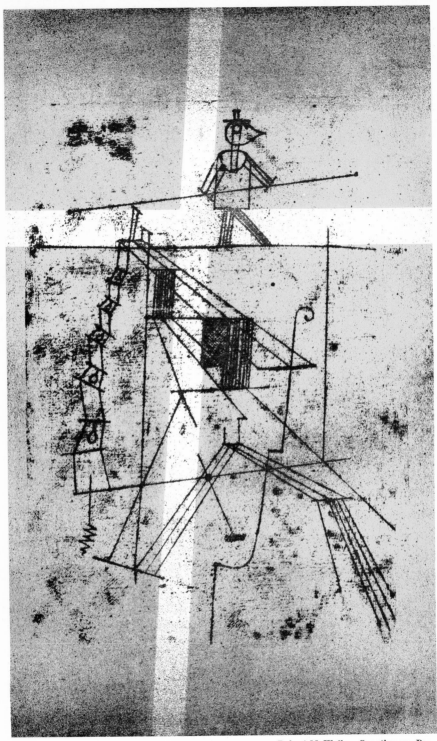

PAUL KLEE / *Man on a Tight Rope*

AESTHETICS

PROBLEMS IN THE PHILOSOPHY OF CRITICISM

Monroe C. Beardsley

SWARTHMORE COLLEGE

HARCOURT, BRACE AND COMPANY *New York*

To E. L. B.

PREFACE

Seldom, I think, has a book whose subject exposes it to inspection by experts in several fields been so blessed with readers and advisers. Though I have cursed them at times for making me think harder about a loose point or recast an uncertain paragraph, now is my chance to confess my great and fortunate debt to them. Whenever it was in their power, they saved me from myself. The faults that survive their scrutiny have been preserved by my stubbornness alone.

I cannot name all those who have helped me in one way or another, but I give my heartfelt thanks to my wife, Elizabeth Lane Beardsley, of Lincoln University, whose latest reading of the manuscript, at once rigorous and affectionate, was the most indispensable; to Richard B. Brandt, of Swarthmore College, whose wisdom in ethics and value theory forced many improvements in the chapters on normative criticism; to Robert M. Daniel, of the University of Tennessee, who saw the chapters as they came from the typewriter and was ever ready with valuable recommendations; to Henry Gleitman, of Swarthmore College, whose conversations have much clarified my understanding of the relevant psychological problems; to Albert Hofstadter, of Columbia University, who read the manuscript with generous care and gave me the benefit of numerous critical reflections; to John Hospers, of Brooklyn College, who also read the chapters as they were ready, and whose comments guided and heartened me as I went along; to Samuel L. Hynes, of Swarthmore College, with whom I had most fruitful discussions of the examples and principles in the chapters on literature; to Hedley H. Rhys, of Swarthmore College, who read the sections on painting and showed me how to make them sounder in various ways; to Richard Rudner, of Michigan State University, with whom I discussed several of these problems when he was my colleague, and whose thinking about them has influenced my own; to Peter Gram Swing, of Swarthmore College, who read the sections on music and showed me how to make them sounder in various ways; to Robert M. Walker, of Swarthmore College, who has taught me much of what I know about the fine arts, and who helped me choose the illustrations; to William K. Wimsatt, Jr., of Yale University (as if my footnote references to his work and my acknowledgments in earlier books did not already make this plain), for all the richness in ideas and persistence of inquiry into critical problems that have over the years been a constant stimulus and model for me; and, finally, but no mere gesture, to my students in aesthetics at Swarthmore College, who—because of their habitual unwillingness to accept statements that are not reasonably defended, and their eagerness to discover for themselves what statements can be reasonably defended—have been my collective Socrates.

I should like to express my appreciation to the John Simon Guggenheim Memorial Foundation, whose Fellowship (1950-1951) enabled me to make a study of metaphor, some of the results of which appear in Chapter III. I should also like to thank Robert M. Walker and Solomon Asch, of Swarthmore College, for generously allowing me to use prints from their collections. And I acknowledge my debt to Miss Lydia Bucknell, a tower of strength in preparing the manuscript; to Mark Beardsley, an expert alphabetizer who saved me time and trouble with the index; and to Philip Beardsley, my authority on one branch of contemporary music, who muted his drums.

While writing this book I have many times been reminded of my old teacher, the late Wilbur Marshall Urban, of Yale University, who awakened my interest in the problems of Aesthetics and guided my first studies. I should be happy if this book can stand as a memorial to him.

MONROE C. BEARDSLEY
Swarthmore, Pennsylvania
October 1, 1957

CONTENTS

PLATES

I am uneasy to think I approve of one object, and disapprove of another; call one thing beautiful, and another deform'd; decide concerning truth and falshood, reason and folly, without knowing upon what principles I proceed.—DAVID HUME

INTRODUCTION

There would be no problems of aesthetics, in the sense in which I propose to mark out this field of study, if no one ever talked about works of art. So long as we enjoy a movie, a story, or a song, in silence—except perhaps for occasional grunts or groans, murmurs of annoyance or satisfaction—there is no call for philosophy. But as soon as we utter a statement about the work, various sorts of question can arise.

For example, a fine arts magazine's review of a showing by a British painter remarks upon the variety of shapes that appear in his paintings, including

> perfectly overt numerals, thrown in for good measure. Sometimes these merely signify the date—although they are not for *that* reason included so boldly in Davie's design; but rather, because they are, very simply, such primary, such obvious *symbols*. They stand, in the composition, as symbols of symbols—and Davie is, like so many other important contemporary artists, more concerned to express the fact that his work comprises symbols than to make these symbols symbolize something specific. This is not strange: it is simply the outcome of possession by that profound sense of reality which the truly creative artist in any age is always assailed by. . . . To celebrate his perception of the reality of whatever it is he is perceiving—that is the artist's object in painting. There is therefore nothing esoteric in the undecipherable crypto-symbols which force their way past Alan Davie and onto his canvases.

How can the numerals be "symbols," if they symbolize nothing "specific," and how can they be "crypto-symbols" if they are not "esoteric"? What *is* a symbol in a painting, and especially what are "symbols of symbols"? How are the painter's symbols connected with his "profound sense of reality," and what does the word "reality" mean in such a context? If this sense of reality, and the goal of "celebrating" the perception of it, are common to painters of all ages, how does it happen that the desire to be somehow symbolic without caring much *what* you symbolize is a peculiar characteristic of contemporary artists?

A reviewer in a literary magazine comments upon a new novel:

> When an American writer attempts to enter the mind of an alien culture it is important for his reader to know whether or not the writer is scrupulous. Is the novelist truly writing, as Hemingway might say, or is he merely seeking picturesque (and irrelevant) symbols for his own private fantasies?
>
> Now, in reading Robert Ramsey's admirable novel [*Fiesta*] about contemporary Mexico the reader need have no fears. Mr. Ramsey's novel is authentic. It is not about the author's own experience. It hews to Mexican experience, and the author's presence is sensed only as a conscience at work. This is a reassuring sort of presence.

Why is it important for the reader to know whether or not the writer is "scrupulous," and to be assured that the novel is "authentic"? Indeed, how can the reader (or the reviewer) possibly find out? What does it mean to say that the novel contains a "conscience at work," and what is the evidence for this statement?

A record reviewer discusses the symphonies of Anton Bruckner:

> Bruckner is quite capable of stopping dead at the end of his first theme and then taking up his second without any polite or cajoling bridge passage whatever. He often uses long stretches of unison without harmonic trimmings, a process which strikes the confirmed Bruckner lover as extremely daring, but which sometimes sounds crude on first hearing. When Bruckner comes to the finish of a big, baroque movement he often hammers it home quite unabashedly with periods and exclamation points, and he is a great user of sequences in the building of his powerful climaxes. In a composer of less genius, these habits might seem either unsophisticated or arrogant. But they are part and parcel of Bruckner's musical personality, and their very lack of sophistication is closely related to the earnestness, the great honesty, and the painstaking effort to communicate noble and simple ideas that endear Bruckner to those who are well acquainted with his music.

What is meant by "harmonic trimmings," "baroque," "sequences"? Why should daring be considered a desirable thing in music? How can musical habits that the reviewer would apparently consider faults in other composers be transformed into merits by Bruckner's earnestness and honesty? And in what conceivable way can music without words be expected to "communicate noble and simple ideas"?

It would be easy to think of many other questions about these quotations, which are fairly rich in unclear terms and challengeable assumptions. They are not offered as Horrible Examples, and we need not consider at this point how far they are typical: that would be hard to decide, for discourse about art ranges from passages that embody the subtlest insight and finest judgment to passages that achieve a level of pretentious unintelligibility that would not be tolerated, much less praised as profound, in other fields. But the three passages above, and the questions about them, do exhibit some of the puzzles that may trouble a thoughtful reader. It is such puzzles that give rise to the subject of aesthetics.

Aesthetics and Criticism

Most of the statements in the passages just quoted are about objects called "works of art." For the present, we shall use the term in a rough sense that will have to be sharpened later.

Works of art fall into a number of readily distinguishable subclasses, and so, correspondingly, do the statements about them. Statements about literary works are called "literary criticism"; there is also music criticism, dance criticism, and so on. I will use the term "critical statement," very broadly, to refer to any statement about a work of art, that is, any statement about such objects as poems, paintings, plays, statues, symphonies. A critical statement is not necessarily critical in the sense of condemning the work—it need not be a value judgment at all—nor is it necessarily a statement made by a professional critic. "*Romeo and Juliet* is in five acts"; "Smetana's *String Quartet in E Minor* is autobiographical"; "Yves Tanguy's painting, *Mama, Papa Is Wounded!* (1927, Museum of Modern Art, New York) has a sinister air"—these are critical statements, whether true or false, and no matter who makes them. Thus critical statements are answers to questions like these: How does the representation of space in Van Gogh's *Night Café* (1888, Stephen C. Clark Collection, New York) contribute to its nightmarish quality? Are there defects in the orchestration of the finale of Schubert's *Symphony in C Major (No. 7)*? What metaphysical outlook is reflected in Shelley's *Adonais:*

The One remains, the many change and pass?

Is *The Cherry Orchard* a better play than *The Wild Duck?* Questions like these are for the critic, amateur or paid, to deal with.

When, however, we ask questions, not about works of art, but about what the critic *says* about works of art, that is, about his questions or his answers, then we are on another level of discourse. What can the word "autobiographical" mean when applied to music? By what method does a critic determine the metaphysical outlook of a poem? What would be a good reason for saying that one play is better, or worse, than another? Questions like these are questions of aesthetics.

As a field of study, aesthetics consists of a rather heterogeneous collection of problems: those that arise when we make a serious effort to say something true and warranted about a work of art. As a field of knowledge, aesthetics consists of those principles that are required for clarifying and confirming critical statements. Aesthetics can be thought of, then, as the philosophy of criticism, or *metacriticism.*

The aim of aesthetics may be clearer if we compare it briefly with two other fields of philosophy: ethics and philosophy of science. "It is wrong to kill," is a moral statement, true or false. Ethics, or at least one branch of ethics, undertakes the examination of moral statements. For example, we might ask, "What does the word 'wrong' mean?" or "How can we know that a certain kind of act is wrong?" These questions are about the meaning and proof of moral statements, but they are not themselves moral questions. Again, it is one task of the physical scientist to provide us with true theories about the properties of subatomic particles, electrons, protons, mesons, etc. But as philosophers we are interested in other questions: Do these particles really exist, independently of the human mind, or are they logical constructs? Does the inquiry into nature presuppose any metaphysical propositions, such as the principle of causality or induction? Can scientific method be applied to all of human behavior? These questions are about science itself; they are not physical, but philosophical, questions.

At a very fundamental level, of course, all the fields of philosophy, including ethics, philosophy of science, and aesthetics, converge upon certain very broad and very fundamental problems. And in the course of this book we shall encounter several problems that would take us, if we pursued them, into other branches of philosophy: metaphysics, theory of knowledge, theory of value. But there is nevertheless a reasonable justification for dividing up philosophical problems, if the fences are not raised too high. Whenever we think about anything, there are some very general principles of reasoning we take for granted, and it is the business of general logic to investigate these principles. But besides the problems involved in this investigation, there are special problems that arise when we try to think hard and well about, say, right and wrong, or about unobservable physical entities, or about history, or God, or sense experience— or works of art. And in this book we shall be concerned with the problems that are peculiar to reflection upon works of art.

If we conceive of aesthetics in this way, we can, in principle, make a clear separation between aesthetics and criticism. Studying ethics may not make you more moral than you were before, and studying philosophy of science certainly does not qualify you to be a scientist. So, too, studying aesthetics does not make you a critic, and still less a painter or a poet. Yet it is demonstrable that neither aesthetics nor criticism can be carried on independently of the other; though each has its own tasks, they depend upon each other.

In the first place, we can't do aesthetics until we have some critical statements to work on. In this book we shall have to make assertions about particular works of art, in order to raise questions about the criteria of their meaningfulness and the tests of their truth. Hence there will be discussion of particular arts, drawing upon what has been discovered by critics. But just because the arts themselves are so interesting, we must be careful not to lose sight of our main purpose, which is not primarily to increase our knowledge of the arts, but to improve our thinking about them. Thus if someone says that Bruckner was earnest and honest, and you don't agree, there is material here for a lively argument; he is one of the most controversial of composers. But the aesthetic problems involved are of a different order. Not: Was Bruckner honest? But: How do you *tell* whether a composer is honest or not? Is biographical evidence relevant here, or is the honesty audible in the music itself? And if we could prove that he was honest, would it have anything to do with the value of his symphonies?

Second, it is clear that, for the sake of reasonable criticism, these aesthetic questions must be asked. To be a good critic, it is not enough to accumulate a vast amount of information about, and a rich experience of, the art you are interested in: you must be able to organize those data in a fruitful way, and you must formulate them so that they can be understood. And this is where aesthetics comes in. Sooner or later, for example, in talking about almost any art, a word like "reality" is bound to crop up: Yes, in some sense, of course, painters are interested in reality. But in *what* sense? Two art critics who have known each other for years may develop such intellectual sympathy that when one speaks of a "profound sense of reality" in a painting, the other understands exactly what he means. Much more often, I am afraid, people think they understand what is meant when they really don't at all. And sometimes they don't really care whether they understand what is meant, if they have a vague feeling that something profound is being said. The critic himself may be more concerned to express the fact that his words are symbols "than to make these symbols symbolize something specific."

Thus "reality" may mean the surface appearances of things, the sense qualities that are open to immediate inspection: smells, tastes, textures. A "profound sense of reality" could then be a strong interest in sense appearance, a fascination with it, a desire to reproduce it. It is not at all clear that in this sense, however, "the truly creative artist in any age is always assailed by" it, or rather by the "possession" of it. This description fits the French impressionists, but not the medieval Gothic or Byzantine artist. Moreover, if the painter is interested in sheer sense appearance, why does that make him use symbols? Surely when the numeral 6 is recognized as symbolizing a number, the perceiver's attention is distracted from the sheer sense qualities of the numeral to the abstract entity that it signifies. Now, of course, "reality" has other important senses; it may mean, for example, a world behind the qualities immediately sensed: a supernatural world known not through sense experience but through intuition or pure reason. The Gothic and Byzantine artist is interested in reality in this sense, and such an interest would explain a

6

painter's use of symbolism; but that is not the same as "to celebrate his perception of the reality of whatever it is he is perceiving."

This cluster of questions about the term "reality" will come up again in its appropriate place. I have dwelt on it here in order to show a little more fully what sort of inquiry we must be prepared to engage in. It is quite possible to be a good scientist without ever philosophizing about science, but the progress of science depends upon *someone's* pausing at some times to think deeply about its methods, the meaning of its basic terms, and even its role as a human enterprise among other enterprises. If the scientist himself does this, he is at that time asking philosophical questions; in the long run, the clearer scientists are about what they are doing, and why, and how, the better our science will be. Again, it is possible for a person to lead a morally blameless life without asking himself what is the nature of the ultimate good, or what is the basis of moral responsibility; but in the long run the clearer we are about what makes life worth living, the more successful we can be in pursuing it; and the sounder our conception of the correct way to decide what is right or wrong, the more rational our decisions are likely to be. In the same way, it is indispensable, in order to keep criticism from degenerating into sheer burbling, nonsensical jargon and maverick evaluations, that someone consider, and consider with care and persistence, the foundations of criticism. We must ask what presuppositions critics make about perception, about value, about knowledge, about reality, and we must examine these presuppositions to see whether they are justified. We must consider the meaning of their basic terms, and the logic of their arguments, and subject them to analysis and test. It is not up to the critic to justify his own assumptions, but he must believe that they *can* be justified or he would be dishonest to make them.

In the course of this book, then, we shall think of aesthetics as a distinctive philosophical inquiry: it is concerned with the nature and basis of criticism—in the broad sense of this term—just as criticism itself is concerned with works of art. Now it must be admitted that this way of staking out the boundaries of the field does not correspond exactly to that of all other aestheticians. Indeed, it is one of the inconveniences in this field that its scope is subject to so much difference of opinion. The chief difference is this: it is customary to include among the problems of aesthetics the nature of the creative process itself; what social and psychological conditions move the painter and poet, and how they go about their work. Now, I do not consider all the problems one can raise about art and artists as problems of aesthetics; I take as central the situation in which someone is confronted with a finished work, and is trying to understand it and to decide how good it is. He will encounter many problems, if he reflects with persistence on what he is doing, but probably he need not inquire into the psychology of artistic creation.

The question, What makes the artist create? is a psychological question, in my view, not a philosophical one. And it is, I think, useful to make a distinction between *psychological aesthetics,* which deals with questions about the causes and effects of works of art, and *philosophical aesthetics,* which deals with questions about the meaning and truth of critical statements. "Aesthetics" in this book is an abbreviation for "philosophical aesthetics." Nevertheless, we shall see that we cannot ignore psychology; its data and conclusions will bear upon ours at many points. For example, when we consider the logic of evaluation, we are led to ask about the nature of aesthetic experience, and this is a psychological question. Where the psychological data are as yet too sparse to answer the question decisively, we can at least analyze the question, and formulate it as clearly as possible, so that we can see what sort of psychological data would be required in order to answer it.

The Problems of Aesthetics

It would be possible to make out a case for saying that it is neither necessary nor desirable for people to talk about works of art. Such talk can be harmful. Some books about poetry are so interesting that they distract people from reading the poetry itself. Sometimes the remarks of critics, even bad and ignorant critics, have enough prestige-value to spread false conceptions of painting and music, so that people miss what is most precious in these arts because they go to them with the wrong expectations. For example, much that is put into the usual notes given out at symphony concerts would be better left unwritten, for it leads the audience to sentimentalize over the composer instead of listening attentively to the music.

But something can be said on the other side, too. There is considerable evidence that teachers of literature, fine arts, and music can help people increase the pleasure they get from poems, paintings, and concertos. Perception can be sharpened, and taste refined. Even some parts of the creative process can apparently be taught in fine arts and music schools, or at least usefully encouraged by instruction. The newspaper reader has reason to be grateful to the reviewer who warns him away from poor plays. And, quite apart from all these considerations, a work of art, like a rare plant, a pile of prehistoric bones, a revolution, or the human brain, is a phenomenon in our environment of some considerable interest in itself, about which we may legitimately feel a persistent curiosity. The great critics have wanted to know, pretty much for the sake of knowing, what makes a poem work, what general features distinguish good melodies from bad, what are the possible modes of visual representation.

In any case, people won't stop making statements about works of art. The question is not whether we shall talk, but whether we shall do it well or badly. We must try not to talk too much or too soon, or trivially, or incorrectly, or irrelevantly, or misleadingly. If it is true, as I believe it is, that the arts have a place in the best human life—a question to which we shall return in the last chapter—then they are worth a good deal of effort. We cannot all be poets or composers, but we ought to take some pains to ensure that what we say about art helps, rather than hinders, the fulfillment of its purpose. And this is a continuing task. For new kinds of painting, new kinds of poetic speech, new sounds in music, are always coming into existence, and they provide the critic with new problems. Moreover, there are always plenty of silly, stupid, or vicious things being said about art, things that need clearing up and clearing away.

For example, a fourteen-foot bronze sculpture, representing a father, mother, son, and daughter, is set up in a new police facilities building in Los Angeles. The figures are attenuated, small-headed, faceless; they are said to symbolize the police-protected family. A City Councilman, speaking for a horrified group of citizens, calls it "probably the most scandalous satire and caricature of the American people that I have ever seen," and suggests that it be torn down and replaced by a realistic sculpture showing a policeman and policewoman apprehending a malefactor. The Hollywood Association of Artists urges that the group be composed of "easily recognizable figures" modeled from actual police personnel, and executed by an artist who has taken a loyalty oath. It can easily be seen that though this complex issue is partly political, there are also woven into it disagreements about the nature of sculpture, its values, and its place in the life of the community. If we could straighten out these disagreements, the conflict would at least become more manageable. There may not be, in these times, quite as pressing a need for sound ideas about works of art as for sound ideas about the great moral and political issues of the day. But to have a good philosophy of art is, after all, no inconsiderable part of having a good philosophy. And philosophy is our ultimate concern here.

The problems of aesthetics are opened up by the basic question that can be asked of any statement about a work of art, as, indeed, it can be asked about any statement whatsoever: What reason is there to believe that it is true? This question, as we shall see more fully later, leads to subordinate questions, e.g., What does the statement mean?

What sorts of thing do we want to say about works of art? I do not wish to raise here the question, What is the *function* of criticism?—whether it is more important, say, for critics to judge works of art, or promote and puff them, to act as a barker or as an entrepreneur between artist and public. The critic, if he has any use at all, may play several social roles, and at a late stage of our inquiry we shall be able to discuss these more effectively. Most critics, I suppose, would in the end justify their activity by the claim that it is auxiliary to appreciation, to the full or proper enjoyment of art, whether or not it assists artistic creation. In any case, whatever the critic may have in mind as an ultimate purpose, he tries to achieve that purpose by telling us something about the work, and it turns out that there are three basically different kinds of thing he can tell us, each of which raises aesthetic problems peculiar to itself.

First, we must distinguish between *normative* statements and *non-normative* statements about works of art. Normative statements are *critical evaluations.* You are evaluating a work of art when you say it is good or bad, ascribe to it beauty or ugliness, recommend it as an object to be sought after or avoided. I know no thoroughly satisfactory way of defining "normative statement," but for the present it will be sufficient to indicate the class in a rough way: critical evaluations are those that apply to works of art the words "good" or "beautiful," their negatives, or other predicates definable in terms of them.

The problems that arise in considering the meaning and logical justification of critical evaluations are the hardest problems we have to face, and they will be reserved for the last chapters of the book. This procedure is, I hope, a sign of circumspection rather than timidity; the task of dealing with them will be much easier if some other matters are taken up first. In this sector we encounter the most puzzling and unsatisfactory concepts. For example, we can approach the problems of critical evaluation by asking what sorts of reason people give for praising a work of art. One reason often given is that the work is *beautiful:* the *Sistine Madonna* (ca. 1515, Gallery, Dresden), Keats' *Eve of St. Agnes,* Fauré's *Requiem.* But suppose one person says it is beautiful and another says it is not; how can the question be settled, or, short of violence, *is* there any way of settling it? The first question is surely what is meant by "beauty," for perhaps the two disputants are using the term in different senses. Is beauty a quality of some sort, inherent in the object, or a tendency of the object to affect people in certain ways, or is there no such thing at all? Is beauty in literature the same as beauty in music? And what sort of evidence about the work is required to prove that it is beautiful? Is beauty common to all good works of art, or only to some? Some people think that a work of art can be great even if it is ugly; others think not. These are some of the puzzling questions raised by the word "beauty," and they await us later.

A second distinction should be made between two kinds of non-normative statement, those that *interpret* and those that simply *describe* works of art.

A *critical interpretation,* for the purposes of this book, is a statement that purports to declare the "meaning" of a work of art—this is not to be confused with the quite different sense in which, for example, a pianist is said to "interpret" a sonata in playing it a certain way. I use the term "meaning" for a semantical relation between the work itself and something outside the work. Suppose it is said that a tone poem contains a joyful affirmation of life, or that it "refers to" something in the life of the composer; or that a dance "represents" the awakening of young love; or that a bridge in a novel "symbolizes" or "signifies" the crises of life; or that a modern office building "expresses" the functional efficiency of modern business. These statements are critical interpretations.

Though the act of interpreting a work is less complicated than the act of evaluating it, it is complicated enough, and raises its own set of problems. Consider, for example, the term "express." How do we determine whether a building "expresses" something? What, if anything, does this term imply about the experience of the architect in designing it, about the relation between the qualities of the building and the purposes it serves, and about the experience of the observer? What connection, if any, is there between the expressiveness of the building and its beauty as an architectural design?

But before these questions can be considered, we must deal, more briefly, with some problems that arise merely in describing the characteristics of works of art. Statements that inform us about the colors and shapes of a painting, or summarize the plot of a motion picture, or classify an operatic aria as being of the *A B A* form, are critical descriptions. The central problems in this sector of the field involve the concept of *form*. Probably no word occurs oftener in the language of criticism. It is opposed, in different contexts, to "expression," to "representation," to "content," to "matter," to "meaning." The possession of form is regarded sometimes as a distinguishing feature of works of art in general, and sometimes as a mark of artistic excellence within this class. But again: How is the term used? Which of its uses are worth preserving and which must be rejected as misleading? What is important to know about the form of a work of art, in whatever sense of "form" is adopted?[1]

Plans of Attack

The problems of philosophical aesthetics, then, however various, fall into three main groups, to which there is a natural order of approach. The problems raised by descriptive statements are the simplest ones, and their solution is presupposed by the rest, so they must be taken up first, in Chapters II to V. The more debatable problems raised by interpretative statements will be taken up in Chapters VI to IX. Finally, Chapters X to XII will come to grips with the problems raised by the critic's value judgments. Now this last set of problems is undoubtedly the most interesting of all; these are the problems that critics would most like to see solved. Moreover, our view of these problems and possible solutions to them will be a guiding influence throughout the whole book. For often critics are interested in describing and interpreting works of art because

---

[1] Some lively examples of critical puzzles and confusions that demand aesthetic examination (and will be examined later) are given by J. A. Passmore, "The Dreariness of Aesthetics," *Mind*, N.S. LX (1951): 318-25, reprinted in William Elton, ed., *Aesthetics and Language*, New York: Philosophical Library, 1954, pp. 36-55.

they want to evaluate them; they use the descriptive and interpretative statements as reasons for, or partial reasons for, normative statements. So when in early chapters I select certain kinds of description for special examination, I shall sometimes have in mind the relevance of this kind of statement to certain critical evaluations that will be discussed in later chapters. However, I do not want to suggest that description and interpretation are important only as grounds for evaluation. Even if we were able, or willing, to refrain from all value judgments about works of art, it could still be interesting and useful to analyze their qualities and inner relations, and to discover what they mean or signify—for, after all, describing and interpreting are the two halves of understanding.

It can be seen from the sample problems reviewed a moment ago that our task will require a certain amount of verbal analysis—defining and making distinctions—especially in the early chapters of the book. This concern with the meanings of words, though it may at times seem remote from our main goals, is by no means trivial. It is for the sake of the more substantive problems. The subject of aesthetics is in such a state today that there is no hope of making progress in it by any more casual, free-and-easy approach.

Indeed, aesthetics has long been contemptuously regarded as a step-sister within the philosophical family. Her rejection is easy to explain, and partially excuse, by the lack of tidiness in her personal habits and by her unwillingness to make herself generally useful around the house. It is plain to even a casual visitor that aesthetics is a retarded child, and though no doubt this is in no small part due to neglect, we must try to forget the past and look to the future. We have come to accept her backwardness, not demanding as much of her as we demand of her brothers and sisters—in fact, we demand too little, much less than with coaxing she can be made to perform. At the same time, we must be prepared to put out more care and effort than we do with a normal child, just to teach her her ABC's.

Considering the present state of the subject, then, a general book like this ought to mingle in precise proportions modesty and ambition. I think it is time to try to bring together, more systematically than has been done in quite a while, the various problems of aesthetics, to collect the scattered work done separately on some of the problems, to see how they look and how much they can aid each other when treated side by side within the same general framework, to push some of them farther toward solution where that can be done, but most of all to try to clarify and connect the problems themselves. I should like to see whether the problems cannot be formulated better than they usually are; whether some of them are not in fact already much farther toward solution than appears in the pervasive terminological confusion; whether a satisfactory technical vocabulary of aesthetic terms cannot be provided, on which most parties can be persuaded to agree. And it seems to me that by work along these lines the quality of our criticism can be made both more sensible and more significant. This is the ambition.

I have therefore tried throughout to be as clear and rigorous as I can, but without passing up opportunities to reach toward a promising idea even when I could not formulate it exactly. Some of our working distinctions have been mulled over for some time by careful thinkers, and they can, I think, be put in fair shape for general use. But there are other things, vague or loose, that seem true and helpful to say about works of art, and we ought, in my opinion, to take a chance on them, even though we don't yet know how to separate out of them what is false or misleading. For at all times one eye must be kept on the object that really matters most: the work of art itself. No matter how coolly analytical and abstract critical discourse must sometimes become if it is to be apt and warranted, it must not lose affection and respect for the things it is about. No matter how proud we may become at unraveling a particularly knotty and annoying bit of terminological or logical confusion, we must remain basically humble before the work itself, and before that precious human power that brought it and all its characteristics, meanings, and values, into existence. This is the modesty.

There is one feature of this book that may require explanation. The "Notes and Queries" at the end of each chapter should generate further reflection upon the problems dealt with in the text, and also related problems that are barely touched upon. They focus on subjects for group discussion and for written essays, and they contain a fairly wide-ranging but selective bibliography to guide the reader, with occasional questions and critical comments. Moreover, by assuming the scholarly burden, they make it possible in the text itself to develop issues and discuss tenable positions and important points of view without debating the merits or defects of individual thinkers. When I present, for defense or attack, a proposed solution to a problem, I make it as clear and reasonable as I can, so that what is most helpful in it can be used; I mention no names, but refer in a footnote to the end-of-chapter Note that cites the main books or papers in which particular versions of the theory are to be found. The Notes and Queries are thus an integral part of the book; they make contact with the currents of discussion in the field of aesthetics.

———————————

It is a good idea, before beginning Chapter I, to collect some examples of critical writing, like those cited at the beginning of this Introduction, from magazines, newspapers, conversations, and books. Analyze them carefully, looking for words that need further clarification and for statements that need further logical justification. Which statements are, or imply, description, interpretation, evaluation? If possible, discuss them with someone else; try to discover which words mean different things to different people, and which underlying assumptions are disputed or disputable.

Here are some sample passages from critical writings, which can serve as a basis for preliminary discussions:

1. It may be doubted whether there are any lines so sincere and so passionate, and yet so direct and impressive, in the whole of English poetry as in Richard Crashaw's "The Flaming Heart." But when instead of a particular object or symbol, passion is directed to ideas and essences, all the intangible universals of thought or meditation, then the passion drives the poet to the expression of innermost opacities and obscurities. Such complex entities cannot, of course, be expressed in direct language or discourse. The poet resorts to emotional analogies—to words which give, not *meaning* which cannot be given, but an equivalence of tone, of color, an equivalence of the *pattern* and contour of thought. Even in the relatively simple passage which I have just quoted, there are phrases like "thy large draughts of intellectual day" and "the full kingdom of that final kiss" which do not permit a logical analysis; they are inviolate phrases, to be accepted wholly and in that mood of emotional enhancement which the poem induces. The two terms of the metaphor they contain are so fused that no discursive or rational meaning can, or should, be precipitated in the mind of the reader. (Herbert Read, *Phases of English Poetry*, London: Faber and Faber, 1948, pp. 90-91.)

2. Hague, a sculptor, does not work in metal, and apparently no longer in stone. His mature medium is wood, filling his gallery with dark brown brooding, as after a B minor chord. . . .

His undulant, ovoid shapes seem at first to suggest much that was seen before. But they are more concretely physical, far less involved with ideal essences than Brancusi's. And unlike Arp's or Viani's biomorphs they do not seek to imply forms in transition. They are stilled and collected and content in their own mass. . . .

All of them, I believe, refer to the human body, especially the elegant *Mount Marion Walnut* and *Log Swamp Pepper Wood*—both of them torsos, and both female, to judge from the warm lifted swell of their surface. But they are depersonalized by their headlessness; by their lack of limb, inactivated; and by their catastrophic breaks, denatured.

In view of their partial humanity, the abrupt breaks that define the ends of his forms are at first vaguely disturbing. A hasty suspicion of sadism is quickly dispersed, for these knifed, arbitrary terminations were present at the work's inception. What they do is to italicize, to put the chosen form in quotes. And so it dawns on one that these are not in fact images of human bodies, but of sculptures of bodies. And their inspiration is a novel form of classic revival, a new way of imitating the antique. (Leo Steinberg, "Month in Review," *Arts*, July 1956, p. 25.)

3. Whereas in the music of most composers it is a case of content *and* structure, it is with Mozart a case of structure only, for there is no perceptible content—*ubi materia ibi geometria*. This is strikingly shown in the overture to *The Marriage of Figaro*. . . . There is no melodic

content as such. You cannot even hear the music in your memory apart from the rush of the strings and the accents of the woodwind. It cannot be played upon the piano. Take away a note of it and the whole is completely disintegrated. Nor can anyone put his hand upon his heart and say what feeling that music arouses in his breast. It is completely without expression, as expression is vulgarly understood; but the oftener you hear it, the more excited you become, the more passionate grow your asseverations that there was never music like this before or since. Its effect upon the mind is out of all proportion to its impingement on the senses. (W. J. Turner, *Mozart: the Man and his Works*, Garden City, N.Y.: Anchor, 1954, p. 317.)

· I ·

AESTHETIC
OBJECTS

What is a work of art? What sort of thing are we referring to when we speak, for example, of *The Rape of the Lock,* or *Le Déjeuner sur l'Herbe* or *Eine Kleine Nachtmusik?* If the problems of aesthetics are problems about statements about such things as these—literary works, works of fine art, musical compositions—we can't be sure what the problems are until we know which statements *are* statements about these things. To put it another way, if a critic is defined as someone who talks about works of art, then we have to know how to tell when something is a work of art before we can tell who is a critic.

Some of the implications of this broad question will be clear if we compare critical statements briefly with other kinds. We would ordinarily say that it is the business of physicists to talk about physical objects; that a mathematician talks about abstract entities, such as numbers and functions; that when you tell the doctor your toe hurts, you are talking about a psychological state. Of course there are some very difficult philosophical problems about all these: In what sense is an "electron" a physical object? How can there be such things as "abstract entities"? What is the relation between the psychological pain-in-the-toe and the toe itself? But for the time being let us assume that these distinctions can be made. Now, when a critic praises Pope's poem for its wit, Manet's painting for its composition, or Mozart's music for its proportions, is he talking about something physical, like a stone, or something abstract, like the number 6, or something mental, like a pain in the toe—or something still different?

It is disconcerting that we should be confronted so early with so

tough a question—and one that has not been very thoroughly or satisfactorily dealt with by writers on aesthetics. Probably we can't be quite
content with any answer to it until we have considered other questions
that come up later in this book, but it has to be encountered at the start,
and we may as well make the best of it. It will be clear as we go on that
some of the troubles of aesthetics come from unwillingness to face the
basic question: what are we talking about? If we are not sure, we are
likely to talk about different things without knowing it, and this doesn't
make for fruitful discussion.

It is convenient to formulate the general question of this chapter—
there are several subordinate questions—with the help of a special term.
As we shall see, critics make many statements that are not strictly critical
statements, for they are not really statements about works of art. After
all, each of us finds it hard to stick to the point sometimes, and even a
critic reviewing the latest Broadway play may talk not only about the
play, but about the audience, the weather, the economics of the theatre,
the international situation, or himself. But I think we could make up a
list of statements that we will all agree are unquestionably statements
about the play itself. For example,

> The first act is slow.
> The irony at the end of the second act is overstressed.
> The confrontation scene in the third act is dramatic.

Suppose we set aside the doubtful cases for the moment; we still
have plenty of typical ones. And let us introduce the term *"aesthetic
object"* for whatever it is that those typical statements are about. Our
question is, then: what is an aesthetic object?

Now, it could be argued right at the start that we are begging an
important, and perhaps fatal, question: namely, whether it is proper to
speak at all of an "object" in this context. When we look over the whole
career of a work of art, it appears as a more or less continuous *process,*
in which shifts and transformations are constantly going on. Take Ibsen's
play *Ghosts* for example. In November, 1880, while he was in Rome, some
feelings and thoughts occurred in the mind of Ibsen, as a result of which
he wrote down some words. A year later, when they were published, other
people read these words—usually with alarm and anger. After two more
years, a producer dared to have them spoken aloud in a certain public
place in Sweden by various people dressed in certain ways, against a
background of a particular sort. Other people later decided to translate
those words into English, and into other languages, and to have those
words spoken in different countries, by different people, against different backgrounds, with different gestures and movements and tones of
voice. Then still other people went to the theatre, where their brains
registered the light-impulses and sound waves that their senses picked up,
and they had certain feelings and thoughts of their own—the London

Daily Telegraph called the play "an open drain; a loathsome sore un- bandaged; a dirty act done publicly; a lazar house with all its doors and windows open." Now, where, you might ask, is there an *object* in all this? Does anything stand still long enough to be called an "object"? Is the French Revolution an object? Is a puff of smoke? Is a wave in the ocean?

We shall use the term "object" to refer to any entity that can be named and talked about, that characteristics can be attributed to. State- ments like "the play is tragic" seem to be about *something* (people have certainly argued whether *Ghosts* is a tragedy or not); let us call that something an "aesthetic object." The term is somewhat artificial, but it helps us get on with our question.

For it does seem to be presupposed by critics, and by each of us when he discusses plays and poems and statues, that there is something that can be discriminated out from the process of creation and contempla- tion, something that can be experienced, studied, enjoyed, and judged. If this assumption cannot be justified, then criticism must either be aban- doned or drastically reformulated. So the main purpose of this chapter is to find out whether there can be such an object: what sort of thing it is that the critic can talk about. We may not be able to give a complete definition of the term "aesthetic object," but perhaps we do not need one. The serious difficulties that critics get into because they are not clear what the object of criticism is, can be readily sorted, and the term "aesthetic object" will be safe to use, providing we can be reasonably clear about five respects in which aesthetic objects are to be distinguished from other things.

§1.   THE ARTIST'S INTENTION

The things that naturally come to mind when we think of works of art are the products of deliberate human activity, sometimes long and arduous—think of the Ceiling of the Sistine Chapel, *Elegy in a Country Churchyard, Wozzeck,* and the Cathedral at Chartres. To put it another way, these things were *intended* by someone, and no doubt they are largely what they were intended to be by those who made them.

The artist's intention is a series of psychological states or events in his mind: what he wanted to do, how he imagined or projected the work before he began to make it and while he was in the process of making it. Something was going on in Chaucer's mind when he was planning *The Canterbury Tales* and in Beethoven's mind when he was considering vari- ous possible melodies for the choral finale of his *D Minor Symphony* (*No. 9*). And these happenings were no doubt among the factors that caused those works to come into being. One of the questions we can ask about any work, but probably not with much hope of a conclusive answer, is: What was its *cause?* And of course a good deal of writing about works of art consists in describing the historical situation, the social, economic and political conditions, under which they were produced—including the domestic affairs and physical health of the artist—in an attempt to explain, if possible, why they were created, and why they turned out the way they did.

Let us not stop to discuss the general metaphysical problems that might be raised at this point. Can a work of art be accounted for as the effect of some set of antecedent conditions? Philosophers who believe in freedom of the will, in the sense in which this theory denies that all psychological events are causally determined, would, I suppose, argue that there is an element of spontaneity, or indeterminism, in the creative act, and therefore that even *in principle* it is impossible to explain any work of art in sociological, historical, or psychological terms. Other philosophers—and I believe them to be sound—cannot see why *Tristan and Isolde,* the Hermes of Praxiteles, *Swan Lake* or the Pyramids are necessarily different in this respect from, say, Hurricane Hazel of 1954, the Second Punic War, the outcome of this year's World Series, or the first hydrogen bomb explosion. Like *Tristan and Isolde,* hurricanes and wars are extremely complicated, and to give a complete account of all their causal factors might not be practically feasible, but there seems to be no good reason for saying that it is *in principle* impossible.

Those who practice what they call "historical criticism" or "sociological criticism" of the arts are engaged in the same explanatory enterprise. And though I think there are good reasons to be doubtful of many explanations of particular works of art, or of general movements such as Romanticism, Impressionism, or the Baroque, this is presumably due to the complexity of the thing to be explained and to the scarcity of available evidence. It is a great field for half-baked speculation, which can often not be disproved and is thus allowed to stand. And perhaps this is why more critics concern themselves, not with the remoter antecedents of the work, but with its proximate or immediate cause in the mind of the artist. These are the critics who are fond of inquiring after the artist's *intention.*

The Evidences of Intention

Two sets of problems appear when we consider the connection between the aesthetic object and the artist's intention. One set of problems concerns the role of intention in *evaluating* the object; these problems we shall postpone to Chapter X, §24. The other concerns the role of intention in *describing* and *interpreting* the object: these we shall consider here. It is the simple thesis of this section that we must distinguish between the aesthetic object and the intention in the mind of its creator.[1]

When you state the distinction that way, it seems harmless enough, and perfectly acceptable. Yet there are some rather serious and interesting difficulties about it, and we shall have to look into them. First, however, it is worth noting that even critics who would perhaps grant the distinction verbally are quite often not able to see the implications of it, both in their critical theory and in their critical practice. Here is part of a paragraph, for example, from a literary critic who generally blurs the distinction in his writing. He is discussing André Malraux' novel *La Condition Humaine:*

> The handling of this huge and complicated subject must have given the author a good deal of trouble. He evidently sat down like an engineer to the problem of designing a structure that would meet a new set of conditions; and *an occasional clumsiness of mechanics appears. The device of presenting in dramatic scenes the exposition of political events,* to which we owe Garin in *Les Conquérants* and his eternal dispatches, *here appears as a series of conversations so exhaustive and so perfectly to the point in their function of political analysis as*—in spite of the author's efforts to particularize the characters—*occasionally to lack plausibility.*[2]

The clauses in italics are about the novel, the rest are about the novelist; and the paragraph passes from one to the other as though there were no change of subject. But, not to be invidious, we must add that equally good examples of the shift back and forth could be found in numerous critics of all the arts.

The consequences that follow from making a distinction between aesthetic objects and artists' intentions are very important, but they are not all obvious, because they depend upon a general principle of philosophy that is often not kept steadily in mind. If two things are distinct, that is, if they are indeed two, and not one thing under two names (like the Vice President of the United States and the Presiding Officer of the Senate), then the evidence for the existence and nature of one cannot be exactly the same as the evidence for the existence and nature of the other. Any evidence, for example, that the Vice President is tall will automatically be evidence that the Presiding Officer of the Senate is tall, and vice versa. But evidence that the Vice President is tall will have no bearing on the height of the President.

This point is obscured where the two things, though distinct, are causally connected, as are presumably the intention and the aesthetic object. For if Jones, Sr., is the father of Jones, Jr., then any evidence about the height of either of them will be *indirect* evidence about the height of the other, in virtue of certain laws of genetics, according to which the

---

[1] As far as I know, the importance of this distinction was first clearly pointed out by W. K. Wimsatt, Jr.; see references in Note 1-A at end of chapter.

[2] Edmund Wilson, *The Shores of Light,* New York: Farrar, Straus and Young, 1952, p. 570. My italics.

tallness of the father at least affects the probability that the son will be tall, though it does not, of course, render it certain.

Thus, in the case of aesthetic object and intention, we have direct evidence of each: we discover the nature of the object by looking, listening, reading, etc., and we discover the intention by biographical inquiry, through letters, diaries, workbooks—or, if the artist is alive, by asking him. But also what we learn about the nature of the object itself is indirect evidence of what the artist intended it to be, and what we learn about the artist's intention is indirect evidence of what the object became. Thus, when we are concerned with the object itself, we should distinguish between internal and external evidence of its nature. Internal evidence is evidence from direct inspection of the object; external evidence is evidence from the psychological and social background of the object, from which we may infer something about the object itself.

Where internal and external evidence go hand in hand—for example, the painter writes in an exhibition catalogue that his painting is balanced in a precise and complicated way, and we go to the painting and see that it *is* so balanced—there is no problem. But where internal and external evidence conflict, as when a painter tells us one thing and our eyes tell us another, there *is* a problem, for we must decide between them. The problem is how to make this decision. If we consider the "real" painting to be that which the painter projected in his mind, we shall go at it one way; if we consider the "real" painting to be the one that is before us, open to public observation, we shall go at it another way.

We generally do not hesitate between these alternatives. As long as we stick to the simplest descriptive level, we are in no doubt; if a sculptor tells us that his statue was intended to be smooth and blue, but our senses tell us it is rough and pink, we go by our senses. We might, however, be puzzled by more subtle qualities of the statue. Suppose the sculptor tells us his statue was intended to be graceful and airy. We might look at it carefully and long, and not find it so. If the sculptor insists, we will give it a second look. But if we still cannot see those qualities, we conclude that they are not there; it would not occur to us to say they must be there, merely because the sculptor is convinced that he has put them there. Yet it is well known that our perceptions can be influenced by what we expect or hope to see, and especially by what we may be socially stigmatized for not seeing. Though no doubt the sculptor cannot talk us into perceiving red as blue, if his words have prestige—if we are already disposed to regard his intention as a final court of appeal —his words may be able to make us see grace where we would otherwise not see it, or a greater airiness than we would otherwise see. If this works on everyone, then everyone will see these qualities in the statue, and for all practical purposes they will be in the statue. Thus the intention, or the announcement of it, actually brings something to pass; what the statue is cannot be distinguished from what it is intended to be. So the argument might go.

But it is precisely this argument that presents a strong reason for not making intention the final court of appeal. Suppose there is an experimental physicist who becomes so emotionally involved in any hypothesis that he cannot help seeing the outcome of his experiments as confirming the hypotheses: he even sees red litmus paper as blue if that is predicted from his hypothesis. No doubt his prospects for a scientific future are dim, but if he is handy around a laboratory, we can still find a way to use him. Let him test other people's hypotheses by performing the experiments called for, but don't tell him until afterward what the hypothesis is. The scientist is wholly imaginary, but the principle is sound. And we shall adopt an analogous rule: If a quality can be seen in a statue *only* by someone who already believes that it was intended by the sculptor to be there, then that quality is not in the statue at all. For what can be seen only by one who expects and hopes to see it is what we would call illusory by ordinary standards—like the strange woman in the crowd who momentarily looks like your wife.

When it comes to *interpreting* the statue, the situation is more complicated. Suppose the sculptor says his statue symbolizes Human Destiny. It is a large, twisted, cruller-shaped object of polished teak, mounted at an oblique angle to the floor. We look at it, and see in it no such symbolic meaning, even after we have the hint. Should we say that we have simply missed the symbolism, but that it must be there, since what a statue symbolizes is precisely what its maker makes it symbolize? Or should we say, in the spirit of Alice confronting the extreme semantical conventionalism of Humpty Dumpty, that the question is whether that object can be made to mean Human Destiny? If we take the former course, we are in effect saying that the nature of the object, as far as its meaning goes, cannot be distinguished from the artist's intention; if we take the latter course, we are saying it can. But the former course leads in the end to the wildest absurdity: anyone can make anything symbolize anything just by saying it does, for another sculptor could copy the same object and label it "Spirit of Palm Beach, 1938."

The Problem of Correct Performance

The problem of distinguishing the object itself from the psychological processes that produced it becomes more difficult, however, with those arts that involve the process of *performance* between the creator and the perceiver. To experience a musical composition or a play, we must ordinarily begin with a score, or script, containing the creator's directions to his performers, and these directions, in the nature of the case, can never be as specific as the performance itself. The score does not settle in advance every decision about dynamics and phrasing that must be made by the players and conductor; the script cannot describe every gesture, movement, intonation.

Indeed, in music the area of uncertainty may be very great. Bach does not even say what instrument is to perform *The Art of Fugue*. There is no sure indication in the score that Mozart wished his minuets played as slowly as Beecham plays them or as fast as Toscanini and Cantelli did. It is not even agreed which of the widely different versions of Bruckner's *C Minor Symphony* (*No. 8*) he wanted performed: the 1887 original, the 1890 version, the 1892 version—or some compromise like that reflected in the Hass version of 1935.

The performer's problem, then, is to decide how the work is to be performed, in matters where the score gives no instructions. And it is natural to say that the solution consists in determining how the composer intended the music to sound, though the score cannot fully report that intention. The "real" music is what the composer heard one time in his head: the aesthetic object *is* the intention. It follows that if the composer is alive, like Stravinsky or Hindemith, we must consult him, and perhaps persuade him to conduct the orchestra; if he is dead, the musicologists must search his letters and notebooks for the answers. And where blanks still remain, the conductor must fill in to the best of his ability, guided by reverence for the imagined wishes of the composer.

No doubt some performers operate upon this principle, but it can easily be shown that most of them do not, and in fact it would be impossible to operate only on this principle. In fact, when the modern performer decides how to perform a work, he is primarily guided not by reference to supposed intention, but by other and more important principles. Since he must choose among possibilities left open by the score, the criterion he uses must be something besides intention, or in most music he would never be able to decide upon a way of performing it at all. Consider some of the typical problems involved in performing Beethoven's *C Minor Symphony* (*No. 5*). The second phrase in the first

movement ends in two tied half-notes, with a fermata which in the auto-graph is one bar long, but in the first edition became two. The question is how long this is to be held. It will make some difference to the continuity of the whole passage, the degree to which these phrases will sound like part of the melody that follows. But it is evident that intention is of no help here; the conductor must decide how it fits in best with the rest of the movement. Again, what is the rhythm of the opening of the scherzo? If it is a four-bar rhythm, with the main stress on the first note of every fourth bar, there is still a subtle but important choice to be made, as I have indicated in the quotation: shall the strong beat fall on the C in Bar 3 or on the G in Bar 5? It is done both ways. But again, there can be no appeal to Beethoven; the conductor is after the intensification of some quality, a blend of playfulness and sinisterness, which it seems to him is best brought out one way or the other.

An even more interesting example is the phrase that leads into the second subject in the first movement. In the exposition section, Bars 59-62, it is in E flat, and is given to the horns, but in the development section, Bars 303-06, it is in C major and is given to the bassoons. Most conductors now assign the second passage, like the first, to the horns, without hesitation. Why? It is argued that if Beethoven's horns had had valves, so that they could play in both keys, instead of being limited to one, he would have let them do so; hence, the decision is based upon an appeal to intention. But the ground of this appeal is not intention; it is the supposition that, had Beethoven been free to choose, he would have recognized, as we do, that the phrase is better when played on the horns, more solemn and momentous. We don't decide what should be done after deciding what Beethoven wished, but the other way around.

The performer, in such cases as these, is then trying to determine what details of performance are most appropriate to the broader features of the music that the score does prescribe. And in so far as this appropriateness can be determined at all—of course, there is disagreement among conductors, who may make different but equally appropriate decisions— it involves relations to be found within the music itself. Of course, it is another question whether there is such a thing as greater or less appropriateness within music: we shall consider it in Chapter IV, §12.

The analogous situation for dramatic performance is well brought out by a passage in an excellent book on play production. The writer has just pointed out that the art of the theatre is "essentially a group art," to which the director, actors, painters, musicians, stage crew and audience all contribute.

> No amount of technical knowledge or facile craftsmanship will take the place of a true grasp of the author's purpose. Not infrequently a new play is half rewritten at rehearsals . . .[3]

[3] John Dolman, *The Art of Play Production*, New York: Harper, 1928, p. 2.

If the first sentence were thought to endorse the view that the playwright's intention acts as a kind of standard at which the director aims, the second sentence shows this is not so: it is not what the playwright intended, but what he ought to have intended, that the rewriting serves to discover. Chekov told Ivan Bunin he did not write his plays "to make people cry"—it was Stanislavsky's direction that made them sad. The famous "Quarrel of the *Cid*" arose because people were shocked by the marriage of Chimene to Roderick in Corneille's play, as setting a bad example for the young. When in 1660, twenty-four years afterwards, Corneille wrote his *Examen* of the *Cid*, and claimed that since his heroine never explicitly consents to marry Roderick, her silence in the last scene is a refusal, it is highly doubtful that he really convinced people by this lame excuse: no matter what Corneille says he intended, the internal tensions of the play allow no other interpretation.

Intention, then, does not play any role in decisions about how scores and scripts are to be performed. But this is not to deny that scores and scripts are written in a language that has to be learned. To recover plainsong in its original sound, we must of course learn the notation in which it has been preserved, and we must know the rules used by medieval singers for reading that notation. To restore Bach's cantatas to the way they were heard when his singers and players performed them—only, of course, we would like to do a better job of it than they usually did— we must investigate the techniques of performance, vocal and instrumental, that were used in his day. But in conducting these investigations, we are not seeking for the intentions of an anonymous plainsong composer or of Bach. We are asking what the music sounded like at a particular time, not what sounds the composer heard in his own mind. The rules for reading the notation, the customs of baroque performance, were public conventions, historically discoverable, at least in principle; they did not depend upon the intentions of a particular individual.

Meaning in Literature

This distinction may seem oversubtle, but we shall find it of the highest importance, especially for those arts in which the distinction between object and intention seems most difficult, that is, the verbal arts. In literature, the distinction is most often erased by a principle that is explicitly defended by many critics, and tacitly assumed by many more: since a poem, in a sense, is what it means, to discover what the *poem* means is to discover what the *poet* meant. This principle implies that the dramatic speaker, the "I" in the poem, is always the author of the poem, so that any evidence about the nature of either of them is automatically evidence about the other. In

When I consider how my light is spent,

we have Milton talking about his blindness, a fragment of autobiography. The problems involved in this notion are many and interesting, but we shall have to set them aside for Chapter V. At present we are concerned only with the possibility of the distinction between what words mean and what people mean.

Suppose someone utters a sentence. We can ask two questions: (1) What does the *speaker* mean? (2) What does the *sentence* mean? Now, if the speaker is awake and competent, no doubt the answers to these two questions will turn out to be the same. And for practical purposes, on occasions when we are not interested in the sentence except as a clue to what is going on in the mind of the speaker, we do not bother to distinguish the two questions. But suppose someone utters a particularly confused sentence that we can't puzzle out at all—he is trying to explain income tax exemptions, or the theory of games and economic behavior, and is doing a bad job. We ask him what he meant, and after a while he tells us in different words. Now we can reply, "Maybe that's what you meant but it's not what you said," that is, it's not what the sentence meant. And here we clearly make the distinction.

For what the sentence means depends not on the whim of the individual, and his mental vagaries, but upon public conventions of usage that are tied up with habit patterns in the whole speaking community. It is perhaps easy to see this in the case of an ambiguous sentence. A man says, "I like my secretary better than my wife"; we raise our eyebrows, and inquire: "Do you mean that you like her better than you like your wife?" And he replies, "No, you misunderstand me; I mean I like her better than my wife does." Now, in one sense he has cleared up the misunderstanding, he has told us what he meant. Since what he meant is still not what the first sentence succeeded in meaning, he hasn't made the original sentence any less ambiguous than it was; he has merely substituted for it a better, because unambiguous, one.

Now let us apply this distinction to a specific problem in literary criticism. On the occasion of Queen Victoria's Golden Jubilee, A. E. Housman published his poem "1887." The poem refers to celebrations going on all over England. "From Clee to Heaven the beacon burns," because "God has saved the Queen." It recalls that there were many lads who went off to fight for the Empire, who "shared the work with God," but "themselves they could not save," and ends with the words,

> Get you the sons your fathers got,
> And God will save the Queen.[4]

------

[4] From "1887," from *The Collected Poems of A. E. Housman.* Copyright, 1940, by Henry Holt and Company, Inc. Copyright, 1936, by Barclays Bank, Ltd. By permission of the publishers. Canadian clearance by permission of The Society of Authors as the Literary Representative of the Trustees of the Estate of the late A. E. Housman, and Messrs. Jonathan Cape Ltd., publishers of A. E. Housman's *Collected Poems.*

Frank Harris quoted the last stanza to Housman, in a bitterly sarcastic tone, and praised the poem highly: "You have poked fun at the whole thing and made splendid mockery of it." But this reading of the poem, especially coming from a radical like Harris, made Housman angry:

> "I never intended to poke fun, as you call it, at patriotism, and I can find nothing in the sentiment to make mockery of: I meant it sincerely; if Englishmen breed as good men as their fathers, then God will save the Queen. I can only reject and resent your—your truculent praise."[5]

We may put the question, then, in this form: Is Housman's poem, and particularly its last stanza, ironic? The issue can be made fairly sharp. There are two choices: (1) We can say that the meaning of the poem, including its irony or lack of it, is precisely what the author intended it to be. Then any evidence of the intention will automatically be evidence of what the poem is: the poem is ironic if Housman says so. He is the last court of appeal, for it is his poem. (2) Or we can distinguish between the meaning of the poem and the author's intention. Of course, we must admit that in many cases an author may be a good reader of his own poem, and he may help us to see things in it that we have overlooked. But at the same time, he is not necessarily the best reader of his poem, and indeed he misconstrues it when, as perhaps in Housman's case, his unconscious guides his pen more than his consciousness can admit. And if his report of what the poem is intended to mean conflicts with the evidence of the poem itself, we cannot allow him to *make* the poem mean what he wants it to mean, just by fiat. So in this case we would have the poem read by competent critics, and if they found irony in it, we should conclude that it is ironical, no matter what Housman says.

Intentionalistic Criticism

With the help of test cases like this one, we can draw a pretty clear distinction between two types of critic, in any of the arts. There are those critics who talk steadily and helpfully about the aesthetic object itself, and who test their statements about it by what can be found within it. They may take advantage of external evidence, where it is available, to suggest hypotheses about what may be in the work: for example, if a poet refers to his poem in a letter he may suggest a further meaning in the poem that readers had missed. But the proof, the confirmation, of the hypothesis is the poem itself; it is just as important not to read something into a poem as it is to overlook something. There are other critics who tend to shift back and forth between the work and its creator, never quite clear in their own minds when they are talking about the one or the other. They mingle the evidences of intention with the evidences of

---

[5] Frank Harris, *Latest Contemporary Portraits*, New York: Macaulay, 1927, p. 280.

accomplishment, and sometimes decide what the work is or means primarily on external evidence. This is to practice intentionalistic criticism.

As examples of the first type, I will cite Cleanth Brooks, Sir Donald Tovey, and A. C. Barnes—all of whom are on the whole remarkably consistent in their observance of the distinction. Even when they seem to ignore it, the appearance is merely verbal. Tovey writes, for example, of the sixteenth variation in Bach's *"Goldberg" Variations:*

> Lastly, it is, after all, not Bach's *object* to give the impression of a fully developed overture on a large scale at the expense of the proportions of what is, after all, only one of thirty variations. His *intention* is that after the fifteenth variation has closed the first half of his work with a chapter of sadness and gloom the sixteenth variation should usher in the second with promise of a larger and fuller life than anything the listener has yet learned to expect from it. For this *purpose* the audacious indication of the main facts of the two-movement overture form is more effective than a complete working out.[6]

Anyone who is familiar with Tovey's style, and who reads this in its context, will have no difficulty whatever in translating this passage into non-intentionalistic language. "After the fifteenth variation . . . the sixteenth variation *does* usher in the second with promise of a larger and fuller life. . ." etc.

When Barnes writes of Cézanne,

> His primary *purpose* was to make color the essential material of all his forms, and he *strove* to build up everything with color,[7]

he is really talking about what Cézanne *did*. Indeed, Barnes' analyses of paintings are almost perfectly free of any references to the painters as such. And when Brooks writes of the fourth stanza of Wordsworth's "Ode: Intimations of Immortality from Recollections of Early Childhood,"

> The metrical situation of the stanza, by the way, would seem to support the view that the strained effect is *intentional*,[8]

he makes plain his chief concern in a footnote:

> Whatever Wordsworth's intention, the sense of strain fits perfectly the effect which the poem as a whole demands.

Thus many apparently intentionalistic statements can be regarded as misleading ways of talking about the work itself. There are certain common ellipses that are so convenient they are hard to avoid, even when

---

[6] Donald F. Tovey, *Essays in Musical Analysis: Chamber Music,* New York: Oxford U., 1949, pp. 57-58. My italics. Compare a similar use of "intention" in a discussion of Schubert's orchestration, *Essays,* Vol. I: *Symphonies,* p. 202.

[7] Albert C. Barnes, *The Art in Painting,* New York: Harcourt, Brace, 1937, p. 322. My italics.

[8] Cleanth Brooks, *The Well Wrought Urn,* New York: Reynal and Hitchcock, 1947, p. 124. My italics.

reiterated use of them leads us to neglect the distinction; we speak of "Rembrandt" when we mean Rembrandt's paintings; we speak of "Robert Frost" or of the "author" of "Birches" when we mean the *dramatic speaker* of the poem; we speak of the "intent" of a musical composition when we mean only its main structure or prevalent quality; we may say, very carelessly, that a part of a painting does not carry out the "intention," when we mean only that it is not what seems to be called for by the rest of the painting. Such modes of speech are often harmless, but it is a good idea to avoid them as much as we can, even if it is awkward to do so.

For there are other critics who persistently make the confusion, and whose criticism hinges on certain terms that are inexpugnably intentionalistic. Or, if part of the meaning of such terms can be translated into a direct description or interpretation of the work itself, there is a residue that cannot. Hence it is hard to know how much of the term refers to the work and how much to the artist, and it is pretty clear that those who use the terms do not know how they would carry out the translation if they were asked. Yet if we do not know whether a critic is talking about the work or about the artist, how can we know whether what he is saying is true, for how can we know what sort of evidence is required to confirm it?

Take, for example, the following statement about a novel by Thomas Wolfe: "In this work there is an unsuccessful effort to particularize the characters." This could be understood intentionalistically: Wolfe wanted to particularize his characters very much, but was unable to. But how does the critic know this? He cites no evidence outside the novel itself. We must ask then what it is that he finds in the novel that he is tempted to describe in this fashion. When we see what he thinks would *test* his statement, we then have dug out its *non*intentionalistic meaning; we have discovered what it actually says about the novel itself. We may judge from the context that what the critic has in mind is (a) that the characters are not very fully particularized, as characters in novels go; (b) that the degree of particularization is spotty and irregular throughout the novel; and (c) that the novel would have been better if the characters had been more fully particularized. *These* statements are about the novel, rather than about Thomas Wolfe, and the first two of them at least can be tested by going to the work itself.

But suppose a critic writes of a play that it is "unintentionally funny"; it might be a good deal harder to say in this case how he *knows* that it was not intended to be funny, if it is. Perhaps it is funny in some respects but not in others, or perhaps the humor is of a peculiar and irritating kind. Another critic says that in a certain poem there is too much "elegance," by which he says he means "excessive attention to outward form." Can this be translated into nonintentionalistic terms? We can decide only if the critic goes on to point out specifically what features or elements of the poem he is referring to.

The recurrent key terms of intentionalistic criticism are such terms as: "sincere," "artless," "spontaneous," "facile," "contrived," "forced," "subjective," "personal," and "authentic." All these terms have the capacity to shift their reference from art to artist; in their primary sense they describe intentions, but they can all be used in derivative senses to describe *results* of intentions. You can't define them in any universal way; it is precisely their variability of meaning that makes them handy for critics who do not want to bother to be clear what they are talking about, and therefore you can only decide in each particular case how a critic is using one of these terms. The relevant and deciding question is: what sort of evidence does he offer for saying that the work is "sincere" or "contrived"? If he goes on to say that a love poem is insincere because he has discovered a letter written by the poet at the same time he wrote the poem, privately confessing that he didn't really care for the young lady at all, then the critic is talking intentionalistically. If, on the other hand, he points out that certain phrases in the poem suggest that the dramatic speaker is aware of his own hypocrisy, then the critic is talking *objectively*—that is, about the aesthetic object.

To put the difference colloquially, and no doubt oversimply, the objective critic's first question, when he is confronted with a new aesthetic object, is not, What is this supposed to be? but, What have we got here?

§2. THE PERCEPTUAL AND THE PHYSICAL

Consider what a variety of statements we can make about a painting:

1. It is an oil painting.
2. It contains some lovely flesh tones.
3. It was painted in 1892.
4. It is full of flowing movement.
5. It is painted on canvas.
6. It is on a wall in the Cleveland Museum of Art.
7. It is worth a great deal of money.

Now ordinarily anyone who made these statements about the painting, for example, a critic writing in a museum bulletin about a new acquisition, would suppose that in all of them he was talking about the same thing—say, *Three Bathers* (1892, Cleveland Museum of Art) by Renoir. The pronoun "it" seems to have the same referent throughout.

Yet there is a fundamental distinction that can be made among the statements.[1] Suppose we should ask about each statement, "How do you

---

[1] This distinction has been proposed by C. I. Lewis and Stephen Pepper; see Notes 2-A and 4-B.

know it is true?" In other words, suppose we should ask about the method of *verifying* the statement: What sort of evidence is required to justify us in believing it? In the case of Statements 2 and 4, the answer would be, I suppose, that we can *see* that they are true: we can look at the painting and observe the flesh-tones and the flowing movement. But this answer will not serve for the other questions. To verify Statements 1 and 5, we would have to undertake a chemical analysis, of the paint and of what it is applied to. To verify Statements 3, 6 and 7, we would have to go far beyond the painting itself, into history, or geography or the auction room.

It appears, then that there are at least two sorts of thing you can learn about a painting (leaving out Statements 3, 6 and 7 for the time being). There are the statements whose truth can be decided by direct perception of the painting itself—its shapes and colors as they appear to sight. And there are the statements whose truth can be decided only in a more roundabout way, by scraping off a layer of pigment to see what is underneath, by putting the painting under ultraviolet light, by dissolving a piece of it in a test tube, etc. And it is this distinction that raises the crucial question for us to consider now: Should we say that Statements 1 and 5 are statements about the same object as Statements 2 and 4? No one will doubt, I think, that Statements 2 and 4 are statements about an aesthetic object, but are Statements 1 and 5 about an aesthetic object?

There is one way you might think to settle this question. According to Statement 4, there is movement in the picture, but Statement 6 says that it is hung, apparently quiescent, on a wall. These two statements appear to contradict each other, and if they are both true they cannot be true of the same object, for no object can have contradictory characteristics. However, there is a way[2] to get around this argument: one need only say that these two statements don't really contradict each other. When we assert that there is movement in the picture we don't mean that part of it has a positive velocity relative to the wall of the museum, as though it were a mobile. Therefore this argument does not show that there are two distinct objects involved here.

The question becomes sharper, and easier to answer, when we direct it to music. For it seems very clear that it is one thing to talk music, another to talk acoustics. Sound is one thing, sound *waves* are another. And even if the word "sound" is used both in a book on harmony and in a physics book, it means utterly different things in the two contexts. When you speak of the tone-color of an orchestral composition by Debussy, or the sensitivity of phrasing in a performance of a Schumann piano composition, or the harshness of certain passages in Bartók's *Third String Quartet*, you are talking about something you can *hear*. The number of vibrations per second produced by the middle C key of the piano, the

---

[2] Suggested by Paul Ziff; see Note 2-A.

mechanical action of the harpsichord, the width of the grooves in a long-playing record, are not things you can hear, however much you can study them as a physicist and describe their behavior in rigorous mathematical terms; they are therefore not part of the music they produce.

When we talk about the sound waves and say, for example, that at such and such a point they increase in amplitude, we are talking about the physical conditions under which the music is to be heard. When we say that there was a crescendo in the music, we are talking about what *is* heard. Of course there is a causal relation between the perceived music and its physical conditions: when the amplitude of the sound waves increases, a crescendo is heard. But a musician who can read a score well does not need to have sound waves battering his eardrums in order to experience the music, and most of us can remember a tune and sing it silently over in our minds. Probably we would never become acquainted with any music unless at some time or other our ears were stimulated by sound waves; but if some way were discovered to make people hear music by giving them drugs or passing radio waves through their brains, the music critic would not have to change anything he says, though the physiologist would.

There is, moreover, seldom any doubt in our minds whether or not we are talking about the music. Perhaps the names of instruments are ambiguous in this way, but not dangerously. When we say that the clarinet has a cylindrical bore that causes it to produce the odd-numbered partials, we are referring to the physical instrument. When we describe the way the clarinet sounds as it skips about from one register to another in the first variation of the finale of Mozart's *Clarinet Quintet,* we are

FOURTH MOVEMENT, BARS 22-24
Clarinet (as it sounds)

Mozart, *Quintet in A for Clarinet, K. 581*

referring to the clarinet tone quality, which we can *hear.* And we could go on referring to this tone quality in exactly the same way even if it were produced electronically.

Aesthetic Objects as Perceptual Objects

In the case of music, then, we must clearly distinguish between the audible thing, which I shall call a *perceptual object,* and its *physical basis.* A perceptual object is an object some of whose qualities, at least, are open to direct sensory awareness. Indeed, we should all agree, I

31

think, that all of the qualities of a musical composition can be heard in it, though not all at the same time, and that any quality that cannot even in principle be heard in it does not belong to it as music.

The physical basis of the music consists of things and events describable in the vocabulary of physics. "Physical" may be misleading here, but it is hard to get along without it. We call a chair a physical object, but the chair, considered as being brown, hard, smooth, etc., is a perceptual object: it is perceivable. Besides the perceptual chair, there is the physical chair, the chair whose properties are discovered not by direct sensation but by weighing, measuring, cutting, burning, etc.

Take the case of the psychologist's reversible figures: the cube that turns inside out, the stairway, the profiles that face each other and turn suddenly into the background of a vase. The peculiarity of these figures is that in them we have one physical basis—the pattern of the light waves striking the retina—but two preceptual objects, the perception of which depends to some extent upon choice.

When we turn to those objects that involve words, it becomes much harder, as we shall see, to say exactly what the aesthetic object *is*, but it is no less obvious that it is *not* something physical. We would not be tempted to identify a poem with the sound waves that carry it when it is read aloud, or with the electrical processes in the brain when it is read silently, or with the ink marks in the book when it is printed. There would be no poems unless there were brain processes, no doubt, and none could be shared by several people unless there were sound waves or ink marks. But when a literary critic writes about *The Waste Land* or *Four Quartets*, he is not writing about any of those things.

The literary historian may, of course, be concerned in an auxiliary way with ink marks. Bibliography is the science that deals with the material transmission of literary texts. It may be of interest to discover, for example, that certain quartos of Shakespeare dated 1600 and 1608 were actually printed in 1619, or that the printing of the First Folio was interrupted. But these questions are not critical questions: the bibliographer's work is preliminary to criticism, for he offers not to talk about the play or poem, but to determine the "authentic text," that is, to decide what it is the critic will talk about.

Again, suppose we tried to give an exhaustive description of a television play. There is some question what it is that we are describing, but surely we are *not* describing the electrons in the picture tube. Or, for one more example, in a movie the scene depicted appears to stretch out on each side—we see it as part of a whole, though in fact the room may be in the middle of a sound stage, and come to a stop just outside the range of the camera. When we talk about these things, however, we recognize that we are talking about different things: (1) the presented picture, as it appears, and (2) the set used in making it.

When we turn back to the fine arts, the distinction between the perceptual and the physical may seem less clear, and less important. You could say that a statue, for example, is always the same object, whoever talks about it, and it has both perceptual qualities, which can be directly observed—such as its smoothness, its way of taking the light, the round-ness of its form—and also physical ones, which cannot be directly ob-served—such as its being made of marble, being solid, or weighing a quarter of a ton. The distinction would still be made, only it would be a distinction not between two objects, but between two aspects of the same object. To speak of the sculpture as an aesthetic object would be to speak of it in respect to its perceptual qualities; to speak of it as a physical object would be to speak of it in respect to its other characteristics.

I don't see that it makes much difference which terminology we choose here, so long as we are as clear as we can be about the distinction. It is convenient, wherever it does not distort the truth, to find a termi-nology that will serve for various types of works of art—statues and plays, paintings and musical compositions—and this is what I shall do here. But I don't think it would be fatally misleading to say that what I have called two objects are really two aspects of the same object.

To make the distinction between the perceptual object and the physical object is not, of course, to deny the importance of the physical stuff involved in the process of painting, or sculpturing, or building. So far as we now know, the only way to obtain perceptual statues is by working on stone or bronze or other materials, and it takes tools and pigments to make paintings. The sculptor must be on the most intimate terms with his physical materials, and the painter must undergo an arduous ap-prenticeship. Creation in the fine arts is, no doubt, not a process in which an idea springs forth in the artist's mind, to be mechanically worked out in some material; it involves feeling out the possibilities inherent in the stone or the pigments. Moreover, it might be argued that if we want to achieve the fullest appreciation of works of fine art, we, too, must know something about the characteristics of oil and water colors, about the methods of color-mixture, about the methods of cleaning and repairing paintings. It is a nice question exactly how such knowledge is relevant to the perception of the painting as aesthetic object, and perhaps a de-batable question. But the distinction between the aesthetic object and the physical object still remains.

When a critic, then, says that Titian's later paintings have a strong atmospheric quality and vividness of color, he is talking about aesthetic objects. But when he says that Titian used a dark reddish underpainting over the whole canvas, and added transparent glazes to the painting after he laid down the pigment, he is talking about physical objects. And this distinction is quite important. For to describe the perceptual painting as such is to say nothing about how its physical basis was pro-duced—whether the colors were painted on, dripped on, splashed on, blown on, thrown on, photographed, engraved, drawn, or merely spilled. What matters is the visible result.

The source of confusion here is that the terms we use to describe differences in the perceptual object are all physical terms derived from the *processes* by which these differences were produced. What really concerns the critic about a print is not its method of production— whether it is a woodcut or a wood engraving—but its appearance. The terms "carving" and "modeling" can refer to two techniques of making sculpture, or to two kinds of sculpture, for one can see the difference in the statue even if he knows nothing of sculptural techniques. When Arthur Pope[3] distinguishes between "drawing" and "painting," he makes no reference to physics or chemistry at all; except for a minor qualification, it depends on "whether the element of color (hue and intensity) is included."

It is one of the hazards of fine arts criticism that most of its ordinary classificatory terms are physical: "painting," "engraving," "lithograph," "water color," etc. We need a term that will include them all, as objects that are experienced as bounded portions of the visual field, no matter what their physical basis: they are *visual aesthetic objects*.

§3.   *PHENOMENAL OBJECTIVITY*

We have seen that it is important, though sometimes difficult, to distinguish statements about aesthetic objects from statements about their causes and conditions, psychological or physical. It is no less important, but it involves us in a different set of problems, to distinguish statements about aesthetic objects from statements about their *effects*. It is one thing to say what an aesthetic object *is;* it is another thing to say what it *does* to us.[1]

In general, as far as ordinary physical and psychological processes are concerned, we have no great difficulty in distinguishing causes from effects: the scratch of the match from the burning flame, the tickle in the nose from the sneeze, the insult from the angry retort. Where the process is closely continuous, we can raise philosophical questions about where the line is to be drawn—when the fire heats the water and it boils over, which part of the event is cause and which is effect? And where we have not made up our mind about the definition of some relevant term, we may be puzzled about how to use it—is the yellow pigment in the skin of someone who has a liver disease an *effect* of the disease, or *part* of the

---

[3] *The Language of Drawing and Painting*, Cambridge, Mass.: Harvard U., 1949, pp. 55, 57.
[1] The importance of this distinction was first made clear to me by W. K. Wimsatt, Jr.; see Note 3-B.

disease itself? But usually our common-sense practical approach avoids such perplexities.

In regard to aesthetic objects, too, there is often no difficulty in deciding whether we are talking about the object or about its effects. A. E. Housman says that Milton's line,

> Nymphs and shepherds, dance no more,

can produce tears, spinal shivers, and a constriction of the throat.[2] Beethoven said that he wept during the composition of the Cavatina of his *String Quartet in B Flat Major (Op. 130)*. Haydn predicted that the sudden loud chord in the Andante of his *"Surprise" Symphony (G Major, No. 94)* would make the ladies sit up and take notice, and no doubt his prediction came true. Whittaker Chambers has told us that his early reading and rereading of *Les Misérables* had a profound effect upon the two great decisions of his life, his entering and leaving the Communist Party.[3] Daumier's caricature of Louis Philippe as Gargantua, swallowing bags of money, must have irritated someone, for he was put in jail for it in 1832. And the pleased monks in Browning's poem reported to Fra Lippo Lippi the impact of his fresco of St. Laurence being roasted:

> "Already not one phiz of your three slaves
>   Who turn the Deacon off his toasted side,
>   But's scratched and prodded to our heart's content,
>   The pious people have so eased their own
>   With coming to say prayers there in a rage."

In all these examples, the cause is easy to distinguish from the effect. But in other cases, the distinction is not easy at all.

Consider, to begin with, the three following statements, which are drawn from a large class: "Some passages in Byron's *Don Juan* are *funny.*" "This Moorish interior by Matisse is *cheerful.*" "The slow movement of Debussy's string quartet is very *sad.*" These statements all purport to be statements about the qualities of aesthetic objects, but, on second glance, it may seem that they cannot be. For example, some philosophers would hold that when I call *Don Juan* "funny" I am really saying something like, "It makes me laugh," or, "I feel amused when I read it." But these are statements about the *effect* of *Don Juan* upon me. So, according to these philosophers, when I say that an aesthetic object is funny, cheerful, or sad, I am really not talking about the aesthetic object at all, but about myself. If I think I am talking about the aesthetic object, that is merely because I confuse the object with my response to it.

If we really are mixed up on this point, and are half the time talking about ourselves under the mistaken impression that we are talking about

---

[2] *The Name and Nature of Poetry*, New York: Macmillan, 1933, pp. 45, 46.
[3] *Witness*, New York: Random House, 1952, pp. 133-138.

something else, it would be well to know it. Therefore we had better consider this view very carefully.

Now, there are two lines of thought that converge upon the issue, and two corresponding distinctions that will enable us to resolve it. The first of these we have already dealt with in the preceding section. Imagine the following little dialogue:

> A: Isn't that Matisse painting cheerful?
> B: You mean, I take it, that it makes *you* cheerful?
> A: No, I mean the *painting* is cheerful.
> B: Oh, but you must be mistaken, for after all the painting is only a collection of electrons, protons, neutrons, etc., and obviously electrons can't be cheerful.

B's argument brings out one of the reasons why it is often thought that statements like the examples given above cannot really be about aesthetic objects. Of course, if aesthetic objects are physical objects, it would be hard to see how adjectives like "cheerful" could apply to them. But once we clear up this confusion, and see that these statements do not refer to physical, but to perceptual, objects, then *B*'s argument evaporates.

However, *C*, who has been listening in, might come to *B*'s defense with a second argument, of a more sophisticated sort:

> C (after we have replied to *B* on *A*'s behalf): Granting that we aren't talking about electrons when we say the Matisse painting is cheerful, still we cannot be talking about any other kind of object, either. For only *people* can be cheerful, strictly speaking, and thus all statements attributing cheerfulness to something must be statements about people if they are not to be nonsense.

"Strictly speaking" is the crucial phrase here. What else could it mean but "literally—as opposed to metaphorically—speaking"? Yet if this *is* what it means, surely the argument is very peculiar. Suppose *C* should say that *A* was barking up the wrong tree; we could then reply, in his own terms that "strictly speaking" only dogs—and seals—bark, and therefore *C* is not really talking about *A* but about a dog or a seal. Of course, when I say that the Matisse painting is cheerful I cannot mean by the word "cheerful" just what I mean when I say that a person is cheerful; it is a metaphorical extension of the term. There are many problems about metaphor, some of which we shall consider in Chapter III, but even without solving them we can see that *C*'s argument would make metaphorical statements impossible, and this is going too far.

We can't fully clear up *C*'s problem, however, without the help of a further distinction from the psychology of perception.[4] Let us use the general term *"phenomenal field"* to refer to all that one is aware of, or conscious of, at a given time. Thus my phenomenal field at this moment consists of various colors and shapes (the visual field), the sounds of typewriter and nearby birds and cars (the auditory field), my thoughts, memories, feelings, expectancies, and so on. Some of the parts, or ingredients, in my phenomenal field are *phenomenally objective;* some of them are *phenomenally subjective.*

Suppose you are contemplating a single object—something you have just acquired, say, a new LP phonograph record, in its slip-case. As you hold it in your hand, and turn it around, you get various sensations—the case is smooth, firm, square, brightly colored. You are also aware of a pleasurable feeling of expectation—pretty soon you will be able to play the record and hear how it sounds; perhaps you are trying to recollect what you have heard of the composer or the performers; perhaps you are wondering whether to invite someone else in to hear it.

The object appears as something persisting "out there," self-contained, independent of your will, capable of owning its own qualities, and the colors and shapes appear as belonging to it. I do not, of course, want to raise any questions about whether the record case *really* exists independently of human organisms; I am merely trying to describe what we find, or what is given to us in awareness, without any reference to physics or epistemology. This is the way it looks to you; the redness is on the cardboard, and it appears so rooted in, or fastened to, it that it will continue to remain there even if you shut your eyes or go away. It is phenomenally objective.

Your feeling of pleasurable expectation, however, does not appear as a characteristic of any object "over there" in your visual field, but as something going on in your *self.* For in this field you are aware of another thing, an "I," that is distinct from the objects in the room around you, that has its own nature and characteristics. And the pleasure in your phenomenal field you refer to yourself, as something "here" rather than "there." It is phenomenally subjective.

To decide whether something you find in your phenomenal field is phenomenally subjective or phenomenally objective, you must inspect it to see whether it seems to belong to something "outside" you, like an orange, a skyscraper, or a pudding, or to come up from "within" yourself, like slow anger or the effort of recalling a forgotten name. There are degrees of objectivity, and fluctuations of it, so there may be borderline experiences, without a decisive orientation either toward the phenomenal

---

[4] This distinction, and its importance in understanding the character of aesthetic objects, has been discussed by Kurt Koffka and other psychologists; see Note 3-A.

self or away from it. But the distinction is fundamental to our consciousness, and almost omnipresent in it.

A painting is then, of course, phenomenally objective. Its redness, warmth of color, shape, and position within the visual field, we "find" before us; they are "given." And the cheerfulness of the painting, the rhythmic order of its shapes, the sharp contrasts of its hues—these, too, are phenomenally objective in exactly the same sense. They appear as qualities of the phenomenal painting.

It may be thought that the cheerfulness or gloominess of the painting cannot be at all the same as qualities like red and square; the former seem to depend upon past experience in a way that the latter don't. So it may be argued that the former are subjective in a sense in which the latter are not. Now there are, of course, important differences between a quality like red and a quality like cheerfulness, and we shall discuss them in the following chapter. But at this point we are not concerned with the causes of what we perceive, but with the description of it. Experiments with perception may show, for example, that if you are a common seaman in the Navy, a man will look taller to you if you take him for an Admiral than if you take him for an Ensign. Or, to give a different sort of example, if you are confronted with a Rohrshach ink blot, what you take it to represent will depend on psychological conditions in your mind—which is why the test is diagnostically useful. Such experiments show that what we perceive as phenomenally objective needs to be explained, and cannot be accounted for on the basis of the physical stimuli alone. They do not affect the phenomenal character of the perception, however; the size of the Admiral, considered as a phenomenal object, is phenomenally objective. Similarly with the phenomenon known as "projection"—when the psychiatric patient projects his own (unconscious) hostility upon the analyst, the hostility is yet phenomenally objective for him, even if he is mistaken about its true (subjective) *source*.

Thus to say "The Matisse painting is cheerful" is not at all the same as to say "The Matisse painting *makes me feel* cheerful." In one case I am talking about a phenomenally objective quality of the painting; in the other, I am talking about my own phenomenally subjective feeling, which appears to me as an *effect* of the painting. If these two statements meant the same thing, neither could be true unless the other were, but the statements are in fact logically independent. No doubt a cheerful painting will often help to cheer me up. But even when, under some circumstances, the sight of a cheerful painting only increases my own melancholy, by reminding me of what I lack, I can perceive its cheerfulness nevertheless, and in fact it is precisely this perception that makes me sad. Moreover, a picture—say, a photograph of someone I know—may make me feel cheerful even though it is not itself a cheerful picture, in the sense in which the Matisse is.

It is perhaps a little less obvious that a musical composition is also a phenomenal object, distinguishable from the effects it may have upon us. When I listen to the music, it seems closer to me than the performers do as I watch them, or at least spread about more indefinitely through the surrounding space, somewhat as though I were inside it. But I do not hear it as inside *me;* it does appear as something I *encounter,* something that comes to me from "out there." I don't have control over it; it is like standing in a rushing stream and feeling the stream's force. The music is objective in the same way as the rushing stream.

Even when I recall a tune, or make one up, though the *feeling* of effort, or concentration, or satisfaction at success, is phenomenally part of myself as subject, the tune appears as something *found,* or *made,* and with its own individuality and self-existence. It is there, not in a particular place, but isolable, audible, recognizable—only its existence in this case, of course, depends upon my will, as it does in a less definite way when I play a phonograph record.

When we say, therefore, that Debussy's melody is sad, with an unutterably lost and hopeless sadness, we are again talking about something phenomenally objective, not about ourselves, even though it would be strange to find anyone who could hear the sadness of this music without being touched at all by it. We shall return to this problem in Chapter VII, §18.

Of course, we may be mistaken about the qualities we attribute to an aesthetic object. We may, for example, hear a musical composition once as sad—the sadness being phenomenally objective in that experience of the music—and later hear it no longer as sad, and we may conclude that we misheard it the first time. In short, not all the qualities that appear as phenomenally objective in some experience of an aesthetic object are to be counted truly characteristic of that object. This is a separate question which we shall have to tackle in the following section; for the moment, we are concerned only with the distinction between the subjective and the objective itself.

This distinction becomes most puzzling when we apply it to works of literature. For here it might seem as if the boundary between the work and its effect collapses, because no distinction can be made between what is phenomenally objective and what is phenomenally subjective in the literary experience. After all, what is it to *read* a poem or a novel? The marks on paper, or the sounds, are phenomenally objective, but our attention is not, or not entirely, on them, but on the meanings they evoke in us. How can we separate object from response when the experience is *all* response, and no object?

The defining mark of phenomenal objectivity is not immediate presentation to us, but experienced independence of the self. And there is more than one mode of awareness[5] of phenomenal objects. I "see" the apple; I "think of" my childhood home or of the Fiji Islands; I "imagine" Shangri-La. When I see a picture of someone I know, I think of that person; when I see a picture of someone—say Perseus—whom nobody ever knew, because he never existed, I think of that person too.

There are, of course, differences between seeing something and merely thinking of it. And there are also differences between thinking of something you believe to exist and thinking of something you don't believe to exist. It is rather hard to say, however, what these differences are. When you think of someone you believe in, like Queen Elizabeth or Willie Mays, your conception of that person may be no more vivid, or detailed, or interesting, than when you think of someone you don't believe in, like Anna Karenina or Baldur the Beautiful. Probably your conception of Tito or Mao is less vivid than that of Santa Claus; and you know Falstaff better than you know J. Edgar Hoover. For our present purposes, we need not explore this question, though it is an interesting and puzzling one. The main point is that thinking of something is one mode of awareness of it, and even if that which is thought of is non-existent, it is something that can be dwelt upon, contemplated, as if it were or could be before you—though it is not at all necessary that you should have mental images of it—and hence it impinges upon your phenomenal field as an object.

What we find to attend to, then, in literary works are persons and places, and the things that happen to them. There are Camelot, the *Pequod,* 221B Baker Street, Mt. Olympus; there are Jean Valjean, Scarlett O'Hara, Dracula, Peter Pan, Sinbad the Sailor. We also make responses to these characters—affection, contempt, envy, admiration. When you think of Hamlet you can distinguish him from your feelings about him— which, of course, are *your* feelings, not his. He is not before you, as a real person could be, even when you see the play, for it is not Hamlet you see on the stage but someone acting Hamlet. But he is complex and substantial, someone you can study, and reflect upon, and discover new things about.

You might say that though this distinction works for novels and plays, which are large and realistic enough to envelop worlds of their own, it does not work for lyric poems. What, besides the sound, is phenomenally objective about them? The difference is one of degree. When I read, for example, Shelley's "Ode to the West Wind," what I attend to are the feelings of the speaker—his self pity ("I fall upon the thorns of life! I bleed!"), his unsatisfied ambition ("Be through my lips to unawakened earth / The trumpet of a prophecy.") His feelings are not mine; they are what my feelings are about. Hopkins' lovely poem, "Spring and Fall: To a Young Child," contains rich complexities. In the lines

---

[5] The distinction between various "modes" of consciousness of things is made by Karl Duncker; see Note 3-C.

the falling leaves are metaphorically sad, and so, in a different sense, is the mutability they symbolize; there is Margaret's sadness; there is the speaker's sadness about the situation; finally, there may be the reader's sadness about all of these things. In every poem—we shall return to this point in Chapter V, §15—there is some concept, however dim or abstract, of a person and a situation, and so there is always something for the reader to regard and to contemplate.

Affective Terms

The distinction, then, between what is phenomenally objective, and can therefore be ascribed to the aesthetic object, and what is phenomenally subjective, applies whether the aesthetic objects are visual, auditory, or verbal. And we might expect the significance of this distinction for criticism to be so evident that critics would in general keep clear in their own minds whether, on a given occasion, they are talking about aesthetic objects or about themselves. On the contrary, however, very little attention is paid to it, and many favorite terms of criticism in all the arts seem almost designed to obscure and if possible erase it.

Consider, for example, the term "feeling" itself. In ordinary speech, this shifts its meaning about nicely without very often producing serious ambiguity. When you say, "I feel low," you're talking about your feeling; when you say, "The sandpaper feels rough," you're not talking about feelings at all, but about the tactile quality of the sandpaper, which you perceive by the sense of touch. But when critics come to describe the qualities of aesthetic objects, the term "feeling" may become ambiguous. "In this Cézanne landscape there is a *feeling* of solidity." The solidity is not a feeling, nor is it felt in the same sense in which melancholy is felt; it is perceived by the eyes, that is, it is *seen*. And the statement would be much less likely to mislead people into thinking that the solidity must be somehow phenomenally subjective if it were translated, "In this Cézanne landscape there is a quality of solidity," or, "The objects in this Cézanne landscape are solid."

Even the word "effect" can cause trouble. "In Velásquez's portrait of Innocent X (1650, Rome) there is an *effect* of fierce and rugged dignity" —which, if you don't get to Rome, you can also see in the preliminary study in the National Gallery in Washington, D.C. This statement might be understood as describing an effect of the picture, though on reflection that would of course be absurd, since the picture doesn't make the

---

[6] From "Spring and Fall," *Poems of Gerard Manley Hopkins*. Copyright, 1918, by the Oxford University Press and reprinted with their permission.

beholder fierce or dignified. The "effect" is simply a characteristic of the Pope as portrayed by Velásquez; it is something that you can see in the picture. Of course, the picture itself is an effect of Velásquez's activities, but that is another point. The word "effect" has no business in this description at all.

Many other adjectives that are widely used by critics in describing aesthetic objects have this peculiarity of reference. We may call them *affective terms,* and by this phrase I mean any adjective that, as applied to a work of art, contains as at least part of its meaning some reference to the effect of the work upon the percipient. When a critic says, for example, that a musical composition is "irritating," that means that *he* is irritated by it. And this affective term doesn't really tell us anything about the music, for it doesn't tell us what there was in the music that caused his irritation. On the other hand, when he says that a novel is "depressing," though he is saying in part that he is depressed by it, perhaps this affective term also gives some description, however vague, of the novel; we can guess with reasonable security, if he is telling the truth and using the word with care, that the novel contains some misfortunes and little ground for hope.

Thus affective terms differ in the extent to which they give objective information: some of them are entirely, or almost entirely, used to describe phenomenally subjective states; some of them, though at first glance subjective, actually turn out to be objectively descriptive, and whenever we wish we can translate such terms into other terms—as we did with "depressing" above—that will convey the same information without the misleading affective element. It would take us into too many details here if we were to attempt the analysis of a number of such affective terms, to see how much, if any, objective meaning can be found in them. The analysis could not be done well, anyway, unless we described specific uses of each term and often we would have to have the whole context available to see whether the critic, in using the term, is actually saying anything about the work.

Such a long analysis need not be undertaken here. Once you understand the method involved, you can always carry it out yourself when you need to. Here is a random list of other affective terms:

moving	stirring
vivid	powerful
impressive	inspiring
striking	restful
exciting	frightening
gripping	stunning

When you find a critic applying such an adjective to an aesthetic object, you know he is at least—and perhaps at most—recording his response to it. But first, how precisely and in how much detail does he describe his response? For, in general, the more carefully he describes his response, the more he will have to point out those features of the aesthetic object that he is responding *to*, and thus he will indirectly say something about the object. And second, to what extent does he give reasons to show that his response is normal, or suitable, or to be expected? For, in general, in order to defend his response, and show that it is not eccentric, he will have to point out features in the object that others would presumably feel similarly about, and thus again he will at least partially describe the object.

We must not lay down the dogma, of course, that critics should never describe their feelings. Surely we may be sometimes very much interested to know what other people feel about an aesthetic object, and to check our feelings against theirs; and of course such feelings may turn out—we shall consider this in Chapter XI, §28—to be bound up with the process of evaluation. We do sometimes *ask* other people how the object made them feel. But on the other hand, we also ask people what the object is *like*, and when we ask this question we don't want them to reply by telling us about their feelings. So it is well for us if those we ask are capable of telling the difference between the two questions.

§4. *THE OBJECT AND ITS PRESENTATIONS*

Consider a particular musical composition—for example, Béla Bartók's *Music for String Instruments, Percussion, and Celesta*.[1] Suppose that on Monday you hear it played in a concert hall; on Tuesday you hear it on the radio, with a different orchestra and conductor; on Wednesday you go out and buy a recording of it, and play the recording twice under different conditions on two different phonographs; on Thursday, or at some later time, you get hold of the score and with its help run through the music in your mind. You may be running the risk of overexposure if

FIRST MOVEMENT, BARS 1-3   Bartók, *Music for String Instruments,*
Andante tranquillo   *Percussion and Celesta*
Violas (muted)

[1] From *Music for String Instruments, Percussion, and Celesta* by Béla Bartók. Copyright 1937 by Universal Edition. Copyright assigned 1939 Boosey & Hawkes Ltd. Reprinted by permission of Boosey & Hawkes, Inc. Canadian clearance by permission of Associated Music Publishers, Inc., New York. Copyright 1937 by Universal Edition, Vienna.

you do all this, but the composition is such a fine one that it will stand a good deal of listening.

Here are, then, five separate hearings of the composition, and of course they are not exactly the same. The orchestras may perform it at different tempos; the phonographs may give different tone colors. And your own grasp of the composition will grow, too; at first the subject of the fugal first movement may not sound like a melody at all; where the counterpoint becomes complex, you may not be able to hear the voices, so that the texture is a hash of sound; and it may take a few hearings to get the hang of the phrasing and accents in the chief melody of the finale.

FOURTH MOVEMENT, BARS 6-8
Allegro molto

Nevertheless, despite these differences, we would ordinarily say that you have all along been listening to the *same* composition—though you have been listening better, and have heard more of what is in it, and have "understood" it more completely. And it seems very clear that this common-sense way of speaking—according to which there is one composition, but many experiences of it—is the music critic's natural idiom, too. For when, ordinarily, a music critic writes about a symphony, or a tone poem, or an opera, he is writing about some sort of *object*, not any particular *experience* of the object. To put it another way, we do not identify the musical composition itself with what is phenomenally objective in the auditory field in any single hearing of the music; we want to say that some hearings are more adequate than others.

It will help to clarify the problem here if we introduce a new term. An aesthetic object appears in a phenomenal field as a phenomenal object; let us call each such phenomenal object a *presentation* of the aesthetic object. A particular presentation of an aesthetic object is, then, that object as experienced by a particular person on a particular occasion. Each hearing of the Bartók composition by each person is a presentation of it. Common sense and criticism ordinarily assume that an aesthetic object is not identical with any particular presentation of it.

This assumption could, of course, be denied, but at considerable cost. It might be maintained that a critic can talk meaningfully only about his own experience of an aesthetic object, or, in our terminology, only about particular presentations of it. This theory, if it were worked out sufficiently to require a name, could be called *Critical Impressionism*. But although there are no systematic Critical Impressionists,[2] there are certainly Impressionistic critics—that is, critics who often talk about presentations of an aesthetic object rather than about the object itself. "The play *struck me* as too long," "*I felt* at the time that his painting *Bird in Window* was very sentimental," "The sonata *sounded* formless *on first hearing.*" Now, of course, such examples are most likely to occur in the columns of reviewers, and a reporter who is covering the first performance of a play or musical work is sensible to talk about the presentation rather than the work. For he is acquainted with only one presentation, and is not ready, perhaps, to commit himself to an opinion about the work without more chance to know it. His first impression may be wrong. But other critics seem to do it on principle.

In examples like those above, the distinction between an objective statement and an impressionistic one may be not much more than a quibble; they can easily be transformed. "It *seemed* formless to me" might have been put "It was formless." But of course there is a very significant theoretical difference that might come out on occasion. For if we should reply to the critic, "It was *not* formless," he could take refuge in the retort, "I didn't say it *was;* I merely said that it *seemed* that way to me at the time, and I don't believe you can persuade me that it didn't."

The philosophical question here is whether there is any reason for holding that a critic cannot make meaningful statements about anything but his own presentations. It might be said that the burden of proof rests upon the objective critic rather than on the Impressionist. Suppose we agree that I can talk meaningfully about my own experiences and what is phenomenally objective in them; there is still the question whether I can talk about anything beyond them. Therefore, if I propose to talk about aesthetic objects as something distinguishable from their presentations, I may legitimately be called upon to explain how I can do this. And this will require some account of the nature of aesthetic objects and of the connection between statements about them and statements about their presentations.

The scope of the problem needs first to be marked out. What do critics actually assume about the relation between aesthetic objects and their presentations? If we can draw up a list of these assumptions, they may be set forth as the postulates of objective criticism. And the question is whether a reasonable justification of these postulates can be given. If so, then objective criticism is possible; if not, we should have to abandon it in favor of the Impressionistic Theory. Now, I do not promise to give such a justification here, but only to take the first, and most fundamental, step in giving one. Is there a way of conceiving the relation between aesthetic objects and their presentations from which it

---

[2] Oscar Wilde sets forth a view somewhat like this in Part I of *The Critic as Artist.*

would follow that these postulates are true, and which is reasonable on other grounds?

The Postulates of Criticism

When we analyze the sorts of statement that are made about aesthetic objects, we find that many critics, at least, presuppose the following six postulates:

1. The aesthetic object is a perceptual object; that is, it can have presentations.
2. Presentations of the same aesthetic object may occur at different times and to different people.
3. Two presentations of the same aesthetic object may differ from each other.
4. The characteristics of an aesthetic object may not be exhaustively revealed in any particular presentation of it.
5. A presentation may be veridical; that is, the characteristics of the presentation may correspond to the characteristics of the aesthetic object.
6. A presentation may be illusory; that is, some of the characteristics of the presentation may fail to correspond to the characteristics of the aesthetic object.

I suppose it need not be argued at length here that these postulates are all quite widely assumed. When a teacher assures his students that a first reading of a poem will not enable them to understand it completely, he assumes Postulate 4; when he tells them, later on, that they have *mis*understood a poem, he assumes Postulate 6.

Are these, then, reasonable assumptions?

Let us first consider the presentations themselves. And it will be helpful to begin with an example from the visual arts: say, that famous painting of Toledo, by El Greco, that hangs in the Metropolitan Museum in New York. We want to mark off a class of experiences which we call "an experience of seeing El Greco's *View of Toledo* (ca. 1610) and our first problem is to find the boundaries of this class: that is, the class of presentations of this painting.

Of course, the boundaries of the class may be vague; that can't be helped, and need not trouble us. If you stood looking at the El Greco while twilight and darkness came on, it would gradually grow more indistinct, and finally you would see nothing. At what precise point do you cease to have the experience of seeing the El Greco? The answer has to be, at no precise point. There will, of course, be similar types of vagueness in all the arts—a musical composition broadcast over the radio, gradually choked and overcome by static, for example. Or, again, if we transcribe Bach's *C Minor Organ Passacaglia and Fugue* for symphony orchestra, or play Scarlatti on a modern Steinway instead of a harpsichord, we could ask whether it ceases to be the *same* composition, and ought to be called a different one. But these questions can be postponed. The important thing here is that we mark off such classes of presentations—of the El Greco, or the *Passacaglia and Fugue*, or *Romeo and Juliet*—from other experiences, and the distinction is indispensable even if the edges are hazy.

What all the presentations of the El Greco landscape have in common is that they are caused by some exposure to the stimuli afforded by the physical basis of that aesthetic object. The physical basis—the electrons and their radiating electromagnetic disturbances—is, as we have seen, not the aesthetic object. But anyone who (1) satisfies certain minimal physiological conditions—who is not, for example, seriously color-blind—and (2) stands in front of the canvas in a good light with his eyes open, and (3) attends to what he sees, is having an experience of the painting. It might be difficult, and it would surely be tedious, to lay down, and secure general agreement on, *all* the exact conditions that must be satisfied—the degree of astigmatism permitted, the range of distances he is to stand from the wall—for an experience to be classified as an experience of the El Greco. That would only be necessary if a quarrel arose between two people and one claimed that the other had not had such an experience at all—which might happen if the second person had gone to the wrong gallery, or had looked at one of the other El Grecos in the Metropolitan. But of course these contingencies are easily taken care of.

But not everything that happens to you while you are standing in front of the El Greco can be counted as part of your experience of it. If you hear a cough, or the giggling of a troop of children, these do not belong to the El Greco presentation. What *does* belong to that presentation is whatever is caused by, or correlated with, the physical basis of the El Greco. Thus the class of presentations of a particular work of art seems to be definable in terms of exposure to a particular physical stimulus; it is that stimulus, or vehicle, which remains constant, as a condition of each presentation, however the presentations themselves may differ.[3] At least this works for paintings; what about the other arts?

Turn back to Bartók's *Music for String Instruments, Percussion, and Celesta.* Whether one hears it in a concert hall, or in a broadcast, or on a recording, there are certain common patterns of sound waves. These are absent when you read the score, but we can broaden the class to include that sort of presentation too. For a person who can read a score, that is, transform the images into sounds in his mind, is having a presentation very much like one that it would be *possible* to produce by physically performing the score under certain conditions. But what about someone who memorizes the music and merely shuts his eyes and runs through it

---

[3] Compare the discussion by Stephen C. Pepper and his critics, Note 4-B.

in his mind? Is this to be counted a presentation of the music, though no physical stimulus is involved? We could say, if we wished, that in this case he is not enjoying a presentation of the music, but only a *memory* of a presentation of the music. Yet it may be so vivid, so complete, and so much like being in a concert hall that it seems arbitrary not to include this as a presentation of the music, too. We surely want to say that Beethoven, though deaf, heard his last quartets, though he did not hear them *played*. In that case, we shall have to broaden the class of presentations of Bartók's composition, again, to include reasonably close facsimiles of actual presentations, even where the facsimiles are not directly stimulated by sound waves.

Similar questions can be raised about poems, and they can be answered in a similar way.

Now, when the various presentations of an aesthetic object supplement each other, there is no difficulty in ascribing to the object itself the phenomenal characteristics of its presentations. When you go back to the Metropolitan on several occasions and look at the El Greco *View of Toledo* again and again, you will expect to see things in it that you had missed before, for example, the tiny shapes of people on the bank of the river and in the field, or the winding roads in the distance. And you would ordinarily describe this process by saying that you were discovering more and more of what is in the painting. But when two presentations conflict with each other, a new problem arises. Suppose one person reports that the picture seems to him to have depth, while another reports that the menacing sky and the tormented hills and fields seem to him to thrust themselves forward and fill the space. As long as each is content to report his own presentations, there is no contradiction, for they are talking about different things, but if they both claim to be describing the painting, their claims conflict.

Evidently we cannot avoid making up our minds about whether to adopt a seventh critical postulate, one that is stronger than the other six and perhaps more debatable.

7. If two presentations of the same aesthetic object have incompatible characteristics, at least one of them is illusory.

Postulate 7 amounts to saying that an aesthetic object cannot have incompatible characteristics. Even more obviously than the others, this postulate embodies a stipulation, or resolution, about the use of the term "aesthetic object." There is not much use in having the term "aesthetic object" at all unless we insist upon its freedom from self-contradiction, but the question is whether we can secure that freedom for it.

The same problem that arises with the El Greco can of course arise with the Bartók. To one listener the texture of the fugue in the first movement appears muddy; another listener can hear the separate voices much more distinctly. Or the slow movement seems to one listener formless, to another nicely balanced. And, of course, even more striking examples could be found in literature. Consider the opening lines of one of Dylan Thomas's most obscure sonnets:

> Altarwise by owl-light in the half-way house
> The gentleman lay graveward with his furies;
> Abaddon in the hangnail cracked from Adam,
> And, from his fork, a dog among the fairies,
> The atlas-eater with a jaw for news,
> Bit out the mandrake with to-morrow's scream.[4]

This is so very puzzling that to many readers it presents itself as having no meaning, that is to say, no coherent and consistent meaning, at all. But if we approach it with random associations, we come up with at least partial explications, and some of them are inconsistent with one another. The gentleman is dying, that's clear; is he in the "half-way house" because he is middle-aged, or is he already, so to speak, in purgatory, waiting for a final dispensation? Is the "gentleman" the constellation Hercules moving through the autumnal equinox in the direction of Ara? In a very favorable review, Miss Edith Sitwell once said that the lines about the atlas-eater refer to "the violent speed and the sensation-loving, horror-living craze of modern life," but Dylan Thomas said they meant no such thing: they were to be taken in their literal meaning. Who is right?

The impressionist answer to these questions is simple and easy: there is no "real" meaning of the poem; what it means is what it means to you now, to you tomorrow, to me now, to someone else. There is no one poem; there are many poems, indeed as many as there are readings. The unpleasant consequences of adopting such a view as this[5] ought to make us look for an alternative. If we reject it, we must maintain, I think, that there are *principles of explication* for poetry in terms of which disagreements about the correctness of proposed explications can be settled. Whether or not there are such principles is an important question we must consider later, when we are in a position to discuss the language of poetry more fully. It is obvious that some disagreements about the meaning of English words can be settled objectively—that is, by consulting a dictionary. The trouble is that disagreements about the meaning of "half-way house" and "atlas-eater" in this poem cannot be settled by consulting

---

[4] From "Altarwise by owl-light in the half-way house," *Collected Poems of Dylan Thomas.* Copyright 1952, 1953 by Dylan Thomas. Reprinted by permission of New Directions.

[5] Discussed by I. A. Richards and René Wellek; see Note 4-C.

any dictionary. It is my view that they can be settled according to legitimate criteria that are tacitly, and sometimes explicitly, assumed by contemporary literary critics; however, the defense of this view will have to wait till Chapter III, §10.

A good many of the disparities between one presentation and another in the case of music and painting are resolvable in a relatively uncomplicated way. We know that some of the phenomenal characteristics of an aesthetic object may be hard to see, may require close attention and an effort to bring into the field of attention a number of elements at once. When you find in a painting a quality that I cannot see, you can point out to me the colors, shapes, contrasts of colors, repetitions of shape, and so on, and in that way help me to see what I am missing. If we have to choose between divergent reports, we have reliable, though not infallible, independent tests, to tell who is probably the more discriminating, experienced, and judicious observer, and whose perceptions of the object are thus more likely to be correct.

There is, however, even in the case of the nonverbal arts, a curious difficulty that grows out of the distinctions we discussed earlier. In the famous Guarantee Building, Buffalo, built in 1895 by Louis Sullivan, not every pier, but every other one, contains a steel column, and the steel columns in the thick corner piers are no larger than the others. The architect has been reproached for this. Now imagine two people visiting one of our neo-Gothic college campuses, and stopping before a chapel or library.

A: Isn't that a beautiful building? It is so sturdy-looking and yet so graceful.
B: To me it looks cheap, vulgar, insincere, and earth-bound.
A: How can you say that? Has not the stone a handsome grain? Are not the Gothic arches nicely placed and balanced? Do you not think the proportions of the tower very suitable to the rest of the building?
B: I agree with all you say, but I know something that you do not know. Though this appears, on the outside, to be a Gothic building, it is not a Gothic building in one very vital respect. Whereas Gothic cathedrals supported themselves by the weight of their own stone, this building is secretly built around a steel framework, so that though it may look to the uninitiated as though the stone were holding it up, actually the steel is. The building therefore appears phony to me.

Now it is tempting, in reply, to say to B that he is merely falling into the elementary confusion we have discussed in §2. After all, the unseen steel framework is not part of the building as a perceptual object, and aesthetic judgments are bound to refer to what can be presented to perception. If B objects to the way the library is built, that is an engineering matter.

This reply is unfortunately too simple. For it is a fact that our knowledge of the physical conditions of an aesthetic object may in fact affect

the way it appears to us. Because we have that knowledge, its presentations may take on phenomenally objective characteristics they would not
otherwise have. The building may have a different quality to B from what
it has to A. And this could happen in other ways too.[6] Suppose you saw
a massive bronze statue that impressed you with its power; you might
find it harder to see that power if you learned that it was composed of
painted cream puffs or carved out of a hunk of soap. It might actually
look different. Or suppose you tuned in on a piece of music and found it
rather pleasant—perhaps it would sound worse if you were told that it
was being played on a harmonica or a penny whistle.

The question here is not whether this does happen, but whether it
ought to happen. And that is another way of asking whether such characteristics, which may accrue to presentations as a result of knowledge
about their physical conditions, are to be counted as characteristics of the
aesthetic objects themselves, or as illusions. Should we say the Gothic
library really has a dishonest look, and A doesn't know enough to be able
to see its dishonesty, or that B's knowledge is making him see something
in the building-as-perceptual-object that is not really there?

Veridical and Illusory Qualities

Contemporary analytic philosophers have taught us to be wary of
questions in which the word "really" figures prominently; we have learned
that such questions are seldom what they seem, and often invite question-
begging answers. We must be circumspect, therefore, in approaching the
question whether or not dishonesty, as a phenomenal characteristic, really
belongs to the library as an aesthetic object. Fortunately, contemporary
philosophers have also taught us the right methods to use. We begin by
trying out substitute questions that have a more manageable form, to
see how much of what was puzzling us when we asked the original question can be cleared up by answers to the substitute questions. One such
substitute can be constructed in this way. We might look around among
critics of architecture to see whether in general they tend to conceive of
the aesthetic object in their field in such a way that phenomenal characteristics induced by knowledge of physical facts are counted as belonging to the object. Is there a consensus of usage which we can fall back
on, and say, at least, that this is the usual, or normal, way of distinguishing veridical from illusory characteristics in that field?

This would be an arduous task to carry very far, for we should have
to comb through a large bulk of architectural writings to dig out a tacit
usage. We would find few, if any, direct answers to our question. We
would have to keep our substitute question carefully distinct from other
questions that are very easy to mix up with it: for example, architectural

---

[6] Wolfgang Köhler gives some examples; see Note 4-F.

critics would have a great deal to say about the suitability of certain phenomenal characteristics of the building to its function in society, but that is a very different question. And, in the end, we would probably discover, if we came up with any conclusion, that there is no consensus of usage on this point. Phenomenal characteristics of the sort we are interested in are about as often attributed as denied to buildings considered as aesthetic objects.

When a question about what is "really" there cannot be answered by appeal to generally accepted rules of usage, we can try out a second substitute question, which might be constructed in this way. For clarity of criticism in any field, it would seem essential to draw a distinction somehow between veridical and illusory characteristics. If critics don't do this, they run the risk of getting into verbal disputes; and indeed some of the futility of critical debate can surely be accounted for in this way. The question is, What is in the aesthetic object? The substitute question is, How should we decide to distinguish phenomenal characteristics that belong to the aesthetic object from those that do not belong to it? And if there is no accepted answer to this question—if in fact the question has hardly even been asked[7]—then it is up to me to propose a way of making the distinction, and to give reasons for adopting it. And that is what I shall now proceed, briefly, to do.

Leaving aside literature in the present discussion, I propose to count as characteristics of an aesthetic object *no* characteristics of its presentations that depend upon knowledge of their causal conditions, whether physical or psychological. Thus I will say that the dishonesty seen in the library by *B* in the dialogue above is not in the library as aesthetic object, and that to see the object in its true nature, *B* must either forget what he knows about its physical conditions, or learn to abstract from that knowledge. I will say that to hear properly certain kinds of music, it may be necessary for a listener whose phenomenal field is easily affected by his beliefs about the lives and loves of composers to push those beliefs out of his focus of attention: if Schubert's music sounds pathetic to one who sympathizes with his poverty, that is a mistake. And I will say that if a perfect imitation of a bronze statue be carved from cheese, so that to sight and touch no difference could appear—let us ignore the smell—then as an aesthetic object the imitation is exactly similar to the original, and the characteristics in which they may appear otherwise to people who know of their actual physical basis are not *their* characteristics at all.

But unfortunately there is one qualification that must at once be added to these forthright stipulations, if they are not to anaesthetize the aesthetic object completely. We do not come to the object cold, and, as

---

[7] Except in an important essay by Charles L. Stevenson, "Interpretation and Evaluation in Aesthetics," in *Philosophical Analysis*, ed. by Max Black, Ithaca: Cornell U., 1950, pp. 341-83. Stevenson's argument will be discussed, in its application to literary explication, in Chapter III, §10.

will be even more evident later on, our capacity to respond richly and fully to aesthetic objects depends upon a large apperceptive mass. This may include some previous acquaintance with the general style of the work, or of other works to which it alludes, or of works with which it sharply contrasts. All this may be relevant information for the perceiver; what is not relevant is specifically information about the physical basis, the physical processes of creation, and the biographical background.

Now, to defend a proposal such as this, I suppose, one can only point (a) to the conveniences of adopting it, and (b) to the inconveniences of rejecting it. But one must also reply to conceivable objections to it on the ground that it has its own inconveniences. Let us take these in order.

The distinction is at least fairly clear-cut, and it provides a way of settling specific issues. Moreover, it gives to the aesthetic object a certain stability of qualities; it permits us to say that through the years, for example, a painting whose physical basis is not damaged is the *same* painting, its characteristics visible to all, even if the secret of mixing its pigments or other physical facts may be forgotten. Anyone who attributes to aesthetic objects all the phenomenal characteristics induced by the knowledge of the personalities of artists and their techniques is faced with an uncomfortable dilemma. He may say that the characteristics of the object change as historical knowledge changes; which is an odd way of speaking. Or he may say that the "true" object is the one that contains all the phenomenal characteristics that would be seen in its presentations by anyone who knew all the facts about its causal conditions. This would seem to imply that we can actually know little of the "true" nature of all ancient and medieval, and most modern, works of fine art, even works that we can study for years in a good state of preservation.

And what unhappy consequences flow from adopting the criterion I have proposed? It would, of course, make false a good many things that people have said about particular works of art. Yet many such things are generally felt to be fantastic in any case—scraps of half-reliable information that lead the soft-headed critic into pages of gush about the Gioconda smile; or Sir George Grove's romantic discoveries of reference to Beethoven's unhappy courtship in his *B Flat* and *C Minor Symphonies*. You can't attribute to the aesthetic object *everything* that *anyone* thinks he sees in it, even if it is not inconsistent with what others see; and I know of no better place to draw a line. It would also force a much-needed qualification of a widespread theory that it is impossible to see what is there in works of fine art without extensive and exhaustive study of its physical means and techniques. It may be a psychological help in seeing, for example, the difference in qualities between a line engraving and an etching, to know how they are made, but everything that is there in the print is visible, and could be seen by someone who knew nothing of the methods of production.

Classes of Presentations

We now have formed the concept of the *class* of presentations of an aesthetic object, and our original questions remain: What is the aesthetic object, and what is its connection with its presentations? One way of answering these questions would be to say that the aesthetic object—the Bartók composition or the Dylan Thomas sonnet—*is* just the class of its presentations. This answer would distinguish the object from its presentations, all right, for a class is not the same as one of its members—the class of cows is not itself a cow; the United Nations is not a nation. But it is not acceptable. For a class is an abstract entity that can be conceived, but not perceived; and this contradicts our Postulate 1 above. A cow is a perceptual object; the class of cows is not. Nor will it do to substitute for the concept of a class some other abstract object, a "construct," an "essence," an "ideal entity," the "limit of convergence of a series" of presentations; for none of these is a perceptual object either.

Our predicament is this: we have various names of aesthetic objects, which cannot be construed as names of particular presentations of those objects, yet there seems to be nothing else available, either, that they could name. In a predicament like this we must, as before, always turn the question about, to see what other questions might be better asked instead. And there is a way out of it.[8]

While, as we agreed, not all the characteristics of an aesthetic object may be revealed in any single presentation of it, *each* of its characteristics is revealed in *some* presentation. Thus whenever we want to say anything about an aesthetic object, we can talk about its presentations. This does not "reduce" the aesthetic object to a presentation; it only analyzes *statements about* aesthetic objects into statements about presentations. We don't want to do this all the time, of course; it would be too cumbersome. But we may want to assure ourselves that it can be done, in principle, for this takes care of at least the troublesome part of our original question about the relationship between the object and its presentations: where disagreements arise about the characteristics of aesthetic objects they can be verifiably settled by appeal to past or present presentations or to probable predictions about future presentations. When I talk about the El Greco, for example, I am not merely describing my experience of it, but saying something about the experiences that could be obtained by other qualified perceivers under suitable conditions.

Thus, consider again the sorts of statement that critics make about aesthetic objects, and the corresponding presuppositions that we stated above in our six postulates. Suppose a music critic says, "The ending of the Bartók composition is vigorous, but last evening's performance was slack." Statements about the performance are to be understood as state-

---

[8] Pointed out by Richard Rudner, in an important paper, on which I rely in the remainder of this section; see Note 4-A.

ments about the presentations to members of the audience last evening; these presentations had something in common that differentiated them from other presentations that could be obtained on other occasions. The critic's statement then might be restated: "There have been, or will be, vigorous presentations of the end of the Bartók composition; but last evening's presentations were slack." The statement, "Bartók composed the *Music for String Instruments, Percussion, and Celesta*" means "The first presentation of that composition occurred in Bartók's phenomenal field." The statement, "The incidental music to Sophocles' *Antigone* is lost" means "No more presentations of that music will occur."

The philosophical significance of these translations is not perfectly evident, though it is always of philosophical interest that sentences using certain kinds of words can do all or part of the job done by sentences using different kinds of words. Such a discovery may throw light on the verification of these sentences, and it may even bear upon the metaphysical question, What are the entities that make up reality? But our aim here is somewhat less grand than the metaphysician's. There is one peculiar problem, it must be noted, about the process of translation from object-statements into presentation-statements, and it is raised by the word "good." "This is good music" cannot be directly put into the form "Some presentations of this music are good," for, as I shall argue briefly in Chapter X, §25, "good" is not the sort of word one can apply to presentations. Nevertheless, I shall also argue, in Chapter XI, §28, that "This is good music" can be translated into *other* statements about its presentations. But this subtle and complex issue will have to wait.

The "presentation" language is, of course, a rather formalistic way of speaking, and once we have assured ourselves that we *can* express ourselves with such accuracy when we need to, we can resume a more colloquial style. But for the time being we still have a further use for the term "presentation," because we have not yet pinned down sufficiently the nature of the aesthetic object that is responded to with pleasure and described, interpreted, and evaluated by the critic.

When two people listen to a pianist play a sonata, there are three presentations, including the pianist's; when the pianist plays it to himself, there is only one presentation. Let us, then, distinguish, in the case of music, three things: (1) There is the composer's *artifact*—in this case, the score. (2) There is the performance; any rendition of the sonata that is recognizably guided by the composer's instructions in the artifact will be called a performance of that sonata, but there will, of course, be many different performances of the same work. (3) There is the *presentation*— a single experience of the music—and for each performance there may be a number of presentations.

But (2) needs to be divided further, for the term "performance" has two senses here. In one sense, you could say that when you play a particular recording twice, you are giving two performances of it. This is the

56 sense established by Justice Brandeis' decision in *Buch* v. *Jewell-La Salle Realty Co.*, 1931[9]; he formulated the principle of "multiple performance," according to which when a piano concert is broadcast, there is the performance to the studio audience, the broadcaster's performance to the radio audience, and there also may be the tuned-in hotel proprietor's performance to his guests. In another sense, you could say that since the pianist was only playing once, he was giving only one performance, and even if he played it twice, but exactly the same, he would be giving only one performance. These two senses are nicely distinguished in the drama: a play—say *Measure for Measure*—may have a number of *productions*— the Old Vic's, a college drama club's, the Stratford, Connecticut, Shakespeare Theatre's—and each production, if it is fortunate, may have a number of *performances*. I shall transfer this terminology to music, and say, for example, that Raphael Kubelik's recording of the Bartók composition is a specific production of it, and all playings of this recording are playings of the same production.

Productions and Performances

We can now face another, and at first somewhat paradoxical, consequence of our adoption of Postulate 7. The recorded production of the first movement of Beethoven's *D Minor Symphony (No. 9)* by Toscanini lasts about thirteen minutes; that by Furtwängler about seventeen minutes. If we ask, How long is the first movement of Beethoven's *D Minor Symphony?* we get contradictory but true answers. By Postulate 7 the answers cannot be true of the same aesthetic object, even if they are true of the same *symphony*. Therefore the name of a symphony is not the name of a single aesthetic object. The word "same" has to be watched here. Toscanini and Furtwängler are producing the same symphony— that is, their productions are productions of the same work—but they are not producing the same aesthetic object. Thus the object we are talking about in the criticism of music, at least usually, is not the symphony in general but some production of it.

I do not think there is really anything disturbing about this conclusion, so long as we do not have illegitimate expectations. For example, critics often ask whether a production is "adequate" to the work, which is different from asking whether a particular person's presentation is "adequate" to the production. This question means, approximately, could there be a better production of the work? This is a legitimate question, and perfectly discussable, so long as we do not let it mislead us into two further assumptions: (1) that there is one and only one ideal production of the work, and (2) that this ideal production is to be sought, if vainly, in the intention of the composer. There may be one actual and possible pro-

---

[9] See Jacques Barzun, *Music in American Life*, Garden City, N.Y.: Doubleday, 1956, p. 99.

duction of the composition that is better than all others. Or there may be several very different, but equally good, ones: you might say that Toscanini's production of the Beethoven movement has fiery tension, whereas Furtwängler's has majestic breadth. Partisans of either conductor may, if they wish, argue that their favorite production is artistically superior; but it serves no useful purpose to dismiss the other production hyperbolically as "not Beethoven at all."

Thus, when we are interested in the characteristics of a musical composition, we must be clear in our own minds whether we are asking about what is common to all, or most, productions of that work, or to a particular production by a particular symphony orchestra under a particular conductor. And the same distinction must be kept in mind for other arts as well.

A play, for example, may be regarded, in one sense, as a work of literature capable of dramatic performance, that is, a work of a sort that everything quoted in it can be spoken by actors, every scene presented, every action acted by actors on a stage, before an audience. It might even be that by this definition some novels—for example, Steinbeck's *Of Mice and Men*—are plays, since they require practically no change to be presented. The artifact in this case is the script. But in a narrower sense, the play is a particular production, with its own sets, business, and costuming —as when *Measure for Measure* is done in modern dress, or *The Tempest* is presented as the wreck of a space ship on a distant planet. Again, two productions of the same play, though differing immensely, may be equally good aesthetic objects. There is not necessarily an ideal production.

As regards literature, the poem as written down or printed may be considered the artifact; the poem as read silently or aloud is the production of it. The reader performs the poem just as the pianist performs the sonata; and the reading as well as the piano playing may be a single private presentation, or a public group of presentations. The only odd consequence of this way of speaking comes from the fact that poetry is most often read silently. If each reading is a new production, so that each production has only one presentation, and each production is a numerically distinct aesthetic object, it looks as though we have too many aesthetic objects to be convenient. I don't know whether this really ought to be embarrassing, if it can't be helped. Certainly teachers attempt to correct their students' readings: their stressing of words—"*Who* brought you?" means something different from "Who brought *you*?"—and their grasp of figures of speech. We shall ask in Chapter III, §10, how much it matters whether we say the student is learning how to produce the poem or how to perceive his production. They coalesce into one, just as when the musician reads a score to himself; it is not philosophically significant that public performances of music happen to be more usual than public performances of poetry.

In the fine arts the distinctions work out a little differently. In architecture, the architect's plans are the artifact; the completed building is the production. Perhaps there is usually less leeway for the builder than for the musical performer: blueprints can give more complete instructions than a score. There may be only one production of the building, or there may be several, as in housing projects. The relation of an engraved plate to its various impressions, is like the relation of the play script to its productions, or the blueprint to the building. The impressions of a print do not differ so greatly as productions of a play, but they differ significantly as each impression wears away some of the metal.

In painting and sculpture, the distinction between the artifact and the production almost disappears. You could think of the artist's sketch for his painting—for example, a sketch by Rubens—as analogous to score, script, and blueprint. But this would be a mistake. The Rubens sketch is a work of fine art in its own right, and it is valued as such; but the score is not music, the script drama, or the blueprint architecture. However, between the artist's completion of his painting or statue and the audience's perception of it, there is, or may be, a process of *exhibition,* and to some extent this process, the arrangement of suitable conditions for the perception of the work, hanging, framing, lighting, is analogous to the performance of music or the construction of a building.

These comparisons are illuminating, and lead into other interesting questions, which, however, will not detain us now. The main thing to bear in mind, throughout this book, is that we must know, when we use names like *Le Bain* (Manet's original title) or the *"Moonlight" Sonata* (not the composer's title at all), whether we are referring to aesthetic objects, their artifacts, or their presentations. In general, where the context gives no special warning, when I speak of a play or a sonata, I shall mean some production of it, even though it will usually not be necessary, for the issue in hand, to specify which production is meant.

§5. *THE RANGE OF CRITICAL STATEMENTS*

The problems that are to engage our attention in this book are, as I have said, problems about the meaning and truth of what I have called "critical statements," or "statements of criticism." Since there are few subjects in which it is, at the present stage of knowledge, more important to make explicit from the beginning exactly what the inquiry is to be about, we have taken some pains to narrow down the range of statements that we are concerned with, and to set aside other sorts of statement that we are not concerned with. But there is one further distinction to be made.

Aesthetic objects are perceptual objects, but so are other things, for example, cows, weeds, and bathroom fixtures. Not all statements about perceptual objects are statements we would ordinarily want to count as critical statements—at least, not without some argument. This is, then, one point at which we might try to narrow the scope of our inquiry, by asking: what distinguishes aesthetic objects from other perceptual objects?

This question is often answered by recourse to a term that we have sedulously avoided so far in this chapter: the term "work of art." We might agree to sort out works of art from all perceptual objects that are not works of art, and then agree to say that statements about works of art—or at least, some subclass of these statements—are critical statements. If we were to do this, the next step would be to define "work of art," that is, to state the criteria by which people who are interested in such things as paintings, poems, and musical compositions, distinguish works of art from other things.

Now, in the first place, usage is so variable that this task would prove a very difficult, and perhaps impossible, one.[1] And even if we carried it out to our satisfaction, we might still feel that by confining our attention to statements about works of art we were unduly narrowing our inquiry. Whatever other criteria we would need to use, a work of art is certainly something deliberately fashioned by human effort—it is a *work*, it is the product of *art*, or skill, at least in the traditional sense of the term. But some of the things we can say about a painting by Van Gogh we could say about a living cypress tree; the beauty of a flower would presumably be explainable, if at all, by some of the same principles that apply to a still life by Chardin; and there is no good reason why we may not discuss the sculptural qualities of a rock formation even though the sculptor was wind and water instead of Moore or Maillol. Of course, I do not mean that the natural objects are, or are ever likely to be, as good works of art as the artificial ones—perhaps you recall Oscar Wilde's sunset that turned out to be "simply a very second-rate Turner, a Turner of a bad period." Nor do I mean that all kinds of things one can say about the latter can also be said about the former. But it seems arbitrary to leave out at the beginning perceptual objects that are not works of art, in the strict sense, if they have something else to recommend their inclusion.

Even if we agreed, however, to restrict ourselves to works of art, there would still be an almost ineradicable inconvenience in the term itself. For it has a persistent normative, or value, component in its meaning. Expressions like, "It's clever, but is it art?" or, "His verse is fun to read, but it's not art," bring out this element clearly: to call something a "work of art" in this sense is to say, among other things, that it is good, or aesthetically valuable. We could agree to purge this normative meaning, and use the term neutrally; but the normative meaning might slip by us at times without our being aware of it. And if we retained the normative meaning, the term would be of no use to us at all at this stage of

---

[1] See the papers by Paul Ziff and Morris Weitz, Note 5-F.

our inquiry, for even before we decided what species we are talking about, we would have to decide what constitutes a *good* member of the species.

Let us, then, keep the term "aesthetic object" as our most general one—though there will be no confusion if we occasionally use the term "work of art" when we are speaking about aesthetic objects that everyone would agree to *call* works of art. The question is, then, how to distinguish aesthetic objects from other perceptual objects. And this seems usually to have been done in four different ways, of which the fourth is, in my opinion, the best.

Psychological Definitions of "Aesthetic Object"

1. We might define "aesthetic object" in terms of *motive,* and limit its scope, like that of "work of art," to objects deliberately produced by human beings. This might be called a genetic or intentionalistic definition of "aesthetic object." For example, we might say that a perceptual object is not an aesthetic object unless it is the result of an act of "self-expression." There could, of course, be other varieties of intentionalistic definition. According to this proposal, we would first distinguish an "aesthetic motive" from other motives, which would then usually be called "practical" in a broad sense, including intellectual, religious, and moral purposes. Thus a steam locomotive, *The Wealth of Nations,* a menu, a Zuñi rain dance, a kitchen stove, the Ghent altarpiece, and a sailing boat would not be aesthetic objects, because they were not produced by an "aesthetic motive."

Whether or not there is such a thing as "self-expression," or some other distinct and isolable aesthetic motive, is an interesting question. It does not, however, need to be asked in order to talk clearly and sensibly about aesthetic objects. Therefore we shall not ask it in this book. But if we were going to ask this question, it might be best to put it in the form, "What psychological states and processes are generally, or universally, involved in acts by which aesthetic objects are produced?" And if we wanted to ask this question we would obviously have to define "aesthetic object" independently of any reference to its psychological conditions, or we would beg the question.

There are other uncomfortable consequences of this proposal. First, we would not be able to decide at all whether or not, say, the paleolithic cave paintings of bison and mammoths at Les Combarelles and Altamira are aesthetic objects. For we do not know whether they were created for "self-expression" or for magical—hence, practical—purposes. Second, we would have great difficulty in deciding whether or not to call religious paintings "aesthetic objects." An altarpiece, a devotional object, or a painting of the martyrdom of a saint has surely a pious aim. We could say that there must have been an aesthetic motive mixed with the religious one. But note that our only evidence for this is that the result is highly satisfactory; we are tacitly arguing that if it is a good aesthetic object, it must have been created by an artist with an "aesthetic motive"; but this presupposes that we have already defined "aesthetic object" in a nonintentionalistic way. And third, the intentionalistic definition, even where it can be applied, is arbitrary. If we can weigh the value of a Mondrian painting, why not the top of a Kleenex box? If a surrealist painting by Tanguy or Dali, why not a book jacket or a record slip-case? If an abstraction by Braque or Pollock, why not a photograph of lunar craters or a microscope slide, a modern chair or a pattern of frost on the window pane?

2. We might, on the other hand, define "aesthetic object" in terms of its *effects*. This might be called an affective definition of "aesthetic object." For example, we might say that a perceptual object is not an aesthetic object unless it produces a certain kind of experience—say, a feeling of intense repose. There could, of course, be other varieties of affective definition. According to this proposal we would first distinguish an "aesthetic experience" from other experiences, such as, for example, the experience of "entertainment." *Oklahoma!*, a television sketch by Sid Caesar, wallpaper, jewelry, "Maple Leaf Rag," Pogo, and *The Murder of Roger Ackroyd* would be entertainment, and these objects would therefore not be aesthetic objects, because they do not produce the "aesthetic experience."

Whether or not there is such a thing as "aesthetic experience," and if so, how it is to be characterized, are interesting questions, and they are questions that have to be asked in exploring the problems of critical evaluation. We shall discuss them in Chapter XI, §28. But when we do discuss them, we shall find that it is best to put the question in this form: "What psychological states and processes are generally, or universally, found in responses to aesthetic objects?" And we must evidently define "aesthetic object" independently of its psychological effects, or we will beg the question. It is mainly to leave the question open, and askable, that I want to avoid an affective definition of "aesthetic object."

There is another reason, too. If you study almost any writer who defines "aesthetic object"—or "work of art," if he takes that as marking the scope of his inquiry—affectively, you will see how difficult it is for him to keep the normative element out of his discussion. In one sentence he will be talking about the objects, and in the next about good objects. And this is easy to do, for if you define "aesthetic object" by its effect, and hold that the effect is valuable, then you won't have room left in your terminology for the term "worthless aesthetic object." The Tariff Act of 1930 defined "antiques," which are allowed into the country without a duty, as "objects with artistic merit made before 1830." But we will do better to define "aesthetic object" in such a way that there may be—the question is left open—good ones and bad ones. And this is what I propose to do.

3. There is a third way of defining "aesthetic object": that is, in terms of our approach to it, or our attitude toward it. This might be called an "attitudinal definition" of "aesthetic object." According to this proposal, we would first distinguish a certain sort of attitude toward things, the aesthetic attitude, and then we would say that any perceptual object may be an aesthetic object if we take it that way, or treat it as such by approaching it with an aesthetic attitude.

For example, you might say that there are at least two ways of regarding an apple. You might take a "practical" interest in it: you might want to judge its economic value, or worminess, or estimate the success of an apple harvest, and so on; that would be taking the apple as a clue for the manipulation of the physical environment. Or you might be interested only in savoring its "surface qualities," its color, texture, and taste. If you approach it in the latter way, it is for you, at that time, and in that respect, an aesthetic object. An analogous distinction can be made with respect to, say, Darwin's *Origin of Species*. If you are interested in learning facts about natural and artificial selection, or the history of biological theory, you are taking a practical attitude. But, if you wish, you can read it as an enormously patient and sustained argument, or as a masterpiece of style, or as the record of a dedicated and selfless pursuit of an important truth about the world. In that case, you are after its "aesthetic qualities," and considering it not *qua* biological treatise, but *qua* literary work.

The attitudinal distinction is then a relational one; nothing is aesthetic or nonaesthetic in itself. Of course, some objects will be more likely to be approached with an aesthetic interest than others—a Brancusi more than a baseball bat, a sports car more than a dump truck, a Dior gown more than an old bathrobe—but since any perceptual object by definition has some "surface qualities"—that is, phenomenal qualities that can be contemplated—there are no a priori bounds to what a painter might be interested in staring at, or even in painting. Again, of course, some objects will be more rewarding when approached with an aesthetic interest than others. To look for valuable qualities in an object doesn't insure their being found, and a reader who turns with an aesthetic attitude to Aristotle's *Metaphysics*, a speech in *The Congressional Record*, a singing commercial, or an elementary logic textbook, will soon turn away.

The attitudinal definition of "aesthetic object" has much to recommend it. In its tolerant way it offers the widest possible scope for critical statements, and is therefore least likely to beg any questions at the start. Moreover, anyone who defended this definition along the lines I have suggested could truthfully point out that if we make any distinction at all between aesthetic and nonaesthetic perceptual objects, and if we then

later on give an account of aesthetic value in terms of the sort of experience afforded by aesthetic objects, it will almost certainly turn out that
some of the nonaesthetic objects have some slight aesthetic value, too.
And if this seems like an intolerably paradoxical way of speaking, the
attitudinal definition shows us an easy way of avoiding it.

It does not, however, seem to me an intolerably paradoxical way of
speaking, and it seems to me we should be quite prepared to accept
that consequence. It is only saying that sometimes people will use perceptual objects that are not aesthetic objects by our definition *as if they
were* aesthetic objects, and sometimes these objects serve moderately
well in this unexpected capacity—just as sometimes people sit on tables
rather than chairs, in an emergency or for the fun of it, and use pennies
in fuse-boxes, no matter how often they have been warned. But being
able to serve as a makeshift fuse is no part of the definition of "penny,"
and we can quite well distinguish pennies from other things by criteria
that make no mention of this extra talent.

The Objective Definition

4. The safest and most informative way of distinguishing aesthetic
objects from other perceptual objects would not be by their causes or
effects or relations to people, but by their own characteristics. This is,
after all, the way we distinguish cows from horses, men from women,
and bread from stones—in terms of shape and substance. Such a definition
of "aesthetic object" would be an *objective* definition.

But there are two ways of trying to construct such a definition. Of
these two ways, the simpler and more convenient one, if it can be carried
out, would consist in selecting a set of characteristics that all aesthetic
objects possess, though no other objects have them all. It may turn out
that aesthetic objects have some noteworthy features in common; for
example, they present themselves as bounded segments of phenomenal
fields, and have internal heterogeneity but with enough order to make
them perceivable as wholes. Perhaps there are, as some philosophers
think,[2] even more important common, and exclusive, characteristics, that
can serve as the basis of a definition.

The point is that to discover such characteristics is itself the result
of a considerable inquiry, and we shall not be in a position to decide,
with confidence, whether these proposals are true until we have considered various arts in some detail and with some care. What we require
at this stage is something less informative, but more achievable, namely,
a type of definition that will mark out an area for study without presupposing an intensive knowledge of that area. Therefore, we may consider
an alternative type of objective definition.

To construct this definition, we must first divide perceptual objects

[2] For example, Susanne Langer and Morris Weitz; see Note 5-D.

according to their sensory fields: some are seen, some heard. When we review the basic distinctions within the auditory field in Chapter II, §8, we shall try to agree on the point at which we shall mark off musical compositions from noises, bird songs, and an orchestra's tuning up. It won't be necessary to draw a fine line, though we can make it as fine as we wish.

Again, once we have considered the basic properties of the visual field, we can distinguish visual aesthetic objects from other visible objects (see Chapter II, §7). And once we have considered the basic elements of language and meaning, we can distinguish literary works from other discourses, philosophical, scientific, and practical (see Chapter III, §9). The point of breaking the question up this way is that each of these distinctions raises its own problems; the difference between an opera and the noise of barrels rolling down a chute is not the same as the difference between *Paradise Lost* and a Burma-Shave ad. Some of the distinctions will be more difficult than others, and all of them will, of course, be somewhat vague, since general usage draws no sharp lines.

But if we want to carry out this project, we can then group together disjunctively the class of musical compositions, visual designs, literary works, and all other separately defined classes of objects, and give the name "aesthetic object" to them all. Then an aesthetic object is anything that is either a musical composition, a literary work, and so forth. We cannot actually carry this out until later, when we talk specifically about vision and hearing and language. But we are in no danger of defining in a circle, for although we shall, for example, be speaking about the elements of music in the next chapter (§8), we do not need to introduce the term "music" in order to define "music"—we need only introduce terms like "pitch," "loudness," and "melody."

By such a method, then, we can distinguish aesthetic objects from other perceptual objects, and consequently we can distinguish statements about aesthetic objects from statements about other perceptual objects. Consider, now, the class of statements about aesthetic objects. Some of them are statements about the causes and effects of the aesthetic object; let us call these "external statements." The others are statements about the aesthetic object as such: its blueness, its "meaning," its beauty; let us call these "internal statements." From now on, I shall mean by "critical statement" an *internal statement about an aesthetic object.*

Statements about the writer's unconscious, or the influences of one painter upon another, or the social conditions that were improved by a novel, are statements that belong to the history, or sociology, of art. There are, of course, problems involved in verifying them; but these problems are not peculiar to aesthetic objects, and they belong to the methodology of history and the social sciences, not to aesthetics. But statements about the characteristics of aesthetic objects, statements describing, interpreting, or evaluating them, do raise special problems that are peculiarly the domain of aesthetics. We will therefore ignore external statements, except as they turn out to be relevant to the verification of internal statements. We have already seen that there are good reasons to doubt that external statements are relevant to the verification of descriptive, or of some interpretative, statements about aesthetic objects; the question about their relevance to other interpretative statements and to evaluative statements will have to wait.

We have now reached an agreement about the meaning of "aesthetic object," and therefore about the range of critical statements whose problems will in this book be considered the subject matter of aesthetics. It may be in order here to remind ourselves that this is all that we have done, even though the chapter has been long and wide-ranging. One of the practices that spread confusion in the introductory chapters to books on aesthetics is that of jamming together a definition of "aesthetic object," or an alternate term, with a theory about aesthetic objects. When writers speak of art "as" this or that—"art as expression," "art as wish-fulfillment" —they often do not make clear to themselves whether they are proposing a way of using the word "art" or a generalization about the thing "art."[3] In this book, we shall try to keep these quite distinct. Theories and generalizations will come later; up to this point, we have been occupied with what is surely the first order of business, that is, agreeing upon the agenda.

It is now feasible to divide our task into manageable units. Setting aside the external statements about aesthetic objects, we are left with three large groups—descriptions, interpretations, and evaluations, to place them in order of increasing difficulty. One other division is desirable. There is a monistic approach to the arts that is committed from the start to the axiom that they are completely parallel, and that every distinction that must be made in each can also be made in all. This generally leads to confusion. It forces the evidence as far as it can, and when that fails it achieves apparent symmetry at the cost of equivocation in basic terms. We shall do well to start out as pluralists, though prepared to note parallelisms where they can be established. Now, there are certain complexities and perplexities that turn up in literary works, or verbal aesthetic objects, that have no parallel in music or in painting. Literature differs from both of them more than they differ from each other. Throughout the treatment of descriptive and interpretative statements, therefore, we shall take up literary problems in separate chapters. In the treatment of descriptive statements, music and painting will be discussed side by side, but they, too, will diverge when we come to the problems of interpretation.

---

[3] When I speak of "an art" in this way, I mean "the class of aesthetic objects in a particular field."

§1

Note: I have used the following abbreviations for periodicals:

JAAC	*The Journal of Aesthetics and Art Criticism*
J Phil	*The Journal of Philosophy*
PAS	*Proceedings of the Aristotelian Society*
Phil and Phen Res	*Philosophy and Phenomenological Research*
Phil R	*Philosophical Review*
PMLA	*Publications of the Modern Language Association*

1-A INTERNAL AND EXTERNAL EVIDENCE. Can a satisfactory distinction be made between internal and external evidence of the meaning of a literary work? Does external evidence ever outweigh internal evidence? See "Intention," *Dictionary of World Literature,* ed. by Joseph T. Shipley, New York: Philosophical Library, 1943, pp. 325-29; W. K. Wimsatt, Jr., and Monroe C. Beardsley, "The International Fallacy," *Sewanee Review,* LIV (1946): 468-88, reprinted in Ray B. West, Jr., ed., *Essays in Modern Literary Criticism,* New York: Rinehart, 1952, pp. 174-89, and in W. K. Wimsatt, Jr., *The Verbal Icon,* Lexington, Ky.: U. of Kentucky, 1954, pp. 3-18. Compare Leslie A. Fiedler, "Archetype and Signature: A Study of the Relationship Between Biography and Poetry," *Sewanee Review,* LX (1952): 253-73; the very judicious paper by T. M. Gang, "Intention," *Essays in Criticism,* VII (1957): 175-86; R. Jack Smith, "Intention in an Organic Theory of Poetry," *Sewanee Review,* LVI (1948): 625-33; William Empson's remarks in a group review, "Still the Strange Necessity," *Sewanee Review,* LXIII (1955): 475-77.

1-B TRANSLATING INTENTIONALISTIC TERMS. Analyze a critical essay in the art you are most familiar with to discover where the writer shifts from talking about the aesthetic object to talking about its creator, and vice versa. Which statements about the creator can be translated into statements about the object, and which cannot? Look out especially for intentionalistic terms like "artless," "spontaneous," "contrived," and "forced," and approximate synonyms of "intention," such as "aim," "purpose," "design," "plan," and "tried."

1-C THE WRITER AS EXPLICATOR OF HIS WORK. Is a writer necessarily the best explicator of his own work? Various points of view are represented in Robert W. Stallman, ed., *The Critic's Notebook,* Minneapolis, Minn.: U. of Minnesota, 1950, ch. 8, Bibliography (pp. 289-93). See particularly Hart Crane's explication of his poem "At Melville's Tomb"; the question is how much of what he says is in his poem is really there. Compare R. P. Tristram Coffin, *The Substance That Is Poetry,* New York:

the poem he writes there is another poem "which did not get written" that is "a part of it," and that may be important for the understanding of the poem that did get written.

1-D THE PAINTER AS INTERPRETER OF HIS PAINTING. Look up what some painters have written about the way in which the "meaning" of their paintings is to be interpreted, e.g., the letters of Van Gogh, in one of which he says, "I have tried [in the painting *Le Café de Nuit* (1888, Stephen C. Clark Collection, New York)] to express the terrible passions of humanity by means of red and green." For other examples see Robert Goldwater and Marco Treves, *Artists on Art*, New York: Pantheon, 1945. Does it make sense to say that something is actually "expressed" in a painting but that we could not discover it unless the painter told us?

1-E THE CRITERION OF CORRECT MUSICAL PERFORMANCE. Find examples of objections to a musical performance on the ground that in one respect or another it failed to carry out the composer's supposed intention. Analyze each example carefully: (a) What evidence does the critic have that the intention was what he claims it was? (b) Is the critic really arguing that the music would sound better if played the way he suggests? Consider the theory and practice of conductors and performers, e.g., in Roger Sessions, *The Musical Experience*, Princeton, N.J.: Princeton U., 1950, ch. 4, and David Ewen, *Dictators of the Baton*, Chicago, New York: Alliance, 1943, esp. Introduction: to what extent do they actually appeal to intention in deciding how music is to be performed?

1-F INTENTION AND PERFORMANCE IN THE DRAMA. What is the proper role of the playwright's intention, or supposed intention, in the staging of a play? Examine critically the views of famous directors and producers (e.g., Stanislavsky, Otto Brahm, Copeau, Meyerhold) on this point. See Toby Cole and Helen Chinoy, eds., *Directing the Play*, Indianapolis, Ind.: Bobbs-Merrill, 1953; John Gassner, *Producing the Play*, rev. ed., New York: Dryden, 1953, pp. 272-300, 436-44.

1-G BIOGRAPHICAL CRITICISM OF LITERATURE. Can you think of any literary works of which part of the meaning would not be discoverable unless we knew something about the writer—his personal experiences, domestic problems, relationships to his friends? Analyze your examples to determine (a) whether the information is really needed, and (b) whether if it is needed, it is not already provided by the work itself. E.g., when we read Milton's sonnet on his blindness, we do not need to know Milton's age when he wrote it; and though we do need to know that the speaker in the poem is blind, we do not require biographical evidence for this, for the speaker tells us so in the first two lines. On the other hand, it might be argued that we cannot understand Milton's sonnet on his dead wife unless we know that he was blind when he married her. See George Boas, "The Problem of Meaning in the Arts," *University of California Publications in Philosophy,* XXV (1950): esp. 318-25. See also René Wellek and Austin Warren, *Theory of Literature,* New York: Harcourt, Brace, 1949, chs. 7, 8, Bibliography; and E. M. W. Tillyard and C. S. Lewis, *The Personal Heresy: A Controversy,* New York: Oxford U., 1939. What precisely does Lewis mean by "the personal heresy"? How can we resolve the issues between Lewis and Tillyard over the relationship between the "personality" of the poet and the "personality" of the dramatic speaker in his poems? In the case of Yeats, who used in his later poetry a number of private symbols whose meaning he explained in a prose work, *A Vision,* there is the question how much of the meaning of the poems can be discovered in them independently of his explanation. See the discussion of "Two Songs from a Play" in Cleanth Brooks and Robert Penn Warren, *Understanding Poetry,* rev. ed., New York: Holt, 1950, pp. 457-64.

See also Wayne Shumaker, *Elements of Critical Theory,* Berkeley, Cal.: U. of California, 1952, chs. 5, 6, 7. "What horrible crime provoked the remorse of Byron's Manfred? A solution cannot be found on the printed page; therefore it has been sought in the circumstances of the author's banishment from England" (p. 42). Shumaker is not shocked, but he ought to be. This is a perfect parallel to the old joke about the drunk who loses something in a hedge one dark night and is later found across the street on all fours under a lamppost; when asked why he is looking for it there, he replies, "Because there is more light here."

Some literary critics hold with Stanley E. Hyman, *The Armed Vision,* New York: Knopf, 1948, pp. 121-22, that to "understand" a literary work it is "vital" to know whether the author was a homosexual (Whitman, Sophocles), repressed and frigid (Emerson, Thoreau), impotent (Henry James?), insane (Nietzsche), alcoholic (Fitzgerald); but what can the word "understand" mean here?

1-H LITERARY SOURCES. In what way, if any, is the study of the sources of a literary work relevant—or what types of source can contribute—to our understanding of the work itself? Does the use of such sources involve a tacit appeal to intention? See Robert W. Stallman, "The Scholar's Net: Literary Sources," *College English,* XVII (October 1955): 20-27; René Wellek, "Literary History," in N. Foerster et al., *Literary Scholarship, Its Aims and Methods,* Chapel Hill, N.C.: U. of North Carolina, 1941.

Note that the importance of bibliographical research does not bear upon the problem of intention: the bibliographer is trying to discover, not what Shakespeare intended, but what he actually wrote. Similarly, the restorer of old paintings, though he may say that he is trying to re-

cover the artist's intention, is in fact trying to restore the painting to the
condition it was in when it left the artist's studio (unless he is unethical
and wants merely to give it a fashionable brightness or a Rembrandt
glow).

1-I THE BODY OF A WRITER'S WORK. One method used in understanding a literary work is to appeal to other works by the same writer:
a poem by Robert Frost may be taken to have a certain meaning because
some of his other poems obviously do; a novel by Dostoyevsky or a play
by Shakespeare may be taken to have a certain theme because this theme
can be found in other works by the same author. One way of justifying
this method of argument would be to say that what an author intends
once or twice he is likely to intend again, because it is part of his system
of beliefs—a debatable generalization which might lead us to misread
a writer by putting something into one of his works that is not there at
all. Can you find examples of this mistake? Is there any way of justifying
this method of explication without appealing to intention, or must the
method be rejected?

1-J SOCIOLOGICAL CRITICISM. To give an explanation of something,
Y, is (roughly) to discover (1) some conditions, X, that occurred antece-
dently to Y, and (2) a general law of the form, "Whenever conditions X
occur, Y also occurs." To verify such a law, you must find a number of
examples of X and Y, unless you can deduce the law from some more
general law. Now, considering the complexity of works of art and of
their antecedent conditions, and considering the uniqueness of good works
of art (they are, so to speak, only one of a kind), how high a degree of
probability is to be expected from historical and sociological explanations
of literary works? See Wellek and Warren, *op. cit.*, ch. 9, Bibliography.
Look around in Arnold Hauser, *The Social History of Art*, New York:
Knopf, 1951. For example, speaking of Flemish painting in the sixteenth
century, Hauser writes: "Restored Catholicism allowed the artist more
freedom here than elsewhere, and it is owing to this liberal attitude that
Flemish art was less formalistic and more spontaneous than court art in
France, and also more natural and cheerful in its general mood than
Church art in Rome" (Part I, p. 457). Is this just a plausible guess, or
does he present adequate evidence of a causal connection between the
religious situation and the qualities of the painting?

1-K MEANING AND INTENTION. Is the poem's meaning just the poet's
meaning, or can these be distinguished? Are there poems that mean more,
or mean less, than the poet meant to mean? There is a rather technical
discussion of the distinction in Karl Aschenbrenner, "Intention and Understanding," *University of California Publications in Philosophy*, XXV
(1950): 229-72.

2-A THE DISTINCTION BETWEEN THE PERCEPTUAL AND THE PHYSICAL. See C. I. Lewis, *Analysis of Knowledge and Valuation*, LaSalle, Ill.: Open Court, 1947, ch. 15, secs. 5-7 (pp. 469-78). Compare Paul Ziff, "Art and the 'Object of Art,'" *Mind*, N.S. LX (1951): 466-80, reprinted in William Elton, ed., *Aesthetics and Language*, New York: Philosophical Library, 1954, pp. 170-86. How would you describe the difference of opinion between these two writers on the question whether the aesthetic object is distinct from its physical conditions? Apart from the confusions that Ziff exposes in the book by Samuel Alexander, does Ziff prove that in the case of a painting "there are two descriptions, not two objects," and that therefore "that ghost of aesthetics, the mysterious aesthetic object" is to be exorcised? Could his conclusion be extended to music as well? Ziff's treatment of Alexander has been pointedly attacked by Francis Sparshott, "Mr. Ziff and the 'Artistic Illusion,'" *Mind*, LXI (1952): 376-80. See also Harold Osborne, *Theory of Beauty*, London: Routledge and Kegan Paul, 1952, ch. 5, esp. pp. 91-101.

2-B CRITICAL TERMS WITH A DOUBLE MEANING. Find, in your reading about music or the fine arts, examples of terms that have a physical sense and a perceptual sense—e.g., "light" in painting may mean the light waves or the visible lightness. Do any of the terms lead to confusion because of a failure to distinguish the two senses clearly? R. F. Creegan, "The Significance of Locating the Art Object," *Phil and Phen Res*, XIII (June 1953): 531-41, has pointed out the importance of being clear about the "location" of the "art object."

2-C THE RELEVANCE OF TECHNICAL INFORMATION. In what ways, if any, does it help us to experience an aesthetic object if we know certain things about its physical conditions? For example, could we say that knowing about the various ways in which oil paints are ordinarily applied to canvas is likely to help us make finer discriminations in looking at the finished product? Discuss the relationship between appreciating a painting or a musical composition and possessing technical information about pigments, varnishes, acoustical theory.

2-D AESTHETIC OBJECTS AS "IMAGINED OBJECTS." See R. G. Collingwood, *The Principles of Art*, Oxford: Clarendon, 1938, ch. 7, pp. 125-53; W. B. Gallie, "The Function of Philosophical Aesthetics," *Mind*, LVII (1948): 302-21, reprinted in William Elton, *op. cit.*, pp. 13-35. What does Collingwood mean by saying that a "work of art" is not something perceived, but "something imagined" that "exists in the artist's head"? Is his argument clear and convincing?

3-A PHENOMENAL OBJECTIVITY. On the distinction between phenomenal objectivity and phenomenal subjectivity, see Part I of Kurt Koffka, "Problems in the Psychology of Art," *Art: A Bryn Mawr Symposium*, Bryn Mawr, Pa.: Bryn Mawr College, 1940, esp. sec. 3, pp. 190-209; Wolfgang Köhler, *Gestalt Psychology*, New York: Liveright, 1929, pp. 224-33. Are there elements in awareness that might be borderline cases, impossible to classify? Does the distinction disappear in some experiences? Compare the two ways of seeing described in James J. Gibson, *The Perception of the Visual World*, Boston: Houghton Mifflin, 1950, ch. 3; but note that he distinguishes the "visual world" from the "visual field," while both of these are covered by the term "visual field" as used in this book. See the discussion in David W. Prall, *Aesthetic Analysis*, New York: Crowell, 1936, pp. 141-57: how does Prall's account square with Koffka's? Prall denies (p. 149) that in this chapter he is using the term "to feel" in more than one sense; does his argument confuse "functional" and "phenomenal" subjectivity? See Ivy G. Campbell-Fisher, "Aesthetics and the Logic of Sense," *Journal of General Psychology*, XLIII (1950): 245-73.

3-B AFFECTIVE CRITICAL TERMS. See W. K. Wimsatt, Jr., and Monroe C. Beardsley, "The Affective Fallacy," *Sewanee Review*, LVII (1949): 458-88; the relevant parts have been reprinted in Robert W. Stallman, *Critiques and Essays in Criticism*, New York: Ronald, 1949, pp. 401-11; it is reprinted in full in W. K. Wimsatt, Jr., *The Verbal Icon*, Lexington, Ky.: U. of Kentucky, 1954, pp. 21-39. Find examples of affective terms used by critics, and analyze them in their contexts to bring out their objective descriptive content, if any.

3-C THE WORLD OF THE LITERARY WORK. On the phenomenal objectivity of literary characters, see sec. 1 of Karl Duncker, "Phenomenology and Epistemology of Consciousness of Objects," *Phil and Phen Res*, VII (June 1947): 505-42; Duncker refers to the Faust legend as an example, (p. 516). How does the mode of our consciousness of fictional events differ from our mode of consciousness of actual ones (see also p. 533)? Describe as fully and objectively as you can the phenomenal status of the events of some well-known novel, as you think about them. See Richard Rudner, "Some Problems of Nonsemiotic Aesthetic Theories," *JAAC*, XV (March 1957): esp. pp. 306-08.

§4

4-A THE AESTHETIC OBJECT AS AN ABSTRACT ENTITY. See Richard Rudner's criticism of C. I. Lewis (*Analysis of Knowledge and Valuation*, LaSalle, Ill.: Open Court, 1947), "The Ontological Status of the Aesthetic Object," *Phil and Phen Res*, X (1950): 380-88, and his alternative proposal that the names of aesthetic objects are "syncategorematic." Note that he uses the term "rendition" instead of the term "presentation." Rudner's position is also defended by Donald F. Henze, "The Work of Art," *J Phil*, LIV (1957): 429-42, esp. 438-42.

4-B THE AESTHETIC OBJECT AS A CONSTRUCT. Consider the following controversy: Stephen C. Pepper, "Supplementary Essay on the Aesthetic Work of Art," *The Basis of Criticism in the Arts*, Cambridge, Mass.: Harvard U., 1949; Nathan Berall, "A Note on Professor Pepper's Aesthetic Object," *J Phil*, XLVIII (November 22, 1951): 750-54; Pepper, "Further Considerations of the Aesthetic Work of Art," *J Phil*, XLIX (April 10, 1952): 274-79; J. L. Jarrett, "More on Professor Pepper's Theory," *J Phil* XLIX (July 3, 1952): 475-78; Pepper, "On Professor Jarrett's Questions," *J Phil*, XLIX (1952): 633-41; Stephen C. Pepper, *The Work of Art*, Bloomington, Ind.: Indiana U., 1955, chs. 1, 4. Pepper's view has been most thoroughly criticized by Henze, "Is the Work of Art a Construct?" *J Phil*, LII (1955): 433-39, and "The Work of Art," *J Phil*, LIV (1957): 429-42, esp. 434-38. Does Pepper's account of the aesthetic object as a "construct" and as a "dispositional object" square with the account given in this chapter? Compare Andrew P. Ushenko, *Dynamics of Art*, Bloomington, Ind.: Indiana U., 1953, pp. 18-25, 42-51. How does his view that an aesthetic object is an "essence" with the "status of potentiality" differ from Pepper's? See also Stephen C. Pepper and Karl Potter, "The Criterion of Relevancy in Aesthetics: A Discussion," *JAAC*, XVI (December 1957): 202-16.

4-C THE POEM AS A CLASS. See I. A. Richards, *Principles of Literary Criticism*, London: Routledge and Kegan Paul, 1925, ch. 30; René Wellek, "The Mode of Existence of the Literary Work of Art," *Southern Review*, VII (Spring 1942): 735-54, largely reprinted as ch. 12 of René Wellek and Austin Warren, *Theory of Literature*, New York: Harcourt, Brace, 1942; and in Robert W. Stallman, ed., *Critiques and Essays in Criticism*, New York: Ronald, 1949, pp. 210-23. What obscurities do you find in Wellek's theory of a literary work as a "stratified system of norms"? Does it help to explain how disagreements about interpretation of literary works are to be settled? The objections to Wellek by S. J. Kahn, "What Does a Critic Analyze?" *Phil and Phen Res*, XIII (December 1952): 237-45, seem to be based upon a general rejection of all the useful distinctions.

4-D THE OBJECT AND ITS PRESENTATIONS. Can the relationship between (a) a musical composition or play and (b) its "interpretations" by conductors or actresses, (c) "translations" and "transcriptions," (d) "renditions" or "performances" of it, be clarified by the terminology of the present chapter? For example, is the translation of a poem still the same poem? Is a transcription of a musical composition still the same composition? Is the distinction between the "performing" and the "non-

performing" arts fundamental? See Stephen C. Pepper, *The Work of Art*,
ch. 4.

4-E THE PROBLEM OF CHANGE. Does a poem or painting change in the course of time? Or should we say that it remains the same, but partly becomes lost to us? How can the distinction here be clarified by stating it in terms of "presentations," along the same lines as those suggested at the end of §4?

4-F THE VARIABILITY OF PHENOMENAL CHARACTERISTICS. See Wolfgang Köhler, "Psychological Remarks on Some Questions of Anthropology," *American Journal of Psychology*, L (Golden Jubilee vol., 1937): 271-88, esp. 275-82; also Karl Duncker, "The Influence of Past Experience upon Perceptual Properties," *ibid.*, LII (1939): 255-65. Do these facts that show the effect of the perceiver's beliefs upon his perception entail the impossibility of coming to interpersonal agreement about the nature of an aesthetic object?

§5

5-A DEFINING "AESTHETIC OBJECT." Discuss the relative merits of the alternate types of definition, intentionalistic, affective, attitudinal, and objective. Notice how other writers seem to be making the distinction (some of them use the term "work of art" instead of "aesthetic object"). See, for example, the selections from Jacques Maritain, Benedetto Croce, DeWitt H. Parker, and Charles Morris in Eliseo Vivas and Murray Krieger, eds., *The Problems of Aesthetics*, New York: Rinehart, 1953, Part II, esp. pp. 51-57, 77-78, 94-105, 109-11 (when are they defining "art"? "work of art"? "artistic activity"? "aesthetic experience"? "aesthetic value"? or some other term?).

5-B INTENTIONALISTIC DEFINITIONS OF ART. Can aesthetic objects be distinguished from other objects, clearly and conveniently, by reference to the activities and experiences involved in making them? This type of definition is used by C. Hillis Kaiser, *An Essay on Method*, New Brunswick, N.J.: Rutgers U., 1952, ch. 3; T. M. Greene, *The Arts and the Art of Criticism*, Princeton, N.J.: Princeton U., 1940, pp. 5-12; C. J. Ducasse, *The Philosophy of Art*, New York: Dial, 1929, ch. 8, and *Art, the Critics, and You*, New York: Piest, 1944, ch. 2; L. A. Reid, *A Study in Aesthetics*, New York: Macmillan, 1931, pp. 52-53; DeWitt H. Parker, *The Principles of Aesthetics*, Boston, New York: Silver, Burdett, 1920, ch. 2, and *The Analysis of Art*, New Haven: Yale U., 1926, ch. 1; Thomas Munro, *The Arts and Their Interrelations*, New York: Liberal Arts, 1949, ch. 3. See also John Hospers, "The Croce-Collingwood Theory of Art," *Philosophy*, XXXI (1956): 3-20.

5-C AFFECTIVE DEFINITIONS OF ART. Can aesthetic objects be distinguished from other objects, clearly and conveniently, by reference to their effects upon percipients? This type of definition, sometimes combined with intentionalism, is used by Thomas Munro, "Form and Value in the Arts: A Functional Approach," *JAAC*, XIII (March 1955): 316-41; David W. Prall, *Aesthetic Analysis*, New York: Crowell, 1936, ch. 1; Harold N. Lee, *Perception and Aesthetic Value*, Englewood Cliffs, N.J.: Prentice-Hall, 1938, ch. 9; E. M. Bartlett, "The Determination of the Aesthetic Minimum," *PAS*, XXXV (1935): 113-36.

5-D OBJECTIVE DEFINITIONS OF ART. Can aesthetic objects be distinguished from other objects, clearly and conveniently, in terms of characteristics that they all—including borderline cases like landscape gardening, flower arranging, tattooing—have in common, but which other things lack? For example, are they definable as "organic complexes"—see Morris Weitz, *Philosophy of the Arts*, Cambridge, Mass.: Harvard U., 1950, p. 44? "Semblances"—see Susanne Langer, *Feeling and Form*, New York: Scribner's, 1953, ch. 4; Arthur Berndtson, "Semblance, Symbol, and Expression in the Aesthetics of Susanne Langer," *JAAC*, XIV (June 1956): 489-502?

5-E NORMATIVE DEFINITIONS OF ART. Can the term "aesthetic object," or a synonym, be defined nonnormatively, or must aesthetic objects be distinguished from other objects by their possession of aesthetic value? See Harold Osborne, *Aesthetics and Criticism*, London: Routledge and Kegan Paul, 1955, pp. 18, 40-47, especially his discussion of the quotation from R. G. Collingwood, *Principles of Art*, 1938, p. 280. What is the fallacy in the argument, "The definition of any given kind of thing is also the definition of a good thing of that kind: for a thing that is good in its kind is only a thing which possesses the attributes of that kind"?

5-F THE DEFINABILITY OF "WORK OF ART." See Paul Ziff, "The Task of Defining a Work of Art," *Phil R*, LXII (January 1953): 58-78. Ziff points up the shifting senses of the term "work of art." Does he make out a convincing case for his view that musical compositions and poems cannot be said to be works of art "in the same sense of the phrase" as paintings and statues? Morris Weitz, "The Role of Theory in Aesthetics," *JAAC*, XV (September 1956): 27-35, also argues that the term "art"—as well as other critical terms—designates an "open concept," so that in its ordinary use no necessary and sufficient conditions for its application can be discovered. But of course he does not deny that for technical purposes one can stipulate a definition that may correspond to some of its familiar uses.

· II ·

THE CATEGORIES
OF CRITICAL
ANALYSIS

The critic's first task, when confronted with an aesthetic object, is to see what that object is. Everything else he may do with it depends on this, for, though he does not expect to discover all its manifold features and aspects, he cannot even fully enjoy it until he has a good grasp of its main features and primary aspects. Now, the critic may be content to observe and to enjoy, but if he plans to interpret or to evaluate the work, then he must be prepared to give at least a partial description of it—to point out clearly those characteristics upon which its interpretable significance or its aesthetic value depends. And to describe an aesthetic object is by no means easy.

Critical descriptions are of all levels of precision and specificity, but they are most helpful when they discriminate and articulate details, and thus give us an insight into the inner nature of the object. Such a description is called an analysis, and in this chapter we shall consider the problems that arise in analyzing aesthetic objects. But first something needs to be said about analysis itself, and some of the persistent misunderstandings of it.[1]

Two objections are often made to critical analysis: first, that it is somehow impossible in the case of aesthetic objects, that they resist it or will not yield themselves to such a consideration; and second, that even if it were possible to analyze aesthetic objects, it would be undesirable, because it would spoil our pleasure in them, by getting in the way of our emotions. The first objection is based on certain assumptions about the nature of aesthetic objects, the second is a reaction to modern critics of painting and music, and especially to the so-called "New Critics" of literature—they are said to be overintellectual, overingenious, and given to missing the woods for the trees.

As far as the second objection is concerned, the reply is simple. To analyze is not to enjoy; you can't always do both at the same time. But to analyze at one time does not preclude enjoyment at another time; how could it? A dietician or a chemist has to study food. To study it is not to eat it, but why should the study spoil one's appetite? This analogy must not be pushed too far; aesthetic analysis is not the same as chemical analysis. To analyze an aesthetic object is precisely to get acquainted with its finer details and subtler qualities, to discover, in short, what is there to *be* enjoyed—to be responded to emotionally. The alternative to analysis is a half-cocked, crude emotional reaction to the gross, obvious features of the object.

The doubts underlying the first objection are somewhat more sophisticated. It is sometimes thought that analysis "destroys" the object, or does away with its important characteristics. If a color analyst said that green is "really" nothing but yellow and blue, what would happen to the green? But of course that would be a most ridiculous thing to say, and in any case it is not what we mean here by "analysis." To analyze in the chemical sense means to take apart, and after the chemist is through analyzing your blood, it is of no use as blood. But to analyze in the critical sense is only to see or hear or read better; the analysis does not hurt the object. A chemist can analyze a cake and find a small quantity of arsenic in it, but if the arsenic can't be tasted, then it's no part of the *sensory* analysis of the taste, as when a cake critic might report, "There's too much salt" or "not enough vanilla." To say that by mixing blue pigment and yellow pigment you can produce green pigment is not to "analyze" green; you don't see the yellow *in* the green, unless it is a yellow-green. This is a statement about the physical causes of green, and it is no part of critical analysis. To say that the figure eight may be constructed of two tangential circles *is* to give an analysis, in our sense, but it does not imply that the eight is "really" not an eight after all, and it need not blind us to the figure.

It is also sometimes said that analysis is bound to "distort" the aesthetic object, and force us to make false statements about it. If this objection could be sustained, it would be serious, for the analysis would be self-defeating, but it is based upon a misleading way of describing certain important facts about perception. These are the facts that show

---

[1] See the defenses of critical analysis by David W. Prall, *Aesthetic Analysis,* New York: Crowell, 1936, ch. 1, pp. 12-31; ch. 2; and Edmund Gurney, *The Power of Sound,* London: Smith, Elder, 1880, pp. 40-41.

that if there is a change in the context of a part of the sensory field, the qualities of that part may be changed without any change in the physical stimulus corresponding to that part. Thus, to take a few random examples, a gray circle on a piece of paper looks darker when contrasted with a white background than when contrasted with a dark background, though the amplitude of the light waves emanating from the paper does not change; if a gray patch is surrounded by an intense color, it will take on a tint of the complementary color; a light-colored circle on a dark background seems larger than a dark-colored circle on a light background, even though a ruler will show them to have the same diameter. And of course there are countless similar examples available from each sensory field.

It might then be argued that if we observe in a painting a gray patch surrounded by red, and then consider the patch by itself, it will lose its green tint, and no longer be what it was. But again this is a misconception of analysis. If we were to cut up the canvas into its separate patches of color, and put them in separate places, why then of course they would mostly look different. But analysis is not chopping. We analyze what is given—what appears. And there is nothing to prevent us from pointing out that in this part of the painting there is a green-tinted gray—even though the tint is partly a function of its relation to surrounding colors, not solely of the pigment.

Finally, it is sometimes said that analysis is bound to leave out too much, because "the whole is more than the sum of its parts"—especially in an aesthetic object. Taken in a plain sense this maxim means that some things may be true of a whole that are not true of any of its parts—for example, your weight. This is correct. But a critical analysis is not committed to denying it. In fact, it is precisely the purpose of analysis to discover, first, what *is* true of the parts, and, second, how the parts contribute to the peculiar qualities of the whole.[2]

To analyze, then, is to distinguish, to discriminate, to describe in detail. And analysis proceeds on certain assumptions about what kinds of detail it is important for the critic to note. The analyst employs certain *categories,* or basic distinctions. And this is what creates the central problem for us now: what are the proper categories of critical analysis? We must examine briefly some widely employed categories, and show what is wrong with them. And we must propose some more usable alternatives. To illustrate these alternatives in this chapter, we shall confine our discussion almost wholly to painting and music, leaving to the reader the question how well these categories may be applied to sculpture and architecture.

---

[2] Compare Charles L. Stevenson, "On the 'Analysis' of a Work of Art," *Phil R,* LXVII (1958): 33-51.

An aesthetic object usually has certain obvious and emphatic features, its dominant patterns or qualities, that we are likely to notice first about it. These features may not be its best, for what we discover on closer inspection may be far more worthy of attention, but they stand out clearly and can be perceived without much effort or sensitivity. By an easy, though fallacious, transition of thought, these obvious features are sometimes inferred to be the ones the artist hit upon first, or set most store by, and in this way they come to be regarded as his main intention. The rest of the work is then considered to be subordinate, a mere means of carrying out that intention. Thus if you ask some critics what they look for when analyzing an aesthetic object, they reply that it is first essential to discover what in it is its *end*, or aim, and to distinguish that from its *means*, or execution.

Let us examine this puzzling pair of terms. They have important uses, of course; our question is whether they can serve as categories for critical analysis. "End" and "means" natively apply to processes in which we can discriminate different stages, one causally dependent upon another. Thus the end-means relation is temporal and asymmetrical, at least as far as a particular process is concerned: the hammering is a means of driving the nail, but not vice versa. Now suppose we pick up an object—a piece of sculpture by Lehmbruck, a pack of cigarettes, an old shoe. How do we decide which part of the object is the end, and which part the means?

This question clearly has something silly about it. And it would probably never get itself asked if it were not for the sliding nature of the end-means distinction, which leads to vagaries of usage in careless hands. In some cases it is perfectly clear that a critic is using the term "means" to refer to the activities of the artist before the work was completed—and then, of course, the work itself is all "end." In other cases it is clear that the critic is using the term "end" to refer to the effect upon the beholder —and then, of course, the work itself is all "means." In neither case do the terms mark a distinction *within* the work between an end-part and a means-part. But the notion persists that such a distinction can be made, and should be made.

Consider a typical statement: "In Rembrandt's drawing, *Girl Sleeping*, PLATE II, the end has been attained by very economical means." The writer does not go on to point out that Rembrandt, being hard up at the time, bought cheap materials, or made the drawing lying down to conserve his energy. He shows us the drawing as evidence and plainly thinks of his statement as confirmable by inspection of the drawing itself.

In all such cases as this, our method is to ask first what could sensibly be meant, and second whether it could be less misleadingly stated. And in the present case, the meaning is clear: the brush strokes that outline the girl's body and the folds of her garment are few and have a casual air, yet the body stands out with an amazing soft solidity, and there is a great deal of tenderness in the picture. The means, then, are the individual lines and shaded areas, and the end is the general character of the picture; and the critic is praising Rembrandt because the picture has that general character though the strokes are so few and so simple.

The oddness of this way of speaking can be brought out if we recall briefly one other feature of what might be called the normal uses of the end-means distinction. You need this distinction when you have alternative means to the same end, abstractly conceived. For example, if your end is getting to a certain city—and you are for the moment not interested in other related ends, such as cutting down expenses or saving time— then as far as this abstract end, getting to the city, is concerned, there is more than one means: you can take the train, or the bus, or a plane, or drive, or walk. If you now introduce a *second* end, say, cutting down expenses, you can compare all the means to the first end with respect to the second end: you can ask, for example, which is the most economical, that is, least expensive, means of getting to the city.

Now let us apply this to the Rembrandt drawing. Suppose we could find another drawing of a sleeping girl that has exactly these same qualities of solidity, softness, and tenderness, but in which there are many more lines, so that there are no large blank spaces as in this drawing. Then we could say that this is more economical than the other. But it is clear that we do not have alternative means to the same end, for without these blank spaces, without sparing strokes, the light in the picture would not fall so sharply upon the girl, and some of her solidity or softness would be lost. If the lines were different, if they were longer or shorter, or thicker or thinner, or there were more or fewer, then the general character of the whole drawing would be different. It makes no sense to say that the "means" were most economical when no less economical means would have achieved the *same* end.[1]

The terms "end" and "means" are so familiar in critical description that this succinct rejection of them may appear overhasty: I do not wish to be dogmatic here, and we could not clear up all the puzzles about these terms without a great deal more discussion. For example, there is a sense in which you might say that you have alternative means to an end in a painting. There are several ways of representing one figure as farther away than another: superposition, linear perspective, atmospheric perspective, etc. It is natural to say that these are different means of representing distance. And perhaps we need not always avoid these terms, so long as we make clear by the context what we mean, and refrain from

---

[1] The concept of economy, and its application to music, painting, and literature, is more fully discussed in M. C. Beardsley, "The Concept of Economy in Art," *JAAC*, XIV (March 1956): 370-75; see also the letter by Martin Steinmann and reply, XV (September 1956): 124-25.

hypostatizing them into basic categories, for that is what leads to unfortunate questions like: "How well do the artist's chosen means achieve his end?" We must not assume, in other words, that when an artist uses perspective he wants much depth or little, and praise or blame him because he got what he wanted or failed to. The degree of depth, and its own special quality, will depend on the way the color areas are related in the painting. Very likely there were ends and means in the artist's mind. Perhaps he wanted the depth and then found the right perceptual conditions; perhaps he wanted those conditions and was willing to accept the consequent depth. But this is of no moment to the perceiver, and need not govern his perception. The end-means terminology is a vestige of intentionalistic ways of speaking, and it is objectionable because it tends to foster notions about intention that cannot be verified and that draw us away from the work itself.

Other Misleading Idioms

A second pair of terms is also very common in critical writing, and a troublesome pair of terms it is: "what" and "how."[2] According to those who use these terms, the critical analyst is to discover in the aesthetic object first "what" was done, and second "how." The term "how" has, of course, two very different senses that must be disposed of first. We can ask: "What did he do?" He cut down the tree. "How (by what means)?" With an axe. In this sense, the how-what distinction is the same as the means-end distinction, and subject to all the distractions of the latter. But we can ask: "What did he do?" He swung the axe. "How (in what manner)?" Gracefully, smoothly, forcefully, skillfully.

The first thing to note about this second distinction is that it is thoroughly relative and arbitrary. Swinging an axe and chewing gum are two different actions. But when he swung the axe, the grace with which he swung it was not another action, it was the *same* action, only more specifically described. When you first ask *what* he did, you don't get a full description, but an abstract classification that might apply to many actions. For example, "He moved his arm." When you ask "How?" you are asking for more details about the *what:* "He moved it wood-choppingly, or baseball-throwingly"—in ordinary speech, we would say, "as though he were . . ." If you are still unsatisfied, you can ask "How (in what manner) did he chop the wood?" "Gracefully" describes the same action more precisely.

The distinction between "how" and "what," then, in its home-application, does not separate an action, and much less an object, into two parts, any more than it follows that if a man has three names each name

---

[2] In Chapter V we shall discuss these terms in their application to literary works, most sharply analyzed by A. C. Bradley in his lecture, "Poetry for Poetry's Sake"; see Note 14-A.

must name a separate part of him. The distinction is relative to a particular information-inquiring context, and it will not serve at all as a critical tool. Nor will other terms that are often introduced as close synonyms to "how," such as "treatment," "handling," and "technique."

Each of these familiar terms has so many uses and senses that it would be impossible to clear them up briefly. All we can do here is to notice some of the most important points, and illustrate a method for dealing with troublesome terms.

The word "treatment" is sometimes used to describe a relation between the aesthetic object and something else. When a critic speaks of Dvořák's "use" of folk music, or Titian's "use" of a composition by Giorgione, he may say, for example, "Titian has treated the composition differently." In this sense the term "treatment" has no function; it means, "Titian's composition is different in some respects." But the suggestion is that taking Titian's painting alone, you could distinguish the composition from the treatment of it—which you cannot do.

Consider these examples: "In the finale of Ernest Bloch's *Concerto Grosso*, the subject is *treated* by inversion and augmentation." "The *treatment* of space in Mannerist painting is different from that in the classic Renaissance period." They are fairly harmless, for they are easy to translate into other terms. The inversion of Bloch's melody is a melody in its own right; one is no more a "how" than the other, and if the second had come first, we would have called the other the "treatment." And we can just as well speak of the *space* in Mannerist painting, and drop the term "treatment." The trouble with "how" and its synonyms is that they are, again, intentionalistic. They suggest that the artist started with something, then did something to it, which may be true, but then they invite us to try to determine from the work itself what came first and what was done second. This task is impossible except in peculiar cases—when we can see that a line in a drawing has been almost erased, for example—and it is useless.

The term "technique" has a habit of skipping lightly back and forth from the aesthetic object to its physical basis. In the fine arts, it often refers to such things as the movements of the painter's hand, his method of applying pigment; in this sense, there is no such thing as a composer's technique, though there is a performer's technique. Where, on the other hand, "technique" refers to things that can be heard in the music itself, to certain kinds of dissonances or the relations between voices in counterpoint, then, in this sense, it will also refer to what can be seen in a painting—say, size, direction, or width of brush strokes, or thickness of paint. A critic can always take the trouble to make his context show what he is talking about when he uses the term "technique." The main objection to the term is that its use claims that there exists a distinction that has, in fact, never been made. Suppose you copied out a thousand descriptive statements about paintings and musical compositions; by what criteria could you decide which of them are to be classified as statements about technique instead of about something else?

There is one other widely used term that we should consider briefly here: "medium."[3] This term has so many different, and yet easily confused, senses, that it is now almost useless for serious and careful criticism. Even if we set aside all the senses that have nothing to do with aesthetic objects—the newspaper as a mass medium, air as a medium of transmission of sound, Mrs. Beauchamp as a spiritualistic medium, the United States mail as a medium of communication—we have still a bewildering variety of senses. The sense in which oil or tempera is a medium is not the sense in which words are a medium; neither is the sense in which line engraving is one medium and aquatint another; still different are the sense in which a newspaper—in a review of a concert by Duke Ellington's band and the Symphony of the Air—once referred to the jazz band and the symphony orchestra as two "musical mediums," and the sense in which a comedian was once described on the radio as "an outstanding success in every comic medium, including night clubs," and the sense in which Oscar Wilde said that Browning "used poetry as a medium for writing in prose."

It is not necessary for us to try to clear up all these distinctions, and rescue for the word "medium" some saving sense in which we might agree to use it. It would be easy enough to assign it a use, but that would not confer immunity to confusion. For in any likely sense it will still cling to a suggestion of its root meaning, the concept of a "means" or a "that by which." And moreover, in no likely sense will it mark a distinction that is of use to critical analysis.

I take it "This is a water color" is a statement about the medium. Then either the medium is not part of the painting at all, as an aesthetic object, but only its physical basis, or else the medium is simply a set of visible qualities—the thinness, flatness, transparency of the colors. There seems to be no useful way of dividing descriptions of aesthetic objects into those that refer to its medium and those that do not.

Elements and Complexes

We must now turn, therefore, to the question what *would* be a good set of categories for aesthetic analysis. It is clear that in so far as the disputable terms we have just discussed do refer to something verifiable about aesthetic objects, they refer to parts of those objects and their relations to one another. And it is the part-whole relation that we shall take as our basic category of analysis. In the remainder of this section, I shall lay out, rather abstractly, a small set of categories connected with the part-whole relation, leaving it to the next two sections to show that they are usable and useful.

---

[3] T. M. Greene has made much use of this term; see Note 6-B.

There can be no quarrel, I think, about the meaning of the relational term "part of" when it is applied to the visual field. In a reasonably clear and obvious sense, the figure of a nude, or a patch of pink, is a part of the whole painting. It is perhaps a little less familiar to speak of a note or a melody as part of a symphonic composition, though we usually say that an entire movement, or a section of a movement, is part of it. In these cases, so long as there are heterogeneities in the object, distinctions can be made within it, between a pink part and a blue part, or between a part in the key of D minor and a part in the key of F; and whatever we find between such points of distinction is a proper part of the whole.

Any part of a sensory field is then itself a *complex* if further parts can be discriminated within it. An absolutely homogeneous part of the field is partless, and such a partless part may be called an *element* of the field. Analysis stops with the elements. You can distinguish the light and dark parts on the surface of the moon, but if within a dark patch you can find no differences, then that patch is elementary.

Such an elementary part must have some qualities, otherwise we could not perceive it: its darkness, its shape. Let us call such qualities *local qualities*. The white area inside the "O" in the word "local" is an element of this printed page, and its whiteness is therefore a local quality. But some complexes have qualities that are not qualities of their elements: the word "local" has five letters, but none of its letters does. And some complexes have qualities that are not qualities of any of their complex parts: the preceding sentence has twenty-four words, but none of its phrases or clauses does. Let us call a property, or characteristic, that belongs to a complex but not to any of its parts a *regional property* of that complex. Notice then that your having weight is *not* a regional property, in this sense, because your parts—arms and legs, for example—also have weight; but your property of weighing 150 pounds, if you do, *is* a regional property, for none of your parts weighs that much.

Some regional properties can be perceived by the senses; some cannot. Your weighing 150 pounds is not directly perceivable—it has to be measured on a scale, or inferred in some other way—but your being heavy-set or thin *is* perceivable. In our descriptions of aesthetic objects we are interested in the perceivable properties, for which we shall reserve the word "qualities." Thus when I speak of the regional qualities of a complex, I mean its perceptual regional properties.

It may seem that we should make a further distinction between two sorts of regional property, which are sometimes called *summative* (or additive) and *emergent*. For example, if two one-pound weights are combined on a scale, the combination will have a weight of two pounds, which, by our definition, is a regional property, since it does not characterize either part by itself. But the weight of the whole is a simple arithmetical sum of the weights of the parts. On the other hand, the saltiness of sodium chloride that is not present in its separate elements, or the wetness of H_2O when neither hydrogen nor oxygen is wet by itself, is not describable as a sum; something new and different seems to emerge from the combination. Again, we might say that the brightness of a white light made up of two white lights is summative; the color of a light made up of two different colored lights is emergent.

Intuitively, this distinction seems defensible. But unfortunately no attempt to analyze it and define it in a general way has been quite successful. You can't say, for example, that the weight in the first case could be predicted from knowing the separate weights, whereas saltiness could not be predicted from the separate properties of sodium and chlorine. Actually, neither can be predicted merely from a knowledge of the parts, but both can be predicted once you have added the weights together and weighed the sums, and once you have combined sodium with chlorine. Perhaps the difference lies merely in the degree of surprisingness, and is not a fundamental difference at all. For example, if you have nine equal cubes you can fit them into a larger cube; there is nothing very remark-

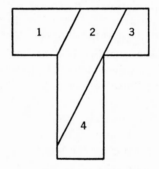

able in this. But though in the well-known puzzle the four pieces combine into a T, when you are presented with them separately this is not obvious.

In certain fields of science, emergence can be defined with reference to prevailing explanatory theories. Suppose there is an accepted theory, T, and a property, P, whose presence cannot be explained by T; then P is emergent with respect to T. But this distinction does not seem to be the one we are after in analyzing aesthetic objects. In any case, it is quite certain that if the distinction between summative and emergent properties is ever satisfactorily formulated, this will be done by rather complicated methods, and with the help of some technical symbolic apparatus.[4] Therefore, it will be convenient for us if we can say, as I think we can, that the distinction probably does not matter greatly for our purposes. What is important for discourse about art is that the regional qualities of a complex have two aspects: they have novelty, in that they are not to

---

[4] See especially the articles by Ernest Nagel, and E. H. Madden, and N. Rescher and P. Oppenheim, referred to in Note 6-C.

be found in the parts when separated, but they also depend upon the parts and their relations.

The categories that we now have on hand can be illustrated by a simple figure. Here are four small circles, lettered for convenience of reference.

Ⓐ   Ⓑ

Ⓒ   Ⓓ

The question is, what basically different types of thing can we *say* about this figure?

First, we can describe the elements: *A, B, C,* and *D* are circles; the background is white.

Second, assuming, for convenience, a geographical coordinate system, we can describe the relations between the elements: *A* is 1″ west of *B, C* is 1″ west of *D, A* is 1″ north of *C, B* is 1″ north of *D*. There are other relations we could describe, of course—for example, *A* is northwest of *D*. The first four, however, are sufficient, for once they are given, they determine the figure uniquely, and consequently all the other relations among its parts.

Third, we can describe the regional qualities of the figure as a whole: this figure has a squarish character. The squarishness is a regional quality because it belongs to the complex but not to any of its parts, and a complete description of the figure would have to include the statement that this quality is present.

Is there anything we have left out? We could describe the elements more precisely: they are outlined in thin black lines. We could enumerate more relations: circle *B* is $\sqrt{4\frac{1}{2}}''$ northeast of circle *C*. We could say more about the qualities of the whole: the figure has a certain amount of stability, but not very much tendency to hold together. But there seems to be no new *kind* of thing that ought to be part of the description: no matter how complicated we made the figure, the true statements describing it would fall into the same basic categories. There are statements about the number and local qualities of elements, about complexes and their regional qualities, about relations between elements or between complexes.

Regional Qualities and Perceptual Conditions

There are some points that should be noticed at once. A regional quality may be more or less *extensive,* that is, it may prevail over a larger or smaller portion of a sensory field. For example, we might make the figure and its circles larger or smaller, keeping the proportions the same. A regional quality may be more or less *intensive*. For example, we might insert more circles between the others to make the squarishness more pronounced,

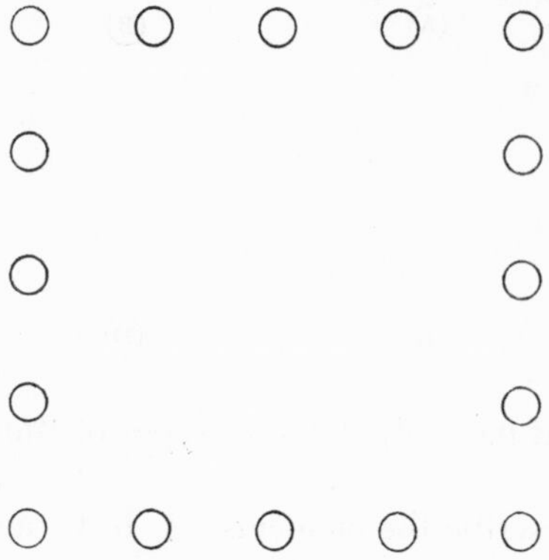

O   O   O   O   O

O   O

O   O

O   O

O   O   O   O   O

or on the other hand, we might increase the distances between the circles so that the squarishness becomes more and more indistinct until it disappears. A regional quality may be more or less *persistent* in time. That is, it may characterize an object, as above, or an event, or a series of events regarded as a whole in time. For example, it is not a single event on a stage, but a series of events that has a dramatic quality.

We are now in a position to introduce two other terms that will be useful in the remainder of this chapter, and later. When two elements or complexes, A and B, are both parts of a larger complex that has a relatively intense regional quality, then A and B seem to belong together in an important way. Without losing their individuality, they take on, if one may speak very metaphorically, a kind of awareness of each other; in that case, let us say they are perceptually joined. They do not merely accompany each other, but *fuse*. The four circles in our diagram, for example, take on this fusion, for each appears not just as a circle but as the corner-of-a-square-having-three-other-corners, though the fusion is less than, say, in the second figure, where each circle is even more apparently and decisively an element-in-a-row-that-forms-the-side-of-a-square-having-three-other-sides.

When the complex A-B has its own regional quality, it may be said to be a *whole*. It segregates itself for perception from its environment; it takes on individuality. Wholeness is another regional quality, which a complex may possess in various degrees, depending upon the intensity of the other regional qualities that bind its parts together; the second figure above, for example, has squarishness and stability to a higher degree than the first, and consequently it is, so to speak, more whole-ish. "Wholeness," like the names of all regional qualities, can only be ostensively defined, that is, the quality must be pointed out in examples.

It will be important for our future purposes—and it will be made clearer later on—that the existence of the regional quality of a complex depends upon the elements and their relations: they are the *perceptual conditions* of the quality. This is obvious enough in the diagram: it is because the four circles are placed in the relations they are in that the whole figure has its squarishness. If A had been southwest of B, B northwest of C, C northeast of D, and D southeast of A, then the figure would not have been squarish, but diamondish. But when we *say* that it is squarish, we are not talking about the relations between the parts; we are reporting on the consequent character of the whole. In other words, it is not a tautology, but a synthetic empirical statement, to say that the figure is squarish because of the spatial relations among A, B, C, and D.

Generally speaking, we may say two things about regional qualities and their perceptual conditions. First, if the perceptual conditions are altered, there will probably be some change in the total set of regional qualities, or in some one quality. But second, a given regional quality may persist through radical alterations of the conditions. It is possible for the same regional quality to turn up in very different perceptual conditions—as a kind of scowling look may appear on a human face or on the radiator grillwork of a car.

There are, then, two important confusions to be avoided. First, it is important to keep perceptual conditions distinct from what was in the previous chapter called the physical basis. The statement, "Normal eyes exposed to light having a frequency of 600 mμ or over will perceive red," is a statement about the relation between a sense quality and its physical basis. But the statement, "Alternating bands of highly saturated red and green will have a flickering, restless, uneasy quality," is a statement about the relation between a regional quality and its perceptual conditions. Second, statements about perceptual conditions of regional qualities do not imply anything about ends and means. A critic may say of the Rembrandt drawing, "Rembrandt put a dark area in the upper left-hand part of the drawing, but left a light edge next to the girl's dark hair, in order to bring the head forward in space." The objective content of this statement can be rendered in the form: "The spatial orientation of the figure, with the upper part advancing (a regional quality), depends in part upon the shading in the upper left-hand part of the drawing (a perceptual condition)."

For convenience in laying out the basic terms, I have used the simplest possible diagram. How far the terms so introduced are serviceable in talking about more complex visual figures, I shall try to show in the next section. Also for convenience I have begun with an example from the visual field; it is yet another question how far the same distinctions can be applied, in the same senses, to the auditory field.

It is customary to make a distinction between two classes of art: the "space arts" of painting, sculpture, architecture; and the "time arts" of music, poetry, drama, dance. Now we must surely be prepared to find that some things that are very important in painting do not occur at all in music, and vice versa, and all the way along we must be on guard against overfacile transfers from one art to another. But we must not overstress the difference, either, for there are two general reflections that make this difference less absolute than it may seem at first: On the one hand, just as it takes time to listen to a musical composition, so it takes time to see a painting; and though that seeing-a-painting process is not so fully controlled as musical audition, it has some of the same characteristics: contrast, and a cumulative intensity based upon the recall and synthesizing of earlier stages. On the other hand, though the early bars of the music, once past, cannot be gone back to, like a part of the painting, yet to one who knows the music well all its parts are available for contemplation and comparison, and the having of them helps to give significance to every part that is heard, the parts-to-come to the parts-gone-by, just as the parts-gone-by to the parts-to-come.

There is prima-facie evidence, then, that our basic categories of description can be fruitful for music as for visual art. But we shall have to consider more carefully whether there are musical elements, relations, complexes, regional qualities, fused complexes, wholes. This inquiry we shall resume in §8.

§7. THE ANALYSIS OF A VISUAL DESIGN

It is surprising that there is no single term in general use among students of the fine arts to refer to all such things as paintings, drawings, etchings, engravings, lithographs, photographs, and finger-paintings—but excluding sculpture and architecture. To talk about any of these without regard to the method by which it was produced, we shall have to invent a name; let us call it a *visual design.* And as a visual design, it belongs to the same class as frost on a window pane, cracks in a section of sidewalk, shadows on a wall, or the zebra's stripes. Visual designs are one kind of aesthetic object.

Not every part of one's visual field is, strictly speaking, a visual design. First it must be bounded or framed in some way, marked out for perception from its background, so that what is within its boundaries can constitute a limited picture-plane. If we arbitrarily think of a couple of square feet of sooty brick in the middle of a wall, for example, we don't have a bounded area. Second, a design must contain within itself some heterogeneity, some difference in color or—like the Jensen *Composition,* PLATE I—in light and dark. A blank sheet of paper is not a design.

Some would regard this definition of "visual design" as undesirably narrow, and would prefer to leave out the requirement that it contain some degree of heterogeneity. Does a clear blue sky, a single note on a French horn, or a whiff of perfume constitute an aesthetic object? To say so would trivialize the concept. There is, of course, the painting *White on White* (ca. 1918, Museum of Modern Art, New York) that Malevich, in his search for the essence of painting, finally arrived at in 1918, five years after he had declared that a black square on a white ground was that essence. But even that painting is heterogeneous, for the tilted white quadrilateral is faintly outlined, and is lighter than its background—which means that the background must appear as a light gray, so that the title is doubly ironic. A painter could hardly exhibit less—though he could do less work—by hanging up an empty frame on the wall, for the wall would probably have variations of quality, in which case the design within the frame would be more complex than *White on White*. This does not mean, of course, that the wall-area would be as good a painting, for it would lack the controlled contrast that is interesting in *White on White*.

Others would regard our definition as too broad, and would prefer to include a further requirement. A random scrawl, or a bagful of groceries spilled on the floor, is certainly not a design in one sense; not only because it was not in fact designed—which is true of a snowflake—but because it does not look as though it could be designed, or planned, or arranged. In short, it lacks order. The concept of order is one that we shall have occasion to consider in Chapter IV, §13; it, or some related concept, will evidently be important in saying what constitutes a *good* design. But at this stage, when our purpose is still purely descriptive, it is perhaps best to leave out any reference to this notion. Scrawled lines on a sheet of paper will be a design by our definition, because they are bounded—by the edges of the sheet—and heterogeneous—because of the contrast between the lines and the background.

What, then, are the parts of a visual design?[1] Not just any fragments that you might cut it into with a knife or scissors, but its actual parts, as perceived. Considered in one way, a visual design is a spread of elementary patches, which may be called *areas,* and its surface, the set of all its areas, is the *picture-plane.* This description is perfectly apt for paintings or prints in which the areas are sharply distinguished—the Jensen *Composition*, PLATE I, or even the Dürer woodcut of *The Last Supper*, PLATE VI, in which the individual lines can be clearly seen. It is more artificial for works in which there are continuous gradations of tone, so that one area merges into another—the Rouault lithographs in *Miserere et Guerre*, PLATE V, or Goya's *The Colossus*, PLATE VII. But even in the latter case the terminology is a convenient one for analysis, providing we keep its limitations in mind.

Two areas can differ from each other in *shape, size, position,* and *tone,* or color quality. "Size" means scale, not as measured by the ruler

---

[1] This question is raised and discussed by Rudolf Arnheim, *Art and Visual Perception*, Berkeley, Cal.: U. of California, 1954, pp. 53-64.

but as relative to the frame, or boundaries of the whole picture-plane. It is not the actual size, for example, of Max Beckmann's *Self-Portrait,* PLATE IV, that gives it its force and dominance, so much as the way it crowds and nearly bursts out of the frame; some of the humility and spiritual anguish in Rouault's picture of the sower, PLATE V, comes from the way the figure is folded so close to the side and top. On the other hand, the expanses in the background of Käthe Kollwitz's *Municipal Lodging,* PLATE III, help to give the group its isolation. Position is also relative to the boundaries of the picture-plane: it includes both the *location* of the area—the Rouault sower on the left, the Goya colossus in the upper right—and the *lie,* or orientation, of the area—the angle of Rembrandt's sleeping girl, PLATE II, or the horizontality of the table-covering in Dürer's woodcut. In Paul Klee's *Man on a Tight Rope,* FRONTISPIECE, the lines are nearly all slightly askew from the vertical or horizontal, and this is one of the most important things about them.[2]

Shape, size, and position are not merely respects in which areas can differ; they involve intrinsic relations in terms of which areas may be serially ordered. Positions are related to each other in that one is to the left of, to the right of, above, or below, another. One size is larger or smaller than another. And one shape is more or less regular than another. But shape, size, and position—and also, of course, color—are independent properties of areas: each can be varied, within limits, while the others are kept constant. Two concentric circles only slightly different in size may still have the same position, but if the larger circle is gradually expanded, it will come to crowd the picture-plane, and will no longer have the same position as the smaller one.

The Qualities of Color

Now consider two areas of the same shape and size and approximately the same position; they may still differ from each other in their tone. And this difference is complex, for there are several ways in which two tones can differ from each other: one may be lighter or darker, brighter or duller, heavier or less heavy, warmer or cooler, more or less forward (advancing or receding), gayer or less gay, and livelier or flatter in timbre (a silkish red rather than a woolish red). Other qualities that some investigators have claimed to discriminate—such as wildness and tameness—might be added to this list.

In the tone of a particular area we can distinguish, though not separate, a variety of qualities: it is yellow, light, bright, warm, advancing, and so on. But for the purpose of classifying and cataloguing tones, it is customary to select three of the ways in which they differ and treat

---

[2] It is interesting to compare this lithograph with Klee's remarks on the tightrope walker and the vertical dimension in his *Pedagogical Sketch Book,* trans. by Sibyl Peech, New York: Nierendorf Gallery, 1944, secs. 21-24.

these as the basic tonal dimensions. For it turns out that when each of these has been specified the tone and its relations to other tones is uniquely fixed, and all its other qualities are determined. These three basic dimensions are familiar. Two tones may differ in *hue*, as red differs from green, or garnet from maroon, claret, and crimson. Two tones of the same hue may differ in *lightness* or darkness, as one part of the wall differs from another where there is less light; this is sometimes called "value," sometimes "intensity," sometimes "brightness." Two tones of the same hue and lightness may differ in *saturation*, or color strength, as pastel shades from richer tones; this is sometimes called "hue-intensity," sometimes "chroma." Black and white and shades of gray are tones, but hueless, "achromatic," ones; in other words, they have zero saturation.

To *name* a tone in such a way that it will not be mistaken for another tone, it is only necessary to refer to the three basic dimensions, for a tone of a certain hue, lightness, and saturation will always have the same specific degree of warmth, advancingness, brightness, and so forth. But to *describe* the tone fully, you must mention these other characteristics. For they are no less "in" the tone than the basic ones. Hue, lightness, and saturation are convenient to select as basic for two reasons. First, they are among the most obvious color qualities to most people—though a painter may first notice, and be more conscious of, the warmth-coolness difference—and they are therefore relatively easy to discriminate, so that a comparison in terms of them is more likely to be accurate. Second, they are most directly correlated with the physical processes by which they are produced, and therefore most easily controlled. This correlation is not perfectly exact, for various reasons, but in general, if two gray circles, for example, appear on the same black background, to the same observer under normal conditions, the lighter circle will be the one that corresponds to the wave lengths of greater amplitude, as measured physically.

It is important to be clear about this point. For once the distinction between basic and dependent qualities is made, it is easy to think of a particular tone as constituted merely by its basic dimensions, and then to ask, "How did it acquire the dependent ones?" Thus, people ask why it is that we see orange as a warm color, or why blue has a receding character. Such questions seem to presuppose that there was a time when people saw orange as *not* warm, and blues that did not recede, and that somehow those colors later took on those qualities, so that the process of acquisition needs to be explained. There is no evidence, however, that there ever was such a time, and the question does not arise.

There is a second form of the same question that might seem more defensible. "Why do *we* see orange as a warm color?" might be completed as: "when the Chinese don't," or "when the people across the street don't." If there were variability in the perception of the warmth-coolness dimension, with no corresponding variability in the hue-lightness-saturation dimensions, we should then be justified in wondering why some people see orange as warm and some as cool. But again, the evidence does not appear to justify the question. It is true that the warmth of the tone, as compared with other tones, may not be as obvious at first glance as its yellowness, but its degree of saturation may not be obvious either. After a quick glance we might be able to report that it was yellow, without being able to report whether it was a green- or an orange-yellow, and hence whether it was cool or warm. But no one, I think, who stops to contemplate orange in full saturation, and who knows how to use the words "warm" and "cool" in this context, will report that orange is a cool color.

There are interesting psychological problems about the characteristics of color.[3] But some of the puzzles reflect only a misleading terminology. Instead of newly invented technical terms, we use terms like "warm," "exciting," "gay," to describe some of the dependent characteristics of color, and these terms are not clear or precise because the characteristics are rather elusive and hard to discriminate. Therefore some writers have called such characteristics "affective qualities" or "feeling qualities." But once we lose the distinction between the quality as phenomenally objective and our emotional response to it, other confusions are likely to ensue. The dependent qualities, phenomenally speaking, are no more subjective than the basic ones. The pink, for example, that contributes so much to the general liveliness and even uneasiness of Paul Klee's *Man on a Tight Rope*, FRONTISPIECE, cannot be divided—though it can be distinguished—into two sets of qualities, its basic tone and its vivacity or transparency. Any of these qualities is present in the picture in exactly the same sense as the rest.

There is a linguistic question about the six basic characteristics of areas, shape, size, position, hue, lightness, and saturation. In ordinary language, our color names and shape names are borrowed from familiar objects. Hence we get "flesh pink," "cherry red," "grass green,"—and also "doughnut-shaped," "tree-shaped," "wedge-shaped." Terms constructed like these, however handy, are prescientific, for they are not very exact, at least until we specify the standard of comparison: Whose flesh? Which tree? Now that a systematic nomenclature of color names has been supplied,[4] it is clear that if, for convenience, we speak of an area in a painting as "blood-red," this involves no necessary reference to blood as such, for we could name the color by its position on the color chart, which makes no mention of blood. Hence when we recognize an area as blood-red, this recognition does not commit us to the assertion that in some way it must represent or symbolize blood. There is no such system of shape names, but they, too, are similes; we shall revert to this point in Chapter VI, §16.

───────────
[3] See Charles Hartshorne and others, Note 7-A.
[4] See A. Maerz and M. Rea Paul, *A Dictionary of Color*, New York: McGraw, 1930, and *The Science of Color*, Optical Society of America, Committee on Colorimetry, New York: Crowell, 1953, ch. 9; see also references in Note 7-A.

Now that we have reviewed the primary terms for describing visual designs, it will be illuminating to consider the meaning of two other terms that are of considerable importance in fine-arts criticism: "line" and "mass." Though we cannot hope to be exhaustive in this account, the discussion will be useful in two ways: it will illustrate the problems that arise in trying to construct a clear vocabulary for describing visual designs, and the methods that are needed to solve those problems; it will also remind us of some important features of paintings that we shall need to bear in mind in the argument of the following chapters.

In the analysis of visual design, the word "line" can refer to any identifiable link between one position and another that establishes, in however slight a degree, a *path* between them. There are three types of visual line. (1) If an area is stretched in one dimension or narrowed in another, as the disproportion between length and width increases, it gradually takes on a line-like, or linear, character. Where this character is pronounced, we have something that is commonly called a line, but that we shall call a *line-area:* for example, the line you make when you sign your name in cursive. (2) Where there is a fairly sharp edge between one area and another, there is a *boundary-line:* for example, the edge of this page. (3) And where a number of small disconnected areas are so disposed in relation to each other that they form a row, the whole set of them takes on a linear character, and may be called a *broken line:* for example, the line-up of letters on a page of print. If we put down a single dot, and then quite close to it another, there appears not only the pair of dots, as a pair, but a slight linkage between them. If we now put more dots beside them, all in a row, each of the dots comes to appear more strongly as part of a whole including them all: the dots, in other words, fuse into a broken line that may possess many of the characteristics of line-areas.

The distinction between the types of line is made in terms of local conditions prevailing along the route of the line. And of course these conditions determine the *strength* of the line, that is, the intensity of its linearity. Some line-areas are thin or faint, others black and assertive; some boundary-lines are vague and soft, others sharp and clear; some broken lines are just barely perceivable as lines at all, while some are unmistakable and quite as strong as most line-areas. The strength of a line is dependent, then, upon various characteristics that may vary from locality to locality in a line: for example, its thickness (except in the case of boundary-lines), its contrast with the background, the closeness and similarity of the distinguishable areas in a broken line.

The characteristics of lines as lines are of infinite variety, but once more it is convenient to distinguish a small set of them as basic. In order to identify a line in a visual design it is only necessary to specify three things: its length (relative to the frame), its orientation (or slope, or posture) with respect to the frame (whether it is horizontal, vertical, or at an angle), and its curvature from place to place. Upon these three characteristics all the others are dependent. Thus, for example, slanted lines have a certain instability, while horizontal lines are quiet and peaceful. Other lines are jagged, wiry, billowy, droopy, or nervous.

It is these striking and unmistakable qualities of line that we come to know and value in the master draftsmen and painters: in a line etched by Rembrandt or engraved by Dürer, drawn by Picasso or Schongauer, painted by Rouault or Botticelli. They are part of what we may call the *significance* of line. A line is significant partly in so far as it functions representationally in conveying information about the properties of the figure it outlines, like the softness of Hendrickje, if it is she, in Rembrandt's drawing, PLATE II, the surface planes and recesses in Max Beckmann's *Self-Portrait,* PLATE IV, and the boniness of the figures in Daumier's *The Witnesses,* PLATE VIII. But it is also significant partly because it has strong regional qualities of its own—the tenderness of Rembrandt's brush strokes, the sharp bite of Beckmann's knife, the tortured rhythms of the lines in the Daumier—rather than being characterless, inane, uninteresting. We cannot of course find words in any language to capture exactly the qualities of a good line, but words like "steely," "soft," and "flowing," come naturally to our lips. And such words raise one of the apparent problems in the description of visual design.

As in the case of color, it has seemed to some people not only that the restlessness, sweepingness, boldness, or calmness of a line is *distinguishable* from its length, orientation, and curvature, but that the former qualities must have been superadded to the others, or have been acquired by the line in some different way from the way it acquired the latter qualities. Thus they have attempted to explain, by principles of "association" or the theory of "empathy,"[5] how lines came to be restless or calm. But again, we do not know that there is an acquisition to be explained. The facts are (1) that we use these metaphorical words to describe some of the characteristics of lines, (2) that the descriptions are intelligible and appropriate, and (3) that the metaphorical extension of these terms from human beings to lines does presume a similarity between the two—more is to be said about this in Chapter III, §10. But there is nothing surprising here. A line that changes its direction frequently is like an uneasy or unsettled mind, wavering between alternatives, or subject to contrary impulses; to call the line "restless" is to borrow the term on good collateral.

The general quality I describe as "billowiness" would be differently described by one who has had no experience of waves; or he might be at a loss to describe it at all. It does not follow that he cannot *perceive* that quality merely because he has never perceived the waves.

---

[5] For references see Note 7-D.

A line that turns upon itself so that its ends are fused, and is therefore endless, defines a *figure*, or what is often called a form. It may be a continuous, unbroken, line-area—that is, an outline—or a circular row of dots, or a group of sketchy line-areas that fuse into a broken line and make a triangle, a pitcher-shape, or an elephant-shape. Consider, for a moment, a square, each of whose sides is a line-area. It does not matter much whether you call this outline a single line, or say that it consists of four lines, one for each side. If we speak in the latter way, we shall want to say that when two lines—as any two sides—fuse together in such a way that they both become parts of a single figure, then they "go with" each other. Line X goes with line Y when they are parts of the same figure.

To explore this concept a little further, we may consider the *multiple relevance* of lines—a phenomenon much exploited in modern nonrepresentational painting, but one that also throws light upon principles that have always been important in painting. Suppose we draw a large goblet bulging at the top, and a small decanter bulging at the bottom, in such a way that the same line-area serves as the right-hand side of the goblet and as the left-hand side of the decanter. This line belongs to two distinct figures

at the same time, or, in other words, goes with two distinct sets of lines. It binds the two figures in a particularly intimate way, by guiding the eye from any point on the outline of either figure continuously to any point on the outline of the other. It is interesting to distinguish varying degrees of intimacy in the connection between two figures, depending upon the connections of their outlines. (1) The figures may be entirely separated, as in Italian primitive painting. (2) There may be a broken line that goes from one to another, as in a painting by Rubens or El Greco, where the line of one figure's leg or back will be picked up by the arm or side of another figure. (3) The same line may belong to both figures, as in the decanter-goblet example, or in paintings by Ozenfant, Gris, Braque, or Picasso in one period—see his *Seated Woman* (1927, Art Institute, Chicago). (4) There may be strong lines that cut across both figures, throwing their actual outlines into the background, so that in fact the figures are actually submerged and tend to lose their character as figures. This is the principle of camouflage.

Every area in the picture plane, simple or complex, stands out to a certain degree for attention, or makes its presence known, so to speak, in comparison with other areas. It has a degree of *dominance,* or subordination. This quality depends partly on its position within the picture plane— for the framing of any area automatically sets up a kind of field, in which certain positions, at or about the middle, are more dominating than others. But it also depends on what might be called the *visual density* of the area, its quality of impenetrability or of opacity. One area has more to it than another. The degree of visual density is a resultant of size, brightness and saturation of tone, contrast with the background, and other local qualities. We are still on the two-dimensional surface, not yet in the realm of three-dimensional objects. Even if a design is flat, or nearly so—like the Jensen *Composition,* PLATE I—its areas differ in visual density.

But it is almost impossible for a complex design to remain completely flat: some of the colors will thrust themselves before others; some of its shapes, on account of their stability or regularity, will push others into the background; the superposition of one figure upon another will create a differentiation and recession of planes; there may be modeling, or linear or atmospheric (aerial) perspective.

What emerges under such local conditions is a new regional quality— *depth.* The space of the picture takes on a third dimension, and becomes more than a picture-plane; it is a *picture-space.* It may appear as an indefinite space, going back without visible limit into the distance, or it may have a definite boundary, like the back walls of a room. In either case, the painting is now said to possess *visual volume,* and that volume consists partly of filled space—solid, or three-dimensional, mass—and, for the rest, of void—the mountain seen at a distance has nothing, visually speaking, in front of it. Mass is therefore a regional quality.

We are not yet, I think, necessarily in the realm of *representation,* though I have just referred to a represented object, a mountain. Even in paintings that would normally be called abstract or nonobjective there may be solid figures, related within the design by means of their mass and positions within the deep space. But of course when there is perspective, there is, in a stricter sense, representation; the depth is pictured, not merely presented as a regional quality. This is a fine point, and it involves a nice question about the best definition of "representation"—a question to which we shall return in Chapter VI, §16.

Lines and figures, when they have certain characteristics—certain shapes and orientations—take on a kind of directed instability. They ap-

pear to be moving, or to be about to move, or to be straining in a direction in which they could move. A row of arrows with their heads all pointing the same way has this characteristic to a high degree. A field of cows
all facing the same way has it to a lesser extent, but not because they are
cows and cows are known to be slow-moving; it results from the bluntness
of their shape, compared with the arrow's. A slanted shape has a falling
tendency whether it is part of a Modigliani woman or a Christ carrying
the cross.

This *implicit movement,* as we may call it, to distinguish it from the
actual movement of a car or train, is not a matter of imagination, but
something presented in the visual field. A series of such movements, each
of which leads to its successor, may complete a cycle within the picture-
space. Or the movements may be counteracting. In the Jensen *Composition,* PLATE I, the sharply left-slanted white shaft opposes, and indeed
strikes a very delicate balance with, the two less sharply right-slanted
shafts. In the Daumier *Witnesses,* PLATE VIII, the angle of the figures,
and the pointed wedges made by their knees, set up a strong rightward
movement that drives the attention to the open doorway, even without the
accusing finger—but this rightward movement is blocked by the vertical
lines of the doorway. This opposition of movements, or of movement and
obstacles to movement, sets up the quality of tension in a visual design.
Tension, then, is a regional quality of a design in which implicit movement is checked or counteracted. Many post-Cézanne paintings are organized around such a tension between the deep parts of the design and the
picture plane. André Derain's painting, *The Window on the Park* (1912,
Museum of Modern Art, New York), is a very clear example of this—the
window scene with its color and light is only just held back and in by the
room, with its drab colors and reversed perspectives, so that the design
pulsates with repressed energy.

§**8.**   *THE ANALYSIS OF A MUSICAL COMPOSITION*

From one point of view, a musical composition, or auditory design, is
a complex event, and its elements are smaller events, little—though sometimes momentous—changes that are occurring simultaneously and succes-
sively. For the purposes of critical analysis, these changes can be
described by their termini, for a change is always *from* something *to*
something—from loud to soft, from low to high, from sweet to harsh. The
termini of musical changes are sounds, and these we shall here regard as
the elements of music.

Sounds have many properties, all of which can be of musical significance, but like the properties of visual areas they are conveniently divided
into two groups: basic and dependent. Every sound has (1) a certain *dura-*

tion, that is, it lasts a certain length of time, (2) *intensity,* or degree of loudness and softness, (3) *timbre,* or quality—for example, shrillness, smoothness, scratchiness, hoarseness. Some sounds also have (4) *pitch,* that is, they are high or low; and these sounds are called *tones,* the rest *noises.* Silence may be defined as sound of zero intensity. Music consists of sounds, including noises and silences, for silence is present in music not only as a background against which it happens, but in its pregnant pauses, such as Haydn's—for example, in the first movement and minuet of his *C Minor Symphony (No. 95)*—and in the interstices of contrapuntal lines of melody, as in a madrigal of Weelkes.

Duration, intensity, timbre, and pitch are the basic qualities of tone, but tones also have dependent qualities: they differ in dullness and light-ness, as a thud differs from a squeak, in location in phenomenal space—the low tones seem to come from lower down—and in volume, for they may be described as thin, thick, heavy, confused, as taking up more or less of phenomenal space.

We may think of the totality of all audible tones as a four-dimen-sional array that contains within itself all the elements of all music. It is limited, first, by physiological and psychological conditions: the range of human hearing and the threshold of auditory discrimination. For ex-ample, a few composers, like Alois Haba, have divided the half-tone into three distinct pitches and have written music in this scale of thirty-six pitches to the octave, but to most of us a tone that is a sixth-tone lower than middle C does not sound like a distinct pitch, but like a flat C. But perhaps this may be remedied by training. The range of musical tones is limited also by social and technological factors: the variety of timbres available to a composer depends on the instruments that have been in-vented by his time. With ingenuity, of course, he may create new sounds, as when Stravinsky opened *The Rite of Spring* with a bassoon playing in an impossibly high register, or when Henry Cowell extorts novel sounds from the piano by doctoring the strings and then plucking or rubbing them—as in *Banshee.* If the R.C.A. Electronic Music Synthesizer, which is already remarkable, develops to the point where it can produce any conceivable sound without the use of musical instruments or performers, then musical sounds will be technologically limitless.

The four-dimensional array of musical tones, like the six-dimensional array of visual areas referred to in the preceding section, is ordered by the intrinsic relations among the tones themselves. Of any two different pitches, one must be higher than the other; similarly, tones can be ar-ranged in a serial order of loudness or of duration. As with color areas, it is these intrinsic relations that make it possible to combine musical tones into the larger structures that we are familiar with in music.

Visual areas and tones are different in this respect from smells and tastes. Smells and tastes can of course be classified in certain ways, and basic dimensions have been proposed for them analogous to the dimensions of color and sound. But we cannot, at least not yet, arrange them in series, and so we cannot work out constructive principles to make larger works out of them. We are told by Fanny Farmer[1] that "cooking may be as much a means of self-expression as any of the arts," but that only goes to show that there is more to art than self-expression.

Suppose you were trying to construct a scent-organ with keys by which perfume or brandy, or the aroma of new-mown hay or pumpkin pie could be wafted into the air. On what principle would you arrange the keys, as the keys of the piano are arranged by ascending pitch? How would you begin to look for systematic, repeatable, regular combinations that would be harmonious and enjoyable as complexes? No doubt there are vague principles of cooking appetizing meals, such as the ones Fanny Farmer recommends: include foods different in flavor, texture, shape, and color. Creamed fish, mashed potatoes, cauliflower, and vanilla pudding are a combination to put off a hungry diner, no matter how well cooked. And some smells are certainly more pleasing than others. But there does not seem to be enough order within these sensory fields to construct aesthetic objects with balance, climax, development, or pattern. This, and not the view that smell and taste are "lower senses" compared with sight and hearing, seems to explain the absence of taste-symphonies and smell-sonatas.

The Movement of Music

Not every random collection of sounds, however, is music—not even every collection of tones. Rain on the roof, coal going down a chute, an office full of typewriters, may become parts of a musical composition, but they do not make one. For they lack the essential quality of music, which is a special *auditory movement*.[2] This movement, or quasi-movement, is very difficult to talk about, but it is perfectly apparent to the attentive ear. Certain sounds or sound complexes seem to call for, or point toward, other sounds to come—they have what has been called a vector-quality. This is putting the point in phenomenally objective terms; the corresponding subjective statement would be that they arouse our expectations or anticipations of further developments, and make us care about those developments sufficiently so that we can be surprised, pleased, or disappointed by the later sounds. The series of sounds fuses into a single process, and exhibits direction and momentum.

Some degree of musical movement can be generated by very simple perceptual conditions, and we can, if we wish, adopt a very broad defini-

---

[1] *The Boston Cooking-School Cook Book*, Boston: Little, Brown, 1937, p. 3.

[2] Edmund Gurney, in his valuable book, *The Power of Sound*, London: Smith, Elder, 1880, pp. 165 ff., called it "Ideal Motion." One of the best descriptions is that of Grosvenor Cooper; see Note 8-A.

tion of "music." For example, a little Cheremis children's song[3] is sung entirely on one note, and uses only two values, eighth and quarter notes, but it is still a musical composition, however simple. Some sense of musical movement can be set up by a regular or rhythmic drum beat, and indeed many musicians would be willing to accept a definition of "music" that would make a drum solo a musical composition: music is rhythmic sound. It does not matter a great deal where we draw the line, but I think it convenient to include in the definition the requirement that there be at least some tones. This definition would have been objected to, no doubt, by the Italian Futurists of the First World War and early twenties, who wrote for purely percussive orchestras of "Bruiteurs," or noisemakers, and called their art "the art of noise." It would not rule out, however, such a work as Edgard Varèse's *Ionization,* which, though scored for percussion and sirens, does have some tones produced by piano and chimes.

In any case, we do not, I think, have musical movement in a high degree and in its purest form until we have *melody.* A melody is, no doubt, a series of tones, but not every series of tones is a melody. Consider two notes of different pitch; the pitch distance between them is called their *interval.* Now, suppose one is followed immediately by the other. Under certain conditions—that is, given certain local qualities of the notes and certain relations between them—they fuse together into a single line of movement. They are heard, not as two successive tones, but as something moving from one pitch to another—sinking, swooping, climbing, shooting up. We speak of a melody as rising or falling, but what is the "it" that rises or falls? Something comes into existence besides the tones themselves, and the latter become points of stability, or of acceleration, or of change of direction, within a continuous process. It is the same thing in "Swanee River" that steps gravely downward by seconds from E to D to C, jumps up a major third to E and goes down again, leaps an octave to the C above, dips a minor third to A, and rises to C again. This fusion into a single movement will not happen if the intervals are extremely large, or the time interval between the tones very great, or the timbres in violent contrast. Some contemporary composers, Webern for example, have made sequences of tones that are not melodies, in this sense, or not quite; they are still in motion, however.

When a series of tones becomes a melody it acquires some further regional qualities that are of the greatest importance in music. First, it acquires direction: it moves upward or downward or remains steady, grows louder or softer, and tends toward an implicit goal, even though the goal itself may be constantly changing. And second, it becomes a *whole,* in which the parts, without losing their identity, fuse together. The wholeness of the melody seems to depend upon two other regional qualities, cadence and contour.

---

[3] Quoted by Bruno Nettl, *Music in Primitive Culture,* Cambridge, Mass.: Harvard U., 1956, Example 8 at end of book.

Musical movement, from moment to moment, has always a certain
degree of propulsion. At one extreme, it presses forward urgently, insistently, straining against the tempo; it need not be fast, though speed
contributes to its thrust. At the other extreme, the movement tends to disappear; the music comes to a standstill, its energy seems at least momentarily exhausted, or, if it still moves, it moves only in a meandering and
hesitant manner, as if it has no clear idea where it is going or why. Let us
call these *degrees of musical drive*. Cadential quality is the lessening of
musical drive. The closes and half-closes that punctuate a musical composition are points of marked cadential quality. The contour of a melody is
its continuous curve of pitch and dynamic changes. It makes no difference
that there may be rests in the middle of the melody; the contour reaches
right over them, and embraces all the tones within the melody, making
them parts of a single whole. This regional quality is, indeed, the most
easily recognizable thing about a melody; sometimes when you cannot
quite recall a tune, you can remember that it went up and then down, or
got slower or louder.

When a melody consists of a series of melodies, each of which is itself
a whole, or almost a whole, because it is fairly detachable and has a firm
and memorable contour, then these subordinate melodies are its *clauses*,
or periods. "Au Clair de la Lune," for example, consists of two main
clauses, each of eight bars, but the first clause is itself made up of two
clauses that are exactly the same. A clause itself may consist of two or
more segments which have a lesser, but still noticeable, degree of wholeness: these are its *phrases*. Any group of two or more notes within a
phrase, if it is a fragment that has some character of its own and can be
recognized even in isolation as a part of the melody, is a *figure*, or motive. Thus in "Au Clair de la Lune," we have

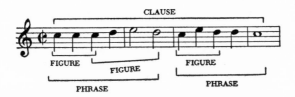

A figure is not a melody, but only an abstraction from one, and it
takes its character primarily from its context. For example, consider the
following familiar strain:

Here, by itself, it is a little phrase, but it is also a figure with which a remarkable number of melodies in different keys begin[4]—melodies of extremely different kinds, that would not even remind us of each other. But when a figure is taken from one melody and made a part of another in the course of the same composition, as in the development section of a movement in sonata form, it can carry with it a reminiscence of its former context, so that in its new one it may be surprising and dramatic. This aspect of melody, and related ones, we shall deal with more fully when we come to discuss musical form, in Chapter IV, §12.

The foregoing statements about melodic movement, necessarily brief and sketchy, will do quite well as a description of what is often found in our phenomenal fields when we listen to music, but a problem nevertheless lurks behind them. Suppose two people hear the same series of tones, and one reports that it is a melody, while the other reports that it is not. This is not merely a theoretical possibility; it happens both in the development of one person's aptitude, and even more strikingly in the history of music. When we consider Western music alone, from plainsong to Schönberg, we must conclude that the ability to hear a series of notes as fused into a melodic line depends not only upon the local qualities of tones and their relations to each other but upon the auditor's training and experience. Most of the original composers, Beethoven, Brahms, Wagner, Debussy, and Stravinsky, for example, have composed melodies that many of their contemporaries could not at first hear as melodies at all, but only as detached tones. They were not used to such large intervals, or to such long, unpunctuated phrases. And obviously we can make no safe prediction about what series of tones people of the future will be capable of hearing as melodies: perhaps even those odd electronic whinings, slithers, zings, and burps that are now used to accompany science fiction movies—for example, that excellent one named *Forbidden Planet*.

This variability in the perception of melody affects both contour and cadential quality. With respect to the former, it is a matter of being able to hear the melody as moving continuously through certain intervals. We have no trouble with melodies that rise an augmented fourth—the *Dragnet* theme; Jerome Kern's "All the Things You Are," at the word "winter"—or fall a seventh—the same Kern song, in several places, for example, at "I'll know." But these intervals seem like breakdowns in the process to those who are trained to follow only seconds, thirds, fourths, and fifths.

---

[4] For example: Bach's *Wachet Auf!* (*Cantata No. 140*); Bach's aria, "Ich esse mit Freude mein weniges Brot" (*Cantata No. 87*); Bach's "Et Resurrexit" (*B Minor Mass*); Beethoven's *Symphony in D Major* (*No. 2*), slow movement; the slow movement of Schubert's *Cello Sonata in A Minor*; the minuet of Mozart's Serenade, *Eine Kleine Nachtmusik*; the "Seguidille" from *Carmen*; the main theme from Strauss's *Death and Transfiguration*; the hymn "Lead, Kindly Light"; Humperdinck's *Hansel and Gretel* ("I know a little house in the forest green"); The "Merry Widow" Waltz; Lecuona's "Andalucia"; Dmitri Tiomkin's "Ballad of Frank Miller," from the movie *High Noon*; the South African song, "Brandy, Leave Me Alone."

With respect to cadence, the difference is quite as great. To one who is used to hearing melodies that end on the tonic tone, a melody that ends on the third or on the sixth—like some folk songs—will seem unfinished, and lacking in wholeness. And the same may be said about harmonic sequences.

The question is, then, whether "melody" does not have to be defined in a relative way: a series of notes is a melody at a certain stage in the history of music, or in a certain culture, if it can be heard as fusing together by people at that place or time who have had whatever training and experience is available. This is not an individual matter, for the word "can" makes the definition interpersonal. When Brahms' contemporaries complained that some of his series of notes were not melodies, they were mistaken, for others, and perhaps later they themselves, could hear them that way. It follows, of course, that we cannot be dogmatic about saying that certain series of notes will never be heard as melodies by anyone, though of course this may very well be true. However, the distinction between what is a melody and what is not is objective and discoverable within the context of a given musical period or the music of a given culture.

Rhythm and Tonality

A melody also exemplifies another fundamental characteristic of music, that is, rhythm. There can, of course, be rhythm without melody, but in music the important rhythms are for the most part derived from melody. For example, the rhythmic figure *a* is omnipresent in the first

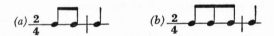

movement of Mozart's *G Minor Symphony* (*No. 40*); it is recalled as the rhythm of the first notes of the restless and insistent opening theme. The rhythmic figure *b* plays a similar role in the first movement of his *Piano Concerto in C Major* (K. 503), and, at a somewhat faster tempo, in the first movement of Beethoven's *C Minor Symphony*. These rhythmic figures are abstractions from melody.

The rhythmic aspect of music involves three distinct though related characteristics. The first is *pulse*. When sounds of any sort regularly recur, so that they divide the flow of time into nearly equal intervals, there is the impression of a continued serial order. This is pulse: for example, the dripping of a faucet. If the sounds are of markedly different degrees of loudness, however, even if they are of several degrees, they tend to sort themselves into two main classes, strong accents and weak accents. When a pulse consists of a regular recurrence of accented and unaccented beats, there is *meter:* the clackety-clack of the train wheels, for example. *Rhythm* is distinct from meter and pulse. When one or more unaccented beats group themselves in some relation to an accented beat, there is a rhythmic unit. It may be relatively weak in distinctness, or relatively strong; it may occur once, or be repeated. It may occur against a background of a pulse, or without it. The rhythmic figures from Mozart are examples.

When the pitches in a melody are fairly definite and stable, and it moves from pitch to pitch by regular and repeatable steps, certain intervals begin to appear as native to the melody; and if it returns often to a certain tone and gives it rhythmic emphasis, or dwells upon it, that tone will take on the character of being central to the melody, like a home base. It will become a tonic tone. There emerges that sense of a systematization of tones which we call scale. Some melodies, such as the songs of birds and human wailing and keening, are scaleless, or practically so, because the intervals are not fixed.[5] But musical melodies in Western civilization have nearly always been, in a broad sense, scalar. Oversimplifying somewhat a complicated matter, we may say that the scale of a melody is determined in somewhat the following way: list all the notes that it contains, in ascending order, beginning with the note that appears as the most final, has the greatest cadential quality. There is a little more to it than that, however, for scale comes to be a regional quality not only of single melodies, but of whole sets of melodies, and can be abstracted and can exist independently of any particular melody written in that scale. Thus one of the ecclesiastical modes, for example, or the major scale in Western music, is an infinite potentiality of different melodies. Even though a particular melody may not use all the notes of that scale, if it uses enough to sound in that scale, the other notes will be heard as in the background, and as part of the scale of that melody.

Certain kinds of scalar melodies take on a further characteristic: they sound as though they called for other tones to be sounded simultaneously with them. In other words, they imply a *harmony.* For the psychologist and music theorist the subject of harmony bristles with important technical problems—its nature, its correct analysis, its physical and psychological bases, but our present task is not to take up these problems. Harmony occurs whenever two or more tones are sounded together: the resulting chord fuses into a whole with a quality of its own. For example, the augmented fifth has a restless and expectant air, of which Puccini made memorable use in the famous theme from *Madame Butterfly:*

Puccini, *Madame Butterfly*

---

[5] But I am told that this is disputed in the case of the wood thrush's phrases and the ovenbird's nuptial song.

And there is a tenseness and wildness about the diminished seventh chord in which Bach, in the *St. Matthew Passion,* has the crowd scream out for the release of Barabbas. But perhaps not much of importance musically can be said about chord qualities in themselves; after all, Puccini's chord would not have much to it apart from the melodic phrase, which itself has a questioning and doubtful quality.

Once it was thought that chords could be divided into consonant and dissonant ones, but the development of music in the nineteenth and twentieth centuries put an end to that. Nevertheless, it is still a *relative* property of chords that one is more or less dissonant than another, and this appears to be a fairly fundamental musical fact. Every chord has some degree of stability or instability, from which progressions of chords take on a directionality simply as chords, quite apart from the directionality of melody. Thus a musical composition that contains no highly cadential chords, like the major triad, will still have to reach a *comparatively* cadential chord, in terms of the degree of dissonance that prevails within it, if its ending is to sound at all like a conclusion.

There is one more regional quality that we must touch upon, for it plays a fundamental role in a great deal of music. Suppose a certain scale is used in a number of melodies, so that it comes to be recognizable as distinguishing and defining that class of melodies; suppose its keynote, or tonic tone, takes on a high degree of finality, or cadential quality, in the melodies written in that scale; and suppose this finality is reinforced by the cadential quality of some favored highly stable chord that accompanies that tone, so that other chords are felt as tending toward, or pressing toward, that chord. Then a melody based upon such a scale and system of harmony will have *tonality.* It will have the air of being in a key, and this air will pervade and circumscribe and govern its flow, giving it a strong internal continuity and a kind of gravitational orientation in terms of which the direction of its movement becomes decisive and clear.

Tonality is a quality that, like a particular sort of weather, can be present in various degrees, and the degree will depend on various local and subordinate regional qualities of the melody. In "Pop Goes the Weasel" tonality is very strong, partly because the melody strikes the tonic or keynote on the first strong beat, and comes back to it at the end; partly because the harmony is clearly implied all the way through, and both beginning and end are in the tonic major chord; partly because the contour of the melody is such as to bring out clearly the importance of the tonic note:

But in, say, the first movements of Bartók's *Fourth String Quartet* or Ernest Bloch's *Third String Quartet,* tonality is almost lacking. Not quite—for in some passages there is a sense of being at least in some one of a limited group of keys. A melody may be ambiguous in tonality, like the famous opening bars of Beethoven's *D Minor Symphony,* in which it is not at first clear whether the key is A major, A minor, D major, or D minor. The "Danse Russe" theme in Stravinsky's *Petrouchka* is notated in C major,

Stravinsky, *Petrouchka*

but it has a strong air of being in the key of G, even though it is not in that key with perfect definiteness. If this theme contained an F natural moving to an E, it would go into the key of C; if it contained an F sharp moving to a G, it would go into the key of G; but it does neither.

It is possible to prevent tonality from emerging at all, or at least to prevent it from establishing itself. This possibility is exploited by the composers in the "twelve-tone" system, whose music is called atonal, meaning that it is lacking, not in tones, but in tonality—for example, Schönberg's *Third String Quartet* and Alban Berg's *Lyric Suite.* But there are some well-known passages in classical music where the tonality is temporarily destroyed, as in the slow passage before the finale of Mozart's *C Major ("Dissonant") Quartet* (K. 465), or the dramatic passage opening the development section in the finale of his *G Minor Symphony,* where the melody leaps about erratically for a few bars, using most of the twelve tones in the octave, almost as if it were a Schönberg twelve-tone row. If the melody avoids highly consonant intervals, like fourths and fifths, and if the various melodic lines are very independent of each other harmonically, and if no particular tones are permitted to assume special noteworthiness as tonal centers, then, even if at some points the music starts to settle into some key, that key is quickly dissipated by developments that are quite incompatible with it.

Modulation is the change from one tonality to another. In the modulatory passage, there is a sense that the tonality is weakening, and a moment when it seems suspended, but in classical modulations these moments of suspension are few, and even when the keys are changing fairly frequently, as in the course of a Mozart piano concerto, the music remains in each key long enough to get it established, and the transitions are smooth and decisive. Some modern composers have, however, developed a type of melody which itself modulates as it goes along. For example, consider the fugue theme that opens Hindemith's *Third String Quartet:*

FIRST MOVEMENT

Without being very insistent about any of them, this melody moves from C to D to A.

The purpose of this brief and selective review of some musical fundamentals is not to take the place of such introductory or technical treatments as are referred to below in the Notes and Queries. Like the review in the preceding section of some of the basic terms in fine arts criticism, it has had a few limited aims: (1) to recall some terms that will be useful when we come to discuss the form of music, in Chapter IV, §12; (2) to show how these terms may be fitted into the general scheme of categories proposed in §6, especially the distinction between regional qualities and their perceptual conditions; and (3) to exhibit, without claiming to resolve, some of the difficulties that arise in trying to describe even the most obvious and unmistakable features of music—for, as the references below will show, there are subtle puzzles that remain for the musician and musicologist even in such concepts as melody, rhythm, and tonality, though the technicality with which they can alone be fruitfully discussed has kept me from exploring them very fully here.

NOTES AND QUERIES

§6

6-A   MISLEADING IDIOMS.   Find examples of descriptions of aesthetic objects using such terms as "end," "means," "how," "manner," "treatment," "technique," and "handling." If possible, determine from the context, or from examples given, what part or aspect of the object is referred to in each case, and translate the description into less misleading terms. For example, "The idea of combining a whole family in one sculpture was a plausible one but it is not carried out very well," may mean, "The sculpture represents a family, but the design is not coherent."

6-B   "MEDIUM."   See T. M. Greene, *The Arts and the Art of Criticism*, Princeton, N.J.: Princeton U., 1940, Part I, esp. chs. 1, 2, 5. Compare Thomas Munro, *The Arts and Their Interrelations,* New York: Liberal Arts, 1949, ch. 7. Examine Greene's definition of the term "medium": note that he cannot apply it in the same sense to all the arts. Is his distinction between "primary raw material" and "primary medium" of any utility to the critic of music or the fine arts, considering that it is not a distinction *within* the aesthetic object, but outside of it? Consider his distinction between "primary raw material" and "secondary raw material," and the corresponding one between "primary medium" and "secondary medium": are they clear? Should not the "secondary raw material" be classified under what the object does rather than what it is?

6-C REGIONAL QUALITIES. For problems about identifying, describing, and classifying such qualities, see Kurt Koffka, "Problems in the Psychology of Art," *Art: A Bryn Mawr Symposium*, Bryn Mawr, Pa.: Bryn Mawr College, 1940, pp. 209-12; Koffka calls them "tertiary qualities," of which "physiognomic characters" are a subclass. Heinz Werner, *Comparative Psychology of Mental Development*, New York: Harper, 1940, pp. 67-103, distinguishes "physiognomic qualities" from "geometrical-technical qualities" (p. 69). Wolfgang Köhler, *Gestalt Psychology*, New York: Liveright, 1929, chs. 5, 6, uses the terms "*Ehrenfels*-quality" (p. 190), "supralocal" (p. 188), and "*Gestaltqualität*" (p. 192). On the meaning of "*Gestalt*," see Harry Helson, "The Psychology of *Gestalt*," *American Journal of Psychology*, XXXVI (1925): 342-70, 494-526, esp. 364-68; XXXVII (1926): 25-62, 189-223, esp. 201-14. C. D. Broad, *Examination of McTaggart's Philosophy*, Cambridge, Eng.: Cambridge U., 1933, Vol. I, pp. 268-69, reprinted in H. Feigl and W. Sellars, *Readings in Analytical Philosophy*, New York: Appleton-Century-Crofts, 1949, pp. 474-75, divides "collective properties" into "reducible" and "emergent" properties; the latter he expands in *The Mind and Its Place in Nature*, London: Routledge and Kegan Paul, 1925, pp. 59-67. For more technical discussions, see E. H. Madden, "The Philosophy of Science in Gestalt Theory," *Philosophy of Science*, XIX (1952): 228-38, reprinted in H. Feigl and M. Brodbeck, *Readings in the Philosophy of Science*, New York: Appleton-Century-Crofts, 1953, pp. 559-70; Ernest Nagel, "Wholes, Sums, and Organic Unities," *Philosophical Studies*, III (1952): 17-32; N. Rescher and P. Oppenheim, "Logical Analysis of Gestalt Concepts," *British Journal for the Philosophy of Science*, VI (August 1955): 89-106; Paul Henle, "The Status of Emergence," *J Phil*, XXXIX (1942): 486-93.

6-D FIELDS AND VECTORS. The concepts of field and vector are used in the description of aesthetic objects by Andrew Ushenko, *Dynamics of Art*, Bloomington, Ind.: Indiana U., 1953, ch. 2; how do these concepts differ from the ones in this chapter? Note Ushenko's basic categories: whatever in the sensory field is not at once perceived, but requires attention, is said to be "implicit" and to exist in a state of "power" or "potentiality," rather than actuality. Thus a row of dots is an "implicit" line; its linear character is "latent," not present to the senses but "reconstructed" by the "imagination," because drawing a line through the dots would make the linear character more explicit. To what extent does Ushenko's terminology reflect a different assumption about the facts of perception?

6-E DESCRIPTION. Give in your own words a detailed description of a painting or a musical composition, without any reference to its causes or effects, and without any mention of what it might "mean" or "represent." This exercise will help to make clear the difficulty of sheer description, and it will help you to think out the sorts of information that ought to be included.

§7

7-A COLOR. For discussions of the dimensions and qualities of color, see Arthur Pope, *The Language of Drawing and Painting,* Cambridge: Harvard U., 1949, chs. 1, 2, Appendices 1-3; Stephen C. Pepper, *Principles of Art Appreciation,* New York: Harcourt, Brace, 1949, ch. 8; Rudolf Arnheim, *Art and Visual Perception,* Berkeley: U. of California, 1954, ch. 7; David Katz, *The World of Color,* London: Routledge and Kegan Paul, 1935, esp. Part I; George H. Opdyke, *Art and Nature Appreciation,* New York: Macmillan, 1933, pp. 75-330; Committee on Colorimetry of the Optical Society of America, *The Science of Color,* New York: Crowell, 1953, ch. 2; Ralph M. Evans, *An Introduction to Color,* New York: Wiley, 1948, chs. 8, 10; Charles Hartshorne, *The Philosophy and Psychology of Sensation,* Chicago: U. of Chicago, 1934, sec. 13 (pp. 117-26); Robert M. Ogden, *The Psychology of Art,* New York: Scribner's, 1938, ch. 8; Albert R. Chandler, *Beauty and Human Nature,* New York: Appleton-Century, 1934, chs. 5, 6 (see also his bibliographies).

One of the chief problems here is about the relations between the basic and the dependent qualities of color. Note, for example, that *The Science of Color* regards the dependent qualities as modes of appearance of physical objects; Evans places the warm-cool quality under "emotional response to color" (p. 180); Hartshorne says, "The 'gaiety' of the yellow is its yellowness" (p. 123). See the excellent article by Jeanne Wacker, "Hartshorne and the Problem of the Immanence of Feeling in Art," *J Phil,* LIV (1957): 635-45.

See also Ivy G. Campbell-Fisher, "Aesthetics and the Logic of Sense," *Journal of General Psychology,* XLIII (1950): 245-73, esp. 258-66.

7-B LINE AND SHAPE. For discussions of the kinds of line and the qualities of lines and shapes, see Pepper, *op. cit.,* ch. 9; Arnheim, *op. cit.,* chs. 8, 9; James J. Gibson, *The Perception of the Physical World,* Boston: Houghton Mifflin, 1950, chs. 10, 11; Lois Bingham, *How to Look at Art: The Search for Line,* Washington: National Gallery of Art, 1946; Chandler, *op. cit.,* pp. 46-50; Opdyke, *op. cit.,* pp. 382-417, 467-77. Examine Pepper's distinction between "primary" and "secondary" characteristics of line, its legitimacy and utility. Collect and classify some important regional qualities of lines and shapes: for some interesting examples, see Leo Steinberg, "Month in Review," *Arts,* June 1956, pp. 42-45.

See Paul Klee's distinction between three kinds of line, *Pedagogical Sketch Book*, trans. by Sibyl Peech, New York: Nierendorf Gallery, 1944, secs. 1-5. His "passive" line corresponds to my "boundary line." His "active" line—a line that changes direction—and "medial" line—a line that encloses a space, such as the circumference of a circle—can be either line-areas (his examples) or broken lines.

7-C VISUAL MASS AND DEPTH. For discussions, see Pepper, *op. cit.*, chs. 10, 11; Arnheim, *op. cit.*, chs. 5, 6; Evans, *op. cit.*, ch. 9. On visual movement, see Ivy G. Campbell-Fisher, "Static and Dynamic Principles in Art," *Journal of General Psychology*, XLV (1951): 25-55.

7-D EMPATHY. For explanation and defense of the theory of empathy, see Herbert S. Langfeld, *The Aesthetic Attitude*, New York: Harcourt, Brace & Howe, 1920, chs. 5, 6, partly reprinted in Eliseo Vivas and Murray Krieger, eds., *The Problems of Aesthetics*, New York: Rinehart, 1953, pp. 315-25; Vernon Lee (Violet Paget), *The Beautiful*, Cambridge, Eng.: Cambridge U., 1913, chs. 8-11. Compare the criticisms by Kurt Koffka, "Problems in the Psychology of Art," *Art: A Bryn Mawr Symposium*, Bryn Mawr, Pa.: Bryn Mawr College, 1940, pp. 213-29. What is meant by "the merging of the perceptive activities of the subject in the qualities of the object"? What questions is the empathy-theorist trying to answer, and which of them make illegitimate assumptions?

7-E "VIRTUAL SPACE." Susanne Langer, *Feeling and Form*, New York: Scribner's, 1953, chs. 5, 6, argues that the essential nature of a visual design—she says of all "plastic art"—is that it is a construction and articulation of "virtual space." How does she think pictorial space differs from ordinary phenomenal space? Is she right? Note her use of the term "scene" (p. 86); when she says that a visual design is a "virtual scene," is she simply saying that a visual design is a bounded space that is internally complex?

§8

8-A THE DEFINITION OF MUSIC. See Grosvenor Cooper, "The Nature of Music," *Journal of General Education*, VII (1953): 176-82. On musical movement, see also Ivy G. Campbell-Fisher, "Static and Dynamic Principles in Art," *Journal of General Psychology*, XLV (1951): 25-55, esp. 49-53; George S. Dickinson, "Aesthetic Pace in Music," *JAAC*, XV (March 1957): 311-21. Compare the view of Susanne Langer, *Feeling and Form*, New York: Scribner's, 1953, chs. 7-9, that music is "virtual time." Is she talking about time itself or about *processes* in time? For example, consider her discussion of the difference between musical time and time in ordinary life.

8-B THE QUALITIES OF SOUND. See Albert R. Chandler, *Beauty and Human Nature*, New York: Appleton-Century, 1934, ch. 10; James L. Mursell, *The Psychology of Music*, New York: Norton, 1937, pp. 49-80; Carroll C. Pratt, *The Meaning of Music*, New York: McGraw-Hill, 1931, pp. 1-8, 28-62, 104-26; Robert M. Ogden, *Hearing*, New York: Harcourt, Brace, 1924, chs. 3, 5, 6; Edmund Gurney, *The Power of Sound,* London: Smith, Elder, 1880, ch. 12; Charles Hartshorne, *The Philosophy and Psychology of Sensation*, Chicago: Chicago U., 1934, Appendix B.

8-C THE AESTHETICS OF SMELL, TASTE, AND TOUCH. Are smells and tastes and tactile sensations so lacking in intrinsic order that they cannot be regarded as materials for aesthetic objects? Would you argue that a meal can be a work of art? Besides the argument from the lack of order, there are two other lines of argument that these senses are aesthetically unsuitable: (1) The lower senses are utilitarian in function, and strongly connected with self-preservation, so that they do not lend themselves to detached contemplation as colors and sounds do. (2) Reactions to the data—preferences in tastes and smells—vary so greatly from person to person, and change so much over a period of time, that no stable objects of enjoyment can be constructed of them. Are these convincing arguments? Remember that an expert tea-taster can discriminate as many as 1500 kinds of leaf. See David W. Prall, *Aesthetic Judgment*, New York: Crowell, 1929, pp. 57-75, reprinted in Eliseo Vivas and Murray Krieger, *The Problems of Aesthetics*, New York: Rinehart, 1953, pp. 182-93; Edmund Gurney, *op. cit.*, chs. 1, 2, and pp. 48-49, 243-44; Thomas Munro, *The Arts and Their Interrelations*, New York: Liberal Arts, 1949, pp. 136-39; Hartshorne, *op. cit.*, sec. 36; Frank A. Geldard, *The Human Senses*, New York: Wiley, 1953, chs. 14, 15.

Sidney Zink, "Esthetic Contemplation and Its Distinction from Sense Pleasure," *J Phil*, XXXIX (1942): 701-11, argues that "aesthetic pleasure" should be defined as pleasure derived from the contemplation of relations, so that the pleasure taken in single colors or tones or smells, etc., is not aesthetic. His argument is discussed by C. J. Ducasse, "Esthetic Contemplation and Sense Pleasure: A Reply," and Carl Thurston, "Is Our Pleasure in Single Colors Esthetic?" *J Phil*, XL (1943): 156-59, 320-23.

The problem whether it is possible to construct orders of sense qualities, even of hues, in which each distinct quality is assigned a unique position in virtue of its relations to other qualities, is discussed by Nelson Goodman, *The Structure of Appearance*, Cambridge: Harvard U., 1951, Part III; W. C. Clement, "Quality Orders," *Mind*, N.S., LXV (1956): 185-99; see also Goodman's note, *ibid.*, LXVI (1957): 78.

8-D MELODY. There is an excellent discussion of melody in Leonard B. Meyer, *Emotion and Meaning in Music*, Chicago: Chicago U., 1956, pp. 92-102. We shall consider the general theories of this important book in Chapter IV. See also Robert Erickson, *The Structure of Music*, New York: Noonday, 1955, pp. 3-69; Donald F. Tovey, "Melody," *Encyclopaedia Britannica*, 14th ed., Chicago: U. of Chicago, 1929, reprinted in *The Forms of Music*, New York: Meridian, 1956; Aaron Copland, *What to Listen For in Music*, New York: Mentor, 1953, ch. 5; Gurney, *op. cit.*, ch. 9; Douglas Moore, *Listening to Music*, rev. ed., New York: Norton, 1937, ch. 5; Ebenezer Prout, *Musical Form*, 4th ed., London: Augener, 1893, chs. 1-8; Chandler, *op. cit.*, pp. 180-84; Mursell, *op. cit.*, pp. 99-107.

8-E RHYTHM. There is an excellent discussion of rhythm in Leonard B. Meyer, *op. cit.*, pp. 102-27, to which I am especially indebted. See also Donald F. Tovey, "Rhythm," *op. cit.*; Copland, *op. cit.*, ch. 4; Chandler, *op. cit.*, pp. 193-96; Robert M. Ogden, *The Psychology of Art*, New York: Scribner's, 1938, ch. 4, sec. 19; Mursell, *op. cit.*, chs. 4, 5; Gurney, *op. cit.*, pp. 127-39, Appendix B; Douglas Moore, *op. cit.*, ch. 4; Matyas Seiber, "Rhythmic Freedom in Jazz?" *Music Review*, VI (1945): 30-41, 89-94, 160-71; Curt Sachs, "Rhythm and Tempo," *Musical Quarterly*, XXXVIII (July 1952): 384-98.

The term "polyrhythm" sometimes covers two things that ought to be differentiated. (1) There is *change of meter*, from one bar to the next, or within the bar. In the first minuet of Mozart's *Divertimento in E Flat Major for String Trio* (K. 563), the three instruments play in duple time for the first two bars, though the signature is 3/4; in the third bar the minuet tempo is established. Striking examples are also Beethoven's shift from a four-bar to a three-bar swing in the scherzo of the *D Minor Symphony* (*No. 9*), and the displacement of accent in the presto (Bar 109) of his *String Quartet in C Sharp Minor* (*Op. 131*). In the trio of the scherzo of his *Fifth String Quartet* (1934), Bartók uses a 10/8 tempo, in which the eighth notes are grouped sometimes 3 + 2 + 2 + 3 and sometimes 2 + 3 + 3 + 2; Beethoven, again, does something of the sort with the 9/4 tempo in the sixth variation of the fourth movement of the *C Sharp Minor Quartet*. (2) But in the minuet in Mozart's *G Minor Symphony*, though the melody is partly in duple time, the accompaniment keeps up the triple time, and the harmony changes at the beginning of the bars, so that there is a clear contrast of simultaneous meters, of which one is perhaps more fundamental. This is syncopation, which we are sufficiently used to in compositions like "Twelfth Street Rag" and "I Can't Give You Anything but Love, Baby." It may also be called "polymeter," though this term is perhaps most appropriate where the two meters are nearly equal in stress.

8-F SCALE, HARMONY, TONALITY. See Erickson, *op. cit.*, pp. 71-107; Donald F. Tovey, article "Harmony," *op. cit.*; Copland, *op. cit.*, ch. 6; Chandler, *op. cit.*, 184-93; Ogden, *Psychology of Art*, chs. 3, 4, secs. 16-18, 20; Ogden, *Hearing*, chs. 7, 8, 10; Mursell, *op. cit.*, pp. 81-148;

Pratt, *op. cit.*, pp. 62-71; Gurney, *op. cit.*, pp. 139-49, ch. 11, Appendix
C; Moore, *op. cit.*, chs. 6, 8; John Myhill, "Musical Theory and Musi-
cal Practice," *JAAC*, XIV (December 1955): 191-200; Mark Brunswick,
"Tonality and Perspective," *Musical Quarterly*, XXIX (1943): 426-37;
Donald F. Tovey, "Tonality [in Schubert]," in the Schubert issue of
Music and Letters, IX (1928): 341-63, reprinted in *The Main Stream of
Music*, New York: Oxford U., 1949, pp. 134-59; C. Hubert H. Parry, *The
Evolution of the Art of Music*, ed. by H. C. Colles, New York: Appleton,
1941, chs. 2, 15; Igor Stravinsky, *Poetics of Music*, Cambridge: Harvard
U., 1947 (reprinted New York: Vintage, 1956), ch. 2.

On "atonal" music, see: Richard S. Hill, "Schönberg's Tone-Rows
and the Tonal System of the Future," *Musical Quarterly*, XXII (January
1936): 14-37; George Perle, "Evolution of the Tone-Row: The Twelve-
Tone Modal System," *Music Review*, II (1941): 273-87; William Hyman-
son, "Schönberg's String Trio (1946)," *Music Review*, XI (1950): 184-94.

The tonality situation in present-day music, and the probable and
desirable directions of future development, are discussed profoundly in
Joseph Yasser's remarkable book, *A Theory of Evolving Tonality*, New
York: American Library of Musicology, 1932. Yasser has presented the
most searching and elaborate explanation of recent developments in
scales, such as the whole-tone scale, the twelve-tone system, and various
subdivisions of the semitone, and pointed out what is significant and what
is mistaken about them.

· III ·

THE
LITERARY
WORK

What is a literary work? Like most questions of the what-is-it form, this question may reflect several different, though overlapping, concerns.

For example, we may want to know what it is that the literary artist creates, what sort of entity is the product of his labor. We have seen that the painter creates a visual design, and the composer an auditory design; what sort of design is it that the writer creates? Or we may want to know what the basic constituents of literary works are. If we say that a visual design, in the last analysis, consists of color areas, and a musical composition of sounds or of movements from one sound to another, what are the elements of literature? Or we may want to know how literary works are to be marked out from other things in the world that resemble them in some ways: from newspaper advertisements, scientific treatises, and medicine-bottle labels. What is the general definition of "literary work"?

Suppose we should find, in a review of a recent novel, the following statements:

1. It is tragic.
2. It is complex.
3. It contains a good deal of sharp nature imagery.
4. It has three main characters.

5. It has thirteen chapters.
6. It takes place in Trinidad and Tobago.
7. It is written in Portuguese.

These could all be true. Moreover, they are descriptive statements; they do not interpret. But though they are all statements about the novel, they are not all of the same order; in fact, they seem to be about two rather different kinds of thing.

To the question, What does the writer create? we can give this answer: he creates characters, that is, he conceives of people who are given to acting in certain ways; he invents settings for their actions; he constructs plots, or sequences of actions. He makes, or *makes up*, Raskolnikov, Mrs. Micawber, the Forsyte family; Erewhon, Zenith, the island of Circe; the marriage of Figaro, the fall of the House of Usher, the case of the Speckled Band. From this point of view, the literary work is a set of human actions, imagined or conceived. Actions involve actors and settings; this totality of persons, places, and things I shall call the *world of the work*. It is this entity to which Statements 1, 4, and 6 apply; and so can Statement 2.

But we can also give another answer to the question. The writer puts words together in a new order; he constructs phrases and sentences and paragraphs; he writes chapters and verses. From this point of view, the literary work is a verbal design, or *discourse*—an intelligible string of words. It is to this entity that Statements 3, 5, and 7 apply; and so can Statement 2.

About the world of the work we shall have to say more in Chapter V, §15. Since it exists as what is meant, or projected, by the words, the words are the things to consider first. And in this chapter we shall approach the literary work as a discourse, or design of words.

§9. THE LANGUAGE OF LITERATURE

Since a literary work is a discourse, its parts are segments of language: a sentence is a part of a paragraph, a word of a sentence. Not that the relation of sentence to paragraph is the same as the relation of word to sentence, but *being a part of* is common to both relations.

When we ask what the ultimate parts, or elements, of literature are, we can give a variety of defensible answers, and must choose between them with reference to the purpose we have now in mind, that is, the purpose of the critical analysis. We could say that it is the sentence that is the smallest complete unit of discourse, and parts smaller than sentences are to be defined and understood in relation to actual or possible sentences. Or, we could say that the elements are the minimal particles of meaningful language, the roots and affixes that make up words: "un-law-ful" contains three of these particles. It is more convenient, however, to count as our elements something between sentences and particles, namely *words*. A word is, roughly, a unit of language such that any division of it will produce some part that cannot stand alone, at least not without a change of meaning: "law" can stand alone, but "un" and "ful" cannot.[1] This definition is imperfect, but fortunately it need not be refined here. A more pressing task confronts us.

Since they are meaningful sounds, words present two aspects for study. Later on, in Chapter V, §14, we shall discuss the sound-aspect of words; it is their meaning-aspect that we must consider now. Though a good deal of interesting and helpful work has been done on the problem of meaning in recent years, there are still many unanswered questions. To review in detail the present state of the problem would involve us in issues from which we could extricate ourselves only with considerable difficulty. We shall have to be contented with a general framework of distinctions that are well established and important to the literary critic.[2]

Import and Purport

Under certain conditions, a piece of voluntary human behavior—a gesture, grunt, or cry—acquires the tendency to affect perceivers in some fairly definite way, and this capacity may be called the *import* of that behavior. Since we shall be concerned only with linguistic behavior— spoken sounds, or written marks that stand for such sounds—we can limit the scope of our definitions. A linguistic expression has import *for* a certain group of people, namely those who have been prepared by previous experience to respond to the utterance, spoken or written, of that linguistic expression.

Two basic types of import are to be distinguished. On one hand the linguistic expression may have a tendency to cause certain beliefs about the speaker; it may be so connected with particular mental states that its utterance permits the hearer to make an inference about what is going on in the speaker's mind. This capacity I shall call the *cognitive import* of the linguistic expression—or, for short, its *purport*. For example, when an English-speaking person says "Ouch!" we infer that he has felt a sharp pain. Of course the inference is sometimes not correct: the speaker may be only pretending. But in general the inference will be made and will be correct. The speaker doesn't necessarily intend to communicate information about himself when he says "Ouch!" He is merely giving vent to his feelings. But his exclamation does convey information, and therefore has a purport.

[1] See Edward Sapir, *Language*, New York: Harcourt, Brace, 1921 (reprinted New York: Harvest, 1956), chs. 1, 2.

[2] In this account of meaning I draw heavily, despite some differences in terminology, upon Charles L. Stevenson's *Ethics and Language;* see Note 9-A at end of chapter.

On the other hand, the linguistic expression may have a tendency to evoke certain feelings or emotions in the hearer. This capacity I shall call its *emotive import*. For example, among a certain group of people, an Anglo-Saxon four-letter word may tend to arouse a feeling of horrified shock or disgust; certain sentences about Home, Mother, or Alma Mater may tend to arouse a warm glow of affection.

Since the purport of a linguistic expression is its capacity to evoke a certain belief in the hearer, we can make a further distinction. The utterance of that linguistic expression may lead the hearer to believe something about the *beliefs* of the speaker; or it may lead the hearer to believe something about the *feelings*, or emotions, of the speaker. Thus, when A says "Alas!" this has a tendency to make B think that A feels sad. But when A says, "It's growing dark," this has a tendency to make B think that A believes it is growing dark. When a linguistic expression affects the hearer's beliefs about the beliefs of the speaker, I shall say that it has *cognitive purport,* which I take to be the same as *meaning*. A sentence's meaning is thus part of its purport, but it does not exhaust it. For, in the first place, it may also affect the hearer's beliefs about the speaker's *feelings*—"Oh, dear, what can the matter be? Johnny's so long at the fair"—and this I shall call its *emotive purport*. And, in the second place, it may affect the hearer's beliefs about other characteristics of the speaker, his nationality, social class, religious affiliations, state, status, or condition, and this I shall call its *general purport*. For example, if you use a technical term of sailing, speleology, herpetology, polo, witch-doctoring, or electronics, your mere use of this term, apart from what you say, will give information about you. And under the same heading we may place the informativeness of upper and lower class speech habits, colloquialisms native to one or another section of the country, and even the clichés that get to be the stereotyped responses of people with certain social or political attitudes—"Operation Rathole"—though most of these are also heavily charged with emotive purport.

Now, of course, when someone says, "It's raining," we do not take this to mean merely that he *believes* it is raining. It means that it *is* raining; it refers, truly or falsely, to something going on in the world outside the speaker's mind. This referential capacity of sentences—their semantical aspect—is by no means completely understood. I think we can say, however, that it is based upon, and in the last analysis explainable in terms of, the capacity of a sentence to formulate beliefs. When we hear the sentence spoken, we may not think of the speaker at all, but only of the rain, and of course we can understand the sentence perfectly well even if we happen to know that the speaker does not believe what he is saying. But to understand the sentence is to know what beliefs it *could* formulate. And this is the same as knowing what it would be like to believe it ourselves: what we would expect to see if we looked out the window, or feel if we went out without a hat. Hence, after we learn the meaning of a sentence, we can speak of its meaning as independent of what any particular speaker does with it.

It will, I think, be helpful at this point to draw up a table of these distinctions, so their relations will be perspicuous:

Import: capacity to affect the hearer.

Cognitive import = purport: capacity to affect the hearer's beliefs (i.e., to convey information).

Emotive import: capacity to affect the hearer's feelings.

Cognitive purport = meaning: capacity to convey information about the speaker's beliefs.

Emotive purport: capacity to convey information about the speaker's feelings.

General purport: capacity to convey information about other characteristics of the speaker.

The meaning of a linguistic expression, then, is its capacity to formulate, to give evidence of, beliefs. But we must make still another distinction for this scheme to serve our needs. Normally it is declarative sentences that formulate beliefs; this is their primary role, as when someone says, with earnestness, "The stock market is basically sound." Other kinds of sentence, whose primary role is different, can also be informative; when the broker says, "Hold off before buying stocks," although this is an imperative, it lets us know something about his probable beliefs.

But both of these examples are sentences, and it is not only sentences that have meaning, but words and phrases. Perhaps not *all* words; for example, "is" and "the" do not have meaning by themselves, but they are indispensable parts of linguistic expressions—"God is" and "the man in the moon"—that do have meaning. Now, if I suddenly say "moon," just by itself, I cannot ordinarily affect people's beliefs about my beliefs, though I might affect their beliefs about my sanity. In what sense, then, can we say that "moon" has a meaning? Only in a derivative sense; to say that "moon" has a meaning is to say that it can appear as a functional part of linguistic expressions—e.g., "Jupiter has nine moons"—that do have a meaning. To say that "lorph" has no meaning in English is to say that there is no sentence in English that contains it. In more familiar terms, "moon" has meaning in that it tends to call up an "idea" in the mind of one who knows the language. But this idea is not necessarily an image. You can understand the word "moon" even when it does not occur in a sentence, but you don't understand it unless your beliefs can be affected by some sentence in which it occurs.

Bearing in mind these general remarks about meaning, we can now inquire, more specifically, into the nature of literature. It would be convenient if we could find criteria to distinguish literary discourses from all other discourses—criteria which would then afford us a definition of "literature." The central question of this section is whether literature can be identified by its language, by the way language is used in literature as opposed to nonliterary discourses.

It is not universally conceded that this attempt can be carried through; perhaps we cannot even define "poetry." Literary theorists do often speak of the "language of poetry," implying that "poetry" can be defined as discourse written in a certain kind of language. In some periods of English poetry this was not very difficult; a poem could be recognized by its poetic diction: it said "finny tribes" or "scaly breed" instead of "fish," and "fleecy flocks" instead of "sheep." But we are used to poems with fish in them, alive and dead, plain and fancy, sensuous and symbolic—such poems as Yeats' "Sailing to Byzantium," in which

> The salmon-falls, the mackerel-crowded seas,
> Fish, flesh, or fowl, commend all summer long
> Whatever is begotten, born, and dies.[3]

The old criterion no longer suffices. Nevertheless, we ordinarily speak as though we can distinguish poems from other things.

Even if there is a good definition of "poetry," there may be no good definition of "literature": perhaps when we call a poem a literary work we have a different sense in mind from that required for calling a novel a literary work, because different distinctions are involved. Even so, it would be clarifying to see how close we could come to ordinary uses of the term "literary work" by a definition, and for some purposes it might be worthwhile to abandon the ordinary uses in favor of a better one.

Literature and Emotive Language

The attempts to define "literature" by its language are of two types: those that hinge on the emotive aspect of language, and those that are stated entirely in terms of meaning.

The first type of definition is very neat—in fact, too neat to be acceptable. But it raises some fundamental questions, and calls for careful discussion. It would usually, I think, be offered as a definition of "poetry," rather than "literature" in general, so we shall consider it in this narrower form. Even in this form it is not very plausible, but it has to be considered, for it represents a point of view familiar and frequent enough among those who have thought a little, but not a great deal, about poetry.

The general formula for an emotive definition of "poetry" is: "Poetry

---

[3] From "Sailing to Byzantium," William Butler Yeats, *Collected Poems.* Copyright 1951 and reprinted with the permission of The Macmillan Company.

is emotive language." And emotive language is further explained as language that has *independent emotive meaning*. The term "emotive meaning" is one that I plan to do without in this discussion; it is precisely when we search about among the distinctions just made for suitable substitutes for this term that we become aware of the confusions it sometimes fosters and hides. Making a vertical cut in our table of tendencies, above, we can distinguish the cognitive force of words, including cognitive import and cognitive purport, and the emotive force of words, including emotive import and emotive purport. Now a very fundamental and far-reaching question arises about the relation between the emotive force of words and their cognitive force, and especially about the extent to which the former is dependent upon the latter. The Independence Theory of this relation is that there is emotive force that is not causally dependent upon cognitive force.

But stated in this broad form, of course, the Independence Theory is hardly discussible; it needs to be broken down in terms of the relevant cross-relations that can be found in a table of imports and purports. There are two Independence Theories, completely distinct from each other; and the questions to which they lead should certainly be dealt with separately. But before we tackle these questions, the notion of Independence is itself in need of clarification. For present purposes, there are two points to be noted. Given any two things, X and Y, we may say that X is independent of Y if (a) X can occur without Y, or (b) X can change without Y's changing. Thus the Bulgarian representatives at the United Nations are independent of the Soviet representatives whenever (a) they vote but the Soviets don't, or vice versa, or (b) they vote differently from the way the Soviets do.

The Independent Emotive Import Theory, as it may be called, is the broader of the two, and the less interesting to us here, but it requires some consideration. According to this theory there is emotive import that is independent of cognitive import—that is, purport. Two questions arise. (a) Are there words or sentences that have emotive import—that is, arouse the hearer's feelings—without having any purport at all—that is, without conveying any information at all about the speaker's beliefs or feelings or other characteristics? This seems in the highest degree improbable. You may use shocking words, which have strong emotive import, but their effect certainly depends to some extent upon their meanings, however vague. The same may be said of words of endearment like "Darling" and "Beloved" at the other end of the emotive spectrum. (b) Then does emotive import vary independently of purport? To test this part of the thesis we would look for a pair of terms that have exactly the same purport but differ in emotive import—that is, convey the same information but arouse different feelings, say, one arouses negative feelings and the other positive ones or none at all. It is safe to say, I think, that no such pair of terms has been produced. This is not merely because in a living language any two words have their different histories and therefore differ to some extent in their total purport. For we do not even find two words very close to each other in their purport and yet markedly different in emotive import. The usual examples, like "house" and "home," "liberty" and "license," "politician" and "statesman," won't do at all. The nearest you can come is probably a pair like "sister" and "female sibling," for they are fairly close in purport, though the first one has some positive emotive import that the second one lacks. But their purport is not the same, for we can think of poetic contexts that would lose purport if "female sibling" were substituted for "sister": for example, "Ye learned sisters" in the first line of Spenser's "Epithalamion."

But even if no unquestionable examples can be produced, this does not, of course, refute the Independent Emotive Import Theory. There are theoretical reasons in favor of it. Suppose Southerners and Northerners react in different ways emotionally to the same word. A plausible case can always be made out for the view that the word has some range of import that is at least a little different for the two groups. Yet it does not follow that the difference in emotional response can be completely explained in terms of the difference in purport. After all, two people can feel very differently about the same thing, and even if the word purports exactly the same thing to both, they might feel differently about that sort of thing, so the word would have a different emotive import. Moreover, suppose the word "foreigner" has a negative emotive import for a person afflicted with xenophobia; he could come to feel differently about foreigners, and consequently respond differently to the word, even if his understanding of its purport did not change.

We are entitled to conclude, I think, that the purport of a discourse, though not the only factor on which its emotive import depends, is the predominant one. I do not say it is impossible to dissociate them, for a particular person, under special circumstances, may be conditioned to respond in a certain way to the sound of a word, but not to its approximate synonym. But this response is idiosyncratic; it does not count as part of the emotive import of the word, which is a settled and fairly regular tendency to produce a particular feeling among a certain group of people. As far as public responses are concerned, the way the word "mother" becomes a bad word in Aldous Huxley's *Brave New World* shows that words can change their emotive import—but that change is not independent of certain changes in belief.

The Independent Emotive Purport Theory holds that there is emotive purport that is independent of cognitive purport, that is, meaning. Again we have two questions. (1) Are there words or sentences that have emotive purport—that is, reveal the speaker's feelings—without having any meaning at all—that is, without revealing the speaker's beliefs? There is a small class of such expressions, simple expletives like "Hell!" and "Ouch!" that probably can qualify for this description, though even their situation is not wholly clear. When you say, "Ouch!" you do show how you feel, and perhaps you don't show what you believe, though it is hard to draw an exact line, of course. (2) Are there pairs of words or sentences that are identical in meaning but different in emotive purport? Similar considerations arise here as in the problem of the independent variability of emotive import, and, oddly enough, the same examples are often quoted, though if they are relevant here, they are not relevant to the former question. But if "sister" and "female sibling" have a different emotive purport, it is partly because of a subtle difference in their meaning. The same is true of "Southern Democrat" and "Dixiecrat," and of "Northerner" and "Yankee."

Even this rather hasty discussion of independent emotive force is enough to show, I think, that anyone who seeks the defining characteristic of poetic language in this region will have a variety of subtly different versions to choose from, and it would be tedious to distinguish and discuss them all here. At one extreme would be a conception of poetry as pure emotive language, that is, of language with emotive purport but no cognitive purport. Such a poem would consist entirely of exclamations —"Damn!" "Oh dear!" "Ah!" and "Mmmmm!" Presumably no one would maintain such a conception, for as soon as these vague exclamations are filled out so that they can show precise and definite feelings, as a poem does—"I am aweary, aweary, I would that I were dead!"—they are no longer merely emotive, and the emotive purport they have seems to be determined and controlled by their meaning. At the other extreme would be the conception of poetry as simply language with a good deal of emotive purport, and perhaps a good deal of emotive import. This is innocuous, but also insufficiently defining, for of course a great many discourses that are not poems at all—cries of help or of alarm, announcements of births and deaths—have greater emotive purport or import than poems are likely to have. It may be that between these two extremes there is an emotive conception of poetry that is both applicable and distinctive, but I do not think so.

An alternative to the Emotive Definitions, then, is to seek for the defining characteristics of literature in the meaning of its language. And the most promising line of thought is that which distinguishes between two levels of meaning, sometimes called *explicit* and *implicit* meaning. There are really two distinctions here, which we must now state as succinctly as possible.

Primary and Secondary Meaning

Consider sentences first. With some exceptions, which will be noted in Chapter IX, §22, every declarative sentence has a *primary meaning* by virtue of its grammatical form: it presents a complex of meanings of such a sort that it can be said to be true or false. In short, it is a statement. Declarative sentences normally give utterance to beliefs; if one says, "Napoleon was a great general," we usually take him to be saying something he believes to be true. An imperative sentence is not a statement, and therefore does not give utterance to a belief, on its primary level of meaning, but indirectly it may show that the speaker has a belief even though he does not state it. Thus, if one says, "Please shut the window," we may infer that he believes the window should be shut, or perhaps that he believes it is chilly. These beliefs are not *stated*, but they are, in a technical sense of the term, *suggested*. What a sentence suggests I shall call its *secondary sentence meaning*.

A declarative sentence can state one thing and suggest another, and what it states may be true or false, and what it suggests may be true or false. Consider the following sentence: "Napoleon, who recognized the danger to his right flank, himself led his guards against the enemy position."[4] This complex sentence states (1) that Napoleon recognized the danger to his right flank, and (2) that Napoleon led his guards against the enemy position. If either of these statements is false, the sentence is false. But the sentence says more than it states, for it suggests (1) that Napoleon's maneuver occurred *after* the recognition of danger, and (2) that it occurred *because* of the recognition of danger, or in other words that the recognition of danger was the reason he led his guards against the enemy position. Now suppose we should discover that his decision to use his guards had already been made before he recognized the danger to his flank; we might still say that the original sentence was true, "strictly speaking," but we would also want to add that it was misleading, since it suggested something that is false.

What a sentence suggests, then, is what we can infer that the speaker probably believes, beyond what it states. One test for suggestion is that of misleadingness. Suppose there is something meant by the sentence that, if we should discover it to be false, would not lead us to call the sentence false, but only misleading, then that something is suggested, but not stated. The suggestion is part of the full meaning of the sentence, but its presence is not felt to be as central or as basic as the primary meaning, on which it nevertheless depends. That is why I call it secondary meaning. It is usually less emphatic, less obtrusive, less definitely and precisely fixed than the primary meaning, but it may be no less important, even from a practical point of view. What a sentence suggests it says implicitly, rather than explicitly, in the form of insinuation, innuendo, hint, or implication. The difference between "Mrs. Smith is

---

[4] This example is from Gottlob Frege, "Sense and Reference," trans. by Max Black, *Phil R*, LVII (1948): 227-28; I also borrow Frege's analysis. (Another translation of this paper, called "On Sense and Nomination," is in H. Feigl and W. Sellars, *Readings in Philosophical Analysis*, New York: Appleton-Century-Crofts, 1949, pp. 85-102.)

prettier than Mrs. Jones" and "Mrs. Jones is uglier than Mrs. Smith" is a difference of suggestion. If either is precisely correct, the other is misleading. But, "On a scale of beauty, Mrs. Smith would rank somewhat higher than Mrs. Jones, and both would rank very high," approaches scientific language. It may be false, but it cannot be misleading, and therefore suggests nothing.

We shall not stop to consider here the varieties and uses of secondary sentence-meaning. The important point for our purposes is that a great number of rhetorical and compositional devices used in literature can be subsumed under this general heading. Any deviation from what is felt to be the normal grammatical order is a case of secondary sentence-meaning. So is any juxtaposition of ideas that, as in the Napoleon example, implicitly claims a connection between them, but leaves it to the reader to supply the connection himself. When we cannot supply such a connection, we have either obscurity or one kind of nonsense: "Napoleon, who was short in stature, was born in the eighteenth century."

Whatever part of the meaning of a poem depends on syntax, then, or upon the order of lines and sentences and stanzas, is suggestion. And this may constitute an important part of its meaning. If there is bourgeois propaganda in Gray's *Elegy*, it is because it is suggested by comparing the rural genius, frustrated by lack of opportunity, to a desert flower, which after all does not really want to be picked. If there is implicit paganism in *Paradise Lost*,[5] it is because the lines

> In shadier Bower,
> More sacred and sequestered, though but feigned,
> Pan or Sylvanus never slept, nor Nymph
> Nor Faunus hunted,

suggest that the pagan bowers had *some* degree of sacredness, just as the sentence, "Jack never had more money than Joe" suggests that Jack had *some* money. Or consider the first stanza of Housman's poem:

> Crossing alone the nighted ferry
> With the one coin for fee
> Whom on the wharf of Lethe waiting
> Count you to find? Not me.[6]

The answer to the question asked is "Me," not "Not me"; the question that "Not me" answers ("Whom *will* you find?") is not asked, but it is nevertheless implicitly there, as the second stanza shows.

---

[5] These two examples are from William Empson, *Some Versions of Pastoral*, London: Chatto and Windus, 1930, pp. 4, 190.

[6] From "Crossing Alone the Nighted Ferry," from *The Collected Poems of A. E. Housman*. Copyright, 1940, by Henry Holt and Company, Inc. Copyright, 1936, by Barclays Bank, Ltd. By permission of the publishers. Canadian clearance by permission of The Society of Authors as the Literary Representative of the Trustees of the Estate of the late A. E. Housman, and Messrs. Jonathan Cape Ltd., publishers of A. E. Housman's *Collected Poems*.

When we turn from sentences to parts of sentences, we can make a corresponding distinction between the standard, or central, meaning of a word and its marginal or accompanying meanings. The word "sea" *designates* certain characteristics, such as being a large body of salt water; this is its primary word-meaning. It also *connotes* certain other characteristics, such as being sometimes dangerous, being changeable in mood but endless in motion, being a thoroughfare, being a barrier, and so on. These are its secondary word-meanings. "Sister" and "female sibling" have the same designation, but they differ in connotation, for two women who are not literally siblings may be "sisters under the skin."

The distinction between these two levels of term-meaning is not sharp, but it is operative in all our ordinary speech. Some of the commonest and most important feats of language, especially those carried to a high degree of subtlety and power in literature, depend upon our feeling that the total meaning of a word divides in this fashion. The word "wolf," for example, designates certain characteristics that define a class of animals; it also *denotes* the animals that have those defining characteristics in common. But besides having the characteristics that make them wolves, many wolves have certain other characteristics, or are widely believed to have them: fierceness, persistence, and predatory clannishness. And these characteristics have been ascribed to wolves in contexts that contain the word "wolf," whereas the contexts that contain its technical synonym, *Canis lupus*, have not so commonly ascribed such characteristics to them. Hence, when a person now uses the word "wolf" in certain contexts, we can infer that he probably believes that the entities referred to have some of the characteristics connoted by the term. And these characteristics, unless ruled out by the context, are part of what I call the full meaning of the word, though not of its strict, or dictionary, meaning —that is, its designation.

What a word connotes, then, are the characteristics that it does not designate but that belong, or are widely thought or said to belong, to many of the things it denotes. This is the word's range of connotation. But what it connotes in a particular context—its contextual connotation— is always a selection from its total range; indeed, the range may include incompatible connotations—"sea" connotes both being a barrier and being a highroad. In some contexts, all, or nearly all, its connotations may be kept out by the other words; these are contexts whose meaning is fully explicit, not likely to mislead, as in the best technical and scientific writing. In other contexts, its connotations are liberated; these are most notably the contexts in which language becomes figurative, and especially metaphorical, but this kind of language we shall consider more fully in the following section. It goes almost without saying that it is the language of poetry in which secondary word-meaning is most fully actualized. For example, in the first stanza of Thomas Carew's "Song,"

> Ask me no more where Jove bestows
> When June is past, the fading rose;
> For in your beauties' orient deep
> These flowers as in their causes sleep,

the word "causes" is freighted with a large chunk of Aristotle's metaphysics.

A discourse that has both primary and secondary levels of meaning may be said to have *multiple meaning:* for example, if it contains puns, *double-entendre,* metaphor, ironic suggestion. Multiple meaning is often called "ambiguity," and ambiguity is said to be a special characteristic of the language of poetry. I reserve the term "ambiguity" for linguistic expressions that are doubtful in meaning because they could have either, but not both, of two possible meanings and provide no ground for a decision between them. Where there is suggestion or connotation, no choice is called for; several things are meant at once.

The Semantic Definition of "Literature"

From the foregoing discussion we can now draw some general conclusions. Discourses may be arranged, roughly, in an order with respect to their reliance upon secondary meaning, that is, the proportion of meaning presented *implicitly,* by suggestion and connotation. Toward one end we put discourse that is highly charged with meaning, that condenses, so to speak, a great deal of meaning into a small space. Of course this spectrum is fairly continuous, but we can choose some standard discourses to mark off certain points along it, if we want to take the trouble. Moreover, we can draw a line, even if a somewhat vague one, between discourse that has a good deal of secondary meaning and discourse that has not. We may now try out a definition: a literary work is a discourse in which an important part of the meaning is implicit. This is a Semantic Definition of "literature," since it defines "literature" in terms of meaning.

All literary works fall into three main classes: poems, essays, and prose fiction. The *Spectator* papers and the sermons of Donne are in the second class. Play-scripts and motion-picture scenarios may be counted as fiction. A play as produced consists of a series of human, or humanlike, movements on a stage; it may involve the speaking of words, but it is not a literary work, but something more complicated that is related to literature. In this book we shall not have room to discuss the drama as such. But a play as read, that is, the script of the play, is a literary work, and falls within our classification; it is either a poem, like *Hamlet,* or a prose fiction, like *Ghosts.*

Each of the three classes of literary works presents us with its own problems of definition, that is, of distinction, and we cannot clear them up until we have investigated several other matters that await us in

Chapters V and IX. But let us see what can be said at this stage. With respect to the *essay,* to take that first, the problem is to distinguish essays, in the literary sense, from technical writings, articles in the *Journal of Philosophy,* news stories, and so forth. This is certainly a matter of degree, but the question is, Along what scale is the degree to be measured? I think it is the proportion of the total meaning that occurs on the second level, that is, in suggestion and connotation. The literary essay is higher in stylistic reliance upon secondary meaning, and in such qualities as wit, humor, and irony that depend upon it. The line will be rather arbitrary, and of course even after it is drawn we may still look for, and find, what may be called "literary qualities" in nonliterary discourses. But at least we know what we are about.

The distinguishing mark of *fiction*—what marks it off from narrative that is nonfictional—is basically its lack of a claim to literal truth on the first level of meaning; but this definition will have to be amplified and defended in Chapter IX, §22. It might be convenient to include all fiction, so defined, in the class of literature, though some critics, I think, would want to reserve the term "literature" for something a little more substantial than mere statements that are not expected to be believed. In any case, in comparison with history and psychological case studies, fiction tends not merely to describe character abstractly but to leave it partly to be inferred from action, and its judgment upon the significance of events is suggested rather than overtly stated. And this is secondary meaning.

Poetry presents a more complicated problem. First, no doubt, there is a distinction in *sound,* and this we shall explore with some care in Chapter V, §14. Poetry is, at least, organized sound, and one problem is to analyze that organization which defines "verse." But not all verse is poetry. Now suppose that "verse" has been defined; which verses are, in the stricter sense, to be called "poems"? A poem is a verse that carries a large part of its meaning on the second level. It is almost possible to define "poem" in terms of figurative language—metaphor, simile, symbol. But though this will include nearly all poems, it will not include quite all. Consider, for example, the well-known anonymous ballad, "Edward": it has no figures of speech, unless we count "the curse of hell" in the last stanza, but what makes it a poem is all it suggests about motives and consequences of murder, about hate and guilt.

Tentatively, therefore, we may say that "literature" is well defined as "discourse with important implicit meaning." This definition not only draws a useful distinction by calling attention to noteworthy characteristics of the language of literary works, but it corresponds reasonably well with the reflective use of the term "literature" by critics.

It may, nevertheless, be felt that the Semantic Definition of "literature" is too formal, or, in one sense, merely nominal, like the definition of "man" as "featherless biped." And there is indeed another way of defining "literature," which we perhaps ought to consider briefly to round out the present topic; I argue that in the end it practically coincides with the linguistic definition.

Suppose we seek the defining characteristics of literature not in its language but in the world it projects. To put the view first in intentionalistic terms, which can easily be translated into objective ones, the essential thing that the literary creator does is to invent or discover an object—it can be a material object or a person, or a thought, or a state of affairs, or an event—around which he collects a set of relations that can be perceived as connected through their intersection in that object. For example, he might see, or imagine, a young boy's cast-off winter coat on the grass one sunny day in early spring. He creates the substance of literature if he can invest that coat with what I shall call, in a special and somewhat guarded sense, *multiple relatedness*. He sees it as, or makes it into, an indication of the eternal boyish struggle to be free of confinement and out running around unencumbered, or of the end of winter, or of the conflict between parents and children over chills and colds; he makes it function in a plot, as a symptom of motives and character, or as a cause of tragic events; or he may ruminate upon the exquisite carelessness of a crumpled, red-lined snowsuit on the feeble grass, one arm perhaps hanging over into a damp gutter.

I do not mean, of course, that he merely draws *inferences*. If he is interested in only one or two of these things, and is turned aside by curiosity about correlations and explanations—What proportion of American children get colds in March?—he moves toward abstraction, generalization, and science. But if he can hold the individual object in view as a focus of some pattern of human behavior, reflecting a quality of human nature, he has a contemplatable literary object.

My somewhat loose speculation touches already upon some matters that we shall have to deal with more systematically in Chapters V and IX; I venture it here only with reservations. But see what follows from it. We can conceive of the writer going off in different directions toward a lyric poem, a work of fiction, or a light literary essay. But all of them have in common the concern with multiple relatedness, the concrescence of patterns, different from the manner in which the trained botanist sees swampy ground as a likely habitat of certain mushrooms, or the trained political scientist sees the deliberations of the Senate Foreign Relations Committee as a symptom of incipient conflict with the State Department.

But the key words in this account are words like "invest" and "make"; *how* does a discourse—switching back now to objective language—invest the objects it refers to with these characteristics? Only, I should suppose, by means of the secondary levels of meaning; only through connotation and suggestion. So that, even if we start with the world of the literary work, we come back in the end to its language, and that is the reason the Semantic Definition was put foremost.

Because it contains deep levels of meaning that are only hinted at through connotation and suggestion, a literary discourse has a kind of semantical *thickness* when compared with mathematical and technical discourse. This is not to be equated with mere vagueness, looseness, flabbiness, or wildness; it is compatible with precision and control. But it gives the discourse an air of being more than it seems to be at first glance, or even, sometimes, after prolonged contemplation; as if dwelling on it further would turn up new meanings, as if it were, for all its liberality, always holding something in reserve. Hence the experience of coming to understand a literary discourse is a kind of growth; not, as with a simple symbolism, that either we have it or we don't, but a matter of more or less, of depth or shallowness. All this is especially true of poetry.

Moreover, we can be helped to understand a poem; there are meanings that we do not see unaided, but acknowledge to be present as soon as they are pointed out to us. To point out a meaning in a poem is to *explicate* the poem.

We can certainly understand a great deal of some poems without any explication, by ourselves or others: "O Mistress mine, where are you roaming?" for example. Other poems yield up their meaning only after thought: they are more obscure. But even those that make very good sense on first reading do not exhaust themselves in that reading; we find more the next time. It is a difference of degree that leads from Shakespeare's songs, Shelley's lyrics, or Byron's *Don Juan,* at one end, to Hart Crane, Wallace Stevens, or Dylan Thomas at the other. Explication merely does for us in a shorter time what we can do for ourselves in a longer time, if we have the right training. The explicator gives us information that we need to understand the poem but haven't already acquired. Not that he claims to point out all the meaning in a poem. He will say, " 'Liquefaction' in this poem means, among other things . . ." or " 'Knot intrinsicate' in this context means, among other things . . ." These are partial explications. The fundamental question before us in this section is this: how are such statements known to be true?

To explicate a linguistic expression is to declare its meaning. It will be convenient, however, to restrict the term "explicate" by distinguishing it from another way of declaring meaning, definition. If you ask what a word means in a specific context, you are asking the kind of meaning-question that the explicator answers. But you can ask a different sort of question about the *general* meaning of the word; this is the kind of question the lexicographer answers. He investigates meaning that is relatively invariant throughout most contexts, or most contexts of a certain sort—for example, legal writings or chess books. This intercontextual meaning of the word—there may, of course, be several—is a kind of standardized meaning; it is what in the preceding section was called *designation.*

To make explicit a standard meaning of a word, by presenting a term that is synonymous with it, is to define it: the word "hinny," as used by animal breeders, means the same as—designates the same characteristics as—"offspring of stallion and she-ass." In many contexts this is what "hinny" means, and in some contexts it is all that "hinny" means—"The hinny is in the barn." Definitions are evidently very useful, but they do not do everything that explications are called upon to do, for they are not designed to report the full meaning of the word in any particular context.

Although explication is often—more often than not—called "interpretation," I propose to reserve the latter term for something different, which is to be discussed in Chapter IX, §22. The distinction is not sharp, but a critic is explicating when he talks about relatively localized parts of a poem, the meaning of a metaphor, the connotations of a word, the implications of a fragment of ambiguous syntax. Since, from one point of view, a poem is a complex of meanings, explication-statements can be counted as part of the description of the poem.

There is no doubt that literary critics utter numerous statements that are, or claim to be, explications of poems; but there may be doubt whether they can give good reasons to justify these statements. Suppose two critics give incompatible explications of a poem—"incompatible" in the sense that they are not just supplementary explications, one pointing out something missed by the other, but logically contradictory ones. Is there some proper and objective way in which the disagreement can, at least in principle, be settled? Is there, in short, not only explication, but a *method* of explication?

Consider for a moment the word "method." For some things you do, there is a method of doing them, for others not. It makes sense to ask, "By what method do you separate whites of eggs from yolks?" or ". . . get *your* children to go to bed?" But it makes no sense to ask, "What is *your* method of sneezing?" An action can be methodized only if (a) there are alternative ways of performing the action, (b) it is possible to keep in mind general principles, or rules, while performing the action, and (c) a good reason can be given for following those rules rather than others. When the action is one that, like the act of thinking, but not like the act of batting a ball, issues in a claim to truth, the method of doing it may in a broad sense be called a "logic." Thus there is such a thing as drawing deductive inferences, which you can do without ever studying how to do it; but there is also a logic of deduction, that is, a set of rationally justifiable general rules in terms of which we can say when deduction has been done correctly and when it has been done incorrectly. There is also a logic of induction, and perhaps more specific subordinate logics of historical inquiry and moral reasoning. The question before us now is whether there is a logic of explication.

When we reflect upon the practices of those contemporary critics who have helped us most with the understanding of poetry, we can, I think, draw the outline of a general procedure that is very often followed, more or less explicitly. If it can be systematically worked out and justified, it is the logic we are after. So let us begin by considering it.

The meaning of any complex linguistic expression, such as a sentence, is a regional meaning. In many sentences it is clear that this meaning is a unique function of the meanings of the constituent words plus their grammatical relations. You have probably never seen the sentence, "The crocodile is on the piano," before, but you have no difficulty in construing, that is, understanding, it. For if you know the dictionary meanings of "crocodile," etc., and their syntax, and the rules of English grammar, you can read the regional meaning of the whole from the local meanings of the parts. Of course, an ambiguous sentence, such as "Jack owes John more money than Jim," is like an ambiguous visual design—the figure of the stairs, for example—in that two different regional meanings can be constructed from it. But a great many sentences are quite determinate in sense.

There is another large class of sentences, however, in which the relation between the regional meaning and the local meaning is more complex. If we had been able in the preceding chapter to give a good definition of the term, it would be tempting to call this "emergent meaning."

> In the metaphysical streets of the physical town
> We remember the lion of Juda

(Wallace Stevens, "An Ordinary Evening in New Haven"[1]). If we try to construct a regional meaning for this sentence out of the separate words and their grammatical relations, as if it were like "The cat is on the mat," we are balked. The contextual meanings of "metaphysical" and "physical" here are certainly much more novel and puzzling, and go far beyond the point where the dictionary leaves off. If there is a method of explication to be brought to bear in cases like this, it will have to be more than the one we use for ordinary sentences.

The Relativistic Theory of Explication

And of course critics do have another method. In essence it has two parts, each of which may require a good deal of thought and sensitive judgment. The first step is to ask about the potential range of connotations of such words as "metaphysical" and "physical"; this we discussed in the previous section. The second step is to discover which of the potential ones are *actual*, by selecting those that can be fitted into the context. The conditions to be met in the explication are set by the standard senses of

---

[1] From "An Ordinary Evening in New Haven." Reprinted from *The Collected Poems of Wallace Stevens*, by permission of Alfred A. Knopf, Inc. Copyright 1931, 1954 by Wallace Stevens.

the words, including words like "town" that have a fairly plain sense, limited to their designation, even in this context. Thus, given "town" and "street," which *possible* connotations of "metaphysical" and "physical" can be meaningfully applied to them? And when "metaphysical streets" and "physical town" are further combined into a larger phrase, which of the possible meanings of each can be fitted together? In such a manner, roughly speaking, the explicator may be said to work. Of course his mind may do this far more rapidly and more subtly and richly than my description shows. Nevertheless, we may say that what he does is to try to work out the regional meaning of the whole as a semantical function of the meanings—including secondary meanings—of the parts, in their grammatical relations. And his work involves two different procedures: determining the ranges of connotation, and selecting from these the actual ones.

On deeper reflection, however, we may become skeptical about the decisiveness of this method. A method is decisive, we may say, when two people who apply it to the same problem correctly and have all the relevant information will reach the same conclusion. Thus the method of measuring a table by a tape measure is in this sense decisive. But suppose the application of the method depends not only upon having information and following rules, but upon something else that varies from person to person, or from time to time for the same person—in that case, the method is not decisive. It cannot be expected to give results that are interpersonally valid; it is a relativistic method. For example, if the tape measure is elastic, and has to be stretched in order to be used, then the result of the measurement will depend in part on the individual's strength and momentary inclinations, and if two individuals get different results, we cannot say either of them is wrong.

There is an analogous theory about explication, which can be given a strong defense.[2] If it is true, then there is no logic of explication, and a good deal of criticism becomes pointless, except as an enjoyable form of free association. The skeptical view can be based upon two complementary arguments, either of which, if conclusive, is fatal to the logic of explication.

The first argument concerns the first step in the explicative method, which is to determine the potential range of connotations of the words in the poem. The argument is that this question admits of no objective answer. According to this view, we can ask what a word connotes to a particular reader on a particular occasion, which depends upon his own experiences and personality traits; we cannot ask what it connotes in general. In short, connotation cannot be distinguished from personal associations, and is therefore relative.

This first argument clearly comes into conflict with a claim that I

---

[2] See the paper by Charles L. Stevenson, Note 10-A.

made in the preceding section, and it is rebutted if that claim can be made good. I say that the connotations of such words as "fire," "desert," "moon," "steel," "stone," to take easy ones for brevity's sake, are objective parts of the meanings of those terms as they belong to a certain speech-community, just as much as their dictionary meanings, though somewhat less obvious. Their connotations come from the way these objects appear in human experience. "Desert" connotes unfruitfulness and death, whether a particular reader is aware of it or not; he can correct and improve his reading by recalling the real effects of deserts. Thus, to put it more abstractly, the connotations of "desert" are a function of the *designation* of "desert," and in principle if two people know the designation of "desert" and have all the relevant facts about the nature of deserts, and the current beliefs about them, and the past verbal contexts in which deserts have been spoken of, by explorers, engineers, and historians, then they can, within narrow limits, agree on which characteristics are or are not connoted by the word. Moreover, maverick readings—"It reminds me of a pretty little sandpile I knew as a child"—can be spotted as such.

But if the first argument can be answered, the second is much more dangerous. Suppose that two critics agree completely about the potential range of connotations of the words in a poem; they still have to decide which of those connotations are actual. Some of the connotations have to be excluded, as we say, by the context. But, the skeptic might say, a context can neither admit nor exclude a connotation, apart from the writer's express intention, which is generally unavailable; therefore, the admission or exclusion calls for a decision on the part of the reader. All he can do is read the poem both ways, *with* the particular connotation and without it, and then decide which of the two poems he prefers. If he likes the poem with it better than the poem without it, that is the way he will choose to read the poem, though another reader may choose differently. Of course, he may disguise the normative element, the element of preference, in his decision, by saying he chooses the meaning that "fits" best, or is most "coherent," but, according to the argument we are now pursuing, these terms cannot be objectively defined, either. The explication-statement, "This poem means such-and-such," then, means, "I prefer the poem when read this way (rather than some other way)."

In this view, all explication-statements refer implicitly to the speaker himself, and his personal preferences. When Empson asserted, and his critics denied, that "bare ruin'd choirs" refers to the Destruction of the Monasteries,[3] they were not really contradicting each other, though they seemed to be, for one was saying he liked the poem with that meaning, and the other that *he* liked it better without it. This I shall call the Relativistic Theory of Explication.

The Relativistic Theory implies that no explication is wrong, for an

---

[3] *Seven Types of Ambiguity*, New York: Meridian, 1955, p. 5.

explication makes no claim of objective validity, when properly understood. That is because it depends at two vital points upon the idiosyncrasies of the individual reader: his personal associations with words, and his personal preferences about poems. To refute the Relativistic Theory it is sufficient to show that explication is independent of both sets of idiosyncrasies, in other words, to produce a nonrelativistic logic of explication. The first argument of the Relativistic Theory—the argument for the relativity of connotation—I shall suppose to have been taken care of. It is the second argument that will concern us now. And the problem is, again: how do we know which potential meanings to attribute to a poem, and which to leave out?

To reduce this large and searching question to manageable proportions, while at the same time not neglecting any important aspects of it, we must select a sample problem of explication, a kind of model that will serve as a test case. There is a large variety of explication-problems, but I shall take the problem of explicating metaphors. If we can give a satisfactory account of what is involved in such nuclei of poetic meaning, and if we can then show in a general way that what holds for them holds also for larger entities, like whole poems, then we shall be in a position to give a reasonable reply to the Relativistic Theory of Explication.

Theories of Metaphor

What is a metaphor? The theory I shall propose, tentatively and for the sake of discussion, because I am aware of its incompleteness, though I believe it gets somewhere near the main truth, will appear in its clearest light if we first contrast it with alternative theories of metaphor, of which I distinguish three. It is hard to find clear-cut examples of writers who defend one or the other of these views,[4] and perhaps that does not matter. They are, at least, possible and defensible views, and, more or less explicitly, they have all been held at one time or another.

The first theory of metaphor I shall call the *Emotive Theory*. It is a commonplace that metaphorical combinations of words in some way violate our normal expectations of the way words are put together in English. A metaphor is perceived as a dislocation, or misuse, of language, though it differs from other ways of misusing language in having a peculiarly valuable and interesting character, so that this sort of misuse is often called a supreme use of language. It is this character that the Emotive Theory aims to explain.

To make this theory most plausible, we must conceive the meaning of a word more narrowly than we did in the preceding section; according to the Emotive Theory, a word has meaning only if there is some way of confirming its applicability to a given situation—roughly, only if it

---

[4] The chief writers are sorted out somewhat in Note 10-C.

has a clear designation. For example, the sharpness of a knife can be
tested by various means, so that the phrase "sharp knife" is meaningful.
We may also suppose that "sharp" has some negative emotive import,
deriving from our experience with sharp things. Now, when we speak of
a "sharp razor" or a "sharp drill," the emotive import is not active, because
these phrases are meaningful. But when we speak of a "sharp wind," a
"sharp dealer," or a "sharp tongue," the tests for sharpness cannot be applied, and therefore, though the individual words are meaningful, the
combinations of them are not. In this way the emotive import of the
adjective is released and intensified.

A metaphor, then, according to the Emotive Theory, is an example
of what we looked for earlier but could not find: an expression that has
emotive import but no meaning. But clearly it is not an example of such
an expression, and therefore the Emotive Theory is wrong. There are, in
fact, at least two things wrong with it. First, it rests upon too narrow a
concept of meaning, and also of testability. The connotations of "sharp"
can still, some of them, apply to tongues, even if its designation does
not. And therefore it is not correct to say that there is no test for sharp
tongues. Anyone who often scolds and finds fault sarcastically can be
said to have a sharp tongue; these are the tests. Of course the tests for
sharp tongues are not the same as the tests for sharp razors, but the tests
for sharp razors are not the same as the tests for sharp drills, either.
Second, it will not do to explain metaphor in such a way as to entail that
all metaphors are emotive. They can be emotive, and many of them are;
they don't have to be. Perhaps a sharp wind is a wind we don't particularly care for, but "sharp wind" is not highly emotive, like "birdbrain" or
"stinker." Moreover, if in "sharp wits," "sharp" is not pejorative, but
honorific, this must be because its meaning is being changed in the new
context, so that it cannot be meaningless. Finally, phrases like "sharp immortality" and "sharp indolence" *are* meaningless, but in them "sharp" has
no emotive import at all.

The Emotive Theory differs from the other three theories in denying meaning to metaphors; the others are all cognitive theories.

The second theory of metaphor I shall call the *Supervenience Theory*.
The defense of this theory begins with the observation that poetic language, and metaphor in particular, is capable of conveying meanings that
literal language cannot convey. Why else, indeed, would we have need
of metaphor, unless it supplied a mode of speech for which there is no
substitute? Proponents of the Supervenience Theory would generally, I
think, brush aside examples like "sharp wind" as not "true" metaphors, or
not the important sort: but in Plato's metaphor of the Cave or Dostoyevsky's metaphor of the Underground, they would say, the natural becomes
capable of bearing a supernatural meaning. Only through metaphor—and
its extensions in myth and ritual—is language freed from the restrictions of
literal speech and permitted to range abroad at will.

According to this theory, the meaning of a metaphor does not grow out of the literal meanings of its parts, but appears as something extraneous to, and independent of, them. The literal meanings are overridden and lost; the metaphorical meaning is inexplicable in terms of them.

There is a familiar analogy. A phrase in a language that has a special meaning all its own, not depending upon the meanings of its words, is an *idiom;* a foreigner cannot figure out the meaning of *"chez lui"* or "by the way," just working from a grammar and dictionary. The Supervenience Theory regards a metaphor as a species of idiom. Like the Emotive Theory, but for a different reason, it denies that metaphors can be explicated. In this respect these two theories differ from the two yet to be considered.

Just because an idiom is an idiom, its meaning has to be learned all at once; it is, in effect, a new word, and is listed as such in the foreign-language dictionary. But when we read a metaphor, we can figure out at least part of its meaning without having such a dictionary. How is this possible? Here the Supervenience Theory has to make a fundamental distinction: there is a method by which we come to understand "The cat is on the mat"; but this has nothing to do with the way we come to understand William Blake's

> Tyger! Tyger! burning bright
> In the forests of the night,
> What immortal hand or eye
> Could frame thy fearful symmetry?

("The Tyger"). A metaphor cannot be construed from the interactions of its parts; it calls for a special act of intuition.

The implications of this theory now appear: it presupposes a theory of knowledge, and that raises problems that we are not yet prepared to deal with. We shall take them up in Chapter IX, §23. Meanwhile, we can justly regard the Supervenience Theory as a last resort. If, in other words, a reasonable theory of metaphor can be given, which accounts satisfactorily for its peculiar characteristics, and if this theory implies that metaphorical meanings can be analyzed and explicated, then, though the Supervenience Theory will not be refuted, it will be rendered unnecessary.

The third theory of metaphor I shall call the *Literalist Theory.* The term "literal" has two common meanings. (a) It is opposed to "figurative," as excluding metaphors, similes, and other tropes. (b) It is opposed to "metaphorical"—which is the sense in which I use it here. A simple comparison ("His house is like my house") is a literal expression, in that it uses none of its words metaphorically. And this is also true of one sort of simile:

> his frosted breath,
> Like pious incense from a censer old

(Keats, "Eve of St. Agnes"). The Literalist Theory is that metaphor is a disguised or telescoped simile. "Our birth is but a sleep and a forgetting" is to be construed as "Our birth is like a sleep and a forgetting"; the metaphor "passion spins the plot," from

> In tragic life, God wot,
> No villain need be; passion spins the plot;
> We are betrayed by what is false within,

(Meredith, "Love's Grave") is to be construed as "passion *is like some-thing that* spins *and* the plot *is like something spun*," for this is a double metaphor, in that passion only metaphorically spins and plots are only metaphorically spun.

The concept taken as fundamental by the Literalist Theory is that of *ellipsis.* This is a notion that modern grammarians are uneasy about; if nowadays people nearly always say, "She is the one I adore," it seems artificial to regard it as elliptical for "She is the one *whom* I adore"—they are not conscious of leaving out anything. But there are sentences where we could say with some confidence that certain words are implicit, though not uttered, because they are needed to complete the sense by ruling out other possibilities. "If he's going, I'm not" requires another "going," rather than "staying," to be understood after "not." The Literalist Theory, then, holds that metaphors are elliptical similes. Since there is no funda-mental difference, they can be understood the way similes are, by the ordinary rules of language, and present no special problems for explica-tion. For the only problem with a simile is that of assembling enough factual information to determine how far it goes:

> Like as the waves make toward the pebbled shore,
> So do our minutes hasten to their end

(Shakespeare, Sonnet LX). It is true that we have to work out the com-parison ourselves, but that is not strictly part of the *meaning* of the simile, which only says that the waves and minutes resemble each other in some respect.

Now metaphors and similes are in some ways not very different, and the view that one can be reduced to the other is rather ancient. Neverthe-less, it is a mistake.

First, note that there are two kinds of similes: (1) An *open simile* simply states that X is like Y—the minutes are like the waves. (2) A *closed* simile states that X is like Y in such and such a respect. In the lines

> And custom lie upon thee with a weight,
> Heavy as frost, and deep almost as life

(Wordsworth, "Ode: Intimations of Immortality from Recollections of Early Childhood") custom and frost are compared in "heaviness," custom and life in "depth." Closed similes work like metaphors, and can be re-stated fairly satisfactorily as metaphors—"Custom is frost-heavy"—but not

all metaphors, I think, can be satisfactorily restated as closed similes--
for example, in "The moon lies fair upon the straits," what is it that the
moon lies like? But a metaphor cannot be reduced to an open simile,
either, for they work very differently in poetic contexts. The open simile
is empty and uncontrolled without a context: A is like B, but in what
relevant respects the context has to inform us. The metaphor is full and
rich, apart from any context; indeed, the function of the context is rather
to eliminate possible meanings than to supply them. A metaphor is not
an implied comparison.

Logical Absurdity

The fourth theory of metaphor I shall call the *Controversion Theory*.
This odd name is the best I have been able to discover for either the
theory of metaphor or the general rhetorical strategy of which it is a
species. Consider first a certain kind of discourse, to be called *Self-Controverting Discourse*. Its essential principle is that the speaker or writer
utters a statement explicitly but in such a way as to show that he does
not believe what he states, or is not primarily interested in what he states,
and thereby calls attention to something else that he has not explicitly
stated—"If he wins, I'll eat my hat." It is discourse that says more than it
states, by canceling out the primary meaning to make room for secondary
meaning. The principle has extremely broad application, for it underlies a variety of tactics. Irony is a clear example: when you make a statement ironically, you show, by tone or in another way, that you are withdrawing your statement in the act of making it, and thereby suggest the
opposite. There are many other ways of doing the same thing: you can
label your statements a "joke" or a "story" or a "parable"; you can put
them into verse, which carries the suggestion that your chief purpose is
not to give useful information. You can use names that don't name anything, like "Huckleberry Finn" or "Yoknapatawpha County," or say that
any resemblance to actual persons, living or dead, is purely coincidental.
You can put in obvious exaggerations, or violations of the laws of nature.
You can be evasive about the details, and thereby show that you aren't
really prepared to verify your statements or submit them for verification.

In all these cases, the strategy is similar: the reader can see that you
are not asserting the statement you make (to assert is to evince and to
invite belief), but since the statement is made, and something is presumably being asserted, he looks about for a second level of meaning on
which something *is* being said. And in poetry the chief tactic for obtain-
ing this result is that of *logical absurdity*. In other words, it is the logical
absurdity of statements in poems that gives them meaning on the second
level.

Let us use the term "attribution" for any linguistic expression containing at least two words, one of which denotes a class and also charac-

terizes it in some way, and the other of which qualifies or modifies the characterization. I shall call an expression an attribution whether it is merely a phrase, "large dogs," or a complete sentence, "The dogs are large." But when I require the distinction, I shall speak of "phrase-attributions" and "sentence-attributions." The term that is modified in either case, "dogs," I shall call the *subject* of the attribution; the other term, "large," the *modifier*. Notice that I do not say dogs are the subject, but the *word* "dogs."

Consider now those attributions that have the peculiarity of being *logically empty attributions*. I do not say they are meaningless attributions; they simply have a certain logical property: they are, or contain parts that are, inapplicable to the world. And these logically empty attributions are of two fundamental sorts.

A *self-implicative attribution* is one in which the meaning of the modifier is already contained in the meaning of the subject, and therefore the modifier adds nothing to the whole expression. If the self-implicative attribution is a phrase ("two-legged biped," "old harridan"), it is *redundant;* the entire attribution is not logically empty, but the modifier is useless. If the self-implicative attribution is a sentence ("Bipeds are two-legged," "Harridans are old"), it is *tautological.*

Now, it is possible to utter self-implicative attributions unwittingly, from ignorance or haste—some people don't know that harridans are old by definition. But it is also possible to utter them wittingly, giving clear evidence that you know what you are doing. Then the utterance controverts itself. The astute reader (or listener), seeing that you are apparently serious about what you and he both know is logically absurd, must look about for another possible meaning. If he can find it among the connotations of the modifier, he can give a meaning to the whole expression. It becomes no longer a bare self-implication, but a *significant self-implication:* that is, an attribution that is self-implicative, and therefore logically empty, on the level of what the modifier designates, but not on the level of what the modifier connotes.

I shall give a few examples. First, redundancy:

> Seven years we have lived quietly,
> Succeeded in avoiding notice,
> Living and partly living.

(Eliot, *Murder in the Cathedral*[5]). This is a double redundancy—taking the words literally—since "living quietly" entails "living," and "living" entails "partly living." The second and third times "live" turns up, we understand its redundancy on one level, but we instantly turn to reflect upon the rich connotations of this word to see which of them we can bring into the context. Another type is a pair of synonymous terms: "Th'inau-

---

[5] From *Murder in the Cathedral* by T. S. Eliot. Copyright, 1935, by Harcourt, Brace and Company, Inc., and reprinted with their permission.

dible and noiseless foot of time" (*All's Well That Ends Well*, V, iii, 40); Empson[6] gives this example and several others. The reader, seeking to circumvent the apparent repetitiousness, pays more attention to the subtle connotations that make the slight differences in meaning than he would if each word were alone.

For an example of tautology, the Eliot passage may be matched with

> I cannot live with you
> It would be life

(Emily Dickinson[7])—that is to say, "If I should live with you, I would be living." Empson, again,[8] has shown in detail how rich is the meaning of "Let me not love thee, if I love thee not" (George Herbert, "Affliction"). Compare:

> This Jack, joke, poor potsherd, | patch, matchwood, and immortal
> diamond,
>> Is immortal diamond

(Hopkins, "That Nature Is a Heraclitean Fire and of the Comfort of the Resurrection"[9]).

It may seem strange to apply to poetry the cold machinery of formal logic. But poetic statements, like all statements, have a logical form, and I am arguing that it is just their peculiarities of logical form on which their poetic power depends. There is not room here to dwell in detail upon the full meaning of all the lines I quote—to consider, for example, the way "immortal diamond," and its implicit conception of the soul, is given a kind of resurrection in the Hopkins lines, by first appearing, in the subject, among a handful of humble things, and then suddenly coming to the fore, by itself, in the predicate. This is rare and rich. But our present concern is only with the elementary point that, on the literal level, this clause is a tautology, and it is the recognition of its tautological character that forces us to read its higher-level meanings out of it.

Metaphorical Attributions

A *self-contradictory attribution* is one in which the modifier designates some characteristic incompatible with the characteristics designated by the subject—"four-legged biped," "Circles are square." A bare self-contradiction is just that; but when the modifier connotes some characteristic that can be meaningfully attributed to the subject, the reader jumps over the evident self-contradiction and construes it indirectly, on

---

[6] *Op. cit.*, pp. 108-11.

[7] From "I Cannot Live with You," *The Poems of Emily Dickinson,* ed. by Thomas H. Johnson. Reprinted with the permission of the Belknap Press of the Harvard University Press.

[8] *Op. cit.*, p. 207. He calls this "ambiguity by tautology"; cf. the discussion of his seventh type in ch. 7.

[9] Reprinted from *Poems of Gerard Manley Hopkins,* 3d ed., N. Y. and London: Oxford University Press, 1948, by permission of the Oxford University Press.

the principle that the writer knows he is contradicting himself and wouldn't utter anything at all unless he had something sensible in mind. Then the expression becomes a *significant self-contradiction*.

The simplest type of significant self-contradiction is *oxymoron:* "nasty-nice," "living death" (Milton, *Samson Agonistes*), "unkindly kinde" (Donne, "Song"), or "These my feet go slowly fast" (Lovelace, "The Snayl"). But it is easy to find examples of larger ones:

> And what you do not know is the only thing you know
> And what you own is what you do not own
> And where you are is where you are not

(Eliot, "East Coker"[10])—or Wordsworth's description of the London masses,

> melted and reduced
> To one identity, by differences
> That have no law, no meaning, and no end

(*The Prelude*, Book VII, ll. 726-28). We might even include Marianne Moore's "imaginary gardens with real toads in them" ("Poetry").

But there is another kind of self-contradiction that is more indirect, in the sense in which "male female" is a direct contradiction but "female uncle" an indirect one. To call a man a "fox" is indirectly self-contradictory because men are by definition bipeds and foxes quadrupeds, and it is logically impossible to be both. To call streets "metaphysical" is indirectly self-contradictory, because streets are by definition physical, not metaphysical. And these are two examples of metaphor. "The man is a fox" says that the man has the characteristics connoted by "fox"; "metaphysical street" attributes to the street characteristics connoted by "metaphysical." It is easier to decide what characteristics are connoted by "fox" than to decide what characteristics are connoted by "metaphysical." Metaphysics flourishes in New Haven, to be sure, even on an "ordinary evening," but more in Linsly Hall than in the streets. If "metaphysical streets" is meaningful at all, it must be because some connotations of "metaphysical" can be found to apply to it: for example, they may—compare them with Prufrock's streets—wander like a metaphysical argument, or they may—like Berkeley's physical world—have no existence outside the mind. In any case, I propose that whenever an attribution is indirectly self-contradictory, and the modifier has connotations that could be attributed to the subject, the attribution is a *metaphorical attribution*, or metaphor.

But this generalization, though I think true, does not go both ways, and so it does not yet provide a complete theory of metaphor. It is probably too strong to say that in D. H. Lawrence's lines,

> You who take the moon as in a sieve, and sift
> Her flake by flake and spread her meaning out

10 From *Four Quartets*, New York: Harcourt, Brace, 1943. With permission.

("The Sea"[11]), it is self-contradictory to speak of spreading a meaning out. Yet there is evidently something queer about this expression that shows us it is metaphorical, not literal. For another example, it is a saying among theatrical people that "Outside Broadway, everything is Bridgeport," which evidently applies the connotations of the name of my much-maligned native city to the hinterlands in general. We know how to construe this sentence, though it is not self-contradictory, but merely absurd; that is, it is so obviously false, and so obviously known by the speaker to be false—since if he knows what "Bridgeport" refers to, he knows it has city limits—that we know it is not merely a literal statement.

One way of resolving the problem is this. Most words, quite apart from their standard meanings, have certain *presuppositions*. These are the conditions under which we regard the word as correctly applied. For example, "Barbara" does not designate sex—indeed, it has no designation at all, being a proper name—but it presupposes *being a girl*, which is what is meant by saying that it is a girl's name. "Bridgeport" is a city's name. "Loan" is correctly applied to money; that is one of its rules. So "spread," we might say, requires that what is spread be a physical stuff, and *being physical* is its presupposition, though not part of its definition. When, therefore, it is applied to something that is not physical, it is misapplied, and can make a metaphor.

We may then restate the Controversion Theory as follows: a metaphor is a significant attribution that is either indirectly self-contradictory or obviously false in its context, and in which the modifier connotes characteristics that can be attributed, truly or falsely, to the subject. It may be helpful to exhibit the distinctions we have been making by a diagram:

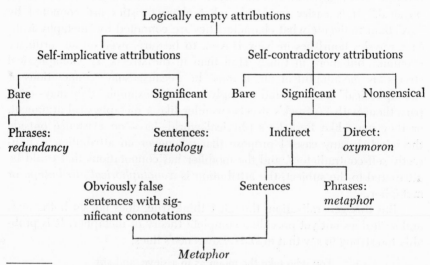

11 From "The Sea," *Collected Poems of D. H. Lawrence*, copyright 1929 by Jonathan Cape & Harrison Smith, Inc. Reprinted with the permission of Jonathan Cape, Ltd., The Viking Press Inc., and the Estate of the late Mrs. Frieda Lawrence.

The more difficult it is to work out connotations of the modifier that can be attributed to the subject, the more obscure is the metaphor—but this obviously depends upon the powers of the reader. As long as there are such connotations, it is still a metaphor, however obscure. But if there are no such connotations, we have not a metaphor, but *nonsense* of a particular kind. It is not as easy as it might seem to discover clear-cut examples of nonsensical attributions; even if we put all English adjectives in one hat, and all nouns in the other, and drew them out at random, we would find that the strangest combinations yield possible meanings upon reflection; and this is a significant feature of living language that has a bearing on another point I shall come to in a moment. Moreover, it must be admitted that we cannot know with certainty that a given attribution is nonsensical, because someone may find a meaning in it that we have overlooked, perhaps by inventing a line of poetry in which the attribution works.

Thus, for example, I once made up the expression "laminated government" in class, on the spur of the moment, as an example of nonsense. A student later pointed out to me a very similar expression in a book on government that gives it, in context, a definite meaning.[12] I should think "participial biped" and "a man in the key of A flat" are very probably incapable of being explicated, and also such old philosophical favorites as "Consanguinity drinks procrastination."[13]

The Controversion Theory explains one of the most puzzling and important features of metaphor, its capacity to create new contextual meaning. Sometimes we have an idea and search for a metaphor to mean it—though even in this case we don't know fully what we shall decide to mean until we find the metaphor. But sometimes we invent, or hit upon, a metaphor and find that it gives us a new idea. The reason is that the connotations of words are never fully known, or knowable, beforehand, and very often we discover new connotations of the words when we see how they behave as modifiers in metaphorical attributions. The metaphor does not create the connotations, but it brings them to life. For example, suppose we take the modifier from the metaphor "rubber questions" (E. E. Cummings), and combine it with a variety of nouns:

> rubber cube roots
> rubber melody
> rubber joy

12 "In contrast to the monolithic state, the strength of American political, economic, and social organization is its laminated structure . . . In this laminated society of pluralistic loyalties, it is obvious that the country is able to preserve its strength and unity, literally its integrity, so long as each of the constituent organizations makes only such demands upon its members as can rationally be reconciled with their obligations to other organizations." George A. Graham, *Morality in American Politics*, New York: Random House, 1952, p. 302.

13 See Bertrand Russell, *An Inquiry Into Meaning and Truth*, New York: Norton, 1940, p. 209.

rubber garden
rubber cliffs
rubber hopes

Some of these are quite certainly nonsense; in others, the combination yields a strange new meaning because the subject singles out for attention a hitherto unnoticed connotation of the modifier.

In this way a metaphor is able to mean something that no literal combination of words in existence at a given time can mean. It augments the resources of our language, just as the Supervenient Theory insists. But the Literalist Theory is right in saying that metaphor is nevertheless analyzable.

Congruence and Plenitude

It must be admitted that it is a long leap from simple attributions to the complex texture of actual poems. Therefore the Controversion Theory worked out here is only a framework. We have, however, something to which we can appeal in trying to resolve the problem with which we started in this section: whether there is a logic of explication. For a metaphor is a miniature poem, and the explication of a metaphor is a model of all explication. The problem of construing the metaphor is that of deciding which of the modifier's connotations can *fit* the subject, and the metaphor means *all* the connotations that can fit—except those that are further eliminated by, because they do not fit, the larger context. Consider "O frail steel tissues of the sun" (G. H. Luce), which some of I. A. Richards' protocol-writers in *Practical Criticism* had so much trouble with. It is a multiple metaphor, and its total regional meaning is the resultant of a number of clashes and interlockings of words. We think in what connotative senses the sun may be said to have tissues, and a tissue to be steel, and steel to be frail. Or, to put the words in right order, "frail" prepares us to respond in a variety of possible ways; "steel" can only accept some of the connotations of "frail"; "tissue" further rejects and limits; and when the metaphor completes itself in "sun" only certain of the originally possible meanings of the separate words still survive—except that some of them, too, may be pushed out by the larger context.

In explicating the metaphor we have employed two principles—and the same may be said of whole poems. First, there is the Principle of Congruence. "Laminated" can connote the isolation of parts, but not in "laminated modulation," for modulations cannot have isolated parts. This is what "fitting" has to mean, I think; in assembling, or feeling out, the admissible connotations of words in a poem, we are guided by logical and physical possibilities. But second, there is the Principle of Plenitude. All the connotations that can be found to fit are to be attributed to the poem: it means all it *can* mean, so to speak.

The two principles of explication constitute the method, or logic,
that we have been looking for. But two fundamental questions about
them remain.

First, is the method decisive? There can be no doubt that the method
produces agreement among critics in a large number of cases. And when
a poem is very complex, and different readers work into it from different
angles, so that each finds things the others have missed, their explications
supplement each other and converge as they expand—consider, for example, the many readings of Keats' "Ode on a Grecian Urn." A proposed
explication may be regarded as a hypothesis that is tested by its capacity
to account for the greatest quantity of data in the words of the poem—
including their potential connotations—and in most poems for which alternative hypotheses can be offered it will turn out in the end that one
is superior to the other.

Nevertheless, it remains theoretically possible that even such a complex discourse as a poem is radically ambiguous, in the strict sense. For
the sentence "He rents the house," two incompatible explications can be
given, and, without a context, there is no way to choose between them.
Suppose—a far-fetched analogy—we have six odd-shaped pieces of cardboard and are asked to fit them together into a simple symmetrical figure.
It may be that *A* fits them together into a triangle, and *B* into a diamond.
Both have solved the problem; it simply has two solutions. Neither is
wrong, though any other would be wrong. The sort of ambiguity we find
in "He rents the house" is unlikely to occur in complex and controlled
discourse. Gray's *Elegy* contains the line "And all the air a solemn stillness holds," which is syntactically ambiguous because "air" can be either
the subject or object of "holds." But we do not need to make a choice;
the ambiguity suggests that it is hard to distinguish between the air and
the solemn stillness. Therefore this line does not make the poem as a
whole ambiguous. Whereas in "He rents the house," we do have to choose,
because a man cannot both pay rent for and accept rent for the same
house at the same time.

Where a poem is as a whole ambiguous, in the strict sense, it has no
single correct explication, though it has a limited number of equally correct ones.

There is another way of regarding the process of explication. To read
a poem—that is, to sound the words, not necessarily aloud, and understand them—is to perform it, or, in my technical sense, to give it a production. A reading usually begins with the printed marks, and is analogous
to the violinist's reading of a score. We found in Chapter I, §4, that unless
we take the aesthetic object in the case of music to be the particular production, contradictions result. But if we take explication-statements as descriptions of particular readings of the poem, we are back with relativism,
for every explicator is talking about his own private production. Yet if

explication-statements are not descriptions of particular readings, what are they?

I think they are statements about how productions are to be carried out—how, in the colloquial sense, the poem is to be performed. The explicator is something like the music teacher or coach. The list of potential secondary meanings of the words shows what *can* be produced from them. The explication, under the Principles of Congruence and Plenitude, shows what constitutes a *correct* performance. But we doubted in the case of music that there *is* a single correct performance; why, then, should there be a single correct performance of poetry?

In some cases, as we have agreed, there may not be: an ambiguous poem is one of which two or more equally congruent and plenary explications can be given. But if explication is subject to these two principles, what it can make of the words, with their connotations and in their syntactical relations, is generally fixed and focused. The explicator cannot make so free with his marks on paper as the violinist with his marks. For the explicator's marks are not arbitrary signals for specialized items of behavior—this note to be stopped, the bow to change its direction at this point—but parts of a living language deeply implicated in the thoughts and experiences of many human beings.

There is still the second of our two final questions: what is the justification for adopting the Principles of Congruence and Plenitude as a general method of explication? They might, of course, be given an instrumentalist justification, on certain assumptions that we shall have to consider in Chapter XI, §28. Adopting these principles tends to make us read poems as complexly and coherently as possible—though the Principle of Congruence, since it only rules out impossibilities, does not guarantee that poems read by it will necessarily turn out unified. If the value of a poem depends in part on its coherence and complexity, then in the long run adopting the two principles will maximize poetic value. This makes the principles depend upon a theory of value, but they are not relative unless value is relative, and once the principles are adopted, questions of value can be ignored in the explication itself.

The instrumentalist justification may be the answer, but I think our problem may be part of an even deeper one for which no perfectly adequate solution has yet been found. In all empirical inquiry, when we choose among alternative hypotheses that explain a certain body of data, we are guided by a general principle, the Principle of Occam's Razor, which enjoins us always to adopt the simplest hypothesis. The simplest hypothesis will be the one which explains the most by the least; it is a principle of intellectual economy. But though we use this principle, and indeed make it almost part of the definition of "rationality," we do not know how to justify our use of it—or at least many philosophers today are much puzzled by the problem. Some, however, would say that the very notion of empirical explanation, when we consider it, involves the accounting for much by means of little—unless a hypothesis is at least somewhat simpler than its data, it is not really an explanation at all. Therefore any good reason we have for explaining things is also a good reason for explaining them as simply as possible.

The Principles of Congruence and Plenitude play in explication a role analogous to that played by the principle of simplicity in scientific inquiry; and perhaps at bottom they may even all be special cases of some broader principle of economy. The very notion of critical explication seems to involve getting as much meaning out of the poem as possible, subject only to some broad control that will preserve a distinction between "getting out of" and "reading into." In the preceding section we found that "literature" seems to be definable in terms of its second-level meaning as supremely significant language, and surely poetry is the kind of literature that exhibits this multiplicity and resonance of meaning to the highest degree. But if this is so, then the most appropriate approach to poetry would seem to be that which is fully open and alive to all its semantical richness, however subtle or recondite.

NOTES AND QUERIES

§9

9-A MEANING. Charles L. Stevenson's account of meaning is in *Ethics and Language*, New Haven: Yale U., 1944, ch. 3. Note the difference between his terminology and that adopted here: his "emotive meaning" covers both emotive import and emotive purport; his "descriptive meaning" is my "designation"; his "cognitive suggestion" is my "connotation."

On understanding, or construing, words and sentences, see Gustaf Stern, *Meaning and Change of Meaning*, Göteborg: Elanders Boktryckeri Aktiebolag, 1931, ch. 6, esp. pp. 155-57; C. H. Whiteley, "On Understanding," *Mind*, N.S., LVIII (1949): 339-51 (he analyzes understanding in terms of expectation); Bertrand Russell, *The Analysis of Mind*, London: Allen and Unwin, 1921, ch. 10.

9-B EMOTIVE FORCE AND ITS RELATION TO COGNITIVE FORCE. (I) The outstanding statement and defense of the Independence Theory is in Charles L. Stevenson, *loc. cit.* Stevenson's view is further defended, qualified, and criticized in two symposia: "A Symposium on Emotive Meaning," with papers by Stevenson, Max Black, and I. A. Richards, *Phil R*, LVII (1948): 111-57 (Black's paper, with comments on the others, is reprinted in Black, *Language and Philosophy*, Ithaca, N.Y.: Cornell U., 1949, pp. 203-20, 254-57; Richards' paper in Richards, *Speculative Instruments*, London: Routledge and Kegan Paul, 1955); and papers by Stevenson,

"The Emotive Conception of Ethics and Its Cognitive Implications," and R. B. Brandt, "The Emotive Theory of Ethics," *Phil R*, LIX (1950): 291-318, with replies, 528-40.

An early and influential version of the Independence Theory was put forth by C. K. Ogden and I. A. Richards in *The Meaning of Meaning*, London: Routledge and Kegan Paul, 1923. They distinguished an "emotive use of words," under which they classed poetry (pp. 147-58; see also ch. 10), but the "symbolic use of words" was far too narrowly defined as "statement" (p. 149). A similar oversimplification underlies the thesis of Richards' *Science and Poetry*, 2nd ed., London: Routledge and Kegan Paul, 1935, reprinted in Mark Schorer, Josephine Miles and Gordon McKenzie, eds., *Criticism*, New York: Harcourt, Brace, 1948, pp. 505-23; the important section is also in Ray B. West, Jr., ed., *Essays in Modern Literary Criticism*, New York: Rinehart, 1952, pp. 167-74, and Robert W. Stallman, ed., *Critiques and Essays in Criticism*, New York: Ronald, 1949, pp. 329-33. Poetry is not "statement," but "pseudo-statement," a pseudo-statement being "a form of words which is justified by its effect in releasing or organizing our impulses and attitudes" (p. 65). The difficulty in dealing with this thesis comes from its mixing up of several distinct issues, some of which we shall deal with in Chapter IX, §§22, 23. For example, Richards sometimes talks as though pseudo-statements are —like exclamations—not statements at all, sometimes as though they are true or false but simply not asserted, sometimes as though they are true or false but their "scientific truth or falsity is irrelevant to the purposes at hand"; sometimes he talks not about what poetry is, but about "the business of the poet," meaning what the poet ought to do. Nevertheless this essay is a classic and indispensable discussion of the problem. Richards' later views are set forth in the symposium with Black and Stevenson, *loc. cit.*, and in "Emotive Language Still," *Yale Review*, XXXIX (Autumn 1949): 108-18.

See also Gustaf Stern, *op. cit.*, pp. 54-60, on "emotive elements of meaning," by which he means (approximately) emotive purport; S. I. Hayakawa, *Language in Thought and Action*, New York: Harcourt, Brace, 1949, ch. 8; Irving Lee, *Language Habits in Human Affairs*, New York, London: Harper, 1941, ch. 8, pp. 132-33.

(II) For criticism of the Independence Theory, see: W. K. Wimsatt, Jr., and Monroe C. Beardsley, "The Affective Fallacy," *Sewanee Review*, LVII (1949): 458-88, sec. 1, reprinted in W. K. Wimsatt, Jr., *The Verbal Icon*, Lexington, Ky.: U. of Kentucky, 1954, pp. 21-39; William Empson, *The Structure of Complex Words*, New York: New Directions, 1951, ch. 1, and pp. 56-64; Monroe C. Beardsley, *Thinking Straight*, 2d ed., rev., Englewood Cliffs, N.J.: Prentice-Hall, 1956, secs. 27, 30; and the symposia on Stevenson, *loc. cit.*

(III) A third aspect of language, often called "pictorial meaning," has been analyzed by Virgil Aldrich, "Pictorial Meaning and Picture

Thinking," *Kenyon Review*, V (1943): 403-12, reprinted in H. Feigl and
W. Sellars, *Readings in Philosophical Analysis*, New York: Appleton-
Century-Crofts, 1949, pp. 175-81; it is the tendency of a linguistic expression to evoke an image in the mind of one to whom it is uttered. I question whether this tendency is regular and constant enough to be called a
third kind of import, "pictorial import"; the effect, when it occurs, is
clearly dependent upon meaning, and therefore the term "pictorial meaning" is misleading.

9-C MULTIPLE MEANING. (I) On the distinction between primary
and secondary sentence-meaning (or, in the case of declarative sentences,
statement and suggestion), see Monroe C. Beardsley, *op. cit.*, sec. 28, where
various types of suggestion are distinguished. Otto Jesperson has an interesting definition, *The Philosophy of Grammar*, New York: Holt, 1924,
p. 309: "Suggestion is impression through suppression." Suggestion is
sometimes called "implication" (as opposed to "entailment"); cf. P. F.
Strawson, *Introduction to Logical Theory*, New York: Wiley, 1952, p. 48.

On the distinction between primary and secondary word-meaning
(designation and connotation), see Monroe C. Beardsley, *op. cit.*, sec. 25,
where the sources of connotation are classified; John Sparrow, *Sense and
Poetry*, London: Constable, 1934, ch. 1 (his distinction between "meaning" and "association" corresponds to my distinction between "designation" and "connotation"); William Empson, *op. cit.*, pp. 15-38 (his "Implication" means "range of potential connotations"; his "Sense" means
"designation"); Lascelles Abercrombie, *The Theory of Poetry*, London:
Secker, 1924, ch. 4; Richard D. Altick, *Preface to Critical Reading*, rev.
ed., New York: Holt, 1951, ch. 1; T. M. Greene, *The Arts and the Art of
Criticism*, Princeton, N.J.: Princeton U., 1947, ch. 6. Under connotation
we should also include the word's cross-references to other words, through
sound-similarities; see I. A. Richards, *Philosophy of Rhetoric*, New York:
Oxford U., 1936, ch. 3, on "interinanimation."

Secondary meanings are sometimes called "pragmatic meaning" or
"psychological meaning." But the connotations of a word are no more
"pragmatic"—i.e., related to, or tending to produce, action?—than its designation, and no more "psychological"—i.e., irrelevant to belief? The distinction is sometimes made in terms of rules: there are "rules" of designation but not of connotation. This is puzzling too, but "rules" can
presumably refer only to dictionary definitions—what other rules are
there in general use?—and, if so, the distinction is misleading. For no one
would say that a dictionary can tell *all* the meaning of a word in any
particular context, and so the meaning cannot be reduced to what is reported in a dictionary. The term "obliqueness" might have been used for
secondary meaning, as suggested by E. M. W. Tillyard, *Poetry Direct and
Oblique,* rev. ed., London: Chatto and Windus, 1948, since Tillyard agrees
that all poetry is more or less oblique, though differing in degree (p. 10);

but his correlative term, "statement," is so oddly used—"Alastor" seems to be statement because it reports "things seen," and books read, by Shelley (pp. 29-30)—that his terms are too loose for critical purposes.

The distinction between the primary and secondary meaning of words is based on the commonly held view that for most general terms (e.g., "horse") there are certain characteristics that are necessary conditions for the application of the term (a horse must be physical, must have a certain shape, etc.), and these are its defining characteristics, i.e., its designation. This view has been effectively criticized by Michael Scriven, "Definitions, Explanations, and Theories," in Herbert Feigl and Scriven, eds., *The Logic of Scientific Concepts and the Mind-Body Problem*, Vol. II of *Minnesota Studies in the Philosophy of Science*, Minneapolis: U. of Minnesota, 1958, who holds that most general terms have no necessary, but only sets of sufficient, conditions. If Scriven is right—the matter is in dispute—then there is at least a difference in the degree of centrality or peripherality of meaning: having a certain shape belongs to more sets of sufficient conditions of being a horse than, say, having a tail. And this difference of degree will probably suit the main purpose for which the distinction between primary and secondary meanings is made here: the analysis of metaphor in §10, below. We do not have a metaphor at all, as far as I can see, unless some fairly central characteristic associated with the word is excluded by the context.

Empson's highly original and valuable analysis of what he calls "statements in words"—*op. cit.*, ch. 2; but the whole book is part of the argument—opens up an important type of secondary meaning. The covert statement in the word is that two of its senses—designations or connotations—somehow belong together, because they are both in the word. If "design" can mean both "something that has an order" and "something planned," its use, with certain tones or supporting words, can implicitly claim that what has an order must have been planned. Empson's numerous examples are more subtle than this. It is not fully clear how his discoveries can be assimilated to the principles of this chapter, but one point of connection is evident. The implicit claim can only be worked where there is a strong overlapping of denotation—it would be impossible for the word "post" to make it seem plausible to believe that fence posts are ordinarily sent through the mails. And where one of the two senses is a connotation, its being so presupposes that there is, or is generally believed to be, a large proportion of the relevant objects that has the connoted characteristics. Thus to make a statement merely by using a word—at least the statements Empson calls "equations"—is somehow to call attention to some empirical generalization that connects its designations or one that underlies one of its connotations.

(II) The chief problems in defining "connotation" are (1) the problem of distinguishing public connotations from personal and private associations that grow out of individual experiences like being afraid of

spiders or allergic to cat's fur, and (2) the problem of distinguishing connotations from designations, that is, of deciding at what point a characteristic connoted by a word in many contexts comes to be counted as a part
of its standard meaning. Neither of these distinctions can be made with
absolute precision, but perhaps further investigation can sharpen them.
Unfortunately these inherent difficulties are further complicated by variations of terminology and certain confusions: What I have called "designation" is usually, in literary criticism and by teachers of literature,
called "denotation," but this latter word is needed for the relation between
words and things they refer to. The term "connotation" I have defined in keeping with prevailing critical usage, but logicians often use it
in a sense equivalent to the way I have defined "designation." The connotations of words, which are characteristics of things, must not be confused with the emotional effects of words; the common expression "emotional connotations" smudges an important difference.

The problem of distinguishing connotations from personal associations is pointed up by an odd controversy over a word in a poem by Edith
Sitwell. The first shot was apparently fired by John Sparrow, *op. cit.*, p.
81, who cited "Emily-colored hands" as a purely private reference; later,
Philip Toynbee, in an article defending James Joyce against obscurity,
conceded that "Emily-colored hands" was "clearly cheating"; the consequent series of letters in the London *Observer* is summarized in *Time*,
November 12, 1951, p. 31. The figure of speech was strongly condemned
and just as strongly defended by those who said they knew "quite well
what [they] are like, thin, pale, yellowish, and faintly freckled." Miss
Sitwell herself commented:

> I did not write "Emily-colored hands," a hideous phrase. I wrote "Emily-
> colored *primulas*," which to anyone who has progressed in poetry reading
> beyond the *White Cliffs of Dover* calls to mind the pink cheeks of young
> country girls.

(She has discussed this example further, and several other amusingly
Sitwellian metaphors, like "hairy sky" and "furred is the light," in "Some
Notes on My Own Poetry," *The Canticle of the Rose, Poems: 1917-49*,
New York: Vanguard, 1949, pp. xii-xxxviii.) See also the discussion by
Geoffrey Nokes and Kingsley Amis, *Essays in Criticism*, II (1952): 338-45.

(III) The term "ambiguity," as a general term for all kinds of secondary word- and sentence-meaning, was first installed in the critic's
vocabulary by William Empson, *Seven Types of Ambiguity*, London:
Chatto and Windus, 1930—but see also the Preface to the 2d ed., rev.,
1947. He defined it as "any verbal nuance, however slight, which gives
room for alternative reactions to the same piece of language" (2d ed., p.
1). His attempt to classify these nuances in seven categories broke down
—no one could really follow the distinctions or apply them himself—but
the great subtlety and fruitfulness of his discoveries about multiple mean-

ing, both syntactical and semantical, in poetry had an enormous influence, even though he said that the method he used had been invented by Robert Graves. The distinction between the sort of multiple meaning he was concerned with and doubtfulness of meaning, is so important that I have reserved the term "ambiguity" for the latter—for a fuller explanation see Beardsley, *op. cit.*, secs. 17, 18. Instead, however, one could adopt the set of technical terms recommended by Abraham Kaplan and Ernst Kris, "Aesthetic Ambiguity," *Phil and Phen Res*, VIII (March 1948): 415-35, reprinted in Ernst Kris, *Psychoanalytic Explorations in Art*, New York: International Universities, 1952, who use the term "disjunctive ambiguity" for ambiguity proper, and the terms "conjunctive ambiguity" and "integrative ambiguity" for two not very clearly distinguished species of multiple meaning. This valuable article also deals with a number of psychological questions about multiple meaning in poetry.

W. B. Stanford, *Ambiguity in Greek Literature*, Oxford: Blackwell, 1939, Part I, esp. ch. 5, uses "ambiguity" to cover various types of multiple meaning, which he discusses and illustrates in an interesting way, and distinguishes from vagueness and obscurity.

Philip Wheelwright, *The Burning Fountain*, Bloomington, Ind.: Indiana U., 1954, p. 61, has proposed the term "plurisignation" for multiple meaning.

9-D THE LANGUAGE OF POETRY. (I) The Semantical Definition of "poetry" is apparently supported in Cleanth Brooks' statement, "The language of poetry is the language of paradox." See his essay, "The Language of Paradox," in Allen Tate, ed., *The Language of Poetry*, Princeton, N.J.: Princeton U., 1942, also in Schorer, Miles, and McKenzie, *op. cit.*, pp. 358-66; it became ch. 1 of *The Well Wrought Urn*, New York: Reynal and Hitchcock, 1947, but without the two footnotes connecting metaphor with paradox (Tate, *op. cit.*, pp. 45, 57; without the footnotes it also appears in Robert W. Stallman, *op. cit.*, pp. 66-79). See also Brooks, *The Well Wrought Urn*, chs. 2, 11, p. 223: "The essence of poetry is metaphor"; cf. I. A. Richards, "The Interactions of Words," in Tate, *op. cit.*

See also the very suggestive article by Dorothy Walsh, "The Poetic Use of Language," *J Phil*, XXXV (1938): 73-81: poetry is language that "means all it says." Also Richard von Mises, *Positivism*, Cambridge, Mass.: Harvard U., 1951, ch. 23.

Empson's profound remark, *Seven Types of Ambiguity*, New York: Meridian, 1955, p. 30, makes the "essential fact about the poetical use of language" to consist in suggestion:

> Lacking rhyme, meter, and any overt device such as comparison, these lines are what we should normally call poetry only by virtue of their compactness; two statements are made as if they were connected, and the reader is forced to consider their relations for himself. The reason why

these facts should have been selected for a poem is left for him to invent; he will invent a variety of reasons and order them in his own mind.

Compare the example from Frege in the text; but note also that the reader's "invention" is controlled by the conditions of the explicit discourse itself.

Coleridge's famous distinction between "poem" and "poetry," *Biographia Literaria,* ch. 14, reprinted in Schorer, Miles, and McKenzie, *op. cit.,* pp. 249-53, is intentionalistic and psychological, but his "balance or reconciliation of opposite or discordant qualities," when translated into objective terms, is not far from the Semantic Definition. For a good discussion, see Meyer H. Abrams, *The Mirror and the Lamp,* New York: Oxford U., 1953, pp. 114-24. This book contains much interesting material on various historical definitions of "poetry," chs. 1, 4, 5, 6; cf. his comments on Wordsworth's puzzling remark, in the 1800 Preface to *Lyrical Ballads,* that there is no "*essential* difference between the language of prose and metrical composition."

D. G. James, *Scepticism and Poetry,* London: Allen and Unwin, 1937, pp. 87-97, seems to define poetry semantically; note also his example (p. 260): "A thing of beauty is a joy forever" is poetry, but "A thing of beauty is a constant joy" is not.

Kenneth Burke, "Semantic and Poetic Meaning," *Southern Review,* IV (1939): 501-23, reprinted in *The Philosophy of Literary Form,* Baton Rouge, La.: Louisiana State U., 1941, pp. 138-67, contrasts "poetic meaning" with "semantic meaning," by which, curiously, he means the language of science; but his description of the "semantic ideal" (*The Philosophy of Literary Form,* p. 141) is open to criticism.

See Ezra Pound, "Literature Is Language Charged with Meaning," *ABC of Reading,* London: Routledge and Kegan Paul, 1934, p. 14.

Warren Beck, "The Boundaries of Poetry," *College English,* IV (1943): 342-50, has some interesting remarks about the minimal requirements for a discourse to be a poem.

Charles L. Stevenson, "On 'What Is a Poem?' " *Phil R,* LXVI (1957): 329-62, has argued very persuasively that in the actual usage of literary critics there is no single set of necessary and sufficient conditions for a discourse to be a poem, and he has proposed an interesting way of representing fluctuations in the meaning of "poem" by a diagram that weights various characteristics for their relative requiredness. This need not, however, in my opinion, dissuade us from proposing to solidify or stabilize usage if reasons can be given for adopting a new definition.

(II) A. E. Housman, *The Name and Nature of Poetry,* New York: Macmillan, 1933, has said that simile and metaphor are "things inessential to poetry" (p. 11), the "peculiar function of poetry" being "to set up in the reader's sense a vibration corresponding to what was felt by the writer" (p. 8); but his first example of a verse that has a "tinge of emotion" is metaphorical (p. 8). And when he says that "Take O Take Those Lips Away" is "nonsense" but "ravishing poetry" (p. 40), it is clear that "nonsense" is hyperbole, not exact language. In support of the same thesis, John Hospers, *Meaning and Truth in the Arts*, Chapel Hill, N.C.: U. of North Carolina, 1946, pp. 117-38, cites as examples of nonfigurative language (a) the last stanza of Wordsworth's "She Dwelt among the Untrodden Ways"—but it is the middle stanza that lifts the first and last into the poetic dimension—and (b) the first stanza of Matthew Arnold's "Dover Beach"—but this is full of personification, e.g., "the sea meets the moon-blanched land," "the waves draw back, and fling," which I judge to be metaphorical, even though not as obviously so as, say, Oscar Williams' line, "The ocean slobbers on the shore."

Hospers and Housman are nevertheless right in saying that there are poems that are not figurative, but their emphasis is wrong, for these are relatively rare. It might be worthwhile to try to work out the following scheme: (A) Metrical discourses that are not poems because they have no secondary meanings as a whole: "Thirty Days Hath September"; the medieval listing of the valid figures of the syllogism, "Barbara, Celarent, Darii, Ferioque prioris," etc.; perhaps Bentham's listing of the factors of the hedonistic calculus, which begins

> Intense, long, certain, speedy, fruitful, pure—
> Such marks in pleasures and in pains endure

(*An Introduction to the Principles of Morals and Legislation*, New York: Hafner, 1948, p. 29n). (B1) Poems that are nonfigurative, but carry important secondary meaning via connotation or suggestion: "O Western Wind, When Wilt Thou Blow"; Robert Frost, "Neither Out Far Nor In Deep"; Wordsworth, "We Are Seven"; Hardy, "The Man He Killed"; Robert Louis Stevenson, "Requiem." On the borderline of A and B1 are perhaps Robert Frost, "The Pasture"; William Carlos Williams, "Silence"; Masefield, "Cargoes." Parts of some poems, e.g., Frost, "Two Witches," do not deviate at all from ordinary language, but even these parts are given a secondary meaning by other parts of the poems in which they occur. (B2) Poems that contain figures of speech; these are the vast majority. On the borderline of B1 and B2 are some short Imagist poems, like many of the Japanese Hokku and Arthur Waley's translations from the Chinese (see Po-Chü-i, "The Cranes"); most of the cinquains of Adelaide Crapsey are definitely, though very vaguely, metaphoric or symbolic.

(III) Charles W. Morris, *Signs, Language, and Behavior*, Englewood Cliffs, N.J.: Prentice-Hall, 1946, pp. 136-38, offers a definition of "poetic discourse" as "primarily appraisive-valuative," using these terms in his own sense: poetic discourse contains a high proportion of "appraisors" used for the purpose of "inducing valuative attitudes." If we leave out the second criterion, as involving a reference to intention that is not open to test with most poems, we are left with the first, and this seems far from affording a distinction between poems and other discourses. "That was a good movie" is appraisive-valuative; it is not poetry.

The definition of "poetic discourse" as a species of "expressive discourse" systematically formulated by Philip Wheelwright, *op. cit.*, chs. 2-4, is connected with an Intuitionist Theory of Knowledge, and will therefore engage our attention in Chapter IX.

See also Max Rieser, "Language of Poetic and of Scientific Thought," *J Phil*, XL (1943): 421-35, for poetry as the language of value that endows things with "life-meanings." This article is commented upon by M. Whitcomb-Hess, "The Language of Poetry," *Phil R*, LIII (1944): 484-92, whose own view is unclear.

Owen Barfield, *Poetic Diction,* 2nd ed., London: Faber and Faber, 1952, chs. 1, 2, offers an affective definition, which is developed in the direction of Intuitionism (see Chapter IX, §23, below).

Marguerite H. Foster, "Poetry and Emotive Meaning," *J Phil*, XLVII (1950): 657-60, says that poetry does not "convey" information, but neither is it "meaningless" or "purely emotive."

Solomon Fishman, "Meaning and Structure in Poetry," *JAAC*, XIV (June 1956): 453-61, objects to the Semantical, which he calls the "structuralist," definition of "poetry," but his strictures do not seem fatal to the version given in this chapter.

There are some interesting, though inconclusive, reflections in Bernard Mayo, "Poetry, Language and Communication," *Philosophy,* XXIX (1954): 131-45.

9-E THE DEFINITION OF "LITERATURE." The problem of defining "literature" is discussed in René Wellek and Austin Warren, *Theory of Literature,* New York: Harcourt, Brace, 1949, chs. 2, 12; their distinction depends in part upon the concept of "aesthetic function," which we have not yet defined. Thomas C. Pollock, *The Nature of Literature,* Princeton, N.J.: Princeton U., 1942, defines "literature" in terms of "evocative symbolism" (pp. 96-97, 141), which is capable of inducing in the mind of the reader a "controlled experience" similar to the writer's (see also chs. 8, 9). This definition, and the distinction between "literature" and "pseudo-literature" (p. 180), seem to me intentionalistic. Nor does Pollock give an adequate account (chs. 6, 7) of the specific features of evocative symbolism; but I should judge that such an account would correspond fairly well to that given in the present chapter.

Albert Hofstadter, "The Scientific and Literary Uses of Language," *Symbols and Society,* 14th Symposium of the Conference on Science, Philosophy and Religion, New York: Harper, 1955, ch. 10, distinguishes poetry from science by its "function": to produce an effect that is "intrinsically interesting" (p. 307).

Lascelles Abercrombie, *op. cit.*, chs. 3, 6, says that poetry—literature in general?—is what does not merely describe, but imitates what is happening in the author's mind.

Another attempt to define "literature" in the sense we are after is De Quincey's: he calls it the "literature of power"—because its "function" is "to move"—as distinguished from the "literature of knowledge"; see his review of Pope, partly reprinted in Schorer, Miles, and McKenzie, *op. cit.*, pp. 473-76.

9-F THE EXISTENCE OF THE LITERARY WORK. Since a literary work exists, so to speak, in the habit patterns of people who belong to a certain speech-community, it may be said to change as the meanings of its words change. If we ask for the meaning of a certain Shakespeare sonnet, we can ask what it meant in 1650, in 1750, in 1950; this does not involve an appeal to intention, but only (see §10, below) to usage at a given time. Some discourses probably gain new richness of meaning with age, as their words are used in notable contexts by other writers: the King James version of the Bible is an example. Others are ruined by changes, and their original quality almost irrecoverable; for example, in Tennyson's "Edwin Morris" there are the lines

> And this is well,
> To have a dame indoors, that trims us up,
> And keeps us tight

(see Wellek and Warren, *op. cit.*, p. 180). A modern American reader can hardly exclude the slang meanings. In general, however, one might say that the more tightly organized structures of meaning, like the best Shakespeare sonnets, are remarkably resistant to language changes; it is the looser ones that are most at the mercy of time, though of course no foresight could have protected Tennyson's lines against their fate. Even without being told, a reader of Hamlet's "I'll make a ghost of him that lets me," could probably guess that "lets" had in Shakespeare's time a meaning exactly opposite to that which it has now—except for its survival in tennis and in "without let or hindrance."

§10

10-A THE PRINCIPLES OF EXPLICATION. (I) For the Relativistic Theory of Explication, see Charles L. Stevenson, "Interpretation and Evaluation in Aesthetics," in Max Black, ed., *Philosophical Analysis*, Ithaca, N.Y.: Cornell U., 1950, pp. 341-83. Stevenson's argument, as applied to explication, might be stated this way: "The poem means M" can be defined as "The poem will be understood as meaning M when *properly* explicated"; but "proper" is irreducibly normative here, and cannot be given purely nonnormative specification in terms of methods of explication. Now Stevenson grants that in "X is red," which means "X

appears red under *proper* conditions," "proper" *can* be given nonnorma- 157
tive specification (p. 353), in terms of bright lighting, etc. Probably he
would also grant the same for standard meanings of words: "'Uncle'
designates maleness" means "'Uncle' will be understood as limited to
males, when *properly* construed," but here "proper" can be given nonnormative specification, in terms of the methods of linguistic investigation. But when it comes to the *contextual* meanings of words, as in his
example from Donne (p. 358), he denies that criteria of "proper" explication can be given; "proper" contains an "imperative" element ("The
poem *is to be interpreted in this way*"), so the "proper" explication can
only be "justified" in the way imperatives are justified—that is, in terms of
consequences desired.

W. K. Wimsatt, Jr., "Explication as Criticism," *English Institute
Essays, 1951,* New York: Columbia U., 1952, reprinted in *The Verbal
Icon,* Lexington, Ky.: U. of Kentucky, 1954, pp. 235-51, holds that many
useful explicative terms are inherently normative as well as descriptive;
he suggests that the explicator, in trying to settle on the correct explication of a poem, is to some extent guided by his conception of what a
good poem would be. But Wimsatt's normative theory is not relativistic
like Stevenson's.

Isabel Hungerland, "The Interpretation of Poetry," *JAAC,* XII
(March 1955): 351-59, takes the aim of explication, which she calls "interpretation," to be "the aim of achieving maximum aesthetic satisfaction for the individual interpreter from the work in question" (p. 356),
which is a relativistic standard; she uses intention and "correspondence"
as criteria of acceptable explications, but thinks that "the concept of
coherence in general is almost without content" (p. 359).

On the principles of explication in general, see Cleanth Brooks, "The
Poem as Organism," *English Institute Essays,* New York: Columbia U.,
1941; his general point of view is that explications are interpersonally
testable. Compare R. S. Crane, "I. A. Richards on the Art of Interpretation," in *Critics and Criticism,* by Crane et al., Chicago: Chicago U.,
1952, pp. 27-44.

See also the discussion by F. W. Bateson, John Wain, W. W. Robson,
"'Intention' and Blake's Jerusalem," *Essays in Criticism,* II (1952): 105-14.

10-B PROBLEMS OF EXPLICATION. For further investigation of methods actually used, and principles tacitly or explicitly assumed, by literary
critics, I cite below some examples of explications and disagreements
about the correct explication of poems.

What is meant by "numbers" in the lines from Hart Crane's "Faustus
and Helen" beginning "The mind is brushed by sparrow wings"? Yvor
Winters' explication in "The Experimental School in American Poetry,"
In Defense of Reason, New York: Swallow, 1947, pp. 41-43, was withdrawn after attack; see pp. 153-55; the essay, with explanatory footnote,

is reprinted in Mark Schorer, Josephine Miles and Gordon McKenzie, eds., *Criticism,* New York: Harcourt, Brace, 1948, see p. 294. Compare Crane's own explication of his poem "At Melville's Tomb," in Robert W. Stallman, ed., *The Critic's Notebook,* Minneapolis: U. of Minnesota, 1950, pp. 242-47; also ch. 4.

In Yeats' "Among School Children," stanza 5, who is "betrayed" by "honey of generation," mother or child? How is this question to be settled? See the discussion by John Wain, *Interpretations,* ed. by John Wain, London: Routledge and Kegan Paul, 1955, pp. 198-200.

William Empson, "Marvell's Garden," *Some Versions of Pastoral,* London: Chatto and Windus, 1935, ch. 4, reprinted in Schorer, Miles, and McKenzie, *op. cit.,* pp. 342-52, and in Ray B. West, *Essays in Modern Literary Criticism,* New York: Rinehart, 1952, pp. 335-53, is very instructive. Rosamund Tuve's learned essay on Herbert's "The Sacrifice," and her criticism of the explication of this poem given by William Empson, *Seven Types of Ambiguity,* New York: Meridian, 1955, ch. 7 (see *A Reading of George Herbert,* London: Faber and Faber, 1952, Part I), raise some good questions about the logic of explication, especially the relevance of literary history. See also Chapter I, Note 1-H.

It is hard to see what plausible principles would justify the method of explication used by Elder Olsen, *The Poetry of Dylan Thomas,* Chicago: U. of Chicago, 1954; for example, he says that "And from the windy West came two-gunned Gabriel" refers to the constellation Perseus, for Perseus had two weapons, his sword and the Medusa's head; two guns recall the Wild West, the West recalls poker, poker is a game of cards, cards suggest trumps, and trumps suggest the Last Trump, hence Gabriel (p. 74). Is there any limit to explication by this method? See Theodore Spencer, "How to Criticize a Poem," *New Republic,* CIX (December 6, 1943): 816-17; but it is a nice question at what point his attack becomes unjust.

One interesting problem of explication arises in connection with key words that a particular writer uses in a number of his works: e.g., Yeats' "rose" and "ceremony," or Blake's "lamb." In different contexts, these words have different connotations, but the question is whether, or to what extent, the different poems support each other. Two general principles of explication might be stated: (1) A word means in each poem all that it means in other poems by the same author, except for those ruled out by the context. (2) The word carries over specialized senses from earlier poems by the same writer only if these senses are supported by the present context. Some critics would argue for the first, or broad, principle, on the ground that short lyrics by Blake or Yeats become much more meaningful if we give some words all the richness they have in larger poems. Others would argue that this makes the poems lean on each other too much, and leads to reading things into poetry.

Some examples of alternative discussions of poems are given in

David Daiches, *Critical Approaches to Literature*, Englewood Cliffs, N.J.: Prentice-Hall, 1956, p. 300. See also the useful bibliography, George Arms and Joseph Kuntz, *Poetry Explication*, New York: Swallow, 1950.

10-C METAPHOR. After Aristotle (see below), I. A. Richards' *Philosophy of Rhetoric*, New York: Oxford U., 1936, chs. 5, 6, is one of the two most fundamental contributions to the theory of metaphor; the other is Gustaf Stern's. Richards unfortunately elected to use the term "metaphor" very broadly, and in such a way as to smudge the important distinction between a live metaphor and a "dead metaphor," which is precisely *not* a metaphor but an attribution that has passed from a metaphorical to a literal state because some of its former connotations have become fixed as part of its current designation. (See also his *Interpretation in Teaching*, New York: Harcourt, Brace, 1938, ch. 2.) It is also unfortunate that he did not go further in introducing the two terms, "tenor" and "vehicle" for the parts of the metaphorical attribution. Such a distinction was needed, but his definition of them is not fully explicit, and neither he nor anyone else has been able to use these terms consistently and unwaveringly (even those who have pointed out their ambiguities): for example, Richards himself speaks of tenor and vehicle as two "things" that may resemble each other (p. 118), and also says "we can extract the tenor and believe that as a statement" (p. 135). In other words, in the metaphor "dusty answer" sometimes dust—the physical stuff —is said to be the vehicle, sometimes the *word* "dusty"; sometimes the answer is said to be the tenor, sometimes the word "answer," and sometimes the characteristic connoted by "dusty" (unwanted, unsatisfying, unacceptable, etc.)—"the underlying idea . . . which the vehicle . . . means" (p. 97). It seems more satisfactory to have terms explicitly for the verbal components of the metaphor ("answer" is the subject, "dusty" the modifier). Richards does not propose the Controversion Theory, but that theory can assimilate what is fruitful in his account.

C. S. Lewis, "Bluspels and Flalansferes: A Semantic Nightmare," in *Rehabilitations and Other Essays*, New York: Oxford U., 1939, proposes an interesting theory of the way metaphors might be transformed into literal expressions. Compare Owen Barfield, "Poetic Diction and Legal Fiction," in *Essays Presented to Charles Williams*, New York: Oxford U., 1947.

On metaphor in general, see: René Wellek and Austin Warren, *Theory of Literature*, New York: Harcourt, Brace, 1949, ch. 15, Bibliography (pp. 373-74); D. G. James, *Scepticism and Poetry*, London: Allen and Unwin, 1937, pp. 94-108; F. W. Leakey, "Intention in Metaphor," *Essays in Criticism*, IV (1954): 191-98.

(I) The Emotive Theory. Max Rieser, "Analysis of the Poetic Simile," *J Phil*, XXXVII (1940): 209-17, and "Brief Introduction to an Epistemology of Art," *J Phil*, XLVII (1950): 695-704, holds a semi-emotive Theory: in the simile, of which metaphor is a "transformation," "the link is not factual but emotional" (XXXVII: 210); the "poetic comparison is not a proposition at all" (XLVII: 701). The theory of Max Eastman, *The Literary Mind*, New York: Scribner's, 1931, Part IV, ch. 1, secs. 5, 6 (compare *The Enjoyment of Poetry*, New York: Scribner's, 1913) is not exactly an Emotive Theory—if indeed it is a theory at all—but it is close to being one. A metaphor is an "impractical identification" (p. 187) which "heightens consciousness" by applying an adjective that is not "habitually" applied (p. 164). But metaphorical statements are not identities, and habit will not distinguish metaphorical from nonmetaphorical attributions; Eastman does not really explain metaphor, but only describes its usual, or occasional, effect.

(II) The Supervenient Theory. As an example of this theory, I would cite Martin Foss, *Symbol and Metaphor in Human Experience*, Princeton, N.J.: Princeton U., 1949, pp. 53-69, esp. 61-62; he seems to hold that in a metaphorical attribution, the separate terms lose all sense of their original designations, and that "the metaphorical sphere . . . realizes a simple and indivisible unity" (p. 61). I do not think this can really be defended; see the excellent discussion of Foss by W. K. Wimsatt, Jr., "Symbol and Metaphor," *Review of Metaphysics*, IV (December 1950): 279-90, reprinted in Wimsatt, *The Verbal Icon*, pp. 119-30. And it seems to me unfortunate that, in his effort to draw a broad contrast between two methods of knowledge, Foss has stretched the term "metaphor" to the point where all verbs (p. 64), the word "being" (p. 65), and even causality (p. 67) are "metaphorical." Less extreme than Foss's view is that of Philip Wheelwright, *The Burning Fountain*, Bloomington, Ind.: Indiana U., 1954, chs. 5, 6. He asserts "the ontological status of radical metaphor" (p. 97); it embodies a unique kind of knowing that is "paralogical," and hence is a species of poetic discourse. Wheelwright's views are also set forth in a review of several books (including Foss), "Symbol, Metaphor, and Myth," *Sewanee Review*, LVIII (1950): 678-98.

(III) The Literalist Theory. A pretty thoroughly Literalist Theory is set forth by Scott Buchanan, *Poetry and Mathematics*, New York: Day, 1929, ch. 4. Aristotle, in his *Rhetoric*, III, 2-10 (see Lane Cooper, trans., New York: Appleton, 1932), says that the difference between metaphor and simile is "but slight" (1406b); he holds (see *Poetics*, ch. 21) that a metaphor expresses a comparison and that its "ground" is a "proportional analogy." But his idea that a metaphor is the "application of an alien name" can be developed into a Controversion Theory, though Aristotle does not really explain in what consists the alienness of the name. Andrew Ushenko, "Metaphor," *Thought*, XXX (1955): 421-39, follows Aristotle pretty closely, but adds the notion of "bearings" (pp. 428-29), or contextual control. It is objectionable, I think, to define "metaphor" in such a way that by definition it must have a larger context (an isolated metaphor he calls a "pseudo-metaphor," p. 424).

(IV) The Controversion Theory as developed in this chapter is not to be found elsewhere, except for a bare outline in Monroe C. Beardsley, *Practical Logic,* Englewood Cliffs, N.J.: Prentice-Hall, 1950, pp. 94-105. But some other discussions of metaphor are close to it or consonant with it. For example, Max Black's excellent paper, "Metaphor," *PAS* (1955): 273-94, sets forth an "interaction view of metaphor," which he opposes to the "substitution view" and the "comparison view." His "system of associated commonplaces" (p. 287) is the set of beliefs that determine the range of connotation of the metaphorical modifier. He has some valuable things to say, but I judge his theory incomplete in not explaining what it is about the metaphorical attribution that informs us that the modifier is metaphorical rather than literal. Abraham Kaplan, "Referential Meaning in the Arts," *JAAC,* XII (June 1954): 457-74 (esp. 469-73), follows Richards; his position is, I think, compatible with the Controversion Theory. See also the very subtle and rewarding discussion of William Empson, *The Structure of Complex Words,* New York: New Directions, 1951, chs. 17-19; Scott George, *The Eighteenth Century Philosophy of Metaphor,* Nashville: privately printed, 1945—but he uses "metaphor" in a very broad sense.

I take the Controversion Theory to give an account of what it means to say that a metaphor consists in "using a term normally signifying an object or concept in such a context that it must refer to another object or concept"; this formulation by W. B. Stanford, *Greek Metaphor,* Oxford: Blackwell, 1936, p. 101, is more careful than usual (see chs. 1, 5, for a judicious discussion of metaphor), but the key word that requires analysis is "must." Why "must" the term refer to another object? Because its combination with the other words in the context creates an impossibility on one level of meaning. Another, and I think in the last analysis, equivalent, account of metaphor is that it is "a word transference from one universe of discourse to another" (Wilbur M. Urban, *Language and Reality,* London: Allen and Unwin, 1939, p. 433); the "universe of discourse" of a word is either a general class that includes the things denoted by the word or else a class to which application of the word is restricted; and the "transference" is effected by the incompatibility between the universes of subject and modifier. One of the most careful and thorough discussions of metaphor, fruitful despite a number of errors, is that in Gustaf Stern, *Meaning and Change of Meaning,* Göteborg-Elanders Boktryckeri Aktiebolag, 1931, ch. 11, pp. 390-93. He calls the intentional transfer of a name from one referent to another "Nomination" (p. 167-68), of which figures of speech are a subclass: they are Nominations that involve "emotional factors" (p. 296). Metaphors are a subclass of figures; Stern's emphasis on the "fusion of disparate elements" (p. 300) in a metaphor, and on the "tension between the actual context and the primary meaning" of the modifier (p. 307) are in line with the Controversion Theory.

One way of sharpening the Controversion Theory of metaphor is to examine metaphors that lie on or near the borders of metaphor and other kinds of attribution that it must be distinguished from. For example: (1) Eliot's "shape without form" lies near the line between bare self-contradiction and significant self-contradiction; it does not quite reduce, however, to "shapeless shape." (2) Certain attributions can be either literal or metaphorical in different contexts. To call a lion a cat, or the heart a pump, or to speak of "the slow smokeless burning of decay" (Robert Frost), is to make this sort of attribution: there are technical senses of "cat," "pump," and "burning" (the chemist's combustion), in which these are all literally true, but if something in the context limits "cat," for example, to the domestic variety, then the attribution becomes a metaphor. See Milton's "darkness visible" and the ambiguous question, "Is black a color?"

10-D SIMILE. Though similes are not metaphors, they can, I think, be brought under the general heading of Self-Controverting Discourse. First, consider *open similes*. "A is like B," means, "There is at least one characteristic that A has and B has"; this is logically true, for whatever A and B are they are both members of unit-classes, so the simile is tautological. Even Edith Sitwell's "The stars were like prunes," though remote, is true: stars and prunes are both physical. So with E. E. Cummings' "Spring is like a perhaps hand." Second, consider *closed similes*. "The wind is as sharp as a knife" suggests that the wind is sharp, which is a metaphor; a closed simile, in other words, suggests a metaphor. "Custom lie upon thee . . . deep almost as life," from Wordsworth, suggests that life is deep, which is a metaphor. This is another reason why metaphors cannot be reduced to closed similes; the reduction would be circular, for what gives the closed simile its figurative power—"Jane is as optimistic as a cow" vs. "Jane is as optimistic as Joan," which is a plain comparison—is that it suggests a metaphor.

10-E IMAGERY. The two main, and often confused, senses of this term are clearly distinguished by Josephine Miles in "The Problem of Imagery," a review of R. H. Fogle, *The Imagery of Keats and Shelley*, *Sewanee Review*, LVIII (1950): 522-26: (a) if it means a general term that denotes an object perceptible to the senses, then there are nonmetaphorical images; (b) if it is synonymous with "figure of speech," then some images are abstract rather than concrete, which is an odd usage. It seems best to confine the term "image" to the first sense, but there are still a number of problems about the term, which Professor Miles points out. Caroline Spurgeon, *Shakespeare's Imagery*, Cambridge, Eng.: Cambridge U., 1952, uses it in the second sense (p. 5).

Edith Rickert, *New Methods for the Study of Literature*, Chicago: U. of Chicago, 1927, contributed a great deal toward the quantitative study of imagery in literature; see her classification of "figurative imagery" (pp. 47-49). See also C. Day Lewis, *The Poetic Image*, New York: Oxford U., 1947, chs. 1, 2; Louis MacNeice, *Modern Poetry*, New York: Oxford U., 1938, ch. 6 (note his interesting distinction between the images of a poem and its "properties," in the stage-sense, p. 91); Lascelles Abercrombie, *The Theory of Poetry*, London: Secker, 1924, ch. 4; J. M. Murry, "Metaphor," *Countries of the Mind*, 2nd Series, London: Oxford U., 1931; Elder Olson, "William Empson, Contemporary Criticism, and Poetic Diction," in R. S. Crane et al., *Critics and Criticism*, Chicago: U. of Chicago, 1952, pp. 79-82; Una Ellis-Fermor, *The Frontiers of Drama*, 3d ed., London: Methuen, 1948, ch. 5.

10-F OBSCURITY IN LITERATURE. Contemporary poets are often blamed for their obscurity, as a "failure to communicate," and this charge is taken as a ground for condemning the poem as well as the poet. But until the obscurity is penetrated, we do not know what the poem *is,* or indeed whether we have one. It would be helpful in coping with the issues, and it would also clarify that area where obscurity shades into unintelligibility, to have a classification of the factors in literature that make for obscurity, and hence of the types of obscurity—for example, not knowing who Asoka was, when the name appears in a poem, is very different from not being able to fill out an elliptical expression, as in Auden's sonnet, "Petition":

> Sir, no man's enemy, forgiving all
> But will its negative inversion, be prodigal.[1]

See "Emily" in Note 9-C, above. Obscurity has been discussed by John Sparrow, *Sense and Poetry*, London: Constable, 1934, chs. 4, 5; Louis MacNeice, *op. cit.*, ch. 9; Julian Symons, "Obscurity and Dylan Thomas," *Kenyon Review*, II (1940): 61-71; Max Eastman, *The Literary Mind*, New York: Scribner's, 1931, Part III, chs. 1, 3; Randall Jarrell, "The Obscurity of the Poet," *Poetry and the Age*, New York: Knopf, 1953.

10-G NONSENSE, or unintelligibility, is of various sorts, but in discourses that are likely to come to the attention of the literary critic, the constituent expressions are all likely to be words; or at least recognizable parts of speech with connotations, even if they are made up—e.g., "chortle," "galumphing," "bandersnatch." Syntactical relations that are so disordered they cannot be reconstructed by the reader produce one sort of nonsense—"Chocolate kilowatt striving an, / Barometer within aging." This is the asymptotic limit of ellipsis. Syntactically correct expressions that are nonsensical—"The chocolate kilowatt strove to age the incredulous barometer"—are the limit of rapidly moving metaphor.

For philosophical discussions of these types of nonsense, see A. C.

---

[1] From "Petition," *The Collected Poetry of W. H. Auden.* Copyright 1945 and reprinted with the permission of Random House, Inc. and Faber and Faber Ltd.

Ewing, "Meaninglessness," *Mind,* N. S. XLVI (1937): 347-64, esp. 359-64 (he holds that "Virtue is a fire-shovel" and "Purple quadratic equations go to race-meetings" must be meaningful because we know that they are false); Max Black, "Philosophical Analysis," *PAS,* XXXIII (1932-33): 237-58 (he holds that "succulent substantives" and "Adjectives love analysis" are not meaningful); Wilbur M. Urban, *op. cit.,* pp. 197-203, 221 (he holds that "Caesar is a prime number" is not meaningful); also the symposium on "Negation," with J. D. Mabbott, Gilbert Ryle, and H. H. Price, *PAS,* Suppl. vol. IX (1929). Whether a nonsensical expression is to be called "meaningless" or not is an interesting question; the fact that its *parts* are meaningful does not guarantee that it is as a whole. In any case, it is not explicable.

· IV ·

ARTISTIC
FORM

One feature of aesthetic objects in which critics take a great interest is their *form*. It is often said, indeed, that their possession of certain forms, or of form in a high degree, is exactly what distinguishes them from other objects and gives them their special value. If this is true, it is important to know; but unfortunately such positive statements are too rarely accompanied by an adequate explanation of what can be meant by "form" in this context.

If, for example, the "form" of a statue is its shape, how can one statue have more form than another, and how can any statue have more form than any other object, such as a basketball or a turnip? If, on the other hand, we want to say that the statue has a *better* form than the turnip— is as superior in shape as it is inferior in edibility—does this mean simply that its shape is preferred, or is there something more involved, something that would enable us to say, for example, that Haydn's *String Quartet in F Major (Op. 3, No.5)* and Tennyson's "Lady of Shalott" also have better forms than the turnip?

To talk about the form of an aesthetic object is at least to imply a distinction between its form and its other aspects. And it is this distinction that raises puzzling problems for aesthetics. Out of it come some of the most debated questions. Can form be separated from content? Is the form of an aesthetic object more, or less, important than its content, or its meaning? What makes the form of one object aesthetically better than the form of another? It is sometimes said that great art differs from poor art in that in the former, but not in the latter, form is *identical* to content, and cannot be distinguished from it; but in that case, what can the words "form" and "content" signify? So long as the relevant senses of the word "form" are not fixed, but are allowed to wander, every such question is really a bundle of questions lumped together, some of which are serious and searching, some verbal and trivial.

There is a fairly neutral, that is, a non-question-begging, way of approaching these puzzles. Among the terms that critics use to describe aesthetic objects, are there some that ought to be labeled "form-terms"? Or, equivalently, is it possible, and is it useful, to mark out a class of statements about aesthetic objects as "form-statements"? We might say, for example, that the statements, "This painting has a spiral composition" and "This musical composition is a rondo" are form-statements, but "This painting is gloomy" and "This music is gay" are not form-statements, but some other kind.

Whenever we face questions like this, there is a good method to follow. It has two steps. First we ask: what is the general usage, if any? Most critics, I think, would agree about the words "rondo" and "gay"; the former refers to form, the latter does not. And if we could make two lists of descriptive terms, and obtain general agreement on which belong to each list, it would then be possible for us to work out a distinction and obtain a definition of "form" that would accurately reflect prevailing usage. But unfortunately, when we look about, we find our hope disappointed by the extreme vagaries of the word. Some art critics use the word "form" to mean approximately the *composition* of a painting—"It is a pointillist painting" would not be a form-statement in this usage. Others, to mean the whole design, in contrast to what the painting *represents*—"It contains a red patch" would be a form-statement in this usage. Others, to mean "how" the objects are arranged on the picture-plane—"thickly" and "gracefully" would be form-terms in this usage. And there are other varieties.

If we are going to require at the least that our own way of using the term shall be clear and unequivocal, we cannot hope to frame a definition that will correspond to all common usages. Therefore, we must consider the second step. Let us single out the usage, even though it is not exact, that seems most worth preserving. For example, we already have the term "design" for the bounded visual surface itself: all statements about its elements, relations, and regional qualities are statements about the design. It would therefore be an unnecessary duplication of terms to assign the term "form" to the same thing; it would be more interesting to see whether there was some subclass of statements about the design that it is useful to distinguish from the rest. And in terms of the categories we have already introduced, there is a clear distinction that can be made between (1) those statements that describe the local qualities of elements, and the regional qualities of complexes, within a visual design or a musical composition, and (2) those statements that describe internal *relations* among the elements and among the complexes within the object. These latter statements we may call "form-statements."

This distinction is exact enough, I think; in fact, with the help of some logical apparatus it could be made more exact than it probably needs to be. If I say that in a certain musical composition one note is higher or louder than another, or that one section of a movement is in a brighter key, or that one movement is longer than another, these are relational statements. That is, they are statements of the type: "X has such and such a relation to Y." And so, by the above definition, they are form-statements. Similarly, if I say that in a visual design one side contrasts with another, or one area is darker than another, or one part of the picture space is deeper than another, I am talking about form.

If from the class of critical descriptions we abstract all the form-statements, what remains? First, there will be statements about the elements and complex parts to be found in the work: the musical composition begins with the note A, and has four movements; the painting contains some patches of coral red, or two main solids. Second, there will be statements about the regional qualities of the work or of its parts: the music is in the key of F, or is violent, or its opening is serene; the painting is bright and lively. It is convenient to have a name for these descriptions that are not formal descriptions, but there is no thoroughly satisfactory one available. "Form" naturally takes "content" as its complement, and we may accede to this custom. "Content-statement" is a poor term in one respect, for among the things that musical compositions and visual designs contain, in a perfectly good sense, are the relations among the parts as well as the parts and their qualities. For the most part I shall get along without using the word "content" at all, but when I do it will be in this sense: a content-statement is a description that is not a form-statement.

Now, once we get such a distinction, it is also important not to be carried away by the sheer beauty of its precision; we must again look around to see whether it is useful. Plenty of precise distinctions are not worth making, because there is nothing you can do with them. If we single out certain aspects of an aesthetic object and give those aspects a special name, this can only be justified by the fact that they have a special function or importance, that something depends on them in some way. Hence the task of the present chapter. We must try to show that important things that critics want to say can be best said in the terms we adopt, the term "form" and other terms defined by means of it. We must show that it is important to single out form in this sense for special notice, because it plays an important role in art.

Meanwhile, it is plain that some of the familiar puzzles about form disappear if we adopt the proposed definition. Can form be distinguished from content? Certainly it can, in the sense that we can talk about one without talking about the other. Are form and content connected? Certainly they are connected, since some of the relations that hold between two notes, say, depend on their qualities, and some of the qualities of a given color area in a given design depend on its relations to neighboring areas. Are form and content separable? Surely not, and it is a serious mistake to confuse distinguishability and separability. As was pointed out in Chapter II, §6, the quality of a complex is a function of the elements *and* their relations, or, as we might say, both its form *and* content, and if either of these is changed—if different notes or colors are substituted, or if the music is speeded up or the color areas are rearranged—that particular quality will change or disappear.

Is form more important than content, then, according to this usage? This question gets in very deep, and indeed opens up more than one avenue of inquiry. On the face of it, it does seem as if we value the regional qualities of aesthetic objects very highly: the qualities, for example, of the first two movements of Mozart's *G Minor Quintet for Strings* (K. 516) are about as precious as anything in music can be. And one might want to say that this is the main or only value; the form is important only because it is indispensable to the achievement of those qualities. Or one might want to say that the form is what we should chiefly cherish about music, and that it would be valuable even if it had no such profound anguish. This is an issue we must be prepared to face farther along; but we are not ready for it yet, and part of the preparation consists in disposing first of some more manageable problems about form.

§11. *STRUCTURE AND TEXTURE IN VISUAL DESIGN*

If we agree to say that the form of an aesthetic object is the total web of relation among its parts, then we are in a position to make another distinction that is of some moment to the critic.

For an aesthetic object may have certain main parts, or chief segments, like the movements of a symphony or the two halves of a painting that is divided by a clear axis. These parts will be related in some ways—the second movement may be in the key subdominant to the key of the first movement; the halves of the painting may be approximately equal in visual density. And the object will contain smaller parts—its elements and minor complexes—like the melodies in the symphony or the solids in the painting. And these smaller parts will be related in some ways—one melody may be more animated than another; one solid may be deeper in space than another. The distinction between the main parts and the subordinate parts will sometimes be vague, and perhaps arbitrary; but usually it will be palpable to the eye or ear. In either case it will be useful.

Thus there are relatively large-scale relations among the main parts and relatively small-scale relations among the subordinate parts—or, in

other words, there are relations among large, and perhaps distant, regions,
and there are relations among neighboring regions, of the object. Hence
we shall distinguish two species of aesthetic form: *structure* and *texture*.
In this section we shall apply this distinction to visual designs.

The term "texture" is often used by fine-arts critics in a sense that is
not exactly the one I propose. When they say, for example, that silk and
burlap, or pine and maple, differ in texture, they sometimes mean that
these *look* as though they would *feel* different if you rubbed your hand
over them: there is a difference in tactile quality. That is true. But if we
analyze what it is that we see, the differences in the way they look are
differences in the way they vary in quality from point to point: one wood
is close-grained, the other not; one cloth consists of tiny overlapped
squares, the other is tight and varies smoothly and by the subtlest degrees
in the sheen or color it takes from the light. This is what I mean by
"texture": the texture of the visual design at any location within it consists of the relations among the small parts at that location. We can also
generalize about the texture of the whole, that is, certain small-scale
relations that turn up at various locations.

It is possible to have a design with structure but no texture, or with
texture but no structure. Imagine, in the first case, a large rectangle containing two large red circular areas on a white background. This design
clearly has certain main parts, and these parts are related: the circles
stand out from the background, and they balance each other in a simple
symmetrical way. The relations "stand out from" and "balance" are structural relations in this case, for they relate the main parts. Suppose that
within the main parts, however, there are no visible differentiations, and
so there are no smaller parts to be discriminated and compared. Then
there is structure, but no texture. In fact, however, the areas of a visual
design will always have some heterogeneity—as, for example, in the Jensen, *Composition*, Plate I, which would otherwise be an example of
structure without texture.

Now imagine a field of white covered with small red spots, equally
spaced—tiny polka dots, such as you might find on material for a simple
dress or a kitchen curtain. If the whole field consists of such dots, there
are no major divisions within it; the design does not fall into any large
sections for the eye, and so it has no structure. But it has texture, indeed
it has the same texture throughout, for each dot is related in the same way
to its white background and to its neighbors. Different textures may be
seen in the backgrounds of Rouault's lithograph, Plate V, in the top
right-hand corner; in the Dürer woodcut, Plate VI, the floor and rear
wall; in the Goya aquatint, Plate VII, the upper left side. Of course the
distinction between structure and texture is relative; if we start to mag-
nify a texture, or make the whole field smaller, we will come to the point
where the elements are major, rather than minor, parts of the design. But
that will be a different design. It is perfectly clear that when you look at

a painting it almost always has certain large divisions, and when you look at bathroom tiles or a brick wall there are no large divisions, though there are small ones.

Composition and Style

Consider now the term "composition." Suppose we say that Käthe Kollwitz's *Municipal Lodging*, PLATE III, has a triangular or pyramidal composition. This can be understood in two ways, and though the distinction in general is not to be overlooked, I think we may consider the definitions as equally good in this context. In one sense, to say the composition is triangular is to map the large-scale relations among some of the most notable areas within the picture: the mother's head is in a certain direction from the child's foot, for example. That would be to analyze statements about composition into large-scale relations. The other way would be to introduce the term "dominant pattern" for any large shape that stands out within the picture, emerging from the subordinate patterns because of certain strong lines between them—the mother's or the child's back. The dominant pattern of a design is not a set of relations, but a regional quality that depends upon those relations. It will not matter greatly whether we say that the composition is the relations themselves or the pattern that is determined by them. In any case, if the relations are there, so will the pattern be. We shall want to say that composition is at least part of structure in a visual design. In other words, any statement about the composition of a design is a statement about its structure.

It may be helpful to review these points by referring to the simple diagrams on the opposite page.

Note, first, that *D* differs from the other three in many of its elements: it consists mostly of crosses instead of little circles. Second, *B* differs from the others in its *dominant pattern,* which is triangularish instead of squarish, because in *B* the large-scale relations between the elements—the prevailing directions of the rows of elements, and the relations of the large circles to each other—are different. Thus, *B* is different in *structure* from all the others. Third, while *A* and *B* are alike in *texture,* in that the neighborhood relations between the little circles are similar—they form right-angled zig-zags—*C* differs from both *A* and *B* in texture, in that its little circles are related so that they form rounded waves.

The term "composition" is, then, definable in our categories of analysis. When it means, as it does to some writers, the "arrangement" of all the areas in the design—that is, their relations—then it is synonymous with "form." If it is limited to large-scale relations and/or dominant pattern, it is synonymous with "structure."

With the help of the terms "structure" and "texture," we can clarify another term that plays a considerable role in the vocabulary of criticism: "style." This is one of those terms that make good sense if we pay attention only to what critics do with them—that is, what they say about particular aesthetic objects—but lead into extraordinary confusions if we ask critics how they would define them. Usually such definitions, as often as not copied from popular dictionaries, refer to the artist's "manner of

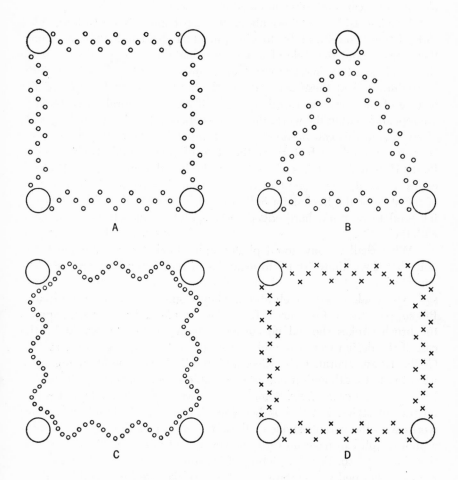

A   B

C   D

expression" or his "personal contribution to the work," and these are of no help. For it is surely requisite that, however we use the term "style," we use it in such a way that we can tell by empirical observation what *is* the style of a work.

That the term has a widely varying and fluctuating usage is obvious enough. A photographer who is also a painter, Steven Trefonides, has said that his photographs show some of the same stylistic traits as his paintings. But a well-known book on painting[1] says quite flatly that

---

[1] H. Ruhemann and E. M. Kemp, *The Artist at Work*, Baltimore: Penguin, 1951, p. 10.

photographs have no style, apparently because there is nothing in them that one can trace back to the direct handiwork of an artist. There is need for some analysis here, and, as usual, we shall in the end have to make our own decision about the term: to choose the definition that would make it most useful to us, and least misleading, to fix that definition as clearly as we can, and to recommend it to others.

Leaving aside questions about the artist and his operations, what sorts of thing do critics refer to when they talk about style? For one thing, they speak about the style of a particular painting: the brushstrokes are short and close together; or there is much impasto; or the work is a pointillist painting. And these are statements about recurrent features of the texture of the painting. In other words, if certain textural characteristics are repeated within the work, these are singled out and regarded as traits of style. And this can be done without any reference to the artist at all. It is, for example, a feature of the style of Rembrandt's *Girl Sleeping*, PLATE II, that the patches of ink tend to be broad, transparent, soft at the edges, tapered, and—except in the background—separate. It is a feature of the style of the Beckmann *Self-Portrait*, PLATE IV, that the patches of ink tend to be dark, hard-edged, sharp-pointed, and starkly contrasted with the white.

What shall we say about photographs, in that case? We must first note that if we allow "style" to mean "recurrent features of texture," it is conceivable that there could be visual designs without style, or whose style you couldn't say much about. They would have texture, no doubt. But suppose the texture varied from place to place; for example, suppose the brush strokes showed no constant characteristics, as would be the case if the design were assembled from pieces of works by Rubens, Van Gogh, Titian, Seurat, Gris, Klee, and Raphael. We might in that case want to say that though it had a remarkable variety of textures it did not have any style *as a whole*. Sometimes we would rather say that it was a mixture of styles, but that is because we are already familiar in other works with the various styles of those painters. This does not mean that a photograph can have no style, however, and indeed it is unlikely that this should be so. For if a picture of certain objects is taken in a certain light and finished in a certain way, there is likely to be something about the sharpness of contrasts between light and dark, the shininess or dullness of the surface, the clarity or dimness of its lines, that is common to much of the picture. And those would be its style.

We could say this of a particular visual design even if no other visual design in the whole world had the same, or a very similar, style. But of course the art historian is more interested in an extension of the term to *groups* of visual designs. Thus he will want to distinguish stages in the development of Rembrandt's style, and say that the last stage is characterized by stronger and richer chiaroscuro, or contrasts of darks and lights, by bits of black in the color areas, by a variety of strokes—some made with the handle of the brush. Or he will want to speak of period styles: the Gothic or the International, the Florentine or Venetian, the Flemish or Baroque. Again, a style is a collection of recurrent characteristics. But in these cases, art historians usually broaden the term somewhat, and perhaps without serious risk of confusion, if we know what they are up to. Suppose a historian says that the Baroque "style" is characterized by open, rather than closed, forms, by extreme contrasts of light and dark, by compositions built upon a diagonal receding into space. Some of these are recurrent features of texture, some are recurrent features of structure. It is a little odd, if a painter is fond of using spiral compositions, to say that this is a feature of his style, but perhaps it is not too odd, and the habit is deeply rooted in art history.

We may summarize our discussion of style in visual design, then, as follows: First, when this term is applied to individual objects, it is best used to refer to recurrent features of texture, and this usage corresponds fairly well to that of art critics, if one ignores their tendency toward intentionalism when they offer to define the term. Second, when the term is applied to groups of objects, to the *oeuvre* of a given age or of a given painter, it usually refers to recurrent features of texture and structure.

One qualification perhaps should be added. Some fine arts historians would hold out for a stronger definition of "style," in one respect. For sometimes when they speak of a style they do not mean just any set of recurrent characteristics, but a *system* of characteristics. Cubism, for example, is said to be a "strong" style, because the characteristics that define it are not merely associated with each other, but belong together; they are, in the sense to be discussed below in §13, a *coherent* set. The high Baroque and, to a slightly lower degree, mannerism are very strong, whereas "synthetic" cubism and surrealism are not. It is best, however, I think, to use "style" in the broader sense, allowing, of course, for a further distinction between more or less coherent, and therefore more or less distinctive but exhaustible, styles.

Classification-Terms

A good part of what critics have to say about visual designs, and the greater part of what art historians have to say—in so far as they talk about the aesthetic objects instead of the biographies of the artists—consists in comparing and classifying them. Sometimes it is a question of determining the correct attribution of an unsigned painting, or of dating a signed painting, by stylistic analysis, where external evidence is lacking. Sometimes it is a question of grouping painters and their works into schools or movements, so that inferences can be made about their connections with social and political changes. Sometimes it is a question of proving the influence of one painter upon another, by similarities so close as to suggest direct borrowing. Indeed, as we shall see later, some critics hold that until you have correctly classified an aesthetic object, you cannot evaluate it.

Yet aesthetic objects, musical compositions as well as paintings, are thought to be unusually resistant to comparison and classification. They are often said to be highly individual objects, each in a class by itself, unlikely to permit of very successful generalizations. This view has a *prima facie* plausibility. Even if it may sometimes be a help in improving people's appreciation of aesthetic objects to point out their similarities to other objects, it may be even more important, according to some critics, to emphasize their irreducible differences.

It is not clear what it means to say that one object is more highly individualized than another, but, without pausing to consider that question at this point, we may take it for granted, I think, that aesthetic objects are no more highly individualized than human beings. There is no good reason to suspect that the general principles of classification do not apply to aesthetic objects as they apply to metals, butterflies, economic systems, or mental diseases, though the difficulties of applying those principles may be unusually great in the arts. It is, however, fairly evident that many of the most popular terms used in classifying aesthetic objects are in a poor state of definition. Thus we get such hopelessly verbal arguments as whether a certain twentieth-century composer, say Schönberg, is a "romantic" or "anti-romantic," or whether a certain painter, say Manet, is a "realist" or an "impressionist." These are not idle questions, for they can arise from a genuine interest in perceiving clearly the works themselves, and making articulate the subtle differences between those works and other works. And so, though debate about such questions may unfortunately become a substitute for close study of the works themselves, it is too harsh and radical a cure to banish all such general terms from the critic's vocabulary. Words, for all their deficiencies, are the best tools we have for making explicit to ourselves and others how aesthetic objects differ and what is noteworthy about them; but if we are going to use words, we ought to make them as clear as we can.

Some of the classification-terms in the fine arts are clearly definable in terms of representational subject matter—"landscape," "still life"—and we shall not discuss them now. There are other terms that refer to form alone, and still others that are mixed or puzzling in certain ways—"surrealism." Let us consider some of the purely formal distinctions first, and then deal briefly with a few sample terms that seem to be conspicuously in need of analytical shaping.

What are the possible relations that can subsist among parts of the visual design? The main ones we can conveniently divide into two groups. First there are *dual* relations, that is, relations that hold between two parts of the design. These are in the logical sense symmetrical; that is, if they hold from *A* to *B*, then they hold from *B* to *A*. These relations are chiefly important as constituting structure, that is, in so far as they hold between relatively large segments of the object.

The dual relations may be further subdivided. Suppose we single out two parts of the visual design that are both in view at the same time—for example, two figures on a background—and compare them with respect to their similarity or difference of various characteristics. If we consider a particular characteristic—say, shape, color, orientation, or size —there are three possibilities to distinguish. They may be *similar* in that respect, though not exactly; or they may be *contrasting* in that respect, as dark vs. light, or large vs. small, or smooth vs. jagged, or they may be *indifferently different*, that is, they may not stand out as either much alike or much opposed. A capital *P* is similar in shape to a capital *R*, for the *R* contains a *P;* a capital *X* contrasts with a capital *O*, for one is all open and the other all closed; a capital *P* and a capital *M* are neither very similar nor in clear contrast.

Among these dual relations, there are three in particular that have great structural significance in visual design. The first appears when we compare two parts of the design with respect to their visual density. They may be similar in density, that is nearly equal, in which case they are said to be in *balance;* they may be contrasting, or they may be neither. Balance implies a point, or vertical line, of reference, an axis that divides the two comparable areas. For example, in Dürer's *Last Supper,* PLATE VI, the round window at the top and the empty plate at the bottom set up a strong vertical axis, a broken line, and though there are seven figures to the left and only five to the right, the sizes and groupings of these figures are such that they balance perfectly on the two sides of the axis. A more subtle example is Rembrandt's *Girl Sleeping,* PLATE II, in which the heavy vertical stroke that marks the shadow just to the left of the top edge of her upper arm defines an axis about which the upper part of the body and the lower part are in delicate balance.

The second appears when we compare two parts of the design with respect to their color, or *color-tonality.* They may be *harmonious*—the colors go well together. They may be *clashing* or conflicting—the colors are disturbed by each other's presence. Or they may simply be indifferent. Color-harmony is one sort of similarity, like shape-harmony or size-harmony.

The third dual relation arises when we compare two parts of a design with respect to their movement, including not only the amount of thrust in the movement but the direction as well. Two black figures on a white background may, for example, seem to move in the same direction, say toward the upper left-hand corner. Or they may seem to move together, as if pulled by internal forces, or to drive each other apart, depending on their shape, size, position, and so on. Or there may be other figures that counteract these tendencies, so that a stable tension is generated, and the figures appear to be held in position. Thus, two such figures are either in *equilibrium* or in *disequilibrium*. The Jensen *Composition,* PLATE I, is a simple and clear example of such equilibrium, with the two rightward-leaning white areas pitted against the leftward-leaning one. Rouault's picture of the man sowing, PLATE V, is more complex. Here the inclined head and forearm, and the roads in the distance, set up a strong clock-wise movement, but this is held in check and given vital poise by the angle of the right thigh, which sets up a counter-clockwise movement at the bottom of the picture. Compositions like the Rouault and the Beckmann are said to be in unstable equilibrium, for their equilibrium comes from a tense opposition of strong opposing forces; compositions like the Kollwitz and the Dürer are said to be in stable equilibrium.

Besides the dual relations, there can be *serial* relations within a visual design. Consider any three or more figures, whether complex or simple, in relation to each other. And set aside for the moment the dual relations that may hold between any two of them. There are three possibilities that remain. First, they may all have some characteristic in common, their color, shape, size, orientation, position, etc. In that case we shall say that they form a series by *repetition,* for each is similar in the same way to all of the others. Second, they may vary in some regular way, in color, shape, size, orientation, or position: for example, A may be darker than, larger than, to the left of, B, and B darker than, larger than, to the left of, C. In this case, the relation between A and B is similar to the relation between B and C, and we shall say they form a series by *directional change.* Or third, there may be no serial relation that connects all of the figures. Some of the little groups of lines in the Beckmann *Self-Portrait,* PLATE IV, are examples of such series. He avoids any simple directional changes, but within each group there are variations in length and thickness, and sometimes a prevailing direction—as, for example, at the upper right, on the figure's left forehead.

These purely formal distinctions can be either structural or textural, of course, depending on whether we are considering major or minor parts of the design. For example, figures along the wall of an Egyptian temple may form a series of some kind, and that would be structural; the interlaced lines around the border of a page of illuminated manuscript may form a series, and that would be textural.

Words like "cubism" and "impressionism," that have been brought in to name whole movements in painting, are much more difficult to define than to learn to use in a somewhat knowledgeable fashion. One of the difficulties with them is that they often have to serve two purposes at once, which are not necessarily in harmony. They provide criteria for distinguishing one type of painting from another—for saying whether or not a particular painting is a cubist painting, or, more flexibly, in what ways it is cubist and in what ways not. That is really the first and more important task. But they also get attached to the aesthetic theories of certain painters, including, sometimes, the most remarkable talk about the metaphysical or mystical ideas that are supposed to be conveyed by a particular mode of painting.

We will leave these notions for Chapter VIII, §21, and consider how such terms are to be used when they are used descriptively. It may be said that the impressionist painter "attempts to record the shifting appearances of things, the impression they make on his senses," or that the cubist painter "abstracts certain essential shapes from solid objects, the cube, the sphere, the cylinder, the pyramid, the cone, and pictures those objects in terms of various planes." But we can distill out the intentionalistic idioms. If to classify a visual design as impressionist means, among other things, that it contains small adjacent areas of pure—that is, highly saturated—hues, that there is a great variety in the shape, direction, and size of the discriminable brush strokes, then impressionism is a type of texture. And if to classify a painting as cubist means that it contains a number of simple and sharply defined masses, related in deep space, then "cubism" refers to both structure and texture.

There is another puzzling term that we may look at briefly here, though it cannot by any means be briefly cleared up. Critics sometimes speak of "decorative art," not as a term of praise necessarily, but in contrast to "expressive" or other art. It would presumably be said, for example, that wall-paper, fabrics, manuscript illuminations, and some paintings by Matisse are decorative designs, but the paintings of Giotto, Rubens, and Cézanne are not. In the most clear-cut sense, we could define "decorative design" as "design that has texture but not structure," and in fact this will fit prevailing usage pretty well. But not perfectly; for sometimes when a critic labels a design as "decorative," he means, not that it has no structure, but that the interesting or aesthetically valuable thing about it is its texture. The distinction between structure and texture is certainly basic to the concept.

This is brought out in a newspaper account of a contemporary painter by the remark,

> cubism is too uncompromising a style to be employed decoratively. It is architectural or it is nothing.

I take this to mean—note that cubism is called a "style," though opposed to "decoration"—that the space-relations and mass-relations that cubist paintings operate with can make a good painting if they are used as structural ("architectural") relations among relatively large masses, but that if the masses are small so that their relations are textural ("decorative"), the painting will not be a very good one. Of course we are here touching upon questions of value for which we are not yet prepared; but without discussing the truth or falsity of what this writer says, we can make fair sense of it. And this bit of linguistic analysis may serve to illustrate the way in which you can clarify critical statements by analyzing them in terms of the categories we have been using.

The distinction we have made between statements describing the structure, and statements describing the texture, of aesthetic objects is just as important in music as it is in the visual arts, and perhaps even clearer, though it is just as relative to size. If the composition is a short melody, it will be in order to call the relations between its main clauses its structure; if the melody occurs in the course of the finale of a piano concerto, then relative to the whole movement the relations between its clauses are part of the texture.

It is clear that the word "sonata" is a structure-word, though of course it was not so originally. When you say that a movement is in sonata-allegro form, you are implying that its main sections—exposition, development, recapitulation—are related in certain important ways: in the development some figures of the exposition-melodies appear; the recapitulation is all, or largely and finally, in the same key as the first part of the exposition. These are large-scale relational statements. On the other hand, when you say that a composition or a passage of it is in canon, this means that one voice repeats, or imitates, the same melody as another voice, but at some distance behind, and not necessarily at the same pitch. The voices are all at the same pitch in a round, such as "Frère Jacques" or "Row, Row, Row Your Boat." Here are two simple but eloquent canonic passages from Josquin des Près:

Josquin des Près, *Ave Maria*

In the first one the tenors imitate the sopranos an octave below and two bars behind; in the second the imitation is a fifth below and only one quarter-note behind.

These examples show that by the definitions proposed here the distinction between structure and texture is not the same as the distinction between the horizontal and vertical dimensions of music. Musical texture is often divided into monophonic, homophonic, and polyphonic, depending on whether it consists of a single melodic line; a melodic line accompanied by chords or by arpeggios, which are figured chords; or two or more melodies, that is, counterpoint. These are textural distinctions, of course, but the term "texture" is broader than this. When we say that the passage is canonic, we are talking not only about the vertical dimension, but, so to speak, about diagonal features of the music. And when we say that there is a certain harmonic progression, or a repetition of certain melodic intervals, we are talking horizontally, but we are still talking about texture, which, in this more convenient sense—a sense that corresponds to the usage of some of the best critics—refers to anything going on at a given moment that can be described in terms of relations among nearby parts. The difference between barrelhouse and Dixieland is a difference in texture.

Musical structures are often classified by reference to the number of their main parts, or sections. The ordinary thirty-two-bar popular song, for instance, is a binary, or two-part, structure, of which the first sixteen bars form one part, and the last sixteen the other; and the classical minuet-with-trio movement is a ternary, or three-part, structure. But this description raises a problem: what constitutes a section, or main part, of a musical composition? What marks the dividing line between one section and another?

As far as popular songs and minuets are concerned, there is little likelihood of dispute. But where the principle is not clear and explicit, disagreements can arise, and in fact there has been disagreement about such a familiar matter as the classical sonata-allegro movement: is it a binary or ternary structure?[1] It appears that the disagreement arises from the fact that critics have used two different criteria of what might be called *musical punctuation,* and these criteria, though they often would give the same results, sometimes give different ones.

The first criterion makes the division in terms of *stopping-places.* When we ask whether a movement is binary in structure, we may be asking whether there is one point in it that has a much more intense cadential quality than any other point before the end. The classical sonata-allegro movement has just such a point, where the music could stop without sounding as though it had been interrupted—namely, the end of the exposition, just before the development begins. The end of the development, or beginning of the recapitulation, is no such point; indeed that point is likely to be one of the most intense, with the music rushing ahead urgently and inevitably to find its way into the tonic key again for the last stretch. Therefore, by this first test, the classical sonata-allegro movement of Mozart and Haydn is binary in structure.

But when later composers, such as Beethoven and Brahms, expanded and developed the sonata-allegro structure, they aimed at greater continuity and they found ways of moving from the exposition into the de-

---

[1] This question is discussed briefly but pointedly by Donald F. Tovey, *Essays in Musical Analysis,* London: Oxford U., 1935-39, Vol. I, pp. 10-12.

velopment with no pause, and with less of a break in the musical flow. In such a case, it is not possible to pick out any one outstanding point of cadence within the movement, and so by the first criterion the movement does not divide at all, but is unary. However, the movement can be divided by means of a second criterion. Let us select the *points of greatest change:* that is, points where the contrast between the preceding passage and the passage that follows is perceived to be most striking and evident. And indeed there are often two such points, generally speaking: where the music plunges into a relatively remote and contrasting key at the beginning of the development, and where it suddenly arrives back in the home key at the beginning of the recapitulation. So, if you like, you can say that the sonata-allegro movement consists of three main parts, and is ternary in structure. But this method is going to lead to rather unexpected results if we apply it without prejudices or prior theoretical commitments to certain large movements in sonata-allegro structure—for example, the first movements of Beethoven's *E Flat Major ("Eroica")* and *D Minor Symphonies*—for it may turn out that there are more than two such notable turning-points, some indeed right in the middle of the development itself.

Concerning the relation between structure and texture in music, we may raise the same question we asked earlier about visual design: can either exist without the other? It is pretty clear that there can be no structure without texture, for there is no structure unless there are main sections, and for the musical movement to develop some momentum there must be local changes going on, rise or fall of melody, thickening or thinning of harmony, variations in rhythm or tempo, and these are its texture. On the other hand, there could theoretically be music that has texture but no structure. The pure case would be an unaccompanied melody like that sung by a child to himself, one that goes on and on for a time, always changing and wandering about, never repeating itself or coming to a pause until the end. But the possibility of structureless texture can be made plausible in another way. Consider a "Gloria" or "Credo" in a mass by Palestrina, or the motet by Des Près quoted above, a beautiful setting of the *Ave Maria.* Such music has a remarkably steady flow, always subtly changing with the words, but because of its modal melodies and harmonies, never approaching extremes of urgency or of finality. It divides into parts, with half-closes, though often not sharply, because one voice is taking up a new theme as the others are finishing the old one. But the sections do not, *as sections,* have definite and clear-cut relations to each other. There may be thematic echoes: for example, in Palestrina's *Pope Marcellus Mass* the "Agnus Dei" begins like the first "Kyrie"—he does this in other masses, such as the *Ad Fugam* and *Aspice Domine.* And the second passage from the motet by Des Près might be regarded as a variation of the first. Moreover, there are important contrasts in the motet, as when the second passage changes from duple to triple time, or when at the words "Ave praeclara omnibus" there is a sudden access of poignancy.

But, on the whole, it seems correct to say that such music does not have much that you can talk about by way of structure, though it has a great deal that is significant in its texture.

Thus, if we were comparing the mass by Palestrina with the motet by Des Près, it would be the recurrent features of the texture that interest us most; for example, the mass has in general a more complex texture, the motet has greater contrasts of texture. In short, we would be concerned with *style*. Indeed, the analysis of the term "style" proposed in the previous section fits even better the usage of music critics than that of fine-arts critics.

Thus a critic would refer to the style of Debussy's piano music or Duke Ellington's jazz. Or he would say that Beethoven's late quartet style is different in certain ways from his earlier styles: there is much canonic imitation, there are sudden contrasts of tempo and loudness, the voices, especially in slow movements, often range widely over the tonal space, with several octaves between the first violin and the cello. These are evidently recurrent features of the texture. And similarly when music historians compare Baroque music—say, Handel or Bach or Scarlatti or Tartini—with post-Wagnerian nineteenth-century music, they point out many differences, but generally speaking they limit the term "style" to the textural differences. It is not a part of Baroque *style* that Baroque composers wrote concerto grossos. But some music historians would say that it is a part of Baroque style that the concerto grosso movement is typically built on the *ritornello* principle, in which a certain passage recurs at regular intervals, and this is a kind of structure. In this usage, "style" is not limited to texture.

Musical Structure-Types

We must now consider the fundamental relations by means of which musical structures are built, and in terms of which they can be classified. Some of them are relations of tonality—similarity, nearness, contrast—some are melodic or thematic relations; and both of these are involved in the meaning of the technical terms for types of musical structure. In discussing musical structure, it is extremely important to bear in mind that in classifying music we are abstracting *some* of its formal relations, and ignoring others, for special purposes. Thus, to say that a musical composition has a sonata-allegro form is to describe only part of its structure, for the total structure consists of all the large-scale internal relations, not just those that are included in the definition of "sonata-allegro structure." The sonata-allegro structure is really a *structure-type*. And other familiar terms stand for structure-types, too: "rondo," "theme-and-variations." Sometimes they are called *procedures*.

This way of regarding the structure-terms has important consequences, and guards against certain errors. In the first place, these types are not to be thought of as *a priori* forms, or moulds, that are filled in by particular composers. Sometimes, it is true, the sonata-allegro structure has exerted such an artistic compulsion upon composers, and has been able to determine the very way in which they thought of melodies and harmonic progressions. But from the critic's point of view, this structure is something that is abstracted from a number of concrete individual compositions, each of which would be what it is even if the rest were destroyed; it is simply their common features. It does not exist prior to, or independently of, those works that exemplify it, any more than the shapes of objects exist independently of them.

It is this derivative character of such structure-types that explains the strong tendency of their names to wander in meaning. For music never stands still, and as soon as a term is used to refer to a structure-type that is found in a good many compositions, someone will write another composition that differs from it just a little bit, and then it will be tempting to broaden the meaning of the old term so that it will take in the new music too. Thus, for example, "sonata-allegro" has a very restricted meaning in the works of Haydn and Mozart, and enough of that meaning still applies in the works of Schubert and Brahms to make the extension convincing. Some things have to be remarked as "irregularities," as when Schubert sometimes begins his recapitulation in a key different from the home key, but one related to it in such a way that the same modulation which in the exposition took him *out* of the home key will now take him back into it. But there are still many common features: the contrast of keys or themes in the exposition, the central section that goes into distant keys before it returns. When contemporary critics, however, describe any movement that involves a kind of recapitulation—for example, the first movements of Bartók's *Fourth String Quartet,* Bloch's *Second String Quartet,* or Schönberg's *Third String Quartet*—as "free sonata form" or "modified sonata form," even though there is no strong tonality, if any, then the terminology becomes perhaps too confusing.

In the second place, a musical work can have structure even if it belongs to no hitherto-recognized and named structure-type. It is an elementary, but not unknown, mistake to overlook this. There are in contemporary music very interesting departures in musical structure—for example, Samuel Barber's *First Symphony,* which is in one movement but has several main sections, each of which works out one of the themes stated at the beginning—that have not been baptized, and of course there are some famous classical movements that cannot be analyzed very convincingly in terms of the classical types, for example, the slow movement of Mozart's *Sinfonia Concertante in E Flat Major for Violin and Viola* (K. 297b), the third movement of Beethoven's *String Quartet in B Flat (Op. 130),*[2] the first movement of Haydn's *String Quartet in D Major (Op. 76,*

---

[2] See the interesting analysis by Donald MacArdle, "Beethoven's Quartet in B Flat: An Analysis," *The Music Review,* VIII (1947): 15-24.

highest order, have no structure.

Although there is something accidental and arbitrary in the structure-types that have come to be picked out of classical practice in composition and handed down as the basic ones, still they are not wholly
arbitrary, for they reflect certain fundamental principles of musical structure. These principles have not yet, to my knowledge, been fully worked
out, formulated, and well-named, but the kind of inquiry involved here
can be briefly indicated. Suppose you have a melody, harmonized or not:
what are the possible things you can do with it, after you have played
it once? You can repeat it, perhaps several times; this would be the
simplest monadic structure. Evidently no very complicated musical movement can be generated in this way. Or, to make the repetition more desirable by building up some interest in it before it arrives, you can introduce a second melody in between, by way of contrast. If the contrasting
section is a complete melody in itself, you will have a ternary structure,
A/B/A. But if the point of the contrasting section is that, while it takes
off in a new direction, it leads back inevitably and without pause to the
first section, as does the third eight-bar clause in a popular song, then
you have a binary structure, *A/BA*. The popular song is likely to repeat
the *A* before the *B*, so you get *AA/BA;* this gives more balance to the two
sections, but is not a fundamental structural difference. Or you can follow the melody with a second melody that is recognizably similar to it,
and sounds derived from it in some way, in its rhythm, or intervals, or
harmony, or general contour—one that sounds like a stretching or twisting
of it, or like a commentary upon it; and this second melody will be a
variation of the first. Or you can combine the first melody with itself
canonically, or with another melody or with a variation of the first
melody: this is the essential principle of the various polyphonic forms,
such as the *fugue*. Or you can break up the melody, or its rhythms and
harmonies, into figures, and recombine the figures, with other figures, into
new melodies or nonmelodic passages: this is *development*.

Notice that here we are talking about the way one part of the music
is related to another—it is a repetition of it, or a variation of it, or a development of it—and to speak of "what you can do" with the melody is
only a colloquial idiom. Furthermore, we are not talking about types of
movement, a "variation-movement," for example; we are reviewing certain essential musical relations. Thus a set of variations may involve fugal
passages, or even contain fugues—like Beethoven's *Grosse Fuge* (*Op.
133*)—and it may contain other interludes of various sorts, including contrasts and development, as in his variations in the slow movements of
Op. 127 and Op. 131. And a large development section of a symphony,
for example, Mozart's last three symphonies and Haydn's "London" symphonies, may contain repetitions in different keys, fugal passages, variations of themes, as well as development in the strict sense.

These fundamental musical relations are important, but in a way it is a misfortune of music criticism that it is so relatively easy to explain them in a mechanical way. The usual definitions of "scherzo" and "rondo" can be quickly memorized. But there is another aspect of musical structure that is equally important, especially when we come to problems like those to be discussed in the following section. So little has been done to clarify it that the suggestions I am about to make must be rather tentative. I propose to say that a musical composition has, besides the formal relations already described, what I shall call a *kinetic pattern:* it is the pattern of variation in its propulsion, or intensity of movement. We saw in Chapter II, §8, that music, as a process in time, has varying regional qualities that can be described, metaphorically, by terms borrowed from physical motions: the music is rushing, hesitating, pausing, picking up speed, becoming calm, driving ahead, overcoming resistance, building up inertia, insisting, going pell-mell, dragging, exploding, withdrawing, creeping, fading. These are only approximate, though sometimes very apt, descriptions of what is going on from moment to moment. In some music the main pace and intensity are steady, without striking changes, though as long as the melody is moving about, there are subtle developments in the kinetic pattern. In other music, there are abrupt and profound changes. In either case, the kinetic pattern is the most fundamental aspect of musical form.

Kinetic quality, and some of the perceptual conditions on which it depends, can be illustrated in the simplest melodies. Consider, for example, this old folk tune, which is in the form *AA/BA,* each clause taking eight bars. And let us describe some of the notable intensifications and diminutions of its kinetic quality.

Notice first that the melody consists almost entirely of four figures, or

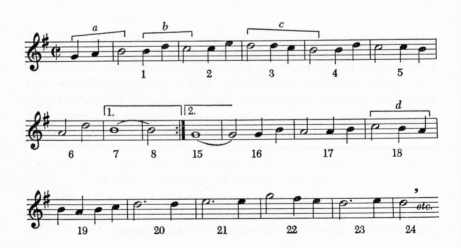

motives, two of which, *a* and *b*, are three-note rising figures, and two of which are falling figures, *c* with four notes and *d*—which does not appear until the contrasting clause, Bar 18—with three. The movement of the first clause is first upward from G, touching on E, its highest note, and then downward to B in Bar 7. It contains the four figures, sometimes overlapping, in this order: *a, b, b, c, b, c,* with a final two-note cadence—the rising figures predominating in the first four bars, the falling ones in the second four bars. The melody has a very firm and clear contour, from which any deviation later on will sound especially intense and important. Moreover, it moves within a limited tonal range, the interval of a sixth, and this is further intensified by the repetition of the first clause, so that it seems like a rather unambitious melody, content to lie within its bounds, and if, later on, it breaks out of these bounds, there will be strong tension and a sense of overcoming obstacles, even if self-imposed.

In its first eight bars, the melody begins on the tonic tone, from absolute rest, and rises in urgency and propulsion, but not in pace, to Bar 3, when it begins to settle down once more. But its first close is only a half-close, on the B, and its energy is therefore not exhausted; it promises a repetition of itself, and that is what happens. The second time around, it reaches home with the original G, and at this point we can see that the melody must either stop for good or else turn in a new direction. It follows the latter course. The new clause is partly constructed out of the same figures, but in a different order, and though it too strives upward, it does so more deliberately and with a greater gathering of strength for the assault. Its figures are *b, a, d, a, d,* but with a new pattern of movement in Bars 21 to 24. In Bar 19 we get, for the first time in the song, a bar-rhythm of four quarter-tones, which have in this context great decisiveness and march upward as though striving for higher notes. This striving is held in check and increased, first by a dotted half-note on D, Bar 20—the first dotted note in the song—then by another one on E, Bar 21. Finally there is the leap to the G, the highest note in the song, and the climax of the melody, which sings out lyrically here. There is a slight pause, a sense of suspended animation, and then the first clause comes round again. Notice, too, that though in general the odd-numbered bars are stressed, as against the even-numbered ones, the climactic note comes in Bar 22, in what otherwise would have been an unstressed bar, and this rhythmic subtlety increases the tension of this moment.

If we could diagram the fluctuations of intensity in this melody, we would be mapping its kinetic pattern, and what can be said about this melody can also be said, though perhaps with much more subtlety and complexity, for great melodies of Beethoven and Mozart and Schubert. When we turn to larger musical forms, we find the same sort of movement, but on a larger scale. For a large work divides into phases, or passages, and though there is an infinite variety of kinetic qualities, we can hear, I think, four main kinds, or degrees of movement, each of which may qualify a whole passage. The scheme I would like to suggest may seem like a considerable over-simplification, and no doubt it is simplified. Yet there is, I think, an important and useful truth in it.

Sometimes the music sounds strongly introductory, or promissory: it has the air of an announcement, as though something important is to come; and, up to a point, the longer it continues, the more it leads us to expect and to require. The quality is a waiting and expectant quality. It may be a few bars of arpeggio accompaniment, as, for example, just before the first subject in Schubert's *String Quartet in A Minor*. It may be a long, and profound, passage, such as the classical composers some-times put before their major symphonies: see Mozart's *E Flat Major Symphony* (K. 543) and Beethoven's *A Major Symphony (No. 7)*. But the *Introduction Quality* I refer to appears not only in actual introductions: the classical composers wrote important passages with this quality in the last parts of their development-sections, just before the recapitula-tion—the first movement of Beethoven's *String Quartet (the "Harp") in E Flat Major (Op. 74)*, Bars 109-138, is a good example. And, indeed, large stretches of music in the "tone poems" and other program works of romantic composers have this same quality, sometimes continued beyond endurance—for a promise whose fulfillment is constantly postponed grad-ually ceases to sustain our interest.

Other passages have a *Conclusion Quality*, or sense of approaching finality; they seem to be winding things up, as if things will soon be over. The codas of classical symphonies have this quality to a high de-gree, though sometimes—as in Beethoven's *Symphony in F Major (No. 8)*—they generate a good deal of new vitality and put off their conclusive-ness as long as they can. But passages with a Conclusion Quality to a lesser degree may turn up at various strategic points in a classical move-ment. Or a movement, like the finale of Mozart's *E Flat Symphony*, may wind up with only the lightest hint of conclusiveness, and surprise us with its abruptness.

But a melody in itself, like a song or much of the exposition of a classical symphony, has neither an Introduction nor a Conclusion Quality: it is simply present. After the slow introduction to a late Haydn sym-phony—for example, the *"Military" Symphony in G Major (No. 100)*—the allegro melody seems to say, "This is it; this is what you've been waiting for; here I am." But some themes need no introduction; a few strokes of the lower strings by way of accompaniment, and then, after two notes of the opening theme of Mozart's *G Minor Symphony*, we are off: this is clearly the main business on the agenda. Any real melody, a well-rounded theme, has this quality; let us call it *Exhibition Quality*, for such a pas-sage does not sound as if something has just happened or will happen, but as if the important thing is happening right now.

Finally, there are passages that have a *Transition Quality*. The pas-sages, usually not of great intrinsic melodic interest, that serve to carry through the modulation from the home key to the second key in, say, the sonata-allegro movements of Haydn's string quartets, are generally called "bridge-passages." They have the sound of being on foot from one Exhibition to another. They suspend the proceedings, and introduce a note of temporary uncertainty or inconclusiveness, which is resolved when we catch sight again of a new passage with Exhibition Quality.

We could, then, roughly map out the *dominant kinetic pattern* of a musical movement in terms of these four qualities—provided we take care to note that they emerge in different degrees, sometimes insistently, sometimes just slightly. There is an Exhibition passage, followed by a Transition passage, followed by another Exhibition passage; there is a sudden halt, and the brief silence that follows also sounds a little Transitional. Then we hear a rather ambiguous passage that could be an Introduction; its Introduction Quality increases in definiteness, and it leads into another Exhibition passage. This develops momentum and begins to slacken; gradually we find ourselves clearly in a Conclusion passage, which rounds itself off, and the movement is over. Such would be an over-all view of a dominant kinetic pattern of a musical work, or perhaps of several.[3]

In describing the kinetic qualities of music, I have spoken the language of phenomenal objectivity. That is, I have used words like "tension" and "relaxation," "tendency" and "striving," "hesitancy," "slackening" and "closure"; and these words name regional qualities of the musical process. Now there is also a language of phenomenal subjectivity, which can be spoken instead, and, indeed, for some purposes it is very useful. In this language we would talk of "arousing expectations" and "disappointing" them, of "anticipations" and "fulfillments," that is, the corresponding phases of the listener's attitudes as they are evoked by the music. For the experience of music is one in which the listener's feelings are constantly guided and manipulated. If he hears the notes without forming any expectations about what will happen next, he is not enjoying them as music, for they have no direction for him. And when people say they do not "understand" a certain piece of music, they usually mean that as they listen to it they are unable to form any expectations that *can* be disappointed or fulfilled. Everything that happens is equally indifferent, neither surprising nor anticipated. They cannot feel their way into the musical process, or get the hang of it.

---

[3] I think what I call the "kinetic pattern" is similar to what Arnold Elston refers casually to as the "energy curve," in his interesting article, "Some Rhythmic Practices in Contemporary Music," *Musical Quarterly*, XLII (1956): 329. The nearest thing I have found to a detailed description of music in terms of dynamic pattern is in ch. 2 of the excellent *Handbook for Music* used in Humanities One at the College of the University of Chicago, 5th ed., Chicago: U. of Chicago, 1955, recently revised by Grosvenor Cooper, *Learning to Listen*, Chicago: U. of Chicago, 1957.

One problem that arises, then, is this: what is it that arouses our expectations about music? And we can make an important distinction between two kinds of expectation. First, there are those such as we have just noted, which are tied to the qualities of the music itself. We expect a dominant seventh chord to be resolved, because the chord seems to need that resolution. We expect a melody that ends on a half-cadence to repeat itself. We expect a melody that has circumscribed a tonal space of a sixth in its first clause to remain within that space, because it seems to have marked out its own range; of course, intellectually, we realize that it probably won't stay in that space, but we have got to feel when it doesn't that something special and unheralded is happening, and this is what the music itself makes us feel. As we saw in analyzing the folk song, to form these expectations is nothing more than to enjoy the music.

But second, there are other expectations that play a role in our musical experience, and these are of a more intellectual sort. If we know, for example, that the music about to be played is either the second or third movement of a Mozart string quartet, and it begins in triple time, not fast, we can predict that it will turn out to be a minuet with a ternary structure. Or if it is the finale of a classical symphony, we listen to the opening theme and say to ourselves that it is behaving more like a rondo theme than a sonata-allegro theme, and this leads us to expect certain general features of the ensuing movement, for example, that the theme will recur two or three more times in a relatively intact form, with intervening passages. These expectations are based on generalizations from past experience of certain types of music.

Even the expectations of the second sort are of course generally not mere statistical predictions, as when someone says he is going to play a three-voice fugue by Bach, and even before he begins we know the chances are that the second voice will enter in the dominant. If a theme is recognized as a rondo-theme, it is partly because of the nature of the theme itself. It has a four-square quality, a wholeness and self-sufficiency, and a certain bounce, and it is in no danger of modulating into another key; these are the qualities that make it suitable for a rondo, and not so suitable for a sonata-allegro movement. So, too, if the theme has a firm and striking contour and rhythm that will show up even in a thick contrapuntal texture, and if its second half is made up of shorter notes than the first half, we prepare ourselves to hear a fugue, even if we haven't read the program.

The problem, however, is not raised by this distinction between the internal and the external grounds of expectation, but by a strong line of reasoning that might seem to wipe out that distinction. For we have been assuming that some of the expectations that constitute an experience of musical form are a function of the kinetic qualities of the par-

ticular music itself, and therefore independent of statistical information
about other musical compositions. But what if the perception of those
very kinetic qualities, that is, their appearance in someone's phenomenal
field, itself depends on his previous experience of other, similar, music?
Then the kinetic pattern of the music is relative to that experience, and
to individuals who have had it. I shall call this the *Relativistic Theory
of Musical Form*.[4]

According to this view, a musical style, in a broad sense in which
it includes both structural and textural features, is a system of probabilities, and to become acquainted with a style, by hearing music in that
style, is to become aware of the relative probabilities of certain developments—for example, that certain chords will follow others, that certain
melodic figures are likely to be endings or beginnings, that certain intervals belong to certain scales. Knowing these probabilities is not necessarily conscious; they are embodied in the listener's habit-patterns, and
become a set of latent expectations. To understand a musical composition is to bring to it habit-patterns relevant to its style. Thus, according
to this view, the kinetic qualities of music would be analyzable into, or
dependent upon, certain probabilities. Instead of saying, for example, that
a certain passage has a strong Conclusion Quality, we should have to
say that at such-and-such a time, and in such-and-such a place, considering the frequencies of occurrence of similar passages in music at the end,
rather than at the beginning, of various compositions, there is a high
probability that this passage is a conclusion.

Now, of course, the Relativist need not go so far. He may concede
that within certain limits the kinetic qualities of music are internal, that
is, a function of the local qualities, rather than learned. But he will also
maintain that some of the expectations that form an essential part of
musical enjoyment are responses to kinetic qualities that depend not
only on local conditions in the music, but on the way the music follows
or deviates from certain norms established by previous compositions.

There is not room here for adequate treatment of this view; but I
should like to offer some comments. First, the problem of estimating
musical probabilities is complicated, and it won't work to calculate them
simply in terms of frequencies.[5] The tonic triad is still the chord to which
the *Tristan* sevenths strive, even if Wagner doesn't let them attain this
goal; it is still the most "probable" chord to follow, even if it hardly ever
does. Of course, this may be because Wagner's harmonic style is set
against a background of other music in which the tonic triad is a frequent conclusion. Still, we do not have examples, I think, of other musical
systems in which, by constant repetition, people have come to expect

---

[4] It has been most cogently developed and argued by Leonard B. Meyer, in his
extremely important book, *Emotion and Meaning in Music;* for references, see Note
12-B.

[5] This point has been well made by Meyer in his later article, "Meaning in Music
and Information Theory"; see Note 13-C.

tonic triads to resolve themselves into dominant sevenths, because the latter seem more stable and cadential. Second, there is a problem of clarifying the notion of "understanding" a style. It is not the case that once you have formed the habit-patterns appropriate to Mozart, you can no longer hear Palestrina without the constant irritating expectation that the harmony will get thicker, or that once you have caught on to Wagner's idiom you can no longer make sense of Mozart. Apparently one can live in a variety of style-systems, and this seems to suggest that there is more to the matter than habit-patterns.

It may be that we shall have to say something like the following: the kinetic qualities, and hence the form, of a musical composition is to be defined by its place in the development of music, just as a poem has to be defined with reference to the language in which it is written. And music may conceivably change, or lose, its form. The kinetic qualities it possesses at a given time are those that would be heard in it by a listener who not only attends to all the local events within it, and follows its course with the closest attention, but who has heard all the music composed up to that time. This is, of course, an idealized definition, to which no actual listener conforms. But one does not have to hear all the music in a style in order to know that style. And there is good reason to suppose that some listeners are well qualified to speak, though not infallibly, of the kinetic qualities of music they know well, and consequently of its form.

§13.   *UNITY AND RELATED CONCEPTS*

There is an important sense of the word "form" very different from those we have considered so far, though not always carefully kept distinct from them. Critics often speak of a visual design or a musical composition as "formless" or "lacking in form." There are other phrases, more or less equivalent: it is said that a painting by Jackson Pollock or William Baziotes "has no structure" or "is not well organized;" a symphony by Bruckner or Sibelius "does not hang together" or "falls apart." Never mind for the moment whether or not these judgments are true; the first question is what they can mean, and how they could be known to be true.

In this sense, form is something that an aesthetic object can have in different degrees; perhaps it must have some, but it may have very little. Form in the sense defined earlier in this chapter is a different sort of characteristic: in that sense you may ask of an aesthetic object what form it has, but not *how much form* it has. In the new sense, however, you do ask how much form it has, or in other words, how well formed it is. And the importance of this question comes from the fact that almost all critics suppose that the answer given to it will have something to do with the value of the aesthetic object. It is almost always accounted a merit in the object if it has good form, or is "highly organized." Whether it is a merit or not is a question we shall come to in Chapter X, §24; but first, we must consider the notion of "good form" itself.

The two senses of "form" involved here can be made clearer by comparing the two correlative senses of "order."[1] Suppose someone spills a bag of marbles on the floor, and they roll at random until they stop in an untidy sprawl. We might ask for a description of the order in which they lie, for in one sense they have an order, no matter if by chance: there are definite relations of distance and direction, on a Cartesian co-ordinate system, connecting every marble with every other, and these relations can be measured and stated. But we would also say that they are not "in good order," or "well ordered," or "orderly," and this is quite a different sense of the term. They are in an order, but not in order. The word "design" goes through the same mutation: according to some theologians the world not merely *is* a design, but was *designed*.

It is obviously an advantage to keep these two ideas distinct by choosing different sets of terms to mark them. And once we have them well marked, it is a further precaution against error to stick to a fairly limited vocabulary, just so it be sufficient to mark all the distinctions we require, without falling into elegant variation through the lavish use of nearly synonymous terms—which abound in English and are much favored by writers on the arts. A certain terminological asceticism is called for, however incongruous it may seem with the rich sensuous nature of the subject we are talking about.

The word "form" we have already found a use for, and pretty well fixed that use: from here on, I shall not use it in the sense of having more or less form. But for this latter sense there is a perfectly good word that presents little danger of confusion. When we speak of the *unity* of an aesthetic object, or say that one object is more or less unified than another, we mean to refer to a quality that different objects can possess in different degrees. Let us see whether we can make empirical sense of such statements.

Some students of aesthetics prefer not to talk about "unity" as such, but about "organic unity," as a special kind of unity peculiarly germane to aesthetic objects. But it is not clear what this adjective adds. We could say that an object has organic unity if and only if it is a complex—in other words, reserve "organic unity" for unity that is a regional quality. This would be clear, but unnecessary. In critical discourse, we are not concerned with the unity possessed by elements of aesthetic objects, but only of complexes; in this context, unity, if it is a quality at all, will always be a regional quality. According to the way others use the term, to say

---

[1] The two senses are not exactly the same as, but connected with, the two senses distinguished by Bergson in his penetrating analysis of the concept of disorder, *Creative Evolution,* trans. by Arthur Mitchell, New York: Holt, 1911, pp. 220-236.

that an object is organically unified is to say that the removal of any part would change it. This is, of course, too loose a way of defining it; in a trivial sense, any change in a complex changes that complex. We might try to make it more specific, then, by saying that the whole is organically unified if any change in its parts or their relations would make it less unified. The test of organic unity would then at least be clear; you would try changing the colors in a painting, or shifting the masses, to see if every change lessens the unity. Of course the number of possible changes is considerable, so you could never be sure; however, it is doubtful if there exists a single painting in the world, however unified, that would pass this test.

Visual Completeness and Coherence

The safest way of analyzing the term "unity" is to consider first its use in visual design, and then its use in music; after that, we can compare the uses to see whether, or in what respects, they are the same.

There are two distinguishable components in the concept of unity. Though they tend to go together, they are not the same, and within limits they can vary independently of each other, but the word "unity" seems to apply to both. This will not necessarily lead to any confusion, provided we are aware of it. Otherwise, we might compare two objects and find that their unities seem different in some subtle way, though we cannot say which has it in a higher degree. And we might be unnecessarily puzzled unless we are aware that one object has one of the components of unity to a higher degree than the other, but the other has the second component to a higher degree than the first. In such a case one cannot say that either is more unified; one can either talk about the components instead, or say that the objects are about equal.

One component I shall call *completeness,* the other *coherence.*

As we have seen, a visual design is by definition marked out from other parts of the visual field; it is framed. Hence it appears as a definite and limited part of the field, with its own picture-space tied to its picture-plane. To say that it has completeness is to say that it appears to require, or call upon, nothing outside itself; it has all that it needs; it is all there. This is not a definition: completeness is a simple quality that must be pointed out. All we can do here is to talk around it, give examples, and try with the help of synonymous expressions to show where to look. There is no reason in principle why we should not be able, with care, to make sure that we mean the same thing by the term—indeed, we may already mean the same thing. But completeness is not going to be analyzable into any simpler qualities.

We can, of course, talk about some of the conditions under which a visual design will have a high degree of completeness: in other words, some of the characteristics of the parts of the design, and their relations, that tend to increase completeness. For example, other things being equal, the stronger the frame the more it will tend to cut off the interior from the rest of a wall, and the more the picture-space will be driven in upon itself. On the other hand, if the painting is placed on a wall painted in various gay colors some of which are the same tones as those found in the painting, these color-harmonies will inevitably connect the interior of the painting with the exterior, and reduce its self-sufficiency and independence. If there is no strong dominant pattern in the design, as in some contemporary paintings, or in the big Monet (*Water Lilies*, ca. 1925) in the Museum of Modern Art, they may look as though they could as well be continued in any direction and would not be seriously lacking if cut in two. Or if the harlequin in a painting steps forward, out of the picture-plane, so that he seems to be moving into the space of the room in which the picture hangs, the completeness will be lessened. But if all the masses in the picture-space are clearly and definitely related to each other, they will not drive the eye beyond the frame or need anything to supplement themselves for visual completeness.

We are talking here basically about design, though of course representational elements may complicate it, as in the example of the harlequin. But the completeness in question now is independent of representation. A piece of sculpture that is merely a torso, or even a classic statue with arms or legs missing, may be nevertheless quite complete as a design, though from a physiological point of view there is evidently something missing. Thus Rodin did not destroy the completeness of his statue *The Inner Voice*—later used for the Victor Hugo monument—when he left off the arms because arms, he said, imply action, and action is the enemy of meditation. But a painting with a strong diagonal that runs to the edge of the picture, with nothing to lead the eye back into the picture space, and no balancing lines to soften its eccentric movement, will appear incomplete, whether the diagonal line is an arm, a rope, or a road.

In Kollwitz' *Municipal Lodging*, PLATE III, and Goya's *Colossus*, PLATE VII, a high degree of completeness is obtained by keeping the interesting figures away from the frame. The foot of Rembrandt's *Girl Sleeping*, PLATE II, and the hair and ear of Beckmann's *Self-Portrait*, PLATE IV, run outside the picture plane, and this introduces a slight incompleteness, but very slight. In Daumier's *Witnesses*, PLATE VIII, there is a strong suggestion that the group we see is the vanguard of a larger unseen group, and this gives the picture a good deal less completeness, though of course it increases its power in another respect.

The great unfinished works of art—for example, the late Cézannes, Bach's *Art of Fugue*, Kafka's *Castle*—have a powerful incompleteness—so much so that some people feel compelled to try to complete them.

For the term "coherence" there are roughly synonymous expressions that we can use to help direct attention to this quality where it is to be found: the coherent design contains nothing that does not belong; it all fits together. But the quality is itself simple; therefore the term cannot be given the sort of definition that analyzes a concept into parts. We can say something, however, about the phenomenal conditions of coherence, and in this indirect way make reasonably sure that we are talking about the same thing.

Not that we can lay down an exhaustive list of conditions that will tend to make a design cohere or that will tend to make it incoherent. For one thing, progress in the fine arts consists just in the fact, not that greater works are produced, but that great painters discover quite new and profoundly valuable ways of making designs cohere. We can set up some broad categories, and perhaps in a way make room for all possible types of coherence-conditions, but we must remember this is only a convenience for the critic, and in no way reflects upon the originality of painters or restricts the future of painting.

We might speak here of "principles" of coherence; such a principle is a statement that, other things being equal, such-and-such a set of elements or of relations will tend to produce, or to increase, coherence. And these principles may be grouped in three large classes.

Coherence is promoted by *focus*. A focus is the dominant pattern, or compositional scheme, if it stands out clearly from the whole painting, or it may be that part of the painting that has the greatest perceptual strikingness or to which the eye is led from various directions by the convergence of strong lines. The unity of a late Rembrandt—and indeed of much of Baroque painting—is partly dependent upon having such a central focus. But not all unified paintings are unified in this way. The principle of focus may be seen in the dominant patterns of the Kollwitz, PLATE III, and the Goya, PLATE VII; in the pointed hand to which the eye constantly returns in Daumier's *Witnesses*, PLATE VIII; and in the figure of Jesus in Dürer's *Last Supper*, PLATE VI, on whom many lines converge, and at whom every one of the disciples is looking, except the one in front of him, and one other who is, nevertheless, pointing at him.

Coherence is also promoted by balance and equilibrium, of which examples were given in the preceding section. There is a nice problem in the history of painting: given two standing figures, how to connect them. The painters of Adam and Eve have faced this problem from earliest times of Western painting, and it still is fascinating to painters. To some degree they can be unified by being made to balance each other, if a fairly strong axis can be provided—and it is fortunate that the story in Genesis supplies a handy tree for this purpose. If the painter, like Picasso in some of his paintings of harlequins, wishes to get along without a tree, there are other things he must do, if his design is not to fall apart into two more or less complete wholes.

The concept of balance can be extended to relations in depth within the picture-space. If there are lines with strong movement that take one back into deep space, then they may be balanced by lines that bring one

back to the picture-plane—as in many of Cézanne's landscapes. Otherwise, the rear of the picture and its front will tend to divide, to become
independent, and the picture will lose coherence.

Third, coherence is promoted by *similarities* among the parts of the
design. This principle is often called the principle of *harmony*, and I
think it is also what many people mean by "order" in this context. Thus,
generally speaking, if two areas are similar in color tone, in lie, or in
shape, they appear as if connected; there is cross-reference, and a tendency toward coherence in the design of which they are a part—a tendency
that may, of course, be counteracted by strong contrasts. As a rough generalization, we may say that, other things being equal, the more similarities there are among the parts of the design, the more coherent the design will tend to be.

Similarity of texture, or, in other words, consistency of style, throughout the design, is one of the most powerful perceptual conditions of coherence. The designs reproduced in this book are all excellent examples
of this; each one has its outstanding and unforgettable qualities of line
and local shape, in tones of gray or black, that are carried through the
whole design.

These brief notes on completeness and coherence in visual design
are only a summary of many complex and subtle matters. Our problem
here is, however, not to discover exactly what conditions tend toward
unity in painting, and what do not. That is the critic's task. We want to
see, if we can, what he is doing, and assure ourselves, if not him, that it
can be done. And it is an empirical question that we are dealing with.
It is easy to see in simple cases that we are making sense. Given a piece of
yellow paper, a blue triangle, a green star, and a red square, we might
set up a problem: to arrange the figures on the yellow paper in such a
way that despite the contrast in hues the whole will be as unified as it
can be made. Maybe there is no single ideal solution of the problem, but
there are certainly better and worse ones, and you need not be a creative
artist at all to think up solutions that would be extremely poor—if they
were put in three different corners, for instance. Now it seems clear that
when we compare two such solutions, we can sometimes clearly see that
one design is more unified than the other, either because it is both more
complete and more coherent, or more of one though about equal of the
other. And we can say such things as, "A is more coherent because the
triangle and star are closer together," or "A is more coherent because the
three figures are put in a roughly triangular pattern." This won't make
them great works of art, but we are not concerned here with their value:
we are only concerned to note that it is an empirical question whether
one visual design is more or less unified than another. When we jump
from this artificial exercise to a large work by Paolo Veronese or Tintoretto, the matter becomes infinitely more complicated; but what we are
looking for when we look for unity is apparently the same sort of thing.

The *Las Meninas* of Velásquez (1656, Prado) exhibits many of the unifying features that have been reviewed above: a focus in the figure of the Infanta Margareta, serial orders among the other figures, balance, clearly defined planes of space, a harmonized tonality due to controlled value-intensity relations throughout.

Musical Completeness and Coherence

In music, the concept of completeness can be even more readily and strikingly exhibited. We have seen that it is part of the definition of "melody" that a melody has some cadential quality at the end, and is therefore somewhat complete in itself, just as it is part of the definition of "visual design" that a visual design is in some way bounded. But the experience of breaking off a melody in the middle, as in a game of Musical Chairs, affords an even clearer idea of incompleteness than does cutting a visual design in half with scissors. And not only does an unfinished melody sound incomplete, but so does an unfinishable one: someone working at a monotonous task who is trying to whistle a tune, without thinking much about it, and constantly returns to a half-cadence that leads back to the same melody over and over again, without ever finishing a final cadence, offers a powerful and exasperating example of incompleteness in music.

When we consider larger melodies that have their own phrases and clauses, the completeness depends on subtler aspects of the dynamic pattern. For example, "Swanee River" is of the $A_1/A_2/B/A$ type, but A_1 ends differently from A_2. If we imagine it played in the key of C, the A-clauses begin on E, with the tonic chord; the clause A_2 ("Dar's where my heart . . . the old folks stay") ends on the keynote, C, and on the tonic chord, so that the two clauses A_1/A_2 together form a double clause, or sentence, with considerable completeness, though A_1 by itself (up to "far, far away") is incomplete, because it ends on D and the dominant seventh chord. "Au Clair de la Lune" is also of the $A_1/A_2/B/A$ type, only in this case all of the A-clauses end on the keynote and the tonic chord, so that A_2 is exactly like A_1. In this song, then, A_1 is itself highly complete, though short, but when we repeat it (A_2) we decrease the completeness slightly, because the repetition creates a greater need for some sort of contrast, and leads to the expectation that it will be followed by something different (B).

The completeness of larger-scale musical works, such as the movements of symphonies, is a function of their kinetic pattern. If, for example, a composition moves at some point into a passage with Introduction or Transition quality, and then comes to a stop, there will be anticlimax, and a destruction of completeness. Tovey has given a wonderful description of Liszt's tone poem *Ce Qu'on Entend sur la Montagne* in terms of its dominant kinetic pattern:

This work consists of an introduction to an introduction to a connecting link to another introduction to a rhapsodic interlude, leading to a free development of the third introduction, leading to a series of still more introductory developments of the previous introduction, leading to a solemn slow theme (which, after these twenty minutes, no mortal power will persuade any listener to regard as a real beginning), and so eventually leading backwards to the original mysterious opening by way of conclusion.[2]

This is a kind of incompleteness: it promises a passage with Exhibition Quality, but never really gets under way, and when it stops it is still promising something that never arrives.

The concept of kinetic pattern affords a means of exploring in detail the completeness component of unity in large works. Compare, for example, the first movement of Shostakovitch's *Fifth Symphony* with the first movement—to take one at the opposite extreme—of Beethoven's *B Flat Major Symphony (No. 4)*. The suspense in the opening bars of the spacious slow introduction in Beethoven's symphony promises that something noteworthy is going to happen, and the introduction works up to a headlong rush into the allegro; from that point on every let-up is only a way to build up higher tension and the demand for further passages, and the demands are, in the end, satisfied: the climax of the development, with echoes of the upward sweeps that brought in the exposition—a diminuendo (Bar 265), a hushed air of expectancy, the long drum roll (Bars 311-335), and the sense that the strings are catching fire—is a tremendously satisfactory preparation for the recapitulation, and the whole movement is one of the most tightly knit, self-contained, and complete in all of Beethoven.

On the other hand, Shostakovitch's symphony begins with a fairly decisive four-bar phrase, which immediately yields to a sort of vamp-till-ready (Introduction) passage in the lower strings, and a slow melody that has Exhibition quality, but not very strongly. This soon fades out into a hesitant Transition passage, and though fragments of the slow melody are woven into a new theme, the whole thing fails to build up any drive or tension; it has always the air of being in danger of petering out. The fanfare (#7 in the score) sounds like a conclusion, but we are suddenly back in the introduction, with more vamp-till-ready, and a new slow melody—a dull square theme that for all its limitations does sound more definite and Exhibition-like than anything since the first four bars. This is the way the movement goes. The most promising fff climax (#38), which sounds like the Conclusion, is followed by a delayed end, a letdown, and further anticlimax. In general, build-ups are thrown away because there are no strong Exhibition melody-passages to which they lead, and Conclusions are followed by anticlimactic hesitant passages. The movement has a loose and indecisive and incomplete quality.

---

[2] Donald F. Tovey, *Essays in Musical Analysis*, London: Oxford U., 1935-39, Vol. II, p. 7.

A similar contrast could be made between the movements of Beethoven's ("*Kreutzer*") *Sonata for Violin and Piano in A Major* and, say, the second movement of Bartók's *Second Violin Sonata* (1920) with its stops and starts, speedings and slowings, little melodies and perky pizzicato phrases.

Musical coherence is most easily seen in contrast to its opposite. If you can imagine a few bars of "Stormy Weather" or "Tiger Rag" inserted in the slow movement of Beethoven's *A Minor String Quartet (Op. 132)*, you have an example of wild incongruity. Without being dogmatic about the limits of coherence—allowing the greatest possible latitude for discoveries by future composers that things can be made to cohere in ways we know not of—it is highly doubtful that these could ever be combined in the same composition and perceived as belonging together, as part of the same work. On the other hand, in the first movement of Dvořák's *Cello Concerto in B Minor* there is a rousing little theme that appears at the end of the opening *tutti* and then is never heard again. Yet it is not heard as utterly irrelevant because of several things: for example, something of that quality is called for at that point, to mark off sections of the movement; and it is stylistically in keeping with the character of the rest of the work. The same may be said of the little theme that makes its first appearance in the development section of Mendelssohn's ("*Italian*") *Symphony in A Major:* it is perfectly in keeping with the context. Indeed, the music of Dvořák and Mendelssohn, despite its other limitations, is in general characterized by a high degree of coherence in the clarity and continuity of its kinetic pattern; they know how to manage preparations and climaxes.

What conditions contribute to the coherence of music? Again, as in visual design, we can never hope to set forth all the conditions that might be combined to make music cohere: this is something that composers discover and critics take note of. We know that the coherence of a melody is enhanced by certain factors: if it is all in the same key, it will tend to be more coherent than if it changes key; if the intervals are mostly small, it will tend to be highly coherent; if there are similarities, parallelisms, and echoes in its melodic and rhythmic figures, they will tend to make it cohere. Music that is not melodic, or whose melodies are not highly coherent, can still be made coherent in other ways: rhythmically, for example, or in over-all regional qualities.

Some music is made coherent largely by its structure: for example, a movement of a Haydn symphony, which is built on certain main dynamic contrasts held together by firm tonality relations and melodic repetitions and developments. Other music is made coherent largely by its texture: for example, a movement of a Baroque concerto grosso, which may develop a considerable continuity and constancy of drive that keep it going to the end. The first movement of Bach's *Third Brandenburg Concerto in G Major* has a structure—its *ritornello,* and its modulations into related keys, and back again. But it is more remarkable for its constancy of texture, partly because it has the same instrumentation throughout, and hence the same tone-colors, and partly because the melodic lines are based on the same recurrent figures. Every passage in it sounds as if it belongs to the same composition. Such works as these can perhaps achieve a higher degree of coherence than works built around the sonata-allegro structure-type, but they do not achieve, as a rule, such a high degree of completeness. They would not sound very much less complete if stopped at the penultimate cadence.

One of the most puzzling problems about musical unity arises in connection with compound, or several-movement, compositions. It is reasonably clear in what the unity of each movement consists. But what makes a group of movements, as in a sonata or suite, constitute a coherent whole? The movements offer contrasts in tempo and key, and may make an interesting pattern in sequence, but so do the various numbers on a concert program, and a concert is not a single composition. But Beethoven's *C Minor Symphony* is one composition, and so is Handel's *Water Music,* and Brahms' *Clarinet Quintet.*

It has recently been argued[3] that the unity of a compound composition is secured chiefly by a special sort of thematic affinity that goes beyond theme-development and theme-variation and such canonic devices as inversion. According to this view, the themes of two movements may be significantly related by certain features, even though they are of an entirely different, and even contrasting, character. For a simple example, consider the openings of the first, second, and fourth movements of Mozart's *Eine Kleine Nachtmusik.* These melodies are entirely distinct, and would not be confused with each other, yet they share a pattern of notes that would be regarded as significant by those who hold the theory we are now considering:

Mozart, *Serenade: Eine Kleine Nachtmusik,* K. 525

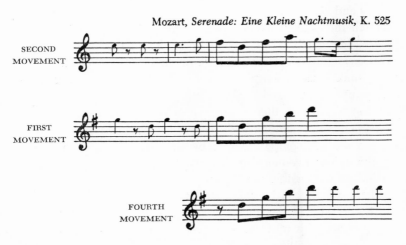

SECOND MOVEMENT

FIRST MOVEMENT

FOURTH MOVEMENT

---

[3] By Rudolf Reti, *The Thematic Process in Music;* see Note 13-B for reference.

The same sort of relationship can be traced on a larger scale in Bach's *St. Matthew Passion,* for in at least fifteen of its numbers the melody contains a figure of a rising second followed by a falling second, or by a slight variation of this figure.

This "thematic transformation" theory offers some fruitful possibilities of further inquiry, especially on account of its psychological assumptions. There is no doubt, I think, that the movements of *Eine Kleine Nachtmusik* seem to go very well together; the question is whether this can be accounted for by the theory, which proposes that we are affected by thematic affinities even where we do not notice them, so that we perceive two movements related by thematic transformations as connected even though we do not hear their melodies as in any way derived from one another. This thesis could be tested, of course. On the one hand, we might ask whether the third movement, which also seems to belong to the composition quite well, though perhaps not so intimately as the other three, can be analyzed to reveal thematic affinities. On the other hand, we might try in its place a suitable string quartet minuet—chosen with care, for *Eine Kleine Nachtmusik* is not, either in scoring or style, a string quartet—in which we have found thematic affinities, to see whether it sounds more suitable than the present one.

Forms Common to the Arts

I have talked about unity in visual design and unity in music, and used the same word for both, but it may well be thought that this begs a crucial question: am I in fact talking about the same thing? Is it really the same quality? Without trying hard, in fact, one can make out a fairly skeptical case on this point. When you say that something is unified, and you wish to use this term in a sense that will apply to both auditory and visual fields—not to mention poetry and the drama—it seems as though the concept has to be watered down to the point where you aren't saying much. Sight is one thing, hearing is another; reds and squares belong to one, slow and high-pitched to the other; how can there be any quality that belongs to both? The test of whether there is a common quality is easy and conclusive: if you mean the same thing by "unity" in both cases, then you ought to be able to compare a musical composition and a painting with respect to this quality, just as you compare two musical compositions or two paintings. Finally, if you do let unity through as a common quality, what will you not let through? There is no limit to the possible absurdities.

These doubts can be answered, it seems to me, although I do not wish to suggest that the question is settled. If we keep clear about the distinction between unity as a compound regional quality and its perceptual conditions, there is nothing inherently implausible in saying that

a similar quality can arise from two very different sets of conditions. And
this is, indeed, what often happens.

Nor need we turn down the challenge of comparison. Obviously there is a range of what might be called indeterminacy in all comparisons. Where the quality in terms of which the comparison is made is measurable, the range of indeterminacy may be very slight. If we weigh two stones on an accurate balance, the difference in weight can be detected down to tiny amounts. On the other hand, if we try to tell by hefting two stones whether they are equal, we cannot detect small differences in weight; we may find them indiscriminable in weight even though they differ by a few ounces. Now the degree of unity in a visual design is not a magnitude; that is, we do not know how to construct a scale for measuring it. Consequently, we must expect it to be vague.[4]

In order to show that unity is the same quality in music and painting, it is not necessary to be able to compare with assurance *any* music with *any* painting, but only that there be some reasonably clear-cut cases where the comparison is possible. And the extreme cases are clear-cut. Show us a painting with some unity, and we can find a musical composition, or movement, that is more unified than that painting, and we can find, or invent, a musical composition that is less unified.

There was one other objection to the generalized concept of unity, the last one mentioned above, though rather casually. If we concede that music and visual design can possess unity as a common quality, is this the only characteristic they can share, or are there others? Where can we draw a line?

It is asking too much, of course, to require some general principle here: all we can do is to consider the sorts of comparison that critics have made or might make, to see which of them are plausible, and which are not. And these comparisons can, I think, be divided into three main groups. First, some critics have looked for basic structure-types common to the arts, including literature. Second, critics have looked for common regional qualities—for similarities in "mood" or "feeling" or "spirit." Third, critics have looked for basic similarities in structure and style that will define period-types, and reveal underlying connections among various works of man, including other things than works of art, at a given point in history.

Considered at a rather abstract level, musical designs and visual designs exhibit common structural features that might be made the subject of a General Theory of Design, which would underlie the Theory of Visual Design and the Theory of Musical Design. For example, there are certainly important similarities, as we have seen, between one part of a visual design and another, and between one part of a musical composi-

---

[4] It has been suggested that unity would be measurable if it could be defined in terms of the concept of *redundancy*, which is taken over from Communication Theory; see Note 13-D.

tion and another. Could we not say, then, that they both exhibit *repetition*, or recurrence, though each in its own way? And when there are not only similar parts, but similar relations between the parts, could we not say that they both have *rhythm?* The regular recurrence of beats in music is rhythmic; why not the figures on a frieze or the disposition of masses in a cubist painting?

Some difficult problems of analysis are turned up by this line of thought, and they have not yet been satisfactorily resolved. This is one of the places where I propose rather to raise questions than to try to settle them. Whenever something is clearly identified in a particular art, as rhythm in music, it is tempting to see whether it is not a species of some broader and more basic characteristic that that art has in common with others, and then make the same word do for both. The early paintings of Juan Gris (e.g., *Guitar and Flowers*, 1912, Museum of Modern Art, New York) are sometimes said to be "polyphonic" because certain shapes recur at "rhythmic" intervals and there are distinct "axes," something like the voices of a fugue. The word "rhythm" comes from the auditory field, and there does seem to be at least a prima-facie case for applying it to such things in the visual field as repetitive patterns and wavy lines. On the other hand, the word "balance" has its home meaning, so to speak, in the visual field, but it is often applied also to music. A phrase that ends on a half-cadence is said to call for another phrase to balance it. This seems to be quite a different sense. It is less clear how this term could apply to larger musical segments. If a symphonic movement has both an introduction and a coda, there may be important relations between them, but there does not seem to be any respect in which they sound equal, so that one could speak of them as balancing each other.

More ambitious attempts have been made to distinguish certain basic design-types that run through all the arts. For example, as we have seen, the theme-and-variations structure is an important one in music. So it might be said that in a painting where a certain curve or a certain hue appears in various places with slight alterations, but recognizably similar, we have basically the same structure-type. Now, if we consider them abstractly enough, we can of course find similarities, but perhaps the differences are more important and would only be obscured by lumping them together. In a musical set of variations there are two essential features that are quite lacking in visual design: first, there is an original air, or theme, that acts as a kind of central reference-point, to which all the variations, however remote, are related; second, there is a dramatic order in which the variations are unrolled, so that the composition would have a very different character if the order were changed, while in a visual design the eye is not fully controlled and can wander about almost at will over the parts.

The attempt to compare music and visual designs in terms of their qualities raises another interesting question. We are all familiar with the easy transfers of quality-terms from one of these fields to another: "tone-color" in music and "color-tonality" in visual design, blue areas and blue notes, cheerful wallpaper patterns and cheerful tunes. Music has been composed ostensibly to capture in sound the outstanding regional qualities of visual designs—for example, Moussorgsky's *Pictures at an Exhibition*. And such painters as Whistler have produced "nocturnes" and "scherzos" ostensibly embodying the regional qualities of music.

The gist of the problem can be put somewhat colloquially in this way: can music sound the way a design looks? The elements of music are not the elements of visual design; the relations among them are not the same. They may be analogous in some way, as loud noises are to bright colors, but to be analogous is not to possess common characteristics. Is it possible, then, for the same regional qualities to emerge from different perceptual conditions?

There are two statements about the relation between regional qualities and their perceptual conditions that must be kept clearly distinct. First, the sum total of all the regional qualities of a visual or auditory complex is fixed by its perceptual conditions—that is, the discriminable parts and relations—so that any notable change in the parts or their relations will produce a change in some of the regional qualities, at least in their intensity. But second, a change in the parts or their relations may leave other regional qualities unchanged, so that a particular regional quality can be present in two complexes that differ in their parts or relations or both. This is plain in visual design: see, for example, the diagrams above, p. 171. Similarly a melody that is transposed to a different key or is played on a different instrument may be the same melody as before, though its elements are changed; and the melody played a little faster or augmented to twice its length, or even played somewhat out of tune, may still be recognizable, though the relations between the elements are slightly changed.

There is no theoretical reason, then, why we should doubt the possibility that the same regional quality can attach to different perceptual conditions, though the greater the difference in the conditions, the more likely it will be that there is some difference in the regional quality. And it seems clear that some qualities do in fact appear in both music and visual designs. We are not deceived when we hear in a musical composition a quality of boldness, or of gentleness, or of boisterousness, or of serenity that we also see in a visual design. This does not imply that *all* the qualities that music can exhibit are also exhibited by visual designs, or vice versa. But that there are some sharable qualities I think we must grant, however difficult it is to describe them, or verbally call attention to them.

The third sort of comparison between music and visual designs is that which is often attempted by the historian. They are first grouped in certain style-categories or period-categories within each art, and then put together in groups that cut across the arts. The terms "Baroque," "romantic," "Gothic," "modernistic" have been used for such a purpose.

Now there are two very different purposes to which such terms have been put, and in considering the question whether they can safely be used, the two purposes should be separated. Consider the term "Baroque." First, we may note certain traits of style or structure that turn up frequently in paintings of a certain period: in, say, the paintings of Rubens, Rembrandt, El Greco, Vermeer, Poussin, despite the enormous differences between them. It is convenient to group them together as constituting a similar group in these respects, and to give them all a label.

But here a problem arises. The ordinary way of defining a general term, like "table," "centipede," or "proton," consists of listing a set of characteristics that are to constitute the necessary and sufficient conditions for the application of that term: in other words, an object is properly called a "table" if, and only if, it has *all* the characteristics on the list. But this will not do for words like "Baroque" at all. For if we restricted our definition to characteristics found in *all* the paintings of these painters— or even of any one of them, or all paintings painted between 1615 and 1620—the term "Baroque" would mean nothing, for there would be no absolutely universal characteristics. On the other hand, if we picked out a list of say ten characteristics we were interested in and made them the definition of "Baroque" we should hardly find more than a very few Baroque paintings, and the term would not be very useful.

There is a logical way out of this, and it is probably what art historians for the most part actually do, though they may not put it clearly to themselves, and do not always respect its consequences. We can lay down the ten characteristics and say that we shall call a painting a Baroque painting if it has any five, or more, of them. We then get a class of paintings any two of which will probably have some of the ten characteristics in common, though none will have them all. And if we do not make the mistake of forgetting how we have defined the term, we shall be able to work with it rather conveniently.

But there is a second step that some historians of culture have wished to take, and this is the one that bears most directly upon our problem here: the comparability of music and painting. They want to see whether some of their characteristics defining "Baroque" are not also to be found, or close analogues of them at least, in other aspects of culture: in music, in literature, as well as in sculpture and architecture. Indeed, some of the more imaginative and speculative cultural historians have not been content with "Baroque music" and "Baroque drama," but have discussed "Baroque politics," "Baroque military tactics"—as in the Thirty Years' War, which is said to resemble Milton's prose—"Baroque mathematics" and "Baroque philosophy"—Hobbes or Leibniz, perhaps.

Of course, to verify such generalizations would be difficult indeed, and when terms like "Baroque" and "romantic" get used in this vague way, it is all too easy to be impressed by what are really superficial analogies. In such a case, we ought to be rather hard-boiled, I think, for everybody's good. What does Baroque music after all have in common with Baroque painting? A painting by Rubens is full of large and dramatic contrasts, organized around a strong dominant pattern strongly focused; in these respects, at least, it is more like a Beethoven symphony than like a Passion by Heinrich Schütz or a Handel concerto grosso.

Not that we must rule out the possibility of finding interesting and illuminating similarities; we must only insist that they be tested. Most of those cultural historians who have emphasized the common spirit or style of the arts and their similarity to other aspects of culture[5] have done so in pursuit of certain broad theses about the nature of history or of culture: the thesis, for example, that in each age there is a *Zeitgeist*, or Spirit of the Age, that underlies and manifests itself in every activity, or the thesis that what happens in a culture at any age is determined by the state of development of that culture's inner soul. It would lead us too far afield to consider these theories on their own merits; we will all agree, however, that it would take a great deal of evidence to establish them, once they are adequately formulated, and the evidence ought to be clear and definite.

Complexity

Before we set aside these problems about the comparability of the arts, there is one more concept that we should deal with, though briefly, and it comes in appropriately enough here because it often plays an important role in the description and comparison of visual designs and musical compositions, as a correlative term to "unity." It is the term "complexity." The two notions need to be distinguished with care, for though the opposite of "unity" is "disunity," and the opposite of "complexity" is "simplicity," it will occasionally be found that critics use the term "simplicity" when they mean what I have chosen to mean by "unity." Thus, a black outline-circle on a white page is both simple and unified, but its simplicity—that is, its lack of complexity—is not the same as its unity—that is, its lack of incompleteness and incoherence. Complexity is, roughly, the number of parts, and of differences between them, to be found within the aesthetic object.

It might be useful to have a more general concept here, which could be called the magnitude of an aesthetic object, its perceptual size, so to

---

[5] For example, Lewis Mumford, Egon Friedell, Oswald Spengler; see Note 13-H.

speak. A circle with a dot in it is greater in magnitude than a circle the same size that has no dot, and a square is greater in magnitude than a circle, for it has more changes in change-of-direction. But magnitude seems to reduce (as in these two comparisons) to complexity. Perhaps not wholly. Rembrandt's etching, *Goldweigher's Field* (1651, Hind catalogue 249) is printed on a small-sized paper, but the amount of space it encompasses and keeps in order is tremendous; it is, in this respect, a big work.

We might try to distinguish magnitude and complexity in this way. Suppose we photographed our circle-on-white and blew it up to twice the original size. We could say that its magnitude has been increased, though its complexity has not, for no more parts are distinguishable than there were before. Of course, when you blow up an ordinary photograph, things become visible that were too small to be seen before, so you increase its complexity. And there is perhaps a factor of absolute size—or rather size of the whole design relative to the real world, as against the size of its parts relative to the whole—in some works of fine art that would have to be taken account of. Especially, of course, in architecture; as has been remarked, a pyramid an inch high is inane. And in painting, if the area could be multiplied many times, without anything else being changed, something would undoubtedly happen to it as an aesthetic object, for good or ill; it is an essential part of the character of a Renaissance mural painting that it is large and broad. Nevertheless, for the time being, let us concentrate on complexity as a measure of magnitude. That presents problems enough.

In music, magnitude is perhaps a subtler but an equally important thing. The scale on which a symphonic movement or the first movement of a concerto opens out at the beginning sets up internal proportions for it, as does the frame of a painting, and it must keep to that scale if it is not to sound incomplete. A slow movement may have fewer notes or fewer changes in pitch or volume than a fast movement, and yet it may last longer, and appear a vaster and nobler edifice. But again, let us speak only of complexity in music, and mean by it what we meant by it in painting: one musical composition or section is more complex than another if it has a greater number of discernible elements, complexes, and differences—that is, changes. But only roughly speaking.

This caveat, "roughly speaking," calls attention to the first problem here, the same problem that arose for "unity." It might sound as though we could count the factors that make for complexity, and then assign a numerical measure, if it came to a dispute whether X is more complex than Y. In a visual design—even in such a vast one as Michelangelo's *Last Judgment* (1541, Sistine Chapel, Vatican)—we could conceivably count the areas, though where they shade into one another we should have to mark off somewhat arbitrary areas to show least distinguishable differences, and we could count the number of complex parts that are composed of them. In a musical composition we could count the notes in the score, and we could count the number of melodies, melodic sentences, clauses, phrases, and possible figures. But when we come to relations among the parts, we get beyond the realm of numerical reckoning, even if we are not already exhausted. For we could never be confident that we had thought of *all* the relations between any two parts, or even all that might be important, even if we ignored all relations of the parts to the outside world, and confined ourselves to the object itself.

Fortunately, such a numerical measure is not at all necessary to permit us to speak empirically and testably, even if sometimes vaguely, of the complexity of visual objects and musical compositions. There can be no doubt at all that Masaccio's *Tribute Money* (1428, Brancacci Chapel, Florence) is more complex than the circle-on-white, or that Bach's *B Minor Mass* is more complex than "Pop Goes the Weasel"—and that is enough to show that we mean something by the term "complexity," even if we run into difficulties deciding whether, say, Masaccio's *Tribute Money* is more or less complex than Piero della Francesca's *Visit of the Queen of Sheba* (ca. 1460, San Francesco, Arezzo), and whether Bach's *B Minor Mass* is more or less complex than his *St. Matthew Passion*. Because the levels of complexity are in these cases so high, we are not confident of our rough estimate, though it is the best we can make—it is the same sort of trouble we have estimating whether there are more beans in a jar than cars passing a certain point on a Labor Day week-end.

But the complexities must be genuine complexities when we take them into account in describing the magnitude of a given work. The real complexity, for example, of musical texture is determined by the ear, not by its appearance in score. Some pages of the score of Stravinsky's *Petrouchka* are of the highest visual complexity, yet on the whole it is rather simple music, though produced with great difficulty by an enormous orchestra; for in many places where the instruments are all going their own ways in rapid arpeggios, the individual voices do not appear as such. There is just a shimmering background for a simple folk tune. Some pages in the coda of the finale of Mozart's (*"Jupiter"*) *Symphony in C Major* require only a few staves for the score, but their texture is more complex, for they have counterpoint for five independent voices, each of which retains its individuality while combining with the rest.

The same may be said of visual designs; very subtle differences, as in stippling or mottling, will contribute to the complexity of the design, but not necessarily as distinct areas: for example, the background in the Rouault lithograph, PLATE V, and the shading in Dürer's woodcut, PLATE VI. The figures in the Dürer count, however, and so do the subtle variations in the lines of the Rembrandt drawing, PLATE II, and the Beckmann woodcut, PLATE IV. We can surely say that the Dürer is a more complex design than the Beckmann, and the Beckmann more complex than the Jensen *Composition*, PLATE I. It is a more delicate matter to discriminate between the Rembrandt and the Beckmann, because the one is so much subtler and yet so much more unified. It seems to me that the Rembrandt is more complex, but the complexities of the Beckmann are likely to strike us first and most forcibly, while the complexities of the Rembrandt reveal themselves more slowly.

Though we cannot define "aesthetic complexity" as a magnitude, so that we could say that one musical composition or visual design is twice as complex, or 2.3 times as complex, as another, we can be reasonably sure we know what we are talking about. It should be clear, now, that unity and complexity are distinct things, and can vary independently within limits. Within limits, because, first, the simplest things cannot but have a fairly high degree of unity; and, second, the most complex things will be difficult to unify, and perhaps cannot be as completely unified as less complex things. Unity and complexity are set over against each other: very broadly speaking, the former is increased by similarities of parts, the latter by differences. Thus if we take, say, a design of a given sort, with several distinguishable areas, we can always change it in two directions. If we cut down on the variety of color-tones, we will, other things being equal, increase its unity but decrease its complexity; if we make every area of a different color-tone, we will increase its complexity, but decrease its unity. If we wish to increase its complexity, while preserving its unity, we shall have to introduce further similarities along with the new differences—by adding shape-similarities, for example, or by making the color-tones, though distinct, harmonize in brightness or saturation. This kind of experimental dabbling with designs is far removed from the actual process of painting pictures; the point is only to illustrate operationally, so to speak, the difference between, and the independence of, the two characteristics, unity and complexity.

Rembrandt's famous painting, *The Shooting Company of Captain Cocq* (1642, Rijksmuseum, Amsterdam)—the so-called *Night Watch*—is a highly complex, yet highly unified painting; a rococo ceiling by Tiepolo is highly complex, and much less unified. A still-life by Cézanne and a landscape by Van Gogh may both have a very high degree of unity, but the Cézanne is likely to be more complex as a design. Beethoven's *Missa Solemnis* is much more complex than, say, Fauré's *Requiem Mass*, but it is probably not much less unified. On the other hand, Liszt's *Les Préludes* is much simpler than the first movement of Beethoven's *Symphony in F Major (No. 8)*, but it is also less unified.

Finally, we can perhaps agree that comparisons of complexity can, in principle at least, be made to cut across the divisions of the arts. We might hesitate to say whether Beethoven's *Missa Solemnis* is more complex than *The Shooting Company*, but it is surely more complex than the Cézanne still-life or the Van Gogh landscape. And *The Shooting Company* is more complex than *Les Préludes*. These may seem like odd comparisons, and I do not press them; but it is imperative that we raise the question at this point, and pause to reflect upon it. For it will make some difference later on in our concept of critical evaluation whether we hold that terms like "unity" and "complexity," first, have adequately well-defined senses when applied to aesthetic objects, and, second, can be applied in these senses to aesthetic objects of various fields, without being so diluted in meaning as to be trivial.

NOTES AND QUERIES

§11

11-A   THE DEFINITION OF "FORM."   Morris Weitz, *Philosophy of the Arts*, Cambridge, Mass.: Harvard U., 1950, ch. 3, discusses some of the variations in the meaning of "form," and proposes his own definition, which makes form indistinguishable from content (pp. 47-48). This decision, he says, "is no *mere* stipulation" (p. 49) for it is "more consonant with [the] actual organic character [of art]" and therefore "a more adequate language" for talking about art. How could the refusal to make a distinction, or to mark it by a particular word, make it possible to say something about aesthetic objects that could not otherwise be said, or said so clearly?

See D. W. Gotshalk, *Art and the Social Order*, Chicago: U. of Chicago, 1947, pp. 117-18, reprinted in Eliseo Vivas and Murray Krieger, eds., *The Problems of Aesthetics*, New York: Rinehart, 1953, pp. 201-03; T. M. Greene, *The Arts and the Art of Criticism*, Princeton: Princeton U., 1947, chs. 7, 8 (note the circularity of his definition, p. 32); C. J. Ducasse, *The Philosophy of Art*, New York: Dial, 1929, pp. 202-06; John Dewey, *Art as Experience*, New York: Minton, Balch, 1934, ch. 6. The notion that form and matter are "identical" is criticized by Milton C. Nahn, *Aesthetic Experience and Its Presuppositions*, New York: Harper, 1946, ch. 8. Dewey shows how many different questions that need to be separated are mingled in this broad formulation of the issue.

11-B   THE DISTINCTION BETWEEN STRUCTURE AND TEXTURE IN VISUAL DESIGN.   Albert C. Barnes, *The Art in Painting*, 3rd ed., New York: Harcourt, Brace, 1937, pp. 25-31, 38-42, distinguishes "form"—opposed to "matter"—and "technique," and this distinction appears to correspond, in so far as it is clear, to the structure-texture distinction. Barnes does not adhere strictly to this meaning, however, for "form" sometimes (p. 27) becomes "plan of organization" and thus easily slips over to mean "intention" (pp. 29-30; see the references to Claude and Manet, and the statement: "Unless we have seen what the artist intends to show [i.e., his form] we cannot tell whether the means [i.e., technique] are appropriate or inappropriate"). See also his discussion of composition, pp. 102-08.

Does Roger Fry's distinction, *Last Lectures*, New York: Macmillan,

1939, ch. 2, between the structure and the "sensibility"—which he also calls "texture"—of a painting correspond to the distinction made in the present chapter? Note that his distinction, which he says is very important, is stated intentionalistically, but with enough clues to show its translatability into nonintentionalistic terms.

See T. M. Greene, *op. cit.*, chs. 9, 10. Examine critically his distinction between "manners of treatment" and "compositional patterns." In what respects does this distinction correspond to the texture-structure distinction? Note that it is not consistently carried through, and that it is mixed up with intentionalistic notions—e.g., "handling." In what sense can the "primary medium" be "handled"?

11-C THE DEFINITION OF "STYLE" FOR VISUAL DESIGN. Collect some examples of the use of this term by fine-arts critics, and analyze them in their contexts to determine in what respects they correspond to, and in what respects they differ from, the analysis of the term proposed in this chapter. Compare Thomas Munro, "Style in the Arts: A Method of Stylistic Analysis," *JAAC*, V (September 1946): 128-58, whose definition in terms of "significant trait-complexes" is quite close to it.

See also Henri Focillon, *The Life of Forms in Art*, trans. by C. B. Hogan and George Kubler, New Haven, Conn.: Yale U., 1942, ch. 1; Meyer Schapiro, "Style," in A. K. Kroeber, ed., *Anthropology Today*, Chicago: U. of Chicago, 1953, esp. secs. 1-4.

11-D STRUCTURE IN VISUAL DESIGN. On structure in general see Rudolf Arnheim, *Art and Visual Perception*, Berkeley, Cal.: U. of California, 1954, ch. 1; Gyorgy Kepes, *Language of Vision*, Chicago: Theobald, 1944, chs. 1, 2. Hilaire Hiler proposes some interesting distinctions, which could be further analyzed, in "The Origin and Development of Structural Design," *JAAC*, XV (September 1956): 106-16.

On composition see Erle Loran, *Cézanne's Composition*, Berkeley, Cal.: U. of California, 1946, also critical comments by J. M. Carpenter, "Cézanne and Tradition," *Art Bulletin*, III (1951): 174-86.

On color harmony see Arnheim, *op. cit.*, pp. 283-303; Arthur Pope, *The Language of Drawing and Painting*, Cambridge, Mass.: Harvard U., 1949, Appendix I; Ralph M. Evans, *An Introduction to Color*, New York: Wiley, 1948, chs. 20, 21.

On balance see Albert R. Chandler, *Beauty and Human Nature*, New York: Appleton-Century, 1934, pp. 51-54.

11-E CLASSIFICATION-TERMS FOR VISUAL DESIGN. Collect examples of some terms used in distinguishing schools of fine art, e.g., "realism," "expressionism," "dadaism." Which are structural, which textural, which mixed, which neither?

On the term "decorative," see Albert C. Barnes and V. de Mazia, *The*

Art of Henri Matisse, New York, London: Scribner's, 1933, ch. 5; Sir
Charles Holmes, *A Grammar of the Arts*, London: Bell, 1931, ch. 3;
Walter Abell, *Representation and Form*, New York: Scribner's, 1936, pp.
152-58.

11-F THE DESCRIPTION OF PAINTING. Read the contexts of the following quotations from Heinrich Wölfflin, *Principles of Art History*, trans. by M. D. Hottinger, London: Bell, 1932 (reprinted New York: Dover, 1950):

a. "The style of open form everywhere points out beyond itself and purposely looks limitless" (p. 124).
b. In the open (a-tectonic) style, the whole is "meant to look like a piece cut haphazard out of the visible world" (p. 126).
c. "The final question is not one of full-face and profile, vertical and horizontal, tectonic and a-tectonic, but whether the figure, the total picture as a visible form, looks *intentional* or not" (p. 126).
d. "Even the repetition of a color at various points in the picture manifests the intention to weaken the objective function of color" (p. 203).
e. "The real intention envisages a total impression distinct from the objective content" (p. 220).

All of these statements are intentionalistic, but they have some objective meaning that can be made explicit; wherever possible, with the help of the terms introduced in Chapters II and IV, translate the statements in such a way as to bring out what they say about the work itself.

§12

12-A MUSICAL TEXTURE AND "STYLE." See Donald F. Tovey, "Contrapuntal Forms," "Counterpoint," "Fugue," *Encyclopaedia Britannica*, 14th ed., Chicago: U. of Chicago, 1929, reprinted in *The Forms of Music*, New York: Meridian, 1956. Aaron Copland, *What to Listen for in Music*, 1939, New York: Mentor, 1953, chs. 8, 9, limits the term "texture" to the vertical dimension of music, but Willi Apel, "Texture," *Harvard Dictionary of Music*, Cambridge, Mass.: Harvard U., 1950, does not support him. There is an interesting distinction between two "styles of progression" in W. S. Newman, "Musical Form as a Generative Process," *JAAC*, XII (March 1954): 301-09. The discursive survey by C. Hubert H. Parry, *Style in Musical Art*, Oxford: Clarendon, 1900, chs. 1, 6, 10, 11, illustrates some interesting confusions, e.g., "style is mainly an external attribute—a means to an end," pp. 1-2.

Robert Erickson, *The Structure of Music*, New York: Noonday, 1955, pp. 116-201, has an excellent discussion of counterpoint.

I take it that the words "repetition," "development," and "variation" are structure-type words because they designate fundamental relations between sections of music. But the term "fugue" is not. When we say that a passage is *"in* fugue," this is a statement about its prevailing texture: there is a constant imitation. When we say that a composition is *"a* fugue," we are saying at the least that it is entirely *in* fugue. Perhaps we are saying more. According to the precepts of some of the eighteenth century theoreticians, there are rules for fugue, specifying that a fugue must, for example, move through at least so many keys, and must have at least two entries, and wind up with a stretto—that is, a passage in which the voices crowd in close behind each other—as it returns to its home key. If all fugues followed such rules—and it is an interesting question whether there are any structural features common to all the fugues of Bach's two books of the *Well-Tempered Clavier*—then "fugue" would be in part a structure-term. But I think we would ordinarily call a composition a fugue without implying anything about its main passages or key relationships. Of course every fugue has a structure, but that is not, I think, part of its definition.

12-B STRUCTURE-TYPES IN MUSIC. See Copland, *op. cit.,* chs. 10-14, Appendices I, II, III; Donald F. Tovey, "Sonata Forms," "Variations," "Rondo," "Scherzo," *op. cit.;* Albert Gehring, *The Basis of Musical Pleasure,* New York, London: Putnam, 1910, ch. 2; Carroll C. Pratt, *The Meaning of Music,* New York: McGraw-Hill, 1931, pp. 77-114; Douglas Moore, *Listening to Music,* rev. ed., New York: Norton, 1937, chs. 10, 11; Albert R. Chandler, *Beauty and Human Nature,* New York: Appleton-Century, 1934, ch. 11, pp. 196-209; Ebenezer Prout, *Musical Form,* 4th ed., London: Augener, [1893], chs. 9, 10; Edward J. Dent, "Binary and Ternary Form," *Music and Letters,* XVII (1936): 309-21; Colin McAlpin, "Concerning Form in Music," *Musical Quarterly,* XV (1929): 55-71; M. D. Calvocoressi, *Principles and Methods of Musical Criticism,* London: Milford, 1923, pp. 132-38. Hugo Leichtentritt, *Musical Form,* Cambridge, Mass.: Harvard U., 1951, gives a thorough review, but a very conventional treatment, of the types.

Compare also the definition of "form" given by D. J. Grout, "Johann Sebastian Bach: An Appreciation," *The Music Review,* VI (1945): 132.

See Herman Reichenbach, "Gestalt Psychology and Form in Music," *Journal of Musicology,* II (1940): 63-71.

One of the most fruitful approaches to the study of musical form is that of Leonard B. Meyer, *Emotion and Meaning in Music,* Chicago: U. of Chicago, 1956; see also Note 13-C below. Meyer unfortunately uses the term "embodied meaning" for the basic constituent of musical form: a musical event means (or "points to") other musical events that are about to happen (p. 35). His work deals mostly with musical form, and his theory is very carefully and judiciously worked out, with many excellently analyzed examples of the way expectations are manipulated by melody and harmony and rhythm; see esp. ch. 2.

Look up the definitions of some terms commonly used in classifying musical compositions, e.g., "chaconne," "march," "gigue," "gavotte." Which are defined in terms of style, or structure, or quality, or some combination of these? See also Donald F. Tovey, "Symphony," "Concerto," "Suite," "Overture," "Serenade," *op. cit.;* Douglas Moore, *op. cit.*, chs. 12-14.

There is an interesting problem of characterizing the difference in form between the exposition of a sonata-allegro movement in a symphony and the orchestral exposition of a concerto; see Tovey, *loc. cit.*, also his essay "The Classical Concerto," in his *Essays in Musical Analysis,* New York: Oxford U., 1935-1939, Vol. III; Arthur Hutchings, "The Keyboard Concerto," *Music and Letters,* XXIII (1942): 298-311; Abraham Veinus, *The Concerto,* Garden City, N.Y.: Doubleday, Doran, 1944.

The term "symphony" sometimes refers not only to structure, but to regional quality. The definition that works for the classical composers is simple and very clear: a symphony is a sonata for orchestra, just as a string quartet is a sonata for four strings. But once we decide, as modern composers have done, to apply the term to works that no longer follow any particular pattern of movements, or contain any movements in sonata-allegro form, it is in order to ask whether we can any longer distinguish symphonies from other compositions. Now, however they differed, classical symphonies—even many of Haydn's and Mozart's early ones—developed a breadth, by the contrast between their movements, so that they seemed to exhibit a range of qualities; and even if some of the movements were light and easy-going, they contained at least one or two movements in which some power was generated, a considerable degree of tension and dramatic force. Thus the over-all quality of a Mozart serenade, for example, such as the *Serenade in B Flat for Thirteen Wind Instruments* (K. 361) is generally different from the quality of one of his symphonies, even though they both have sonata-allegro movements, minuets, slow movements, and rondo finales. Now, if Irving Berlin put four of his songs, minus words, together, marked them Allegro, Andante, Presto, and Allegro, and called them "Symphony No. 1," we would all, I think, recognize this as a joking use of the term. If he called them "Song Suite," that would be tolerable. And the distinction is one of quality: unless at least one movement has a firm enough structure, with a strong dynamic pattern, and a texture rich and complex enough so that the whole takes on a "symphonic" quality, a weightiness, a drive, a sense of importance and consequence, it is not, at least in one useful sense, a symphony. This symphonic quality is hard to describe, but it is there; and it is sometimes described as "profundity." I think this quality can be heard in Samuel Barber's *First Symphony,* in Roy Harris's *Third Symphony,* in Walter Piston's *Second Symphony,* and in Vaughan Williams' *Sixth Symphony;* but not, except perhaps in the opening bars, in Randall Thompson's *Second Symphony,* Milhaud's *First Symphony,* or Douglas Moore's *Second*

Symphony. Prokofieff's *Fifth Symphony* has it in the first movement, but lacks it conspicuously in the finale, which sounds more like a movement of a suite or like ballet music. The first movement of Carl Maria von Weber's *Symphony in C Major (No. 1)* is interesting in this respect; like his overtures, it is a series of passages with Exhibition Quality, with transitions from one to the next; there are no long buildups or developments such as give tension and climax to symphonic movements. It is extremely difficult to be sure about these distinctions, for the danger of subjectivity is great, but the difference seems to be there.

§13

13-A UNITY IN VISUAL DESIGN. For further descriptions of visual unity, and discussions of the factors that make for it, see Denman W. Ross, A *Theory of Pure Design*, New York: Smith, 1933 [note that Ross defines "design" (p. 1) in terms of "order," so that his whole book is concerned not with form in general but with unity]; Stephen C. Pepper, *Principles of Art Appreciation*, New York: Harcourt, Brace, 1949, chs. 3, 4, pp. 249-58; Mateo Marangoni, *The Art of Seeing Art*, London: Castle, 1951, pp. 59-87, 122-79; R. W. Church, *An Essay on Critical Appreciation*, London: Allen and Unwin, 1938, ch. 4; Walter D. Teague, *Design This Day*, New York: Harcourt, Brace, 1940, chs. 7, 8; E. A. Batchelder, *Design in Theory and Practice*, New York: Macmillan, 1910, ch. 3; George H. Opdyke, *Art and Nature Appreciation*, New York: Macmillan, 1933, pp. 487-547; Hermann Weyl, *Symmetry*, Princeton: Princeton U., 1952; Herbert S. Langfeld, *The Aesthetic Attitude*, New York: Harcourt, Brace and Howe, 1920, chs. 9, 10; W. R. Sickles and G. W. Hartmann, "The Theory of Order," *Psychological Review*, XLIX (1942): 403-20; W. R. Sickles, "Psycho-geometry of Order," *Psychological Review*, LI (1944): 189-99; Ivy Campbell, "Factors Which Work Toward Unity or Coherence in a Visual Design," *Journal of Experimental Psychology*, XXVIII (1941): 145-62. Compare Rudolf Arnheim, *Art and Visual Perception*, Berkeley, Cal.: U. of California, 1954, ch. 2, pp. 37-51. For the most part Arnheim seems to mean by the term "simplicity" what is meant by "unity" in this chapter, but perhaps not at every point—for example, when he says (p. 39), "A straight line is simple because it uses one unchangeable direction."

On unity in general, see T. M. Greene, *The Arts and the Art of Criticism*, Princeton, N.J.: Princeton U., 1947, ch. 11; L. A. Reid, *A Study of Aesthetics*, New York: Macmillan, 1931, pp. 187-95; José I. Lasaga, "Outline of a Descriptive Aesthetics from a Structuralist Point of View," *Psychological Review*, LIV (1947): 9-23.

13-B UNITY IN MUSIC. For further discussions of the factors that make for musical unity, see Edmund Gurney, *The Power of Sound*, London: Smith, Elder, 1880, chs. 9, 10; W. H. Hadow, selection from *Studies* *in Modern Music* in Eliseo Vivas and Murray Krieger, eds., *The Problems of Aesthetics,* New York: Rinehart, 1953, pp. 262-76; Douglas Moore, *op. cit.,* chs. 7-9; C. Hubert H. Parry, *The Evolution of the Art of Music,* ed. by H. C. Colles, New York: Appleton, 1941, ch. 3.

For discussion of the problems of unity in Bruckner and Sibelius, see Robert Simpson, "Bruckner and the Symphony," *The Music Review,* VII (1946): 35-40: W. G. Hill, "Some Aspects of Form in the Symphonies of Sibelius," *The Music Review,* X (1949): 165-82.

See Rudolph Reti, *The Thematic Process in Music,* New York: Macmillan, 1951, esp. Introduction, chs. 1, 5, 9, 12. Is his concept of "indirect affinity" (p. 240) so broad that almost any two themes have this relation, or can a reasonably restricted definition of this term be collected from Reti's examples and analyses? See also Leonard B. Meyer, *Emotion and Meaning in Music,* Chicago: U. of Chicago, 1956, esp. chs. 4, 5.

There is also much of interest in Joseph Kerman's analysis of Beethoven's *A Minor Quartet (Op. 132),* "Beethoven: The Single Journey," *Hudson Review,* V (Spring 1952): 32-55.

13-C UNITY AND COMPLEXITY. Are these two concepts independent of each other? Find a number of critical statements comparing visual designs or musical compositions with respect to these two characteristics; try to obtain clear-cut examples that differ decidedly in one of the characteristics but not noticeably in the other. What further questions about the analysis of these terms (questions not taken up in this chapter) are raised by your examples?

George D. Birkhoff has attempted, in *Aesthetic Measure,* Cambridge, Mass.: Harvard U., 1933, esp. pp. 1-11, to give numerical definitions of the terms "order" and "complexity" and combine them in a formula for the calculation of aesthetic value, which he calls "aesthetic measure": M equals O/C. Putting C in the denominator may appear puzzling, since it would make the least complex designs tend to be the best, but it appears —especially from his remarks on p. 211—that O in his system really means what I have called "complexity" (he sometimes equates it with "variety") and that C really means "disunity," the inverse of unity, so that his formula, expressed in terms of this book, would be: M equals $C \times U$. But it is not at all evident that Birkhoff's interesting methods could be applied to any but fairly uncomplicated designs.

On complexity in music see Carroll C. Pratt, *The Meaning of Music,* New York: McGraw-Hill, 1931, pp. 77-87. On "organic unity" see Harold Osborne, *Aesthetics and Criticism,* London: Routledge and Kegan Paul, 1955, pp. 238-48.

13-D REDUNDANCY. *The New York Times,* December 31, 1955, p. 7, reported some discussion at the fifth conference of Princeton Graduate School Alumni, Princeton, New Jersey, of the possibility that unity might be defined in terms of redundancy, and this has also been suggested by Benbow Ritchie, of the University of California, and Henry Gleitman, of Swarthmore College. Some of the problems are well discussed by Leonard B. Meyer, "Meaning in Music and Information Theory," *JAAC,* XV (June 1957): 412-24. The essence of the proposal might be summarized as follows. Information Theory deals with the transmission of messages, in a very broad sense of "message," and the term "redundancy" also has a very broad use. In writing this book, I use letters of the Roman alphabet. And to some extent, when I begin a word, you can guess what is coming even before I complete the word. This may partly depend on the *sense* of the sentences: if I write "communicate wi," you can bet the "wi" will be followed by "th," because only a very few English words beginning with "wi" will make sense after "communicate."

But to simplify our example, let us set aside meaning, and consider only the letters as they appear in English words. If I start a word "th," there is a definite probability of its being followed by every other letter, depending on the frequency of these combinations in English. The probability of "th" being followed by a "z" or a "k" is zero; the probability of its being followed by an "a" or "i" is high, and by "e" even higher. Now, the higher the probability that a given letter will follow, the more unnecessary it is to write that other letter—in fact, you would understand me perfectly if I never wrote "the," but always "th" followed by a space. Since "q" is *always* followed by "u," the "u" is utterly unnecessary, that is, 100 per cent redundant. The less redundant the message, the shorter and more efficient it is, but the higher the likelihood of being misunderstood, especially if the book contains typographical errors.

Notice that if I wrote the message out in a series of letters, hitting the typewriter keys by chance, so that the result would not be English at all, but a random series of letters, then there would be complete absence of redundancy, because you would never be able to predict the next letter, and you would have no way of knowing what it is until you see it. Thus redundancy is opposed to randomness, in one sense. But so is coherence in a visual or auditory design.

This suggests the following possibility: if a series of notes were played by chance, there would be no redundancy, and also no coherence; the degree of coherence is a function of repetitions of intervals and melodies and keys, and other elements and relations: could we not then say that the measure of coherence in music is the degree of redundancy? And in a visual design, coherence depends on similarities of various sorts: could not the number of such similarities—which we can count—serve as a precise measure of its coherence? This line of thought, very little explored as yet, has some promising aspects, but I think we need not be troubled if it does not go far. It is not clear that all the factors connected with coherence in visual design—for example, focus—can be defined in terms of similarities, and hence of redundancy in this broad sense; and it is even less clear that completeness can be handled in the same way, even if coherence can.

For a more detailed account, see R. C. Pinkerton, "Information Theory and Melody," *Scientific American*, February 1956, pp. 77-86.

13-E GOOD PROPORTION. One of the concepts often applied to visual designs—and somewhat less often to music—is that of proportion, especially the concept of *good* proportion. What does this term mean? How, if at all, is it connected with the concept of unity? See Jay Hambidge, *Dynamic Symmetry: The Greek Vase*, New Haven: Yale U., 1920; he speaks of "the perfection of proportion" (p. 44) in the Greek vase, which seems (p. 142) to consist in its being unified through an over-all mathematical scheme, but this is not developed and there are puzzling paragraphs on pp. 59 and 89. See also Erwin Panofsky, "The History of the Theory of Human Proportions as a Reflection of the History of Styles," in *Meaning in the Visual Arts*, Garden City, N.Y.: Anchor, 1955; Rudolf Arnheim, "A Review of Proportion," *JAAC*, XIV (September 1955): 44-57; Albert R. Chandler, *op. cit.*, 54-56.

13-F COMPARATIVE FORM AND QUALITY IN MUSIC AND VISUAL DESIGN. On the possibility of identifying basic structure-types in various arts, see DeWitt H. Parker, *The Analysis of Art*, New Haven, Conn.: Yale U., 1926, ch. 2, partly reprinted in Rader, *op. cit.*, pp. 357-70; D. W. Gotshalk, *op. cit.*, ch. 5, reprinted in Vivas and Krieger, *op. cit.*, pp. 194-208.

On "rhythm" in fine arts, see Ross, *op. cit.*, pp. 2-3, 25-36, 56-89, 120-29; W. D. Teague, *op. cit.*, ch. 9.

See C. A. Harris, "The Element of Repetition in Nature and the Arts," *Musical Quarterly*, XVII (1931): 302-18, for an attempt at a basic classification. Compare Joseph Yasser, "The Variation Form and Synthesis of Arts," *JAAC*, XIV (March 1956): 318-23. See Doris Silbert, "Ambiguity in the String Quartets of Joseph Haydn," *Musical Quarterly*, XXXVI (1950): 562-73; is there anything in visual design analogous to what she calls "ambiguity" in musical texture?

See Meyer Schapiro, "Style," in A. L. Kroeber, ed., *Anthropology Today*, Chicago: U. of Chicago, 1943, esp. secs. 5-8; Wolfgang Stechow, "Problems of Structure in Some Relations Between the Visual Arts and Music," *JAAC*, XI (June 1953): 324-33.

On intersensory qualities, see E. M. von Hornbostel, "The Unity of the Senses," in W. D. Ellis, *A Source Book of Gestalt Psychology*, London: Routledge and Kegan Paul, 1938, pp. 210-16. It is instructive to inquire how successful, or unsuccessful, composers have been in attempts to recapture in sound the regional qualities of vision: for example, Arthur Bliss's *Color Symphony*, and the musical sketches of various paintings by Henri Rene (see the RCA Victor LP recording, *Passion in Paint*).

13-G THE CONCEPT OF STYLE PERIODS. See René Wellek, "The Concept of Baroque in Literary Scholarship," *JAAC*, V (September 1946): 77-108; Wellek, "The Parallelism Between Literature and the Arts," *English Institute Annual 1941*, New York: Columbia U., 1942, pp. 29-63; Paul L. Frank, "Historical or Stylistic Periods?" *JAAC*, XIII (June 1955): 451-57. Examine Frank's argument in the light of Wellek's criticisms of spurious parallelisms: for example, Frank says that the transition from "linear" Renaissance painting to "painterly" Baroque painting (see Wölfflin, *op. cit.*) "is comparable to the shift of emphasis from rhythm to harmony and tone color" in the music of 1600-1750; are these really analogous? Compare various articles on the Baroque in *JAAC*, XIV (December 1955): 143-74, especially M. F. Bukhofzer, "The Baroque in Music History," pp. 152-56, and comments by Wolfgang Stechow, pp. 171-74. See also J. H. Müller, "Baroque—Is It Datum, Hypothesis, or Tautology?" *JAAC*, XII (June 1954): 421-37; Austin Warren, *Richard Crashaw, A Study in Baroque Sensibility*, Baton Rouge, La.: Louisiana State U., 1939, ch. 3.

Wylie Sypher, *Four Stages of Renaissance Style*, Garden City, N.Y.: Anchor, 1955, esp. pp. 1-35, is mostly concerned with the comparison of literature and the fine arts, and his argument can be reconsidered after we have dealt with literature. It is interesting to consider, though, how far his style categories—Renaissance, mannerism, Baroque, and late Baroque—can be applied to music. For example, he says (p. 11) that a minuet, a rococo panel, a painting by Watteau, the verse of *The Rape of the Lock*, and a sculpture by Falconet have "kindred" "tempos"; what could this mean? Though he holds that comparison of the arts in terms of "subject" is much less significant than comparison in terms of style (p. 12), a careful examination of his book will show, I think, that the comparisons in terms of subject tend to be the more convincing ones. But cf. Sypher's mannerism with the characteristics of "early baroque" in M. F. Bukhofzer, *Music in the Baroque Era*, New York: Norton, 1947, chs. 1, 2, 10.

Look up definitions of other period terms, e.g., "romanticism" and "neoclassicism," that are applied to both painting and music; what common elements are really there?

13-H THE UNITY OF CULTURE. For attempts to find correspondences in "style," or in regional quality, between aesthetic objects and other manifestations or artifacts of culture, see Lewis Mumford, *Technics and Civilization*, New York: Harcourt, Brace, 1934, esp. chs. 2, 6, 7; Mumford, *The Culture of Cities*, New York: Harcourt, Brace, 1938, esp. ch. 2; Egon Friedell, *A Cultural History of the Modern Age*, trans. by C. F. Atkinson, 3 vols., New York: Knopf, 1930-33, esp. Introduction and Book II; Oswald Spengler, *The Decline of the West*, trans. by C. F. Atkinson, 1 vol. ed., New York: Knopf, 1932, esp. Vol. I, chs. 7, 8.

For a style study that is very illuminating and full of significant observations about works of art themselves, despite its being couched in terms of "the Gothic will to form," see Wilhelm Worringer, *Form in Gothic,* trans. by Herbert Read, New York: Putnam, 1927, esp. chs. 18-21, in which Gothic architecture is compared with scholastic philosophy.

· V ·

FORM
IN
LITERATURE

When the word "form" is applied to literary works, it is subject to certain vagaries. Sometimes the world of the work is called its "content," and the verbal design the "form." Sometimes, within the world of the work, the characters and events are called the "content," and the plot or sequence of events the "form." We will stay with the basic usage adopted in the preceding chapter, and confine the word "form" to relationships within the work, either in its language or in its world of action. For example, critics commonly speak of the novelist's "method"—the point of view he chooses, or the manner of transition from scene to scene, or the proportion of description to dialogue. And though the word "method" could be misleading if it were taken to refer to the process of composing the work, here it clearly refers to discoverable features of the work itself, and these features are aspects of form.

There is, however, an extra complication in literature, since it is both sound and meaning, or, in other words, has both a *phonetic* and a *semantic* aspect. The distinction between sound and meaning cuts across the distinction between structure and texture, giving us, in theory, four categories of form to deal with.

But these categories can be somewhat reduced. It is clear enough, I think, what we should include under the texture of sound in literature, just as in music: details of sound-change, the relations among neighboring sounds. But since there is nothing in literature corresponding to tonality or to the recurrence of a large section, there is nothing quite corresponding to musical structure. When certain types of texture are combined and maintained throughout a poem, however, we get large patterns that may be called sound-structures: the Spenserian stanza, the villanelle, the ballad. The term "sonnet" is completely definable in terms of sound: approximate number of syllables (140) and lines (14), meter (iambic), and rhyme; it makes no reference to meaning. We shall deal with the problems about the sound-texture of literature in the first section of this chapter. But these are most fruitfully approached in connection with problems about meaning.

The distinction between the texture of meaning and the structure of meaning in a literary work is much less apparent, and indeed it may be questioned whether these terms are legitimately applied to meaning at all. But I think they are not only legitimate but illuminating. In a discourse of some length, there will be some meanings that depend upon, or are a function of, the whole discourse, or a large section of it. "Raskolnikov murdered and confessed" sums up a long narrative, and you must read it all, or in large part, to know that the summary is correct. Thus if a critic says that the story of *Crime and Punishment* is a story of sin leading to guilt leading to absolution, he is talking about the structure of meaning in that novel. But if he talks about the meanings of certain paragraphs, sentences, phrases, or words, he is talking about its texture of meaning.

The distinction will become clearer as we go on. We shall begin, in the first section, by considering the meaning-texture of literature, and the main problems posed by the attempt to analyze it. Then we shall consider sound-texture, and the relation between sound and meaning. In the second section of the chapter, we shall turn to the structure of literature, and its peculiar problems.

§14.   *STYLE: SEMANTIC AND PHONETIC*

Though the textures of literary discourse are subject to unlimited variation, certain features of texture tend to recur, and one of the traditional aims of rhetoric has been to study these recurrent features, or "devices." Some of the older rhetoricians were mostly interested in naming and classifying them, but perhaps they never wholly lost sight of a more important purpose: to discover the contributions that such devices make to the sense of a passage in which they occur.

There is no good and unambiguous name for these devices. The terms "figurative language" and "figure of speech" seem often to be limited to metaphor and simile and such tropes as metonymy and synecdoche—

these are also often classified under "imagery." But "figure" in a more general sense can include inversion ("so red the rose" instead of "the rose so red"), abstraction (calling the tree a "plant"), and colloquialism ("fix up" for "repair")—in short, any deviation from what is taken to be the norm of diction and syntactical construction. In this second sense, the study of figures is the study of all identifiable textural features of discourse.

It is clear that, though I have so far avoided the word, I am already talking about those aspects of discourse that would usually be called its "style." And our first big problem in this section is to decide what to do with this important critical term. Given a number of statements about a poem or a novel, which of them are statements about its style, and which of them are statements about something else?

What we should like to have is a definition of "style"; but we must first be clear about what we expect of such a definition. For one thing, it would be interesting to know how practicing critics use the word. It will not help very much to ask them, for their explicit definitions are various, high-flown, and only obliquely connected with actual literary works. It is much more helpful to collect examples of various kinds of statement that critics make about literature when they claim to be talking about its style. Some of these turn out on analysis not to be very sensible; for example, the statement that Bishop Berkeley's style fully expresses his thought—for how do we know what his thought is except by what he says? When such ways of speaking have been eliminated, we are left with some important and testable statements and we can then frame a definition to cover them. This definition will correspond roughly to actual usage, but not completely, for it will be based upon a screening. Hence it has a kind of recommendatory status, as well: in proposing the definition we are partly saying that certain things are possible and desirable for critics to talk about, and that these are most conveniently referred to as "style."

In a literary work there is nothing we can talk about but the sound, and the sense, and the relations between them. Now, style is often taken to include certain features of sound, as when it is said that a writer is given to using long sentences or short ones. And in this sense, style seems to consist of recurrent features of the sound-texture. But let us set this sense aside for the moment. For it would also be said that a writer is given to using compound sentences rather than simple ones, and that this is a characteristic of his style. Our immediate problem is to see what "style" means in contexts like this.

Style as Meaning

"Style" can be defined, tentatively, in some such way as this: the style of a literary work consists of the recurrent features of its texture of meaning. We shall have to sharpen this a little to make it work, but that is not the first task confronting us. For the definition may appear at first to run counter to a very usual way of speaking. Critics often say, for example, that in poetry it does not matter so much *what* you say—and this they call the "meaning"—as *how* you say it: the same thing can be said in two different ways, or, in other words, two sentences may have the same meaning but different styles. Style is thus contrasted with meaning. They say that some literary works are interesting primarily on account of their style, and the style of a writer like Bertrand Russell, for example, can be recognized and valued for its crystal clarity whether he is writing about the logical paradoxes, the nature of sense data, or what to do if your husband runs around with another woman—as he once did for *Charm* magazine. Style seems separately discussible, and indeed rules are often proposed for good style, and for the avoidance of bad style, independently of the relation of the style to anything else: be concrete, be vivid, be economical. So it seems that style is a detachable aspect of a literary work. Yet on analysis, the more carefully we analyze a style or discuss its goodness or badness, the more we seem to be led back to meaning. This is the paradox of style analysis.

Suppose, then, we consider seriously the definition of "style" in terms of meaning: style is detail of meaning or small-scale meaning. I shall call this the Semantical Definition of Style.[1] To make it clear and plausible, let us consider some simple examples. The sentences

> The baby is a boy
> The baby is a girl

differ in meaning, but in a basic way; we would not describe their difference as a difference in style. At the opposite extreme,

> She sells cakes and pies
> She sells pies and cakes

do not seem to differ in meaning—or, if they do, it is only slightly—though they are different sentences; but they do not differ in style, either. In between,

> I am here
> Here I am

do differ in style, and this difference is a difference in meaning—in what they suggest about the situation and the speaker's relation to it: "Here I am" suggests that I have been long awaited or searched for. Again,

> Go home
> Return to your abode

differ in style, but this difference is, once more, a difference in meaning;

---

[1] This has been best defended by W. K. Wimsatt, Jr.; for his argument, and for references to the opposing view of style, see Note 14-A at end of chapter.

for the connotations of "abode" are not the same as the connotations of "home."

Of course, with these fragmentary examples we are not able to explore the richness of larger stylistic differences; between Bertrand Russell and William Faulkner, Sir Thomas Browne and George Santayana, or Karl Marx and Carlyle. But the essential points can perhaps be made even with scale models. Where there is either no difference in meaning at all, or else a gross difference, we do not say there is a difference in style; where the difference in meaning is relatively subtle and is present along with some basic similarity on the primary level, we call the difference in meaning a difference in style.

But is this completely satisfactory? We must admit one qualification. We saw in Chapter III, §9, that certain words, and certain syntactical constructions, show the speaker to be of a particular region of the country, or trade, or social level. From the fact that a speaker says "thee" instead of "you," and "First-day" instead of "Sunday," we can infer that he is probably a member of the Society of Friends. This is part of the information given by these words. Shall we count it among their connotations—shall we say "First-day" connotes *being a Quaker?* This is awkward. But if not, we could say the sentences

> I will meet you at Church on Sunday
> I will meet thee at the Meeting House on First-day

do not differ in meaning, though they do differ in style. The difference in style is, however, a difference in what I have, in Chapter III, §9, called *general purport.* Recognition of the difference—knowing that Quakers use certain expressions—would certainly be a part of understanding a poem, for example, by Walt Whitman, in which these expressions occurred; you would not know that the difference *was* a difference in style unless you knew that it was a difference in purport.

Let us modify the Semantical Definition, then, to take account of this: style is detail, or texture, of secondary meaning plus general purport. Or, in another way, two discourses differ in style when they differ either in their details of meaning or in their general purport. There are not, then, two things, knowing what to say and knowing how to say it; but there is knowing, in general or in outline, what to say, without knowing what other things to say along with it, through suggestion, connotation, and general purport. If you want to invite someone to lunch and have trouble finding the right words—that is, choosing a style—the problem is one of meaning; for the only ground on which you could make a sensible choice between, say, "Would you join me for lunch?" and "How about a sandwich in the drugstore?" is the difference in what they purport about you, about your beliefs, about your attitude toward the other person.

The features of discourse that make up style are conveniently divided into two parts, diction and syntax. Consider, for example, some of those features that define the style of Samuel Johnson. First, there is a tendency to use words that are Latin derivatives, rather than their Anglo-Saxon synonyms: "crepitation" for "crackling," "concinnity" for "fitness," "deglutition" for "swallowing." These words tend to have certain types of connotation, or rather to have less connotation than their synonyms; this is a difference in meaning. But they also have a different purport, a scientific or technical aura that comes from the fact that they would normally be used in scientific or medical books, and they contribute a solemn and rather pompous quality to the sentences in which they occur.

This quality is reinforced by the second tendency of Johnson's style, the frequent parallelism and antithesis.

> As this practice is a commodious subject of raillery to the gay, and of declamation to the serious, it has been ridiculed with all the pleasantry of wit, and exaggerated with all the amplifications of rhetoric.[2]

Four clauses, the first contrasted with the second, the third with the fourth; the first parallel to the third, the second to the fourth; the first pair conditional to the second pair. Whatever the subject of the discourse, sentences like these give a sense of balance of one idea against another, and an air of judiciousness, of having considered things from both sides. This air may be an illusion. But, like the orator who claims to recommend a mean between extremes, or a middle-of-the-road policy, no matter what he recommends, the Johnsonian syntax claims a certain attitude and capacity in the speaker, and thus has both meaning and general purport of its own.

The qualities of style, then, that we find in different writers—learned, spare, lean, archaic, terse, tortuous, flowing, witty, ironic—are its detailed meaning and general purport. And this is the kernel of sense in the rather mushy statements that writers usually make when invited to offer a definition of "style"—most of which are of no help at all until pinned down by analysis. "The style is the man" gets us nowhere, unless perhaps it may send us off in the wrong direction romanticizing biographically about the writer. Whether the style of Ernest Hemingway, Jowett's Plato, the King James Bible, Trollope, Proust, or Heine is really the man does not concern us; but the *speaker* of the work, which we shall discuss in the following section, reveals, advertises, or betrays himself partly through those very features of purport and meaning that we call "style." So much is true, and important.

If the Semantical Definition of "style" is correct, it would seem to

---

[2] From *The Rambler*, No. 2; quoted in W. K. Wimsatt, Jr., *The Prose Style of Samuel Johnson*, New Haven, Conn.: Yale U., 1941, from which I have borrowed in this discussion.

follow that the goodness or badness of style cannot be judged independently of the work, any more than any other part of its meaning and general purport. And this consequence may seem to be contradicted by practical criticism. Now, we are not yet prepared to tackle questions about value directly, and yet something must be said about this problem in relation to style. Let us consider, somewhat briefly, that part of the issue which can be stated in neutral terms.

In a review of a collection of literary essays, in the *Saturday Review*,[3] Howard Mumford Jones once quoted two passages from the book he was reviewing, of which I offer one sentence:

> All those occasions on which the term has been used with opprobrium or forced into a loaded synonymity with Mme. de Staël's ceremonials at courts, Mrs. Vanderbilt's hypocrisies at tea, or Mr. Eliot's "pleasing archaeological reconstructions," we must now assume to have been improper occasions, the work not of disinterested minds but of those in whom the very suggestion of manners evokes nightmares of class distinction and minority group, pogrom and ghetto, and whose willed misunderstanding of their meaning is politically requisite to a continued rational engagement of contemporary life, the preservation of what we tend to think of as the liberal-egalitarian or "whole" view of reality.[4]

"Surely," said the reviewer, "phrases like these are the very ecstasy of bad prose." And it does seem clear that the style of this passage is somewhat censurable.

But what is wrong with its style? What reasons could be advanced for the censure? I take it that the critic of style would say such things as the following: "Willed," applied to "misunderstanding"—of the "meaning" of "manners"—is not the *mot juste* for "intentional" or "willful"; somehow it suggests that the willing took place before the misunderstanding, and this is a distraction. "Loaded synonymity" is baffling, but apparently the writer simply means that people have taken the word "manners" to denote social graces. "Synonymity," however, is simply misused, for a word is not synonymous with the things it denotes, but only with other words. And "loaded" is redundant, because it only repeats "used with opprobrium," but since it is there it makes us look, in vain, for something it might mean in addition to what has already been said. "Engagement of contemporary life" is thoroughly loose, yet it is led up to as though we were going to be told what it is that the misunderstanding is requisite for. "Politically" seems to derive from "politic" rather than "political," but it requires a double look at the context to discover this.

In short, the connotations and special designations of many of the words are such as to cut across, or work counter to, the main lines of meaning. What results is, first, incoherence of meaning, and second, am-

---

[3] May 26, 1956, p. 33.

[4] John W. Aldridge, *In Search of Heresy: American Literature in the Age of Conformity*, New York: McGraw-Hill, 1956, pp. 70-71.

biguity, in the strict and pejorative sense. Bad style, as critics discuss it, might then be tentatively described in these terms: the diction and syntax of a discourse are such as to produce an incoherence between the primary and secondary levels of meaning, or such as to produce ambiguity or obscurity. Perhaps there is more to be said: I am mainly concerned to point out the kind of objective analysis that the evaluation of style ought to be. So far as the faults of a literary work may be called faults of *style,* they will turn out to be faults that proceed from a poor management of the details of meaning, connotation, general purport, and syntactical suggestion, in relation to the larger and more prominent parts of meaning. On the other side, a style may be said to be appropriate to, or coherent with, the rest of the work's meaning if, so to speak, the eddies of meaning it sets up work together with the main streams.

This brief discussion is far from an adequate treatment of this complicated problem; but one objection that is bound to arise should be answered, if it can be. Some critics who have seen the impossibility of setting up specific and general rules of style have retreated to a position at the opposite extreme. What is good style in a poem may be bad style in an essay, and vice versa, they say; thus there is nothing one can advise about style in general, for the kind of style that is right depends upon the "intention." Now, apart from intention, which I should, of course, like to set aside, this view seems to rest upon a mixture of truths and errors. For example, sometimes this view is defended by saying that in poetry ambiguity is a good thing, but in prose a bad thing. But I take it that "ambiguity" is used in two senses here. The uncertainty and flabbiness of meaning that we object to in prose is just as objectionable in poetry; this is the strict sense. But if we use the term "ambiguity" in the sense of multiple meaning, then we cannot say it is a bad thing in prose—nor can we even say it is a good thing in poetry, since it is a defining characteristic of poetry, and therefore indispensable to it: we do not say that being female is a good thing in sisters. Or again, sometimes a critic will say that obscurity is a bad thing in prose, but permissible in poetry. But if obscurity is difficulty of comprehension, there is surely only one standard for both prose and poetry, and that not a strictly literary one: if we have to puzzle a long time to understand what a discourse says, and then find that what it says is not worth the trouble of understanding, we will object to it, whether it is prose or poetry. If, on the other hand, our effort is sufficiently rewarded, what right have we to complain? "Forced into a loaded synonymity with" is more objectionable than "taken as referring to" not just because it is more difficult to unravel, but because the extra difficulty does not pay off in extra dividends of relevant meaning.

Let us now turn to the auditory texture of literature. It takes a considerable effort of abstraction to consider a literary work merely as a series of sounds. But it is an effort we can make, since there is no necessary connection between the meaning of a word and its sound, and it is an effort we must make in order to understand the way literature works. For there are important, even if not necessary, connections in literature between sound and sense, and to be clear about this connection we must first distinguish the aspects that are connected.

There are three factors to concern us. First, there is *sound-quality*, or timbre. We speak of words as soft, smooth, rough, sonorous, harsh, guttural, explosive. About individual words not much can be said—even about "cellar-door," which is reputed to be one of the most beautiful-sounding words in our language. With a sequence of words, especially one that shapes itself into a meaningful sentence or line of verse, the sound becomes more determinate and controlled.

The still, sad music of humanity

(Wordsworth, "Lines Composed a Few Miles above Tintern Abbey") naturally calls for a grave and quiet reading. The sound-quality of a discourse is, then, a regional quality that depends in part upon the qualities of its words, and also upon the two other factors of sound that we have not yet mentioned.

Second, there is *sound-similarity*, which we may call "homophony." It includes rhyme, consonance ("wind," "wound"), assonance (*"music,"* "humanity"), alliteration ("still," "sad"). It is not necessary for us to deal with homophony in detail; we shall return later to the ways in which it becomes involved in the meaning of a poem.

Third, there is *sound-pattern*, that is, meter and rhythm. Here we reach one of the most problematical aspects of poetry, a field still fertile in misunderstanding and disagreement. And so we shall have to be brief and cautious. Let us see what the main problems are, and what principles of methodological or general aesthetic interest they involve.

The meter of a discourse is a regional quality of it, and consists essentially, as is generally agreed, in some sense of regularity or recurrent pattern—not absolute, but prevailing and normal despite all deviations. The difficulty arises when we inquire about the perceptual conditions of this quality, the local features of linguistic sound upon which the regularity depends. Syllables, the units of linguistic sound, have, besides their individual tone-color, or timbre, and pitch-contour, two other qualities that are metrically of great moment: relative length—the syllables in "canebrake" take longer to say, normally, than those in "very"—and relative stress—depending on their being in an accented or unaccented position in a word or phrase. Length, stress, and pitch of course occur in various degrees, but when two syllables are placed side by side, the comparative degree can be taken by the ear as an absolute, and a string of syllables can be heard, more or less distinctly, as dividing into two classes. Which of the qualities can serve as the basis for such a division depends upon the language, but we shall be concerned only with English.

In English, the decisive determinant of meter is stress. Not all stressed syllables are equally emphasized, but a syllable is stressed if it is stronger than another that is before or after it. And in this way a series of English syllables usually divides quite distinctly into the strong and the weak, or stressed and unstressed. In

>That time of year thou mayst in me behold,

the stress on "mayst" and "-hold" is stronger than that on "me," but in contrast to their neighbors they are all in the strong group, and the line as a whole is apprehended as an alternation of five weaks and five strongs.

A stressed syllable introduces a kind of phonetic punctuation in the flow of speech, and breaks up that flow into groups, or *feet*. The weaker syllables are dominated by, and attach themselves to, the strong ones. And in this way we get the two main types of English verse. In the first type, called *accentual* verse, each unit-group of syllables contains one strong syllable and a number of weak ones, but the number of weak ones varies from foot to foot. This is the verse of *Beowulf*, *Piers Plowman*, much of Hopkins and Eliot, and Coleridge's "Christabel":

>From | her ken-·| nel beneath | the rock
>She mak- | eth ans- | wer to | the clock,
>Four | for the quart- | ers, and twelve | for the hour.

In the second type, called *syllabic* verse, a constant number of weak syllables is associated with each strong syllable. Here we have *meter*, a regular pattern of stresses.

Syllabic meter is first classified according to the type of foot, that is, the number of unstressed syllables. It is duple, triple, sometimes quadruple. But a further distinction needs to be made—a distinction in *rhythm*—within the purely metrical divisions. There are two kinds of duple meter, for example, and three kinds of triple meter, depending on the position of the stressed syllable in the foot. The difference between "protest too much" and "final protest" is that in the former the two feet have a rising rhythmic quality, but in the latter the two feet have a falling quality. The former is iambic, the latter trochaic.

This difference can be important in poetry, but it is not always plain and certain, for it is a regional quality that depends upon a number of local factors. For example, the division in English speech between one word and another is a little sharper than that between one syllable and another in the same word. Therefore, if a line in duple meter contains a number of two-syllable words accented on the second syllable, this will tend to give the line a rising, or iambic, quality, whereas if it contains a number of words accented on the first syllable, this will tend to give the line a falling, or trochaic, quality. But if the last syllable is stressed, or if the first syllable is unstressed, the line will probably be iambic no matter what. Compare these two lines:

Without | a grave, | unknelled, | uncof- | fined, and | unknown
To fol- | low know- | ledge like | a sink- | ing star

(Byron, "Childe Harold's Pilgrimage" and Tennyson, "Ulysses"). The second line contains more falling words, the former more rising ones, and hence the former line is more definitely iambic; but both are iambic as a whole, and not only because they are in contexts that are prevailingly so.

There is a certain analogy between the foot in verse and the bar in music, and it has often been thought that the study of versification might be considerably clarified by adopting musical notation. For example, suppose we wrote:

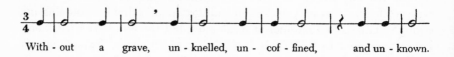

With - out   a   grave,   un - knelled, un -   cof - fined,   and un - known.

And this notation does have some important relation to the verse rhythm. But the question is, what relation? For the musical notation goes beyond the verse rhythm in two important ways.

In the first place, the musical notation assigns equal, or approximately equal, intervals of time to the feet, and this assignment rests upon the assumption that the meter of the verse consists in, or requires, that the feet take equal, or approximately equal, times. But this assumption is, I think, mistaken.[5] We saw in Chapter II, §8, that meter in music depends upon a regular felt pulse, underlying the variations of pitch and stress. But the meter of syllabic verse does not depend upon timing the feet at all; it depends on the regular alternation of stressed syllables with groups of unstressed syllables. And this regularity is perceived as meter despite great changes of pace and tempo in the actual reading. Of course, when verse is set to music, or even when it is just read, a metrical pulse can be imposed upon it. The line from Byron can be read as the notation prescribes. But the pulse is not part of its verbal rhythm.

In the second place, the musical notation assigns particular durations to each syllable; it says, for example, that "-out" is to last twice as long as "with-." And this, of course, can be done. But when we quantify it

---

[5] For the clarification of this and other points about meter and rhythm I am again indebted to W. K. Wimsatt, Jr.

this way we are no longer merely scanning the verse, in the sense of saying what its rhythm is; we are reporting or prescribing a certain way of performing it. The distinction between what belongs to the verse as verse and what is added in performing it is of the utmost importance here, even if it cannot be made with perfect precision. When we scan a line of verse, what is it that we are trying to do? Presumably we are trying to make explicit the prevailing rhythm of the poem, and also the notable deviations from that meter, such as the substitution of an ana- pestic for an iambic foot, or the occurrence of a caesura. The scansion, in other words, points out features of the sound that should be preserved in any reading of it, and must be preserved if the reading is to count as correct or adequate.

But to show the meter of the poem—what is common to various productions of it—is one thing; to describe a particular production is an- other. Musical notation has proved very useful for transcribing poets' readings of their own works, and for recommending readings. But to do this is to go beyond the rhythm of the verse itself. For the word "pri- vately" to be part of a dactylic line, it is only necessary that its first syllable be accented—which it always is. It may be read

pri - vate - ly,   or   pri - vate - ly,   or   pri - vate - ly;

and one may be better than another. But through all of them the verbal rhythm, not the musical rhythm, is the same.

There are a good many complexities about meter, and even some unsettled issues, that this brief account ignores. But perhaps enough has been said to show that questions about the correct scansion of verse are often objective questions, which there is a method for answering. Thus, suppose there is a disagreement between two prosodists about the correct way of scanning a line of verse: say, between Yvor Winters and Robert Bridges about the scansion of Milton's *Samson Agonistes*. In gen- eral, there is a way of settling such disagreements, though sometimes on analysis they turn out to be unreal. For example, the characteristic Shakespearean or Miltonic line is generally regarded as iambic pentam- eter, that is, verse with alternation of five weak and five strong stresses. However, some prosodists say that this is a mistake, and that many such lines are really four-stress lines:

Whether 'tis nobler in the mind to suffer.

This view emphasizes the continuity between blank verse and the accen- tual verse of Old English epic.

The observation upon which the second view rests is that "in" is stressed less than "mind" and "nob-," and it is correct to say that there is a second-order rhythmic pattern in the line that depends on its dominant stresses. But this is not the first-order verse rhythm of the line, which depends not on absolute but only on comparative stress. Indeed, the two rhythms play against each other; in so far as "in" takes a little more stress than "-ler" and "the," it is one of the strong syllables, and therefore the iambic rhythm carries right across the line—though of course it is weaker in the middle than at the extremes. Thus the question, "Is this a five-stress or a four-stress line?" dissolves as soon as the issue is clarified.

But there is a subtler and more troublesome kind of issue. So far, we have been talking about prevailing rhythmic features, and it is to be noted that these do not depend on the meaning of the words, but only on the simplest syntactical considerations, such as the divisions of words and phrases. Thus we can easily scan verse that is made up of nonsense syllables, so long as the rules of English pronunciation guide us in stressing the right syllables.

Descouching hort froomiscious humfle-bun

is also iambic pentameter. But we may sometimes be puzzled about the reading of a poem when we take into account the meaning of its words, and especially the subtle ways in which this meaning is affected by stress or lack of stress. If the printed words constitute instructions for carrying out a production, what are we to do when the instructions seem incomplete or ambiguous?

Consider the following line, from Donne's "Elegy X":

So if I dreame I have you, I have you.[6]

If we adhere to the prevailing rhythm, and stress "I" and "you," we suggest that the important thing is that *I* (rather than someone else) have *you* (rather than someone else). If we introduce a metrical irregularity, and stress "have" instead, we make the poem say the important thing is that I really do have you (rather than only seeming or wishing to). Or perhaps we should, in reading the poem, try to equalize our stress on both "have" and "you," so as to leave the suggestion indeterminate.

The question that concerns us is whether there is a general method for answering such questions. And presumably there is, though we shall not try to work it out here. The procedure is like, or is in part, explication, as we discussed it in Chapter III: we consider the alternatives and choose that which, while still being utterable, introduces the most complexity of meaning with the least incongruity, considering all the rest of the poem. In the present example, the stress on "you" seems to introduce a note that cannot be tied up with other parts of the poem;

---

[6] I take this example from the debate between Arnold Stein and Seymour Chatman in the *Kenyon Review* symposium on meter; for references see Note 14-E at end of chapter.

the stress on "have" makes the most, or the best, sense. In any case the probabilities are on the side of the second reading, and we should have to discover some notable and relevant meaning achieved only by the first reading in order to reject the second. That is because we start with a knowledge of normal stress-patterns for certain kinds of phrases. Whenever we compare thinking, hoping, dreaming, or saying with actuality, the comparison must be conveyed in English by stressing the verb: "I *thought* you could do it and you *did* it"—not "*you* did it" or "you did *it*"—and in the poem it is the reference to dreaming that calls for the stress on "have." Here is a general principle about English stress;[7] it is such principles that guide us in the reading—i.e., the sounding—of poetry.

Verse

We are now prepared to define an important term that has already been used in the definition of "poetry." What is meant, and what is to be meant, by "verse"? The metrical quality of a discourse is a regional quality that occurs in various degrees of intensity, and the boundary that we draw between metrical discourse and nonmetrical discourse is certain to be vague. But that is not surprising or troublesome. It would be simplest if we could define "verse" as "metrical discourse," and probably the term is often used this way. However, it will not quite do—that is, we can find a better approximation to prevailing usage among critics, and one that will provide some further distinctions. For being metrical is neither necessary nor sufficient for being verse. It is not necessary, because critics commonly speak of "free verse" as a kind of verse from which meter may be altogether absent—though in the best free verse there is likely to be more reliance on metrical organization than is sometimes observed. It is not sufficient, because there are metrical passages in the novels of Dickens that lapse into iambics, and there is meter in Starbuck's meditation, in Chapter 38 of *Moby Dick,* but we do not call these passages verse. They could easily be made into verse, but there is something else involved in the making. Passages from Thomas Wolfe have been "arranged" as verse; Yeats did the same with Walter Pater's description of the *Mona Lisa,* and made it the first poem in his *Oxford Book of Modern Verse.* Or take the first definition of Spinoza's *Ethics:*

> By cause of itself, I understand that whose essence involves existence; or that whose nature cannot be conceived unless existing.

That is prose. This is not yet poetry, perhaps, but verse:

> By cause of itself,
> I understand that
> Whose essence
> Involves existence;

---

[7] Proposed by Seymour Chatman, *loc. cit.*

> Or that whose nature
> Cannot be conceived
> Unless existing.

This is even fairly regular verse; but the first sentence of Leibniz' *Monadology* would be freer verse:

> The monad
>   Of which we shall here
>   Speak
>   Is merely a simple
> Substance,
> Which enters into composites;
> Simple,
>   That is to say,
>   Without parts.

Granted that this is just barely verse; it is perhaps not more borderlinish, as far as its sound goes, than some lines of Marianne Moore's or the quotations from official documents inserted in Ezra Pound's *Cantos,* or the passages about the difficulty of using words in Eliot's "East Coker."

What are we doing when we make these divisions? Presumably we are dividing up the flow of prose into rhythmic sections—thereby, of course, introducing new and sometimes very significant emphases and suggestions—slowing it down in smaller units. We are introducing more regularity and control into the normal cadence, or rise and fall of the voice. And this is sufficient to make verse, though not necessarily poetry. But, of course, it cannot be done with all prose.

Verse is, then, discourse whose sound-pattern is more highly organized than prose. And it seems that there are two independent types of organization. The first, and dispensable, one is meter, or organization into rhythmic feet. The second, and indispensable, one is organization into lines, or verses in the older sense. Therefore, there is some approximate truth in the naïve view that poetry can be recognized by its arrangement on the printed page. But only approximate truth; for the divisions on the printed page are not real divisions in the poem unless they correspond in some way to differences that can be performed and heard. Contemporary free-verse writers have, of course, discovered numerous ways in which line divisions and punctuation, or its absence, can make significant contributions to the sound of a poem, and indirectly to its meaning. But it does not follow that all such divisions are really significant. The typographical oddities of E. E. Cummings are quite often not.

The resources of verbal sound are important, but also very restricted, compared with the resources of music—melody, pulse rhythm, and harmony. It is therefore highly misleading to speak of the "music of poetry." For the sound aspect of speech in poetry has much less complexity and variety and interest than music.

It is true that we do not fully understand the effects that verse can have upon us, and it is also true that it is hard to test the conflicting theories about it. Some people say they experience a tremendously moving or hypnotic effect from hearing poetry read aloud in a language they do not understand at all. But this effect, if it occurs, owes something to vague meanings attributed, correctly or incorrectly, to the words, as you can read a passage of Interlingua even though you've never studied the language, if you have some acquaintance with one or two Romance languages, because the roots are recognizable. And it owes something to the emotive purport and general purport of the sounds as they are uttered by the reader in a certain tone of voice. The evidence is debatable, but for my part I believe that practically all of the notable effects of poetic sound come from its connection with meaning or purport.

Sound and Sense

It is often said by critics that in certain poems particularly, and perhaps in all good poems to some degree, the sound "reinforces" or "coincides with" the sense. We must now, to complete our discussion of sound in literature, try to make explicit the nature of this connection. The simplest sort of connection we find in onomatopoeic words, in which the sound designated by the word is also *sounded* by the word. In "snarl," "slither," "purr," "snap," "crackle," and "pop," the sound of the word is, we may say, a *presentational equivalent* of its meaning. It is what it designates.

But we may extend this notion from sounds to other things, and say that the word is a presentational equivalent of its meaning whenever the sound of the word, in its quality or movement, is similar to the qualities or movements of the objects or events it designates. "Swinging" has a swinging movement (so does "winging"); "hollow" has a sort of hollow sound; "disgusted" has a slightly disgusted quality; and so forth. Obviously with a little imagination one can quickly push this far beyond the bounds of testability, while still seeming loosely plausible. It is probably best to claim very little for individual words; but we can still claim a reasonable amount for groups of words. For example, in

> A savage place! As holy and enchanted
> As e'er beneath a waning moon was haunted
> By woman wailing for her demon-lover!

(Coleridge, "Kubla Khan") the sound is also haunting, spell-binding, eerie, and mysterious. In

> sheer plód makes plough down sillion
> Shine

(Hopkins, "The Windhover"[8]), the stresses, the weight of sound, the slow movement, have the quality of push and effort. In Alfred Noyes' "The Highwayman," to take a simpler example, the rhythm is breathless and driving, like the pace of the melodramatic tale it tells.

The relation of presentational equivalence is, then, one relation of sound to sense. We may not miss it when it is absent or weak, but when it is strongly there we notice it and feel it helps the poem to cohere. But there is another relation, which is perhaps an extension of this one, that sometimes plays an important part: it depends on what I have called "homophony." In the state of intense awareness that is induced by a poem, or is at least the state in which it ought to be approached, everything about the words is significant; the reader is keyed up to respond to every verbal cue. The fact that two words sound alike in some way is by itself a suggestion, slight but present, that their meanings are in some way connected; they seem, on some primitive level, to belong together. This notion may be seen in the way children make up unfriendly remarks to a sing-song about each other: "Phil is a pill" and "Josey is nosey" seem somehow right; the fact that the word sounds appropriate is, on this sub-rational level, a kind of "argument" that the attribution is true.

It won't do to push this very far, I suppose, but poetry seems to play with a sense of ideal possibility, as if the right way of speaking would be one in which the sound always dramatized and enacted the meaning-relations. "Enchanted" and "haunted" belong together; the alliteration of "seek" and "shun" makes it easy to suggest that they are part of the same attitude or action. But these are obvious; it is more of a discovery, or exploitation of the language, that Wordsworth can make "music" and "humanity" go together; the claim that humanity has a still, sad music is reinforced by the similarity of sound. And alliteration and internal rhyme especially set up within a poem a web of cross-relations among the words and the concepts and objects they designate; these work toward a thickness of texture by added suggestion, and increase the textual coherence of the poem. Consider

> Past ruined Ilion Helen lives,
> Alcestis rises from the shades;
> Verse calls them forth; 'tis verse that gives
> Immortal youth to mortal maids

(Landor, "Past Ruined Ilion"). The "n" sound in "ruined Ilion Helen" ties them together in a single catastrophe. The "v" of "verse" and the "f" of "forth" bring them together, suggesting that the statement "Verse calls them forth" is naturally true. "Maids" is given irony because its meaning contrasts with the meaning of the two words that are connected with it, "shades" by rhyme and "mortal" by alliteration. The sound-parallelism

---

[8] From "The Windhover," *Poems of Gerard Manley Hopkins.* Copyright 1918 by the Oxford University Press and reprinted with their permission.

of "Immortal" and "mortal" reinforces the slight paradox of the claim that the youth of the maid will outlive the maid.

If the sound of poetry, then, can be appropriate to its sense in some way, can it also be inappropriate? In principle, it would seem so, but convincing examples are not easy to find. Brooks and Warren cite

> Death is here, and death is there,
> Death is busy everywhere

(Shelley, "Death") as a poem in which the "jigging rhythm" has a quality that is incongruous with the solemnity of the subject, and hence tends to trivialize and betray its meaning.[9] This is a good example. Even here it might be argued that with sufficient attention to the meaning one could read the poem so as to minimize the excessive regularity of the meter, but it would be an effort. For the strong accents are all long syllables ("death," "there," "-where"), and the weak accents are all short syllables ("is," "and," "-y"); hence the extreme regularity and heavy beat. This would not be true at all of other poems about death, for example Donne's sonnet:

> Death be not proud, though some have callèd thee
> Mighty and dreadful . . .

We must not stipulate, of course, that all poems about death are to be sad or even solemn. But if the attitude imported by the words is grave, then a sound that is light and tripping will introduce an incoherence into the poem—or, at least, and only with the support of syntax, an ironic tone. There is something of this in William Carlos Williams' "Tract."

A literary work, we may conclude, depends for its unity partly upon its texture of sound and meaning—that is, upon the artificial order of its verse, when it is in verse, and upon a constancy or continuity in its meaning. Moreover, its unity is increased when certain regional qualities of its phonetic style are similar to certain regional qualities of its semantic style. But there is another aspect of its unity that remains to be considered, and this depends upon the structure of the situations and events and human relationships that belong to its projected world. To this structure we now turn.

§15.   LITERARY STRUCTURE

Within the world projected by a literary work we can make certain major distinctions that seem to be universal and fundamental in literature. The primary one is inherent in the nature of discourse, for whatever else it may be, a discourse is a connected utterance in which something

---

[9] Cleanth Brooks and Robert Penn Warren, *Understanding Poetry*, rev. ed., New York: Holt, 1950, p. 112.

is being said by somebody about something. Even if the words happened to be tapped out by a chimpanzee or carved into a cliff by wind and rain, they have this triple aspect.

In every literary work, therefore, there is first of all an implicit *speaker,* or voice: he whose words the work purports to be. He may come forward and reveal much about himself, as in Eliot's "Journey of the Magi," Browning's "Epistle . . . of Karshish," or William Dunbar's "Lament for the Makaris":

> No state in Erd here standis sicker,
> As with the wynd wavis the wicker,
> So wannis this world's vanitie;
> *Timor Mortis conturbat me.*

Or he may stand farther in the background and simply present without giving himself away very much:

> The king sits in Dumferling toune,
> Drinking the blude-red wine . . .

("Sir Patrick Spens")—but even here there is someone telling the story to us, and we know something about the teller from the telling.

Speaker and Situation

The speaker is not to be identified with the author of the work, nor can we learn more of the speaker than he reveals in the poem, say by studying the life of the author. It is not Housman whose heart "with rue . . . is laden," or Frost who has "miles to go before I sleep"; as Ezra Pound once wrote,

> (Of course I'm no more Mauberley than Eliot is Prufrock. Mais passons.) Mauberley is a mere surface.[1]

We have no more justification for identifying the author with the speaker than with any other character in the work—Thomas Wolfe with Eugene Gant, Joseph Conrad with Captain Leggett in "The Secret Sharer," or Katherine Mansfield with Constantia or Josephine in "The Daughters of the Late Colonel." Once we learn from the work itself the character of the speaker, we can, if we wish, ask how similar he is to the author. When we ask, "Is *Stephen Hero* an autobiographical work?" we invite this comparison. But to compare Stephen Dedalus with Joyce is to compare two distinct people—not, in the strict philosophical sense, to treat them as one.

The temptation to confuse the speaker with the writer is greatest with lyric poetry, which almost always contains personal pronouns. Ordinarily, however, we have no reason to regard the "I" of the poem as the writer, just as we have no reason to regard the "you," if there is one, as the

---

[1] Letter to Felix Schelling, July 1922; *Letters 1907-41*, ed. by D. D. Paige, New York: Harcourt, Brace, 1950.

reader. The "I," like the "you," is, in one sense, simply one of the characters in the work, perhaps the only one. Of course the speaker is a rather special, or privileged, character, since it is from his point of view that everything is seen, and in some lyric poems all that happens is what happens in his mind. Now, in some writings, e.g., autobiography, we must take the personal pronoun to refer to the writer. Is there not then ever any good reason for taking a poem as, in the same sense, autobiographical?

First consider some other references in poetry. Suppose a poem contains a proper name—"where some buried Caesar bled," "Great ANNA! whom three realms obey," "Past ruin'd Ilion Helen lives," or, to avoid prosecution for libel, "Immortal S——k, and grave De——re," or Pope's nicknames, "Bavius," "Bufo," and "Bubo." To understand the poem, we must of course know whose name it is, and sometimes we must know a good deal about the person named. Now suppose the speaker of the poem refers to himself by the name of the author; probably in that case we could say the same. But this must be very rare: there is Walt Whitman's "To a Common Prostitute" (I do not count "Song of Myself") and John Ciardi's "Elegy Just in Case":

> Here lie Ciardi's pearly bones,
> In their ripe organic mess[2]

(compare "Landscapes of My Name"); Donne's and Shakespeare's puns on their own names might be added. Something more complex is involved, I think, in the fact that the speaker of Proust's *A la Recherche du Temps Perdu* refers to himself as "Marcel." Though it may hint at autobiographical sources for the work, it does not make the work an autobiography; there is still a difference. But a narrative work in the first person, in which the speaker has the name of the author, and is known to resemble him in certain important respects—especially, to clinch the matter, if it is subtitled "An Autobiography" or "A Memoir"—*is* a work in which the author speaks for himself.

But suppose we have no proper names, only the personal pronoun; what would give us the right to say it refers to the author? Words like "I," "you," "here," "now," cannot be assigned any reference at all unless we know something of the circumstances in which they are uttered— what might be called the *pragmatic context* of utterance. A statement like "Phylogeny recapitulates ontogeny," or "To err is human, to forgive divine," can be understood apart from any pragmatic context. Where we are concerned with the practical consequences of a message containing pronouns, we cannot act until we discover their referents, and we cannot act at all unless there *is* a pragmatic context to give them referents. Now clearly Conan Doyle's use of the word "I" in the Sherlock Holmes

---

[2] From "Elegy Just in Case," John Ciardi, *As If.* Copyright 1955 by the Trustees of Rutgers College in New Jersey and reprinted with the permission of John Ciardi.

stories does not give this pronoun a reference to any actual person (certainly not to himself): "Dr. Watson" did not exist. Why, then, must we assume that when Keats or Shelley uses the pronoun he is always referring to himself? If you write a "Happy Birthday" poem and hand it to someone on his birthday, or send it under your own name, you are giving the message a pragmatic context. If you write a love poem and publish it as a poem, you are not giving the message a pragmatic context; it is from nobody to nobody, it is not addressed to, but rather overheard by, the reader; and though you are the writer, you are not the speaker.

This argument may seem over-nice, but there is evidence enough of confusion on the point. In general, the correct principle seems to be that the speaker of a literary work cannot be identified with the author—and therefore the character and condition of the speaker can be known by internal evidence alone—unless the author has provided a pragmatic context, or a claim of one, that connects the speaker with himself. But we must grant that what constitutes a pragmatic context is not always certain.

In every literary work there is, besides the speaker, a set of objects or events that confront him, which we may call his *situation*. He is faced with, or contemplates in thought, a mouse, a skylark, a Grecian urn, the river Loddon, a churchyard, the death of his beloved, the rape of a lock, the siege of Troy, or the Fall of Man: I use the term "situation" to cover all of these. In this broad sense, the situation is the *subject* of the work —what is found, or met with, what happens or appears, in it. It is, in one sense, what the work is *about*. When the situation is a chain of events, the work is a narrative, and the speaker may be called the narrator.

The situation may be trivial or grand; Browning's "Soliloquy in a Spanish Cloister" or Dante's cosmic tour. It may be projected in vast detail, or only vaguely adumbrated: in some short romantic lyrics we get no more than a dim idea of what is going on—his beloved has left him, or something in the world has produced an inarticulate melancholy—and in some modern poems, while a number of things seem to be happening, they have a dreamlike air of rapidly shifting focus, so the situation is confused and indeterminate. Nevertheless, if the speaker speaks at all, and even if he speaks mostly of himself, there is implicit some concept of an environment, a cause, an object of his concern: somebody he is grieving over, some source of irritation or of despair, some conceivable solution or escape envisioned or hoped for.

The situation of the work must be kept distinct, again, from the occasion of its being written. Some person or event in the writer's life may have inspired, or started him upon, the poem. But what happens in the poem is something else again; of that we only know what the poem itself, directly or indirectly, tells us. It is not Wordsworth, in the poem, but a speaker who may or may not be similar to him, musing near Tintern Abbey; it is entirely irrelevant to the understanding of the poem—though relevant to a causal explanation of its having been written—that Wordsworth himself visited the spot. Similarly, it is interesting to know whether a writer's characters were suggested by his friends or enemies—whether his novel is a *roman à clef* that pays off old scores—or came floating into his ken of their own free will, demanding to be put to work, as Samuel Butler and Henry James have said of their characters. But this, again, has nothing to do with the question of their nature as they are revealed in the work itself.

The substance of literature is human. Even if the chief characters in the work are animal in shape—Mr. Toad, Black Beauty, Chicken-Licken, Pogo, or Babar and Céleste—they are human in nature, with human characteristics, however exaggerated or attenuated.

Given a speaker and a situation, there will in general be an *attitude* of the speaker toward the situation; and in the attitude we may distinguish both feelings and beliefs. In one sort of work—in Ben Jonson's "Drink to Me Only with Thine Eyes," or Byron's "So, We'll Go No More A-Roving"—we cannot say that the speaker reveals any formulable beliefs about the world in general, but he reveals vivid and distinct feelings. In another sort of work—in Johnson's "Vanity of Human Wishes," or Auden's "September 1, 1939"—there is meditation upon general themes, and we can say a good deal about what the speaker thinks. Sometimes the speaker withdraws almost completely, into indifference and detachment; in one sense of the term, and perhaps the most useful sense, such works may be called "realistic." But this does not preclude a certain amount of chilly irony.

> They shot the six cabinet members at half-past six in the morning against the wall of a hospital. There were pools of water in the courtyard. There were wet dead leaves on the paving of the courtyard. It rained hard. All the shutters of the hospital were nailed shut. One of the ministers was sick with typhoid. . . .[3]

The notable thing about the speaker is precisely that he does *not* show any feelings or make any moral judgment about the event. The great French realists, for example Balzac and Flaubert, set their people and events before us like an impresario, and leave the rest to us. By way of contrast, the narrator of *Tom Jones* sometimes walks to the center of the stage to share with the reader his reflections about life and human nature.

Some literary works purport to be addressed to a special audience, and show, by their style or subject, something of the nature of that audience: Leuconoë, Lucasta, Celia, Mr. W. H., the revolutionary proletariat, the British Parliament, the citizens of Concord, Massachusetts, or the Epic Muse. We may say, somewhat awkwardly, that they have an *implicit receiver*. Again, this receiver may not be any actual person or persons: just a group supposedly gathered about a fire or a bar, or a companion

---

[3] Ernest Hemingway, epigraph to ch. 5 of *In Our Time*, New York: Viking Portable Library, 1949, pp. 399-400.

in a boat or Pullman car. Not all literary works have a receiver—unless you say that *Le Rouge et le Noir* is implicitly addressed to people who understand French, or *Finnegans Wake* to people who have read *The Golden Bough, The Kalevala,* and various other things.

When the work has an implicit receiver, we may be able to detect in it the speaker's attitude toward the receiver, as distinct from his attitude toward the situation he faces. This is often called the *tone* of the work, but the word "tone" can be used more generally, and there is no special reason to restrict it so. We find the tone of a poem or novel bitter, gentle, calm, querulous, savage, boisterous, and seem to mean the general quality of the speaker's attitude in so far as it depends, not on introspective description, but on the emotive purport of the diction and syntax. Tone is a regional quality which we may perceive clearly, like the tone of the Hemingway passage above, without being able to describe it well.

The situation in a literary work, or its chain of events if it is a narrative, is always more than the work explicitly states. Certain actions are reported; from them we are to infer other events and states of affairs, including character and motives. Daisy Miller appears at the hotel; therefore, she must have been born. She goes out with men she has barely met; therefore, she is careless of her reputation. Part of what is involved in coming to understand a literary work is this process of filling out our knowledge of what is going on, beyond what is overtly presented. I shall call this process, somewhat arbitrarily, the *elucidation* of the work. It is quite a different thing from explication, which has to do with verbal meaning; like explication, elucidation is often called "interpretation," but I am reserving this term for Chapter IX.

The Elucidation of Literature

The sort of question that the critic attempts to answer by elucidation may be indicated by these examples: Is Hamlet mad? What is Raskolnikov's real motive in killing the old woman? Where is the speaker and what is his situation in "Gerontion" or "Sailing to Byzantium"? What traits are basic to the character of Antigone? Is the "Lydian Stranger" of Euripides' *The Bacchae*—a play that contains several difficult problems of elucidation, and also of explication and interpretation—Dionysus in disguise? In short, the nature of the elucidation question is succinctly summed up in the title of a well-known critical work: *What Happens in Hamlet.*[4]

Elucidation is something we do intuitively and without conscious effort in our ordinary reading; indeed, very little fiction—perhaps only the

---

[4] By J. Dover Wilson, 3d ed. Cambridge, Eng.: Cambridge U., 1956; this book is a mine of elucidation problems, with ingenious, though not always undebatable, solutions.

simplest stories, like those in first-grade readers—would be intelligible at all if we could not constantly supply the links of character and motivation between the words and actions set forth. But about complex works of fiction disputes arise, and here we are forced to consider what we are doing when we elucidate, and whether we are doing it on rational principles. An excellent case in point is Henry James's *The Turn of the Screw*. Here we have two incompatible elucidations, each of which has been vigorously defended: is one right and the other wrong, or are they both wrong, or is neither wrong because there is no method of elucidation that can settle the question objectively?

The issues are too complicated to do justice to here, but it will be worthwhile to sketch them far enough to bring out the basic problem of methodology involved.[5] A central question, on which much depends, is whether or not the children see the apparitions of Peter Quint and Miss Jessel. If they do, then they have concealed something important from the governess and they are in fact, as the governess believes, possessed and corrupted by evil. If they do not see the apparitions, then these are subjective projections of the governess, who is therefore basically neurotic; in this case the evil that destroys the children comes from the governess herself. Now the question admits of only two answers; it seems that a genuine and decisive choice must be made, and what you take the story to be, its quality and point and structure, all depends on how you answer this question.

What are we doing when we elucidate a story; and how do we test our elucidations? Consider the simplest sort of case first. Suppose we read that Homer talked at Bessie for two hours and Bessie yawned; we do not need to be told that Bessie is bored. In the technical sense of the term proposed in Chapter III we may say:

> "Homer talked at Bessie for two hours and Bessie yawned" *suggests* that Bessie is bored.

Obviously the suggestion depends upon our knowledge of certain causal connections. People who are talked at for two hours will probably be bored, and bored people will probably yawn; these are crude psychological laws. To put it in another, but in the end equivalent, way, on the assumption that Bessie has been talked at, the hypothesis "She is bored" is the best available, or the most probable, explanation of her yawn.

It is humorless to dwell upon these obvious points and upon this

---

[5] Edmund Wilson's Freudian interpretation is given in sec. 1 of "The Ambiguity of Henry James," *The Triple Thinkers*, New York: Harcourt, Brace, 1938; reprinted in Mark Schorer, Josephine Miles and Gordon McKenzie, *Criticism*, New York: Harcourt, Brace, 1948, pp. 147-62. This paper is criticized in detail by Robert B. Heilman, "The Freudian Reading of *The Turn of the Screw*," *Modern Language Notes*, LXII (1947): 433-45, and *"The Turn of the Screw* as Poem," *Forms of Modern Fiction*, ed. by W. V. O'Connor, Minneapolis, Minn.: U. of Minnesota, 1948, pp. 211-28; see also A. J. A. Waldoch, "Mr. Edmund Wilson and *The Turn of the Screw*," *Modern Language Notes*, LXII (1947): 331-34.

trivial example; but it is necessary to see what is happening in the simplest case before we approach the more complex ones. I claim, then, that an elucidation statement is, or is part of, a hypothesis that gains its acceptability from its capacity to account for the explicitly reported events. In this respect, there is no difference *in principle* from the mode of reasoning we employ in ordinary life when we try to figure out motives from actions. There is one important difference, however, for in real life there is always the logical possibility of acquiring further evidence to test our hypotheses, while in the novel the set of facts we are trying to explain is forever complete and closed. (This is what makes it possible to invent fantastic elucidations that are absurdly overcomplicated but not conclusively refutable, for example, "Watson was a woman.") We shall return to this point shortly. But first notice how the method applies to the case of Henry James. It is a noteworthy and valuable feature of *The Turn of the Screw* that most of the events up to the final scene *can* be explained on either of the two hypotheses: (1) The apparitions are real, and are seen by the children; (2) The apparitions are only in the mind of the governess. This leaves a lingering doubt, even in her mind, that helps to keep the story moving and give it complexity. But the final scene cannot be explained by Hypothesis 2, for in that scene Miles shows that he has seen Peter Quint's ghost before, and would not be surprised to see it again; he is destroyed by the fact that he can no longer see it. And several events in earlier scenes, hitherto not played up, come to the reader's mind as further points that are explained only, or more simply and directly, by Hypothesis 1: that the governess sees, and accurately describes, Peter Quint's ghost, before she has heard a word about him; that Miles has been sent home from school for some mysterious reason; that the children never talk about their past; that the little girl rows a large rowboat across the lake, and so forth. In the final analysis, one hypothesis is far more probable than the other, and there is therefore no "ambiguity of Henry James" in this story.

Clearly elucidation is simply causal inference, but the difference between fiction and life must not be lost from view. In any work of fiction, it will always be possible to ask questions about the characters that are not answered by the work itself. What did Hamlet study at Wittenberg? What is the minister's secret sin in Hawthorne's short story, "The Minister's Black Veil"? What is the real name of Nora, in *The Doll's House?* (Ibsen actually had an answer ready for this, but he did not put it into the play.) Who was Mrs. Dalloway's great-grandfather? How many years does Tom Jones live after the story ends? Was it Mr. Bazzard that John Jasper murdered in the dark, instead of Edwin Drood? Or—what has now become the archetype of all such questions[6]—how many children

---

[6] Because of the famous article by L. C. Knights, "How Many Children Had Lady Macbeth?" *Explorations*, London: Chatto and Windus, 1951, pp. 1-39, a general attack upon the confusion of literature with life.

had Lady Macbeth? She evidently had *some* children, for she refers to them, and if some, then one, or two, or three, or some other definite number; it is tempting to wonder how many, and of course it is legitimate to seek in the play any clue, however subtle, that will give some probability, however slight, to some hypothesis. But a great deal of Shakespearean scholarship, especially in the past, has gone beyond this; where no evidence is available, critics have felt free to speculate. "I picture Lady Macbeth with two stalwart sons, who resemble their mother, but . . ."; this is no longer elucidation, it is invention.

When, for example, Stanislavsky prepared his *Regiebuch* for *Othello*,[7] he provided an elaborate past history of the relations among Iago, Roderigo, Cassio, and Othello, and there is evidence that this brilliantly imaginative construction, perfectly coherent as it is with the actual play, helped him to direct it and helped his actors to develop three-dimensional roles. The production of a play, in any case, is part invention, or supplementation of the script, but staging the play is different from elucidating it as a work of fiction. The questions that the work of fiction does not answer are unaskable questions. Nor is this ambiguity; it is simply one of the boundaries of the work, in time and space. We may know a great deal before we are through about David Copperfield or Odysseus or Swann, but the subject of the work is only that part of their lives and characters which is explicitly reported or inferrable from that report, and these characters have no existence outside the work.

We must therefore conceive of a line beyond which elucidation cannot go. And it is easy to say that this is where the evidence runs out. However, whether a given fact F is evidence for a hypothesis H does not depend upon F alone; to put the matter very simply, it depends also upon the law, or generalization G, that connects F with H. The inference of motive from action relies upon psychological laws. Therefore, as new laws are accepted, new inferences become feasible, and new elucidations, or new directions of elucidation, are opened up. A test case for the method of elucidation is provided by the celebrated Freudian elucidation of *Hamlet*.[8] The question is: why does Hamlet delay his revenge? Following Freud's suggestions, Ernest Jones shows clearly the difficulties of explaining this delay either in terms of the external obstacles or in terms of some weakness of character, and his solution is, briefly, that Hamlet is kept inactive by an ambivalence in his unconscious mind, arising from a partial identification of himself with Claudius, as his father's murderer and mother's lover. This "hyperinterpretation" makes Hamlet a "hysterical subject."

---

[7] See Konstantin S. Stanislavsky, *Stanislavsky Produces Othello*, trans. by Helen Nowak, London: Bles, 1948, esp. on Act I, Scene I (this part is also in Toby Cole, ed., *Acting*, New York: Lear, 1947, pp. 131-38).

[8] See Freud's *Interpretation of Dreams*, in *Basic Writings*, ed. by A. A. Brill, New York: Modern Library, 1938, pp. 309-11. The argument was further developed by Ernest Jones, *Hamlet and Oedipus*, New York: Norton, 1949.

The interesting question is whether this method of elucidation is legitimate. Let us consider, first, what might be said in favor of it. As we learn more about the world, we can infer more from what we find; therefore, the implications of events and actions in a work of fiction are bound to expand, and the play grow deeper and more complex. Suppose a character in a novel has certain symptoms that could not be diagnosed when the novel was written, and suppose we can now diagnose them as, say, virus pneumonia. Doesn't the character in the novel have virus pneumonia, even though neither he nor the other characters, nor the author, knows it? This would seem to be merely a logical deduction: X has these symptoms; anyone who has these symptoms probably has virus pneumonia; therefore X probably has virus pneumonia. Now, similarly, neither Hamlet, Claudius, Gertrude, nor Shakespeare could know that all human beings have unconscious minds in which are repressed their deep desires to kill one parent and mate with the other; however, if all men have unconscious minds and Hamlet was a man, then Hamlet had an unconscious mind.

But against this sort of argument some strong objections can be advanced. Is this not to treat Hamlet as if he were a real person in the world, and thus make the great confusion between literature and life that gives rise to the silly questions about Lady Macbeth's children and the girlhood of Shakespeare's heroines? If the characters and speaker in the novel cannot conceive of viruses, then viruses do not exist in their world, even if the symptoms do. Freudian unconsciouses no more belong to Hamlet's world than washing machines, proportional representation, marginal utility, or atomic fission. It is an anachronism to put into the play concepts that could not have been in it in Shakespeare's day, and the Freudian "elucidation" is, then, not an elucidation at all, but an ingenious piece of elaboration, or expansion.

The case for the Freudian elucidation is complicated, but not, I think, strengthened, by treating the play and its situation as symptoms of Shakespeare's own unconscious conflicts, which Freud does by bringing in biographical data: for example, that the play was written soon after the death of Shakespeare's father in 1601. It might be argued that Shakespeare unconsciously endowed Hamlet with an unconscious mind—that Shakespeare's unconscious recognized, even if his conscious mind did not, that Hamlet's inability to kill Claudius, though he was able to kill others, was caused by his unconscious guilt. But since Hamlet cannot be psychoanalyzed, and he has no future behavior to observe, the hypothesis seems to be placed beyond the realm of verification.

It is more to the point, I think, to hold that when Shakespeare invented Hamlet and his behavior he was already dimly grasping and revealing the concept of the subconscious inhibition—that the play embodies an insight foreshadowing the Freudian discoveries. At least a case could be made out for this view.

This is nevertheless a knotty problem, and the answer is probably not simple. But two things seem clear. If elucidation is inference according to laws, then the Freudian reading of Hamlet is an elucidation; but then we must certainly distinguish various elucidations according to the laws they assume. One sort of elucidation reads Hamlet in terms of psychological generalizations assumed by characters in the play itself, or assumed at the time it was first produced; this is certainly one legitimate sort. But we can also ask for a twentieth century reading of Hamlet, in terms of generalizations that we now assume, or know. The two elucidations will give two plays, of course.

Perspectival Structures

The *structure* of a literary work can be defined as in the preceding chapter: it consists of the large-scale relationships within the work, the major connections. There are many varieties of possible structure, and a great deal has been written about them. Our problem is to see what might be done by way of a general classification, with the help of the distinctions we have been working with. The major division is clear. We have, first, various possible relationships between the speaker and his situation; let us call these *perspectival structures*. We have, second, where the situation or the speaker's attitude changes in some way, various possible relationships among the major phases of that change; let us call these *developmental structures*.

The perspectival structures are of two sorts, *spatial* and *temporal*. Let us consider the spatial structures first.

It is possible to give a brief and impersonal report of some event, without suggesting anything at all about the speaker's spatial relation to that event: "The Joneses' house burned down." "We watched the Joneses' house burn down," however, claims that the speaker was a witness to the fire, and one of a group of witnesses. "The flames from the Joneses' burning house lit up the midnight sky" does not mention the speaker at all, but it purports a speaker whose post of observation was at some distance from the burning house—as well as one who was at the moment more aware of the visual image than of the danger or the economic consequences.

When what is described is not simply an event, but the action of a human being, it is much more natural to let the description show the describer's spatial relation to the action; and if the description opens out into a longer narrative, it will be almost impossible to keep this relation out. Either the narrator knows directly what is going on in the actor's mind or he doesn't; either he can observe his external appearance or he cannot. Hence arises what is called *point of view* in literature: the spatial perspective from which the speaker observes the events he describes. There are, of course, a number of possible points of view, or of shifts in point of view, and certain general qualities of the work will depend in large part upon this perspective.

There is another relationship that ordinary language carries with it, that is indicated by *tense*. "The Joneses' house burned down" reports the event as in the past, and establishes a temporal relationship between the moment of report and the moment reported. Tense can be more complex: in "Tomorrow I shall have gone," there is the (present) time of speaking, and the (future) time of looking back upon a (still future, but then past) time of going. A literary work has, one might say, a prevailing tense, and in fact some of the main qualities of certain works depend upon this feature. For example, a work of prose fiction is typically in the past tense; it reads like a record of actions and sufferings now over and done with, for the narrator sets himself at a moment of time from which he is always looking back. This may, of course, be varied by having the last event of the book be in the present, or even future: "I write this last page on my last night; tomorrow I am to be hanged." The lyric poem, including the dramatic lyric, is typically in the present tense—the tense we naturally use in describing a play or announcing a baseball game. Something is going on whose outcome is as yet undecided; we are living at the moment, the speaker feels now what he describes himself as feeling. The author may be recollecting in tranquillity, but not the speaker. It is less clear what to say about meditative—religious or philosophical—poetry or prose. It is somewhat like the *tenseless* work of mathematics or science. Consider Newton's third law, that action and reaction are equal, or Fermat's still unproved Last Theorem that there are no integers x, y, z for which $x^n + y^n = z^n$, where $n > 2$. These do not use the words "are" and "is" in the present tense, strictly speaking, but in no tense; the truths they state are not events in the past, present, or future, but timeless. Thus in such sentences as these, the speaker places himself outside, or above, the stream of time. Perhaps the same should be said of the speakers in Pope's *Essay on Man* or in Robert Bridges' *Testament of Beauty*, but this is probably misleading; for in such works there is a progression of thought and feeling, a dynamic development, and hence the speaker is inside the course of time.

Developmental Structures

Developmental structures can be grouped into three main classes: *logical*, *narrative*, and, for want of a more apt word, *dramatic*.

If we pick two sentences or clauses at random from a discourse, and ask what connection between them makes both belong to the same discourse, we may be able to answer in some such way as this: the first provides evidence for the second; the second is among the logical consequences of a set of premises that includes the first; the first provides a definition of a term that occurs in the second, etc. These are logical

connections. What makes it reasonable to utter, in succession, two sentences like "The school equipment needs repairing. The swing is broken,"
is that the second is understood as providing an example of a class of
things referred to by the first. Now, when a large discourse contains a
number of statements that are related in some systematically logical way
—for example, one statement can be deduced from the others, or some
of the statements would, if true, be evidence for others—then the discourse may be said to have a *logical structure*. For example, in the sestet
of Shakespeare's Sonnet 94

> The summer's flower is to the summer sweet,
> Though to itself it only live and die,
> But if that flower with base infection meet,
> The basest weed outbraves his dignity:
>> For sweetest things turn sourest by their deeds;
>> Lilies that fester smell far worse than weeds.

lines 11 and 12 purport to be a conclusion from the premise of line 13.

It is probably incorrect to describe this, however, as an argument,
for it does not in the full sense argue, since the statements are not really
asserted—this distinction we shall deal with in Chapter IX, §23. The
poem "acts" an argument the way one acts Cyrano or Nellie Forbush.
It has the movement and abstract relationships, the articulation, of an
argument. And that is an important thing about such poems as *An Essay
on Man, On the Nature of Things,* Donne's "Canonization," Marvell's
"To His Coy Mistress," W. H. Auden's "September 1, 1939."

It is not, I think, necessary to define "narrative" more exactly than
we have so far done,[9] though it is not so evident what *narrative structure*
is. What sorts of difference between one narrative and another ought to
be counted as difference of structure? For one thing, we can distinguish
between *plot* and *story*: the plot is the sequence of events considered in
the order in which they occurred; the story is the same sequence considered in the order in which they are narrated. To put it crudely, these
two sentences have the same plot, but are different stories:

    1. John kissed his wife and took off his hat.
    2. John took off his hat, after kissing his wife.

But these two sentences have different plots:

    3. John kissed his wife and took off his hat.
    4. John took off his hat and kissed his wife.

A story is not merely a sequence of events, but a sequence that has

---

[9] Gertrude Stein: "Narration is what anybody has to say in any way about any-
thing that can happen, that has happened, or will happen in any way"; Thornton
Wilder has praised the "almost terrifying exactness" of her language (Gertrude Stein,
Narration, Chicago: U. of Chicago, 1935, Introduction, p. vi).

some continuity, because each stage grows out of previous stages and leads with naturalness to the future. But the continuity is not complete, or there would be no structure at all; within the flow of events we can distinguish episodes, and it is the similarities and differences among these episodes that constitute the narrative structure. For example, some episodes are scenes, with attention focused upon dialogue and detail of action, while others are summaries of events, years passing in a paragraph; the proportions in the mixture of these two types are one thing that distinguishes one novel from another in form: *The Forsyte Saga* from *A Farewell to Arms*. The actions of the work differ in the numbers of people involved; a short story may be essentially a story of relations between two people (Sherwood Anderson, "Sophistication") or of a family (Alphonse Daudet, "The Girl in Arles"). A work may differ from another in the number of episodes or sequences of episodes—story lines or "plots" and "sub-plots"—which parallel or contrast with each other, as the Polonius-Laertes-Ophelia family is set against Claudius-Gertrude-Hamlet. A narrative may have the complex, scattered movement of an Aldous Huxley novel or the direct repetitive motion of a shaggy-dog story.

Thus if we were to describe, for example, the narrative structure of "The Three Little Pigs," in a familiar version, we might say it consists of two linear sequences of episodes, most of them scenes-with-dialogue, plus a final episode. In Part I there are three events that parallel each other—the wolf goes to each of the houses—but develop in a certain direction: straw, twigs, bricks; the huffing and puffing gets harder each time and finally fails. In Part II the wolf changes his tactics from force to guile, and there is a reversal from trying to break in to trying to lure the third little pig out; again there are three parallel episodes—the turnips, the apple tree, and the churn—that develop in a certain direction, because each time the wolf is a little more discomfited. In episode 7, the finale, the wolf reverts again to force and tries to go down the chimney, to what end we all know. Considered in this abstract fashion, the plot seems almost to submit to diagramming, but we do not need to insist on that. To take into account other important features of narrative structure even in this simple story, we should have to note, for example, that there is a pattern of two initial successes—I am thinking of the version in which the wolf gets to eat two pigs—followed by deepening failure. There is a pattern of narrowing of the *dramatis personae* from four—not counting the mother pig—to two, with consequent concentration of the conflict. There is in Part I a spatial movement of the action from the other pigs' houses to the third pig's, and in Part II again a movement in the same direction from places outside the house to the house itself, and, in the last scene, to the very hearth.

A literary work as a whole, or a given part of it, cannot have both a logical and a narrative structure at the same time, for the movements are different. And it need not have either. But there is a third type of structure that it cannot help having, for if it moves at all it will vary in certain regional qualities of movement. These qualities, which involve the building and relaxation of tension, we describe in dramatistic terms, and so I shall call this third pattern of development the *dramatic structure* of the work.

Dramatic structure consists of variations in the on-goingness of the work, in its pace and momentum, and it may, I think, be fruitfully compared with what I have called the "kinetic pattern" of music. It is even possible to identify similar kinetic qualities. For example, some episodes or sections of a discourse may have an Introductory Quality: the setting-forth, the appearance of characters, the preliminary descriptive passage, the posing of a puzzle (the finding of the corpse), the arousing of mystery. The truncated newspaper paragraphs that appear in the "Most Fascinating News Story of the Week" section of *The New Yorker* are taken from "human interest" stories, not from straight news stories, whose opening paragraphs do not read like beginnings but like summaries. A short story generally has little room for introduction; it consists mostly of episodes with Exhibition Quality, and this is true also of many novels: the chase, the closing-in, the plot-thickening or complication, the voyage, the scenes of conflict. Where this quality is most intense, and the sense of momentous change most sharp, the scene becomes climactic, and the kinetic curve of a literary work may largely be mapped as developments to and from scenes of greater or less climax: the reversal, the confrontation, the revelation, the showdown, the death. Such scenes may pass rapidly into episodes that have the finality or winding-up character of a conclusion.

Thus "The Three Little Pigs" has a very brief introduction: the pigs are sent out into the world by their mother to seek their fortune, they beg for building materials and build their houses. This is rapidly summarized. Enter the wolf. The wolf's failure to blow down the third house makes the first climax; his threat from the roof, "I'm coming down to eat you," makes the second and greater one. The wolf's death gives finality to the action by resolving the strains introduced originally by his appearance, though of course it does not leave things the way they were originally.

A logical argument has a dramatic structure, or may have: where the premises—introduction—lead on to a conclusion that is in some way expected, or at least looked forward to, however surprising it may be. And of course it is almost impossible for a narrative to lack dramatic structure of some sort, though it may be loose, tedious, overhasty, or anticlimactic. But even a lyric, though it is neither logical nor narrative, often has a sequence of emotions or moods, a rise and fall of tension. The curve is usually simple; we identify the climax of Arnold's "Dover Beach" at the lines

> Ah, love, let us be true
> To one another!

and the climax of Dylan Thomas's "Poem in October" at the lines

> And the mystery
> Sang alive
> Still in the water and singingbirds.[10]

Here the heart turns over. In Shelley's "Ode to the West Wind" we follow the building up toward a climax, which ought to be the line

> I fall upon the thorns of life! I bleed!

—but when it comes it is not enough: the tone is wrong, the feeling is stated but not really *shown,* there is a break in the kinetic pattern.

Unity and Complexity

Classification of structures is one thing; the definition of literary types —the novel, the pastoral, the elegy, the tragedy—is another thing, which depends upon the first. We shall not stop to discuss its problems, but a third question calls for brief attention. We have used two important terms in talking about music and painting, "unity" and "complexity"; the question is whether these terms apply to literary works in the same sense.

That they apply in some sense to literary works can easily be shown. Consider the aspects of unity first.

We can judge completeness easily enough in simple cases. "The Three Little Pigs" without the final scene, where the wolf falls into the kettle, would trail off inconclusively; it would stop, but it would have no consummation or resolution. Some of Dreiser's novels, for example, *The Genius* and *The Financier,* have something of this quality: the action ceases, but you feel that scenes could have been added or dropped without very much difference to the whole; the characters have not reached anything that looks like a final stage of development; indeed, they hardly develop at all. Completeness in the literary work depends primarily upon kinetic qualities; the beginning must sound like a beginning, the end like a conclusion. And if the perceptual conditions of completeness in literature are analogous to—though of course not exactly the same as—the conditions in music and painting, then this affords some support to the immediate and naïve impression we have that the quality of completeness is the same.

Coherence, too, seems to be the same quality in literature as in music and visual design. "The Three Little Pigs" is a fairly coherent story, for the pattern of action is clear, the motivation simple and direct and unchanging, the characters consistent, the climax plain and adequate. It would be less coherent if we introduced at one point an uncle pig to offer avuncular advice, or a domestic scene between Mr. and Mrs. Wolf,

---

[10] From "Poem in October," *Collected Poems of Dylan Thomas.* Copyright 1952, 1953 by Dylan Thomas. Reprinted by permission of New Directions.

for these would interrupt the continuity of the narrative and perhaps set up unsatisfied expectations of further development in other directions. The plot of Dostoyevsky's *The Possessed* is somewhat incoherent—much more so, for example, than *Crime and Punishment* or *The Brothers Karamazov*.

What features tend to make a literary work hang together? We know a good many answers to this question, but there are undoubtedly other answers we do not know. Coherence can be intensified by a clear logical or narrative structure, a decisive dramatic structure with climax but not anticlimax, a single spatial and temporal point of view. *King Oedipus* is one of the most highly unified of all plays, for the action is continuous, the motivation clear, the scene unchanged, the main characters few; moreover, the hero and his antagonist are the same man, and the "discovery" and "reversal of fortune" are the same event. To some extent a discourse is unified merely by being all about the same thing; this is the unity of an encyclopedia article on Korea. More subtly, but importantly, the coherence may be increased by two factors we have not yet much discussed, but will take up in Chapter IX, §22, symbolic convergence and thematic unity, though the latter is perhaps more often a resultant than a condition.

But we also speak of one literary work as being more complex than another, and here we must surely know what we mean. "The Three Little Pigs" is a fairly simple story, but more complicated than "Little Red Riding Hood" or "The Gingerbread Man." *War and Peace* is more complex than *Anna Karenina*. In making such judgments we seem to have in mind both an extensional complexity—the number of characters and events, the range of human experience encompassed, the spatial and temporal scope of action—and an internal complexity—subtlety of discrimination, sharpness of detail, precision of meaning. Shakespeare's best sonnets are more complex than Shelley's, Wyatt's than Merrill Moore's; Faulkner's best novels more complex than Hemingway's. But these are relatively clear and easy judgments; it by no means follows that we can make a decisive comparison of any two poems or any two novels, for the difference may be so slight, or the kinds of elements so fundamentally dissimilar, that we feel uncertain about any judgment of complexity. We cannot expect, and fortunately we do not seem to require, a numerical measure of complexity for literature any more than for painting or music. But there is strong *prima facie* evidence, I think, not undermined by further reflection, that when we speak of the complexity of literary works we are using the term in the same sense as when we speak of the complexity of other species of aesthetic object.

§14

14-A THE DEFINITION OF "STYLE." (I) The best defense of the Semantical Definition of "style"—style is "the surface of meaning, the plane of most detailed organization"—is in W. K. Wimsatt, Jr., "Introduction: Style as Meaning," *The Prose Style of Samuel Johnson,* New Haven, Conn.: Yale U., 1941; in his use, "meaning" includes what I have called "general purport." Wimsatt's view is further developed in two technical essays: (1) "Verbal Style: Logical and Counterlogical," *PMLA,* LXV (1950): 5-20, reprinted in *The Verbal Icon,* Lexington, Ky.: U. of Kentucky, 1954, pp. 201-17; in this paper he clarifies and sharpens the distinction between the "substantial level" of meaning and style as "more like a shadow or echo or gesture." (2) "The Substantive Level," *Sewanee Review,* LIX (1951): 1-23 (*The Verbal Icon,* pp. 133-51); in this paper he tries to mark out a level of abstractness or generality of discourse that is taken to be a kind of norm ("bushes and trees") from which the abstractness of "growing things" and the concreteness of

> the reddish
> purplish, forked, upstanding, twiggy
> stuff of bushes and small trees

(Williams, "By the Road to the Contagious Hospital"[1]) are felt to be deviations. He points out the affinity of his concept of substantive level to that of representation in painting (see Chapter VI). I think it is a mistake to hold that the concept of substantive level is dependent on the theory of "real essences" that was denied by John Locke (essense is discussed in Chapter VIII, §21). See also "Rhetoric and Poems," *English Institute Essays, 1948,* New York: Columbia U., 1949 (*The Verbal Icon,* pp. 169-85).

A. C. Bradley's classic lecture on "Poetry for Poetry's Sake," *Oxford Lectures on Poetry,* New York: Macmillan, 1909, largely reprinted in Eliseo Vivas and Murray Krieger, eds., *Problems of Aesthetics,* New York: Rinehart, 1953, pp. 562-77, and in Melvin Rader, ed., *Modern Book of Esthetics,* rev. ed., New York: Holt, 1952, pp. 335-56, effectually attacked the supposed distinction between the "what" and the "how" of poetry. His argument was also applied to style: "in true poetry, it is . . . impossible . . . to change the words without changing the meaning" (Vivas and Krieger, *op. cit.,* p. 572). The misleading suggestion here that in bad poetry it *is* possible to separate style from meaning was corrected in a later "note" (p. 576). I. A. Richards, in "The Bridle of Pegasus," *Coleridge on Imagination,* London: Routledge and Kegan Paul, 1934, reprinted in Robert W. Stallman, ed., *Critiques and Essays in Criticism,* New York:

---

[1] From "By the Road to the Contagious Hospital" from *Spring and All* by William Carlos Williams. Copyright 1938, 1951 by William Carlos Williams. Reprinted by permission of New Directions.

Ronald, 1949, pp. 289-314, also examines, and rejects, the "what-how" terminology and its several variations; his argument supplements Bradley's in several ways. For a footnote to these writers, see Monroe C. Beardsley, "The Concept of Economy in Art," *JAAC*, XIV (March 1956): 370-75, and exchange with Martin Steinmann, *JAAC*, XV (September 1956): 124-25.

The Semantical Definition of "style" is supported, but hardly ever unwaveringly, by several other authors: J. Middleton Murry, *The Problem of Style,* New York: Milford, Oxford U., 1922, gives a useless definition (p. 71), but adds that "style is not an isolable quality of writing; it is writing itself" (p. 77), and his discussion (esp. chs. 1, 4, 5) is one of the better ones. See also two collections of essays on style: Lane Cooper, ed., *Theories of Style,* New York: Macmillan, 1907; W. T. Brewster, ed., *Representative Essays on the Theory of Style,* New York: Macmillan, 1905. Several of the writers conceive style, more or less clearly, in terms of meaning: Wackernagel (Cooper, p. 10): style is the "surface of linguistic expression"; Buffon (p. 171); Coleridge (p. 206); Schopenhauer (pp. 255-57): the "silhouette of thought"; Lewes (p. 320): "the living body of thought"; Pater (p. 399); Brunetière (p. 422); Newman (Brewster, pp. 9-12). R. L. Stevenson uses the term "texture" (p. 268) but appears to mean by it and by "style" the *sound* of a discourse. In keeping with his general formula that "intuition equals expression," Benedetto Croce, *Aesthetic,* trans. by Douglas Ainslie, 2d ed., New York: Macmillan, 1922, Part I, ch. 9, launches a general attack upon the "philosophical nullity" of all rhetorical categories; he has some penetrating things to say about style, but his denial of all distinctions is not warranted by the facts and is a non sequitur in his own theory.

The Semantical Definition might be tested by various examples. Consider the contrasts of active vs. passive ("John kissed Jane" and "Jane was kissed by John"), formal vs. colloquial ("One never knows" and "You never know"), comma vs. period ("He came, and I went" and "He came. I went"). Are all such differences in style analyzable into differences in meaning?

(II) Most elementary discussions of style, up to quite recent years, and some of the classic discussions, reveal, more or less distinctly, an "ornamental," or detachable, view of style. See Pope's *Essay on Criticism:* "What oft was thought, but ne'er so well expressed" (Part II, l. 298) and "Expression is the dress of thought" (Part II, l. 318). Aristotle's statement (*Rhetoric,* Book III, ch. 1; Cooper, *op. cit.,* p. 53), "it is not enough to know what to say but it is necessary also to know how to say it," appears to separate style from meaning; see also Voltaire (Cooper, *op. cit.,* p. 184) and De Quincey's distinction of "matter" from "manner" (p. 222; Brewster, *op. cit.,* p. 143); there is also a tendency in this direction in Spencer's analysis of good style in terms of "economy" (his *Philosophy of Style* is in both Cooper and Brewster). John Crowe Ransom, *The New Criticism,*

Norfolk, Conn.: New Directions, 1941, pp. 260-81, distinguishes between the "logical argument" of a poem and its "meaning-texture" or style (*cf. The World's Body*, New York: Scribner's, 1938, p. 348); he also uses the term "texture of sound." At that time he tended to think that these two aspects of meaning are in some way necessarily irrelevant to each other in poetry. This view was somewhat softened later; see "Inorganic Muses," *Kenyon Review*, V (1943): 228-54, 446-47, esp. 285 ff. For further remarks on diction, see Louis MacNeice, *Modern Poetry*, New York: Oxford U., 1938, ch. 8.

14-B GOOD STYLE AND BAD STYLE. The true test of a clear and applicable concept of style is the way you talk about *bad* style; for the temptation here is to treat style as something over and above the meaning and general purport. Wimsatt's remark, *Prose Style of Samuel Johnson*, p. 10, "Bad style is not a deviation of words from meaning, but a deviation of meaning from meaning" shows the correct way of talking, and he is almost the only writer who consistently avoids misleadingness. His occasional references to "intention" in this early work can be readily translated into objective terms. His other two important papers are primarily concerned with the judgment of good and bad style; in "Verbal Style," he shows how elegant variation of terms in a syllogism introduces a tension, or incoherence, between the detail of meaning and the general structure; he also gives the first systematic explanation (based partly upon H. W. Fowler, *A Dictionary of Modern English Usage*, Oxford: Clarendon, 1937) of several faults of style often condemned as intrinsically bad—for example, jingles like "he was real*ly* practical*ly* killed," as opposed to "it was done speedi*ly* and efficient*ly*," where the parallel endings reinforce a parallelism of sense. Another article, "When Is Variation 'Elegant'?" *College English*, III (1942): 368-83 (*The Verbal Icon*, 187-99) deals with one of these faults in very convincing detail. (See also Croce's remarks, reference in Note 14-A above.)

14-C IRONY. One important quality of style, not easy to define fully, is irony. There are clearly two major uses of the term, a structure-use and a texture-use, but it is hard to say exactly what they have in common. We apply the term to events, or sequences of events: it is ironic that the temperance society should be supported by funds derived from a brewery; it is ironic that a character in a play, aiming at a goal, does precisely that which, the audience knows, will ruin all his chances of achieving it: this is "dramatic irony." The ironic fact is one which in some way, if fully revealed, would reverse or restructure the whole field. We also apply the term to discourse. An ironic statement is one that suggests something incompatible with, or opposed to, what it states; but perhaps this requires extension. Pope's "When husbands, or when lapdogs, breathe their last" is ironic because the parallelism suggests an equality of value which is opposed to the relative evaluations implicit in the normal uses of these terms. Irony is thus not something distinct from meaning, but a species of meaning: to say "I will love you forever" ironically is to suggest that I know I am probably exaggerating, under the press of emotion, and, like most human things, even this violent love will probably not last, but I am only being human in feeling right now that it is eternal—or some part of this.

These notes may suggest lines for more thorough and systematic study.

14-D MIXED METAPHOR. Some special problems of style are presented by the so-called "mixed metaphor." The first question concerns the distinction between metaphors that are mixed and those that are not. Very often, "mixed" is defined normatively, so that mixed metaphors become bad by definition; but sometimes "mixed" is defined neutrally, so that a second question can then be asked: Are mixed metaphors necessarily bad style, and if so, why? For example, Daniel Webster's remarks on Hamilton (March 10, 1831; *Works*, Boston: Little, Brown, 1857, Vol. I, p. 200), "He smote the rock of the national resources, and abundant streams of revenue gushed forth. He touched the dead corpse of Public Credit, and it sprung upon its feet," probably should not be called a mixed metaphor, but rather a rapid shift from one metaphor to another. Again, the line "Throw hither all your quaint enamelled eyes," from Milton's "Lycidas," would—like the famous examples from *Hamlet* and *Macbeth*—be called a mixed metaphor by some, merely because on its literal level it describes a physically impossible action, but then—as in, "Cast your eye on this,"—all metaphors are mixed, for they involve impossibility at one level. There are certainly different degrees of rapidity in the shift from one kind of object, or one category of thing, to another; hence, degrees of heterogeneity and surprise, and degrees of obscurity and condensation of meaning. But it does not seem possible to draw a satisfactory line between the mixed and the unmixed ones; the question is really what they mean, if anything, and how much meaning, and relevant meaning, they contribute to the poem of which they are a part.

For discussions of mixed metaphor, see I. A. Richards, *Practical Criticism*, London: Routledge and Kegan Paul, 1929, Part III, ch. 2—but his tentative criterion (p. 196) for distinguishing good and bad metaphors amounts to little more than a tautology. Stephen J. Brown, *The World of Imagery*, London: Routledge and Kegan Paul, 1927, pp. 198-202, gives many examples that are instructive to analyze. Some even more grotesque examples, together with some attempt to define mixed metaphor in terms of the impossibility of visualizing the object or event—surely an unworkable criterion—are in John Press, *The Fire and the Fountain*, New York: Oxford U., 1955, ch. 5.

14-E PROSODY. Very useful is Karl Shapiro's annotated *Bibliography of Modern Prosody*, Baltimore: Johns Hopkins U., 1948. See also Lascelles Abercrombie, *Principles of English Prosody*, London: Secker, 1923; René Wellek and Austin Warren, *Theory of Literature*, New York: Harcourt, Brace, 1949, ch. 13. Albert R. Chandler, *Beauty and Human Nature*, New York: Appleton-Century, 1934, ch. 13, reviews a number of psychological investigations, and discusses them judiciously, except that the analyses in musical notation, pp. 266-71, should not be called "scansions." Compare Robert M. Ogden, *The Psychology of Art*, New York: Scribner, 1938, ch. 6; I. A. Richards, *Practical Criticism*, London: Routledge and Kegan Paul, 1929, Part III, ch. 4. John Hollander, "The Music of Poetry," *JAAC*, XV (December 1956): 232-44, stresses the importance of keeping "descriptive" distinct from prescriptive, or "performative," systems of prosodic analysis, and clarifies some of the comparisons between music and verse.

On the analysis of meter: Sidney Lanier's introduction of musical notation into the analysis of poetic meter in *The Science of English Verse*, New York: Scribner's, 1880, was based upon a conviction that poetic meter, which he calls "rhythm," is the same as musical pulse: "Time is the essential basis of rhythm" (p. 65), and accent, or stress, does not have a rhythmic function "until after rhythm is established" (p. 103); see chs. 2, 3 (esp. the argument on p. 65n). Raymond M. Alden, *English Verse*, New York: Holt, 1903, rejects Lanier's extreme view (pp. 391-409), but also holds a pulse-concept of poetic meter: "the accents appear at regular time intervals," though poets use "great freedom in departing from this regularity" (p. 11). Paul F. Baum, *The Principles of English Versification*, Cambridge, Mass.: Harvard U., 1922, regards time and stress as coordinate ingredients of meter (ch. 3), but his conception of the relation between them he does not make clear. The Lanier system is repudiated by Cary F. Jacob, *The Foundations and Nature of Verse*, New York: Columbia U., 1918. See also David W. Prall, *Aesthetic Analysis*, New York: Crowell, 1936, ch. 4. The contributions of linguistics to the analysis of meter are interestingly discussed in a symposium, "English Verse and What It Sounds Like," with papers by Harold Whitehall, Seymour Chatman, Arnold Stein, and John Crowe Ransom, *Kenyon Review*, XVIII (1956): 411-77.

On the definition of "verse": Paul F. Baum defines verse in terms of meter; free verse is "at its best, but a carefully rhythmed prose printed in a new shape" (*op. cit.*, p. 42; see also pp. 150-58). Yvor Winters has an interesting, but debatable, analysis and defense of free verse in "The Influence of Meter on Poetic Convention" (from *Primitivism and Decadence*), *In Defense of Reason*, New York: Swallow, 1947, pp. 103-50. Compare Robert Bridges on the rules of accentual verse, *Milton's Prosody*, rev. ed., Oxford: Oxford U., 1921, Part IV.

14-F THE RELATION OF SOUND TO MEANING IN POETRY. The discussion in Cleanth Brooks and Robert Penn Warren, *Understanding Poetry,* rev. ed., New York: Holt, 1950, ch. 3 is recommended. There are good examples in John Press, *op. cit.,* ch. 4; Paul F. Baum, *op. cit.,* ch. 5. Elizabeth Drew, *Discovering Poetry,* New York: Norton, 1933, pp. 93-144, cites Cowper's "Verses Supposed to Be Written by Alexander Selkirk" as an example of inappropriate meter (pp. 121-22). Wimsatt has explored the contributions of rhyme to the suggested meaning of poetry in "One Relation of Rhyme to Reason," *Modern Language Quarterly,* V (1944): 323-38 (*The Verbal Icon,* pp. 153-66). See also W. S. Johnson's article, "Some Functions of Poetic Form," *JAAC,* XIII (June 1955): 496-506; Paul Goodman, *The Structure of Literature,* Chicago: U. of Chicago, 1954, pp. 192-224, but his scansions are not all reliable; Laura Riding and Robert Graves, *A Survey of Modernist Poetry,* London: Heinemann, 1928, chs. 1, 2; Northrop Frye, *Anatomy of Criticism,* Princeton, N.J.: Princeton U., 1957, pp. 251-81; Lascelles Abercrombie, *The Theory of Poetry,* London: Secker, 1924, ch. 5; Louis MacNeice, *op. cit.,* ch. 7; Gilbert Murray, *The Classical Tradition in Poetry,* Cambridge: Harvard U., 1927, ch. 4; Kenneth Burke, "On Musicality in Verse," *The Philosophy of Literary Form,* Baton Rouge, La.: Louisiana State U., 1941, pp. 369-78; T. S. Eliot, "The Music of Poetry," *On Poetry and Poets,* New York: Farrar, Straus and Cudahy, 1957, pp. 17-33; Albert R. Chandler, *op. cit.,* ch. 14; Robert M. Ogden, *op. cit.,* ch. 5. Edmund Gurney, *The Power of Sound,* London: Smith, Elder, 1880, ch. 19, is good on sound in verse; see especially his skepticism about the pure "melody" of verbal sound, pp. 440-41. See Pope's well-known examples of simple presentational equivalence, *An Essay on Criticism,* Part II, ll. 337-57.

14-G TYPOGRAPHY AND POETRY. The relation of sound to meaning may be compared with the relation of the visual appearance of poetry to its meaning, which raises similar problems. For example, see George Herbert, "The Altar," "Easter Wings," etc.; Dylan Thomas's shaped poems in "Vision and Prayer"; E. E. Cummings' experiments with typography; Francis Quarles, "Sighes at the Contemporary Deaths . . ."; or, for a trivial example, Lewis Carroll's "Tale of a Mouse" from *Alice's Adventures in Wonderland.* Can these arrangements of type be regarded as presentational equivalents to the sense, and as cohering with it, or does the relation remain accidental and merely curious? What happens to a poem when it is printed in italics or small caps, in a large size, or in a special type face, such as Gothic, Caslon Old Face, or Garamond?

One feature of the interaction between the visual and semantical aspects of poetry is the pun that depends on being written: on "will" and "Will" in Shakespeare's Sonnets 135 and 136. These depend upon the poem's existing as written, not merely spoken, words.

14-H VISUAL AIDS IN LITERATURE. When a literary work is accompanied by pictures, what are the possible relations between work and picture? Can they cohere into a single experience? Do they work at cross-purposes to each other? Consider, for example, the illustrations in nineteenth century novels and children's books; the decorations in the *Book of Kels;* experiments in combining words and pictures: Archibald MacLeish, *Land of the Free;* William Blake, *Songs of Innocence* and *Songs of Experience;* Wright Morris, *The Home Place;* James Agee and Walker Evans, *Let Us Now Praise Famous Men.*

§15

15-A THE SPEAKER AND THE SITUATION. (I) The concept of the dramatic speaker—"persona," "mask"—is widely used in criticism, but seldom analyzed. For a brief discussion, see R. P. Parkin, "Alexander Pope's Use of the Implied Dramatic Speaker," *College English,* XI (December 1949): 137-41. Walker Gibson, "Authors, Speakers, Readers, Mock Readers," *ibid.,* XI (February 1950): 265-69, suggests distinguishing between the reader and the implicit or purported reader, whom he calls the "mock reader." See also Albert Hofstadter, "The Scientific and Literary Uses of Language," *Symbols and Society,* 14th Symposium of the Conference on Science, Philosophy, and Religion, New York: Harper, 1955, pp. 327-33; Susanne K. Langer, *Feeling and Form,* New York: Scribner, 1953, pp. 254, 292-301; E. M. Forster, "Anonymity: An Enquiry," *Two Cheers for Democracy,* London: Arnold, 1951, pp. 77-88.

The problem of deciding under what conditions the speaker may or may not be identified with the author (see also Chapter I, Note 1-G) is pointed up by borderline cases, i.e., semi-autobiographical works. For example, Christopher Isherwood assigns his own name to the narrator in *Lions and Shadows,* New York: New Directions, 1947, pp. 45, 60, though in "To the Reader" he says, "It is not, in the ordinary journalistic sense of the word, an autobiography," gives the other characters fictitious names, and advises the reader, "Read it as a novel."

Another question is raised by literary works in which there are two or more speakers, poem-dialogues like "Lord Randall," Housman's "Is My Team Ploughing," Auden's "Ballad" ("O what is that sound which so thrills the ear"), and narratives told by more than one person (Browning, *The Ring and the Book;* Faulkner, *As I Lay Dying*): are we to understand that another speaker is standing behind these voices, and quoting them?

(II) Susanne Langer, *op. cit.,* chs. 13, 14, gives a good, though I think partly misleading, description of the world projected by the literary work. She says the poet makes an "illusion, a pure appearance" (p. 211), "a piece of *virtual life*" (p. 212), or a "*virtual experience*" (p. 215). Note the limited sense she attaches to the term "discourse," according to which a poem is not a discourse (p. 252); it means "statement about actuality" (p. 253).

Charles Mauron, *The Nature of Beauty in Art and Literature,* London: L. and Virginia Woolf, 1927, pp. 61-88, describes the world of the literary work as consisting of "psychological volumes" or "psychological realities." See Eliseo Vivas, "The Object of the Poem," *Creation and Discovery,* New York: Noonday, 1955, pp. 129-43; "What Is a Poem?" *ibid.,* 73-92; Elder Olson, "An Outline of Poetic Theory," in Robert W. Stallman, ed., *Critiques and Essays in Criticism,* New York: Ronald, 1949, esp. pp. 277-78. On the difficulty of attending to, and describing, "the book itself," see Percy Lubbock, *The Craft of Fiction,* New York: Scribner, 1955, ch. 1; what does he mean by "the book itself"? See also Chapter I, Note 3-C.

15-B EMOTIONS IN AND OF THE WORK. Consider the various sadnesses of Hopkins' "Spring and Fall," referred to in Chapter II, §8. It is a question which of these things we might mean when we speak of a "sad poem" or a "sad story." T. S. Eliot's famous but confused remarks on the "objective correlative" bear upon this question; see "Hamlet and His Problems," *Selected Essays,* new ed., New York: Harcourt, Brace, 1950, pp. 121-26, reprinted in Robert W. Stallman, *op. cit.,* pp. 384-88, in R. B. West, Jr., ed., *Essays in Modern Literary Criticism,* New York: Rinehart, 1952, pp. 527-31, and in Mark Schorer, Josephine Miles and Gordon McKenzie, *Criticism,* New York: Harcourt, Brace, 1948, pp. 266-68. More important, see the excellent criticism by Eliseo Vivas, "The Objective Correlative of T. S. Eliot," *American Bookman,* I (Winter 1944): 7-18; reprinted in Stallman, *op. cit.,* pp. 389-400, and in Vivas, *Creation and Discovery,* pp. 175-89. Compare Yvor Winters, *In Defense of Reason,* New York: Swallow, 1947, pp. 469-74, 523-27; Paul Goodman, *The Structure of Literature,* New York: Noonday, 1954, pp. 3-6. See also Chapter I, Note 3-B.

15-C ELUCIDATION. Some problems in the methodology of elucidation are illustrated in Elmer E. Stoll's well-known paper on the character of Shylock, *Shakespeare Studies,* New York: Macmillan, 1927, ch. 6. Stoll's approach is avowedly intentionalistic (pp. 257, 332): "Apart from Shakespeare's opinion, what Shylock is there?" (p. 332). Indeed, he seems to think that the sole alternative to intentionalism is complete impressionism (p. 259). His argument mingles internal evidence, the data in the play itself, with external evidence from Elizabethan dramatic customs and literary history; but these are not two kinds of evidence for the same thing, for there are really two distinct questions: (1) What is the character of Shylock? (2) How did Elizabethan audiences probably feel about Shylock? Stoll's principle that character-elucidation is a matter of "emphasis" (p. 303) is important; it is questionable whether he adheres to it in his reading of the crucial and most problematic speech of Shylock, beginning, "Hath not a Jew eyes?" (pp. 324-29).

The famous Notes to A. C. Bradley's *Shakespearean Tragedy*, 2d ed., New York: Macmillan, 1905, provide other good examples of elucidation problems. See, for example, Note EE, *Macbeth*, pp. 486-92, on the problem of Macbeth's children. Note that the question whether "He" in Macduff's "He has no children" refers to Macbeth or Malcolm does not call for explication but for elucidation, since the question is what is going on in Macduff's mind. So also the problem of understanding the priest's parable of the Law in Kafka's *The Trial* is an elucidation problem, though a fantastic one.

There are some interesting comments on the Ernest Jones reading of Hamlet in Lionel Trilling, "Freud and Literature," *Kenyon Review*, II (1940): 152-73, and *The Liberal Imagination*, New York: Viking, 1950, pp. 34-57, and in Schorer, Miles and McKenzie, *op. cit.*, pp. 172-82.

An instructive problem of elucidation is presented by the ballad "The Three Ravens"; see Cleanth Brooks and Robert Penn Warren, *Understanding Poetry*, rev. ed., New York: Holt, 1950, pp. 44-47; Earl Daniels, *The Art of Reading Poetry*, New York: Farrar and Rinehart, 1941, pp. 133-37; *The Explicator*, IV (June 1946): 54; V (March 1947): 36. The problem is whether the "doe" who buries the knight is a real doe or a woman. Can this question be resolved by appeal to empirical generalizations plus a principle of internal congruence, or must we appeal to the ballad traditions, or must we simply choose the reading we enjoy more?

For further examples see George Arms and Joseph Kuntz, *Poetry Explication*, New York: Swallow, 1950.

15-D POINT OF VIEW. The importance of the narrator's point of view is stressed in Lubbock, *op. cit.*, of which important chapters are reprinted in J. W. Aldridge, ed., *Critiques and Essays on Modern Fiction*, New York: Ronald, 1952, pp. 9-30. See also E. M. Forster, *Aspects of the Novel*, New York: Harcourt, Brace, 1927, ch. 4, pp. 118-25; Susanne Langer, *op. cit.*, pp. 292-301. It would be worthwhile to re-examine the principles underlying the conventional classification of possible novelistic points of view, and to reconsider the question to what extent and in what way a shift in the point of view in a short story or novel tends to lessen its unity.

15-E TENSE. The role of tense in literature has been commented on by John Crowe Ransom, "The Tense of Poetry," *The World's Body*, New York: Scribner, 1938; Thornton Wilder, "Some Thoughts on Playwrighting," *The Intent of the Artist*, ed. by Augusto Centeno, Princeton: Princeton U., 1941, pp. 96 ff.; T. M. Greene, *The Arts and the Art of Criticism*, Princeton: Princeton U., 1940, ch. 9, sec. 6. Susanne Langer, *op. cit.*, chs. 15-17, has made most use of the concept of tense in distinguishing basic literary types. Of "poesis" in general the "primary illusion" is said to be the creation of "virtual history"; "literature proper" presents that history in the "mode of memory" (pp. 264, 266); drama presents a

"virtual future" in the "mode of Destiny" (p. 307). These distinctions are
worth careful examination. A logical analysis of the tenses of verbs is
given by Hans Reichenbach, *Elements of Symbolic Logic*, New York:
Macmillan, 1947, sec. 51.

The importance of tense in literature may be illustrated by such
examples as these: (a) When Arthur Miller printed, but not when he reprinted, his play, *The Crucible,* 1953, he appended a prose passage in
past tense giving more information about the historical prototypes of the
characters; this has the air of being entirely irrelevant to the play itself.
(b) There is a mixture of tense in many ballads—e.g., "Sir Patrick Spens"
and "The Lady of Shalott"—as Susanne Langer, *op. cit.,* pp. 269-73, has
pointed out; one question is whether these shifts in tense have an organic
connection with the rest of the poem or merely create a general weakening of the time sense.

15-F DEVELOPMENTAL STRUCTURES. Most of the problems about
structure in general are briefly reviewed by René Wellek and Austin
Warren, *Theory of Literature,* New York: Harcourt, Brace, 1949, ch. 16.
On story and plot, see E. M. Forster, *op. cit.,* chs. 2, 5; on narrative structures, ch. 8; also Edwin Muir, *The Structure of the Novel,* New York:
Harcourt, Brace, 1928, chs. 1, 2; on the pace of narrative, chs. 3, 4. Aristotle's *Poetics,* esp. chs. 7-12, 18, is still one of the good starting-points
for reflection on structure; some of his main terms, like "reversal," "complication," "unraveling," and "turning point," designate fundamental and
very general, if not absolutely universal, features of narrative. Paul Goodman, *The Structure of Literature,* Chicago: Chicago U., 1954, has presented a set of analytical categories, rather difficult to grasp but, at least
in his hands, very fruitful of discovery: see, for example, his excellent
account of developmental structures in verse, pp. 199-206.

On the nature of *suspense:* In his extremely interesting essay "On
Stories," in *Essays Presented to Charles Williams,* London: Oxford U.,
1947, C. S. Lewis remarks, "In the only sense that matters the surprise
works as well the twentieth time as the first. It is the *quality* of unex-
pectedness, not the *fact* that delights us" (p. 103).

Kenneth Burke has proposed a definition of "literary form" in terms
of what he calls the "psychology of the audience"; see *Counter-Statement,*
New York: Harcourt, Brace, 1931, pp. 38-56, 157-89, reprinted in Robert
W. Stallman, *op. cit.,* pp. 224-49; *The Philosophy of Literary Form,* Baton
Rouge, La.: Louisiana State U., 1941, esp. pp. 73-90. His analysis is closely
connected with his concept of "symbolic action" (see Chapter IX, Note
22-A). But notice that his contrast—in the first essay, "Psychology and
Form"—of the "psychology of form" with the "psychology of information,"
and his apt comparison of literary form with music's dealing "minutely in
frustrations and fulfillments of desire," show that he is talking about
phenomenally objective tendencies and tensions of the work itself, and

its action, or, in other words, dramatic structure. His account of "qualitative progression" in the second essay, "Lexicon Rhetoricae," comes close to a definition of dramatic structure. This term has been taken over by Yvor Winters, "The Experimental School in American Poetry," *In Defense of Reason*, pp. 30-74, reprinted in Schorer, Miles and McKenzie, *op. cit.*, pp. 288-309, and redefined as a kind of free association, though perhaps this is what Burke also means. In any case, it is a good name for a kind of progression in poetry where *A* is associated with *B*, *B* by a different association with *C*, but *A* has no structural connection with *C*—Alice's meditation while falling down the hole, or the conversations of Mrs. Nickleby, are examples. Winters' valuable essay develops and enlarges upon Burke's classification of literary structures.

The concept of dramatic structure may be illustrated by a partial analysis of the movement of Lincoln's Gettysburg Address. There is a movement from distant past (eighty-seven years ago), to recent past (the war), to this day, to the future; there is a movement in space from continent to nation, to the battleground on which we stand, to the nation, to the earth. The now and the here come together in the middle as a focus, and the transition following that point is also a psychological movement from an outward look to an inner resolve, a turn from consecrating to being consecrated ("it is for us the living"), which is the highest emotional point, or climax, of the whole.

Certain other problems of structural analysis, not taken up in the text, may be mentioned here: (a) How do we know which are the main characters of a novel? What are the implicit criteria of the hero? Shall we say that in some novels there is no hero? (b) What features of discourse are the perceptual conditions of the kinetic qualities of narrative movement? For example, suppose we selected a short passage, *A*, from the beginning of a story, and another short passage, *B*, from farther along; even apart from context, *A* might *read* like an Introduction, perhaps because it explains more about the characters, instead of assuming you already know them, or deals with events that usually open rather than close sequences of actions (going away from home vs. coming home; entering a room vs. leaving it; receiving a letter or a phone call, etc.). "Once upon a time . . ." is a beginning of something; ". . . they lived happily ever after" closes an account. (c) To what extent do qualities of movement depend upon established expectations of what is likely to happen, not in life but in novels or plays? This is analogous to the problem of musical expectations (see Chapter IV, Note 13-B); does the very structure of a play change if it is produced years later when different dramatic conventions are in force, and different norms of dramatic movement are in the spectator's mind?

15-G LITERARY TYPES OR GENRES. René Wellek and Austin Warren, *op. cit.*, ch. 17, review the main problems. See also Susanne Langer, *op.*

cit., ch. 16. Benedetto Croce, *Aesthetic,* trans. by Douglas Ainslie, 2d ed., New York: Macmillan, 1922, chs. 12, 15, has attacked the whole concept of literary types, and even the distinctions between one art and another; while his grounds do not seem adequate, his criticisms point up some difficulties in making the distinctions and some tendencies to misuse the categories. No doubt some critical theorists have seriously confused descriptive classifications with normative prescriptions, and some of the classificatory concepts tend to vanish into either useless refinement or vague generality. But Empson's working out of the concept of pastoral, *Some Versions of Pastoral,* London: Chatto and Windus, 1930, is an especially fruitful example of type-analysis.

There are many problems about the nature of type-concepts, and their method of formation. For example, can "satire" be defined nonintentionalistically, or identified as such without external evidence of some person or situation to which it is directed?

For references on analogies, formal and qualitative, between literature and the other arts, see Chapter IV, Notes 13-E and 13-F.

References on tragedy and comedy are given in Chapter IX, Notes 22-I and 22-J, because these concepts are not only structural but thematic.

Christopher Caudwell, *Illusion and Reality,* New York: Macmillan, 1937, chs. 10, 11, has some interesting ideas about the differences between poetry and the novel. See Northrop Frye, *Anatomy of Criticism,* Princeton, N.J.: Princeton U., 1957, pp. 203-14.

15-H UNITY AND COMPLEXITY IN LITERATURE. One good way to test the application of these terms to literary works is to see what would happen to the general character of a poem or story if a certain part were taken out or something else were added. There may possibly be a close reciprocal connection, at least in many works, between coherence and completeness: if the absence of a certain verse in a poem would not make the poem less complete, then does the presence of that verse necessarily make the poem less coherent? The same question can be raised about characters and episodes in fiction.

Paul Goodman's treatment of unity, *op. cit.,* pp. 12-18, chs. 2, 4, 6, is worth careful study; note the light he throws on the conditions of unity in lyric poetry by his comparison of Baudelaire's "La Géante" with the English translation by George Dillon (pp. 199-206). See also W. K. Wimsatt, Jr., "The Structure of the Concrete Universal in Literature," *PMLA,* LXII (1947): 262-80 (*The Verbal Icon,* pp. 69-83), and Schorer, Miles and McKenzie, *op. cit.,* pp. 393-403, esp. secs. 4-5.

Allen Tate has some good remarks about unity in poetry, though he uses a confusing terminology; see "Tension in Poetry," *Kenyon Review,* V (1943): 228-54; reprinted in Stallman, *op. cit.,* pp. 55-65; and West, *op. cit.,* 267-78. C. Day Lewis, *The Poetic Image,* New York: Oxford U., 1947, ch. 5, has an instructive comparison of Hopkins' "Harry Ploughman" and his "Felix Randall," pointing out how much more unified the latter is than the former. See also Lascelles Abercrombie, *The Theory of Poetry*, London: Secker, 1924, Part II, ch. 2; John Sparrow, *Sense and Poetry*, London: Constable, 1934, chs. 2, 3.

On unity in narrative, especially the drama, see Gilbert Murray, *The Classical Tradition in Poetry*, Cambridge, Mass.: Harvard U., 1927, ch. 6. On unity in the novel, see C. H. Rickword, "A Note on Fiction," in W. V. O'Connor, ed., *Forms of Modern Fiction*, Minneapolis, Minn.: U. of Minnesota, 1948, pp. 294-305; Edwin Muir, *op. cit.*, ch. 5; Percy Lubbock, *op. cit.*, chs. 2-4; E. K. Brown, *Rhythm in the Novel*, Toronto: U. of Toronto, 1950.

The concepts of unity and complexity are also used in the analysis of fictional character. (a) Critics make a distinction between "consistent" and "inconsistent" characters; presumably the consistent ones are the more unified, and contribute to the over-all unity of the work. How is consistency to be analyzed? It may be in part conformity to probabilities of behavior, given certain prior behavior, in view of known psychological laws, but this is far too simple. Some perfectly consistent fictional characters, like the Karamazov brothers, behave in no common way; and since we form our idea of a character from his behavior, perhaps we can always form some idea, however complex, to account for any behavior, however erratic. On the other hand, if Jean Valjean were suddenly to be cruel to children, we could say that this action was out of character and would blur or trouble our image of him. This problem needs study. (b) Critics make a distinction between "flat" and "round" characters (see Forster, *op. cit.*, pp. 103-18, and Wimsatt, "Concrete Universal"); presumably the round characters are more complex than the flat ones are, but how is this to be analyzed? Complexity in character may be in part having a greater number of characteristics from which probable actions can be deduced—not merely trivial idiosyncrasies and peculiarities of appearance—but it is a nice question whether you can count characteristics of people, and in any case this is too simple. Perhaps genuine roundness involves unity, or integration at some level, as well as complexity.

·VI·

REPRESENTATION
IN THE
VISUAL ARTS

To most of us a painting is a "picture." The first thing we are likely to notice about a visual design is that it shows the latest model Chevrolet, a plaid shirt, a bottle of whiskey, or a pretty girl. In fact, it takes a certain effort to think of a design *as* a design—as a bounded collection of lines, shapes, and colors—even though it is the lines, shapes, and colors that do the picturing. We see through them, so to speak. But a picture is two things at once: it is a design, and it is a picture *of* something. In other words, it presents something to the eye for direct inspection, and it represents something that exists, or might exist, outside the picture frame.

It is this second aspect of the design that we are after when we ask questions like: What does it portray? What is it about? What does it mean? Or, elliptically, what *is* it? Often, of course, these questions do not arise, for we can see the answer at once. But when we first see Paul Klee's *Man on a Tight Rope*, FRONTISPIECE, we might be puzzled: what is going on in this picture, and how are we to take it? And works of very different sorts may present similar problems. What is the irony in the title of Käthe Kollwitz's *Municipal Lodging*, PLATE III? What is the man doing in Rouault's lithograph, PLATE V? What is the significance of the empty charger on the floor in Dürer's *Last Supper*, PLATE VI? And, most mysterious of all, who or what is the Colossus in Goya's aquatint, PLATE VII?

To answer questions like these is to *interpret* the design. And a large part of interpretation consists in saying what the design represents, or to put it in what we shall count as synonymous terms, saying what its subject is.

It is this dual aspect of visual design that confronts us with our next array of puzzles. What is the connection between what is represented and what is presented? Which of these, if either, is more important? Painters themselves differ rather deeply on these questions, and critics quite as much. Meanwhile the ordinary citizen who wants to know what he can expect of visual art, what to look for and be content with, is confounded worst of all. And this is a pity. For in pining after what he cannot have, he may miss what is really of supreme worth.

The notorious twentieth-century example of misunderstanding of art was the public reaction to the New York Armory show of 1913, which first brought various modern movements to the United States. The most upsetting picture there was Marcel Duchamp's *Nude Descending a Staircase* (1912, Arensberg Collection, Philadelphia Museum of Art), which had a kind of descending movement of overlapping cubist forms: it was called "a hurricane in a shingle factory," "a collection of saddlebags," and other impolite things. We should not say that its detractors failed to grasp what the painter *intended;* they failed to see what he had *done,* because they approached it with mistaken assumptions and expectations.

But one need not go back that far; every year brings a new *cause célèbre* involving violent differences of opinion over "modern" art. The word itself has taken on such negative connotations in many quarters that the Boston Institute in 1948 changed "Modern" in its name to "Contemporary." Early in 1955 the Budget Committee of the Nebraska state legislature burst into protests at a mural painting by Kenneth Evett that had been installed in the rotunda of the capitol at Lincoln a few months before. It is a strong, simple design with four figures, representing a craftsman, a cattleman, complete with large bull, a miner, and a builder.

"That square bull gets me," said a state senator. "The figures appear to have been drawn with a T-square." Two years earlier, one of the many reasons advanced against the murals by Anton Refregier in the lobby of the Rincon Annex Post Office in San Francisco, which were attacked by veterans' organizations and which the House of Representatives in Washington voted should be removed, was "Our ancestors did not have rectangular heads."

What should be our judgment of such reasons as these? First of all, are they relevant to the question whether a mural is good or bad art, or is its goodness or badness quite independent of its distortions of bull and man? If they are relevant, in what way are they relevant—is it, in other words, a conclusive objection to these murals that they involve a misrepresentation of nature, or is it just one of the factors to be taken into account in judging them? Of course, the ordinary citizen does not need to care what a final judgment would be; but he is interested to know whether he should go to see them or give them a wide berth, whether he ought to try to understand them even if they repel him by their strangeness, and especially whether his taxpayer's money ought to be spent on them. Here is a place, surely, where a careful and thorough consideration of an aesthetic problem cannot but be of practical value.

§**16.**   *REPRESENTATION AND ABSTRACTION*

Our first step is to become as clear as we can about what we mean by the term "representation," or, equivalently, what we mean by the "subject" of a visual design. Representation is a relation between a design and something else. In the formula

X represents *Y*,

X is the visual design itself—the painting, etching, photograph—and *Y* is the subject represented. Now we know what kind of thing *X* is—it could be a statue or a building, but we shall confine our attention here to two-dimensional designs. What kind of thing is *Y*?

Consider Rubens' painting, *The Judgment of Paris* (1635-1637, National Gallery, London), of which the central female figure is modeled upon Rubens' second wife, Helen Fourment. We can say a number of things about the subject, or subjects, of this painting. For example:

1. The painting represents three women and two men.
2. The painting represents three Greek goddesses, a god, and a shepherd.
3. The painting represents Helen Fourment.
4. The painting represents Minerva, Juno, Venus, Mercury, and Paris.
5. The painting represents a shepherd offering an apple to one of the three goddesses.
6. The painting represents the judgment of Paris, that is, Paris choosing the most beautiful of the three goddesses.

The question is: how many different senses of the word "represent" do we have here? Not that we should try to spin out as many as ingenuity can devise, but if there are distinctions that are important, we don't want to miss them.

We are not interested in distinctions for their own sake, but only as they are relevant to our main problem of seeing what would be a good reason for accepting any statement about representation. We shall discover what distinctions we need by asking of each statement in our list: how do we know that it is true? If it turns out that two of the statements are confirmed in the same way, then we can put those statements in the same class.

Anyone who has seen women and men can recognize that the shapes and colors of certain complex areas in the painting are similar to the shapes and colors of actual men and women, and if he is acquainted with samples of a number of other biological species, he can infer that those figures in the painting are probably more like human beings than they are like any other objects in the world. It is not necessary for him to be acquainted with any particular person in the world, but only with some members of this class. In this first use of the term "represent," then, what is represented is always some—indeterminate and unspecified—member of a class of material objects, including people. We say the painting is a picture of *a* horse, *a* baby, *a* cross, *an* eye. And this has nothing to do with the intention of the painter: in exactly the same sense, the Great Stone Face represents a man, just as can frost on the window pane or dried and twisted roots.

For convenience, let us introduce the term "depict" for this sort of representation, and it will be worthwhile to state the definition rather carefully, in order to make sure that it is clear and acceptable:

> "The design X depicts an object Y" means "X contains some area that is more similar to the visual appearance of Y's than to objects of any other class."

How will this work out?

We must consider some of the consequences of accepting this definition, and decide whether we are prepared to accept those consequences and adhere to them. Of course, as far as we can, we want to bring out what fine-arts critics mean when *they* talk about representation and subjects, and one of the things I want to claim is that quite often they are talking about depiction. But it will not be surprising to find that sometimes they are talking about something else, which they don't always clearly distinguish because they use the same word for both. Therefore we must be prepared to introduce some new terms and some refinements in usage. For what is most important to us is to decide what *we* shall mean when we discuss these problems here.

In order for us to recognize what a visual design depicts, we must of course have the relevant experience. We might look at a photograph and say, "What in the world is that?" and the answer might be, "A gnu," or, "A phalarope"; the point is that if we were to see such creatures and compare them with the design, we could recognize that the creature and the design have a number of characteristics in common. But of course, even before we recognize that the design depicts a gnu, we may recognize that it depicts a four-footed animal, rather than a bird. Thus, to take another example and look at it from the other direction, suppose we draw a circle outline on a blank white page. Now, we don't say it depicts a

circle; it *is* a circle. That is its shape-name. And it has this shape-character
in common with a number of different sorts of objects in the world: plates,
moons, suns, bubbles, oranges, peaches, apples, artificial satellites. But
it is no *more* like a moon than it is like a plate, and so it cannot really be
said, by our definition, to depict any of these things. If it is modeled, and
the background altered, so that it becomes three-dimensional in appearance, if colors and a stem are added, it will have enough qualities in
common with apples to distinguish it from peaches, plums, and oranges.
We shall then say that it depicts an apple, though perhaps not yet a
Baldwin or a Winesap. It takes several characteristics to distinguish
apples from all other fruit, but an object with a distinctive shape, like a
dumbbell or a human profile, can be represented by a single line.

One important sense of "represent," then, seems to be "depict." But
I think some fine-arts critics would feel that the definition of "depict" is
in one respect a little too broad to capture the required sense of "represent" exactly; they would prefer to strengthen the definition by adding
a further condition. But to do this, we must make a rather tricky, and
perhaps in the end not very satisfactory, distinction.

We may approach the problem first by considering the way we often
use the word "subject." It is natural to say of a painting that its subject
is flowers, clouds, or horses: but we would probably not say that its subject is cubes, cones, or solids. In other words, we would say that a painting represents flowers, clouds, or horses, but perhaps not that it represents
cubes, cones, or solids. "It is a picture of a house" is usual; "It is a picture
of a material object" is not usual. It seems that we are tacitly laying some
further restriction on the classes of things that may be said to be represented—on the *Y*'s in "*X* represents *Y*." But how is this restriction to be
made explicit?

Suppose we were to list a number of classes in order of decreasing
abstractness: cylinder, gray cylinder, slender gray cylinder, hollow gray
cylinder, gray metal cylinder, steel pipe. We can certainly say that a painting represents a steel pipe, and if we cannot correctly say that it represents a cylinder, where and how in this series can we draw a line? There
is one method we might try. Certain classes of things figure in our experience in ways that relate to practical ends and needs, or would if they
could be invented or discovered: knives, knees, houses, horses, clouds,
pipes, and prunes. Let us call these *vital classes*. Other classes are ad-
ventitious, or merely conceptual; they are logically just as good, but they
do not have the same significance: torus, sphere, small red triangle, large
smooth rubber polka-dotted cone. Let us call these *formal classes*. Then,
if we wish, we may revise our definition of "depict":

> "The design *X* depicts an object *Y*" means "The class of *Y*'s is a vital class,
> and *X* contains some area that is more similar to the visual appearance of
> *Y*'s than to objects of any other vital class."

When those who hold the theory that we shall call the Divergence Theory in the following section say that to appreciate a painting we need bring with us nothing from life, and can ignore what it represents, they apparently are using the word "represent" in this sense.

I am not sure that this distinction can be maintained; the line is certainly not very clear. But I shall tentatively assume its validity, adopt the new definition, and accept its consequences—for example, that not every painting of solids in deep space is representational. The difficulties appear when we apply the distinction to paintings like those of Yves Tanguy— see, for example, *Indefinite Divisibility* (1942, Albright Art Gallery, Buffalo). This is a good borderline case. If something is depicted here, it is not anything that we have ever encountered, or are fortunately ever likely to encounter, on land or sea. There are rodlike things, bowl-with-liquid-like things; you can't tell whether some of them are organic or inorganic, though they are evidently material objects. This painting raises a number of interesting questions about matters shortly to be considered, but as far as the present point is concerned, I think we can say that it is in part, though just barely, representational: there is a landscape, there are smooth rocks or pebbles. But there are other areas in it that represent nothing.

The definition of "depict" is formulated, I hope, in such a way that objects can be said to be depicted even though such objects have never in fact existed. When we say that a painting is a picture of an Amazon, a griffin, a chimera, or a city of the future, we mean that *if* such objects did exist, the areas on the design would be more like them than like other objects, and therefore if anyone were acquainted with those objects he would recognize the likeness. Nonexistence does not prevent the class of chimeras from being a vital class, either; for this concept is very concrete and full, and we can imagine some of the ways in which such creatures, if they turned up, could affect our lives and present special problems, even if we are not sure exactly how to cope with them.

Thus we have clarified the first two statements about the Rubens painting, and found that "represents" has the same meaning in both. What makes Statement 1 true is that anyone who can see human beings can recognize the likeness of the figures to them. What makes Statement 2 true is that, from all accounts, anyone who met Greek goddesses and shepherds would be able to tell from their general appearance, including their dress, that this picture is like them, or at least more like them than like Egyptian goddesses and shepherds. Statement 2 is more specific than Statement 1, but it is tested in a similar way. In both cases, if two people disagreed about what is depicted, the disagreement could, at least in principle, be settled, and without consulting the depicter.

The letter *Y* stands for things of a different sort, however, in statements like 3 and 4. Here "represent" is followed, not by "a" or "an," but by "the" or by a proper name. We say a visual design represents Joey at

the age of two months, Napoleon, Mt. Sainte Victoire, the Prince of
Monaco—or it represents the Empire State Building, the Three Graces,
David and Goliath. Each of these subjects is a particular object, or a particular group of objects, either named or referred to by a unique description. Broadening slightly a term already in use, we may call this sort of
representation *portrayal*.

The difference between depiction and portrayal can be brought out
by a comparison. Consider two self-portraits by Rembrandt—you have
about sixty paintings to choose from, more than twenty etchings, and
about ten drawings—say, the one in the Frick Collection, New York (1658)
and the one in the Mellon Collection in the National Gallery of Art,
Washington (1659). The author of an excellent work on Rembrandt discusses both of these paintings. Of the first one, he says, "Here is represented an impulsive, volcanic personality, controlled under a calm exterior," and of the second one he says, "Rembrandt has represented himself
here as most vulnerable."[1] Notice that in one case it is a "personality"
that is represented (compare Statement 1 above) and in the other Rembrandt "himself" (compare Statement 3).

For many contexts, there is no danger in this double way of speaking,
but it can cause unnecessary puzzlement. For suppose we ask whether
those two paintings have the same subject. This could lead to a merely
verbal dispute. If we call Rembrandt the subject, then both paintings
have the same subject. Let us say that they portray the same person. If
we describe the subject of one painting as "a volcanic person" and of the
other as "a vulnerable person," then they have different subjects. They
depict different persons.

Two Kinds of Portrayal

The statement that these paintings portray Rembrandt is much like
the statement that Rubens' painting portrays Helen Fourment. That is to
say, we would verify these statements in the same way. But the verification of a portrayal-statement is more complicated than the verification of
a depiction-statement. For, suppose we tried to define "portray" in this
way:

> "The design X portrays the object Y" means "X contains some area
> that is more similar to the visual appearance of Y than to any other
> object."

That is, we might try defining portrayal as we did depiction, except that
the subject of a portrayal is a class with only one member (Rembrandt)
instead of a general class (old man). And perhaps this definition will
sometimes serve. At least it calls our attention to an important point: to
determine whether the painting does or does not portray Rembrandt, it

---

[1] Jacob Rosenberg, *Rembrandt,* Cambridge, Mass.: Harvard U., 1948, p. 30.

would be sensible, if it were feasible, to compare him with it; or, if he is not available, to search other sources for descriptions of his appearance that we can test the portrait by.

This would be fine, except that there is a possibility that forces us to amend the definition just proposed. For when a painter is interested in something more than accurate portrayal, his self-portrait—or his portrait of any other sitter—is not going to be a very exact likeness. Hence it is theoretically possible that the portrait more closely resembles someone else than it does its ostensible subject. And suppose a man turned up to-day who looked more like one of Rembrandt's self-portraits than Rembrandt did: should we then say, as we are compelled by our tentative definition to say, that the painting now does *not* portray Rembrandt, but the other man? This would make it possible, in short, for the portrayal-subject (though not the depiction-subject) of a painting to change merely because new people happen to get born—an odd consequence.

We probably do not want to say this, and if we do not we must stipulate in our definition of "portray" that whether or not X portrays Y does not depend solely upon their similarity, but upon some further external condition that connects X and Y. And this calls for a couple of distinctions.

When a picture is painted in the presence of a model, and the picture is to some extent similar to that model, the model is called a "sitter." Let us broaden this term in two ways. First, let us say that a person is the sitter even if the painter never saw him, but copied from another painting or a photograph—so long as the series of copies can be traced back to the original. Second, let us apply the term to other objects than human ones, even though it seems peculiar to speak of Mt. Sainte Victoire, for example, as a sitter. I shall mean by "sitter" the object that serves as the original model for the painting.

Now, whether or not a particular painting, of a man or a mountain, *has* a sitter cannot be determined merely from the painting itself. Nor can it be conclusively determined merely by finding in the world a man or a mountain that is the spitting image of the painting; we further require that there be some evidence that the painter saw that man or that mountain or a picture of it. If the similarity is striking, and if we have no conclusive evidence that the painter could *not* have seen the object —because he died too soon, or could never have been to the necessary spot—then we say, with reason, that the object probably was the sitter. If on the other hand we can prove, from records left by the painter or his friends, that the man or the mountain actually posed for the painter, and that the painting is a result of that posing, we will call the painting a portrait of that man or that mountain, even if the actual resemblance is fairly slight. We cannot see the features of Rembrandt's sleeping girl, PLATE II, very clearly, but probably Hendrickje was its sitter.

These considerations so far are entirely independent of another important factor: the title. It seems to me that if a painting has no title, and we want to answer the question what it portrays, we search for evidence that there was a sitter, and if we can find such evidence, we will call that sitter the subject. If we cannot find such evidence, we cannot tell what it portrays, or we may guess that it portrays no particular man or mountain at all, but merely depicts one. But if the painting is called a "self-portrait," we will call it a portrait of the painter, so long as it depicts a human being. And if it is entitled *Mrs. Siddons as the Tragic Muse* or *Napoleon on Elba*, we will again call it a portrait, provided the depiction is not utterly incongruous. Of course if a painting depicts a cow and is entitled *Derby Winner, 1936*, we might well be baffled and wonder how this title got misplaced; but that is not very usual.

But sometimes titles are missing, and then we inquire after the probable title of the picture, i.e., what the artist did entitle it. This is not exactly an appeal to the painter's intention, though it perhaps comes close to it; the question is not what the painter intended to portray, but what he called his picture. There are some classic problems of this sort. The painting by Rembrandt that was given the name *The Jewish Bride* in the nineteenth century (ca. 1668, Rijksmuseum, Amsterdam) shows a pair in Biblical costume—that is its depiction-subject—but does it portray Ruth and Boaz, or Isaac and Rebekah, or two of Rembrandt's contemporaries, Miguel de Barrios and his second wife? Evidently the way to answer this question would be to get evidence of its original title, if it had one. And in fact an indubitable reference to this painting in an early sale catalogue—that is, a reference by title, together with a full description—would satisfy the art historian. Another painting by Rembrandt, *Samson Threatening His Father-in-law* (1635? the Walter P. Chrysler, Jr., Collection, New York, contains one of the two existing copies) was previously known as *Adolphus of Geldern Threatening His Old Father in Prison*. Again, we can be sure that representational accuracy was not the decisive reason for this change: there is no way of determining whether the man in the painting looks more like Samson or Adolphus, and we may suppose that the clothing is neutral. What the art historian wants to know, if possible, is what Rembrandt called it, or acquiesced in its being called by his contemporaries.[2]

Statements 3 and 4 about the Rubens painting are therefore both portrayal-statements, but there is a difference between them, and it concerns the sort of evidence that we can expect to get for each. Since Helen Fourment was an actual person, we might find out how she looked; we know that the figure in this painting resembles her. We may be able to prove that she posed for it, as we know she posed for other paintings. And quite apart from the title, we will say that it portrays her. But at the

---

[2] An excellent example of the portrayal problem is given by Panofsky, in *Meaning in the Visual Arts*, pp. 36-38 (see Note 12-A); it is clear in this case too, I think, that the question at issue is what the (unknown) artist probably called the painting. It is not a question of intention, except in so far as the intention is embodied in a verbal stipulation.

same time, and without contradiction, we will say it portrays Venus. But we say this not because Venus could have posed, or because we know what she looked like; we say it because of the title and the fact that what the painting depicts, including the accompanying Cupid, is not incompatible with its portraying Venus. Perhaps the title is not indispensable, for if an untitled frieze depicting three goddesses and a shepherd were dug up in an ancient Roman ruin, we might guess whom it portrays. But our inference is that the frieze probably was regarded—not merely by the sculptor—as portraying them because it is so similar to other friezes we already know to have been so regarded.

Many paintings are pictures of persons who never actually existed, or may not have existed—mythological characters, characters in novels, folk-heroes who may or may not have had a real basis: Moses, Hamlet, Tom Sawyer, Paul Bunyan. In such cases it would be absurd to say that there is a resemblance between the picture and the person, or that if the person should exist we would see that the picture is more like him than anyone else. Of course, we know some things about Venus, but there could be a great many different portraits of her, no one of which could in principle be proved more accurate than any other. And indeed many people today would prefer to think of Venus as somewhat slenderer than Helen Fourment.

The portrayal of a nonexistent person or one whose appearance is now unknown is a more tenuous and arbitrary matter than the portrayal of an existing and known person. There is an analogy, however. In the one case we connect the picture with an original model; in the other, with a concept of some kind already in existence before the picture was painted —that is, a fiction, a myth, a tradition present in the minds of people. A portrayal of a fictitious character cannot stand on its own feet, however; it requires to be baptized. There has to be some verbal indication to connect it with its object. Thus to acknowledge that the Rubens painting portrays Venus, we must know that such a person was conceived of before the painting was painted, and that a story was told of her that the painting also tells, and we must observe that there is nothing in the painting that is inconsistent with what was thought about her, but more than that we must have evidence that Rubens or someone else named the figure in the picture Venus.

We apply the same criterion to cases where the person portrayed, though real, lived so far back in time, and left so little information, that we do not expect any further evidence of his appearance. This at least seems to have been the principle of the publishers of that famous medieval history, *The Nuremberg Chronicle,* for they economized on wood blocks by letting 645 different ones become 1809 different pictures, portraits, and maps. Thus, for example, they "represented" 198 popes by 28 different cuts, and 224 kings and emperors by 54 different cuts, and 69 cities by 22 different cuts. If all that was known of the appearance of King

Alphonse I and King Alphonse II is that they were both men with black beards, it seemed reasonable to use the same cut depicting a man with a black beard to portray both kings.

And perhaps the same general considerations will excuse one of Veronese's devices for getting out of trouble with the Holy Office. When he painted a *Last Supper* for the refectory of the Dominicans at SS. Giovanni and Paolo in Venice, it contained a large dog, "buffoons, drunkards, Germans, dwarfs, and similar indecencies," as the Holy Office said, and they asked him to change the painting. Instead, he changed the title to *Banquet in the House of Levi,* and I suppose that, in the absence of any further information about the décor and fauna in the vicinity of the Last Supper *or* Levi's banquet, we must admit that Veronese changed the portrayal-subject, though of course not the depiction-subject, when he changed the name. Not that he got away with it completely; he had to remove the head of a Negro from beside Jesus' head; the religious authorities refused to accept his plea that a dark patch was needed there.

However, where the object portrayed is someone living, or a historical personage about whom we know a good deal—in other words, where there actually is, or might be forthcoming, independent evidence of the appearance of the object—we require that there be a fair degree of similarity between painting and object to call it a portrait. It is not possible to say *how* similar it must be, and no doubt people draw the line at different places. The doting mother may have a low threshold for saying, "That's not my Susie *at all*," to the photographer who departs too far from verisimilitude, while anyone lucky enough to be the subject of a portrait by Modigliani or Rouault or Picasso will put up with a good deal of deviation from nature—even if the artist should give him two heads. As long as certain significant features are there, we use the term "portraiture" with very wide latitude in modern painting.

It seems, then, that when we say that a picture portrays Helen Fourment, rather than Suzanne Valadon or Saskia or Gabrielle, this is very different from saying that it portrays Venus, rather than Freya or Scarlett O'Hara or Queen Nefretiti. The painting cannot portray both Helen and Gabrielle, or both Venus and Freya, but it can portray both Helen and Venus. Thus the term "portray" must have two meanings, since Helen and Venus are not the same person. Let us then adopt the following pair of definitions to replace the definition previously offered:

> "The design X *physically portrays* the object Y" means "X is fairly similar to the appearance of Y, and Y was the sitter for X."

> "The design X *nominally portrays* the object Y" means "X has no notable characteristics incompatible with those attributed to Y, and there is a verbal stipulation, either in the form of a title, an oral remark, or an accompanying text, that X is to be called a portrait of Y."

Max Beckmann's woodcut, PLATE IV, physically portrays himself. The figures in Dürer's woodcut, PLATE VI, nominally portray Jesus and eleven disciples.

This may seem excessively precise and cautious, but some of these distinctions have never been adequately cleared up, and consequently there arise unnecessary puzzles about representation-statements. To verify that a painting is a physical portrayal of someone (Statement 3), you need evidence that you don't need to verify that it is a nominal portrayal (Statement 4); and to verify that it is a nominal portrayal you need evidence that you don't need to verify that it is a depiction (Statements 1 and 2).

The distinction between portraying and depicting will help to clarify a somewhat misleading, though familiar, way of speaking. Sometimes critics speak of the artist's "treatment of the subject." Since ordinarily they do not mean his treatment of the sitter—though some sitters have been treated badly—they can only mean his depiction of what is portrayed. But it is not possible within a single painting to distinguish, within what is depicted, between that which is the "subject" and that which is the "treatment"; it is all one or it is all the other. Given two different depictions of the same portrayal-subject, we can compare them, of course, to decide in what respects their depiction-subjects are similar and in what respects different. But it leads only into confusion to describe the difference as a difference in "treatment."

The Elucidation of the Subject

Statements 5 and 6 about the Rubens painting introduce a new aspect. The point about phrases like "a shepherd offering an apple," or "Paris choosing"—or "The Last Supper," "The Raising of the Cross," "The Rape of the Sabine Women"—is that they stand not simply for objects, like "apple" and "woman," but for events. However, the distinction between depiction and portrayal applies to events just as to objects: *a* supper is depicted, *the* Last Supper is portrayed; *a* shepherd offering *an* apple (Statement 5) is depicted, *Paris* offering *the* apple (Statement 6) is nominally portrayed. Plainly we shall want to add to our definitions of "depict" and "portray" that in each case the Y factor may be an event as well as an object, that is, an object in motion, as well as an object *in situ*.

It is easy to effect this amendment—consider it done—but there is still a problem. How can the subject of a painting be not merely such-and-such people in such-and-such positions, but people doing things—the disciples recoiling from Jesus' remark that one of them will betray him, or Jesus walking on the waves? How can a motionless design represent a motion?

Evidently we take the static pose as the cross section of an action by reading it as having causal antecedents and consequents: the baseball near the window *has* been hit by a bat, it *will* break the window. The problem here, it seems to me, is exactly the same as the problem of elucidating a literary work, which we discussed in Chapter V, §15, and we are therefore justified in using the same term here. A design can tell a story because we can elucidate it, that is, fill out the pattern of events to which the relations among its depicted objects belong. We see an advertisement of a man in an open topcoat standing at the ticket window in a small-town railway station. The advertisement tells us that he is "appropriately" garbed in Dacron, but it doesn't need to tell us what he is up to. On the floor beside the pot-bellied stove is a suitcase with a gift-wrapped package on it; he has another package under his arm, and there is a holly wreath in the window. Obviously he is on his way home for Christmas vacation. Let us call this set of motives and actions the *dramatic subject* of the picture.

To know what is going on in a picture is part of understanding it, in the full sense, and may be of the greatest importance. Consider the Dürer woodcut, PLATE VI. It obviously depicts the Last Supper, but what is interesting about it is the exact moment of the Last Supper that it depicts—in this respect it may be unique in the history of art. It is not the moment when Jesus announces that he is to be betrayed, but the moment when he is about to give his "new commandment" of love. In the words of Erwin Panofsky,

> Judas, then, has left the room, and only the faithful Eleven remain, with the sacramental symbol of their union shining from the table. . . . It is the giving of this "New Commandment" which forms the principal content of Dürer's woodcut and after which it should be named. For a human tragedy and the establishment of a sacred ritual it substitutes the institution of the Evangelical community.[3]

In the elucidation of painting, as in the elucidation of literature, we depend on our knowledge of causal laws about human behavior and physical processes. Of course there may be ambiguity, as in Benjamin Franklin's joke about the sun that was either rising or falling. We may not know whether a man is coming or going. In Hieronymus Bosch's satirical painting, *The Ship of Fools* (ca. 1500, Louvre, Paris) there is a woman waving a jug, who may be hitting a man over the head or demanding a drink from the other jug that he is cooling in the water. There is no telling. Rouault's lithograph, PLATE V, is an interesting example. It has sometimes been called *The Beggar*, and of course it could depict a man begging. But the title Rouault gave it, a phrase from his friend André Suarès, is: "In so many different ways, the noble vocation of sowing in a hostile land" (*En tant d'ordres divers, le beau métier d'ensemencer une terre hostile*). We must decide what the lithograph depicts by analyzing it in the light of both hypotheses. The hand with the palm up, for example, fits in with begging, but its angle fits in better with scattering grain; the humility of the pose would go with either, but there certainly

---

[3] *Albrecht Dürer*, Princeton, N.J.: Princeton U., 1948, I. 223.

is a hostile land. In short, this depiction is not ambiguous, though it does require some elucidation.

As this example shows, the limits of testability for picture-elucidation are generally even more stringent than for literature-elucidation, since unless the work portrays a known historical event it cannot supply enough details to enable us to carry the elucidation very far backward or forward in time. There is an enormous amount that we *cannot* say about the man with the Christmas packages—where he came from, and where he is going. Of course the Rouault does not even raise such questions. But a great deal of nonsense has been written, for example, about some of the mysterious paintings of Giorgione, especially *The Tempest*, also called *Soldier and Gypsy* (ca. 1500, Academy Gallery, Venice), and the *Concert Champêtre*, also called *Pastorale* (ca. 1505, Louvre, Paris). The deep and tangible atmosphere of these paintings, with their overwhelming air that something extraordinary or momentous is about to happen, tempts us strongly to regard the scenes as cross sections of a drama. Some fine imaginings have been spun out, and though it is not clear that this is a wrong thing to do, it *is* clear that the paintings do not in any sense represent these stories.

Nonrepresentational Designs

We can now clarify another distinction that plays a considerable role in contemporary criticism of the fine arts. Notice, first, that in order to portray something, a painting must depict something. It can depict without portraying, if it is just a picture of a mountain, but not of any particular mountain. But it cannot portray without depicting, for unless it is a picture of *a* mountain, it cannot be a picture of Mt. Sainte Victoire. But there are also visual designs that do not depict anything, and *a fortiori* do not portray anything; and these nondepicting designs form a special class.

Designs that do not depict are called by many names: "abstract" (and also "concrete," by Kandinsky), "absolute," "pure," "nonobjective," "nonfigurative," (and also "realistic," by Gabo and Arp), "presentational," and "nonrepresentational." Of all these the last seems to me the least likely to be misleading.[4] The question now is, then, whether we can divide visual designs into two groups, representational designs and nonrepresentational designs, where a representational design is one that depicts something, whether or not it portrays anything.

At first glance, this distinction seems not only easy but inescapable. This page of print is a design, but it certainly represents nothing, in the

---

[4] For comments on these terms, see Frances B. Blanshard, *Retreat from Likeness in the Theory of Painting*, 2d ed., New York: Columbia U., 1949, ch. 6, esp. pp. 117-22; but Mrs. Blanshard objects to the term "nonrepresentational" and prefers not to use it.

strict sense—the word-marks have meaning, but the word "cow" doesn't represent cows as a picture of a cow does. A section of cracked sidewalk, or a pattern of plowed and unplowed fields seen from an airplane, is a nonrepresentational design—and many of the things we see in galleries of modern and contemporary art are of the same sort.

There is no doubt of the difference; but there is some doubt about how sharp the distinction can be made, and how useful it is. The second doubt we shall put off to the following section; the usefulness of the distinction, to put it succinctly, comes from the fact that certain problems arise with representational art that do not arise at all with nonrepresentational art. The first doubt, however, we must face now. Not that we need be unhappy if the distinction should prove somewhat vague; that is only to be expected of most of our distinctions in this field, and it does not render them worthless.

Part of the trouble with the distinction comes from a deliberate and systematic misuse of the term "representation" on the part of some contemporary writers on aesthetics. We must especially not confound representation with sheer quality. Thus green is a cool color; but we ought not to say, I think, that green "represents coolness." This is not representation; it is plain description. A zig-zag line is jagged; it only confuses things to say that it "represents jaggedness." Coolness and jaggedness are qualities, not objects or events, and there is much to be gained in intelligibility of communication if we restrict the term "representation" so that only objects and events are represented.

Representation should also be kept distinct from the evocation of feelings by the design. I have read that one of the Italian Futurists, Boccioni, pursuing the Futurist goal of "the simultaneous presentation of states of soul at a given moment," painted a picture of an absinthe addict getting intoxicated. And the picture itself is said to be intoxicating: the restaurant and the lady reel, and the spectator himself sometimes feels as though he had had a drop too many. Now this account is partly about the qualities of the painting, and about the objects represented, and partly about the effect of the painting upon the beholder; and the statement that the painting "represents" a "state of soul" can perhaps be regarded as elliptical for the statement that it represents a person undergoing a certain experience. The famous fur-lined teacup by Meret Oppenheim can produce horribly queasy sensations, but it does not represent those sensations.

There is another source of confusion that is responsible for the idea that "in some sense" *all* art is representational, as is occasionally said. The words in our language whose primary function is to classify shapes are few, and most of them are for the simple shapes studied in geometry: circle, square, triangle, rhombus, ellipse, parallelogram, etc. They fall far short of the endless variety of shapes in nature and in the fine arts. But this is not ordinarily a serious handicap for us, because we can always convert an object-name into a shape-name by adding a suffix: thus "leaf-shaped" (or "white-oak-leaf-shaped"), "spider-shaped," "snaky," "wavy" are coined for certain purposes.

Now, consider the following simple figures:

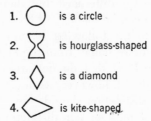

1. ⃝ is a circle

2. ⋈ is hourglass-shaped

3. ◇ is a diamond

4. ⬠ is kite-shaped

When we come to 2 and 4, we simply run out of familiar and available names, so we introduce new ones by borrowing. Statements 2 and 4 are not about representation. The hourglass-shape does not necessarily represent an hourglass; it simply has a similar shape. Nor, of course, do you have to think of an hourglass in order to see the shape of 2. You have to think of an hourglass in order to think of that way of naming the shape; but a person who never heard of hourglasses can see it just as well. If we tried to describe some squiggly figure, for example,

we would find a few common words for parts of it: there is a loop, there are sharp turns. But certain peculiarities of it would elude us, and we would find ourselves trying to think of objects with similar shapes—mushrooms, cushions, or whatnot—to find a description. However, thinking of these other things would not be forced upon us by the design, but by the task of describing it.[5]

---

[5] In his acute paper, "Perception, Meaning, and the Subject-Matter of Art" (see reference in Note 12-C), Arnold Isenberg has shown that the use of shape-names for parts of designs does not commit one to a reference to something outside the work.

And yet doubts may linger. For even though by our definition the squiggly figure is not a representational design, there is a sense in which many critics would want to say it "borders on it," or is "in a broad sense representational." It is not quite representation if a cloud is "very like a whale," or an ink blot can look like a witch or an angel to two different people. Those odd little designs, invented by Roger Price, that are called "droodles" are in the same category: you can't guess what they are, but when the similarity is pointed out to you—man watching TV, or soldier with dog passing a wall, or Mexican sombrero seen from above—you see that it does look like it in some way, though it looks like other things as well. Again, shapes like those in Hans Arp's designs—for example, *Mountain, Table, Anchors, Navel* (1925, Museum of Modern Art)—are like droodles. There are anchor shapes, all right, but not strictly representation of anchors; the "navel" in fact looks more like a doughnut.

If it seems clearer to us not to classify these cases under representation, how shall we classify them? For in many nonrepresentational designs—perhaps not much in the Arp, which is very elementary—there is a connection between the shapes and things in the outside world, and this connection can play a part in the effect of the design. That is, in some cases a full apprehension of the qualities of the design may require that we recognize this connection between, say, a wave shape and the ocean, or a snaky line and snakes, not merely for the sake of naming the shapes, which we seldom have occasion to do, but for enjoying the design as a whole. If the wave shape does not represent a wave, what *is* the connection between them?

According to one view, the connection is association. The wavy line is said to be associated with waves, and the blue color with the sky; to grasp all that there is in a painting, we must associate waves with the line and the sky with an expanse of blue. Now, the basis of this association would presumably be some notable similarity, in shape or color, between the area in the design and the appearance of natural objects. Whether or not the association, as a psychological fact, occurs, will depend on the individual, but whether or not, so to speak, it ought to occur, whether there are grounds for its occurrence, depends on the design itself and on nature. Thus it might be better to use another term, "suggestion." The Jensen *Composition*, PLATE I, is nonrepresentational, but it suggests beams of searchlights cutting across the night sky. The heavy black line, in the shape of a reversed *C*, that starts just under the girl's forearm in Rembrandt's *Girl Sleeping*, PLATE II, suggests the arm of a chair or couch. A design suggests a natural object if it has some notable and quite distinctive characteristic—shape or color—in common with that object, but does not have enough in common with that object to represent it.

"Notable" and "quite distinctive" are very vague here. We would all agree that the guitarlike lines in a Picasso painting do suggest a guitar, though they do not quite represent one. But despite its vagueness, we have to come down rather hard on this phrase, or the definition will be so broad as to be unmanageable. An oval can suggest a watermelon, an eggplant, a head, a circus tent, or the orbit of a planet; but shall we say that in a particular painting it suggests all of these? If to appreciate the painting we have to think of all classes of things with definitely oval or ovoid shapes, we must admit defeat, and, besides, the task of thinking them up can become tedious. Clearly another principle must enter in here somewhere: a Principle of *Suggestion-Congruence*. It is analogous to the Principle of Congruence in literary explication (Chapter III, §10).

Suppose we are trying to decide which of its potential suggestions the oval, or the wavy line, or the blue patch, has in a particular painting. It will depend on the extent to which we can interpret them as suggesting a group of objects that go together or have some natural connection in the world. If there is nothing about the oval that prevents it from being a pond, or the wavy line water, or the blue patch sky, we can fit them together into a generalized suggestion of outdoors, and the critic will very likely say that the design "evokes the world of nature," or "has an out-of-doors feeling, with subtle hints of natural scenes." If, on the other hand, there is nothing about the oval that prevents it from being a cam, or about the wavy line that prevents it from being corrugated iron, or about the blue patch that prevents it from being material for overalls, why then we shall fit them together into a general machine-shop milieu. It is conceivable that both interpretations could be carried through; in which case neither is more nearly correct than the other, for the suggestion is ambiguous.

A good deal of suggestion in visual design we read correctly and readily because it occurs along with definite representation. By itself, the line in the Rembrandt drawing would not suggest a couch or chair, or if it did it would suggest a number of other things equally strongly; but the girl's position limits the relevant suggestions. Here again we are using the Principle of Congruence. Similarly, the house and the road or path in Rouault's lithograph, PLATE V, and the village in Goya's *Colossus*, PLATE VII, are fixed by context: houses and roads go together, and so do villages and plains.

We must keep in mind that in saying these things about paintings we are just about on the borderline of testability; the line between really seeing what is suggested and simply indulging in free association is not well marked, and it is easily passed over in ignorance, carelessness, or conceit. Perhaps it can be made a little more definite, but not without effort, and I suppose any very heroic measures would be out of proportion to the amount of reform they are likely to achieve. So it will have to be enough here to set up these few signposts and let it be known that there *is* a border somewhere in the vicinity.

Thus it is going too far to say of a perfectly nonrepresentational painting, "It conveys a sense of man facing destiny in a somewhat incalculable world"; it is hard to know what could suggest this much. But to say, "The sulphurous greenish-blue shapes convey the sensation of a plane flying into the night," or, "The painting hints at some desolate spot that might be swarmed over any moment by sinister and evil forms"— these make some sense, and can legitimately be taken as reports of suggestion in the work itself.

Now, if there is such a thing as suggestion, in this sense, we should probably make a further distinction between two kinds of nonrepresentational art. In the first kind, there are areas that suggest, however vaguely, such things as insects, female bodies, trees, machinery, and rocks, though without representing them, and the suggestions of different areas cohere to some degree. Such art is sometimes called "abstract expressionism," but both of these words are best avoided here; I shall call it "suggestive nonrepresentational art."

On the other hand, there are nonsuggestive nonrepresentational designs; or, at least, there would appear to be. They are the designs that are mostly limited to straight lines, a few primary colors, and quite regular and simple shapes without depth—those that are frequently called "geometrical": tiles, laces and rugs; designs that alternate black and white squares or hexagons, or interweave various kinds of spirals and ovals. I suppose one could say that a square on the bathroom floor suggests a box, a cabin, or a barn, but this would be an odd and unnecessary way of speaking. If you cannot connect these suggestions with suggestions from other shapes in the pattern, it would be more like reading something into the design than seeing what is there. But designs, however simple, that combine obvious leaf shapes with floral motifs may be said to be suggestive.

Abstraction and Distortion

Nonsuggestive designs are sometimes called "decorative designs," especially if they are unified by their texture rather than by their structure. They are also sometimes called "abstract designs," though this is only one of the many uses of this versatile word. On the whole, it seems best not to use the term "abstract" in this way, for something abstract is, at least in its root, something that has been abstracted. It makes more sense to speak of a suggestive design as abstract, for when we see the bottle shape, for example, and see that it suggests a bottle, we can add that it has probably been abstracted from a bottle, just as the color blue might have been abstracted from the sky. But there isn't really any need for another term for "suggestive"; in fact the needless duplication of terms is the bane of this field. Moreover, there is another idea that we need a word for, and "abstract" is by all odds the best candidate: for some purposes we want to be able to speak of a representational design as *more or less abstract*.

Note that this way of using the term does not distinguish abstract from nonabstract designs; the abstractness is a matter of degree. Suppose we have two representations (depictions) of apples. In order to be representations, they must each have a number of characteristics in common with apples—one will not be enough in this case. But one of the designs may have more characteristics in common with apples than the other; in other words, it may be more like an apple. For example, suppose they both have a rough apple-shape, with stems, and are slightly modeled, but one is red and the other hueless; then the red one has more in common with apples than the hueless one. And in an appropriate and useful sense, the hueless one is more *abstract*.

Thus Cézanne's peaches are more abstract than Chardin's; Matisse's bathers are more abstract than Renoir's, and Renoir's than Boucher's or Bouguereau's. The face of Rembrandt's *Girl Sleeping*, PLATE II, is more abstract than the face of Rouault's sower, PLATE V, the latter more abstract than Beckmann's *Self-Portrait*, PLATE IV, and this in turn more abstract than the faces of the disciples in Dürer's *Last Supper*, PLATE VI. "Abstract" is the converse of "realistic," in one of its senses: to say that A is a more abstract representation than B is the same as to say that B is more realistic than A. So-called *"trompe l'oeil"* art—for example, the paintings of Aaron Bohrod—is least abstract of all. We can say, if we wish, that all suggestive designs are more abstract than representational ones, but the term "abstract" has a primary use for comparing one representation with another. The chief difficulty is that it may unfortunately suggest angularity or linearity. It is true that by our definition, given two maps of the borders of the United States, the one that leaves out some of the little inlets and straightens out the lines is more abstract than the other. But abstractness also applies to colors. Suppose two painters are painting pictures of an object with many varying color tones. Both painters will have to limit the variety of tones they produce and leave out some, but the picture that has a greater reduction in the number of distinct tones is the more abstract in color—compare Cézanne's Mt. Sainte Victoire with Renoir's, or a Manet with a Vermeer.

Along with the term "abstraction," the term "distortion" can also easily be accommodated to our terminology. A distortion, in this context, is a *mis*representation, but you cannot misrepresent something unless you represent it (an ellipse is not a distorted circle). Consider once more the two depictions of apples. They both have a sufficient number of characteristics in common with apples to be recognizably representational. Yet one may report the shape of the apple as cucumber-like, or it may give to the apple a pinkish color that apples never have: these are dis-

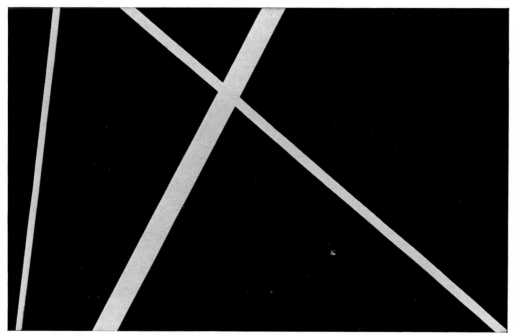

JOHN JENSEN / *Composition*

PLATE I

British Museum, London

REMBRANDT VAN RIJN / *Girl Sleeping*

PLATE II

Solomon E. Asch. Swarthmore, Pa.

KÄTHE KOLLWITZ / *Municipal Lodging*

PLATE III

Museum of Modern Art, New York

MAX BECKMANN / *Self-Portrait*

PLATE IV

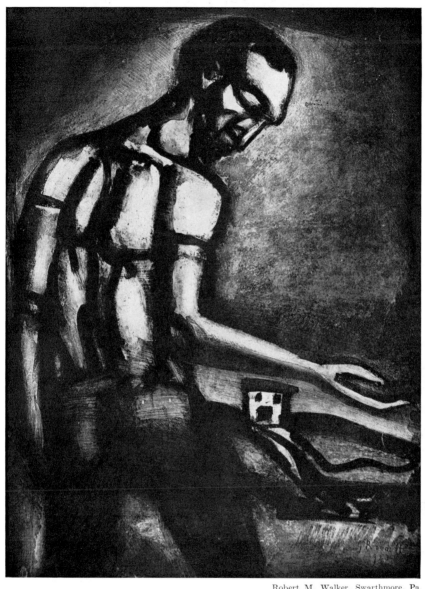

GEORGES ROUAULT / *Miserere et Guerre*, Plate 22

PLATE V

ALBRECHT DÜRER / *The Last Supper*

PLATE VI

Kupferstichkabinett, formerly Staatliche Museen, Berlin

FRANCISCO GOYA / *The Colossus*

PLATE VII

HONORÉ DAUMIER / *The Witnesses*

PLATE VIII

tortions. The deviations from nature in Byzantine saints, Botticellian
ladies and Van Gogh's cypresses, El Greco's and Modigliani's elongated
hands and faces, the proportions of figures in Mannerist paintings—for
example, Parmigianino's *Madonna with the Long Neck* (Pitti, Florence)—
and, in the extreme case, the drooping watches of Dali are distortions.
The normal proportions of legs to torso are distorted in opposite directions in Käthe Kollwitz's *Municipal Lodging*, PLATE III, and Daumier's
Witnesses, PLATE VIII. The one distortion serves to emphasize the protectiveness and suffering of the mother; the other, the gauntness and an-
griness of the headless skeleton.

Note that we have here hit upon a second sense of "realistic," for if
we ask whether Dali's watches are realistic, there are two possible answers: if it means "nondistorted," the answer is No, for they are not
"real" in the sense of showing what exists in the world; but if it means
"nonabstract," the answer is Yes, for the watches are carefully modeled.
Both of these senses of "realistic" are, by the way, different from the sense
in which painters like Courbet are said to be "realists" because they depict low life or the activities of the common man—or the sense in which
Caravaggio was realistic when he painted St. Matthew with dirty feet.

There are special sorts of abstraction and distortion that are sometimes discussed in connection with portraits and depictions of human
beings. It is said, for example, that some persons as depicted have less
individuality than others. The persons in Byzantine mosaics and in some
Gothic painting tend to lack two types of individuality: their facial expressions do not reveal any particular attitudes, and their faces are not
depicted in sufficient detail so that they indicate particular character traits
—you would not be able to pick them out in a crowd. There are some
puzzles here, but part of what we mean is fairly clear. Individualization
is opposed to generalization, and generalization is one consequence of
abstraction: if we draw an apple with only those characteristics possessed
by all ripe red apples, then the class of objects it depicts is larger than
the class of Jonathans or Macintoshes. In this sense the picture is more
general, because it is more abstract.

When an individual is portrayed, the more characteristics he is
given, the richer and fuller his character becomes, as depicted, and the
more of an individual he is, as we would say. Not that we can describe
him in words: it is almost impossible to describe the expressions on some
of Rembrandt's faces—see, for example, *The Listening Christ* (1656, Philadelphia Museum of Art), or *Peter Betraying Christ* (1660, Rijksmuseum
Amsterdam).

It is also said that some painters "idealize" their subjects, whether for
good or ill. Idealization is clearly a type of distortion, but there may be
two notions involved here. We say the painter has idealized the sitter
when we have independent evidence that he has made the sitter appear
better in some way than the sitter really was, as Titian idealized Charles

V in his various portraits, by de-emphasizing the protruding lower jaw and giving him greater presence. This is portrayal-idealization. We also say the painter has idealized human beings, as Poussin sometimes did, or the classic and Renaissance sculptors, by making them appear better in some way than human beings ever do; this is depiction-idealization. It is another question how we would distinguish between noble idealization and the "sentimental" idealization often attributed to, say, Murillo. They are presumably different directions of distortion; but it may also be that the former is more abstract than the latter. In any case, I am afraid we have stumbled upon a *fourth* sense of the term "realistic": it sometimes means "nonidealized."

Symbolism

There is one more term that ought to come in for discussion in this section, though it is one we may well approach with reluctance. Few terms of criticism in any of the arts are less tractable than the term "symbol," but part of what requires interpretation in some works of visual art is their symbolic meaning. I am unable to offer a succinct and adequate definition of "symbol," but it is worth some effort to clarify it as far as may be done briefly.

I think that what we are after is a sense of "symbol" stricter and more useful than one of its familiar senses. In Renaissance painting, the emblems of the saints and of other Biblical persons, which serve to identify them, are often called "symbols": the dove that denotes the Holy Ghost, the four apocalyptic beasts of the Book of Revelation that denote the four gospels, Minerva's owl, St. Catherine's spiked wheel, and St. Lucy's eyes, often held forth on a plate. But though there is a kind of reference in these examples, it is a fairly limited one-to-one correspondence, not very different from having the saints wear lapel-cards with their names, like people at a convention. Of course the objects serve to remind us of their forms of martyrdom, but they are not much more than tokens. They are symbols, if you like, but not in the central and full sense.

For an example of symbolism nearer to the sense we are tracking down, we may consider the eye and pyramid on the Great Seal of the United States (see the back of a dollar bill). They are said to symbolize material strength and duration and the spiritual welfare that is above the material, as the eye is above the pyramid; and the thirteen olive leaves on the branch held in the right claw of the eagle and the thirteen arrows held in its left claw symbolize the nation's power in peace and in war. Or, it would sometimes be said that in a painting of, say, a man behind the barbed wire of a concentration camp there is symbolized the barbarity of totalitarianism or man's inhumanity to man.

One preliminary distinction will simplify matters. There can be

symbolism in a painting of a cross—or of a skull, a mirror, or a balance.
But when we say the painting is symbolic, this can be regarded as an elliptical statement, which is expanded to two: (1) the painting represents a cross, and (2) the cross symbolizes Christianity. In other words, it is objects (the bald eagle, the cross, the flag) or patterns (the red cross, the red star, the fleur-de-lis, the swastika) that symbolize something; a painting is symbolic when it represents or suggests such an object or contains such a pattern. This distinction is a help. For it may be hard enough to discover what we mean when we say, for example, that the Cup is a Christian symbol, but if we do know what we mean by that, then we will know what we mean when we say that Dürer's *Last Supper*, PLATE VI, is symbolic, for that just means it is a picture of, among other things, the Cup.

Though, for convenience, we shall confine our attention to symbolic objects, it perhaps ought to be noted that actions, too, can be symbolic. And not only the ritual actions of devotion—the bended knee, the elevation of the Host—but certain common actions, for example, sowing grain, as in the lithograph by Rouault, PLATE V. Whatever account we give of symbolic objects should be framed in such a way that it can be readily extended to symbolic acts.

If it is, then, an object or pattern or act that does the symbolizing, what is symbolized is always a set of properties or characteristics: faith, hope, charity, courage, wisdom, chastity, decay. A symbolic object can denote a particular thing, but denoting is not symbolizing. The Great Seal denotes the United States, but what it symbolizes are certain characteristics that the United States has or is thought to have or ought to have.

But what makes an object symbolic? How does it come to take on symbolic meaning? These questions have not been satisfactorily answered, but there are some things we can say with reasonable confidence, and they are important. Consider the bald eagle. Three things, at least, seem to be involved in making it a symbol. First, there is a natural similarity in some respects between the eagle and the nation and national qualities it stands for. The eagle is strong, fiercely independent, and has a certain magnificence of form and size; it is possible, at least, to hope that the nation itself has these qualities. Let us call these similarities, actual or believed, the *natural basis* of the symbolism. Second, the bald eagle did not acquire its symbolic function by chance; there had to be a *decision* at some point—namely in 1872—to let it stand for the United States. In other words, there was a kind of agreement or stipulation: let us call this the *conventional basis* of the symbolism. But third, the eagle might have languished on his eminence, or remained a mere token or indication of the nation. A check is a substitute for cash, and stands for the availability of that cash, but it is not a symbol of the cash in any but a pallid sense. In the full sense of the term, it took some *history* for the eagle to become a symbol: it had to be used on the Great Seal and dollar bills, to appear in connection with political gatherings, to acquire the capacity to evoke patriotic emotions, pride and joy. It entered into certain activities, and reproductions of it came to take on some measure of sanctity, so to speak, in themselves. Let us call this the *vital basis* of the symbolism.

Now, many symbols have all three bases, but the third, the *vital*, seems to be the essential or defining one. An object or pattern does not become a symbol in the full sense until it enters into human activities so that it is perceived not as a bare sign of something, but as having valuable qualities in itself, in virtue of its symbolic function. The flag, though a symbol, is protected by rules: it must not be thrown on the floor, and people who see their flag trampled underfoot feel as though the flag were insulted: some of their feelings about the nation have been transferred to the flag itself.

The general principle that I want to propose for consideration, though without supporting it by an adequate array of instances, is this: to acquire a vital basis and become symbolic, an object must have a conventional basis if the natural basis is slight or altogether lacking, but it may acquire a vital basis without a conventional basis if its natural basis is considerable and prominent. This principle I want to illustrate briefly.

The flag, as a symbol of the nation, has a little natural basis for its symbolism: it is not arbitrary that red connects with valor through the color of blood, white with purity and innocence, and blue with the overarching justice of the sky—not to mention the numerical correspondence of the stars and stripes to the states and colonies. The flag has also its conventional basis: it was deliberately chosen. And the vital basis is the sum of human activities that Americans have entered into, in which the flag has played a functional role: wars, parades, rallies, meetings, presidential inaugurations. The cross as a symbol of Christianity has a conventional basis, but little natural basis: there isn't a similarity between the shape of the cross and what it stands for. Its vital basis is the history of Christianity, and of Christian ritual, in which the cross is itself sacred and an object of veneration.

These are examples of symbols with little or no natural basis, but a conventional basis: the red star and the red cross would be other examples. But there is another class of symbols that have no conventional basis, and do not need one. These include various natural objects that have been an important part of the life of man, objects on whose behavior he has often been intent because of what it meant for his safety, security, and well-being: sun, moon, mountain, river, fire. It was not necessary for people to agree to let the sun be a symbol of life, when it shines on a cornfield, or of death, when it shines on a desert; its warmth is the warmth of life, its hotness is the hotness of a fevered death, and its importance for the life of man ensures that these cannot be overlooked.

In the symbolic patterns used by Indian tribes—the lizard pattern that means contentment, or the broken arrow that means peace—there is a conventional element, but it comes in at a different place. The designs are conventional; they are much simplified pictures of lizards or the sun or spiders, and it takes a kind of tacit agreement to let these be understood as indicating those objects—they are not quite representational, though they are suggestive. However, once it is agreed to let the pattern stand for the sun, what the *sun* symbolizes has a natural basis. And I want to say the same sort of thing for the barbed wire. The barbed wire does not stand for totalitarianism because anyone willed it to; there is a natural basis for the symbolism; a totalitarian state is *like* barbed wire in certain ways. And there is, of course, a considerable vital basis.

How, then, do we know what is symbolized in a painting? And where disagreements arise, in what way are they settled? These are the main questions we have been leading up to. As has been noted, it is too easy to reply that we must look for evidence of what the painter intended to symbolize. Even so brief an analysis of symbolism as we have conducted shows that what a painter can symbolize is not subject to his will: no matter what he says, he cannot paint a carrot and make it symbolize the Revolt of the Masses, or a corkscrew the innocence of childhood; and if he tells us that his painting of a black circle on a white background symbolizes the eternal vigilance of divine providence presiding over the aspiring spirit of man, we shall have to reply in a paraphrase of Alice's skeptical words to Humpty Dumpty.

I think what we do in interpreting the symbolism in a painting is first to see whether it contains any symbols with a primarily conventional basis, and second whether it contains any symbols with a primarily natural basis. The first is a study of iconology. To know what the cross or the barbed wire symbolizes, we study not the intention of the painter, but the history of Christianity and of modern governments. To know that in Titian's painting commonly called *Sacred and Profane Love*[6] (ca. 1510, Galleria Borghese, Rome) the nude woman is sacred, and the clothed one profane—instead of the other way about, as we might at first suppose— we have, of course, to consider that the painting was painted before the rise of Puritanism, and in the context of Neoplatonism. It is Neoplatonism that gives us the correct conventional basis of these symbols. The symbols have also a natural basis, of course, but without knowing the conventions, we would find the painting almost as obscure as Bellini's *Earthly Paradise* (ca. 1490?, Uffizi Gallery, Florence) or Rembrandt's etching, *The Phoenix* (1658, Hind 295).

---

[6] According to Panofsky, *Studies in Iconology*, New York: Oxford U., 1939, p. 152, which see on Neoplatonic symbolism, the correct title is *The Twin Venuses* and they are opposed as the eternal Form of Beauty and the force that creates the ephemeral beauties of this world.

It will always be more difficult to agree, and to be sure we know what we are doing, when we interpret those symbols that have no conventional basis, for there is no dictionary of them, no set of rules for decoding them. Here I think it is of considerable importance to separate two questions: How do we know that an object depicted by the painting is a symbol at all? And how do we know what it symbolizes?

The answer to the first question seems to be that we use, often without explicit formulation, a methodological principle of a rather special sort. If the objects in the painting belong together, in the sense that in the normal course of events we would expect to find them in the same vicinity, we are not forced to seek any symbolic significance in them. But if an object stands out in some way, in contrast to its setting, or is brought into focus by the design, then we are invited to dwell on it and treat it as a symbol. In Italian Renaissance paintings—for example, Bellini—you sometimes see the branches of trees lopped off, so that they appear bare. Barren trees are a natural symbol of death and unfruitfulness; they can also symbolize damnation, as perhaps does the tree in the *Netherlandish Proverbs* of Pieter Brueghel the Elder (1559, Kaiser Friedrich Museum, Berlin). But are the Bellini trees symbolic? It is ordinarily regarded as relevant to answering this question to point out that Italian peasants cut off the branches of trees as fodder for their livestock. In other words, there is nothing especially out of the way, or improbable, in their appearance in this landscape, so there is no call to interpret them symbolically.

Let us call this the *Principle of Prominence:* an object that is not already a recognized conventional symbol becomes a natural symbol in a painting only if its presence is in some way unusual or striking. Goya's *Colossus,* PLATE VII, is an excellent example. There he sits, enormous, on the edge of the world, towering over the plain; there is no explanation of his coming or going, he is just a giant out of place. We can hardly refrain from reading him as a powerful symbol. In Rouault's lithograph, PLATE V, the fading out of the background, the strange light, the absence of any coordinate indications of sowing (such as other sowers, or tractors, or tools), and the focus of the design on the hand—all these combine to give a symbolic bearing to the gesture.

The answer to the second question seems to be that we first consider the range of potential symbolic meaning of the objects as they have figured in the life of man. The moon is cool, changeable, remote; the act of sowing is fruitful, chancy, patient, hopeful, humble toward nature and God. But we then see which of these potential symbolic meanings can be fitted into a coherent whole with the other objects in the painting, including their potential meanings, if any. This is the *Principle of Symbol-Congruence.* For example, in the Rouault, there is nothing but the sower and the house and the road, and we can fit most of the potential meanings of sowing into the pattern. In the Goya there is a more subtle problem, for the symbolic significance of giants is far less clear and fixed.

There is something fearful and yet attracting about this creature who towers over the houses at his feet; he does not actually menace us, as he turns to fix us with a shadowed stare, but he is evidently a potential destructive force. He is like something lurking in our own unconscious, an embodied id. But his meaning has never been fully read, probably not even by Goya.

In the Goya we have reason to think there is symbolism, even if we cannot interpret it. But of course, as everywhere in our inquiries, we encounter borderline cases. For symbolism easily shades off into nothing, and where objects are barely suggested, or their symbolic potentialities loose and uncontrolled by the context, it will always be possible to supply, by free association, freewheeling symbolic meanings. But they will be largely subjective and private, and our time might better be occupied in other ways. Consider *Man on a Tight Rope*, FRONTISPIECE. Since this work captures so well in its very design some of the uneasy quality of the tightrope-walker's experience, and of ours as we watch him, it concentrates this quality for our attention. And we say, without serious risk, that it makes the tightrope-walker's act a sort of symbol—though lightly and delicately—of human daring or the risks of the human condition. But to say it symbolizes the particular uncertainties of modern life —or, as has been suggested to me, the predicament of one working his way through the problems of aesthetics—is probably going too far. There is a human being in the painting, at least by suggestion, but there is nothing to show that he is a modern man or an aesthetician—or the heroic rope dancer of Nietzsche's *Thus Spake Zarathustra*.

§17. *THE RELATION OF DESIGN TO SUBJECT*

We are now prepared to deal with one of the most puzzling questions about representational designs—a question posed at the beginning of this chapter: what is the connection between design and subject?

This question is usually formulated in normative terms: it is asked whether the subject is more, or less, important than the design, or whether, in order to be great, a painting must have a subject, as well as be a design; or sometimes whether, indeed, a mere design can be "art" at all, in the sense of that word that makes "art" equivalent to "good art." We are not yet ready for these questions. For hidden in them are certain non-normative questions that don't get answered unless they are brought into the open and examined by themselves. Sometimes critics say that in a particular painting the design and the subject are "appropriate" or "fitting" to each other; but other critics deny that it is possible for designs and subjects to be appropriate to each other. And this is the question for us to deal with now: is there such a thing as appropriateness? In other words, can there be a connection between design and subject that unifies them with each other, and if so, how is it to be analyzed?

Evidently this question rests on a very significant presupposition, which our earlier distinctions aimed to clarify. It does not make much sense to ask whether A is appropriate to B unless A and B can vary independently of each other within certain limits, and A is subject to our control. Thus it is sensible to ask whether a man's weight is appropriate to his height, since he can gain or lose weight voluntarily without changing his height. It does not, however, make sense to ask whether a man's weight is appropriate to his volume, or bulk, unless we can prescribe a method by which he can change his weight and keep his volume constant, or at least produce a large change in one with but a small change in the other. This distinction is not always kept in mind in aesthetic matters. To take an obviously silly example, but not a far-fetched one as they go: suppose someone remarked that the shape of a particular wavy line is appropriate to its quality of billowiness: "In this case, the artist has chosen the appropriate means for the realization of his end." It may be that the shape is the only shape that will have that billowiness, or billowiness to that degree, in which case the question of appropriateness doesn't arise.

The question does arise, however, in the relation of design to subject. Consider first the portrayal-subject. Two different paintings can, as we have seen, portray the same person or object, and yet they may be very different as designs—they may have different colors, different shapes, different dominant patterns, or different textures. Thus Tintoretto portrays the Last Supper differently from Leonardo, and Dürer portrayed it several times in as many different ways; Caravaggio portrays the Supper at Emmaus differently from Piazzetta, Delacroix, or Velásquez, and Rembrandt's engravings portray it differently from his paintings.

Now there is one question that we could ask about these paintings, and I mention it only to point out that it is not the question we shall discuss in this section. We could ask whether the depiction is appropriate to the portrayal-subject. Notice what sort of question this is, and how it would arise. The religious authorities might object to Tintoretto or Caravaggio because they introduced persons into their pictures for whom there was no scriptural warrant, or because they showed Jesus in a way that was objectionable—for example, by making him appear unforgiving, or by not placing him in the center of the scene. These would be objections to the depiction vis-à-vis the portrayal, but they are moral, religious, or historical objections. The objection might be that the painting contained falsehood—in being untrue to the gospel narrative or to Christian doctrine—or that the painting was pernicious and would tend to weaken Christian faith or corrupt morals. These may be serious objections to a painting, and their seriousness and relevance we shall have to deal with carefully later on, the former in Chapter VIII, the latter in Chapter XII. But these issues are not the ones at hand now.

If two paintings depict different things, they must differ somehow in their design; for two designs that are exactly similar—for example, two prints of a photograph—must inevitably be pictures of the same thing. And this works both ways: if two representational designs differ as designs, no matter how little, they must differ in what they depict, even if only trivially. For consider a picture of, say, a village in the distance, and imagine the slightest change in the design, for example, the substitution of green for red in a small patch. Then there will be some change in what is depicted: a green house instead of a red one, or a plot of grass instead of a roof.

Nevertheless, of course, two paintings may be very similar, though not identical, in what they depict, even though they may differ very strongly as designs. Of two photographs of the same bridge taken from different spots, one may bring out the curve of the cables while the other does not. Compare the Titian *Adam and Eve* (ca. 1565-70) with the free copy made by Rubens (1628-29) that hangs near it in the Prado. These are identical in what they portray; and they are fairly similar in what they depict—Rubens has introduced a tropical bird—since they do not tell us very different things about the actions, intentions, or attitudes of the characters. (Rubens makes Adam lean forward more, gives Eve a more intensely desiring expression, and has the baby-faced serpent looking in a different direction.) But the paintings are very different in the qualities of their designs: the differences in angles and directions give Rubens' picture a much more dynamic quality, with the space more filled and the texture more active, though it lacks the perfect balance of curves and the poise of spatial relationships that Titian's picture has.

There are two points that critics are concerned with when they talk about the relation between design and subject. First, there is the unity of the design, as a design, and the factors that make for it. And as regards this characteristic, it is quite clear that two designs that depict almost the same thing—for example, two photographs of the bridge taken from nearby spots, or two paintings of the apple that differ rather subtly in color-tone—may differ enormously in their degree of unity: one photograph may be much more balanced than the other, one apple may harmonize much better with the remainder of the painting. And two designs that depict very different things—a woman and child, and a bowl of fruit—may be very similar in their unity as designs: the composition and color-relations of both may be extremely close, though they clearly have different subjects.

Second, there are the regional qualities of the design. Suppose we take a number of speed photographs of a racing horse; what they represent is very similar, namely, a running horse; and they all represent this by showing his legs in running positions. But in some of them the design, considered merely as a design, will be full of movement, tense and lively; in others the design will be static and quietly balanced. In such a case, we can say that the regional qualities are very different, though the depiction-subjects are not very different. And, again, to refer once more to the woman-and-child and the bowl of fruit, despite the considerable difference in subject, they may, as designs, have similar qualities of grace, calm, or cheerfulness.

The Divergence Theory

Thus we can say that within limits the formal unity or the regional quality of a design can vary considerably without much difference in its depiction-subject, and vice versa. Hence it is not senseless to ask of two different designs that depict a crucifixion or a tea party whether either of them is more appropriate to the subject. This is a question about the coherence of design and subject: is it ever the case that in a painting the connection between the design and the subject is such that they can be apprehended as constituting a kind of whole?

To this question there are evidently two possible answers. Let us consider first the negative answer, which is given by what I shall call the *Divergence Theory* of the relation between design and subject.

The gist of the Divergence Theory is that though a painting may both be a design and have a subject, its subject and its design are always either irrelevant to, or in conflict with, each other.[1] It is not hard to see how a plausible case might be made out for this view. The fact that nonrepresentational paintings exist shows the psychological possibility of abstracting pure design from subject matter, and where the painter doesn't do it, the perceiver can. In the case of a historical painting, it is easy to distinguish the qualities of the design itself, its massive spiral, its flowing lines, its forcefulness and brilliant color, from the patriotic sentiments or feelings of pity or joy that the subject may evoke. And when we are considering these qualities, we ignore the subject—it is of no moment whether it is Washington Crossing the Delaware, some peaches, a side of bacon, or an old shoe. If the artist puts in an old shoe, it is not because he wishes to recall the object, but because he needs that particular shape for his design. Of course, when he uses such shapes he can't help representing, or at least suggesting, the objects. It is up to us to ignore them.

In fact, it might be argued that there are two points of inevitable conflict between design and subject, in the work of an artist and in the mind of the perceiver. The artist's problem in painting a representational picture is to satisfy two demands that may be incompatible. If the question is where the arm or the Christ Child or the horse is to be placed,

---

[1] This theory has been defended by Clive Bell and Roger Fry; see references in Note 17-A.

the aim of accurate and plausible representation may favor one alternative, while the needs of the design favor another. Representationally speaking, the arm is best attached to the shoulder, the Child placed in the Madonna's arms, and the horse stood right side up under the rider; but if the design requires an arm-curve or a child-shape on the other side of the painting, or demands that the horse be upside down, the painter will have to sacrifice either his subject or his design. Poussin had to leave the camels out of his *Rebecca and Eleazer at the Well* (1648, Louvre) because there was no place for such shapes in the design. Defenders of the Divergence Theory admit that in a few cases painters have managed to satisfy both subject and design, but they regard these as *tours de force*, freaks of skill.

For imagine a man juggling plates in the air and whistling "Yankee Doodle." He is doing two things at once, but there is no connection between them; they remain two acts, not one. However, if you sing a waltz while waltzing, there is a rhythmic connection between the two acts, which draws them together, and keeps them from being totally irrelevant and merely simultaneous. The Divergence Theory suggests that the representational painter's task is more like the juggling and whistling.

And it holds that the same is true in the spectator's experience. If the two things, design and subject, do not in any way come together, the spectator's attention is constantly shifting. Instead of seeming to belong together, they may jar and irritate. Of course, if we are insensitive to the design, as are many people who enjoy the humorous situation on a magazine cover or buy cheap religious objects, then it won't bother us, because we won't notice it. Or, with training in visual abstraction, we may be able to go to a gallery and enjoy the designs without really noticing or remembering the subjects at all—at least, that is what some critics say they do.

It is one thing to see a line as jagged, to grasp its jerkiness of movement and sharpness of point; it is another thing to see it as the outline of a rock, a spruce tree, a bolt of lightning. And some defenders of the Divergence Theory seem to hold that it is impossible to do both of these things at once.

I have chosen to formulate the Divergence Theory as an answer to a definite question, and I shall discuss it and the alternative theory with this limitation. But before we come to the alternative, a few broader observations are desirable. For what I have called the Divergence Theory of the relation of subject matter to design was originally set forth under special conditions, where it was not merely an attempt to solve an aesthetic problem but also a weapon in the war to obtain sympathetic understanding of what is called "modern"—in this case especially Impressionist and post-Impressionist—painting. Certain critics realized that what prevented this understanding was a widespread stubborn and uncriticized assumption that the subject of a painting is the thing to notice about it, to study, to remember, and to talk about when a demonstration of cultural competence is called for. They wanted to say: "Stop cataloguing subjects, and look at the painting as a design," and since practical reform, in art as elsewhere, demands positive rallying cries, not merely attacks on the opposition, they wanted a term to single out what people should look for in art. They invented "significant form."

This term had considerable success, and served its purpose rather well. Not that it was ever defined by its users. The first and classic attempt to define it[2] was completely circular, and it was constantly necessary to point out (a) that "significant" was not to be taken as implying that the painting signifies anything, but just that it is significant, and (b) that "form" was not to be limited merely to shapes and shape-relations, but included color, and indeed the entire design. So the term was quite misleading. Yet if we examine not what its original users said about the term, but the way they used it in talking about paintings, we can, I think, offer a pretty satisfactory definition. A painting can be said to have significant form if it is an intensely qualified and highly unified design; in other words, if it has unity and some fairly vivid regional qualities. That is what they seemed to value; that is what they wanted people to look for and enjoy in painting, and what they wanted to distinguish sharply from the subject of painting. I do not believe they wanted to lay any restrictions upon the qualities they had in mind: they praised works for their grace, solidity, power, radiance, delicacy, strength, and many other qualities. They found the same solidity in Cézanne's wine bottles and card players as in his mountains; they valued the brooding uneasiness of El Greco's view of Toledo, the *joie de vivre* in every line of Matisse's bathers, the vitality of Van Gogh's trees and flowers. The essential thing is that the work have some quality that stands out, instead of being vapid, characterless, nothing at all.

However, the term had an unfortunate effect upon aestheticians. It enabled them to label the defenders of the Divergence Theory as "Formalists," and it tempted them to try to stretch this theory into a general "Formalistic Theory of Art," which it has no business being. What could such a theory be? If it means that form is the most important thing about aesthetic objects, or the only important thing, then in any sense of "form" that can be extended throughout the arts, it is clearly false. To be plausible at all, the theory has to be accompanied by some distinction between "form" and "content" in each art, but the meaning of "content" varies from art to art, so the theory is not in fact one theory at all. The only safe thing is to forget the other arts for the time being— it doesn't matter here whether anyone ever held, for example, that the sound of poetry is more important than its meaning, if this is "Formalism"

---

[2] By Clive Bell, who coined the term. Later synonyms were "plastic form" (used by Albert C. Barnes) and "expressive form" (used by Sheldon Cheney); see references in Note 17-B.

in literary theory—and stick to the fairly well-circumscribed and manageable question now before us. This is the question whether or not there can be a unifying connection between design and subject in a work of visual design.

The Fusion Theory

The answer given by what we shall call the *Fusion Theory*[3] is that there can be so close a connection between design and subject matter that the recognition of the subject and the perception of the design become unified, and fuse together into a single experience.

The general principle underlying the Fusion Theory may be formulated in this way: A design and a subject are coherent when the qualities of the subject as *rep*resented (depicted) are *pres*ented by the design. This principle is perhaps stated in too unqualified a way; for example, we might want to extend it a little and add that unity might be present if the design presents some qualities usually connected with the qualities of the subject as represented, not necessarily the same ones. But let us now consider some of the corollaries of this principle, in relation to very simple examples, before applying it to actual works of visual art.

In a line-drawing of a rock, the rock may be represented as brittle and jagged, and at the same time the line itself may have the regional qualities of brittleness and jaggedness. These do not necessarily go together, but when they do there is a similarity, and hence a ground of unity, between the subject and the design. The design contains *presentational equivalents* of its subject, to use a term that was introduced in Chapter V, §14. In a painting of a group of people at a dance or a party, the people may be represented as smiling and laughing and in general having a happy time, and at the same time the design itself may be of a cheerful and lively character. Presentational equivalence is not a one-one relation; a design with a certain quality may be suitable to more than one subject.

Another sort of connection between design and subject is the principle of compositional support. In a painting that informs us by means of representation which person in the painting is the most important, or the central one from the point of view of the subject, the area that represents that person may also be a focus of the design—the hand of Rouault's sower. PLATE V, or the pointing hand in Daumier's *Witnesses*, PLATE VIII. Here again there is appropriateness of design to subject.

Doubts about the possibility of fusion derive in large part, I believe, from a failure to be clear enough about the distinction between the design and the subject. We accept fusion without noticing it a good deal

---

[3] The fullest exposition and defense of this theory has been given by Walter Abell in *Representation and Form*. It has also been defended by D. F. Bowers, Helen Knight, Albert C. Barnes, Rhys Carpenter, Herbert S. Langfeld, L. A. Reid, and DeWitt H. Parker; see references in Note 17-C.

of the time. It is no doubt present to some degree wherever there is representation at all. But in the works of inferior artists and in magazine sketches and photographs we often find something represented without very rich or intense presentational equivalents. The object is depicted, but its quality is not there.

To clarify the concept of fusion, let us begin with a simple sort. Suppose we want to represent a bulky, massive man. We can do so by drawing a small figure at some distance, and setting up the perspective and other objects nearby in such a way that we can read him as a big man, though the shape that represents him is small. But if we bring him up close to the picture-plane, as a portraitist would do, and make him crowd the available picture-space, then the area that represents him will itself be bulky and, if we wish it, massive; here the bulkiness of the man is represented by the bulkiness of the design area. See, for example, Goya's *Colossus*, PLATE VII. We say, colloquially, that we "feel" his bulkiness; we don't merely infer it. This is a very simple case of fusion, but it plays its role without explicit notice—except in such a painting as the unflattering portrait of *Field Captain Alessandro del Borro* (date unknown, Kaiser Friedrich Museum, Berlin) attributed, probably incorrectly, to Velásquez. Here the impression of bulk is further increased by placing the Captain between pillars and setting the spectator's eye level at his feet.

The general principle of fusion can be illustrated in many ways, and it will be desirable to give a variety of examples. I do not insist that you agree with what I say specifically about every painting; it will be sufficient if the presentational equivalence is plain in some of them. The main point is to make the notion itself reasonably clear.

Consider, to begin with, El Greco's *Agony in the Garden*, also called *Gethsemane* (ca. 1604-14, National Gallery, London). Jesus is suffering in advance the ordeal that awaits him, and asking that the cup be taken from his lips. But the emotional qualities he is depicted as having are also qualities of the design itself: of the rocks, whose outlines are twisted in an agonized way, and of the dark and menacing cloud shapes above. Much more can be said about the unity of design and subject in this painting, in which, indeed, the connection is very apparent. The vitality and intensity of its regional qualities as a design, and their eloquent suitability to the subject, suggests some interesting comparisons. In a *Crucifixion* by Murillo we would find a similar subject, but without the presentational equivalents. In a painting called *Agony* by Arshile Gorky (1947, Museum of Modern Art, New York) there are some of the presentational equivalents in the red shapes and irregular black lines, but without the subject, since the painting is nonrepresentational. In El Greco there is a synthesis.

In some landscapes by Hobbema and Ruisdael the peacefulness of human occupations and the gentleness of nature that are represented are also in the smooth and horizontal lines of the design. In Bronzino's *Portrait of a Young Man* (ca. 1535, Metropolitan Museum, New York) the young man is depicted as noble, elegant in dress, self-conscious, disdainful; and the subtle design, with its careful balance on a severe vertical axis, has itself an air of dignity and impersonal aloofness, as well as tension and self-control. In Georges Rouault's *Christ Mocked by Soldiers* (1932, Museum of Modern Art, New York) the constriction of the picture-space, with one of the soldiers' faces crowding the head of Jesus, gives a sense of the pressure on him; the electric quality of the texture, with its many hues and its black lines, gives the design an extraordinary intensity; yet the figure of Jesus comes forward in resignation and serenity, and holds its position in space firmly and clearly, like a man whom nothing will deter from his purpose to do as it was written by the prophets. Rouault's Jesus is not that of Tintoretto, in his *Christ Before Pilate* (1566-67, Scuola di San Rocco, Venice), but Tintoretto's figure of Jesus has inherent design qualities of its own, which are appropriate to the story: chiefly a still but compelling dignity. And in the great *Annunciations* (for example, that of Simone Martini, 1333, Florence, Uffizi Gallery) the shrinking of the Virgin from her glory and suffering is compressed into the lines of her figure and the spatial relations between her and the angel.

In Pavel Tchelitchew's *The Madhouse* (1935, Museum of Modern Art, New York) the distorted perspective and placing of the masses—people and articles of furniture—make the design reflect the patients' state of mind. In De Chirico's mysterious paintings, such as *Nostalgia of the Infinite* (1911), or *Delights of the Poet* (1913, both in the Museum of Modern Art, New York), the desolation and inhuman coldness of the landscapes are depicted by drab and cold patterns of colors.

Finally, consider some examples closer to hand. In *Municipal Lodging*, PLATE III, Käthe Kollwitz has embedded the qualities of the situation in the design itself. The protectiveness of the mother is not merely depicted; the shape that depicts her is itself a looming and enclosing form that draws the child-shapes into it. All the movement in the design is centripetal, just as the figures squeeze together for warmth and comfort, and the warm tones of the broad swaths of gray and black make the white background seem cold and hostile to the group. In no less complex ways, the velvety tones of the Rouault lithograph, PLATE V, hushed, luminous, mysterious, and the softness, tenderness, lightness of touch in Rembrandt's drawing, PLATE II, are perfectly coherent with the subjects depicted.

Such examples, I think, make it plain that fusion of design and subject actually occurs, but of course the general principle as I have stated it—that it occurs when there is presentational equivalence—is rough and vague. It can be made more precise by systematic investigation of the various kinds of equivalence; here is a fruitful problem for psychological study.

It is noteworthy that the connections of design and subject go both ways. Perspective, perceptual mass, and compositional convergence back up the subject by focusing attention on important characters; but also recognition of subject helps in some cases to intensify and stabilize the qualities of the design itself. Here is a triangular shape, for example, in a picture, which in its color and context has solidity; when we take it as representing a distant pyramid, instead of a nearby paperweight, the figure itself will take on a greater solidity, weight, and hardness, unless, of course, this is counteracted by other elements in the painting that may contrive to give it an airy and floating quality. Ostensible size is a function of representation, and the size of the object represented has subtle effects upon the appearance of the area that represents it. It is the same, sometimes, with color quality: the color that is perceived as the color *of* something—plush, silk, corduroy—may appear slightly different from the way it appears when it is just a colored patch. This slight difference may make a very considerable difference to the compositional balance and coherence of the design, just as a design.

Three Dimensions of Form

When a painting has a subject, it exists on two levels, and there are relations between these levels as well as within them. Thus it follows from the Fusion Theory that there are three dimensions of form in a representational painting. Consequently, when we consider the form of such a painting, there are three distinct groups of questions we can ask about it.

First, we can ask about the design itself: is it complete and coherent? How much complexity does it encompass? What are its regional qualities, and how intense are they? These questions we have already considered in Chapter IV, §13.

Second, we can ask about the subject. When it is an event or a situation involving psychological relationships among different people, it can be regarded as the fragment of a drama. A *Deposition*, a *Storming of the Bastille,* a *William Penn's Treaty with the Indians,* has a dramatic subject in this sense, and some of the same questions can be asked about it that are asked about a literary work—questions we discussed in Chapter V, §15. Is the character as represented psychologically consistent? Is the action in which he is engaged consistent with his character as depicted? Is the setting psychologically suited to the action, as—to give a crude example—a stormy night or a blasted heath to a murder? We could ask other questions about the depth and penetration of psychological insight in the painting—but these questions take us into another set of problems, having to do with truth, and they must wait until Chapter VIII, §20.

It is easy to find examples of satisfactory dramatic unity in painting. The work of seventeenth-century Dutch genre painters—Terborch, Jan Steen, Pieter de Hooch—is full of it. Their situations are rich in ironic and amusing contrasts of personality and by-play of action. Pieter Brueghel the Elder's painting *Christ Carrying the Cross* (1563, Staatliche Galerie, Vienna) tells a marvelously complicated and dramatic story, with its distant ring of people on the hilltop, waiting with morbid curiosity for the spectacle to begin.

On the other hand, there are lesser degrees of dramatic unity, or a disruption of it. The various objects and events in Hieronymus Bosch's *Adoration of the Magi* (ca. 1490, Metropolitan Museum, New York) are not all closely related, with the shepherds warming their hands over a fire that is nowhere near the mother and child. The false, melodramatic gestures and postures in David's *Death of Socrates* (1787; Metropolitan Museum, New York) are themselves dramatically disunified, because not fully motivated—apart from the betrayal of the spirit of Plato's *Phaedo,* which is another question. We may similarly object to the melodramatic quality of the raised hands of one of the Marys in Caravaggio's *Deposition* (1602-04, Rome, Vatican)—as presumably Rubens did when he eliminated them in his free copy of this painting (1611-14, Liechtenstein Gallery, Vienna).

We find a high degree of dramatic complexity in two sorts of painting, both of which can be illustrated from Rembrandt. His portrait of Jan Six (1654, Six Collection, Amsterdam) depicts one of the most complex and subtle characters in the history of portraiture; his etching of *Christ Healing the Sick* (also called the "Hundred Guilder Print"; Hind 236) includes a large variety of personalities, attitudes, and human conditions, but all welded together into a pictorial whole.

The third question is about the relation between subject and design: to what degree does the design cohere with the subject by offering presentational equivalents of it? And from the preceding discussion we can see in a general way how the critic would go about answering this question.

When we try to recall paintings in which design and subject are most fully fused, while each is unified and intensely qualified in itself, we think at once of Giotto and Rembrandt. In any of the great Giotto frescoes we have designs that are composed with great coherence and completeness, and, as designs, have strong regional qualities; we have deep psychological portrayal; we have the qualities of the design matching the qualities of the events depicted. The sadness of the event in his *Lamentation over Christ,* for example (ca. 1305, Arena Chapel, Padua), and the sadness of the spectators, is borne out in the drooping folds of garments, the curves of the bent backs, the slanting angle of the composition. In the great Rembrandt portraits of the forties and fifties, such as those in the Widener and Mellon collections in the National Gallery, and in the Metropolitan, there is a remarkable concentration of light that gives the faces their intensity; the designs have the qualities of repose, seriousness, meditativeness, timelessness, gravity, and a fixedness of focus, and also an inner coloristic glow that reflects the vitality and psychological depth of the portrait-subjects; and the surrounding darkness from which the figures emerge is an enclosing envelope that shuts them off from the world, as though they were alone with their souls.

To the third question we may get any of three answers. In many designs, as we have seen, there is a notable unity of design and subject. In others, there is irrelevance. Usually, in magazine illustrations and advertisements, there is very little connection between the design and the subject; they fall apart. There is almost always *some* connection, since a successful illustrator must know how to impart some liveliness and force to his design, but, compared with works of fine art, such illustrations are relatively feeble in regional quality, and hence offer relatively little in the way of presentational equivalents. In other designs, there is a positive incoherence. The gravity, stateliness, and quiet dignity of design in many of Poussin's paintings comports very well with the royalty, classic divinity, or noble rusticity of the characters depicted and idealized in them; see, for example, his *Rinaldo and Armide* (1633, Toledo Museum of Art). But in his *Massacre of the Innocents* (1627-29, Musée Condé, Chantilly), the violence of the depicted action is strangely at odds with the relative stability of the design. And this is especially evident when the painting is compared with the cartoon-study for it, which is far more vigorous and lively as a design.

This sort of incongruity may give rise to a new quality, whether the painter intends it or not: if the subject is trivial or familiar, the incongruity may appear absurd, and therefore funny; if the subject is serious, the incongruity may appear ironic. But perhaps irony is a kind of coherence too; at least, it will not do to be overbearing in analyzing a painting from this point of view. Consider, for example, a puzzling painting, *The Yellow Christ* by Gauguin (1889, Albright Art Gallery, Buffalo). It would be a mistake to say flatly that the pervading yellow is inappropriate to the subject, the large crucifix. That would take us too far outside the picture. The question is not what feelings are appropriate to the Crucifixion, but what qualities of the design are appropriate to the scene depicted here, the kneeling peasant women. And it could be argued that, as far as the subject goes, there is nothing depicted that really conflicts with the color-qualities: in fact, the colors, as well as the lack of modeling and the simplicity of the shapes, help to define a simple, perhaps slightly perfunctory, faith.

All three questions about coherence arise in making a value-judgment of a representational painting, but that does not mean that they automatically settle questions of value. Critics of the visual arts are deeply divided on the problems here. Some hold that representational

painting is of a higher order of value than nonrepresentational painting,
and that a painting with an important and coherent dramatic subject can
be a great painting whether or not it contains much in the way of presentational equivalence. Others say that the presentational aspect of the
painting is the essential one, the representational aspect peripheral. Thus,
they would say that a painting can be great even if it represents nothing;
that a painting that represents but lacks presentational equivalents and
unified design is mere "illustration," not fine art at all.

These are the possibilities; we must keep them in mind when we
come to the problems of evaluation in Chapter X. But at this stage, we
can avoid any sweeping *a priori* judgments that may be troublesome to
defend rationally: for example, that representational paintings are all
poor, or that nonrepresentational paintings are all poor. Evidently a representational painting with no connection of design and subject lacks an
important dimension of coherence; a nonrepresentational painting lacks an
important dimension of complexity.

Design and Function

In order to deal carefully with the problems of representation, we
have had to limit ourselves to visual designs, as defined earlier, without
considering the extension of our conclusions to sculpture and architecture. Some of the extensions are pretty evident; others more puzzling.
However, before we leave the subject, we shall make a brief excursion
into a related set of problems, to see how far those problems parallel the
ones we have been dealing with, and whether they may be handled in
an analogous manner. These problems have to do, not with design and
subject, but with design and use, or, as it is often put, form and function.

What is the relation between the design of an object and its use,
when it *has* a use over and above its use as an object of contemplation
as a design? If it is designed for a practical purpose—as is a stove, a sink,
a spoon, a sword, or an oil refinery—then it is likely to exhibit characteristics that indicate its use. If someone shows us a Buddhist prayer wheel
or a circuit breaker, we will not of course be able to recognize its use
unless we have relevant knowledge; other people might be baffled by
forks and snowplows. But to one adequately equipped, many useful objects show their purpose in their design. Or, as we may say, the spoon
looks like something to stir and dip liquids with; the tent *looks* like a
protection from the weather.

It is not inevitable that this should be so; for sometimes the design
disguises the purpose of an object. The bed may fold back to become a
sofa; the old-style Singer sewing machine may be so elaborately worked
and figured that it looks like a piece of cast-iron furniture; or, to take an
extreme case, the military tank may be camouflaged. This cannot always

be done: it is hard to make a large bridge look like anything but a bridge. But to a lesser extent, all changes in, or additions to, the design besides those that contribute to its capacity to serve its purpose—the chromium on the car, the buttons (once, but no longer, functional) on the jacket sleeve, the engraving on the spoon handle—are partial concealments: they affect the look of the thing without affecting its usefulness.

It would be possible to formulate a Divergence Theory of the relation between design and use: that they are merely distinct aspects of the object, and can have no intimate connection. But a Fusion Theory could also be defended: that in some objects there is a connection between design and use. The problem is: what sort of connection?

To formulate the principle that a Fusion Theory would presumably offer here, we must distinguish two senses of the word "look." When we see an object, we may be able to infer its purpose, or at least one use to which it might be put: it would be good for digging, for clubbing, for swinging on, for swimming in. This is a matter of logical inference, based upon past experience with objects of that sort. It is a practical inference. Suppose, for example, you are examining a car: you might open the hood and say, "It looks as if it will go fast." This is a prediction: if you get into the car, start it, let in the clutch and push down the accelerator, then the car will go fast.

But suppose the car is standing by the curb, and you merely consider its colors, lines, and shapes—it is low and long, the curves sweep backward, and the chromium division between the two colors follows a line that, simply as a design, has forward movement. It has a "fast" look. This is not an inference, and it is not a prediction. For all you know, it may have no motor in it at all, or its motor may be in bad shape. You are simply describing a regional quality of the design itself: it has a clear, swift, flowing, powerful, smooth appearance.

To say "The car is (will go) fast" is to describe a *performance*-characteristic of the object. To say "The car has a fast look" is to describe a *design* quality. The design is appropriate to the function when it contains a quality that is also a desirable performance-characteristic in the object.

Thus suppose a certain make of car is designed to go fast. If it also *looks* fast, then its appearance proclaims its ideal, brings it to direct awareness. It seems to embody, so to speak, the qualities we expect from it; it shows what it is—or ought to be. "The new grille commands attention; it gives an immediate impression of leadership," says a General Motors advertisement. In other words, the commanding appearance of the grille as a design—and in this case it is a rather forbidding and snarling sort of grille—is itself a presentational equivalent of its predicted capacity to get ahead of other cars on the road. "Everywhere you look are the marks of smooth motion . . . vigorous lines that express new engine power"; the design has smooth motion, the car moves smoothly. Or so it

is claimed. Another advertisement says, "Here is beauty without gaudi-
ness, rich yet simple styling without bric-a-brac, long sweeping lines with
purposeful meaning." Even when it's standing still, it looks poised for
instant flight.

The Fusion Theory, as we have stated it, is not a value judgment: it
simply points out a possibility that is sometimes realized. But there is
another theory that is sometimes defended in connection with the Fusion
Theory, and we should consider it at least briefly here. It is called *Functionalism*.[4] The major difficulty in dealing with this theory is that it usually lumps together several distinct and logically independent propositions, which must first be separated. Some of these propositions are not
very debatable. When the functionalist says that buildings should be
"functional," i.e., serve the purpose they were built to serve, it would
be hard to gainsay him. When he says, on the other hand, that function should never be sacrificed to aesthetic value, it would be impossible to justify so sweeping a statement; women's clothes refute it. But
two of the propositions that Functionalists sometimes seem to have in
mind are important and discussible.

First, the Functionalist sometimes asserts that in a useful object the
design ought to be appropriate to the use. Thus, it is the main purpose of a
bank building to keep money and papers safe: it must be strong, secure,
hard to burglarize. Now, with modern materials, it would be possible to
make it secure in actuality, without its looking so at all: it might be made
of glass, and have a kind of soft and floating quality, though it might really
be burglar-proof. Or it can be made to look secure, with a square forbidding front, heavy blocks of marble, and solid-looking doors—even though,
in fact, this one may be less secure than the glass one.

Now, everyone agrees—or nearly everyone—that the bank should be
secure; the Functionalist says that it ought to look secure: its design-
quality should correspond to its ideal, or most desirable, performance. It
is not fully clear what sort of argument could be given for this: in any
case, it takes us into value-questions that are out of our way now. It might
be held that there would be a kind of harmony or unity in our daily
experience if designs and purposes were more closely integrated; this
line of thought could lead into questions about the social effects of art
that we will come to in Chapter XII. Or it might be claimed that if archi-
tects, factory-equipment designers, and furniture-makers would strive to
embody the qualities of their objects in the design, there would be many
more good designs about us. And this argument would bring us to the
second thesis of Functionalism.

For sometimes the Functionalist seems to be saying that the more the
design of an object is appropriate to its use, the better the design will
be. This would apply only to useful objects, of course; they would ordi-

---

[4] This theory has been defended by Horatio Greenough and W. D. Teague; see
Note 17-F.

narily agree that nonuseful objects, like paintings, can have good designs. But they might argue in two ways: (1) If we observe the progress in the development of a certain type of object—from the Brooklyn Bridge to the George Washington Bridge, from the earliest cars and sewing machines and vacuum cleaners to the latest models—we observe that as the object is gradually improved so that it serves its purpose better, its design tends to undergo a corresponding simplification and unification. Unnecessary appendages are lopped off, and the shape grows organically out of the nature of the thing itself instead of being borrowed from elsewhere, like the carriage bodies on the first automobiles. In so far as the value of a design is dependent upon its degree of unity, then, other things being equal, the more the object fulfills its purpose, the better its design will be.

(2) Moreover, there is another tendency that goes along with the first. The more the object is concentrated on its purpose, and nothing else, and the better it serves it, it might be said, the more it will tend to look right: the better the bridge, the more it soars and seems to master and overcome the space it spans; if it is safer, it will look safer. And the better the jug is for pouring, the chair for reclining, the kitchen for preparing food, the more intense and notable their regional qualities will be. And in so far as the value of a design depends upon the intensity of its regional qualities, the more functional the object, the better its design.

It would perhaps not be claimed by all Functionalists that unity and intensity were sufficient conditions for good design, though some would say this, I think, and they would even prefer paintings that looked more like such streamlined useful objects. But there are two questions that we might want to raise about the arguments for the second thesis. First, it is perhaps not *inevitable* that the design of an object should become more simplified as its usefulness increases; present-day oil refineries are not less complex as designs than earlier ones. But as a generalization, there may be much to it. Second, the argument should probably not be allowed to develop a corollary that is often attached to it: the idea that all pure decoration is therefore to be eliminated. For there is an equally important Nonfunctionalist truth that must be kept in mind. Given any object you like, however well it performs its function, the chances are overwhelming that a good designer can add to it a few restrained decorative touches that will make it a more acceptable design and intensify its qualities. Perhaps not every object can be improved in this way: a bullet, or certain jugs, or a ripe tomato. Granted that decorative touches have often spoiled the designs of useful objects; nevertheless it remains true that no matter how well-designed your sports car is for high speed, a few touches of line and color, touches that have absolutely no use at all, and contribute nothing to its performance, can make it look racier. It looks racier in red than in brown, racier with a streak of contrasting hue, but its color does not affect its speed.

In any case, the same, or very similar, principles of fusion seem to

be at work in our experience of useful objects as in our experience of
works of fine art. The aesthetic qualities—unity, complexity, and other
regional qualities—of these objects may be independent of their use, in
which case these will appear most fully when the objects are dissociated
from their use, as when they are taken from their cultural context and
placed in a museum. Or the aesthetic qualities may be the visual embodi-
ments of their use, in which case the perception of them will be fullest
when we understand their significance in the modes of human life they
were made to serve.

NOTES AND QUERIES

§16

16-A THE DEFINITION OF "REPRESENT." On "subject matter" see John
Hospers, *Meaning and Truth in the Arts*, Chapel Hill, N.C.: U. of North
Carolina, 1946, pp. 15-25: note that Hospers chooses to use the term "represent" in a broad sense (p. 29): literature is a "representational art" (p.
23), as is often said. But even though a poem is "about" something, it
seems confusing to use the same terms for that sort of "aboutness" as for
representational designs. Also, note that his two senses of "subject-matter"
(p. 23) are not the same as my distinction between depicted subject and
portrayed subject. Compare Albert C. Barnes, *The Art in Painting*, 3d ed.,
New York: Harcourt, Brace, 1937, pp. 20-21; his distinction between "subject" and "subject-matter" corresponds somewhat to the distinction between what is portrayed and what is depicted.

Morris Weitz, *Philosophy of the Arts*, Cambridge, Mass.: Harvard
U., 1950, supports his "organic theory" by choosing (pp. 56-60) to use the
word "represent"—and other terms that are for him synonymous with it
—in such a broad way that "every constituent in art . . . is representational
in an expressive sense" (p. 60). Thus he would say, not that yellow *is* warm
and sunny, but that it "represents" warmth and sunniness; not that a line
is powerful, but that it "means," or "is a sign of," power. This seems a
quite unwarranted and unbearably loose way of speaking; we shall discuss its specific difficulties in Chapter VII, §18, in connection with theories
of musical meaning.

16-B DEPICTION AND PORTRAYAL. Helen Knight, "Aesthetic Experience in Pictorial Art," *Monist*, XL (1930): 74-83, made a distinction between "abstract" and "concrete" "meaning" in painting, which seems to
correspond to the distinction between depiction and portrayal; it is surprising that her suggestion has not been taken up.

Does the broadening of the concept of portraiture in recent painting
(see introduction to, and reproductions in, Monroe Wheeler, *20th Century*

Portraits, New York: Museum of Modern Art, 1942) raise difficulties for the definition of "portrayal" given in this chapter? For example, is Dali's *Soft Self-portrait* (1941, in the possession of the artist) a portrait?

For material to suggest further problems about portrayal, see Marianna Jenkins, *The State Portrait: Its Origin and Evolution,* Monographs on Archaeology and Fine Arts, the Archaeological Institute of America and the College Art Association, No. 3, 1947.

Erwin Panofsky, "Iconography and Iconology: An Introduction to the Study of Renaissance Art," *Studies in Iconology: Humanistic Themes in the Art of the Renaissance,* New York: Oxford U., 1939, pp. 3-31, reprinted in *Meaning in the Visual Arts,* Garden City, N.Y.: Anchor, 1955, pp. 26-54, seems to classify depiction under the "pre-iconographical description" of the work, and reserves the term "iconography" for the interpretation of "secondary or conventional subject matter," which is apparently portrayal (pp. 30-31); the interpretation of symbolism, along with other statements about the work, he assigns to "iconology" (pp. 30-31).

16-C THE DISTINCTION BETWEEN REPRESENTATIONAL AND NONREPRESENTATIONAL DESIGNS. Richard Bernheimer, "In Defense of Representation," *Art: A Bryn Mawr Symposium,* Bryn Mawr, Pa.: Bryn Mawr College, 1940, esp. pp. 23-30, argues against this distinction on the ground that "Representation in art is ultimately inevitable." Is he, however, using the term in a broader sense than that proposed in this chapter? C. J. Ducasse, *The Philosophy of Art,* New York: Dial, 1929, pp. 206-13, argues that designs are themselves "represented"; but it is a question whether "represented" here means the same thing as above. There is also some interesting discussion in Wolfgang Paalen, *Form and Sense,* New York: Wittenborn, 1945.

See Arnold Isenberg, "Perception, Meaning, and the Subject-Matter of Art," *J Phil,* XLI (1944): 561-75, reprinted in Eliseo Vivas and Murray Krieger, eds., *The Problems of Aesthetics,* New York: Rinehart, 1953, pp. 211-25. What we have when we look at the moon is a moon-presentation (the sense-datum or sense-impression), and in the same sense, says Isenberg, the picture of the moon is a moon-presentation; so why should we speak of the picture as "representing" the moon any more than of the other moon-presentation as representing it? But the picture-moon is, so to speak, not a member of the *family* of moon-representations that belong to, or constitute, the natural moon; we are not seeing the moon when we see the picture of it, and to recognize the picture *as* a picture of the moon does involve something more than recognizing the moon as the moon. Isenberg is concerned "to show how much of what we understand by the subject-matter of art can be rescued for the province of sense perception" (Vivas and Krieger, *op. cit.,* p. 224); but he concedes that not all of what is effective in the experience of fine arts can be reduced to the apprehension of what is presented.

Cubism presents an interesting problem for the distinction between representational and nonrepresentational designs. In *Abstract and Surrealist Art in America,* New York: Reynal and Hitchcock, 1944 (see also its many useful illustrations), Sidney Janis says (p. 4): "All cubist paintings are abstract representations of objects from nature; they are figurative art, as contrasted with nonfigurative." Yet, though some cubist paintings are representational by any definition, there are many that clearly cannot be taken as pictures of any material object that could exist.

To clarify the distinction, I shall list some accessible examples from twentieth-century painting—for convenience, a group in the Museum of Modern Art. Reproductions will serve quite well, and the paintings mentioned are all reproduced in *Painting and Sculpture in the Museum of Modern Art,* ed. by A. H. Barr, Jr., New York: Simon and Schuster, 1948. I should classify as representational Picasso's *Girl Before a Mirror* (1932), Léger's *Three Women* (1921), though both are highly abstract. Some of Marin's paintings, for example, *Lower Manhattan*—also called *Composing Derived from Top of Woolworth*—(1922), and *Camden Mountain Across the Bay* (1922), are borderlinish, but I should be inclined to say they are not representational, though suggestive; and in the same category I would place Braque's *Man with a Guitar* (1911), Picasso's *Card Player* (1913-14), Kandinsky's *Improvisation* (1915) and *Composition VII, Fragment I* (1913), Miro's *Person Throwing a Stone at a Bird* (1926), Baziotes' *Dwarf* (1947). In the category of nonsuggestive works, I would place Mondrian's *Broadway Boogie Woogie* (1942-43), which does not strictly suggest the music but shares with it a nervous quality, Pereira's *White Lines* (1942), and the "suprematist compositions" of Malevich. You may quarrel with some of my examples; perhaps I have overlooked some important suggestion in some of the paintings of the last group. Or you may say that the line between Picasso's girl before the mirror and Miro's bird is pretty arbitrary. Nevertheless there are three rather different types of painting here.

A philosophical puzzle can be designed to confound the attempt to define "representation" narrowly in terms of vital classes. "This painting represents an orange; an orange is a sphere; therefore this painting represents a sphere." Is this argument valid?

16-D SUGGESTION AND SUGGESTION-COHERENCE. On suggestion, see Walter Abell, *Representation and Form,* New York: Scribner's, 1936, pp. 26-35 (but note that "representation" for him sometimes means suggestion). Compare Piet Mondrian, "Plastic Art and Pure Plastic Art" (1937), *Plastic Art and Pure Plastic Art and Other Essays,* New York: Wittenborn, 1945, pp. 50-63, also in *Circle: International Survey of Constructive Art,* London: Faber and Faber, 1937, pp. 41-56. Mondrian's plea for a "really nonfigurative art" (p. 44) seems to mean nonsuggestive designs, as against "figurative fragments" (p. 52); but Mondrian also seems to hold that a balanced composition is somehow the "plastic expression" of "real life," which is "dynamic equilibrium" (p. 46), and this hardly seems possible for nonsuggestive designs.

Find some interpretations of suggestive nonrepresentational paintings, for example, in the critical columns of *The New York Times* on a Sunday, *The Art Bulletin*, or *Arts*. Do these interpretations conform to the principle that a design is not suggestive unless its potential suggestions cohere? In the light of your examples, can you further clarify the formulation of this principle?

16-E TITLES. What are the possible relations between a visual design and its title? For example, in some cases it is a mere label: *Composition #6* or *Harmony in Grey and Gold*—the latter is one Whistler strenuously insisted on when someone suggested that his painting be retitled *Trotty Veck*, after Dickens. In other cases, the relation seems to be more intrinsic. Can you classify the types of relation, with clear examples of each? Does it make any difference whether the title is, so to speak, *with* the painting, or—like the names of the prophets in Michelangelo's Sistine Chapel ceiling—*in* the painting? Is relying on the title for help in interpreting a painting a form of intentionalism? See Abell, *op. cit.*, pp. 106-10.

The works of Paul Klee raise some good questions about the indispensability of titles; see Werner Haftmann, *The Mind and Work of Paul Klee*, London: Faber and Faber, 1954, ch. 8.

16-F ABSTRACTION. The definitions of this and related terms ("distortion," "generalization," "idealization," "realism") proposed in this chapter may help to clarify the distinctions made by Andrew C. Ritchie in *Abstract Painting and Sculpture in America*, New York: Museum of Modern Art, 1951.

Are the "modes" of drawing and painting, distinguished by Arthur Pope in *The Language of Drawing and Painting*, Cambridge, Mass.: Harvard U., 1949, chs. 5, 6, types of representation? See also Stephen C. Pepper, *Principles of Art Appreciation*, New York: Harcourt, Brace, 1949, pp. 238-49.

The distinction made by Jerome Ashmore, "Some Differences Between Abstract and Nonobjective Painting," *JAAC*, XIII (June 1955): 486-95, is overtly intentionalistic, since "original subject matter" in his usage (p. 486) can only mean the object that the artist originally saw or imagined and then put through a "transformation." It is not easy to decide exactly what the distinction amounts to in terms of design and representation when intention and supposed metaphysical implications are set aside.

16-G DISTORTION. Collect some examples of distortion in representation, and discuss the question what in each case the distortion contributes to the work; consider to what extent this contribution depends upon the recognition that it *is* a distortion. For example, if a Martian looked at Parmigianino's long-necked Madonna and assumed that humans were all like that, would the qualities of her figure necessarily be different? See Mateo Marangoni, *The Art of Seeing Art*, London: Shelley Castle, 1951, pp. 115-40.

How should "caricature" be defined? See Bohun Lynch, *A History of Caricature*, Boston: Little, Brown, 1927. Would ludicrousness and exaggeration be part of the defining term? Is it strictly possible to caricature a *class* of people, or only an individual—in other words, can there be depiction-caricature as well as portrayal-caricature?

16-H SYMBOLISM. With the analysis made in this chapter, compare the similar conclusions of Richard Bernheimer, "Concerning Symbols," *Art: A Bryn Mawr Symposium*, Bryn Mawr, Pa.: Bryn Mawr College, 1940, pp. 31-74; he also uses the eagle as an example. E. H. Gombrich, "Visual Metaphors of Value in Art," *Symbols and Values*, 13th Symposium of the Conference on Science, Philosophy and Religion, New York: Harper, 1954, ch. 18, is illuminating; he prefers the term "visual metaphor" for what are usually called "symbols." W. G. Constable, "Symbolic Aspects of the Visual Arts," in the same volume, ch. 14, is not very helpful; he makes too few distinctions in his effort to argue that all paintings are symbolic in some sense. Douglas Morgan, "Icon, Index, and Symbol in the Visual Arts," *Philosophical Studies*, VI (1955): 49-54, makes a number of distinctions in a schematic summary of work in progress.

The analysis of "symbol" needs to be tested by examples of various sorts. See for example George W. Ferguson, *Signs and Symbols in Christian Art*, New York: Oxford U., 1954 (note his distinction between "sign" and "symbol," p. xii); Erwin Panofsky, *op. cit.*; Franz Boas, *Primitive Art*, Cambridge, Mass.: Harvard U., 1927, ch. 4, pp. 88-143; Émile Mâle, *Religious Art from the Twelfth to the Eighteenth Centuries*, New York: Pantheon, 1949, pp. 61-98; J. Huizinga, *The Waning of the Middle Ages*, London: Arnold, 1924, ch. 15. See Gyorgy Kepes, *Language of Vision*, Chicago: Theobald, 1944, ch. 3, on symbolism in modern art. Some very interesting and puzzling questions about the interpretation of Brueghel's paintings are raised and discussed in K. C. Lindsay and Bernard Huppe, "Meaning and Method in Brueghel's Painting," *JAAC*, XIV (March 1956): 376-86. It would be worthwhile to make a careful examination of their method of interpretation, its presuppositions, the kind of external evidence appealed to, and the principle of symbolic coherence employed.

For an example of the Freudian theory of symbolism, see the analysis of the symbol of the ship in Jacques Schnier, "Art Symbolism and the Unconscious," *JAAC*, XII (September 1953): 67-75. The appeal to unconscious desires he considers "the true language of art" (p. 75); is his position an alternative, or a supplement, to the analysis proposed in this chapter? If such unconscious connections between objects and sexual meanings do exist in the mind, are they either necessary or sufficient to account for the interest in those objects or for the power of their emotional effect?

16-I UNANSWERABLE QUESTIONS. Examine critically some standard works about a particular painter for examples of various types of problem that might arise about the interpretation of his paintings. Which problems are in principle unanswerable in a verifiable way? Vermeer is a case in point (see P. T. A. Swillens, *Johannes Vermeer, Painter of Delft*, Utrecht-Spectrum, 1950; Lawrence Gowing, *Vermeer*, London: Faber and Faber, 1952). (a) Assuming that his pictures of rooms are portraits, one can ask how many different rooms he painted (Swillens, pp. 69-70, says five); in what way is this information important for the interpretation of his paintings? (b) Is the painting of the artist and his model, usually called *An Artist in his Studio* (ca. 1665, Vienna), an allegory? If we go by Césare Ripa's definitive *Iconology*, published in Amsterdam, 1644, the trumpet is automatically a symbol of fame, but if we go by the principle of symbolic coherence, and note, for example, that the model doesn't look as though she is going to blow the trumpet, and that to have the painter painting Fame for fame is rather confused (see Swillens, pp. 99-102), then we will probably conclude that it is not a symbol in this context. (c) Is the *Young Woman Standing in Front of the Virginals* (ca. 1670, National Gallery, London) a portrait or not? Can we be certain that she was "no stranger to the painter" (Swillens, p. 103)? (d) Is there any way of deciding objectively whether the girl in *The Sleeping Girl*, also called *The Sad Young Woman* (ca. 1656, Metropolitan Museum, New York), is asleep or sad? Or whether the girl in the *Soldier and Laughing Girl* (ca. 1657, Frick Collection, New York) is holding out her hand for money? And is there any way of testing the correctness of the stories that have been spun about these two scenes (compare Swillens, pp. 1, 105, and Gowing, pp. 50-51)?

§17

17-A THE DIVERGENCE THEORY OF THE RELATION BETWEEN DESIGN AND SUBJECT. For exposition and defense of this theory, see the following: (1) Clive Bell, *Art*, London: Chatto and Windus, 1914, Part I, ch. 1, and pp. 63-68; Part IV, ch. 2, partly reprinted in M. Rader, *A Modern Book of Esthetics*, rev. ed., New York: Holt, 1952, pp. 317-34; *Since Cézanne*, London: Chatto and Windus, 1922, chs. 2, 8; note especially the statement (p. 94) that "it mattered not a straw whether this statue [Epstein's *Christ*, 1919], considered as a work of art, represented Jesus Christ or John Smith."

(2) Roger Fry, *Vision and Design*, London: Chatto and Windus, 1920 (reprinted New York: Meridian, 1956), pp. 16-38 ("An Essay in Aes-

thetics"), 284-302 ("Retrospect"); the essay on Giotto (pp. 131-77) is an excellent discussion of the dramatic subject-matter in his paintings, not quite in keeping with Fry's view (see his note on p. 131); in fact, in some places (e.g., pp. 168-69) it comes close to the Fusion Theory; see *Transformations*, London: Chatto and Windus, 1926 (reprinted New York: Anchor, 1956), pp. 1-43; note his comparison of subject and design with words and music in a song (pp. 27-34).

(3) Hilaire Hiler et al., *Why Abstract?*, New York: Laughlin, 1945, pp. 19-29; N. Gabo, "The Constructive Idea in Art," *Circle: International Survey of Constructive Art*, London: Faber and Faber, 1937, pp. 1-10.

For criticisms of the Divergence Theory, see Morris Weitz, *Philosophy of the Arts*, Cambridge, Mass.: Harvard U., 1950, chs. 1, 2; C. J. Ducasse, *The Philosophy of Art*, New York: Dial, 1929, pp. 213-22; John Hospers, *Meaning and Truth in the Arts*, Chapel Hill, N.C.: U. of North Carolina, 1946, pp. 98-117; L. A. Reid, *A Study in Aesthetics*, New York: Macmillan, 1931, ch. 12, pp. 311-27. Where do these criticisms miss the point of the theory, or misinterpret what Bell and Fry are saying?

17-B SIGNIFICANT FORM. On this concept, see Bell, *Art*, Part I, chs. 1, 2, 3; Part IV, ch. 2; *Since Cézanne*, ch. 2; Fry, "Retrospect," pp. 284-302. Compare Fry's term "vitality," in *Last Lectures*, 1939, ch. 3; Albert C. Barnes, *The Art in Painting*, 3rd ed., New York: Harcourt, Brace, 1937, Book II, ch. 1, pp. 55-71; Sheldon Cheney, *Expressionism in Art*, New York: Liveright, 1934, ch. 5; Susanne Langer, *Feeling and Form*, New York: Scribner's, 1953, pp. 14-15, and ch. 3. C. J. Ducasse's sharp attack, *op. cit.*, Appendix, makes some shrewd points.

17-C THE FUSION THEORY OF THE RELATION BETWEEN DESIGN AND SUBJECT. For exposition and defense of this theory, see (1) Walter Abell, *Representation and Form*, New York: Scribner's, 1936, chs. 7-10. His position is carefully stated, but when he argues (pp. 130-31) that in the Perugino, as compared with the El Greco, *Agony in the Garden*, the color-tonality and composition do not suit the subject, does he partly confuse subject with "point of departure," or depiction-subject with portrayal-subject? It is an interesting exercise to see how many confusions can be found in Lionello Venturi's criticism of Abell's comparison, *Art Criticism Now*, Baltimore: Johns Hopkins, 1941, pp. 42-46. The further comments on Venturi by Bernard C. Heyl, *New Bearings in Esthetics and Art Criticism*, New Haven, Conn.: Yale U., 1943, pp. 129-30, seem beside the point: the issue between Abell and Venturi, if there is one, is not that they are "judging by different standards," but that they are not clear what the subject is to which Perugino's design is to be fitting: whether it is the historical event portrayed or Perugino's own depiction of it.

(2) Albert C. Barnes, *op. cit.*, Book I, ch. 4, sec. 4; Book II, ch. 2; for further examples see pp. 92 (Botticelli's religious paintings), 392 (Giotto),

422 (Giorgione), 477 (Picasso), and Analyses *passim*. Barnes holds the Fusion Theory, despite some statements incompatible with it; some of his inconsistencies are pointed out by Abell (ch. 1). Barnes uses the term "plastic equivalents" (pp. 33, 75) instead of "presentational equivalents."

(3) Rhys Carpenter, *The Esthetic Basis of Greek Art*, Bryn Mawr, Pa.: Bryn Mawr College, 1921, ch. 2, reprinted in M. Rader, *A Modern Book of Esthetics*, 1st ed., New York: Holt, 1935, pp. 272-84; note his argument that lines and shapes that are not recognizable as representational can have neither very intense nor very definite regional qualities.

(4) David F. Bowers, in an excellent article, "The Role of Subject-Matter in Art," *J Phil*, XXVI (1939): 617-30, states the problems very carefully and defends a clear-cut form of the Fusion Theory.

See also the article by Helen Knight, "Aesthetic Experience in Pictorial Art," *Monist*, XL (1930): 74-83; DeWitt H. Parker, *The Analysis of Art*, New Haven, Conn.: Yale U., 1926, pp. 89-100; L. A. Reid, *op. cit.*, ch. 12, esp. pp. 323-26.

Further examples of the connection between design and subject are given by H. S. Langfeld, *The Aesthetic Attitude*, New York: Harcourt, Brace and Howe, 1920, pp. 169-78 and ch. 8; D. W. Gotshalk, *Art and the Social Order*, Chicago: U. of Chicago, 1947, pp. 97-102, 126-30; Matteo Marangoni, *The Art of Seeing Art*, London: Shelley Castle, 1951, pp. 150-236.

17-D DRAMATIC UNITY. What are the different ways in which the dramatic subject of a painting can be dramatically coherent or incoherent in itself? Find some examples and analyze them. What criteria used in connection with the theatre can meaningfully be applied here? See Abell, *op. cit.*, pp. 73-74, and ch. 6; his term "associative form" means approximately "dramatic unity." Roger Fry, *Transformations*, p. 14, uses the term "psychological structure." Charles Mauron, in his brief comparison of painting with literature, *The Nature of Beauty in Art and Literature*, London: L. and Virginia Woolf, 1927, pp. 65 ff., does not appear to use the term "psychological volumes" attributed to him by Fry, but he does refer to "spiritual volumes" in works of literature, not in painting.

17-E SUITABLE SUBJECTS. It is evident from the history of art that certain subjects have been selected over and over again by painters, some of them no doubt for religious and social motives. What other reasons, stated in terms of the sorts of designs that those subjects afford, can be suggested for their frequency of appearance? Discuss some familiar subjects in relation to the designs that can be based upon them, and the unity and quality of the designs. It is also often debated whether there are some subjects that are completely unsuitable for painting (see, *e.g.*, Lessing's *Laocoön*, chs. 2, 3, 24, 25). But apart from political, religious, and moral

objections to certain subjects at certain times, can you think of any subjects that would, if chosen, make it impossible to have a unified design?

17-F DESIGN AND FUNCTION. For defense of functionalism, see essays by Horatio Greenough in *Form and Function*, ed. by H. A. Small, Berkeley, Cal.: U. of California, 1947, pp. 24, 51-86, 113-29, especially the essay on "American Architecture," reprinted in *Theme and Form*, ed. by Monroe C. Beardsley, Robert W. Daniel, and Glenn H. Leggett, Englewood Cliffs, N.J.: Prentice-Hall, 1956, pp. 349-54. The essence of Greenough's position is that "the unflinching adaptation of a building to its position and use gives, as a sure product of that adaptation, character and expression" (p. 62); but each of the key terms in this statement requires careful analysis. The same view is maintained by W. D. Teague, *Design This Day*, New York: Harcourt, Brace, 1940; see ch. 4, esp. p. 53.

For criticism of functionalism, see Herbert Read, *Art and Industry*, London: Faber and Faber, 1934, including his comments on the instructive illustrations; Read denies that there is a "*necessary* connection between beauty and function" (pp. 2, 45).

For examples of functional objects to discuss, see Edgar Kaufmann, Jr., *What Is Modern Design?*, New York: Museum of Modern Art, 1950, and Eugene Raskin, "Walls and Barriers," *Columbia University Forum*, I (Winter 1957): 22-23. It is interesting to compare Lewis Mumford's *New Yorker* essay on the Manufacturers Trust Building in New York, "Crystal Lantern," also reprinted in Beardsley, Daniel, and Leggett, *op. cit.*, pp. 354-58.

·VII·

THE
MEANING
OF MUSIC

Even after we have analyzed a piece of music with some thoroughness, tracing its favored intervals, its melodies and figures, its modulations and developments—in short, exposing the details of its structure and texture—there is, of course, something important we have left out of our description. For we have not mentioned those pervasive regional qualities that are distinctive to it and relished in it. When we list such qualities—it is dramatic, it is turbulent, it is restrained and lyrical, it is boisterous and bluff—we know our description can never be complete. Yet we feel vaguely that even if it were there would still be something further to say about the music.

For it seems as though there is more in the music than what it presents to our attentive ears—an intimation beyond itself, a reference, however indirect, to the world or to the life of man. And this feeling is understandable. The experience of music is sometimes like an experience of revelation: we feel we are discovering something for the first time. Of course, it may be that we are just discovering the music itself, not something else to which the music calls attention or which it mediates for us. To discover a new word, for example "syzygy," is not necessarily to discover a new concept.

It has often been observed that the flow of music bears striking resemblances to the flow of meaningful human discourse. Hence the temptation to speak of music as a "language," and to take over linguistic terms for its analysis: "phrase," "sentence," "paragraph," for example. On the score of the finale of his last string quartet (F Major, Op. 135), Beethoven quoted three short figures from that movement, wrote words under them, and labeled them "The difficult decision":

FOURTH MOVEMENT   Beethoven, *String Quartet in F Major*, Op. 135

"Must it be? It must be!" Some have been led by these words to read into the quartet a philosophical resignation to fate. But if we are looking for the simplest hypothesis consonant with what we know of music and of Beethoven, the chances are that Beethoven was struck by the fact, which we can all recognize, that the first phrase, with its rising inflection and solemn mystery, is kinetically similar to an interrogative sentence; and the other phrases, with their clipped decisiveness and emphatic fall, are kinetically similar to declarative sentences, and have an air of being a reply to the first phrase, of which they are inversions. Now, these phrases do not occur together in just this order in the movement itself, for excellent musical reasons, so Beethoven may have thought it fun to point out this amusing and curious relation.

In any case, the question-and-answer quality, so to speak, is certainly there, at least if you are thinking of German and English questions and answers. And on a larger scale, we detect other discourse-qualities that critics often mention. In a fugue there may be a "conversation" among the different voices, though, considered sheerly as conversation, a rather monotonous one; there is "discussion," "argument," "debate," and sometimes a "coming to agreement." In a concerto the solo voice may "lecture" the rest of the ensemble. Moreover, critics say that music is sometimes "profound," rather than superficial; or that it has "significance" because in it "the composer really had something to say."

Thus arises the view that music has not only qualities of its parts and whole, but a meaning—a semantical dimension, like words and gestures. It is then part of the music critic's task, where apropos, to declare what that meaning is, and to help the handicapped or inexperienced listener find that meaning. To do this would be to *interpret* the music —a different thing from describing it. And the consequent problem for aesthetics concerns this process of interpretation: Does music have a meaning, in some noteworthy sense? If so, how do we know what that meaning is?

These questions are often introduced with a series of reverential bows to the great composers who at one time or another in unguarded moments—when badgered by their Boswells, such as Beethoven's friend Schindler—have tossed off a great variety of confusing remarks about this aspect of music. Tchaikovsky, for example, wrote to Taneev, "I should be sorry if symphonies that mean nothing should flow from my pen, consisting solely of a progression of harmonies, rhythms and modulations."[1] This quotation reveals one of the hazards of the problem. "Does your symphony have a meaning?" is one of those questions that a composer can hardly answer No to lightly, for this is to say that they are meaningless, which sounds as though they were lacking something that symphonies ought to have. Hence the author of the largest extant work on program music remarks earnestly of Beethoven: "In fact, his lofty mind could not but despise mere ingeniously contrived structures of meaningless tone combinations, however sensuously beautiful."[2] Here "meaningless" suggests that the music has no definite regional qualities, just as "tone combinations" suggests that the music doesn't even contain melodies. If the author had written that Beethoven despised "ingeniously contrived and intensely qualified tonal structures, containing melodies of the greatest beauty, though not referring to anything beyond themselves," we should have to conclude that Beethoven's mind was far too lofty to care for music at all. But it is by no means easy to say whether the word "meaningless" adds anything to the quotation besides a generalized disapproval.

Tchaikovsky's remark, in its context, was at least more definite: he was insisting that "most assuredly" his *F Minor Symphony (No. 4)* had a program: it wasn't *just* music, there were words to go with it. This raises some complicated questions about the relations, if any, between music and words, both in song and in program music. These questions we shall come to in the second section of this chapter. Before that, however, in the first section, we must consider music by itself, apart from any words. And we must ask whether musical compositions ever have a semantical dimension, analogous perhaps to the representational dimension of the fine arts: that is, a capacity to *mean*, as well as to *be*.

---

[1] He is so quoted by Marvin Cooper in his essay on Tchaikovsky's symphonies in *The Music of Tchaikovsky*, ed. by Gerald Abraham, London: Duckworth, 1946, p. 27. The letter (March 27=April 8, 1878) as translated by Rosa Newmarch reads: "I do not wish any symphonic work to emanate from me which has nothing to express, and consists merely of harmonies and a purposeless design of rhythms and modulations" (*Life and Letters*, New York: Dodd, Mead, 1905, p. 294; compare the letter to Madame von Meck, February 17=March 1, 1878).
[2] Frederick Niecks, *Programme Music in the Last Four Centuries*, London: Novello, [1906], p. 132.

There are three familiar but relatively trivial ways in which music can remind us of other things. They are trivial in relation to our present concerns because they are quite easily distinguishable as contingent and peripheral aspects of music. It will therefore be well to mention them briefly at once, and then set them aside.

First, of course, the music of a song can remind us of the words if we know it well. The melodic phrase deathlessly associated with the exclamation, "How dry I am!" will make the same comic point as the words themselves if they are played, let us say, in the score to a motion picture as a character pushes his way into a bar and grill. You can say that in this context the notes "mean" the words, in the sense of being a recognizable substitute for them, as well as a kind of mocking comment upon them, but this particular sense of musical meaning is not a very important one, though it is found in the music of Bach, who frequently quotes snatches of hymn-tunes to recall their words.

Second, music that is customarily played on certain occasions can become associated with those occasions. There is dance music, funeral music, military music, religious music—taking these terms not as descriptions of the musical qualities, which they might be, but as indications of the things that are usually done to their accompaniment. If the record companies succeed in their apparent aim to provide *Gebrauchsmusik* for all conceivable occasions, there is no telling to what degree of specialization this second sort of musical association can be carried: we already have Music to Study By, Music to Cook By, and Music to Love By. Soon we shall have Music to Eat French Cuisine By, and Music to Go with Martinis. There are college songs, hillbilly songs, Negro spirituals, barbershop ballads, and other such species—a circumstance of which composers have sometimes made use for topical purposes, for example Brahms with "Gaudeamus Igitur" in his *Academic Festival Overture.* There are historical associations, as with the French and Russian national anthems in Tchaikovsky's *1812 Overture,* or the first four notes of Beethoven's *C Minor Symphony* that were made into a symbol of victory in World War II, because they have the rhythm of a Morse Code V ($\cdot \cdot \cdot -$). Finally, there are associations of a more personal sort: the song that always makes your eyes water because you heard it at the Junior Prom or on shipboard.

That all these are uses of music cannot be denied; they have no bearing upon the central problems of musical meaning, however. If there is such a thing as Music to Study By, which I doubt, its capacity to fulfill this function presumably depends upon its having certain desirable qualities. Whether it also depends upon the music's having a certain meaning is not evident; in any case, the fact that music *can* be studied by is not enough to prove that music has a meaning, much less that it "means" study.

Third, there is the imitative aspect of music. Any event that makes a sound—a battle, a brook, a spinning wheel, an iron foundry, a train, a thunder storm, the bleating of sheep, the croaking of a frog—can be imitated by another sound. And scattered throughout musical literature there are, of course, a great many examples of this imitation of sound by sound. Since a representational painting imitates a sight by a visual design, the imitation of sound by an auditory design—whether the dropping of the guillotine is imitated by pizzicato strings, as in Berlioz' *Fantastic Symphony,* or by an actual guillotine specifically called for in the score by one of our more realistic composers—might be called the "representational" aspect of music. The analogy is close; familiarity with the relevant bird songs is all that is required to recognize Beethoven's imitations of the quail and the cuckoo—or the yellowhammer, as Schindler insists —in the coda to the slow movement of his *"Pastoral" Symphony in F Major (No. 6),* just as familiarity with the visual appearance of the relevant objects is all that is required to recognize a visual representation. However, it will not be necessary for our purposes to press the comparison; we can speak of "sound-imitation," or the imitation of sounds by sounds.

The Image-Evocation Theory

This third preliminary, and relatively trivial, way in which music can remind us of things outside itself prompts a further line of thought that seems to promise more important results. For granted that sounds can imitate sounds, we may ask whether sounds can imitate anything but sounds. Music is sometimes said to imitate sights, too: the sea, clouds, a trout darting silently through the water, a mist lifting from the mountain, a fairy, or moonlight. Honegger said that in his *Pacific 231* he was "depicting" not only the sound, but the "visual impression" of the locomotive. If he succeeded, we can build upon his success one theory of musical meaning that may be worth considering. Consider a certain musical passage, say, from Debussy's *La Mer,* that is said to imitate the sea—not the sound of the sea alone, but the way it looks. Suppose the composer first forms an image of the sea in his mind, and then composes music of such a nature that a qualified listener hearing the music will form the same or similar images. In that case, we could say that the music "means" the sea.

It is doubtful if any serious student of music has ever maintained this theory, which I shall call the *Image-Evocation Theory* of musical meaning. But it is quite certain that many things written about music, especially in reviews and in concert programs, make sense only if this theory, or something like it, is true. Indeed, when people say that they do not "understand" a piece of music, and ask what it means, sometimes their predicament is exactly that they feel they should form some images of objects or historical events to go with the music, and do not know what images to form. "Image" here does not have to mean eidetic imagery, only the concept of a visible thing. If the theory seems plausible only when left vague and half-explicit, that is all the more reason for seeing what it looks like when dragged into the open. And even if it is obviously wrong, its mistakes may be instructive.

People often report that music evokes images, that is, suggests to them some objects or events; in fact, listeners have been classified according to their tendency to respond this way. But the notion of image-evocation requires serious qualifications. If a person takes a hot bath and falls to daydreaming, it would be misleading to say that the bath evokes the daydreams. It provides a favorable condition for daydreaming, to be sure, and perhaps we could say that it stimulates the fantasy. But by itself it exercises very little control over the content of the daydream; it is not sufficiently directive. Similarly, it is misleading to say that music evokes a listener's images if in fact he merely takes advantage of the general musical ambiance to relax his mental control and lapse into reverie.

The answer to the question whether music evokes images, then, depends on the control the music exercises over the images. If it can exercise a high degree of control, the description is apt. If not, not—though no doubt it does exercise more control than a hot bath.

The direct evidence on this matter derives from reports of listeners, and experimental studies support our common experience. Of half a dozen serious people invited to imagine appropriate objects and events while listening to a musical selection that they have never heard before, and whose name and composer they do not know, hardly two of them will come up with the same results. Where one sees a tornado, another will see a fight between a wolf and a wild boar (with tusks); where one sees a white-robed maiden bidding good-bye to her fiancé, another will see a Zen Buddhist priest meditating.

This direct evidence is supported, and its significance explained, by a careful consideration of the question we raised a few paragraphs back and temporarily set aside. Can music imitate the visual appearances of things? For only if the music can, let us say, imitate the white-robed maiden so accurately that she will not be mistaken by a careful listener for a Buddhist priest, is there any plausibility in the Image-Evocation Theory.

We have already, in Chapter IV, §13, found reason to believe that similar qualities can appear in different sensory fields, and our discussion of music and words in the following section will contribute further to this point. But there are serious limits to this correspondence. Consider first physical objects or states of affairs, as opposed to events. Can music sound so much the way the sea looks that we can pick out the sea uniquely as its special object? Tchaikovsky's Sugarplum Fairy, in *The Nutcracker*

Suite, is evidently a different sort of fairy from those that dance about in the Overture of Mendelssohn's *A Midsummer-Night's Dream* music or those that are "tripping hither, tripping thither" in the opening scene of *Iolanthe*. Yet I defy anyone to draw a picture of a fairy—standing still —that will fit Tchaikovsky but not Mendelssohn or Sullivan. The same difficulties arise in distinguishing, by musical means alone, between mist and a light snow, or between moonlight and lamplight.

If we set aside physical objects as such and consider physical events —the things that objects do, or that happen to them—the imitative power of music becomes considerably more notable. Music is at least a process, and certain things can be said of all processes, including physical changes, whether locomotion (change of position) or qualitative change. All proc- esses have such kinetic qualities as pace, tension, momentum, climax, crescendo, dying away. And one process, say a musical one, can be similar to another in its kinetic pattern. Thus music can undoubtedly imi- tate to some extent the kinetic aspects of physical motion: rushing, stag- gering, bounding, creeping, wavering, romping, driving, soaring, gliding, surging, flying, falling, blowing up and collapsing.

And it seems evident that it is just this capacity of music that makes possible the dance-with-music as an aesthetic object. We shall not have space here to deal with the art of dance, though some of the points to be considered in the following section will relate to it. But the existence of such an art depends on the possibility of perceived correspondence between the patterns of music and the patterns of bodily movement.

It does not, however, follow that music can *mean* these processes. For music can never imitate any one of them so precisely that it can refer to that alone. When music is said to imitate the darting of the trout, for example, this is in need of careful restriction: it can present the darting, all right, but not the trout—unless it should happen that trout are the only things that dart. It can present muddying, as when the chords be- come thick at Bar 59 of Schubert's *Die Forelle*, but cannot tell us, with- out words, that the fisherman is stirring the water with a stick to confuse the poor fish. Thus in most cases where musical process is compared with physical processes, several comparisons are sure to be equally apt. Con- sider, for a brief illustration, the scherzo of Beethoven's *A Major Sym- phony (No. 7):*

THIRD MOVEMENT   Beethoven, *Symphony in A Major* (No. 7)
Presto

There is absolutely no need for us to compare this with any physical mo- tion at all. But in order to test the Image-Evocation Theory, let's see what physical processes we can think of that are similar to it in kinetic pattern.

Someone goes up an inclined plane in two quick jumps, and then comes tripping down. Someone squirts water on the roof, and it trickles off. Something is blown up and the air splutters out. Perhaps some of these stories are more enjoyable to contemplate than others; none is very edifying. If *that's* what the music means, you may prefer not to think about it. There is no way of determining whether Beethoven had any of these images, or any images at all, in his mind. It would be silly to encourage people to spend their time trying to think of physical analogues of music instead of listening to the music, and it would be even sillier to say that until the listener has hit upon the correct analogue he has not understood the music.

Now the defender of the Image-Evocation Theory is not, of course, compelled to claim that all music has meaning in his sense. But I think we are in a position to say that *no* music without words has meaning in this sense. It is therefore very misleading to speak of music as "describing" or "narrating" or "depicting." There is no such thing. Vaughan Williams' *London Symphony* does not describe London, nor does Ravel's "Le Gibet," in *Gaspard de la Nuit,* describe a gallows.

The Expression Theory

To get the Image-Evocation Theory out of the way is to set the stage for an examination of two other theories of musical meaning that are more substantial and more fundamental. Strictly speaking, there are several theories, for no two writers agree exactly, but all the theories can conveniently be classified into two main types, based on the two concepts of *expression* and *signification.*

The *Expression Theory* of musical meaning[3] takes as its key concept the formula

$$X \text{ expresses } Y,$$

where X is the musical work, or some part of it, and Y is a psychological state or quality: heroic fortitude, moping melancholy, romping gaiety. For example,

The scherzo of Beethoven's *A Major Symphony* expresses joy.

This may seem like a harmless enough statement—it is certainly a common one. But how do we know what the scherzo expresses: that it is joy rather than fear or fretfulness? What evidence are we to look for in deciding? At this point we find that those who profess the Expression Theory in fact have three very different things in mind.

---

[3] This theory has been held by George Santayana, John Dewey, R. G. Collingwood, L. A. Reid, C. J. Ducasse, T. M. Greene, John Hospers, D. W. Gotshalk, Henry Aiken; for references see Note 18-A at end of chapter.

Sometimes when people talk about musical expression, we can see that they are really talking about the state of mind of the composer; to them,

"The scherzo of Beethoven's *A Major Symphony* expresses joy" means "Beethoven felt joy when composing that scherzo, and was impelled by that emotion to compose it."

This use of the term "express" is familiar in other matters. We say, for example, that a person's face expresses bafflement or bewilderment; he *looks* baffled or bewildered, that is, his face has the sort of look usually accompanying such feelings, so that we can with some probability infer from his look that he has the feeling. The inference depends upon a generalization: "People who look that way are generally baffled." And we are in a position to obtain such generalizations about facial expressions, for we can learn to correlate them with verbal symptoms of bafflement ("I don't understand this at all") and other behavioral symptoms (hesitancy or head-scratching).

It is evident, however, that we know no such generalization as "People who write music like Beethoven's scherzo are generally joyous." For in the first place there is no other music very much like that scherzo; a generalization should not be based upon a single instance. And in the second place, even in this one instance, we have no independent evidence of Beethoven's state of mind. It is true that biographers of the great musicians make this kind of inference constantly, and sometimes offer scraps of not very circumstantial data to back them up. For example, a recent book of psychoanalytical studies has much to say about the inhibitions in Brahms' love life and his unfulfilled longings for love. "We are not surprised to hear longing and woe sound through his music."[4] If this means that we can predict that longing and woe will sound through the music of any composer merely from knowing that he has unfulfilled longings for love, then psychoanalysis is a lot simpler than I had thought. It is a plausible guess, but there is no adequate evidence for it.

The first concept of expression, which identifies it with the venting of emotion, is therefore of no use to us. In this sense, it is very seldom possible for the critic to verify the statement that such-and-such a musical composition expresses joy, since to do that he would either have to know how the composer was feeling at the time, and also that he was relieving his feelings in writing the music, or he would have to be in possession of a general law correlating that sort of music with that emotion. If what the music expresses is something discoverable from listening to the music itself, then expression is not the same as venting emotions.

Other critics who talk about musical expression are really talking about their own state of mind when they listen to the music; to them,

---

[4] Edward Hitschmann, *Great Men: Psychoanalytic Studies*, New York: International Universities, 1956, p. 224.

"The scherzo of Beethoven's *A Major Symphony* expresses joy" means "The scherzo makes me feel joy when I hear it."

This is not the same as saying that the music makes me want to tap my feet or rock and roll: those effects of the music can take place on a physiological level. In this second sense, "express" is synonymous with "arouse": the music makes the listener experience joy or sorrow, calmness or uneasiness.

It is an interesting question whether music, apart from words, can strictly be said to arouse emotions. Anger and fear, curiosity and moral indignation, for example, surely involve a conceptual element, an object to which the emotion is directed, and music can present no concepts. Thus music cannot arouse anger or fear, though it can be angry or fearful. But presumably music may be said to arouse *feelings,* if we mean by this term something more general than emotions: excitement, serenity, lassitude, relaxation, tension. These are feelings about the music itself—not the sort of thing the Expression Theorists usually talk about, such as cheerfulness, human dignity, or heroism. But it is very hard to see how, without the mediation of concepts, any such emotions can really be aroused. Can heroic music make me feel like a hero? Not for a moment.

In any case, the term "expression" is redundant here. We already have a term for arousing emotions, namely the term "arousing"; if that is what we mean when we say the music expresses emotions, it is better to say so. For we can talk about the effects of music upon listeners with no reference at all to the composer and *his* feelings about the matter.

Sometimes when people talk about musical expression, we can see that they are really talking about the regional qualities of the music itself; to them,

"The scherzo of Beethoven's *A Major Symphony* expresses joy" means "The scherzo is joyful."

In this translation we seem to be getting nearer to what some defenders of the Expression Theory have in mind. For, despite the lack of clarity in parts of their theory, they do generally take pains to distinguish the act of expression, in the artistic sense, from simple venting of the emotions, like crying or laughing, and from the calculation of effects, like advertising or political campaigning. In artistic expression, it is said, the artist "puts himself into his work"; he "embodies" or "objectifies" his feelings. This is the difference between art and dreaming or shouting or meditating or cake-baking or knitting to achieve inner calm.

When we ask the Expression Theorists for a fuller account of their concept of objectification or embodiment, which are their occasional synonyms for "expression," we get a number of slightly different answers. But this seems to be the core:

"The composer has objectified (embodied, expressed) joy in his scherzo" means "(1) he has been moved by a feeling of joy to compose the scherzo;

(2) he has given the scherzo a joyful quality; and (3) the scherzo has the capacity to give him the same feeling of joy when he hears it again, and consequently to give it to other listeners, too."

It is this compound theory that I shall call the Expression Theory of Musical Meaning in the strict sense. It involves a statement about the music, plus a statement about the relationship of the music to both the composer and the listener.

It is clear that part 2 of this definition is logically independent of parts 1 and 3, for the music may have a quality even if that quality is neither the cause nor the effect of emotions. If our preceding discussion is sound, we have already found cause to reject the Expression Theory in this compound form, for part 1 is untestable and part 3 is dubious. But part 2 may still be worth considering, and to that we shall now turn. Suppose from "This music expresses joy," we extract the statement, "This music is joyful," which is a description of the music. It is a metaphorical description, to be sure, but it is no less a description for being metaphorical. However, it raises several questions.

As it is most often used, the term "express" does not apply to all regional qualities, but only to some. For music to be called "very expressive," it is not enough that it should be definitely in a key, or have a marked rhythm. Some regional qualities are similar to qualities of human behavior, especially to mental states and processes: somberness, serenity, frolicsomeness, determination, calm, voluptuousness, indecisiveness, for example. Let us call such qualities *human qualities*. The Expression Theory claims, then, that some of the regional qualities of music are *human regional qualities*.[5] The question is whether this is true.

The Human Qualities of Music

You might think that anyone who admits that music has regional qualities at all would have no special reason to balk at the human qualities. But in fact two doubts have often been raised about them even by those who do not raise the same doubts about such regional qualities as tonality or rhythm. The first doubt is whether such qualities are in fact heard as phenomenally objective qualities of the music. On this point, it is argued that our use of such terms as "joyful" shows that we cannot distinguish such qualities but are really talking about subjective feelings. The second doubt is whether such qualities, even if in fact phenomenally objective in the auditory field when they appear, are sufficiently invariant from person to person to be attributed to the music itself as a perceptual object. On this point, it is argued that what one hears when confronted with musical stimuli varies with training, with age, with perceptual sensitivity, with cultural conditioning, and other factors.

---

[5] These qualities are sometimes called "physiognomic qualities," "emotional qualities," or "feeling qualities"; see Note 6-C in Chapter II.

There is ample evidence, from psychological inquiry as well as lay introspection, to quiet the first doubt, but the situation is more complex with the second. To justify the attribution of human qualities to the music we must show that such qualities are a function of—that is, causally depend upon—its local and subregional qualities. In other words, we must show that whenever a person hears and discriminates certain local and subregional qualities of the music—say, melodic leaps, diatonic intervals, or a fast tempo—he will also hear the human regional qualities—say, joyfulness. And this is naturally a difficult thing to show, or to refute. It won't do just to point out that the first time we hear Chinese music we can't tell whether a Chinese hears it as joyful or sorrowful or neither. For without the proper training we don't even hear it as music; we don't really hear, in the full sense, its local and subregional qualities in their true relations.

A certain amount of work has nevertheless been done on the problem by psychologists,[6] varying greatly, to be sure, in care and thoroughness, but giving, on the whole, noteworthy results. The main difficulties have to some extent been overcome. One difficulty is that we cannot be certain that two subjects do in fact hear the same local qualities, independently of their reports about the human qualities. This has limited experimentation with music of other cultures, and we require much more evidence about that. But it is possible to determine that the subject is not tone-deaf and to give him music that is in an idiom not utterly inaccessible to him. Another difficulty is that the subjects must be given correct instructions so that they know what it is they are supposed to report, and here many of the experimenters have multiplied their own obstacles. When the experimenter asks his subjects to describe the music, he tends to get convergent responses. Not everyone will choose the same word to describe it, of course, but the descriptions will tend to correspond very closely, especially if he does not require the subjects to choose single adjectives to describe long passages that may have mixed or varying qualities. On the other hand, when he asks them to say how they think the composer was feeling, or how the music makes them feel, or what pictures it calls to mind, the responses begin to diverge. And no wonder, for these instructions distract their attention from the qualities of the music itself.

Another difficulty is that communication between the experimenter and his subjects is hindered, sometimes fatally, by a linguistic barrier. For where there is no language but metaphor in which to describe the music, there is bound to be some deviation in the understanding of the metaphors, even if all the subjects are in fact hearing the same human quality. The quality one describes as "whimsical" may be the very one that another subject, less gifted in speech, calls "jumpy" or "wild." Or he may say "jejune" when he means "childish."

---

[6] References to these investigations, with further comments, are given in Notes 18-E and 18-F.

This does not mean, however, that such metaphorical descriptions have no objective reference. As we have seen in Chapter III, §10, the minimal condition for applying metaphorically to B a term that applies literally to A is that B is similar to A in some respect connoted by the A term. If there is no term in existence that designates the characteristic in respect to which A and B are similar, the metaphorical term is all we have. It may, of course, be highly misleading unless the context limits its meaning in some way, but it may also be very apt and accurate. In general, we cannot expect to say much about the total quality of a large work. In an essay on Mozart's piano concertos,[7] we are told that K. 414 (A major) has a "fresh, vernal quality," K. 450 (B flat major) is "cheerful, intimate," K. 453 (G major) is "ambiguous . . . generally serious," K. 456 (B flat major) has a "strange ambiguity of mood and character," K. 459 (F major) is "cheerful," and K. 466 (D minor) exhibits "tumultuous and, at times, sinister power." These, I should think, are fair descriptions as far as they go, but they do not go far.

Our descriptions can be made more precise when we confine them to particular movements or to particular passages, but we always feel that the individual quality of the music is something that can only vaguely be indicated by words like "cheerful," which are built to accommodate a wide range of discriminable qualities. Nor does it help much to extend and develop the metaphor itself. If we remark that a certain movement is sad, and we are asked what kind of sadness it possesses, it is not very helpful to say it is the sort of sadness one would feel at losing a relative who is close, but not too close, say, a first cousin you used to spend much time with as a child but haven't seen in several years. It is more helpful to say that it is the sort of sadness that arises from violins playing, in thirds, on their G and D strings, melodies containing many falling minor seconds, in slow triple time. This helps us to imagine the music itself more concretely. But in the last analysis, our descriptions are best when they can be illustrated by pointing to the music itself and simply calling attention to its qualities.

In the absence of the music, then, we make more precise a description of its human quality by analyzing the perceptual conditions of that quality. Such an analysis presupposes that there are perceptual conditions upon which the human qualities depend, and that these conditions can in principle be discovered. The local conditions under which a musical composition tends to be joyous or sad may be called its "joy-making" or "sad-making" qualities. And the statement, if true, that music having such-and-such features—slow tempo, low pitch, chromatic falling inter-

---

[7] By A. H. King, in *The Concerto*, ed. by Ralph Hill, Baltimore: Penguin, 1952. Compare Hermann Scherchen's descriptions of the different qualities of each Contrapunctus in Bach's *Art of Fugue* (*The Nature of Music*, trans. by William Mann, London: Dobson, 1950).

vals, a minor key—tends to be sad, would be an empirical law or generalization.

The difficulty in verifying such laws is that in the incomplete state of our knowledge they have to be quasi-statistical in form. We cannot say that all compositions in a minor key are sad: the song called "The Jolly Miller" and the Rakóczy March from Berlioz' *Damnation of Faust* are both in minor keys, but they are jovial enough; while on the other hand "The Last Rose of Summer" and the Dead March from Mendelssohn's *Saul*, though in major keys, are by no means cheerful. Yet we can still say that being in a minor key is one thing that tends to make a composition sad, though its effect may be overruled by other features. And the same may be said about certain tempos, rhythms, intervals, and pitches. The statement that a composition is sad because it is slow, minor, or falling is not a tautology, but synthetic and testable. Slow cheerfulness and fast solemnity are not logical contradictions, they are just very unlikely or empirically impossible.

There is no methodological error in the project of confirming such general laws about perceptual conditions and human regional qualities. We can recognize, that is, hear, the regional quality of a work before we analyze it in any very detailed way, though the quality may be heard more intensely or subtly after we have made some analysis. Suppose we gather a group of movements that all sound rather joyful or joyous—not only Beethoven's scherzo, but the finale of that same symphony and of the *E Flat Major ("Emperor") Piano Concerto*, the finale of Mozart's *Sinfonia Concertante in E Flat Major* (K. Anh. 9), the finale of Bach's *Italian Concerto*, the opening of Mendelssohn's *Symphony in A Major (No. 4)*—to which we could add such pieces as Tchaikovsky's "Waltz of the Flowers" from *The Nutcracker Suite*, and the dancing theme from Weber's *Oberon* Overture—except that these are better described as "gay." When we then analyze these compositions to see what they have in common, we find a number of features in their tempo, melodic and harmonic progressions, intervals, and so on, that occur with more than chance frequency, and it is probable that they contribute to the emergence of that quality of joyousness.

The Expression Theory has called our attention to an important fact about music—namely, that it has human regional qualities. But in performing this service it has rendered itself obsolete. We now have no further use for it. Indeed we are much better off without it. "The music is joyous" is plain and can be defended. "The music expresses joy" adds nothing except unnecessary and unanswerable questions.

For "express" is properly a relational term; it requires an X that does the expressing and a Y that is expressed, and X and Y must be distinct. When we say that a rose is red, we have only one thing, namely the rose, and we describe its quality; in exactly the same way, when we say the music is joyous, we have only one thing, namely the music, and we describe its quality. There is no need for the term "express."

The same conclusion would be reached for other arts to which the term "express" has been applied. I have taken the Expression Theory as a theory about music, and examined it as such, because I think it makes its best case in this domain. But of course many proponents of the theory set it forth as a general theory about the arts. They would say that the fine arts, too, besides being designs and representations, are expressive. But statements about the expressiveness of works of fine art, when analyzed correctly, turn out, in exactly similar fashion, to be translatable into statements about the human regional qualities of either the design or the subject. Thus, for example, when Lewis Mumford writes that the Manufacturers Trust Building in New York City "expresses the classic qualities of dignity, serenity, and order,"[8] he could as well have used the word "has" instead of "expresses." And though this would not, as we have seen, solve all the problems, it would at least raise the right problems instead of sending us off in the wrong direction.

The Signification Theory

We come now to our second main theory, which I shall call the *Signification Theory* of musical meaning.[9] And though those who defend this theory regard it as a superior substitute for the Expression Theory, from which they want to disassociate it, nevertheless some of the points we have made in connection with the Expression Theory will also apply here.

The Signification Theorists set aside the venting and the evoking of emotions as not properly a matter of meaning at all, but they do not think statements about musical meaning can be reduced to descriptions. For they hold that music does have a referential relation to things outside itself, and they propose to analyze this relation in semiotic terms, that is, using the concept of *sign*. It does not matter for our present purposes that some of them prefer the term "symbol"; I shall consider the theory in what I take to be its most convincing form, leaving it open how my conclusions are to be translated into the terminology of individual writers.

In its broadest sense, in which it can be applied to words, gestures, and semaphore signals as well as markers that direct our way to exits and rest rooms, the word "sign" denotes any object or event that stands for something else, or leads us to take account in some way of something else besides itself. As a matter of fact, the problem of constructing an adequate general definition of signification, or being-a-sign-of, is ex-

---

[8] See reference in Note 17-F, preceding chapter.
[9] This theory has been held by Albert Gehring, Charles Morris, Susanne Langer, L. A. Reid, and others; for references see Note 18-I.

tremely difficult, but fortunately we do not need to attempt it here. For in
order to say whether or not music is a sign of something, we need to
consider only some of the acknowledged defining characteristics of signs.

If, as I have suggested, we use the word "sign" this broadly, we shall
of course want to add that there are very important differences between
traffic lights and words, or between words and flags. But the Signification Theory of music is interested in only one subclass of signs, those that
are in some important way similar to their significata, that is, to the
things they stand for. Such signs are said to be *iconic signs*.

Onomatopoeic words are examples of iconic signs; on a larger scale,
grammatical order can be iconic too. For example, in "The lightning
was followed by thunder" the word "lightning" is followed by the word
"thunder"; but "Thunder followed the lightning," though it describes
the same sequence of events, is not iconic, except in so far as the word
"thunder" is onomatopoeic. The visual analogue of onomatopoea is a
design that exhibits the same pattern as what it signifies. A map is a
sign, in that it maps a certain territory, but it does so by having a structural similarity to the territory it maps: the directional relations and distances between dots on a map of the United States, for example, correspond systematically to the relations between the cities they stand for.
The minimal case of a map might be a road sign:

As every driver knows, this means that there is an S-shaped curve ahead;
the design is a curve, and it calls attention to one.

Is it possible, then, to work out a kind of a map-theory of music?
It would seem so, if there is something that music can map. And this is
what the Signification Theory asserts: music is an iconic sign of psychological processes. It "articulates" or "elucidates" the mental life of man,
and it does so by presenting auditory equivalents of some structural or
kinetic aspects of that life. This theory is sometimes called a *Semiotic
Theory*, because it tries to subsume music under a general theory of

semiosis, or sign-functioning. Like the Expression Theory, it has been set forth as a general theory about all the arts, including literature and painting. Now, certainly literature is a case of semiosis, for words have signification. Representation in the fine arts is more doubtful; a painting of a nude, for example, is not exactly a sign of a nude; at least, it is not a direction for means-end behavior, like a road sign or a map, though a drawing in an anatomy book may be. But our main question is whether music signifies—apart, as we said earlier, from its imitativeness and extramusical associations. The Signification Theorist, like the Expressionist, seems to want to reverse the famous dictum of Walter Pater, "All the arts aspire to the condition of music," by substituting what may be an equally confusing suggestion that music aspires to the condition of literature. It is not at all clear why any art should covet its neighbor's property.

The Signification Theory, then, consists of two propositions: (1) A musical composition can be iconic with a psychological process, that is, it can be similar to such a process in an important way. (2) *By virtue of its iconicity,* the composition is a sign of the psychological process. As the italicized words show, the second proposition depends upon the first, but the first could be true even if the second is false. Therefore, we must consider each proposition separately.

As regards the first proposition, it is perfectly consonant with what I have already said. Still, the Signification Theorists and also their critics have called attention to one aspect of music that has not been stressed above. A musical passage is a *process,* and so is a sequence of ideas and feelings that passes through a person's mind. Qualitatively these processes are very different in many respects: there is nothing in music to correspond to the distinction between the thought of a triangle and the thought of a circle, or between disgust and distaste. But music and mental life both have features that belong to process as such: tempo, variations of intensity, impulsiveness, relaxation and tension, crescendo and diminuendo. These features I have already included under what I have called the "kinetic qualities" of music; sometimes they are called "dynamic qualities." In any case, the same qualities are found in psychological processes.

For example, the opening bars of the Beethoven scherzo can be described kinetically in somewhat this way: there are two increasingly loud explosive bursts, jumping upward in pitch, followed by a lightly tripping stepwise descent. This kinetic pattern could be found in the process of suddenly seeing a joke, with sudden jolts of amusement, followed by its dying down. When we say that the passage is joyful, it is partly this kinetic parallelism that we are relying upon for the metaphor. I do not insist that this particular parallelism is completely apt, or that no better might be found; I only say that the claimed iconicity of some music with some mental processes, and perhaps of any music with some conceivable mental processes, is admissible.

But even if we assent to the first proposition of the Signification Theory, we are not compelled to assent to the second one. For according to that theory, if we recognize the iconicity of the scherzo, we are permitted to go on to say that the music is a sign of joy. To interpret a musical composition would be to say things like "This adagio *means* serene and untroubled contemplation," "This allegro *signifies* a striving for self-control and a final achievement of that goal," and "This alternation between contrasting keys and tempos *indicates* a vacillation and ambivalence of mind, a struggle between hope and despair."

The Nature of a Sign

Does music signify, then, in virtue of its iconicity? First of all, it is clear in general that mere similarity, whether of quality or structure, is not sufficient to make an object a sign. If it were, we should have to say that the territory signifies the map, and that the mental process is a sign of the music, since similarity always goes both ways. One chair may be exactly like another, but that does not make it signify the other. Something more is required.

When we survey the conditions under which an object becomes a sign, we encounter a number of subtle problems. But I think we can say in general that objects do not become signs unless there is either a verbal stipulation (conventional signs) or a cause-and-effect connection met with in ordinary human behavior (natural signs).

Thus a road sign, like the S curve, is a sign only because there is a key to its meaning, a sort of sign-dictionary, in the handbook for drivers published by the State Department of Motor Vehicles. Apart from that verbal explanation, we could not know the first time we saw the sign that it stood for a curve rather than a river. It is a conventional sign. Of course, we might tour the country, taking notes, and discover that every time we pass such a sign, a winding road follows; then it would be a natural sign for us, because we would have established a natural law connecting them. Again, although we can recognize a map if we know the territory well, even without a title, what makes the map a map is, in the last analysis, its title: without it, we might not be able to distinguish between a good map of North Dakota and a poor map of South Dakota. This is one of the crucial differences between signification and visual depiction: we can know that a painting depicts a woman even if there are absolutely no words to help us, but we cannot know what a design signifies—let's say a crude map of a pirate treasure—unless there is at least one proper name or description, such as "Treasure Island." A map is a kind of portrayal, not merely a depiction.

Although, of course, fragments of music may be taken out of context and assigned a signification as theme songs, or elopement signals, or illicit communications between bridge partners, music in general is surely not a conventional sign of anything. Nor is it, in general, a natural sign.

Smoke is said to be a natural sign of fire, the thermometer reading of temperature, and spots of measles, because there is a causal connection between them. In the same way a fingerprint is a sign of someone's one-time presence. Perhaps the canary's song is a symptom of his physical or mental well-being, or of his mating instinct; but with Mozart there is no such simple correspondence. To prove that music is a natural sign, we should have to do what, in our earlier discussion of the first sense of the term "expression," we decided cannot be done, namely correlate musical fragments or passages with specific states of mind of composers.

It is doubtful, therefore, if we can find any good reason for saying that music is an iconic *sign*, either conventional or natural, though it can be iconic. And, indeed, if this theory proved anything, it would prove too much. For if we allow that music signifies every mental process to which it is iconic, then since many qualitatively different mental processes may have the same kinetic pattern, musical signification is bound to be incurably ambiguous. A long crescendo, as in Ravel's *Bolero,* might signify bursting with joy or blowing your top. This consequence is often conceded by the Signification Theorists, who quite properly do not regard it as a fatal difficulty. Perhaps it only shows the limitations of musical signification, but the limitations are severe.

On the other hand, you could say that musical signification is not ambiguous, but highly general: *Bolero* denotes all psychological processes characterized by increasing intensity. This, however, brings out a difficulty in the concept of iconic signification that was hinted at above, in the definition of "iconic sign," by the word "important." If *Bolero*—which I use as my example here because its dominant kinetic pattern is relatively simple—is an iconic sign of those psychological processes that have *all* its qualities, then of course it is a sign only of itself. If it is taken to be a sign of processes that are similar to it in being characterized by increasing intensity, then we cannot tell simply from hearing the music that it is these processes it signifies rather than others. The music must be supplemented by a verbal rule that prescribes which of its qualities are the iconically significant ones. And in the absence of such a rule, we cannot decide among the innumerable possible qualities, so that if the music is a sign at all, it is ambiguous.

Moreover, if similarity alone were a sufficient basis of signification, as the theory declares, we should also have to say that musical processes signify not only mental processes but physical ones as well. For, as we have seen, there is the same sort of iconicity between them. And indeed the psychological and the physical are not wholly separable in this comparison, for music is similar to psychological processes partly by being similar to the behavioral manifestations of those processes: the slow gait of the depressed, the animated and ebullient movements of the happy.

But to make music signify physical processes seems too much of a good
thing.

These considerations do not refute the Signification Theory conclusively, but, as I think, they do show that there is no good reason to hold it and some good reasons not to. The Signification Theory is nevertheless tempting because it offers an interesting possibility, that of construing music as in some sense a special "language of the emotions," a discourse about the tensions and torments of the mind, of a different order from ordinary verbal discourse. Such a language would only be worthwhile, however, if something true and important can be said in it. Here is the point of juncture between this chapter and the next, in which we shall consider whether music is true or false, or contains knowledge of some kind.

The Signification Theory offers an interesting and noteworthy explanation of what we mean when we say, as sometimes most of us may, that we do not "understand" a musical composition: we have not yet discovered what it signifies. But I should think there is another explanation that recommends itself not only by its simplicity but by its correspondence to ordinary experience. To understand a piece of music is simply to hear it, in the fullest sense of this word, that is, to organize its sounds into wholes, to grasp its sequences of notes as melodic and rhythmic patterns, to perceive its kinetic qualities and, finally, the subtle and pervasive human qualities that depend on all the rest. When the music does not make sense to us, on an early exposure perhaps, it is not because we have really heard all that it is—how could that be?—and are casting about for something outside of it to connect or compare it with; the elements or aspects of it that did take auditory shape before us have not yet fitted together, as we hope on further listening they will.

On the Interpretation of Music

It seems that we must tentatively conclude that music does not express or signify. Therefore, interpretative statements about music are false, even though a large part of discourse about music consists of just such statements. Not that all symphonies have been so much interpreted and counterinterpreted as, say, Shostakovitch's *Tenth Symphony*, which Soviet critics have had much trouble with. "The symphony has a clearly expressed tragic character," writes one, but whether its ending is optimistic or not the critics do not agree; nor whether it is the tragedy of a lonely man who feels weak before the powers that threaten him, as other critics affirm and Shostakovitch has himself denied. But other symphonies have been subjected to similar interpretation, especially Mozart's *G Minor Symphony*, Beethoven's *C Minor Symphony* (*No. 5*) and *A Major Symphony* (*No. 7*). And the disputes that arise can never be settled, for they rest upon a mistaken theory.

Now if we grant that such statements as these can at least be taken as attempts to describe the music, it may be questioned whether it matters very much to the music critic whether we allow him to introduce the words "signify" or "express" or their synonyms, instead of advising him to stick with "has" and "is." It may matter a good deal. For listeners who have been exposed to this sort of "interpretation" sometimes come to feel unhappy about music that they cannot talk about in this way, or that no one has talked about for them: they come to feel, quite unnecessarily, that they are missing something important, when in fact they may be hearing, and if left alone enjoying, the very qualities of the music that such statements so poorly report. Or, what is worse, they may feel that when they have learned to make such verbal responses they have got the essence of the music, even before they have made the effort to hear it. When descriptions are put into the form of descriptions, they back up their claims by the music itself, and they lead attention to the music. When they are put in the form of statements about signification, they lead away from the music, very often either into biographical intentionalism disguised as musicological expertness or affective free-associationism disguised as semiotical profundity.

The view of music that we have now arrived at[10] is often called the "Formalist" theory of music. But since, in this context, it is entirely negative—because it consists in the denial of the proposition that music has a meaning—it hardly deserves a special name; and since it is reasonable, it does not deserve a misleading one. Although "Formalism" is a widely used name for a general theory about the arts, it is impossible to discover any theory that it names. The denial of meaning to music may remind us of the Divergence Theory of the relation between subject and design in painting, but there does not seem to be any logical connection between the present view and that. Surely one may hold either without being committed to the other. Nor can I discover any general proposition about aesthetic objects—at least one that is clear, plausible, and unequivocal—from which the Divergence Theory of painting and the "Formalist" Theory of music both follow.

Music, then, is no symbol of time or process, mental or physical, Newtonian or Bergsonian; it *is* process. And perhaps we can say it is the closest thing to pure process, to happening as such, to change abstracted from anything that changes, so that it is something whose course and destiny we can follow with the most exact and scrupulous and concentric attention, undistracted by reflections of our normal joys or woes, or by clues and implications for our safety or success. Instead of saying that music can be no more than this, we ought to say that music can be all of

---

[10] Substantially the one maintained by Eduard Hanslick in his classic work, *The Beautiful in Music* (see Note 18-I), and by Edmund Gurney (Note 18-A) and Carroll C. Pratt (Note 18-E).

this, as nothing else can be. How this makes music valuable, and what value it has, we are to ask later.

§19.   THE RELATION OF MUSIC TO WORDS

Students of the arts have sometimes divided them into two branches, the "pure" and the "mixed." But the principle of division has not been clear or consistent. For example, music may be called "pure" on the ground that it exists only in a single sensory domain, but in that case perhaps sculpture should be "mixed," since it can be both seen and touched. Perhaps more often music, painting, sculpture, and literature are said to be "pure," but song "mixed" because it brings together words and music. However the distinction be made, it is usually introduced to raise two questions. First, are the "pure" arts "higher" than the "mixed" ones? This question I don't know how to answer, unless I take it in a sense that obviously calls for a No: for example, are all pure aesthetic objects better than all mixed ones? Second, are the "mixed" arts possible at all?

This question of possibility must be meant in some sense in which it is not to be answered in the ordinary way: to show that songs are possible, you show that one exists—by singing it. There is a deeper skepticism here, a notion that words and music remain somehow separate and distinct, even when produced simultaneously. Spraying yourself with exotic perfume while listening to Rimsky-Korsakov or looking through a book of Renaissance paintings while listening to Palestrina or Victoria will not necessarily result in a single and unified whole that could be called the art of Odomusic or the art of Musipaint.

The relation of words to music, however, seems to be a rather special one, and it will require arguments much stronger than this general skepticism to destroy the almost universal assumption that some words and music can go together to produce a whole that is a distinct aesthetic object in its own right. If this is called a "mixed" object, it does not matter, providing the mixture be right. In fact, we have already encountered, in the preceding chapter, a sort of "mixed" art, the art of representational painting, which also does two rather different things at once. The comparison is not perfect, because you can have music without words and words without music, whereas in the fine arts you cannot have depiction without design. Nevertheless, the method we followed in dealing with that problem may be helpful to us here.

Whether, and if so in what sense, a particular verbal discourse may be said to be appropriate to, or to fuse with, a particular musical composition or passage, is then the question. And there are two main areas where it arises. First, there is, as I have said, the kind of combination of words and music that we have in song or opera, which is even more mixed. Second, there is the looser kind of combination found in program music, in "symphonic poems" and such compositions. We shall deal with these two separately.

When we ask about the relations of music to words in song, there is a further distinction that we must note, though one of the points will not occupy us long: How is music related to the *sound* of the words? And how is music related to the *sense* of the words?

We can sing only because we can pronounce a word and at the same time produce a tone. If every word, at least in a particular sense, could be produced in only one tone, all speech would be singing, of a sort, but songs could not be *composed*, since there could be only one melody to each meaning. Composition requires that the rules for correct pronunciation are not fixed in certain respects, and therefore leave open possibilities: there is no rule in English that says how fast or how loud or how high in pitch you have to pronounce a word, so long as its dominant phonetic pattern can be recognized.

These commonplace observations are relevant to our first question. For suppose we ask of a particular song whether the sound of the music is similar in some way to the sound of the words. This question is almost unanswerable, for much of the sound of the words, for example, loudness, does not belong to them as words; they only have that sound *as sung*. Still, as we found in Chapter V, §14, there are some qualities that may, very vaguely, be attributed to word-sounds, and we could ask, for example, whether their harshness or smoothness is also exhibited by the music. In this rather limited sense we can compare the word-sound with the music-sound.

But this is not the most important aspect of the relation between word-sounds and music-sounds. A word sung to a note becomes part of the timbre of that note, and thus part of the musical sound itself. Moreover, the movement of the words as sounds—their stresses, pauses, rhythmic groupings, syllabic divisions—affects the movement of the music. Hence the problem of opera translation. One of the high points of *The Magic Flute* is where Papageno asks Pamina, "What shall we say now?" and Pamina replies in a ringing voice:

Mozart, *The Magic Flute*

Die Wahr - heit,   Die Wahr - heit,   wär   sie auch Ver - brech - en!

As Auden and Kallman point out in the notes to their translation of the opera for television,[1] there is no English that substitutes adequately for

---

[1] W. H. Auden and Chester Kallman, trans., *The Magic Flute*, New York: Random House, 1956, p. 107. Compare the amusing and instructive controversy between E. J. Dent and E. W. H. Meyerstein over the translation of Leonora's *"Todt' erst sein Weib!"* in *Fidelio*, *The Music Review*, VI (1945): 64, 128.

the German here. "Truth," which comes closest to *"Wahrheit"* in meaning lacks the sound-movement that the music insists upon, and "truthful," which has the sound-movement, is too insipid and irrelevant in sense.

We ask of a melodic setting that it preserve the important secondary meaning of the original text by adjustment of stresses and pauses so that the suggestion is not lost, and we also note that sometimes the suggestion is intensified, or new and relevant suggestion added, by subtle nuances in the music. Hugo Wolf is one of the greatest masters in this respect, for example in his setting of Goethe's "Prometheus" and in the third Michelangelo song, "Fühlt Meine Seele." But our main problem is not the connection between the sound of the music and the sound of the words, but the connection between the sound of the music and the meaning of the words.

A dispute about this question might be worked up in the following way. At first glance, it is obvious that in some cases words and music have a natural affinity so strong that they seem like inevitable counterparts. Once you learn, say, a song from Gilbert and Sullivan, it is very hard to imagine those words sung to any other music. Some of Schubert's settings for poems have been felt to be so apt and conclusive as to discourage other composers from using the words again. And if it is not clear exactly what "suitable" can designate as a connection between music and words, surely it is easy enough to think of cases of unsuitableness: Schiller's "Ode to Joy" sung to the tune of the "St. Louis Blues," or "Th'expense of spirit in a waste of shame is lust in action" sung to the tune of "Yankee Doodle"—which on metrical grounds alone it perfectly fits.

Nevertheless it can also be shown that there are subjective and private factors involved here, and room for the operation of individual habits. When you learn, say, "Away in a Manger" to one of its three widely sung melodies, or a folk song like "John Henry" or "Lord Randall," which may have numerous versions, and then encounter other people singing different melodies with as much enjoyment as yours, and as great a sense that their melody was made for the words, you may wonder whether the feeling of appropriateness is just familiarity. If the Roman Mass has been set to such an impressive variety of melodies, and some poems over and over again, how can we say that these words call for just one musical setting over all rivals?

The same questions may be asked about songs in which the same music, or very nearly the same music, has been used for very different words. For the "Crucifixus" and the "Qui Tollis" of his *Mass in B Minor,* which seem utterly at one with their words, Bach borrowed music that he had originally used elsewhere for other words. It is said that the Wesley brothers converted sailors by turning the melodies of their bawdy songs into hymn-tunes, a tactic that would seem to depend for its success upon their still enjoying the melodies despite the change of subject. And what, to come to a very simple case, have "Twinkle, twinkle, little star" and "Baa, baa, black sheep" in common that children should sing them to the same tune?

The Fusion Theory

Different words have seemed appropriate to the same music, then, as different music has seemed appropriate to the same words. But can there be a link between words and music, so that we can say that such-and-such music is more or less appropriate to the words than some other music? The theory that there can be such a link might be summarized in this way: A musical passage is appropriate to—coherent with—a verbal discourse that is sung to it when it contains presentational equivalents of the discourse, that is, when it has itself some qualities referred to in that discourse. This theory may be called the Fusion Theory of the relation of music to words in song.[2]

This is a psychological theory: it asserts that the regional quality of coherence will appear, and the words and music become parts of a phenomenal whole, when presentational equivalence is heard with some definiteness and intensity. What we need, as with so many other problems, is careful experimental work to determine within what limits, and with what further qualifications and restrictions, the theory is true. There is evidence on a common-sense level, and testimony by highly qualified and sensitive observers, but there is still much to be done. However, before the theory can be put into a form really suitable for such investigation, some preliminary analysis is in order. Let us try with the help of some examples to clarify the theory and its implications.

1. In Bach's *Cantata No. 106, Gottes Zeit* (also called *Actus Tragicus*), section 2, the three lower voices of the chorus stop while the soprano holds a note on the first syllable of *lange* for ten quarter-notes in ¾ time.

2. In Purcell's *Dido and Aeneas*, whenever the word "storm" occurs in an aria or recitative (see Nos. 5, 19, 26, 30; also "thunder" in No. 25), it is sung to a rapid run or a jerky dotted rhythm.

3. In Handel's *Messiah*, in the bass aria, No. 11, the words "The people that walked in darkness" are accompanied by a wonderfully wandering, uncertain, shifty melody in B minor.

4. In Bach's *Cantata No. 84, Ich bin Vergnügt*, the music for the first aria, "I am content (*Vergnügt*) with my blessings," is set to decidedly contented music; the second, "Cheerfully (*mit Freude*) I eat my portion of bread," is set to decidedly cheerful music; and the two qualities are clearly distinguishable in the music.[3]

---

[2] I take it that this theory, though it has not been worked out as such, is held by most writers on vocal music, even when they merely assume it without explicit statement. For references see Notes 19-B, 19-C, and 19-D.

[3] Compare "My yoke has been broken," from *Cantata No. 56, Ich will den Kreuzstab Gerne Tragen.*

5. In "Gute Nacht," the first song in Schubert's song cycle, *Winterreise*, the music changes from D minor to D major in the fourth verse, at the words, *"Will dich im Traum nicht stören."*
6. Henri Duparc's setting of Baudelaire's poem "L'Invitation au Voyage" has the same sense of timelessness and sensuous satiation as the country referred to in the poem, where *"Tous n'est qu'ordre et beauté: / Luxe, calme et volupté."*

The simplest and most mechanical sort of relation that music can have to words is illustrated by Example 1: the word simply designates some characteristic—here, length—of the note itself. We may notice such things when they occur—the same thing is done with the word "long" in "a long winter's nap" in the familiar musical setting of "A Visit from St. Nicholas"—and they can be exploited for effects with a certain charm, for example, when Roy Harris in his setting of "The Twelve Days of Christmas"—in his version, "A Red-Bird in a Green Tree"—uses a different interval for each day: on the second day, the melody rises a major second, and so on.

But though we may note the presence of such correlations, we do not note their absence; the word "long" does not demand to be treated by a long note any more than by a short one. The relations are external. It would seem, therefore, that such correspondence can contribute very little to our perception of the music and words as coherent.

In Example 2 we have the sort of thing, though simple and naïve, that we discussed in the preceding section, the imitation of physical movement by music. This is a closer sort of correspondence: the music imitates the physical event, the storm, denoted by the word. Again, the presence is notable, the absence is not; we never feel that a melody must include imitations of all the physical movements mentioned in the text. Indeed Bach, whose arias include hundreds of such imitations, never tried to do it line by line. A melodic figure might be suggested to him by a word he found in a verse, but he would use that figure throughout. This sort of imitation can probably not play a very great role in determining the coherence of the words and music.

Handel, in Example 3, has done two things; his passage is partly imitation of physical movement, as in Example 2, but partly imitation of psychological process as well. It has, then, not only general kinetic qualities of physical movement, it has human qualities. Example 4 shows the same thing, more simply and more plainly; here again it is the human regional qualities of the music that correspond to the human qualities designated by the words. And it seems to me that we are now in a realm where we feel a distinct appropriateness of music to words, and where inappropriate music would jar. The words of Handel's aria set to the tune of "Twinkle, twinkle"—the speaker in that rhyme is wondering, but not really wandering in darkness—would be ridiculous. And there would certainly be something peculiar about setting Bach's words, "I am content," to a gloomy and depressed melody.

Indeed, I can't help thinking Bach erred for once in the final alto solo of his *Cantata No. 170, Vergnügte Ruh! beliebte Seelenlust,* where the words "It disgusts me to go on living" are set to a comfortably cozy melody—though I may have overlooked some other connections. The effect is a little like singing to the well-known baritone melody such a parody as "I loathe life, and I hate to live." For another example, take the Fairy Queen's song "O Foolish Fay," in *Iolanthe,* which derives some of its humor, I think, from the incongruity of the words—especially in the second verse, addressed to Captain Shaw of the London Fire Department —sung to so serious and flowing a melody.

The result of incongruous words and music may simply be a falling-apart, or it may be, as in some Gilbert and Sullivan songs, comic; in either case, it is clearly distinguishable at least from the extreme cases of words and music that do have a deep affinity: as in Handel's Example 3, in Bach's "Qui Tollis," in "Dido's Lament" from *Dido and Aeneas,* and in many songs by Schubert, Brahms, Hugo Wolf, Duparc, and others. Our present problem, however, is to try to get at the nature of this affinity.

In Examples 3 and 4, then, the human quality of the music is that designated, literally (Example 4) or metaphorically (Example 3) by the words. In the other examples, the connection is on a broader scale, more remote, yet no less important. In Example 5, the change of key marks the climax of the poem, where the wanderer makes his resolution to pass by the town without disturbing its rest; it brings a sense of purpose out of the previous introspection, a tenderness for others, and a kind of acceptance of the wanderer's destiny; it is a clearing of the emotional atmosphere. In Example 6, Duparc is not at all depicting a territory or tracing out the qualities of any of the single words: he is dealing with the whole moral climate of the poem, and presenting auditory equivalents of it.

We may now try restating the earlier version of the Fusion principle:

A musical passage is coherent with—appropriate to—a verbal discourse sung to it if it has some fairly intense human regional qualities that are either qualities designated by the words or qualities of the events or situation described by the words.

Though not perfectly precise, it is now, I think, in a better form for further investigation; at least it is empirically testable. The examples we have given go some distance to establish it, if we consider them as samples of a numerous class of possible examples. What we should like to know more about, though, is the psychological mechanism involved, and the more detailed conditions under which fusion occurs in some degree. There are some further considerations that might be tentatively mentioned. Music seems to have a remarkable quality of fusing with other things, taking them to its bosom; that is partly why there are so many sorts of occasion when music seems to be appropriate. In some songs, I should think, we might find it difficult to point out any outstanding qualities of the music that especially illuminate the words, but if there is no great incongruity and the music itself is superb—as in Mozart's arias—the song is still a song, and the music carries along the words without trouble. Indeed, the music swallows up the words, and makes their movement a part of its own.

This does not mean that music can combine with anything in the same intimate way as it does with words in song. After all, the words themselves have, as we saw in Chapter V, §15, an implicit speaker, and if the speaker is also a singer, the gap is not so very great as to be unbridgeable. The musical substance of the song can be thought, by extension, to be a further exemplification of qualities of mind that would already be there to some extent in the tone and timbre of the voice if the poem were read aloud. It is not the same as trying to find the right perfume to go with powder-blue crinoline or with "The Skater's Waltz."

In the light of the preceding discussion, then, we can see what answers the Fusion Theory can make to the objections cited earlier. That some people, on familiarity, have come to prefer certain settings of "Away in a Manger" to others does not refute the theory: it may still be possible to show that one melody is better than the rest—if, for example, it has a kind of soothing, cradle-like movement that the others lack—or they may in fact be about equally appropriate, in different ways. And the same sort of thing might be said on a much larger scale about the settings of the Roman Mass.

The second set of examples is equally innocuous. Consider "Twinkle, twinkle" and "Baa, baa." Though one is about a sheep and the other about a star, they have a great deal in common as structures of poetic meaning. They are both four-square in their rhetorical shape. In "Twinkle, twinkle" there is an imperative followed by an exclamation, in simple one-syllable language, one sentence to a line. In "Baa, baa," there is a two-line question followed by a two-line answer, again in straightforward language. This verbal structure is carried out by the simple melody with its rise and fall by plain, decisive, emphatic steps; the melody, like the speakers of both these little verses, is forthright, clear about what it is doing, and very limited in its range and activity. Nevertheless, though it is quite appropriate to both, it is more appropriate to "Baa, baa," because "Twinkle, twinkle" includes a touch of doubt in it ("How I wonder"), and this tune does not wonder about anything.

It would be a complicated task to show, as I think it can be shown, that very similar considerations, though more subtle and deep, apply to Bach's borrowings from himself. The words to which he originally set the melody of the "Qui Tollis" were not, after all, worlds apart from the "Qui Tollis" itself, nor did he take over the melody without some modification, and there can be no question that this music is saturated with rich human qualities, some of which are also qualities of the attitude set forth by the words: "Qui tollis peccata mundi, miserere nobis."

Presentational Specification

There is an even subtler relation between music and words, I think; but we must be very tentative about it. To the concept of presentational equivalence, we may add a concept of *presentational specification,* if the term does not sound too forbidding. What I have in mind is this. Here is a sad verse, and it is set to music that is also sad. So far, so good. But I think we ordinarily do not feel that the union of the two is the fullest possible, or is a complete success, unless there is something more. The music must not merely underline the words, and intensify their meaning, but add to them in some noteworthy way. And this it can indeed do. For suppose the verse is very vague, like some short romantic lyrics: "I am sad because my love has flown away," is about all it tells us. Still the music's sadness will not be sadness in general, it will be of a specific sort, a definite quality, perhaps a little on the resigned or a little on the irritated side, deep or superficial, self-pitying or ironic, sobbing or tight-lipped. I see that these descriptions go too far; they are different qualities of sadness, all right, but music cannot distinguish precisely among them. Nevertheless, I think the music can make some such discriminations, and sometimes it is the music that gives the song its specific quality of sadness.

If this is true, it explains one clear fact about song composition that has often seemed puzzling, namely, why the best poems do not generally make the best songs, and why a good composer can make a very good song out of a poor poem—as Mozart and Schubert and others did many times. If the text is, "I am sad, because my beloved has flown," the composer has room to work in. If it is the precise and sharply balanced, but ambivalent, state of mind shown forth in a Shakespeare sonnet or a poem by Donne, there may be nothing he can do for it in the way of specifying its qualities, but much he can do against it. In that case, he may do well to let it alone. I say this despite Benjamin Britten's settings of Donne's *Holy Sonnets.*

And some songs that might at first seem to fall apart through incongruity come to satisfy us of their unity when we take the music as filling out the words. For example, Hugo Wolf, in "Der Mond hat eine schwere Klag' erhoben," from the *Italienisches Liederbuch,* by Paul Heyse, takes a silly conceit—the moon has counted the stars and found two of the brightest missing, that is, your eyes—and set it to music of the most profound tenderness. The music here does with the words what it will.

The concept of presentational specification can be applied at various levels. The simplest and starkest application might be settings of a passage from the "Credo" of the Mass. Composers of all times, of course, have tended to set the word "descendit" to falling melodic phrases, and "ascendit" to rising ones. Palestrina usually does, though the mass *Aspice Domine* is an exception. In his *Pope Marcellus Mass,* one phrase is this:

Palestrina, *Missa Papae Marcelli*

In Beethoven's *Missa Solemnis in D,* the phrase is this:

Beethoven, *Missa Solemnis in D Major*

There are two descents, so to speak, but what different descents they are! In Palestrina the coming of Christ is a serene passage into the world from a realm not utterly remote; in Beethoven it is a dramatic plunge.

Perhaps I am reading too much into this contrast. I don't say that they contain the whole difference between Catholic and Protestant theology, but they are surely very different in the attitudes and expectations they contribute to the bare statement of the words. This is one of the reasons why those words are so wonderful to set, and can be set in so many different ways. A "Kyrie Eleison" can be a cry of despair, a singing of calm faith, a pleading, or unself-conscious praise; it is the composer who makes it one or the other. It is Fauré in his *Requiem* who tells us what sort of fate awaits the lost ones, by the way he sets the words *"ne cadant in obscurum";* it is Verdi in his *Requiem* who tells us that the day of judgment is more pathetic than terrible by the lyric melody to which he sets the words *"lacrymosa dies illa,"* whereas the music of Berlioz' "Lacrimosa" shows terrifying despair. Or, for one other sort of example, when Handel sets the words "I know that my redeemer liveth," in *The Messiah* it is the music that shows exactly the degree and nature of that serene confidence this aria breathes so fully.

When I use the word "tells us," I am overstating what I am prepared at the moment to maintain. The composer gives the song, which is the union of words and music, a specific quality by making his music supply that quality where the words are vague or abstract; see Wolf's setting of Goethe's "Grenzen der Menschheit." Whether he introduces *propositions,* theological or otherwise, into the song is another question, a question for the next chapter.

The concept of presentational specification can also help to give an account of another aspect of song. We say that the music of Mozart and Wagner, for example, helps to "characterize" the characters in their operas: that is, we learn something about those characters—about Falstaff, Macbeth, or Don Giovanni—that we do not know from hearing their words and seeing their actions alone. The words and actions sketch in the general qualities: Pamina—though *The Magic Flute* is not the best place to search for consistency of character—is pure and virtuous, of course. But the utterly unhesitating and whole-hearted, the emphatic and committed, music to which she sings her answer to Papageno's question tells us the real quality and intensity of her devotion to truth. Music similarly helps portray some very different girls—Carmen, Tosca, Isolde, or the one in the musical comedy song who is "restless as a willow in a windstorm" and "jumpy as a puppet on a string." Considering her special predicament, it is true not only, as the composer has said, that "the tune should be feminine, young, nervous, and, if possible, pretty like the girl,"[4] but also that her problem and her state of mind should be partly given by that tune itself—as they are.

Program Music

Once we conclude that words and music may combine fruitfully in a song, it seems as though it is only a short step beyond to say that the same is true of that other species of word-music composition, program music, including its most important variety, the symphonic poem.

The first step in dealing with this problem, and it is not without risk already, is to agree upon a definition of "program music." I suggest the following: program music is music with a program. No narrower definition will, I am sure, satisfy everyone, and some will hold out for an even broader one. There are good reasons, however, for drawing the line here, as will appear when we are sure we know where we have drawn it. For in the definition above, admirable as it is for its terseness in a subject where few definitions except outrageously misleading ones are terse, there are two problematic terms: "program" and "with."

I propose to count as a program a verbal discourse that narrates a series of at least two events, that has, in short, a plot in the broadest sense, though not necessarily a good one—we are not concerned with literary values here. I do not count titles like *Spring, Parting, Mal de Mer,* or *The Rooster* unless they refer to literary works, such as *Don Juan, A Midsummer-Night's Dream, Les Préludes, Peer Gynt,* or designate plots all by themselves, like that composition by Johann Ludwig Dussek (1760-1812)

---

4 Richard Rodgers, in *Lyrics* by Oscar Hammerstein II, New York: Simon and Schuster, 1949, p. xv.

called *The Naval Battle and Total Defeat of the Dutch Fleet by Admiral Duncan, Oct. 11, 1787.*

There are some interesting problems about titles, which again I must regretfully set aside with a very few comments. It is true that such titles are an indispensable aid, as we saw earlier, in helping the listener imagine specific objects or events while listening to the music. But some of them serve a purely musical function. When a composer writes upon his score such directions to the performers as "plaintively," "passionately," "jokingly," or even "a joyful hymn of thanksgiving," we should not, I think, call these instructions a kind of program. They are merely words that are part of the score itself, the conventional notation being incomplete, to help in performance. Now a title like *Spring,* or even *Mal de Mer,* can serve a similar function: "Play this with a springlike quality," or, "Make it sound a little queasy." Eric Satie wrote on one of his scores, "Like a nightingale with a toothache." And in fact it seems to me that, in the classically debated case, Beethoven's phrases in his *"Pastoral" Symphony* are best understood, if they are indeed anything more than a whim, as a kind of metaphorical suggestion to the conductor. "By the brook" then would not mean, "This pictures a brook," but, "Give the running accompaniment an even, flowing, trickling, brooklike quality." I should say, then, that the *"Pastoral" Symphony* is not program music at all. But note that this says nothing about the music; it just means it has no program.

Of course, you may reply, there are countryfolk dancing, there is a storm, the sky clears; are not these events a simple story that constitute a program of the symphony? They could be, but my objection centers upon the more crucial word in the definition, "with." What does it mean to say that a musical composition has a program? It is not enough that a story *could* be written to accompany it; I should think that could be done with any composition, even Bach's forty-eight preludes and fugues, if you don't mind how silly the story is. It must mean that there exists a story that (a) in some way corresponds to the music and (b) is offered in some way along with it.

After our previous discussions, there shouldn't be any difficulty about the correspondence: the episodes of a story have kinetic qualities that may be matched by the kinetic qualities of the music. It is the offering that raises the problems. If I sit down now and write a story for Bach's *C Minor Fugue* in Book I of the *Well-tempered Clavier,* that is not yet enough to give it a program. I must have the fugue performed somehow and on the same occasion read, or pass out copies of, my story. But more than that, I must give instructions that they are to go together: that the listener is to familiarize himself with the story before he hears the music, and keep the story in mind while he is listening. If I do all this, I have made it into program music; I have given it a program.

Thus, I should say that Berlioz gave his *Fantastic Symphony* a program when he directed that his audiences should be acquainted with his morbid little tale about the poet, and that Tchaikowsky gave his *F Minor Symphony (No. 4)* a program for Madame von Meck when he made up the story, though he neglected to give it a program for the public at large. Leonard Bernstein's *Age of Anxiety,* even apart from the title that refers to Auden's poem, is given a program by the quotation of his own "interpretation" of it on the back of the record jacket—provided you can understand that remarkable passage. As for Rimsky-Korsakov's *Scheherazade,* he first gave titles to the four sections, then withdrew them, and finally remarked in his autobiography that he wanted to give hints to the listener but not regulate his conceptions too precisely. A program of deliberate indecision.

The producer's instructions, as I may call them—it does not matter fundamentally whether it was the composer himself, the conductor, or some bystander who invented the program—are not, of course, binding upon the listener. He can tear up the story or refuse to read the record jacket, just as he can walk out on the music. But the theory that we are primarily concerned with here is just the theory that in program music, as so defined, the music and its program can fuse into a coherent whole so that together they form one single aesthetic object. This theory we may call the Fusion Theory of program music.[5] Though not very clear, and consequently not in very good condition for testing, the theory is discussable, in a tentative and general way. We cannot deal with it thoroughly, but I shall suggest some points to be considered.

That one can expose oneself to music and tell oneself a story at the same time has been conceded. It does not follow that one can follow in detail the movement of the music, and give oneself to it, while simultaneously imagining the story. Where the music is fairly simple in structure and in texture, as song accompaniments tend to be, so that it does not demand sole attention, and where the story-concern consists only in understanding the meaning of sung words, the attention is not divided very much. But where the music is large and symphonic, and the story must be recalled from an earlier reading that has no perceptible connection with the music itself, the correspondence of music to words will probably remain a mere correspondence, and not become a fusion. When admirers of program music report that they experience a fusion, it may be questioned whether they are doing more than noting the correspondence: this is where Don Quixote attacks the sheep, or the windmill; this is Frau Strauss rattling the dinner dishes; this is the broom chasing the sorcerer's apprentice.

Another general principle seems to apply. A short and simple piece of music, with a single main climax and few key changes, and with a fairly constant texture, carries out its destined movement in a plain and easy way, and it does not really distract our attention from that movement

---

[5] It is what I take a number of writers about program music to hold; see references in Note 19-E.

to think, momentarily, or from time to time, while hearing it, of a faun dancing or a train rushing along, or perhaps even of a man dying. But a larger musical work depends for its own musical unity and continuity upon purely musical relations among its parts: it calls for development, for recapitulations, for variations or thematic combination. Now a story depends for its literary unity and continuity upon quite other relations among its parts: motives and fulfillments, character-development and conflict-resolution. If both music and story are complex, then, but must correspond in the main, there is bound to be a tension between them. And the more complex and unified each is, the more they tend to pull apart. This principle, if true, does not deny that there can be relatively simple program music in which some degree of fusion occurs, but it would place a severe limit upon the size of coherent program music. The various versions of Beethoven's *Leonora* Overture are instructive on this point.

Moreover, music that is itself lacking in unity of structure cannot be unified by a program, however unified that program is. When it is said that a symphonic poem, for example one of Liszt's, is itself not very unified music, but that the parts hang together because they are ordered as are the incidents they correspond to, this is probably a misleading way to say it. What happens is that our attention is on the story, and the music falls into the background, or fringe, of attention where, like the music played as background music in moving pictures, it does not appear, and is not heard, in its full nature, but serves only to illustrate the story. I must admit, however, that even here the tremendous vitality and power of music to creep into things and become a part of them is evident. If the music has any similarity at all to the incidents of the story, it hardly ever seems out of place as a quiet background to the story, and it modestly serves; but if the music is fairly intense in its qualities, and highly organized, it can capture our attention, and then we may feel, as listeners often do, that it is the story that is out of place, and has no real business being there.

There is, finally, a more fundamental reason why the art of program music is bound to be a "mixed" art in a sense beyond those senses touched upon at the beginning of this chapter. The coherence of an aesthetic object consists partly, I think, in its seeming to be the product, or the giving-out, of a single human spirit. This is the truth behind the Expression Theory. But note that it is not the Expression Theory itself, for this seeming, which is really another way of describing aesthetic coherence, is quite independent of the question whether in fact the object was made by one, or by many, or by no one. Now, in a representational painting the very same line depicts the world and articulates the design, and in a song the very same voice utters the words and makes the melody. But there can be no such singleness of source in a symphonic poem; the concepts and story-episodes that constitute the "poem" exist as memories in the mind, while the music comes from without. It would be surprising if their association could ever be, to the mind unconfused by fantastic theories, more than a happy accident.

NOTES AND QUERIES

§18

18-A THE EXPRESSION THEORY OF MUSICAL MEANING. (I) For exposition and defense of the Expression Theory, see the following writers:

George Santayana, *The Sense of Beauty*, New York: Scribner's, 1896, pp. 192-208; he says, "In all expression we may thus distinguish two terms": "the expressive thing" and "the thing expressed" (p. 195), yet the latter is supposed to be somehow "incorporated" in the former.

L. A. Reid, *A Study in Aesthetics*, New York: Macmillan, 1931, chs. 2, 3, 4, distinguishes "direct" from "indirect" aesthetic expression. The former, e.g., the eeriness of sounds, he sometimes refers to as "quality" (pp. 75-76); the latter, which he thinks Santayana overlooked or understressed, consists of a "fusion" of past experience with the present datum. For example, the fact that "the tall trees look down upon one with lofty disdain" is accounted for by "association" with past experience of disdainful people. But granted that if we have never experienced such people we would not *describe* the look of the trees this way, does Reid present evidence that we couldn't *perceive* that quality in the trees, or that the perception of the quality presupposes "association"? Note: A statement such as, "The music does not *literally* possess the quality of eeriness," is true; however, it is not the word "possess" but the word "eeriness" that is used non-literally.

John Hospers, *Meaning and Truth in the Arts*, Chapel Hill, N.C.: U. of North Carolina, 1946, ch. 3, discusses both Santayana and Reid. He agrees substantially with Santayana, but emphasizes the variability of expression to the perceiver: "expresses . . . to" implies "arouses . . . from," but not "was intended to arouse . . . from" (compare his later paper below).

John Dewey, *Art as Experience*, New York: Minton, Balch, 1934, chs. 4, 5, gives a vivid description of the act of expression and its mark upon the aesthetic object, but, especially in the absence of any definition of "X expresses Y," his distinction between "statement" and "expression" (pp. 84 ff.) is by no means clear. Expression "does something different from leading to an experience. It constitutes one" (p. 85). This comes close to saying that expression is *not* a relation at all; but he also seems to deny this (pp. 99 ff.), especially when he explains the regional qualities of lines by saying that they "carry with them the properties of objects" (pp. 100-01). Compare Eliseo Vivas, "A Note on the Emotion in Dewey's Theory of Art," *Creation and Discovery*, New York: Noonday, 1955.

T. M. Greene, *The Arts and the Art of Criticism*, Princeton, N.J.: Princeton U., 1940, chs. 12, 15, 19 sec. 3, and "Supplementary Essay" by Roy D. Welch; also "The Problem of Meaning in Music and Other Arts," *JAAC*, V (June 1947): 308-13. Greene's view that art "expresses an interpretation of reality" or of some "subject-matter"—which he has particular difficulty applying to music—is not sharply distinguished from his view that works of art, including music, contain propositions (compare Chapter VIII, Note 20-B).

D. W. Gotshalk, "Aesthetic Expression," *JAAC*, XIII (September 1954): 80-85, analyzes expression into "suggestions of emotion." Compare *Art and the Social Order*, Chicago: U. of Chicago, 1947, ch. 6, esp. his remarks on "universal abstract expressiveness" (pp. 139-40) and "the expression of the personality of the artist" (pp. 140-43).

R. G. Collingwood, *The Principles of Art*, Oxford: Clarendon, 1938, ch. 6, distinguishes carefully between expressing emotions and betraying, arousing, or describing them; expression is at the same time an "exploration." But he appears to hold that just by the examination of a work (esp. p. 123) we can tell whether the artist was really "expressing," and not merely betraying, or attempting to arouse, emotions.

C. J. Ducasse, *The Philosophy of Art*, New York: Dial, 1929, chs. 2, 8, speaks of "the conscious objectification of feeling," but his is an Expression Theory.

On the psychology of music composition, see James L. Mursell, *The Psychology of Music*, New York: Norton, 1937, ch. 7, esp. 268-81.

Henry Aiken argues for the view that works of art are not only "surface" but "express or evoke" emotions, on the ground that the human qualities attributed to music are phenomenally subjective and relative; see "Art as Expression and Surface," *JAAC*, IV (December 1945): 87-95, esp. 91.

F. D. Martin's defense of "expressionism," "On the Supposed Incompatibility of Expressionism and Formalism," *JAAC*, XV (September 1956): 94-99, is weakened by a confusion, in his statement of the issue (p. 94), between what music "should" do and what it does do.

J. W. N. Sullivan's book, *Beethoven: His Spiritual Development*, London: Cape, 1927, reprinted New York: Mentor, 1949, is probably best construed as an overstated and somewhat misleading version of the Expression Theory (see Chapter VIII, Note 20-B).

(II) For criticism of the Expression Theory as a relational theory, see the following writers:

Vincent A. Tomas' examination of the "two-term" theory, as he calls it, in "The Concept of Expression in Art," a symposium in *Science, Language, and Human Rights*, American Philosophical Association, Eastern Division, Philadelphia: U. of Pennsylvania, 1952, pp. 127-44, is excellent. He concludes that to be maintained the Expression Theory must be formulated as a "one-term" theory, which is not, in my terminology, an

Expression Theory at all. Tomas raises questions about the degree of variability of human qualities in music, and the difficulty of testing them (see Note 18-E below); he is criticized on this point in the same symposium by Douglas N. Morgan (pp. 145-65). Morgan supports Aiken, *op. cit.*, on the interpersonal variability of qualities, but not on their phenomenal subjectivity; however, it is difficult to find in his view any support for the two-term Expression Theory. See also comments on the symposium by Charles Hartshorne, "The Monistic Theory of Expression," *J Phil*, L (1953): 425-34; he holds that "sensory qualities" so closely resemble feelings that they are correctly called "feeling qualities," but "feeling qualities" may be more or less objective—" 'agitated' is more objective than 'agitating,' " (p. 433).

John Hospers, "The Concept of Artistic Expression," *PAS*, LV (1954-55): 313-44, distinguishes and examines various senses of "expression" and he argues that expression-statements reduce to description.

O. K. Bowsma, "The Expression Theory of Art," in *Philosophical Analysis*, ed. by Max Black, Ithaca, N.Y.: Cornell U., 1950, pp. 75-101, reprinted in *Aesthetics and Language*, ed. by William Elton, Oxford: Blackwell, 1954, pp. 73-99, also analyzes expression into "having a character"; his argument is roundabout but amusing.

See also Susanne Langer, *Philosophy in a New Key*, Cambridge, Mass.: Harvard U., 1942, ch. 8, reprinted New York: Mentor, 1948, pp. 171-77, a pointed criticism; Stravinsky's famous remark, "I consider that music is, by its very nature, essentially powerless to *express* anything at all" (*Autobiography*, New York: Simon and Schuster, 1936, p. 83; compare pp. 181-86, on Beethoven); Edmund Gurney, *The Power of Sound*, London: Smith, Elder, 1880, ch. 14; Richard Rudner, "Some Problems of Nonsemiotic Aesthetic Theories," *JAAC*, XV (March 1957): 298-310; Harold Osborne, *Aesthetics and Criticism*, London: Routledge and Kegan Paul, 1955, ch. 7.

(III) For views about music and other arts that employ the term "expression," but in such a way as to reduce it to sheer quality, see the following writers:

David W. Prall, *Aesthetic Judgment*, New York: Crowell, 1929, ch. 11, esp. pp. 235-44, and *Aesthetic Analysis*, New York: Crowell, 1936, ch. 5, uses the term "feeling" for "perception" and for "quality," but the gist of his view is stated in this way: "Anything that is expressed is at least qualitative experiential content" (*Aesthetic Analysis*, p. 142).

Charles Hartshorne, *The Philosophy and Psychology of Sensations*, Chicago: U. of Chicago, 1934, ch. 5, uses the term "expression" to talk about qualities, though he sometimes prefers the equally misleading term "objective feelings" (sec. 13, pp. 117-24).

Roger Sessions says music "communicates" (*The Musical Experience of Composer, Performer, Listener*, Princeton, N.J.: Princeton U., 1950, pp. 22-28) or "reproduces" (*The Intent of the Critic*, ed. by Augusto Centeno,

Princeton, N.J.: Princeton U., 1941, pp. 123-24); but his meaning can be translated into the quality terminology.

Lucius Garvin, "Emotivism, Expression, and Symbolic Meaning," *J Phil*, LV (1958): 112-18, speaks of the "feel of the music."

See Ivy G. Campbell-Fisher, "Intrinsic Expressiveness," *Journal of General Psychology*, XLV (1951): 3-24.

18-B IMITATION AND IMAGE-EVOCATION. For discussion of music as imitative of other sounds and also of visual objects, see Edmund Gurney, *op. cit.*, chs. 15, 16 (he uses the term "suggestion"); Mursell, *op. cit.*, pp. 206-10.

There are some amusing pot shots at the fanciful "interpreters" in Winthrop Parkhurst, "Music, the Invisible Art," *Musical Quarterly*, XVI (1930): 297-304.

On the similarity between music and physical motion, see Carroll C. Pratt, *The Meaning of Music*, New York: McGraw-Hill, 1931, pp. 185-90, 221-45 (he argues that it is the "tactile component in music," or "dynamism," that enables it to suggest physical events to some listeners); Mursell, *op. cit.*, pp. 36-42; Edmund Gurney, *op. cit.*, pp. 105-09. Interesting examples are given in Erich Sorantin, *The Problem of Musical Expression*, Nashville, Tenn.: Martin and Bruce, 1932, pp. 104-18, and Albert Schweitzer, *J. S. Bach*, trans. by Ernest Newman, Leipzig, New York: Breitkopf and Härtel, 1911, Vol. II.

Does it make sense to say, when a listener imagines a scene or story while listening to a musical composition and under its general influence, that the music "evokes" the images? One experimenter, Alec Washco, Jr., *The Effects of Music upon Pulse Rate, Blood-Pressure and Mental Imagery*, Philadelphia: privately printed, 1933, played compositions on a phonograph and instructed his subjects to "try to imagine the story of the music" (p. 66) and then afterward write out the story (p. 67). Apparently the subjects, accepting the implied assertion that each composition *had* one and only one story, were able to make them up for the experimenter. But after reading some of them—for example, the stories written to go with Weber's *Oberon* Overture (pp. 175-81) and Liszt's *Second Hungarian Rhapsody* (pp. 194-204)—we ought to have doubts. The subjects knew the title of Liszt's composition, and they gathered that it was gypsy music, so several of them reported gypsies dancing; they did not know that Weber's overture had anything to do with Shakespeare's *Midsummer-Night's Dream*, so their stories ranged all over, from a chariot race in ancient Rome to the raising of the dead. Compare the judicious conclusions of H. P. Weld, "An Experimental Study of Musical Enjoyment," *American Journal of Psychology*, XXIII (1912): 245-308, esp. 254-59, 274-77, and the interesting bit of autobiography in Robert MacDougal, "Music Imagery: A Confession of Experience," *Psychological Review*, V (1898): 463-76.

18-C MUSIC AND EMOTION-AROUSAL. Does music, by itself, arouse emotions or merely feeling-states? This question is well discussed in Eduard Hanslick, *The Beautiful in Music,* trans. by Gustav Cohen, New York: Liberal Arts, 1957, chs. 1, 2, 4, 5. See also Mursell, *op. cit.,* pp. 26-31; Paul Hindemith, *A Composer's World,* Cambridge, Mass.: Harvard U., 1952, p. 49, argues that musical qualities succeed each other so rapidly that the feelings they cause cannot be "real" emotions.

John Hospers, *op. cit.,* ch. 4, proposes to use the term "meaning" for all effects, including emotions caused by the object (p. 75), but I think he does not confine his ensuing discussion of "meaning" in music (pp. 78-98) to this sense; and it is very doubtful whether this is indeed the sense such writers as J. W. N. Sullivan (Note 18-A) have in mind in speaking of the "meaning" of music. Lucius Garvin, "The Paradox of Aesthetic Meaning," *Phil and Phen Res,* VIII (September 1947): 99-106, uses a similar definition of "meaning."

18-D MUSICAL THERAPY. What light is thrown on the problem whether music has a meaning, in any of the three main senses discussed in this chapter, by the ways it can be used for therapeutic purposes? See Edward Podolsky, *Music for Your Health,* New York: Ackerman, 1945; Willem van de Wall, *Music in Institutions,* New York: Russell Sage Foundation, 1936, esp. chs. 3, 4, 7, 13; and the articles in Podolsky, ed., *Music Therapy,* New York: Philosophical Library, 1954.

18-E THE STATUS OF HUMAN REGIONAL QUALITIES. The classic defense of the objectivity and nonrelativity of such qualities in music is that of Carroll C. Pratt, *op. cit.,* pp. 150-215. His occasional use of the term "express" makes it clearly synonymous with "present" (p. 195), though in a later article, "The Design of Music," *JAAC,* XII (March 1954): 289-300, he seems to incline a little toward the Expression Theory. See also his lecture, "Music as the Language of Emotion," Washington: Library of Congress, 1952; Mursell, *op. cit.,* pp. 31-36, 42-46. On regional qualities of human faces and actions, see the excellent discussion in Solomon Asch, *Social Psychology,* Englewood Cliffs, N.J.: Prentice-Hall, 1952, ch. 7.

Ralph H. Grundlach, "An Analysis of Some Musical Factors Determining the Mood Characteristics of Music," *Psychological Bulletin,* XXXI (1934): 592-93, and "Factors Determining the Characterization of Musical Phrases," *American Journal of Psychology,* XLVII (1935): 624-43, found a notable uniformity among listeners asked to describe short musical passages, both in European and in American Indian music; cf. "A Quantitative Analysis of Indian Music," *ibid.,* XLIV (1932): 133-45.

In some experiments, it is hard to estimate the reliability of the results because the instructions generally confuse the description of qualities with the report of subjective feelings or images. For example, con-

sider the various studies in Max Schoen, *The Effects of Music,* London:
Routledge and Kegan Paul, 1927. Myers' subjects were asked to give their
"impressions" of the music (p. 12) and they tended to characterize it (p.
25); but Gatewood's subjects were asked to report their own "feelings"
(pp. 80, 106). Washburn and Dickinson asked for "emotional effects" (p.
122), but some of their subjects must have been attempting to describe
the music instead; some of the words they used, e. g., "confidence," "certainty," "flirting," (p. 128) certainly were not reports of their emotional
states upon hearing the music. Pratt, *op. cit.,* pp. 196-201, comments interestingly on the Washburn-Dickinson experiments, pointing out that
the subjects sometimes said the music "aroused" in them such feelings as
restlessness and sadness, which are unpleasant, and yet they reported
enjoying the music—which strongly suggests that they were not talking
about how the music made them feel, but how it sounded.

The uniformity of response found by Schoen and Gatewood (p. 131)
may derive in part from their somewhat more (though by no means unwaveringly) objective approach: for example, they speak of "types of
music" (p. 135), but also ask the subject, "How did it make you feel?"
(p. 144). Gatewood's study of consistency in metaphorical descriptions of
music obtained positive results (pp. 265-66), but she formulates her problem in a misleading way: "How universal is the tendency to convert the
enjoyment of music, either consciously or unconsciously, into terms of
other personal experiences?" (p. 257). Her study affords no evidence of
such a "conversion."

The earlier, and very interesting, investigation by Benjamin Gilman,
"Report on an Experimental Test of Musical Expressiveness," *American
Journal of Psychology,* IV (1892): 558-76, V: 42-73, led the investigator to
conclude that widely varying reports of a musical composition's "meaning"
or "story" may indicate a considerable agreement about its actual qualities. There is further evidence for this conclusion in June Downey, "A
Musical Experiment," *ibid.* (1897), IX: 63-69; and in Weld, *op. cit.,* pp.
277-85.

The instructions given to his subjects by Washco, *op. cit.,* also illustrate the confusion between qualities and feelings. He gave a list of
words and asked the subject to choose the two that "best describe how
you feel, or how the music affects you," but among his words are "awe-
some," "uncanny," and "oppressive" (p. 66)!

T. M. Greene's examples of "acquired associations and conventions,"
op. cit., p. 332, are all dubious, but require separate analysis. For example,
he speaks of the Greek modes as having different "associations" for us.
However, not modes, but the compositions in them have the qualities he
proposes to reduce to "associations"; for example, when Socrates recommends the Dorian and Phrygian modes as those that best "express the accents of courage . . . and of temperance" (*Republic,* Book III, 398-
99; Cornford trans., Oxford: Clarendon, 1945, p. 87), it is not at all clear

that he is referring to some inherent quality of the modes rather than to the songs, including their words, customarily composed in those modes. See the pointed remarks on the Greek modes by Hanslick, *op. cit.*, pp. 96-97.

See also Glenn Haydon, "On the Meaning of Music," a lecture, Washington: Library of Congress, 1948.

18-F THE PERCEPTUAL CONDITIONS OF REGIONAL QUALITIES. There have been psychological studies attempting to determine some of the local and subregional qualities of music on which the human regional qualities depend. Of these the best-known are those by Kate Hevner, whose objective approach confirmed the importance of such qualities as key (major or minor), rhythm, melodic curve; see "The Affective Character of the Major and Minor Modes in Music," *American Journal of Psychology*, XLVII (1935): 103-18; "Expression in Music: A Discussion of Experimental Studies and Theories," *Psychological Review*, XLII (1935): 186-204; "Experimental Studies of the Elements of Expression in Music," *American Journal of Psychology*, XLVIII (1936): 246-68. Her work was added to by Ivy G. Campbell-Fisher, "Basal Emotional Patterns Expressible in Music," *ibid.*, LV (1942): 1-17. Compare P. R. Farnsworth, "A Study of the Hevner Adjective List," *JAAC*, XIII (September 1954): 97-103.

Erich Sorantin, *op. cit.*, despite a very loose terminology and an unclear line of argument, gives evidence (Part II) to support the thesis that certain local and subregional qualities do contribute to the emergence of certain regional qualities. One test he employs is that in setting words to music composers have used certain intervals, rhythmic figures, etc.: he distinguishes "figures of lamentation," "figures of love," etc. But his thesis is not "in strict contrast" with Hanslick (p. 57). Sorantin's conclusions were tested by Melvin Rigg, "Musical Expression: An Investigation of the Theories of Erich Sorantin," *Journal of Experimental Psychology*, XXI (1937): 442-55; a second article, "Speed as a Determiner of Musical Mood," *ibid.*, XXVII (1940): 566-77, does not add much; but see "The Expression of Meanings and Emotions in Music," *Philosophical Essays in Honor of E. A. Singer*, ed. by F. P. Clarke and M. C. Nahm, Philadelphia: U. of Pennsylvania, 1942.

See also the articles by Grundlach, Note 18-E; C. P. Heinlein, "The Affective Characters of the Major and Minor Modes in Music," *Journal of Comparative Psychology*, VIII (1928): 101-42; Mursell, *op. cit.*, pp. 31-36; also the excellent analysis of the *Tristan* Prelude by Roger Sessions in "The Composer and His Message," *The Intent of the Artist*, ed. by Augusto Centeno, Princeton, N.J.: Princeton U., 1941.

18-G HUMOR IN MUSIC. Some light may be cast upon the problem of the status of human qualities in music by a study of musical humor. It

is possible to distinguish two ways in which music can have humor: (1)
There is humor that depends upon association with human situations (as
in the bassoon part in the trio of the scherzo in Beethoven's *"Pastoral"*
Symphony, which may remind the listener of a player in a village band)
or a parodying of other musical compositions (as in Mozart's *Musical*
Joke). For examples of musical humor based upon quotations from other
musical works, usually a reference to their titles or accompanying words,
see Philip Keppler, Jr., "Some Comments on Musical Quotation," *Musi-*
cal Quarterly, XLII (1956): 473-85. (2) There is humor that is internal,
and depends upon intrinsically incongruous or humanly funny aspects of
the music itself, for example, in Haydn's *D Minor ("Quinten") Quartet*
(Op. 76, No. 2), where the lower voice so faithfully copies the upper one
in the canon of the minuet, and the high violin note at the end of the
opening clause in the finale sounds very playful. If this distinction can
be made, how should we analyze and classify Strauss's *Till Eulenspiegel's*
Merry Pranks and *Don Quixote*, Mahler's *First Symphony*, the "Burletta"
in the third movement of Bartók's *Sixth String Quartet*, Bach's *Variations*
in the Italian Style, and what Donald F. Tovey calls "the Great Bassoon
Joke" (*Essays in Musical Analysis*, New York: Oxford U., 1935-39, Vol. I,
p. 170)? See also Helen Mull, "A Study of Humor in Music," *American*
Journal of Psychology, LXII (1949): 560-66.

18-H   THE DESCRIPTION OF MUSIC.   Some terms used by critics to
describe music may be quite useful and accurate; others may be too
fanciful and remote. In terms of the discussion of metaphor in Chapter
III, §11, we might try to clarify such descriptive terms by making certain
distinctions. Some terms seem to apply literally to all processes, musical,
physical, and mental, e.g., fast, slow, accelerating, smooth, sudden; some
apply literally to mental processes and metaphorically to music, e.g.,
tense, relaxed, gay, depressed; some apply literally to physical processes
and metaphorically to music and mental processes, e.g., creeping, graceful, flowing, wandering; some apply literally to music, and metaphorically
to the others, e.g., crescendo. Do these comparisons help to formulate
criteria for determining what sorts of descriptions are likely to be clear
and not too vague, e.g., "a thundering climax" vs. "hordes of demons
banging tin pans and shrieking in the night"?

Arnold Isenberg, "Critical Communication," *Phil R*, LVIII (1949):
330-44, reprinted in Elton, *Aesthetics and Language*, pp. 131-46, is
skeptical about the description of music: "gracefulness," he thinks, never
means the same thing when applied to a different object or gesture, so
that we cannot verify any general statement about the perceptual conditions under which supposedly the same regional quality of gracefulness
will appear. This is an important argument. However, it is my opinion
that if the descriptive term is introduced by pointing to the music itself,
we can have assurance that it designates very nearly the same quality in

different compositions. We cannot confirm our generalizations about musical qualities to a high degree, but we can attain a useful probability.

18-I THE SIGNIFICATION THEORY OF MUSICAL MEANING. (I) For exposition and defense of this theory, see the following writers:

Charles W. Morris's theory of aesthetic objects as iconic signs is set forth succinctly in two very stimulating articles: (1) "Esthetics and the Theory of Signs," *Journal of Unified Science (Erkenntnis)*, VIII (1939-40): 131-50. Certain crucial statements in this article are in need of critical analysis, e.g.: (a) "The semantical rule for the use of an iconic sign is that it denotes any object which has the properties (in practice, a selection from the properties) which it itself has" (p. 136); this is surely far too broad a rule without verbal stipulation for each musical composition of the *relevant* properties. (b) "In the work of art the sign vehicle is . . . one of its own denotata" (p. 137); but what is to prevent it from being its *only* denotatum, since it is the only object that completely satisfies the above semantical rule and has *all* the properties that it itself has? (c) "Abstract art is simply an extreme case of high generality of semantical reference" (p. 140), i.e., a circle denotes all circular or spherical objects in the world, and a rising musical interval denotes all processes that involve a rise in some characteristic. (2) "Science, Art and Technology," *Kenyon Review*, I (1939): 409-23, reprinted in Eliseo Vivas and Murray Krieger, eds., *Problems of Aesthetics*, New York: Rinehart, 1953, pp. 105-15. Note that Morris cites as examples of "values" (or "value properties")—which are, in his theory, the designata of aesthetic signs—such things as insipidity, sublimity, menace, gaiety (pp. 109-10). Compare also Morris, *Signs, Language and Behavior*, Englewood Cliffs, N.J.: Prentice-Hall, 1946, pp. 190-96, 274n. It is clear that a musical composition or a painting is seldom if ever a "sign" in the sense found for that term by Morris: that is, a preparatory stimulus that under certain conditions causes a disposition in some organism to respond with response-sequences of a certain behavior-family (p. 10). See also the critical discussion of Morris's definition of "sign" by Max Black, "The Semiotic of Morris," *Language and Philosophy*, Ithaca, N.Y.: Cornell U., 1949, pp. 169-85.

For discussions of Morris's theory, see the following writers: Benbow Ritchie, "The Formal Structure of the Aesthetic Object," *JAAC*, III (n.d.): 5-14, reprinted in Vivas and Krieger, *op. cit.*, pp. 225-33, uses the concept of iconic sign as the basis of a very interesting analysis of the processes of artistic creation and aesthetic experience. Compare Isabel Hungerland, "Iconic Signs and Expressiveness," *JAAC*, III (n.d.): 15-21, also in Vivas and Krieger, *op. cit.*, pp. 234-39; C. Amyx, "The Iconic Sign in Aesthetics," *JAAC*, VI (September 1947): 54-60, on Ritchie and Morris.

Susanne Langer's theory has been worked out in two books: (1) *Philosophy in a New Key*, Cambridge, Mass.: Harvard U., 1942 (reprinted New York: Mentor, 1948), chs. 3, 4, 8, 9, 20. The view set forth here

raises several problems that require, and deserve, careful critical attention, e.g.: (a) Music is a "presentational" or "non-discursive" (pp. 75-76,
79), vs. "discursive" (pp. 65-66, 70-71), symbol (presumably in the same
sense in which she holds that a word is a symbol, though it is a different
kind of symbol). I cannot find in her discussion, however, any answer to
the question why we should take the music as referring to anything beyond itself, any more than we take a chair or a mountain that way. (b)
Music has no "vocabulary" (pp. 77, 185), but consists of "unconsummated"
(p. 195) or "unassigned symbols" (p. 209); but how can this be distinguished from saying it contains no symbols at all? (c) Music "articulates"
the "forms" (or "morphology") of feeling (p. 193); what can "articulation"
mean here? (d) To what extent does the plausibility of Mrs. Langer's view
of music depend upon her acceptance (pp. 66-68) of the very misleading
suggestion made—and later abandoned—by Ludwig Wittgenstein, *Trac-
tatus Logico-Philosophicus*, New York: Harcourt, Brace, 1933, esp. pars.
4.01, 4.012, 4.021, that a statement is a "picture" of a fact, so that even in
"discursive symbolism" there is an element of presentational symbolism,
or syntactical iconicity? (2) *Feeling and Form*, New York: Scribner's,
1953, chs. 3, 7-9. This book aims primarily to generalize the Signification Theory of music to the other arts (p. 24). It also develops the theory
of music: music creates an "order of virtual time" (pp. 109, 118). But it
seems to me that it emphasizes the "presentational" aspect of her theory,
and plays down the "symbolic" aspect. She is doubtful, for example,
whether she is talking about musical "meaning" at all, and offers "vital
import" as a substitute (pp. 31-32). And her statement, "The factor of
significance is not logically discriminated, but is felt as a quality rather
than recognized as a function," (p. 32) comes very close to saying that
there is no signification at all, but only quality. See also her article, "Abstraction in Science and Abstraction in Art," in *Structure, Method and
Meaning*, ed. by Paul Henle et al., New York: Liberal Arts, 1951, pp.
171-82. There is even less emphasis on symbolism in her recent collection
of essays, *Problems of Art*, New York: Scribner's, 1957, see esp. p. 139.

Ernst Cassirer's view, of which Mrs. Langer's is a development, is
sketched in *An Essay on Man*, New Haven, Conn.: Yale U., 1944 (reprinted Garden City, N.Y.: Anchor, 1953), chs. 2, 3, esp. 9.

For discussions of Mrs. Langer's theory, see the following writers:
Ernest Nagel, an excellent critical review of *Philosophy in a New Key*,
J Phil, XL (1943): 323-29; Morris Weitz, "Symbolism and Art," *Review
of Metaphysics*, VII (1954): 466-81, a review of *Feeling and Form;* Paul
Welch, "Discursive and Presentational Symbols," *Mind*, LXIV (1955): 181-
99, a very good critical examination of confusions involved in the notion of "presentational symbol"; Arthur Szathmary, "Symbolic and Aesthetic Expression in Painting," *JAAC*, XIII (September 1954): 86-96,
written from the point of view of the Expression Theory.

Compare Albert Gehring, *The Basis of Musical Pleasure*, New York,

Putnam, 1910, chs. 3-5, Appendices C, D, pp. 169-96. I classify Gehring's view as an early version of the Signification Theory, for he not only holds that there is a "parallelism" between some music and mental processes, of which he gives some interesting descriptions, but uses such terms as "symbolization," "indicate," "delineation," "depicting" (pp. 72 ff.), and even proposes the analogy of the map (p. 72). It must be noted that when Gehring asserts that he favors the "formalist" theory, as against the "expressionist" theory, of music, that is not because he denies that music can or often does "express" (in the Signification sense of that term, as is clear from his discussion on pp. 182-96), but because he denies that it is the "office" of music to signify (p. 175); in other words, he understands the Significationist to be saying that music *ought* to signify, because its aesthetic value depends upon its having a signification, and this is what he argues against.

For other (apparent) versions of the Signification Theory, see (1) L. A. Reid, "Aesthetic Meaning," *PAS*, LV (1854-55): 219-50, esp. 240-46; note his peculiar and confusing sense of "meaning": the *idea* of natural selection "symbolizes" the idea of evolution, by belonging to the same system of ideas (p. 222). (2) Max Rieser, "On Musical Semantics," *J Phil*, XXXIX (1942): 421-32; but in his later article, "The Semantic Theory of Art in America," *JAAC*, XV (September 1956): 12-26, a critical review of the Signification Theory, with comments on Langer, Morris, and Kaplan, he seems more dubious of the theory. (3) Norman Cazden, "Towards a Theory of Realism in Music," *JAAC*, X (December 1951): 135-51 (note the odd use of the term "realism"). This article is critically discussed by Paul L. Frank, "Realism and Naturalism in Music," *ibid.*, XI (September 1952): 55-60. (4) Abraham Kaplan, "Referential Meaning in the Arts," *JAAC*, XII (June 1954): 457-74, does not hold a Signification Theory of music, but he does hold a form of that theory for other arts, and proposes an interesting way of reconciling it with, by subordinating it to, an Expression Theory. (5) Lewis W. Beck, "Judgments of Meaning in Art," *J Phil*, XLI (1944): 169-78 (see also criticisms and replies, 513-21), proposes a form of the Signification Theory, but his use of the terms "connotation" and "denotation" requires analysis.

(II) For general criticism of the Signification Theory, including Morris and Langer, see the article by Richard Rudner, "On Semiotic Aesthetics," *JAAC*, X (1951): 67-77, which argues the incompatibility of regarding aesthetic objects as signs and saying that they are immediately responded to in aesthetic experience. This conclusion is briefly criticized by Irving Copi in "A Note on Representation in Art," *J Phil*, LII (1955): 346-49, and by E. G. Ballard, "In Defense of Symbolic Aesthetics," *JAAC*, XII (September 1953): 38-43. See also Eliseo Vivas, "Aesthetics and Theory of Signs," *Creation and Discovery*; Harold Osborne, *Aesthetics and Criticism*, New York: Philosophical Library, 1955, pp. 69-88, 102-09, who uses the term "natural symbol" for "iconic sign."

Eduard Hanslick's penetrating and witty work, *op. cit.*, I interpret as in part a thorough refutation of earlier and less sophisticated forms of the Signification Theory; see esp. Preface, chs. 2, 3, 5, 7. "The forest is cool and shady, but it certainly does not represent [*stellt nicht dar*] 'the feeling of coolness and shadiness'" (p. 4); again "Epithets . . . may be used so long as we remain fully conscious of their figurative sense—nay, we may even be unable to avoid them; but let us never say, This piece of music 'expresses' [*schildert*] pride, etc." (p. 53), and "It is, aesthetically, quite correct to speak of a theme as having a sad or noble accent, but not as expressing [*nicht aber, es sei ein Ausdruck der*] the sad or noble feelings of the composer" (p. 74). Despite terminological lapses, e.g., some puzzling remarks on "symbolism" (pp. 25-26), this position is consistently and vigorously maintained throughout the book.

18-J MUSICAL "UNDERSTANDING." It would be illuminating to analyze the term "understanding" as applied to music in various typical contexts. Does it have various senses? What assumptions underlie its use? What confusions does it betray?

In such an analysis we could take account of a number of writings about music as "symbolizing" something; these perhaps usually reflect an unsystematic and haphazard form of the Image-Evocation or Expression or Signification Theory, and they very often fail to keep distinct the questions about what music can do and what words and music together can do. This is especially true of the most interesting and ambitious study of musical "symbolism," that by Albert Schweitzer, *op. cit.* See the excellent exposition and criticism by Gordon Sutherland, "The Schweitzerian Heresy," *Music and Letters*, XXIII (1942): 265-89. For example, Schweitzer quotes from the aria "God Has Cast Down the Mighty" (*Cantata No. 10*) figures imitating power and the fall, then he quotes a similar theme from the *Organ Fugue in E Minor*, and says: "These motives illuminate for us the gigantic idea that Bach wished to express in the theme of the *Organ Fugue in E Minor*" (Vol. II, p. 90). For further examples see Karl Geiringer, "Symbolism in the Music of Bach," a lecture, Washington, D.C.: The Library of Congress, 1956.

Here are several articles of a similar sort, but of various degrees of sophistication: Paul F. Laubenstein, "On the Nature of Musical Understanding," *Musical Quarterly*, XIV (1928): 63-76; Michael McMullin, "The Symbolic Analysis of Music," *Music Review*, VIII (1947): 25-35, a discussion of the theories of Arnold Schering; Henry Prunières, "Musical Symbolism," *Musical Quarterly*, XIX (1933): 18-23; Edward A. Lippman, "Symbolism in Music," *Musical Quarterly*, XXXIX (1953): 554-75; Edwin Hall Pierce, "The Significance of the 'Trill', as Found in Beethoven's Most Mature Works," *Musical Quarterly*, XV (1929): 233-45; E. H. W. Meyerstein, "The Problem of Evil and Suffering in Beethoven's Pianoforte Sonatas," *Music Review*, V (1944): 96-111; Katharine M. Wilson, "Meaning in Poetry and Music," *Music and Letters*, IX (1928): 211-25; Hugh Arthur Scott, "That 'Finger-Print' of Beethoven," *Musical Quarterly*, XVI (1930): 276-89, a criticism of Ernest Newman's view (*The Unconscious Beethoven*, New York: Knopf, 1927, Part II) that a rising three-note figure common in Beethoven's works always has a "meaning."

§19

19-A MUSIC AND THE SOUNDS OF WORDS. Can you find examples of songs in which the sound of some of the words and the sound of the music appear inappropriate to one another? What general principles do these examples suggest? See Susanne Langer, *Feeling and Form*, New York: Scribner's, 1953, ch. 10, an excellent defense of what she calls "the principle of assimilation," i.e., that words set to music become pure musical ingredients; the music "swallows" the words.

19-B MUSIC AND THE MEANING OF WORDS. What sorts of thing can happen to the meanings of words when they are set to music? For example, does it distort the meaning to sing a one-syllable word in two or more syllables, to sing it to a high note, to sing it to an unaccented note? Can you think of any general principles about the effects of singing upon the meaning of words?

See the interesting remarks of Eduard Hanslick, *The Beautiful in Music*, New York: Liberal Arts, 1957, ch. 2; he emphasizes the "plasticity" of music in relation to words. See also Edmund Gurney, *The Power of Sound*, London: Smith, Elder, 1880, chs. 20, 21, 22; Donald F. Tovey, *Vocal Music*, Vol. V of *Essays in Musical Analysis*, New York: Oxford U., 1935-39, esp. pp. 115, 175, 199, 205; also "Mass" and "Oratorio," *Encyclopaedia Britannica* 14th ed., Chicago: U. of Chicago, 1929 (reprinted in Tovey, *The Forms of Music*, New York: Meridian, 1956); Tovey, "Words and Music: Some Obiter Dicta," *The Main Stream of Music*, New York: Oxford U., 1949, pp. 202-19.

For further examples of the parallelism of verbal meaning in music, see: Albert Schweitzer, *J. S. Bach*, trans. by Ernest Newman, Leipzig, New York: Breitkopf and Härtel, 1911, Vol. II; William Palmer, "Word-Painting and Suggestion in Byrd," *Music Review*, XIII (1952): 169-80.

19-C SONG. To study the problems of appropriateness of words to music, examine alternative settings to the same words: e.g., settings by Fauré and Debussy of Verlaine's poem "En Sourdine" and other examples cited and commented on interestingly by Gerald Moore, *Singer and Accompanist*, New York: Macmillan, 1954, pp. 38-44, 95-96; see also 63-70, 199. How does the music call attention to different qualities of the poem's situation? Compare also alternative words in the same, or approximately the same, setting, e.g., some of Bach's and Handel's borrowings from their own works. How do the different words, by their sound-qualities, change the music? (See Donald F. Tovey, "Bach," *Encyclopaedia Britannica*.)

See Mario Castelnuovo-Tedesco, "Music and Poetry: Problems of a Song Writer," *Musical Quarterly*, XXX (1944): 102-11; Mursell, *op. cit.*, pp. 259-62; Edward T. Cone, "Words into Music: The Composer's Approach to the Text," *Sound and Poetry*, English Institute Essays, 1956, New York: Columbia U., 1957.

There is another interesting problem about songs. When the words set to music are verse, their verse-character (i.e., their meter and rhyme, in the broad sense) may be preserved or destroyed. Now, what independent and intrinsic qualities of music make it possible for the verse-character to be preserved? Quite independently of any reference to words, there is in music itself a rhyming phenomenon, or parallelism of phrases, which makes it possible for the movement of the music to follow the movement of the verse. In the trio of the minuet in Beethoven's *String Quartet in A Major (Op. 18, No. 5)*,

Beethoven, *String Quartet in A Major* (Op. 18, No. 5)

the two notes at the end obviously rhyme, musically, with notes 5 and 6. Can you discover any other such characteristics of music that are relevant to setting verse?

19-D OPERA. What are the special problems about the relation of music and words in opera? For example, in what ways can we say that in Mozart's operas the music helps to characterize Leporello, Masetto, Despina, Dorabella, Papageno, Monostatos, Basilio, Osmin? In what ways, in the operas of Verdi, Wagner, and Puccini, do musical events—climaxes, sudden modulations, recollections of earlier themes—give information about what is going on, or what has happened or will happen? (Some good examples are given here and there in Siegmund Levarie's elaborate critical analysis, *Mozart's Le Nozze di Figaro*, Chicago: U. of Chicago, 1952.)

See Donald F. Tovey, "Opera" and "Gluck," *Encyclopaedia Britannica*, "Gluck," *Main Stream of Music*, pp. 65-102; and problems raised in the following: Winton Dean, "Carmen: An Attempt at a True Evaluation," *Music Review*, VII (1946): 209-20 (note the way in which he defends some of Bizet's songs and his objection to Alban Berg's use of a plain C major chord in root position to accompany Wozzeck's giving money to Marie in the second act of *Wozzeck;* on this chord, cf. Hans

Keller, "The Eclecticism of *Wozzeck*," *Music Review*, XII (1951): 309-15; XIII (1952): 133-37, also correspondence, 252, 332; Edgar Istel, "Gluck's Dramaturgy," *Musical Quarterly*, XVII (1931): 227-33 (especially his remarks about the controversy over Hanslick's observations on *"J'ai perdu mon Eurydice"*); Albert Gehring, *The Basis of Musical Pleasure*, New York: Putnam, 1910, pp. 143-68; Ernest Newman, *Seventeen Famous Operas*, New York: Knopf, 1955; Douglas Moore, *Listening to Music*, rev. ed., New York: Norton, 1937, ch. 16; Joseph Kerman, *Opera as Drama*, New York: Knopf, 1956; H. C. Colles, *Voice and Verse*, New York: Oxford U., 1928.

19-E PROGRAM MUSIC. See the interesting remarks in Hanslick, *op. cit.*, ch. 3, and his analysis of the term "subject" in chs. 6 and 7. See also Frederick Niecks, *Programme Music in the Last Four Centuries*, London: Novello, 1906; Tovey, "Programme Music" and "Symphonic Poem," *Encyclopaedia Britannica*; R. W. S. Mendel, "Beethoven as a Writer of Programme Music," *Musical Quarterly*, XIV (1928): 172-77, and "The Art of the Symphonic Poem," *ibid.*, XVIII (1932): 443-62; James L. Mursell, *Psychology of Music*, New York: Norton, 1937, pp. 262-68; M. D. Calvocoressi, *The Principles and Methods of Musical Criticism*, New York: Oxford U., 1923, Part I, ch. 5; Albert R. Chandler, *Beauty and Human Nature*, New York: Appleton-Century, 1934, pp. 212-19; Ernest Newman, *Richard Strauss*, London, New York: Lane, 1908, pp. 43-88; Douglas Moore, *op. cit.*, ch. 15.

19-F TITLES. What is the relation between a musical composition and its title, if it has a descriptive one: e.g., Schumann's piano pieces, the pieces in Grieg's *Peer Gynt Suite*, Saint-Saëns' *Carnival of Animals;* Paul Creston's *Third Symphony*, subtitled *Three Mysteries;* how does it affect your hearing of these compositions to know the titles? Can you discover by experiment whether your reaction is typical of others'? Should a title be considered a kind of program?

19-G DIRECTIONS FOR PERFORMANCE. Collect examples of unusual directions for performance given by composers: e.g., *"beklemmt"* in Beethoven's *String Quartet in B Flat Major (Op. 130)*; the *"allegro misterioso"* with a *"trio estatico,"* and others in Alban Berg, *Lyric Suite*. Should these be understood as very general programs? Where is the line to be drawn?

19-H THE DANCE. In the light of the discussion of the similarities between musical and physical movement, in §18, it would seem that in the dance a fusion of music and the movement of human bodies can occur. What are the problems in analyzing the possible relationships here? Can one dance be more appropriate to (a better "interpretation" of) a musical composition than another? See Langer, *op. cit.*, chs. 11, 12.

· VIII ·

ARTISTIC
TRUTH

When someone utters a declarative sentence, we need not be content merely to understand what he says; we can, and under some circumstances we must, also decide whether or not to assent to what he says. The sentence has not merely a meaning; it also has the characteristic of being either true or false, and consequently believable or disbelievable. In virtue of having this characteristic, it can record and communicate knowledge. In other words, it has a *cognitive function*.

Paintings and musical compositions are often described in similar terms: they "say" something, they "communicate," they "enlighten." And this way of speaking surely means more than that they represent or imitate the physical world, and more than that they express or signify, though these latter terms have been extended to cover the cognitive function, too. It is one thing to say that music has a meaning, another to say that it is true or false. There seem to be two different concepts here, though they are closely connected. The word "horse" is not true or false. But it was proposed in Chapter III, §9, that the meaning of "horse" is to be understood in terms of its capacity to be used in statements that are true or false: "Richard had a horse." If so, then perhaps the Signification Theory of music, for example, is incomplete unless it goes on to show how musical icons can be combined into statements of some sort: if music is never true, then its parts can never be meaningful, either.

I am not prepared to press this point. I think some people have wished to say that music can signify although it cannot be true or false. If others would extend the Signification Theory or the Expression Theory so that music can be said to be true or false, at least this is clearly an extension. And it is the legitimacy of this extension that we are to consider in the present chapter. We shall still keep the problems of literature on one side—they will engage us in the following chapter—but we shall be concerned with the cognitive status of paintings and musical compositions.

It is worth bearing in mind from the start, what has often been elaborately stressed, that the chief terms we must rely on in this discussion are peculiarly apt to be misleading. Consider the word "say." Horatio Greenough once remarked:

> The obelisk has to my eye a singular aptitude, in its form and character, to call attention to a spot memorable in history. It says but one word, but it speaks loud. If I understand its voice, it says, Here! It says no more.[1]

Greenough was making a distinction between the Bunker Hill monument, which he approved, and the proposed Washington monument, which he disapproved because it was to be placed upon a spot where nothing memorable had happened. I suppose a similar remark might be made about music: a loud crashing chord, or a flourish of trumpets, says "Now!" in the same clear voice. But this sort of "saying" is evidently quite different from "Richard had a horse." An enormous obelisk that calls attention to nothing, or trumpets that announce nobody's appearance, are disappointments, but not exactly lies. They are more like "Look!" and "Listen!" than "This ground is hallowed by the blood of patriots" or "Royal persons are about to enter."

Even the word "true" turns out to have pitfalls enough to keep us constantly on the alert. And although we shall have more to say about it as we go along, it seems very desirable to agree on a few ground rules at the start. (1) When we speak of something as "true," let us keep this word as an epistemic term—that is, a term connected with knowledge—and not let it shift over into one of its other familiar but irrelevant senses, such as loyal, sincere, or genuine. (2) Let us keep truth from getting mixed up with psychological states; the statement "This is true to you, but not to me" means "You believe this, but I don't," and these statements are not about truth at all. (3) Let us agree that truth involves a correspondence of something to reality, but let us not smuggle any assumptions about the *nature* of that reality into our definition of "truth." A person who believes that "The soul is immortal" is true, and "Grass is green" is true, is at liberty to say that souls and grass are different sorts of being, but not that the word "true" is used in different senses.

---

[1] Horatio Greenough, *Form and Function*, ed. by Harold A. Small, Berkeley, Cal.: U. of California, 1947, p. 26.

We may begin by introducing the term "proposition," in no very unusual sense, to mean anything that is either true or false. The first question before us in this chapter, then, is whether some nonverbal aesthetic objects are, or contain, propositions. The affirmative answer to this question I shall call the *Proposition Theory* of the cognitive status of aesthetic objects.[1]

The main outlines of this theory are fairly simple, though, as we shall see, it raises some subtle problems. In linguistic utterances, many philosophers distinguish between the sentence and the proposition the sentence is said to "express"; the sentence is the vehicle of the proposition. The arguments for making this distinction are involved, but perhaps they are chiefly these: First, if two sentences, say "Grass is green" and "*L'herbe est verte*," can express the same proposition, then the proposition they express cannot be identified with either of them. Second, it seems that it is propositions that we believe, not sentences. Third, it seems that a proposition, *that grass is green,* may be true even before anyone writes or speaks a sentence that expresses it; *that Socrates is executed in 399 B.C.* was true before it happened, or even before Socrates was born, though it could not then be known.

If we make such a distinction, it becomes possible to hold that propositions, which we name by "that"-clauses, can have other vehicles than linguistic ones. And indeed there are clearly examples of this. "When I cough, it will be time to turn on the ectoplasm," the medium might say to his assistant before the séance, and then the cough is a prearranged vehicle for the proposition *that it is time to turn on the ectoplasm.* But here there is a specific convention, or agreement, to make the cough an abbreviation for the sentence. The Proposition Theory, however, is that even in the absence of such conventions, at least some paintings and musical compositions can be construed as vehicles of propositions in exactly the same way that sentences in ordinary speech are vehicles of propositions. Not, perhaps, all paintings and musical compositions; I put the theory in the weaker, but by no means trivial or uninteresting, form. In some paintings and in some musical compositions the Proposition Theorist distinguishes two components, a "subject" of some sort and a comment upon it, sometimes called an "interpretation" of the subject. In this way the work "says" something about reality, and what it says can be assented to or dissented from by the spectator.

---

[1] This theory has been maintained by T. M. Greene, Morris Weitz, and Andrew P. Ushenko; for references see Note 20-B at end of chapter.

The Proposition Theory in some form or other is clearly presupposed by numerous statements that critics make about works of fine art, and it is desirable to have a variety of examples on hand for the discussion. It is said that Rembrandt's later paintings and etchings of biblical subjects interpret those subjects with the simplicity, humility, emphasis on personal sincerity, and Biblical literalism of the Mennonites (followers of Menno Simons); that Giorgione's paintings and Rubens' late landscapes are pantheistic; that Velásquez and other Spanish painters have embodied in their works the "tragic sense of life" and a "hunger for immortality," in Unamuno's words; that El Greco's paintings are mystical; that Tintoretto's *Christ before Pilate* (1566, Scuola di San Rocco, Venice) asserts that the individual has dignity but also serves divine ends that pass his understanding; that Courbet's paintings preach humanitarianism and universal brotherhood; that Raphael's *Disputà* (1509, Camera della Segnatura, Vatican) says that the way to Heaven is the Eucharist, and that, placed as it is across from the *School of Athens* (ca. 1508), it also says that there are two forms of knowledge, Reason and Faith; that Ben Shahn's best-known paintings are castigations of social conditions and pleas for social justice. W. H. Auden found a proposition in Brueghel's *Fall of Icarus* (ca. 1555, Musée des Beaux Arts, Brussels) which he put into his poem, "Musée des Beaux Arts":

> About suffering they were never wrong,
> The Old Masters: how well they understood
> Its human position. . . .[2]

When protests were made in 1953 because a section of the Orozco mural at the New School for Social Research was kept behind a yellow curtain, the President of the University said that the painting "does not express the philosophy of the faculty," and by this he evidently meant not that it merely failed to express that philosophy, but that it contained some philosophy incompatible with that philosophy. (The panel shows Stalin in a stiff row with five Soviet soldiers of different races, all armed with hammers and all looking very glum; not even the painter has explained what its philosophy is.)

All these statements illustrate the Proposition Theory, and if any of them are true then that theory is true also. Of course not everyone would accept all these interpretations; if there are propositions embedded in visual designs, they are present in different degrees of clearness and emphasis. Consider three examples from among the reproductions in this book. Dürer's *Last Supper*, PLATE VI, contrasts in some very remarkable ways with his earlier woodcuts of the same subject, the most remarkable

---

[2] From "Musée des Beaux Arts," W. H. Auden, *Collected Shorter Poems 1930-1944*. Copyright 1940 by W. H. Auden and reprinted with the permission of Random House Inc. and Faber and Faber Ltd.

of all being like Sherlock Holmes's dog that didn't bark in the night. The table contains only the chalice, and on the floor in the most prominent position is the charger *without* the sacrificial lamb. At the same time that this woodcut was being made, Luther was arguing that the Holy Mass is not a sacrifice, but a symbolic testament. "In so conspicuously emphasizing the sacramental chalice while eliminating the sacrificial lamb, Dürer appears to profess his adherence to Luther's point of view," says Panofsky.[3] In other words, this picture contains a part of Protestant theology.

Daumier's *Witnesses,* PLATE VIII, is a particularly interesting example, for it may be approached on two levels. On one hand, it seems to belong to a specific political context, in which it would convey a clear and decisive message.[4] It was designed in 1872 for his series of lithographs, *Actualités,* but for some unknown reason was never published; it exists only in the form of a single proof owned by the Metropolitan Museum of Art. On May 16, 1872, a *conseil de guerre* was set up to try Marshal François-Achille Bazaine, commander of the Army of the Rhine in the war with Germany, who had surrendered Metz to the Prussians. Some newspapers had taken the side of Bazaine, who was finally convicted of treason, and had played up the high social position and reputation of those who testified on his behalf. Daumier's "witnesses" are apparently witnesses for the prosecution. Thus if there is a specific proposition in this picture it is something like "Bazaine is a traitor, as those who died in the war would testify." But on the other hand it could be taken in a more general sense by someone who knows nothing of that story as a reminder of the horrors of war, and as an indictment of brass hats and military bureaucrats.

A less definite social comment might be found in Käthe Kollwitz's *Municipal Lodging,* PLATE III. Here, at least, is hunger and weariness; is there also the implication that some unnamed power—society or war or an unjust economic system—is responsible for it?

It is less common, but not unknown, for the Proposition Theory to be applied to music. It is said that certain composers, such as Kodály, Smetana, Dvorák, and Sibelius, are "nationalistic" composers, and that there are strong nationalistic elements in their music; I am not sure that nationalism is a proposition here, however. I have read that Bohuslav Martinu's *Fantaisies Symphoniques* celebrates the indomitable fortitude and bravery of the Czech people, and prophesies a heroic future for them; and that the third movement of Arthur Honegger's *Symphonie Liturgique* attacks the "terrifying imbecility" of "nationalism, militarism, bureaucracy, administrations, customs barriers, taxes, wars which transform human

---

[3] Erwin Panofsky, *Albrecht Dürer,* 3rd ed., Princeton, N.J.: Princeton U., 1948, Vol. I, p. 222. The sentence quoted actually refers to Dürer's drawing of 1523, but it applies also to the woodcut.

[4] My information on this point was kindly given by M. Jean Vallery-Radot, of the Print Room of the Bibliothèque Nationale, and M. Jean Adhémar, editor of Daumier's drawings and watercolors.

beings into robots." And some have held that Richard Strauss's tone poem *Also sprach Zarathustra*, teaches, like the work of Nietzsche after which it is named, the "yea-saying" philosophy of life and the hope of the coming Superman.

The most fundamental objection that may be raised to the Proposition Theory is too complicated to develop very far here. There are serious difficulties in the distinction between propositions and their vehicles—that is, sentences—in ordinary language. In the first place, the arguments for making this distinction do not show that it is really necessary: for example, "Grass is green" can be synonymous with "*L'herbe est verte*" even if there is no third thing, a proposition, that they both express. In the second place, there are serious obscurities in the notion of propositions that are distinct from any proposition-vehicle, that are not themselves perceptual objects of any sort and have a timeless existence or subsistence. I do not believe there are any such entities as propositions, apart from linguistic vehicles. If so, the Proposition Theory is in serious straits, for then a proposition is not something unattached that can have a musical phrase as its vehicle, or a visual design, just as well as a sentence: it is nothing *but* a sentence, or, better, a class of sentences, of a certain sort. And the only way nonverbal objects can substitute temporarily for such sentences is by specific *verbal* stipulation: the medium must use another sentence to make the cough a substitute for one. Of course a composer may provide us with a philosophic program—say a digest of Nietzsche's philosophy—and stipulate that the tone poem is to be an abbreviation for that philosophy. But in this sense anything can be made to mean anything.

Even if the Proposition Theory's theory of propositions can be maintained—and this must be admitted to be an open question in present-day philosophical discussion—there is a further hurdle for it. Apart from arbitrary stipulation, we may ask, what conditions must an object satisfy if it is to be a regular and systematic vehicle for propositions? What does language have that is essential to the making of statements? One thing we can say, I think, with some confidence. In the sentence "Grass is green" we can distinguish between two fundamentally different working parts. The word "grass" has the function of telling what the sentence, in the ordinary sense, is *about*. And the words "is green" have the function of telling what is *said* about the subject. To express a proposition—or to be a statement—an object must have two parts, an *indexical* part, which answers the question "What are you talking about?" and a *characterizing* part, which answers the question "What about it?" Neither of these by itself is sufficient. To utter references, "Grass," "Snow," "Peter Piper," or to utter predicates, "is green," "is white," "picked a peck of pickled peppers," is not to provide anything that one can agree with or disagree with.

It might be objected that not all sentences are of the subject-predicate form; when someone says, "It is raining," we do not ask, "What is rain- ing?" so "it" is not the index. But even here there are parts of the sentence that assume the two basic roles. "It is raining" attributes occurrence, or existence, to a certain event, namely rain; "raining" is therefore the index, and "it is" the characterizer. But in the Latin *pluret*, the inflectional ending *et* is the characterizer.

The question is, then, whether we can discover in nonverbal aesthetic objects parts that function as indexes and parts that function as characterizers.

Saying and Showing

Let us consider paintings first. Suppose we have a representational painting that depicts an object, say, a blue horse, but does not portray. Now, we can distinguish the shape of the horse from its color, but on what ground can we say which of these aspects of the picture is index and which characterizer? There is no way of extracting the proposition "All horses are blue" or even "Some horses are blue," any more than "All blue things are horses." This seems to me a clear-cut case. Perhaps it is so only because I have left out all the interesting complexities. But I think the same principle can be applied to important paintings as well.

At least, it applies to those paintings that depict but do not portray any particular thing as far as we know. The Kollwitz lithograph can be said to depict cold and hungry human beings, and, by abstraction, the sufferings of humanity. Its sympathy is directed to the children, not as individuals, but simply as helpless and homeless and fatherless children. But whatever indictment of society may have been in Kollwitz's mind, or in the mind of many of her admirers, there is no indictment in the paint- ing, for there is nothing that can be read as an index pointing to anything indicted. The Giorgione landscape does not contain the pantheistic propo- sition *that God is immanent in nature,* for no part of it is an index re- ferring to God. But we may perhaps say that it depicts a landscape that looks as though divine force is immanent in it—just as Franz Marc depicts a blue horse without saying that all horses are blue or that there exist blue horses. So with the Brueghel *Fall of Icarus,* forgetting for the moment that it does portray Icarus, and thinking of it as a depiction: it does not contain the psychological generalization that people are indifferent to other people's sufferings. But it does depict a ploughman ignoring a man falling into the sea, and perhaps even shows, as Auden says, that "for him it was not an important failure."

The *Fall of Icarus,* however, raises a somewhat more difficult prob- lem. For it tells a story, or—if "tells" is too strong a word—it reminds us of a story already told elsewhere. Now it is generally held that a story can have an idea or ideology, a "moral," as it is called when the story is simple, and in the following chapter we shall find reason to accept this view. The story of Icarus, for example, might be said to suggest, or imply, that man should not be too proud and ambitious. But if the story contains a proposition about life, and the painting contains the story, then should we not say that the painting contains a proposition? "Contains" cannot mean the same thing in both cases here; the painting depicts the story, and the story suggests the proposition. We can go on to say that therefore the painting suggests the proposition. But this is a very special kind of example, for in this view the painting becomes a kind of illustration of the story, and thus a substitute sign, like the medium's cough; it can only suggest a proposition that is already suggested by a story.

But now suppose we have a picture that portrays an individual person or event. Here we can distinguish two different things in the representation. Let's say it is a cartoon of the President, in which he stands gazing at the Capitol and is made to look like a sheep. Can we not say that the portrayal is the index and the depiction is the characterizer, so that the picture as a whole is the vehicle for some such proposition as *that the President is like a sheep when it comes to getting his bills through the Congress?*

This is an extreme case, I think, and very instructive. For if this is not a proposition-vehicle, then I should think no design can be. I am assuming there are no words, but that both the President and the Capitol are recognizable portrayals, despite the distortion in depiction. And the case for saying that there is a proposition here seems strong. The fact that it is vague is not to the point; it is no vaguer than the verbal simile that I used to translate it, and the Proposition Theorist does not have to concede that it can be adequately translated into words at all, any more than that all English sentences can be adequately translated into French. If this cartoon were placed side by side with another, picturing the President as a Simon Legree whipping his bills through the halls of Congress, we would certainly say they depicted him differently, and we could say that they contradicted each other—which would make them sound even more like proposition-vehicles. And though we would not ordinarily, perhaps, refer to the cartoon directly as true or false, we might call it "unfair" or say it made a "good point," and these expressions seem to imply falsity or truth.

To know what a painting states, then, according to the Proposition Theory, we must first determine what it portrays, then observe the characteristics attributed to the portrayal-subject by the way it is depicted. We can then read off the propositions, and decide, if we wish, whether there is truth in them or misrepresentation. Proposition Theorists would generally hold, too, that the truth and the profundity of the propositions have some bearing upon the ultimate worth of the work.

Nevertheless, I am not convinced. The alternative to the Proposition Theory seems to me simpler and clearer, as well as free from the difficulties raised above about detached propositions, although I do not know how to show decisively from an examination of paintings themselves that the Proposition Theory is wrong. The alternative is suggested by certain very familiar ways of speaking about visual designs. We say "In this painting Rembrandt has represented Saskia as Flora" or "In this painting Sir Joshua Reynolds has represented Mrs. Siddons as the Tragic Muse"; and here the act of "representing as" involves no proposition, clearly. So, too, in a review of recent shows we may read that Matta's paintings "present man as helpless, trapped in mechanism"; that Tamayo "painted man scanning the sky for signs and portents"; that Grosz "shows men reduced to gray nonentities . . . a work full of warning." And I think these phrases[5] are the correct ones.

The two idioms that I want to contrast are: (a) "The painting shows (represents, depicts) the President as sheeplike" and (b) "The painting states (contains the proposition) that the President is sheeplike." I think these are different, and that the first is to be preferred to the second.

The alternative to the Proposition Theory of painting is something like the following. The painting represents the portrayal-subject as having certain characteristics. But it does not itself make a claim to truth or constitute a proposition-vehicle: it simply offers a subject, the President as sheeplike, Napoleon as the savior of his country, Lincoln as an underminer of the Constitution. When we, the spectators, compare that picture with what we take to be the facts, *we* can utter a statement that the picture corresponds or does not correspond to these facts. And this statement may be true or false, but it is a statement *about* the picture, not *in* it. If we say the portrait is true, it is only in the sense in which a sense datum may sometimes be misleadingly called "true," when it corresponds to its object; the proper word is "veridical," for a sense datum is not a statement.

Another way of making the distinction is to say that the painting is not true *of*, or true *about*, its portrayal-subject, in the way a statement may be, but "true *to*" it.[6] "True to" has two different uses, one of which we shall consider in the following section, but the other is relevant here. We can say that the cartoon is true to, or untrue to, the President, as we say that a portrait is true to, or untrue to, its sitter, meaning that the characteristics it depicts are the characteristics he really does, or does not, have. Truth-to is similarity to: the picture is in some important way a likeness. And this likeness is something we may note and point out in a statement, but the picture is not itself a statement that it is like the sitter. Nor, I think, does its title count as an abbreviated assertion of likeness, though even if it did, the painting would not be the whole proposition-vehicle, but only the characterizer.

If we reject the Proposition Theory, we must recast into other, and aesthetically more correct, terms the statements about paintings that

---

[5] Which I borrow from a review by Howard Devree of *The New York Times*.

[6] This has been suggested and interestingly worked out by John Hospers in *Meaning and Truth in the Arts;* see Note 21-D.

were mentioned earlier. Rembrandt's religious paintings show certain events happening in certain ways; they depict forgiveness and humility, and we can say they are in those ways more Mennonite than, say, Calvinistic. But this statement is a description of their representational subject matter, not a statement extracted from the works themselves. There are social and political aspects of the subjects of Courbet and Ben Shahn, of course, but they are simply set forth. It is we who compare them with the world and ask whether they represent it truly or misrepresent it. The Daumier cartoon can be regarded in the same way. It certainly depicts an accusation, and it does more, that is, it shows the accusation as just. We see a group of people—or figures who once were people—set against the cold and empty doorway, and we see that doorway from their point of view. But only by an ellipsis, and a misleading one, could we say that the cartoon is itself an accusation.

The Dürer engraving is more complicated, because of its manipulation of conventional Christian symbols. We can certainly say that the picture, like the two great works of Raphael, embodies a theological concept, even a system of concepts. In this sense it is perfectly correct to say that it is a Protestant work, and shows a certain way of regarding the relation between man and God. But I must confess that we can hardly refrain from adding that in these works there are propositions. And that is understandable. For a symbolic object can by convention come to be the substitute for a verbal formula—just like the medium's cough that was mentioned earlier. The lamb is a reminder that the Mass is a sacrifice. Where a visual design depicts such conventional symbols, there is a kind of language, and the work may be said to be true or false. This tentative conclusion seems to be reasonable. But where there are no such conventional symbols, the work cannot, I think, be true or false.

Of course, from a practical point of view, the choice between saying that the painting states something and saying that it merely shows something is not a momentous one, though I do not see that this should make it uninteresting to a student of aesthetics. A painting that contains a theological error—for example, a painting of *Christ Treading the Serpent* that shows the foot of Christ directly on the serpent rather than on Mary's foot, which touches the serpent—must of course be condemned by a Church that sponsors the painting no less firmly whether it is a misstatement or a misshowing. Presumably it can do just as much harm to the religious believer—unless it is accompanied by a label pointing out that it *is* an error.

On Musical Semantics

When we turn to music in search of a ground for the Proposition Theory, it is evident that no ground is to be had, and indeed it is hard to understand how anyone could have come to believe that music contains

proposition-vehicles. True, a fine musical phrase that sings out with
strength and clarity has an affirmative quality, and it is no bad description
of this quality to say that it seems to call for passionate assent. But we
are not assenting to anything else via the music; we are only giving in to
the music itself and letting it carry us where it will. Music may be nationalistic, in the sense that it uses folk-melodies that remind us of a
certain region; but it cannot be *anti*nationalistic, or internationalistic, in
the sense of urging measures or making predictions. At most it can present qualitative equivalents to nationalistic or antinationalistic program
notes.

This follows from the fact that in the texture of music we cannot distinguish indexical parts from characterizing parts. It is not at all foolish
to consider this possibility seriously, for if music could not only be understood as containing signs, as we saw reason in the previous chapter to
doubt, but signs of different logical form, it would be an interesting aspect
of music, and would give it a new dimension. Therefore I will briefly discuss one way of doing this, the most plausible I can think of, even though
it is not very plausible, and has never been proposed, as far as I know.

Imagine a language with the simplest sort of grammar, designed
for a simple descriptive purpose. All the words in the language are verbs,
or verb-derivatives, and the only rule for combining these words is this:
to put one verb after another is to state that the event referred to by the
first verb was followed by the event referred to by the second verb. Thus
in a pair of verbs like "snowing slushing," the first word "snowing" is the
index and the second word, taken as following it, is the characterizer: in
our language, "snowing is followed by slushing." Or, "House-burning
John-running water-pouring" states a sequence of events.

Now suppose we were to construe musical passages in an analogous
way. Each passage that presents a certain human quality, joy or vigor or
grief, is to be understood as referring to a quality of life or of the experience of man; each sequence of qualities stands for the proposition that
such sequences typically occur in life. And this is just the way some
people talk. They say, "Tchaikovsky's *Pathétique* is a pessimistic symphony because it ends on a tragic note." In our proposal, this means that
when a musical composition presents a cheerful passage followed by a
gloomy one, it implicitly states that gloom usually follows cheer, and if
its last passage is gloomy, it states that this is the way life characteristically is summed up. Again, as some critics have contended, if Beethoven's
last quartet (Op. 135) ends on an affirmative note, it says that life on the
whole is good.

To sketch such a semantics of music as this, even briefly, is to show
how absurd such an undertaking would be. Nevertheless, anyone who
takes seriously the idea that music *is* true or false in a plain, rather than
a maverick or Pickwickian, sense, is, I think, obliged to show that in
music we can discriminate indexes from characterizers, or, in more

familiar terms, a subject matter from the interpretation of it. And this has never been adequately done.

Despite its flaws, which turn up on close examination, the Proposition Theory is an ever-present temptation when we talk about paintings and music. For they have an important characteristic that is so close to being propositional that the distinction is hard to preserve. A visual or auditory design presents itself with every sign of being a human artifact, something thought out intelligently and ordered by a being like ourselves; it has an air of purposiveness and directedness about it. It speaks to us. And when we attend to it, and strain to penetrate its inmost nature, it is as if we were listening for a "message" or trying to catch the voice of its maker. A representational painting has a point of view, in the purely spatial sense that it represents the subject as observed from a certain point: close up, or from a distance, from eye level, or from above, or from several points at once. It has a point of view in a larger sense, which we might call its *attitude;* it represents the subject as regarded by one who has certain thoughts and feelings. Compare the rooms and street scenes of Edward Hopper with those of Balthus, or those of Reginald Marsh with those of John Sloan. We describe the attitude of a painting as cold, detached, hard, sympathetic, pitiless, tender; these words apply to the *implicit viewer* that is present in every representational painting. We may call this viewer by the name of the painter, for convenience, but it is not really the painter we are talking about, for we do not need to go outside the painting itself to compare "Renoir's" attitude toward the nude with "Rubens'," or "Goya's" attitude toward war with "Callot's," or to describe "Toulouse-Lautrec's" attitude toward the prostitutes lining up for medical inspection or the drinkers at the Moulin de la Galette.

A representational painting, then, has an implicit viewer with an attitude—though it may be only dimly apparent—that is shown by the qualities it emphasizes. This concept has something in common with that of the implicit speaker in literary works. I do not think we can extend it fruitfully to nonrepresentational painting or to music, for it becomes too tenuous. Yet it makes sense, even if it is vague to speak of the attitude of such works. In a pure design there may be fun or high seriousness, restraint and discipline or abandon and frenzy. And critics sometimes find in music an out-going and adventurous attitude toward life, or a deep introspective quality.

These descriptions, in the end, are best taken as attempts at a compendious description of the prevalent or dominant human regional qualities of the work. They do not entail, nor do they presuppose, that the work can be, or contain, a proposition.

Though paintings and musical compositions are not, either in whole or in part, statements that we can affirm or deny, this conclusion does not settle the broad issue confronting us in this chapter. For even if an aesthetic object is not itself the bearer of knowledge, like a true verbal statement, it may nevertheless be related to our knowledge in some direct and intimate way. At least this is a view that philosophers have sometimes held, and for important reasons. Most, if not all, of the noteworthy accounts of the relation of art to knowledge can, I think, be collected under two general headings, depending on the concept taken as central, revelation or intuition. In this section we shall consider both of these concepts.

According to some aestheticians, a painting or a musical composition is not to be understood by comparison with a verbal statement, but rather by comparison with a gesture, or a dramatic act, or the moon coming out from behind a cloud. It does not make assertions about, but *reveals,* the nature of reality, and hence, though it may not strictly be called "true," it may well be called "illuminating," "enlightening," or "instructive." This view I shall call the *Revelation Theory* of the cognitive status of painting and music.[1]

Our first task is to try to clarify this theory. To begin with, note that it has affinities with the Expression Theory, though the difference between them is, in my opinion, important enough to justify giving them different names. If a painting expressed anything, it would be something in the mind or spirit of the artist, his feelings or emotions. But what the painting is said to reveal is something in the objective physical world outside the artist, or a reality behind the physical world. It is possible, of course, to hold both the Expression Theory and the Revelation Theory, and it is equally possible to mingle them together without being aware of the distinction, but the problems they raise are rather different, and deserve separate treatment.

The term "reveal" is a puzzling one, in some ways, and its legitimacy in this context is not well established. In common speech, the statement, "His behavior at the party revealed something to me," would usually mean that the behavior afforded observational data that not only (a) suggested a new hypothesis to me, but (b) constituted fairly strong and direct evidence for that hypothesis. I do not think we would ordinarily speak of an event or object as revealing something unless it did both of these things. So might another composer have remarked, after hearing the *première* of Beethoven's *C Minor Symphony,* the first symphony in which trombones were used: "When I heard those trombones, it was a revelation to me," meaning something like, "They made me realize that trom-

---

[1] This theory has been held, in various forms, by Schopenhauer, Hegel, L. A. Reid, Hugo Munsterberg, and others; see Notes 21-A, 21-B, 21-C.

bones could be used with powerful effect in other symphonies as well."

But if this is its meaning, how can the term "reveal" be applied to paintings and music? A painting can reveal things about painting, just as Beethoven's orchestration revealed something about orchestration. But can a painting reveal something about anything else? Consider the sort of thing that might be said about a movie: "It reveals the (shocking!) condition of retarded Southern girls who are kept in unconsummated wedlock." Something of the sort was claimed by author Tennessee Williams and director Elia Kazan for their much-deplored movie of 1956, *Baby Doll*. Even this way of speaking stretches the term from its ordinary use, for though the movie may *suggest* the hypothesis that retarded Southern girls are frequently kept in unconsummated wedlock, it does not present a single authenticated case history (being fiction), and therefore it certainly is not strong or direct *evidence* for that hypothesis.

The distinction between suggesting a hypothesis and giving evidence for it—that is, confirming it—is crucial here, but I assume it to be generally understood and accepted. To give an extreme example, a man may dream that his wife is unfaithful, and this dream, vividly and sharply recalled, may suggest to him for the first time in his married life the hypothesis that she is unfaithful. Here we are speaking of the source, or genesis, of the hypothesis. But the dream is in no way evidence of the truth of the hypothesis, though it may be evidence for another hypothesis, namely that he unconsciously wishes to be unfaithful himself.

Now, in the ordinary sense, then, *Baby Doll* reveals nothing, but it does half of what is involved in ordinary revealing: it suggests hypotheses—at least to some people. And the same may be said about some representational paintings. A painting depicting, let us say, a poor mountain girl scrubbing clothes—since we cannot depict her unconsummated wedlock—may suggest the hypothesis that poor mountain girls have a hard time, though it is again not evidence for that hypothesis. Music, however, cannot suggest any hypotheses at all in this way, since it has no subject. It may suggest hypotheses about music, or about the composer, or perhaps even about the social and cultural conditions under which it was composed, but I do not see how it can suggest any hypotheses about reality in general, as the Revelation Theory claims, much less confirm them.

We are evidently on the wrong track if we take the term "reveal" seriously. If it means hypothesis-suggestion-and-confirmation, no aesthetic objects are revelatory of reality in general, apart from being symptoms of personality or culture. If it means merely hypothesis-suggestion, paintings can be revelatory but musical compositions cannot. But the Revelation Theory purports to be true of all the arts, and therefore it is false.

Perhaps, however, it is a different theory that many Revelationists have in mind, however badly they name it. And the clue to this other theory, which has nothing to do with suggesting or confirming hypotheses, is the word "universal," which they often use. Philosophers commonly distinguish between two sorts of term in our language, singular ("the Washington Monument") and general ("monument" or "monuments"). And most philosophers also distinguish between *particulars,* that is, individual persons, places, and things that are named by singular terms (the Washington Monument) and *universals,* which are repeatable qualities or relations that can appear in various particulars (monumentalness, or monumentality). The particular monument is said to be an "instance" of the universal, or to exemplify it.

The second version of the Revelation Theory to be considered, then, is the theory that aesthetic objects reveal universals. I should like to call this the Universalist version of the Revelation Theory. It is apparently what most Revelationists contend for: a painting or a musical composition discloses, or makes manifest, a universal, and thus calls our attention to it and acquaints us with it. It does not necessarily suggest hypotheses: it may simply present the universal for inspection or contemplation, with no thought of inductive inference at all. Indeed, many Revelationists would make a point of this, and their point might be put as follows: experiences differ a great deal in their puzzlingness; a cigarette butt in the gutter is unlikely to arouse any curiosity, but footprints under the window might. Let us say that the experience is more or less "cognitively open," depending on the degree to which it raises questions, or presents problems, and hence starts up reflective thinking. Now, some Revelationists would say, I think, that the experience of contemplating a universal in an aesthetic object may be cognitively closed, in that it has no tendency to launch an inquiry of any sort; yet at the same time, they would want to say that in this contemplation we acquire knowledge, so that the object makes a cognitive contribution to us. It is this rather paradoxical theory that we have to try to make sense of and test.

Whether there are such things as universals, and whether, if so, they can exist apart from the particulars that exemplify them, are of course old and fundamental questions, no less vigorously, though more fruitfully, debated today than in the Middle Ages. For our present purposes, we must regretfully eschew this debate. If there are no such things as universals, as nominalists maintain, then it is clear that the Universalist version of the Revelation Theory is false. If there are such things as universals, then the Universalist position may or may not be true; that is what we should like to know.

As yet, however, it is not at all clear that the Universalist position says anything very significant. It seems to consist in a trivial statement.

The music is cheerful, i.e., it exemplifies the universal *cheerfulness*, the same one exemplified in some psychological states; in short, it is similar to those states in respect to that universal. This ground we have already trodden. If it sounds more weighty to say that the music reveals the universal *cheerfulness*, then we are obliged to say that a red dress reveals the universal *redness*, and a lump of clay the universal *plasticity*. "Reveals" is just a fancy substitute for "has."

The Revelationist wants to say something more than this. Anything that exemplifies a universal, he holds, may be said in a very broad sense to disclose it, but two different things may disclose the same universal in different degrees of *intensity* and of *purity*. Of two red things, one may be redder than the other; the one that has the specific hue at a higher saturation exemplifies that hue more fully. So, of two cheerful musical compositions, one may be more cheerful than the other; this is a difference in intensity. A crazy-quilt with all different colored patches does not make the red patch show up so clearly as an object that is red all over. And a musical composition that, so to speak, concentrates on being determinedly cheerful, at least in one section, presents that universal in a sort of idealized form, free from accidental and distracting accompaniments, so that it shines forth in its purity and self-identity. Musical compositions and paintings, then, the Revelationist might argue, generally disclose their universals with a higher intensity and greater purity than ordinary objects, and this is what is meant by saying that they don't just *have* the universals, but *reveal* them.

As we have worked it out so far, the Universalist position must be acknowledged to be true, at least of a large number of paintings and musical compositions: many of them do have, as we have seen, fairly intense and fairly pure human regional qualities, and these they force upon our attention, or present for contemplation in cognitively closed experiences. We may balk at calling this "the revelation of universals," but we cannot deny the claim. We can, however, question whether the theory establishes a cognitive status for aesthetic objects by connecting them with knowledge.

There are some good questions here, some of them profoundly difficult. Let us consider them a little. It is sometimes held by philosophers that we have two kinds of empirical knowledge, that is, knowledge based upon sense experience: knowledge by "acquaintance" and knowledge by "description." Roughly, you know the Matterhorn by acquaintance if you have seen it or climbed it, and you know it by description, that is, indirectly, if you have only read about it or seen pictures of it. Now suppose you first read about it. No description you get of it is going to be long enough to list all the statements that are true about the Matterhorn, and therefore when you see it you will discover more about it. These discoveries you might put into words and pass on to other people. However, even if you could give a complete description of your experience of seeing the Matterhorn, that description would not be the same thing as the experience; in other words, to see it and to read about it would still be different.

People say things like, "You don't really know what a toothache is until you've had one." This is presumably knowledge by acquaintance. But is not *having* a toothache different from *knowing* about toothache? It is true that you can't have one until you've had one—the mere description won't give you the toothache. This is trivial. Perhaps the point is that the word "toothache" can only be defined ostensively, so to speak, and therefore until you have had one, you cannot learn the meaning of this word and use it in its full sense. Acquaintance is certainly often required to define words, but defining a word is not knowing something about the world.

We must make a distinction between having an experience and knowing something, and much of what is called "knowledge by acquaintance" is not knowledge but just acquaintance. This applies specially to the Revelation Theory. When we listen to the cheerfulness of the music, or stand with our gaze satisfyingly fixed upon the cheerfulness of the painting, we are *getting* something, to be sure, and when at last we turn away we have *had* something; our experience has had content. Acquaintance is indispensable for knowledge; it provides the raw material. But it does not become knowledge, in the strict sense, until there is inference, until the data are combined and connected by reasoning. Of course, the word "knowledge" can be used in a very general sense, but if we say that a man who feels dizzy has knowledge in the sense that while he has the feeling he knows that he has it, then this sort of knowledge will always be of a peculiar sort, limited to particulars and to the present.

The Universalist version of the Revelation Theory is then, it seems to me, quite right in one respect and wrong in another. It is right in saying that the qualities presented by aesthetic objects may become the data for future knowings, and that aesthetic objects are connected with knowledge in this way. It is wrong in saying that the presentation, or the reception, of such qualities itself constitutes an act of knowledge—or, if this is merely a verbal quibble over the word "knowledge," it is wrong in suggesting that this kind of knowledge is very important before it is turned to account by the mind and confronted with more general and more remote hypotheses.

Essence and Acquaintance

Universalists have frequently developed their position more fully, by proposing further restrictions upon the sort of universals that aesthetic objects reveal. There are several possible ways of doing this. For example, you could say that art reveals the "felt qualities" of experience, rather than intellectual constructions about it. And it would be true that these felt qualities, the gloominess, the *joie de vivre,* the crisp-cold-morning quality, the enervating summer-afternoon-at-the-shore quality, are among the universals that aesthetic objects exemplify. But it would not be true to say that felt qualities—that is, sense qualities—are the only universals that can be exemplified in representational paintings, much less in literature, or that they are the only ones we ought to be interested in.

Two varieties of the Universalist position are common and important enough to deserve some comment, though I shall refrain from calling them by the barbarous names that philosophical exactness would demand —for example, the Essentialist Variety of the Universalist Version of the Revelation Theory.

The first view calls attention to a further distinction that some philosophers would make among universals in relation to particulars. A particular dog, say Fido, may exemplify a vast number of universals, dogginess, shagginess, hugeness, strength, fidelity, and so forth. According to one view, some of these universals are essential to him because he is a dog (quadrupedicity, for example), while others are accidental (fidelity, for example) because even if they were lacking he would still be a dog. According to the theory now before us, musical compositions and paintings sometimes reveal essential characteristics of nature—not just universals, but those universals that are essences of some particulars in the world. It is in this that their cognitive importance consists.

For example, it has been said that Cézanne, in his pictures of trees and buildings, has captured their essential characteristics: what is permanent and abiding in them, such as their fundamental geometric forms, their solidity and palpableness. And it has also been said that in the Prelude to *Tristan und Isolde,* and in the music accompanying the "Liebestod," Wagner has given us the essence of hopeless love and passionate longing.

It would take us too far from our own problems to show in detail why most philosophers have come to reject the distinction between essential and nonessential characteristics as it is made by this theory. The distinction is really verbal: the essential characteristics of dogs in general are just those used in defining the word "dog." And what characteristics are considered essential to Fido in particular depends entirely upon what words you are going to apply to him or, in other words, what class you are going to put him into. Considered as a dog, quadrupedicity is essential to him; considered as a shaggy beast, shagginess is essential to him. No characteristic is essential in itself, apart from human purposes and human classifications. If, then, a painter, let us say, wished to portray Fido in such a way as to call attention to his essential characteristics, all his qualities would be equally essential, from some point of view, which is equivalent to saying that he has no essential characteristics in himself.

There is no essential characteristic of trees or of passionate longing for the creative artist to abstract, intensify, and embody in his work. But even if there were, we would still have to question the cognitive status of the work. For the object that exemplifies the essence, however purely and intensely, is in this respect no different from the original tree or feeling itself, which also exemplifies that essence: it does not give us knowledge unless it informs us *which* of the universals it exemplifies *are* the essences, and which are not. No one can depict a dog without some color, but every particular color will be nonessential, since some dogs don't have that color. But this the picture will not tell us unless it can also embody a proposition—a possibility we came to reject when we examined the Proposition Theory.

The theory that aesthetic objects are especially involved with essences reflects a more basic conviction that they must be especially involved with *important* universals, not just any ones. There is another way of marking out this importance, however, and it constitutes a second— and, for our attention, last—variety of the Universalist position.

A universal is, by definition, repeatable in principle, that is, it can turn up in more than one particular. But not all universals are actually repeated. *Being a Canadian family with quintuplets who survived infancy* is a characteristic of the Dionne family, so far uniquely, and perhaps no other family will ever have this special characteristic. But *being a Canadian family* is a characteristic of many families, past, present, and future. We may say, then, that certain characteristics are recurrent, and of those some are widely distributed, like *redness*, while others are uncommon, like *mauve-and-ochre-stripedness*. According to the theory before us now, some paintings and musical compositions exemplify frequently recurrent characteristics, and thus call attention to pervasive and noteworthy features of the world. In this their cognitive status consists.

Again, it cannot be denied that this is often true. And the examples given just above, from Cézanne and Wagner, though they do not illustrate essential characteristics, may well illustrate frequently recurrent ones. Many natural objects are solid and roughly cylindrical; hopeless love and passionate longing often fall to the human lot. But, unless Cézanne's landscape and Wagner's Prelude contain propositions of some kind, they cannot themselves inform us *how* widespread their universals are, or indeed whether they are widespread at all. That knowledge must be obtained by a process of generalization based upon data observed outside the aesthetic object, and the data *within* the object don't help us at all with this generalization. It would therefore be a mistake to suppose that we can learn, from the aesthetic object itself, anything about the actual distribution of its universals.

The view that aesthetic objects reveal frequently recurrent universals has been formulated in another way, using the phrase "true to" that was briefly discussed in the preceding section. There we spoke of the depiction in a painting as being "true to" the portrayal-subject—"It's the spitting image of Henry." But we could also speak of the depiction as being "true to" classes of things in general—"Ducks do have that peculiar walk," or, "It gives you the feel of a storm at sea." Probably we do speak this way sometimes, but on the whole the more neutral term "similar to" is probably preferable. For I can say that a given painting is similar in its quality to many things in the world, or to only a few, or to none— if it is a quality that can be encountered nowhere outside that painting. But if I use the phrase "true to," I must say either that it is true to reality, if its quality is a common one in experience—however intensified and purified in the painting—or *false* to reality, if its quality is rare or previously nonexistent. But "false to" is likely to be taken to mean more than it legitimately can.

It is surprising, in a way, that those who write about the fine arts and music tend to lay so much stress upon the cognitive value of those arts, even if, driven back from the Proposition Theory and from the stronger version of the Revelation Theory, they are forced to contend that paintings and musical compositions become valuable to us partly because they exemplify for us qualities that we have already found in the world, or that we could find if we looked far enough. It seems vital to such writers that the arts of painting and music composition be subsumed under some broad category that also harbors scientific inquiry and philosophy: they are modes of "discovery" and of "communication."

It is one thing to make a discovery, another thing to create something. Creation and discovery may be combined, of course, in the work of a natural scientist or a mathematician. But note that these thinkers claim to give us discoveries of things that we do *not* encounter among the felt qualities of experience, and since they make good that claim, they give a powerful justification of their activities. But a painter or musician who says his work is justified, and given a high cognitive value, because it makes us acquainted with qualities we have already met with, or could meet elsewhere, is making a very weak case. This cannot be the real reason, or the main reason, for cherishing the work. The truth is much nearer the opposite, it seems to me: considered as discovery, painting and music are of little account, but considered as creation they are great and irreplaceable. What matters most to us, after all, is that they bring into existence new universals, never exemplified in any particulars before those particular paintings and musical compositions. This is overwhelmingly evident to the mind not misled by theory, as far as music is concerned, for nearly everything in music is an improvement on nature, a tremendous leap beyond it; it is practically all invention and the imaginative projection of novel possibilities. We can much more easily trace the colored shapes, and some of the regional qualities, of paintings back to natural origins, and this has historically made it all too easy to think of the fine arts as "imitations" of nature. But if all we can see in the painter's design is that its dominant pattern is something like a dumbbell, or that its quality is like a melancholy mood, we may be missing precisely what is different and precious about the painting.

There is a wise statement in Igor Stravinsky's Charles Eliot Norton lectures at Harvard: "For at the root of all creation one discovers an appetite that is not an appetite for the fruits of the earth."[2] And Paul Klee has eloquently defended the right and duty of the artist to go beyond nature.[3] These two witnesses, I grant, are not exactly a random sample, but I believe they speak for their fellows—at least for what painters and composers did and do, even if they sometimes fall back upon the Revelation terminology when asked to rise and speak about art. It seems to me that what I find in aesthetic objects I find nowhere else, and I go to them looking for qualities they alone afford. Whether I can use those qualities as data in future empirical inquiries is another question. I am inclined to think that some of them in literature, at least, are very useful, and I shall return to this in the following chapter; but I cannot honestly say the same of paintings and music.

Intuitionism

We can now turn to the *Intuitionist Theory*[4] of the cognitive status of the nonverbal arts. It has never, I think, been worked out adequately, so that part of our task here is to see what it would look like if it were, for though it is naturally resistant to explicit formulation, it is surely the theory that a great many teachers and writers hold, in a half-thought-out and uncriticized form.

What philosophers call a Theory of Knowledge is a general statement about the nature and limits of human knowledge, an answer to the question: What can we know? There seem to be, at bottom, three different Theories of Knowledge. Empiricism is the theory that all knowledge consists of propositions that we are justified in believing because of their connection with experience, the data of sensation and introspection. According to this theory, all true propositions except tautological ones are either generalizations induced from experience or hypotheses confirmed by experience because they explain why our experience is what it is. Rationalism is the theory that some knowledge is obtained in an a priori fashion by pure reason itself, independently of experience: there are true propositions we are justified in believing because we grasp their necessity or self-evidence, or deduce them from necessary truths. The rationalist admits that some of our knowledge is empirical, but he denies that all of it is.

---

[2] *Poetics of Music in the Form of Six Lessons,* New York: Vintage, 1956, p. 24; cf. p. 54.

[3] In his Jena lecture of 1924; see *Paul Klee on Modern Art,* trans. by Paul Findlay, London: Faber and Faber, 1948.

[4] This theory has been held by Henri Bergson, Benedetto Croce, and others; see Note 21-F.

Now it is fairly plain that if the Proposition Theory of art were true, it could be maintained by either an Empiricist or a Rationalist, though no doubt the propositions of painting and music would mostly be considered empirical propositions. And the Revelation Theory, in its Universalist version, could also be maintained by either an Empiricist or a Rationalist: the Empiricist would say that the universals revealed by art are those also given in sense experience or introspection of mental processes; the Rationalist might say that these universals also exist, or subsist, in a Platonic realm of Pure Being separate from the world of nature.

The Intuitionist Theory of Knowledge is very different from both Empiricism and Rationalism, however, and it leads to a conception of the cognitive status of art that makes no use of either propositions or universals. According to the Intuitionist, we have a unique faculty of insight that is independent of both sense experience and the rational intellect. It delivers knowledge to us in nonconceptual form, as immediate conviction; there is no inference, or reasoning, so it cannot go wrong. The intuition is more like a feeling than anything else, but it carries with it the inescapable sense that it is trustworthy. In intuition we are in direct communion with the object; since our grasp of it is not mediated by symbolic devices, intuitive knowledge is ineffable, and conveyable, if at all, only by nonverbal aesthetic objects—this is one form of the theory. By intuition we are able to grasp things "internally," that is, sympathetically, not just from the outside: we feel the heaviness of the overhanging rock or the driving life force of the caged tiger. Intuition gives us, not general knowledge or abstractions, but insight into the individual, in all his uniqueness: not rocks and tigers, but *this* rock, *this* tiger. Intuition gives us the indivisible whole; not the town we try to reconstruct from a pile of snapshots of various streets and houses, but the town we get the sense of when we live in it. Intuition alone gives us the understanding of process, of the fluidity of real change, and the flow of our inner life.

If the Intuitionist also holds a metaphysical view that reality, in its inmost nature, is nothing but process, *élan vital*, becoming rather than being, he may then say that it is only in the nonverbal arts that we have knowledge of reality; in science we have only a systematization of the practical approach to reality, which is concerned not with knowledge but with control, not with insight but with logical reconstruction. The artist, with his superior sensitivity, intuits something about the world or about the inner life of man; he creates an aesthetic object; and this object, when we contemplate it, puts us in a special state of mind in which we can share that intuition. Thus when we see Van Gogh's cornfields, we may feel as if we were ourselves inside the corn, full of life and surging power, striving to grow and ripen in the sun. Or when we hear the vast massed repetitive climaxes of Bruckner, as in the finale of his *B Major Symphony* (*No. 5*) or the openings of the first and fourth movements of his *C Minor Symphony* (*No. 8*), we may feel we have gained a new insight into the

Nietzschean Will to Power that lies smoldering under the surface of human nature. Not that we can put these insights into words; words can only witness that we have gained them, and perhaps lead others to try to gain them too.

If we now ask what reason can be found for accepting the Intuitionist Theory, we are confronted with an unusual situation. For this theory is evidently not susceptible of easy refutation; if someone claims to have knowledge of this sort, by what method can we weigh that claim? And some Intuitionists would be affronted by the request for reasons, for they claim to have passed the point at which reason breaks down. This immunity to attack, however, is not really a source of strength, but a ground for suspicion. For if the person who sees the Van Gogh or hears the Bruckner and tells us he has found new knowledge cannot give us any evidence, by his speech or action, that he has this knowledge, we are certainly not justified in assenting to his claim. Not that we must call him a liar; probably his experience was so moving, so overwhelming, and left such a deep and abiding impression, that he felt compelled to describe it in what he took to be the highest terms.

We cannot take occasion here to discuss all the questions that must be raised about the Intuitionist Theory of Knowledge in general. But there are two important points about it that we should consider briefly.

The first point is this: It is fair, I think, to insist that the Intuitionist show that there are certain things human beings know that they could not have known if they had no faculty of intuition. The Intuitionist proposes a Theory of Knowledge to account for some of our knowledge; he must hold that there is something there to be accounted for. "How, except by intuition," he might ask, "could you know that you are fundamentally free from causal determination, or that you have an unconscious will to self-destruction?" To this question, the Empiricist might reply, "I do *not* know that I have a free will, and therefore there is no knowledge here to be accounted for, empirically or otherwise; and even though I may know that I have an unconscious will to self-destruction, I know this empirically, that is, by inference from my behavior, including my actions and my dreams." Now the Intuitionist concedes that we know some things empirically. And if the Empiricist account of a given item of knowledge is adequate, he ought to accept that account on the principle of Occam's Razor, which enjoins us always to choose the simplest explanation that works. The burden of proof is upon him; to make his case, he must supply some examples of knowledge that the Empiricist admits we have and also admits that he cannot account for.

As our two examples show, this is not by any means easy to do. For the Empiricist always has two outs: he can try to account for the knowledge empirically, or he can deny that it *is* knowledge. It is extremely hard to set up a test case. When the Empiricist asks for an example of intuitive knowledge, the Intuitionist, by his own principles, can only point to the music or the painting and ask the Empiricist to intuit its intuitive content. "Look at Goya's *Colossus* [PLATE VII]" he may say, "and feel the insight it gives you into the dark reaches of the human unconscious." Or "Listen to Bruckner's adagios and feel their profound religious understanding." But even these remarks may be going too far, for the dilemma is that there must be some verbal clarification to give reasonable assurance that both parties are really having intuitions, and the same intuitions, but any such verbal clarification must distort, if not wholly conceal, the ineffable intuition itself.

There is a broader strategy adopted by some Intuitionists. This consists of helping us to make a distinction in our own experience between intuition and other things, by forcing upon us a conceptual contrast of a deep and thorough-going sort. Intuition is contrasted with intellect, reason, or science, and a broad attack is launched upon these to show that they have inherent limitations of method or scope and therefore cannot cover the whole of our knowledge. The intellect works by analyzing, and misses syntheses; it abstracts, and is incapable of coping with concrete feelings; it dissects, and is at home in the discontinuous and separate, and so distorts the continuity and flow of mental life; it imposes on things a spatial, logical, or geometrical order; it reduces the novel and emergent to the old and familiar. And so on.

I am afraid it would take far too much space here if we were to attempt to make explicit the profound misconceptions and linguistic confusions that are reflected in such statements as these. Nor is it necessary for our purpose. For the general attack on intellect is futile unless there is an alternative. And this brings us to the second point about Intuitionism in general.

A Theory of Knowledge is fatally incomplete without a criterion of truth: the Intuitionist therefore faces some difficult choices. He must either explain how he distinguishes between true intuitions and false intuitions or say that all intuitions are true. If he chooses the latter, and it is pointed out that intuitions apparently conflict, he must either show that they do not really conflict—Van Gogh's insights into growing things do not conflict with Constable's, Claude's or Salvator Rosa's—or else argue that sometimes when people think they have intuitions, they really aren't having them at all, in which case, again, he may be called upon to provide a criterion to distinguish genuine intuitions from pseudo-intuitions.

Such problems as these the Intuitionist is apt to greet with impatience, but it is unwarranted. To have an intuition is presumably to have an experience of some sort. To call an experience "knowledge," not merely "experience," is to say that something is known *by means of* the experience. In other words, when the experience is over, we must know something more than that we have had the experience. Therefore, there is a distinction between the object known and the experience of knowing it. Therefore, the jump from having the experience to believing something about the object *is* a jump, and involves an act of inference. This inference has to be justified, and by the rules of reasoning. Therefore there is no such thing as *self*-authenticating, or intrinsically justified, intuitive knowledge.

In so far as something is believed intuitively, that is, because of an immediate feeling of truth, it is not yet knowledge, but a hypothesis to be investigated; and when it becomes knowledge it is something more than intuitive conviction. But even if there were intuitive knowledge, and painters and composers had it, it would not follow that paintings and musical compositions could convey it to us. For when you know the caged tiger, in his ineffable individuality, by intuition, you must confront him without mediation by sign or symbol, and worm yourself into his inward nature. But if you come to know him through a painting of him, you are already put off; something interposes itself between, and your knowledge is no longer intuition.

It seems that we must draw this chapter to a somewhat negative conclusion, though we have turned up some positive ideas in the course of rejecting others. Paintings and musical compositions are not, and do not give, knowledge about reality, whether nature or supernature, whether in propositions, by revelation, or for intuition. Nor is this to be regretted, on any just estimate of the arts themselves or of the plural values of life. For knowledge is not the only thing the possession of which can dignify and justify the place of the arts in the life of man.

NOTES AND QUERIES

§20

20-A SENSES OF "TRUTH." For various senses in which the word "true" has been applied to aesthetic objects—most of them have nothing to do with cognitive function—see Bernard C. Heyl, *New Bearings in Esthetics and Art Criticism*, New Haven, Conn.: Yale U., 1943, Part I, ch. 3; John Hospers, *Meaning and Truth in the Arts*, Chapel Hill, N.C.: U. of North Carolina, 1946, pp. 141-45. It would be interesting to discover the sense in which R. G. Collingwood, *The Principles of Art*, Oxford: Clarendon, 1938, p. 287, uses the term in his curious argument that an aesthetic object is true if it is good.

20-B THE PROPOSITION THEORY. (I) This theory of the cognitive status of nonverbal aesthetic objects has been defended by: (1) T. M. Greene, *The Arts and the Art of Criticism*, Princeton, N.J.: Princeton U., 1940, ch. 23. Note his view (p. 454) that the "objectivity of Cézanne's vision" is tested by observing nature; Greene, however, gives no examples of false paintings, and his statement (p. 450) that a painter who uses two different styles in the same painting has "contradicted himself" is surely misleading. Nor does he give a clear description (p. 458) of the way in which musical propositions are to be tested. (2) Andrew P. Ushenko, *Dynamics of Art*, Bloomington, Ind.: Indiana U., 1953, ch. 4, holds that paintings and music can contain "implicit propositions," or "claims to truth" (p. 168) by "presentation through dynamic images or vectors" (p. 172). (3) Morris Weitz, *Philosophy of the Arts*, Cambridge, Mass.: Harvard U., 1950, ch. 8, pp. 147-52, reprinted in Eliseo Vivas and Murray Krieger, eds., *The Problems of Aesthetics*, New York: Rinehart, 1953, pp. 600-04, is doubtful about propositions in music. (4) Douglas Morgan, "On Pictorial 'Truth,'" *Philosophical Studies*, IV (1953): 17-24, stresses the close similarity between the photograph of an event and a statement about it; note that he reserves the term "proposition" for statements in words. (5) See Bertram Jessup, "Meaning Range in the Work of Art," *JAAC*, XII (March 1954): 378-85.

(II) The Proposition Theory has been criticized by: (1) Hospers, *op. cit.*, pp. 157-61. (2) Kingsley B. Price, "Is the Work of Art a Symbol?" *J Phil*, L (1953): 485-503, esp. 485-90, 496-503; he argues very cogently that nonverbal works of art are not "assertive symbols." (3) Max Rieser, "A Brief Introduction to an Epistemology of Art," *J Phil*, XLVII (1950): 695-704; but Rieser seems to have a sort of Proposition Theory himself. See also criticisms of Greene by W. T. Stace, and Greene's reply, *J Phil*, XXXV (1938): 656-61; Vincent Tomas, "Has Professor Greene Proved That Art Is a Cognitive Process?" *J Phil*, XXXVII (1940): 459-69 (but note that Tomas is attacking Greene's view that all art, at least all good art, contains propositions; Tomas himself holds that only some do, and this is what I have called the Proposition Theory); Lucius Garvin, "An Emotionalist Critique of 'Artistic Truth,'" *J Phil*, XLIII (1946): 435-41.

20-C PROPOSITIONS AND SENTENCES. The view that propositions are distinct from the sentences that "state" them is clearly and succinctly presented in Morris Cohen and Ernest Nagel, *Introduction to Logic and Scientific Method*, New York: Harcourt, Brace, 1934, pp. 27-30. The arguments for this distinction are given, and somewhat technically discussed, by Gilbert Ryle, "Are There Propositions?" *PAS*, N.S. XXX (1929-30): 91-126. The alternative view, that it is declarative sentences that are true or false, and that there is no need to postulate subsistent entities, has been cogently argued by Elizabeth Lane Beardsley, "The Semantical Aspect of Sentences," *J Phil*, XL (1943): 393-403. For other criticisms of the subsistent-proposition theory, see Ralph M. Eaton, *Symbolism and Truth*, Cambridge, Mass.: Harvard U., 1925, ch. 5; Paul Marhenke, "Propositions and Sentences," *University of California Publications in Philosophy*, XXV (1950), esp. 275-97; A. D. Woozley, *Theory of Knowledge*, London, New York: Hutchinson's U. Library, 1949, ch. 5; Abraham Kaplan and Irving

Copilowisch, "Must There Be Propositions?", *Mind*, XLVIII (1939): 478-84.

20-D PROPOSITIONS IN PAINTING. Find examples of paintings that might be said, or have been said by fine arts critics, to be or to contain propositions. For example: Do Claude's landscapes imply a different theory about nature from Van Gogh's? Does a landscape in which the human figures are tiny and are dwarfed by the natural scenery say that man is insignificant compared with nature? Does Rembrandt's etching of *Adam and Eve* (1638, Hind 159) as a brutish pair say that this is the way they really were? Does a *New Yorker* cover of a few years back, showing a stained glass window in which the figure is an Easter bunny, say that Easter has been commercialized out of its religious significance? In Brueghel's *Peasant Wedding* we are shown the bride but not the bridegroom; if she is the Bride of Christ, does the picture say that without the true priest the Church is a worldly mockery? See Kenneth Lindsay and Bernard Huppe, "Meaning and Method in Brueghel's Painting," *JAAC*, XIV (March 1956): 376-86. Further examples are given by Weitz, *loc. cit.* Can these paintings be adequately interpreted in the "shows . . . as" idiom, without falling back on the Proposition Theory?

Paul Tillich, *The Religious Situation,* trans. by H. Richard Niebuhr, New York: Holt, 1932, pp. vii-xxii, 52-70, and "Existentialist Aspects of Modern Art," *Christianity and the Existentialists,* ed. by Carl Michalson, New York: Scribner's, 1956, has an interesting analysis and classification of religious painting with respect to "form" and "content."

Edna Daitz, "The Picture Theory of Meaning," *Mind*, LXII (1953): 184-201, clarifies the difference between a picture "showing" something and a sentence stating something. She points out (p. 196) that there are no analogues in paintings for negative, conditional, and disjunctive statements; e.g., you can depict a cat as black, but you cannot depict a cat as not black. Her argument is also directed against the conception of statements as pictures of facts (see Susanne Langer, Chapter VII, Note 18-I).

20-E PROPOSITIONS IN MUSIC. Find examples of musical compositions that might be said, or have been said by fine arts critics, to be or to contain propositions. For example, do Bach's chorale preludes for organ embody theological doctrines in the way they rework the hymn tunes? See references in Chapter VII, Note 18-J. Does Beethoven's *String Quartet in C Sharp Minor (Op. 131)* say that the human will can triumph over all obstacles? Does Berlioz's *Fantastic Symphony* embody a romantic philosophy?

§21

21-A THE REVELATION THEORY OF THE COGNITIVE STATUS OF MUSIC AND PAINTING. Though Plato was arguing against this theory in the *Republic*, Book X, 595-601, when he said that the painting of a bed is at a second remove from "reality" because it is merely an "imitation" of a physical bed, which is itself only an imitation of an ideal Form, and concluded that the artist "knows nothing of the reality, but only the appearance" (see Cornford trans., Oxford: Clarendon, 1945, p. 331), nevertheless it is easy to transform his metaphysics into a Revelation Theory of art: the artist does not imitate the physical bed at all, but tries to get at the same Form the carpenter is after, only with more success, since he does not actually have to make a bed but is free to abstract the "essential" nature. This step was taken by later thinkers.

Varieties of the Revelation Theory have been defended by: (1) Arthur Schopenhauer, *The World as Will and Idea*, 6th ed., trans. by R. B. Haldane and J. Kemp, London: Routledge and Kegan Paul, 1907-09, Book III, a Universalist theory; but Schopenhauer assigns very different cognitive roles to music and painting. On Schopenhauer's theory see Albert Gehring, *The Basis of Musical Pleasure*, New York: Putnam, 1910, pp. 58-68; Israel Knox, *Aesthetic Theories of Kant, Hegel, and Schopenhauer*, New York: Columbia U., 1936; John Stokes Adams, Jr., *The Aesthetics of Pessimism*, Philadelphia: privately printed, 1940. (2) L. A. Reid, *A Study in Aesthetics*, New York: Macmillan, 1931, ch. 10; a Universalist theory. (3) Dorothy Walsh, "The Cognitive Content of Art," *Phil R*, LII (1943): 433-51, reprinted in Eliseo Vivas and Murray Krieger, eds., *The Problems of Aesthetics*, New York: Rinehart, 1953, pp. 604-18. This interesting paper argues that art is the "delineation of the possible"; the artist "reveals" ("presents," "creates") "ideal possibilities" that are "alternatives" to the actual world. But what the aesthetic object presents, first of all, is an actuality; the new quality of the music or the new design of the painting is not a possibility only; it exists as part of the world, in the same sense as anything else, and to say that it is an "alternative" to the world outside the work amounts to saying that the work reveals nothing, but simply is.

See also H. D. Lewis, "Revelation and Art," *PAS*, Suppl. vol. XXIII (1949): 1-29; John Dewey, *Art as Experience*, New York: Minton, Balch, 1934, ch. 12; C. E. M. Joad's paper in the symposium, "Is Art a Form of Apprehension or Expression?" *PAS*, Suppl. vol. V (1925): 190-203.

Hegel appears to have held a form of the Revelation Theory, which he expressed by saying that art is the sensuous embodiment of the Absolute Idea; see *The Introduction to Hegel's Philosophy of Fine Art*, trans. by Bernard Bosanquet, London: Routledge and Kegan Paul, 1886, ch. 3, Part II; ch. 5; W. T. Stace, *The Philosophy of Hegel*, New York: Macmillan, 1924, pp. 443-84. Hegel was evidently an Essentialist: the painter will exclude the contingent features of his subject, such as warts. He had apparently not seen Piero della Francesca's portrait of the Duke of Urbino (1465, Uffizi Gallery, Florence).

J. W. N. Sullivan's book, *Beethoven: His Spiritual Development*, London: Cape, 1927 (reprinted New York: Mentor, 1949), vacillates among several theories. It starts out (Part I, ch. 1) with a defense of a

Revelation Theory of music, but the "personal vision of life" (Preface) that Beethoven is said to communicate turns out to be something more like an emotional response, and the "spiritual content" of his music appears to reduce to an Expression Theory (Part I, ch. 3). There are places where Sullivan comes very close to holding a Proposition Theory, as when he says, "The Beethoven of the last quartets finds that the highest achievement is reached through suffering" (Mentor ed., p. 41; compare his interpretation of the *Grosse Fuge,* p. 129); but he quite clearly also rejects the Proposition Theory: "Nothing that Beethoven wanted to express can be called a philosophy," (p. 70) and, "[Music] cannot express ideas at all" (p. 71). For comments on Sullivan, see John Hospers, *op. cit.,* pp. 227-31.

The views of Victor Bennett in "The Theory of Musical Expression," *Music and Letters,* XVII (1936): 106-17, and "Music and Emotion," *Musical Quarterly,* XXVIII (1942): 406-14, are loosely set forth, but seem to amount to the Revelation Theory: art enables us to "contemplate truth" (earlier article, p. 107).

Herbert Read, *Icon and Idea,* Cambridge, Mass.: Harvard U., 1955, argues for a cognitive role of the arts—they "have been the means by which man was able step by step to comprehend the nature of things" (p. 18; see also pp. 53, 73 ff.)—but his argument is not clear.

See also Arthur O. Lovejoy, "Nature as Aesthetic Norm," *Essays in the History of Ideas,* Baltimore: Johns Hopkins U., 1948, on Eighteenth Century versions of the Revelation Theory.

21-B UNIVERSALS AND ESSENCES. (I) The neoclassic idea that the arts are concerned with the general nature of things is well set forth in Sir Joshua Reynolds, *Discourses on Art,* esp. Discourses 3, 4, 7, 13; contrast the acid comments that Blake wrote in the margin of his copy of the *Discourses,* e.g., "To Generalize is to be an Idiot" (*Artists on Art,* ed. by R. Goldwater and M. Treves, New York: Pantheon, 1945, p. 263; cf. the remark of Maillol, p. 406). T. M. Greene, *op. cit.,* 1940, chs. 14, 16, 17, classifies various kinds of universal that are found in paintings.

The view that art is primarily concerned not with universals but with particulars has been defended by Iredell Jenkins, "The Unity and Variety of Art," *JAAC,* XIII (December 1954): 185-202.

(II) On the nature and existence of universals, see A. D. Woozley, *op. cit.;* Bertrand Russell, *The Problems of Philosophy,* New York: Holt, 1912, ch. 9 (these are both good elementary accounts); H. H. Price, *Thinking and Experience,* Cambridge, Mass.: Harvard U., 1953, ch. 1; Arthur Pap, *Elements of Analytic Philosophy,* New York: Macmillan, 1949, chs. 3, 4, and references. On the concept of essences, and the problem of distinguishing essential from nonessential characteristics of things, see Abraham Edel, *The Theory and Practice of Philosophy,* New York: Harcourt, Brace, 1946, ch. 2.

21-C ACQUAINTANCE AND FELT QUALITIES. The distinction between "knowledge by acquaintance" and "knowledge by description" was made by Bertrand Russell, *op. cit.*, ch. 5; but when he contrasts "knowing truths *about* the color" and "knowing the color itself" (see 1946 ed., p. 47), it seems clear that the latter is not knowing at all, but *seeing*. The point that acquaintance is not knowledge has been well made by Hospers, *op. cit.*, pp. 233-38, who quotes Moritz Schlick, *Gesammelte Aufsätze*. See also C. I. Lewis, *Mind and the World Order*, New York: Scribner, 1929, ch. 5 and Appendix B: "There is no knowledge merely by acquaintance" (p. 118). See also the symposium, "Is There Knowledge by Acquaintance?" *PAS*, Suppl. vol. XXIII (1949): 69-128, esp. the paper by J. N. Findlay, which defends the concept of knowledge by acquaintance in a way that is of some interest to aesthetics. Albert Hofstadter's paper, "Does Intuitive Knowledge Exist?" *Philosophical Studies*, VI (1955): 81-87, is a defense of knowledge by acquaintance.

Hugo Münsterberg, *The Principles of Art Education*, New York: Prang Educational, 1905, Part I (largely reprinted in Melvin Rader, *A Modern Book of Esthetics*, New York: Holt, 1935, pp. 363-76; rev. ed. 1952, pp. 387-400) argues that science gives us, not knowledge of the object itself, which is the "highest truth" about it, but knowledge of its causal connections with other things. But it seems clear that when he says, for example, that science does not give us "understanding" of the ocean, whereas art does, he really means that in art we may *have* (not know) something of the ocean. This is the theme of Browning's "Transcendentalism: A Poem in Twelve Books." Compare A. S. Eddington, *The Nature of the Physical World*, New York: Macmillan, 1928, ch. 15; F. S. C. Northrop, "The Functions and Future of Poetry," in *The Logic of the Sciences and the Humanities*, New York: Macmillan, 1947.

21-D ON "TRUTH-TO." For an analysis and justification of this idiom, see John Hospers, *op. cit.*, ch. 6 (esp. pp. 173-75, 183-96), ch. 8. Hospers' most convincing use of the phrase is in its application to literature; this we shall consider in the following chapter. It is further discussed by Bernard C. Heyl, "Artistic Truth Reconsidered," *JAAC*, VIII (June 1950): 251-58, who agrees with Hospers but adds, "I believe he has exaggerated its importance" (p. 253).

21-E CREATION AND DISCOVERY. Is the artist primarily to be thought of as a discoverer (like an explorer or an astronomer) or as a creator (like an inventor)? Or can he equally be both? Eliseo Vivas deals with this problem, especially in connection with literature, in *Creation and Discovery*, New York: Noonday, 1955, esp. pp. 123, 140, 237. See also Herbert Read, *Icon and Idea*, Cambridge, Mass.: Harvard U., 1955, ch. 7. It is helpful to ask in what sense a mathematical system, or a game of chess, is an aesthetic object as well as a new truth.

21-F THE INTUITIONIST THEORY OF THE COGNITIVE STATUS OF MUSIC
AND PAINTING. (I) For general accounts, expository and critical, of the
Intuitionist Theory of Knowledge, see J. H. Randall, Jr. and Justus Buchler, *Philosophy: An Introduction,* New York: Barnes and Noble (College
Outline Series), 1942, ch. 9; William P. Montague, *The Ways of Knowing,*
London: Allen and Unwin, 1925, Part I, ch. 2; Paul Henle, "Mysticism
and Semantics," *Phil and Phen Res,* IX (March 1949): 416-22, which is
very interesting on the ineffability of intuitive insights.

(II) For Bergson's theory of intuition and its applications to art, see
Henri Bergson, *An Introduction to Metaphysics,* trans. by T. E. Hulme,
New York: Liberal Arts, 1950; *Creative Evolution,* trans. by Arthur Mitchell, New York: Holt 1911, esp. pp. 135-85, where Bergson contrasts intelligence with instinct, and defines "intuition," (p. 176) as "instinct that
has become disinterested, self-conscious, capable of reflecting upon its
object and of enlarging it indefinitely"; *Laughter,* trans. by Cloudesley
Brereton and Fred Rothwell, New York: Macmillan, 1911, pp. 150-71 (reprinted in Melvin Rader, *op. cit.,* 1935 ed. p. 179-91; 1952 ed. pp. 114-26),
where Bergson partly talks the language of the Revelation Theory; *Time
and Free Will,* trans. by F. L. Pogson, New York: Macmillan, 1910, pp.
13-18 (art hypnotizes us into a state of high sympathy and suggestibility);
A. A. Luce, *Bergson's Doctrine of Intuition,* London: Society for Promoting Christian Knowledge, 1922, ch. 1; H. Wildon Carr, *The Philosophy of
Change,* New York: Macmillan, 1914, ch. 2; T. E. Hulme, "Bergson's
Theory of Art" and "The Philosophy of Intensive Manifolds" in *Speculations,* London: Routledge and Kegan Paul, 1924, partly reprinted in Vivas
and Krieger, *op. cit.,* pp. 125-38; Arthur Szathmary, *The Aesthetic Theory
of Bergson,* Cambridge, Mass.: Harvard U., 1937; Bertrand Russell, *Mysticism and Logic,* New York: Longmans, Green, 1929, ch. 1.

(III) Although Croce contrasts "intuitive knowledge" with "logical
knowledge" (*Aesthetic,* trans. by Douglas Ainslie, 2d ed. New York: Macmillan, 1922, ch. 1; also in Vivas and Krieger, *op. cit.,* pp. 69-90), he goes
on to say that intuition is more basic than any distinctions between truth
and falsity or between reality and unreality, so it is rather odd to call it
knowledge at all. For a further account, see his *Breviary of Aesthetic,*
trans. by Ainslie, Rice Institute Pamphlet, Houston, II, *4,* 1915 (partly reprinted in Melvin Rader, *op. cit.,* 1935 ed. pp. 159-78; 1952 ed. pp. 94-113),
and H. W. Carr, *The Philosophy of Benedetto Croce,* New York: Macmillan, 1917, chs. 3, 4; C. J. Ducasse, *The Philosophy of Art,* New York:
Dial, 1929, ch. 3.

William James remarks on the similarity of music to mystical experience ("Music gives us ontological messages"), *Varieties of Religious
Experience,* New York: Longmans, Green, 1902 (reprinted New York:
Modern Library, 1929, p. 412); cf. Rudolf Otto, *The Idea of the Holy,*
London: Oxford U., 1950, pp. 47-49, 20-71.

21-G THE CATEGORIES OF MUSIC CRITICISM. At this point, before we discuss normative statements, or value-judgments, about musical compositions—in Chapters X, XI, XII—it may be helpful to review the distinctions we have already made. We have sorted out the following kinds of nonnormative critical statement about music. The question is whether there are other nonnormative statements that critics would make about music, for which no category is provided here.

I. Description: statements about the characteristics of the music in itself
  A. Statements about the parts of the work
    1. Statements about elementary parts ("It begins with an F")
    2. Statements about complex parts ("It consists of three main sections, of which the first is in F major")
  B. Statements about relations between parts
    1. Statements about relations between elementary parts ("The second note is a half-tone higher than the first")
    2. Statements about relations between complex parts; these are statements about *form*, which include
      a. Statements about large-scale relations ("This section recapitulates that section"): *structure*
      b. Statements about recurrent small-scale relations ("This melodic figure recurs constantly"): *texture* or, roughly, *style*
  C. Statements about regional qualities of the whole or parts
    1. Statements about nonhuman qualities ("This is tonal," "This has such-and-such a kinetic pattern," "This is unified")
    2. Statements about human qualities ("This is vigorous")

II. Statements about the likeness of the music to other things
  A. Statements about the likeness of the music to other sounds ("This is similar to the sound of a fire-engine")—statements about *representation*
  B. Statements about the likeness of the music, in either (a) human quality or (b) kinetic pattern, to
    1. psychological processes ("This music is like a state of depression")
    2. physical processes ("This music is like floating soap-bubbles")

Note that all true statements about the relations of music to other things, other than its causes and effects, are here understood as similarity-statements. These could be called "interpretations" of the music, but that would be misleading in certain ways.

21-H THE CATEGORIES OF PAINTING CRITICISM. We have sorted out the following kinds of nonnormative critical statement about paintings. The question is whether there are other nonnormative statements that critics would make about paintings, for which no category is provided here.

I. Description: statements about the characteristics of the painting in itself

A. Statements about the parts of the work
  1. Statements about elementary areas ("This is blue")
  2. Statements about complex areas ("This is an oval-shaped array of pink dots")
B. Statements about relations between parts
  1. Statements about relations between elementary areas ("This blue is more highly saturated than that")
  2. Statements about relations between complex parts: these are statements about *form*, which include
    a. Statements about large-scale relations ("This side of the painting balances that side"): *structure*
    b. Statements about recurrent small-scale relations ("This shape of brush stroke appears throughout"): *texture* or, roughly, *style*
C. Statements about regional qualities of the whole or parts
  1. Statements about nonhuman qualities ("This has a triangular dominant pattern"—which can also be considered a *structure*-statement—or "This is unified")
  2. Statements about human qualities ("This is vigorous")
II. Statements about the likeness of the painting to other objects in the world
  A. Statements about representation, including
    1. Depiction ("This represents a horse")
    2. Portrayal ("This represents Bucephalus")
  B. Statements about suggestion ("This suggests a windmill") (Symbol-statements are subclasses of representation-statements and suggestion-statements)
  C. Statements about mere likeness ("This line is similar to a line on a human palm")

Note that all true statements about the relation of the painting to other things, other than its causes and effects, are here understood as similarity-statements. Those in groups A and B are generally called "interpretations" of the painting, and there seems to be no serious danger in this usage.

· IX ·

LITERATURE
AND
KNOWLEDGE

Because the most obviously important thing we do with words is to share our information about the world, we do not ordinarily conceive of language except in relation to this use. Of course we know that it is possible to tell a joke, and to enjoy one, without getting involved in anything that could plausibly be called sharing information, but, we might say, joking is a rather special and dispensable use of language. And there is a strong temptation, in giving an account of epic poetry or tragic drama, to emphasize the difference between these serious discourses and the frivolous ones, like jokes, by saying that the difference consists in this very thing: that epic and tragedy do communicate, if not information in a strict sense, then another form of knowledge.

And, far more evidently than painting or music, literature seems to submit itself to such a theory. To make out a case for saying that a painting is true, or that music gives us knowledge, we must find some way in which they can do, without words, what words naturally and essentially can do. But in poems and stories we are already in the realm of language, of indicative moods and declarative sentences. And, if we rule out the view that some words are purely emotive, there is not one word in poetry or fiction that does not, or could not, appear in some other discourse in which it would clearly be used to tell us something about the world.

It is this aspect of literature that we must consider in the present chapter: its cognitive status, or connection with knowledge. A good deal will depend upon our conclusions, including our general view of the significance of literature for human life. Along the way we can profit from ideas that have come up in the discussion of this subject from earliest times. But to make headway we must take two precautions. First, discussions of this subject in the past have too often bogged down because the question has been put in some such form as this: "Is it the purpose—or the *immediate* purpose—of literature to give knowledge?" Let us not talk about purposes, for this term tends to confuse aims with achievements; let us simply ask what literature does do, or what it can do. Second, there must be at least half a dozen distinct questions mixed up here, and they have very seldom been adequately discriminated. Perhaps it will be a good idea to list them now, as a guide through the unavoidable complexities that await us. (1) Do literary works have cognitive meaning? We dealt with this question in Chapter III, §9. (2) If so, can they be true or false? (3) If so, in what respects are they true or false; to what elements in them do these terms attach? (4) If they are true or false, what kind of truth or falsity do they have? (5) Are their truths or falsehoods asserted, or merely presented, by them? This distinction we shall clarify later. (6) Does their truth or falsity have any connection with their being *good* literature? But this last question takes us directly into problems about value, which we shall take up in the following chapter.

§**22.** *THE INTERPRETATION OF LITERATURE*

Assuming a reader who, in a general way, understands the words and grammar of English, we have found that certain problems may still confront him when he tries, in the fullest sense, to understand a literary work. These problems we have so far classified into two types. The problem of *explication* is, briefly, to determine the contextual meaning of a group of words, such as a metaphor, given the standard meanings of the words plus information about their ranges of connotation. But even if a reader has explicated a work, or even if he finds nothing in it that requires explication, he may still face a second sort of problem. The problem of *elucidation* in my special sense is, briefly, to determine parts of the world of the work, such as character and motives, that are not explicitly reported in it, given the events and states of affairs that are reported plus relevant empirical generalizations, that is, physical and psychological laws.

But in every work of literature, at least every work that is somewhat complex, there may remain a third set of questions, even after explication and elucidation have been carried out. Consider, for example, Wallace Stevens' poem, "Thirteen Ways of Looking at a Blackbird," which begins:

I

Among twenty snowy mountains,
The only moving thing
Was the eye of the blackbird.

II

I was of three minds,
Like a tree
In which there are three blackbirds.

III

The blackbird whirled in the autumn winds.
It was a small part of the pantomime.

IV

A man and a woman
Are one.
A man and a woman and a blackbird
Are one.

and so on, including:

VI

Icicles filled the long window
With barbaric glass.
The shadow of the blackbird
Crossed it, to and fro.
The mood
Traced in the shadow
An indecipherable cause.

. . .

VIII

I know noble accents
And lucid, inescapable rhythms;
But I know, too,
That the blackbird is involved
In what I know.[1]

Now, if we ask what this poem is "about," there may be an easy
answer and a hard answer. Or there may be an easy answer that is not the
one we are after, and for the real question no answer at all. The poem is
about blackbirds, snow, shadows, icicles, rhythms: these things are in its
world, because they are referred to by its words; they are, in one sense,

---

[1] From "Thirteen Ways of Looking at a Blackbird." Reprinted from *The Collected Poems of Wallace Stevens*, by permission of Alfred A. Knopf, Inc. Copyright
1950, 1954 by Wallace Stevens.

the subject of the poem. But that is not what puzzles us about the poem. We want to know whether there is some general idea that connects all these diverse references to blackbirds, some concept under which we can relate them: what is the *theme* of the poem? And we want to know whether there is some general statement that the poem may be said to afford, or to contain, some observation or reflection about life or art or man or reality: what is the doctrine, or ideological content, or *thesis* of the poem? The process of determining the theme, or themes, and the thesis, or theses (if any), of a literary work I shall call *interpretation*. And our first problem will be analogous to the problems of explication and elucidation: what are we doing when we interpret literature, and how do we know that we are doing it correctly?

I have given the term "interpretation" a more restricted sense than is customary, because I think the three processes of understanding literature are different enough in method to demand different names. And I use "interpretation" for the third process because I think this is most nearly analogous, though perhaps not identical, to what I have called interpretation in painting and music. (I have argued that there is nothing in music to interpret, but when I said so I used the word "interpret" in the present sense.) To say what a painting represents or symbolizes, to say—I hold, falsely—what music signifies or expresses, is to affirm a meaning-relation or reference from the work to the world; and to say that a poem has a certain theme or a certain thesis is to affirm again that the poem does not merely construct its own world but refers to the real world.

The problem of interpretation might be formulated, then, in these terms: to determine the themes and theses of a literary work, given the contextual meanings of the words and a complete description of the world of the work. This is our problem. Or rather, these are two of our problems, for if we consider a little more carefully the two basic terms, "theme" and "thesis," we shall see that the difficulties with them are rather different.

What sort of thing is a theme? We say that the theme of *Wuthering Heights* is the quest for spiritual contentment through harmony with both good and evil forces of nature; of *War and Peace,* the endless rhythmic alternation of youth and age, life and death, ambition and resignation. We debate whether the theme of Yeats' "Among School Children" is the relationship of matter and spirit, or the human significance of labor, or both. A theme is something named by an abstract noun or phrase: the futility of war, the mutability of joy; heroism, inhumanity.

It may not always be possible to draw a sharp line between theme and subject, but for critical purposes the line is clear enough. We refer to the subject by a concrete noun or nominative construction: a war, a love affair, the Aztecs, the taming of a shrew. The subject of *Oedipus Rex* includes Oedipus, Jocasta, Thebes—the *objects* in the play. Or the subject is the investigation of the cause of a plague—the *action* of the play.

But the themes are pride, divine power, fate, irremediable evil, the driving spirit of man.

A theme, then, is something that can be thought about, or dwelt upon, but it is not something that can be called true or false. What I shall mean by the perhaps awkward term "thesis," however, is precisely something about, or in, the work that *can* be called true or false, if anything can. Critics say, for example, that Shakespeare's *Tempest* embodies a mystical view of life; that Upton Sinclair's *The Jungle* is a protest against the injustices suffered by the poor under a free-wheeling economic system; that there is implicit Platonism in Spenser's "Epithalamion" and Shelley's "Epipsychidion." We speak of the philosophical, religious, ethical, and social ideas in Milton, Shaw, and Sartre. We debate whether Thomas Mann's *Dr. Faustus* is optimistic or pessimistic, how much there is of Schopenhauer and Bergson in Proust. And I take these ideological ingredients to be statable in a form in which we could say, though perhaps only with some hesitation, that they are true or false: even pessimism may be a view of life, not merely a feeling.

There is a terminological embarrassment about these theses. I should like a general term for whatever in the work may be called true or false. In the previous chapter I first proposed the term "proposition" in this sense, which is quite normal, but as we worked out the Proposition Theory of music and painting, it became necessary to conceive of propositions—and this is also normal—as nonlinguistic entities, abstractions of some kind. It is to avoid this second notion that I propose in this context to substitute another word, however odd it may seem at first. Each distinguishable respect in which a discourse or part of a discourse may be said to be true or false I shall call a *predication* in that discourse.[2] Thus a sentence that states one thing and suggests another makes two predications: "Henry is not the *worst* student in the class," which suggests that he is near the bottom. A predication is statable in a "that" clause, though it may not be so stated in the discourse.

To sum up our preliminary distinctions, then, the subject of a novel might be the Compson family, or more generally the Southern aristocracy. A theme of the novel might be the decline of the Southern aristocracy; a thesis might be that the decline of the Southern aristocracy is regrettable, or inevitable. Our first set of questions, then, could be set out as follows: Does every literary work have a theme, or themes? If so, how do we decide what they are? Does every literary work, or does *any* literary work, contain predications? If so, how do we decide what they are?

---

[2] I borrow this term from two articles by Elizabeth Lane Beardsley, "The Semantical Aspect of Sentences" (see Note 20-C), and "Imperative Sentences in Relation to Indicatives," *Phil R*, LIII (1949): 175-85.

We can regard a theme of a literary work as a concept in the mind of the speaker, an abstracted quality or relation that he evidently regards as noteworthy, because in some way he singles it out for attention. Not every characteristic of the objects or events described in the work constitutes a theme, but only those to which some importance is attached in the description itself. Now, whenever anyone says anything, in a serious tone at least, we take him to have something important in mind, or at least something *more* important than other things, and whatever characteristic or characteristics we can attribute importance to, we take as the theme of that utterance. Considered in this broad way, almost any discourse will have some theme or themes, however vague and undeveloped they may be.

Thus even a simple nursery rhyme describes some event or state of affairs, and gives some feature of it emphasis, at least by contrast with what might have been said. In "Little Jack Horner" we have a mildly ridiculous sort of success, and the hero's self-congratulation ("What a good boy am I!") is clearly out of proportion to his achievement; from this we take the theme to be something like vanity. The difficulty arises when we press for precision, and ask how specific or how general we can take this theme to be. Is it the vanity of childhood, because Jack Horner is little? Or do we have here a subtle hint at a broad characteristic of human nature, the endless need for man to think well of himself, the triviality of his accomplishments and powers from a cosmic point of view, the limited perspective—sitting in a corner—from which he makes himself the center of the world and fails to comprehend the providential forces that have provided him with his pie in the first place? To say all this, so bluntly anyway, would certainly be reading things into the verse that are not there. It seems as if we are no longer interpreting, but creating our own work, for even the most elementary work can be made vast and profound by this sort of fancy. Yet in some very remote way some of these reverberations are related to the verse, and the quality and zest of it depends upon these overtones, even when they are not separately discriminated. Where, then, do we draw the line?

At this point we may turn back to the blackbird poem. What is the speaker interested in about the blackbird? Well, for one thing, it appears in various environments, and can be seen in many different lights, as the title points out. Still, this is not yet a theme. We want to know what is important about this multiple-aspectedness of the bird, something special to it as a blackbird, among birds, but common to something else in human nature or human life or the world at large, something that may be said to be on the speaker's mind throughout the poem. But notice that the question (1) What are the themes of this poem about blackbirds, mountains, snow, and icicles? is becoming the same question, or very nearly the same question, as (2) What do the blackbird, the mountain, the snow, and the icicles, *symbolize* in this poem?

Perhaps these two questions are not the same. Or perhaps the broad sense that must be given to "symbolize" in order to make the equation is too high a price to pay for convenient simplification. But they do seem closely related. If the Christmas pie episode may be said to have human vanity as one of its main themes, then we can also say that Little Jack Horner, or his pie, symbolizes human vanity. If Faulkner's tales about the Snopeses have as their theme the overcoming of good by evil, then we can say that the Snopeses symbolize the overcoming of good by evil. There are some sound, though not compelling, reasons, in my opinion, why the "symbol" terminology is, in these days, dangerous and misleading, and the "theme" terminology is better. But we cannot deal adequately with the problems of literary interpretation unless we give some consideration to the analysis of literary symbols.

In Chapter VI, §16, we saw that for any object to become symbolic there must be a vital basis of its symbolism: that is, it must function in some important way in the lives of those for whom it has symbolic meaning. In the present context we may set aside one sort of literary meaning that could be called symbolism, but is perhaps better not, namely, allegory. Any event or series of events *can* be assigned an allegorical sense, with the help of a kind of dictionary: the Red Cross Knight or the Slough of Despond is to stand for such-and-such a thing. The relation here is perhaps similar to that between music and words in program music, neither compelling nor altogether irrelevant; or it is analogous, in painting, to the emblems and tokens of Christian iconography. But the interesting thing is that objects and events—the blackbird or a journey—that are not symbols in their ordinary contexts can become symbols in the context of a literary work. Our problem is to inquire how this can happen, and how such symbols are recognized and interpreted.

The concept of vital basis can readily be taken over; just as the flag or the cross becomes a symbol in a country or a culture, so an object in the world of the work can become symbolic if it plays an important causal role in the lives and fortunes of the characters, or in the mental processes of the speaker. There are really two distinguishable ways in which an object becomes symbolic—either as a *central prop*, in the theatrical sense, or as a *recurrent image*.

The first way is, roughly, this. Suppose any object, a bridge, a door, an animal, appears more than once in a narrative, at crucial times, so that it attracts the attention of characters in the story, and comes to affect them and remind them of other things. Then it takes on symbolic meaning. The Scarlet Letter, in Hawthorne's novel, is in the center of vision in the most climactic scenes; it is a "pearl of great price" and a "burning brand"; and it can cause shame and pride and loneliness. Hence it can embody the leading themes of the novel. In Virginia Woolf's *To the Lighthouse*, there are at least a half-dozen works of art that are important to the story: Carmichael's poetry, Lily Briscoe's painting, the Boeuf en Daube, Rose's centerpiece, Mr. Paunceforte's style, and Mrs. Ramsey herself; one can say that art itself becomes symbolic in this context. We can say something similar of the Wild Duck, the White Whale, the Master Builder's tower, the Cherry Orchard, Blake's Lamb, Yeats' rose, and the mountains and mountain-climbing that have furnished so much symbolic material for writers in recent years. Jack Horner's Christmas pie is a limiting case; it only appears once, but it is the main prop, and hence the focus of all the action there is.

There is a second way in which a literary work becomes symbolic. Suppose there is an object X, whose various characteristics are designated by the modifiers in a number of metaphorical attributions throughout the work. In other words, suppose the same object, or group of related objects, turns up in a number of metaphors. Then we can say that the series of metaphors has established a symbol. I don't know that we could quite say this about "There Was a Crooked Man," though when we have a crooked man, a crooked mile, a crooked sixpence, and a crooked stile, the image of crookedness is well on the way to becoming symbolic. The trouble is that the metaphorical senses of "crooked" in these different lines tend to diverge too far. But when we trace through *King Lear*, or *Macbeth*, or *Antony and Cleopatra*, clusters of recurrent images, astronomical or animal or other, we can, I think, say that the recurrence creates symbols, not through the action of the play but through the texture of the language. And when we find in Allen Tate's "Death of Little Boys" such metaphorical phrases as "terrific as the sea," "crumbling room," "torn in two," "white spars above the wreck," "delirium assails the cliff of Norway," and "rotten skiff," we can say that in this poem a wrecked ship is a central symbol, though it is never named.

What, then, shall we say about the blackbird? First, he is an object that turns up in each of the thirteen paragraphs of the poem, and this harping upon him claims that he is supremely worthy of note, in other words, that he is a symbol. But if he is a symbol, he must symbolize *something*, and this is just the difficulty. In vi, with his crossing shadow, he could be a symbol of death, but that does not seem to fit iv; in i he could be a symbol of watchfulness, but that will not fit iii; in viii he could be a symbol of evil, and also in iv, but that will not fit iii or ii. There does not in fact seem to be anything that he can symbolize throughout, especially if we include the missing sections; in other words, we can trace no definite theme. Yet there is a *claim* to symbolic meaning, and the poem is constantly verging upon it; in other words, possible themes are barely hinted, then withdrawn. And the secret of the poem seems to lie in just the way it toys with these possibilities.

I do not wish to be at all dogmatic about this poem, for it is a famous puzzle. There is always a chance that something has been overlooked, though sometimes there is no way to find out whether others have found it except to tell them that you haven't found it yourself. It is an illuminating example, precisely because it is borderlinish, and it is by no means unique in the respects that concern us here; a great many modern poems, and some fiction as well—for example, Kafka's "In the Penal Colony"—have the same air of being deeply and richly symbolic, without symbolizing anything in particular, or at least anything that you can formulate in other words.

At this point we had better try to draw together the threads of this tentative discussion of the complexities of symbol and theme. What makes an object symbolic in a literary work is its being fixed as the focus of unusual attention either for the speaker or for another character in the world of the work. What it symbolizes is a set of characteristics that it embodies or causes and that are pointed up by the action or the verbal texture. In the course of a novel, it may accumulate symbolic meaning. In some cases we cannot discover what the object symbolizes, though we can see that there is a claim to symbolic status; perhaps it should be called a *quasi-symbol*. In other cases, we can discover some, at least, of its symbolic meaning: the chocolate creams in *Arms and the Man* show the practicality of Bluntschli; the Master Builder's tower shows his self-destructive ambition and pride. But once an object is established as symbolic, it takes on a peculiar thickness and disturbing quality; the central meanings, which are most emphasized, shade off into less and less clearly defined, and more and more remote, ones. We can never say exactly where to stop interpreting it; we feel that the more we search, the more we could find. At a certain point we are, it is true, no longer saying what the symbol means in its context, but exploring its general possibilities; yet we cannot hope to mark this point precisely. In any case, the central meanings of the symbol are generally included among the themes of the work.

It is chiefly the thematic aspect of literature that makes it appear worthwhile to apply to literature the Revelation Theory which was discussed in the preceding chapter. Where the general characteristic—say, vanity in human ambition—pointed up by the work is one that can also be found in life, though seldom in so clear and pure a form, it is natural to describe this fact by saying that the work "reveals" human vanity. This is like holding the mirror up to nature, or scanning the follies of mankind. Not that revelation is limited to themes; the subject may also be revelatory in other respects, as when we say that Tom Jones is true to human nature or that *Cry the Beloved Country*, by Alan Paton, gives an accurate picture of some aspects of life in the Union of South Africa.

In these examples we are speaking, not of predications, but of the matching of characteristics. "Revelation" can belong either to the "shows as" ("true to") mode of speech or the "says that" ("true about") mode. "This novel reveals the vanity of human ambition" is a deeply ambiguous sentence, and we must distinguish its two senses before making a judgment of its truth. In one sense it ascribes a thesis to the novel and may be equivalent to "This novel says that human ambition is sometimes vain." In the other sense it ascribes a theme to the novel, and may be equivalent to "This novel shows vain ambition," that is, it sets forth an instance of vain human ambition, which the reader can meditate upon and compare with his own experience. Probably most statements about revelation in literature are to be taken in the latter sense. The distinction may be pointed up further by this question: A literary work, in its characters, scenes, or themes, may be *true* to human nature or human life, but can it be *false* to them? A predication, that all is vanity, is true or false; it makes sense to call it either. But a quality of human nature exemplified in a literary work is not in the same position; if it can also be traced in real people, we can call it true to human nature; if it cannot, it is not false to human nature, but simply a new invention.

Literature, then, in this sense is a revelation, or can be; some of the universals it exhibits are, as an old critical tradition has claimed, the same universals we find about us, only more intense. The rashness of Hotspur, the self-questioning of Hamlet, the unillusioned realism of Falstaff, as has often been said, are larger than life—though that is not the only important thing about them. But if there are strains of Falstaffishness or Ivan-Karamazovity in human nature, it is not literature itself that proves this. And since the term "Revelation" so easily slides over into a predication theory, it is not, I think, to be recommended.

Theses

At this point we must turn to the second main problem of this section. It seems clear that most literary works have a theme; but it does not follow that they have a thesis—in other words, that they can, in part or as a whole, be sensibly called true or false.

Let us begin with a kind of inventory of the predications, or ostensible predications, that are to be found in literature. The sentences and clauses that occur in a novel can be divided into two broad classes. Class A consists of sentences that report the situation, the objects and events, of the story. Class B consists of sentences, if there are any, in which the narrator generalizes in some way, or reflects upon the situation. Let us say that the explicit predications in the work, then, are either *Reports* (Class A) or *Reflections* (Class B); either like "None of Napoleon's detailed instructions about the disposition of troops for the battle of Borodino were put into execution," or like "The will of an individual king or general has no effect upon the course of history." Doubtless this distinction cannot be made precise, but it is of great use. Where a literary work has an *explicit* philosophy, like *War and Peace,* it will be presented in the form of Class B predications.

But besides the explicit predications in the work, there are implicit ones, which can also be divided into two classes. Class C predications are those derived by elucidation from the Class A predications; they are implicit Reports. Class D predications are those derived by interpretation from the Class A predications: they are *implicit Reflections*.

This classification is preliminary; it does not prove anything. It does not answer our question, but helps us to divide the question into convenient portions. Suppose we find examples of each of the four classes in literature. Then we can put the question this way: Anything that can be true or false may be said to have a *truth-value*—we may know that it has some truth-value before we know which of the two possible truth-values it has. Chairs and tables do not have truth-values, but predications do. Now, then, which of the four classes of *apparent* predications in literature really have truth-value?

Let us consider first the Reports, implicit and explicit. The explicit ones are carried by declarative sentences about objects and events, which make up the greater part of any work of fiction. Now some of these sentences, it seems to me, we can call true or false, if we want to, though we probably do not. For example, *The Romance of Leonardo da Vinci*, by Dmitri Merejkowsky, begins "In Florence, the warehouses of the Guild of Dyers were situated side by side with the Canonica of Or San Michele." This might very well be true of fifteenth century Florence; it could be the beginning of a historical account. Willa Cather's *Death Comes for the Archbishop* begins, "One summer evening in the year 1848, three Cardinals and a missionary Bishop from America were dining together in the gardens of a villa in the Sabine hills, overlooking Rome." Taken by itself this is a perfectly plain statement, and it could be the beginning of a biography, though the odds are thàt it is false. These sentences can be abstracted from their contexts and, in principle, put to a test, though in practice not, or perhaps only with great difficulty. I do not assume here that all predications are in principle verifiable, but surely anything that is in principle verifiable is a predication.

The other sentences that make up the explicit Reports in fiction have a peculiar feature: they contain a reference to a nonexistent person, place, or thing. A novel is about Prince Muishkin or Huckleberry Finn, Shangri-La or Yoknapatawpha County, the Houyhnmhnms or the Green Men of Mars. And a sentence about Huckleberry Finn or the Green Men of Mars is puzzling, for though it is about someone, there is no one for it to be about. The same is true of sentences that contain pronouns without antecedents. "When I consider how my light is spent," let us agree, suggests that the speaker is blind; but the speaker is a fictitious character, too—unless we take the pronoun "I" to refer to Milton, in which case the suggestion has a truth-value, because it is true. We have, in Chapter V, §15, seen why this is unsound.

Let us use the abbreviation "fictional sentences" for "sentences that contain references to fictitious persons, places, or things." Or, if the word "reference" is misleading, let us say that a fictional sentence is one that contains a proper name, or a pronoun, or a descriptive phrase—"the Locri faun" in *South Wind,* by Norman Douglas—that does not denote any-thing. Not all the sentences in fiction are fictional sentences, but our question now concerns these alone. Do they have a truth-value? In other words, are they predications? Three main positions seem to have been taken with regard to this question.

The Analysis of Fictional Sentences

The first position is the least philosophical: it is that fictional sen-tences are all true—but, of course, in an odd and Pickwickian sense. I shall call it the Possibility Theory. It says that the names "George F. Babbitt" and "Zenith" must refer to something, if they are to be meaningful, and that since Babbitt and Zenith do not enjoy a space-time existence, they must exist in some other sense; their "mode of existence" is as a "possi-bility," not an actuality; they are Eternal Ideas subsisting in a World Beyond. And the sentences about them are true of that world, though not of ours.

The motive behind this notion of a realm of fictional reality, in which all the great characters disport themselves forever, is perhaps worth a little scrutiny. Probably there is a childlike fear that one's dearest friends of fantasy, the Three Musketeers and the Rover Boys and Ivanhoe, would lose some of their value if they were denied reality, even the rather thin sort of reality this theory affords.

The chief objections against the Possibility Theory are two. First, it really does not answer the question it is supposed to answer, because its use of the term "true" simply changes the subject. To say that "Paolo loved Francesca" is true because in a World of Possibility there is a possi-bility named Paolo and another named Francesca and there is also the possibility that they loved each other, is just a roundabout way of saying that the sentence is not logically self-contradictory. But that is true of every empirical statement, including false ones. "The United Nations is a World Government" represents a possibility, and one that many people hope for, in exactly the same sense, but it is simply false. So that the Possibility Theory, when we get it clarified, turns out to be no theory at all; it leaves open the question whether, in the usual sense, the story of Paolo and Francesca in *The Inferno* has truth-value.

But second, if it were relevant, the theory would be hopelessly com-plicated in its requirements. For to construct an adequate Fictional Reality, we should have to provide counterparts of our own world. In it, eighteenth century France and twentieth century France would have to exist side by side eternally, along with Egdon Heath, Graustark, Erewhon, the Okefenokee Swamp, and Never-Never Land. It would have to ac-commodate the cosmology of *Paradise Lost* and the chemistry of *Alice in*

Wonderland. It can hardly help being self-contradictory, and so along with all the "possibles," it would contain a good many *impossibles,* which would make it excessively crowded.

The second position I shall call the Falsity Theory of fictional sentences. It is that fictional sentences have truth-value because they are, simply, false. To make this theory clear, we must consider once more the types of fictional sentence. Some of them have as their (grammatical) subjects and objects definite descriptions: "The Gentleman from San Francisco" (Ivan Bunin), "The Man in the Brooks Brothers Shirt" (Mary McCarthy), "The Man Who Was Thursday" (G. K. Chesterton). Others have proper names or pronouns. Now the pronouns can easily be considered as substitutes for proper names. But according to one view of proper names, a proper name has no meaning unless it names something, and therefore a sentence containing a proper name that names nothing is not meaningful at all. It has been shown[3] that this doctrine leads to unacceptable consequences; according to it, we cannot even say, what is certainly true, that "Yoknapatawpha County does not exist," or "There is no such place as Yoknapatawpha County," without falling into either self-contradiction, if it does happen to exist, or nonsense, if it does not exist. We cannot even sensibly ask whether it exists or not. It seems as if we must say that proper names do have meaning even when they have no referent. But how can they?

A very plausible proposal[4] is that proper names are to be regarded as abbreviations for definite descriptions. "Call me Ishmael," begins the narrator of *Moby Dick,* and later occurrences of the name "Ishmael" or the pronoun "I" might be regarded as abbreviations for "the sailor who arrived in New Bedford from Manhattan on a Saturday night in December," thus referring to the first event in the story. Proper names in stories turn up in a continuous narrative, and are generally introduced along with some facts about the person named or events in which he figures, so you can take the first thing you learn about the person as an identification.

There are puzzles about this view, some of them too subtle to deal with adequately here. A proper name is designed to give an absolutely unique reference; two people can have the same name, but what keeps it a name, rather than a general term like "man" or "sailor," is that in each context of use it refers to one and only one person. If a definite description is to be regarded as an adequate substitute for a proper name, it must be sufficient to ensure the same unique reference. And it is doubtful if literary descriptions are unique. Ishmael says his trip occurred "some years ago—never mind how long precisely," and thus prevents us from knowing what December it was when his story began. Moreover, if "Ishmael" is equivalent to some definite description, we must be able to

---

[3] For example, by Willard V. Quine; see Note 22-F.
[4] Made by Quine; see Note 22-F.

find one that can be substituted for "Ishmael" and for "I" in every place
in the book, without producing nonsense.

Suppose that fictional names can be reduced to definite descriptions; the next question is how these in turn are to be analyzed. The classical analysis,[5] the Theory of Descriptions, is that a definite description logically entails the existence of a unique object that it describes: "The gentleman from San Francisco has died" entails that there is one and only one gentleman from San Francisco. "The Locri faun is a forgery" entails that there is one and only one Locri faun. Now since there is in fact *no* Locri faun, and there is *more* than one gentleman from San Francisco— though perhaps none who has done exactly the things done by the gentleman in that short story—both of these sentences entail false statements, and they are therefore themselves false. According to the Falsity Theory, then, all fictional sentences—and this includes most of the sentences in fiction—are simply false, because they entail the existence of certain persons, places, and things that do not exist.

But the Falsity Theory has some odd and unsettling consequences[6] and does not seem a good account of what we actually mean when we talk about nonexistent things. I will mention only one, which is, however, crucial. According to the Falsity Theory, every sentence containing "the Locri faun" is false: the sentence "The Locri faun is a forgery" and the sentence "The Locri faun is *not* a forgery." Now, in ordinary speech, we would certainly regard these as contradictories. In a detective story by Michael Innes one of the characters claims to have the Locri faun. Suppose he does have a statue and it is asked whether this statue is genuine, that is, whether it really is the Locri faun. The correct answer is not that it is false to call it genuine and also false to deny that it is genuine. We should say instead that the question of its genuineness does not arise, because there is no Locri faun for it to be. There are, of course, some false sentences in many works of fiction, especially historical novels; but it is probably a mistake to regard the fictional sentence as false. Rather, we should say that they are neither true nor false.

This is the third position: for want of a better name, I shall call it the Nonpredication Theory of fictional sentences.[7] It is, briefly, that fictional sentences do not really make predications, because their capacity for doing so assumes the existence of something that does not exist. According to the Nonpredication Theory, "The Locri faun is a forgery" does not *entail*, but *presupposes*, that there is one and only one Locri faun. When one sentence S_1 can be true or false only if another sentence S_2 is true, then the former presupposes the latter; but note that the truth of S_2 does not make S_1 true; it merely gives S_1 truth-value. If there is in

---

[5] Made by Bertrand Russell; see Note 22-F.

[6] Pointed out mainly by P. F. Strawson; see Note 22-F.

[7] It has been best presented and defended by P. F. Strawson, but in a slightly different form; see Note 22-F.

France no such village as Digne, then in the first part of *Les Miserables* the sentences have no truth-value at all. Fictional sentences, according to this view are, then, not statements. This does not make them meaningless, because we can perfectly well understand them, and we know what would have to be the case in order for them to become statements. But they are not predications.

The Nonpredication Theory has never been fully worked out, but it seems the most promising of the three positions. It is not altogether free of difficulties, or at least inconveniences, however. For example, it might be said to exaggerate a distinction that, even if it must be made, does not seem as sharp and important in the actual context of literature. A story might begin, "Once upon a time the United States had a Prime Minister who was very fat." Or it might begin, "The Prime Minister of the United States said good morning to his secretaries as he squeezed through the doorway of his office." According to the Nonpredication Theory, if the United States Constitution never changes, the first sentence is false, but the second is neither true nor false. Now there is certainly an interesting literary difference between the two, and it could be argued[8] that it is the difference between "unsophisticated" and "sophisticated" fictional narration; the former has more false sentences, or puts them in key positions, whereas the latter has more sentences that are neither true nor false. *Jude the Obscure* begins: "The schoolmaster was leaving the village, and everybody seemed sorry." That is the sophisticated kind. Henry Green's *Loving*, on the other hand, begins, "Once upon a day an older butler called Eldon lay dying in his room attended by the head housemaid, Miss Agatha Burch." That is the unsophisticated kind, or anyway a highly sophisticated sort of unsophistication. But perhaps the Nonpredication Theory is correct: the key to the difference in style lies in the fact that the existential claim that is overtly entailed in one kind is only suggested by presupposition in the other.

Reflective Predications

To sum up our tentative conclusion about Report-sentences in fiction, then, we may say that some are predications, some—perhaps most—are not. Now we must consider the Reflective elements of literature. The explicit Reflection-sentences need give us no trouble, I think. Tolstoy's philosophy of history, the point made by Chaucer's Pardoner, *"Radix malorum est cupiditas,"* and the morals of Aesop's fables, "The least may help the greatest" ("The Lion and the Mouse"), "One man's meat is another man's poison" ("The Ass and the Grasshopper"), "A liar is not believed, even when he tells the truth" ("The Shepherd-Boy and the Wolf"), are interpretations of the work built into the work itself; they are not fic-

---

[8] This has also been suggested by Strawson.

tional sentences but generalizations, and can clearly be true or false,
though they are very vague.

The hard problem is whether there are *implicit* Reflective predications in literature—and, if so, how we construe them. This problem is closely analogous, of course, to the problem about the Proposition Theory of painting and music. But it is a different problem, and a logically independent one, for here the vehicle is language, and it may quite well be the case that a verbal discourse can make implicit predications, while a picture cannot.

Let us first see how these implicit Reflections could be conceived, and then look about for possible fatal flaws in the view. We have implicit predication, as we saw in Chapter III, §9, in a sentence that suggests as well as states; or, again, when two sentences or clauses are juxtaposed so as to suggest a causal connection between them. What is suggested, or implicitly predicated, is what the speaker purports to believe about the situation he describes, but without saying so in so many words. On a larger scale, then, a narrator of a novel may relate certain events in such a way, that is in such an order and in such a style, as to show that he is *judging* them: reading a generalized significance into them, or making an evaluation of their actors. The theses, or doctrinal content, then, of a literary work, are the set of all Reflective beliefs purportedly in the mind of the dramatic speaker. And the problem of interpreting this content is that of determining what Reflections are suggested by the Reports.

This, I think, is a fair statement of the position generally assumed by literary critics, though they would perhaps not formulate it exactly this way. Let us first consider some objections that might be brought against it.

First, it might be objected that the implicit Reflections in a literary work cannot be regarded as unstated beliefs in the mind of the speaker. For in some fiction, for example Eudora Welty's "Why I Live at the P. O.," John P. Marquand's *The Late George Apley,* Albert Camus' *The Fall,* Browning's *The Ring and the Book,* and Sinclair Lewis's *The Man Who Knew Coolidge,* the story is told in the first person by someone who reveals his own limitations and incompetence in the very act of telling. The total attitude of the work, the basic point of view, extends beyond, and even contradicts, the set of beliefs in the mind of the narrator. In short, the theses of the work are presented ironically.

There is certainly a puzzle here. Nor is it strictly limited to the extreme examples I have given, for in a great many literary works told in the first person the reader can know something about the speaker that the speaker does not know about himself, or can know something about what is happening that the speaker does not understand—as when tragic events are related by a child who is unaware of their tragedy. But I think we must cling to some distinctions here. There are several questions. Can we know more than the speaker does about what is happening? Yes, we can supply inferences from the facts that he does not make; we can elucidate them farther than he does. Can we find in the work Reflections that the speaker does not make? Not in general, for any Reflections we may make on the events of the story cannot automatically be said to be Reflections contained in the work. The story of Jack and Jill might be a warning against stupidity—going uphill for water, when they ought to know that water is always downhill—but I can't say that this is really *in* the verse, any more than I can agree with the critic Thomas Rymer that one lesson of *Othello* is that "Young ladies should look to their linen." Still, there is one exception. It is possible for a speaker to state or suggest a certain Reflection, but in such a way—by revealing his own stupidity or his tendency toward wishful thinking—as to show that he is probably wrong in his Reflection; the effective predication then is the contradictory of the Reflection, and this effective predication is then the real Reflection of the work. So we may say, then, that the implicit Reflections of the work are either predications purportedly believed by the speaker or the ironically suggested contradictories of purported beliefs.

A second objection might be that there is no method for knowing what the implicit predications of a work are, or for settling disagreements when they arise. Consider, to begin with, the simple cases. Aesop's fables always end with a moral; what is the relation between the moral and the fable? The story about the boy who cried "Wolf," for example, illustrates (is an instance of) the generalization that liars are not believed, even when they tell the truth. It does not *prove* this generalization, of course, for that would take more than one instance, and in fact the generalization is not precisely true. On the other hand, the fable is an example of more than one possible generalization, for example, that lying *shepherd-boys* are not believed, even when they tell the truth. Suppose someone were to tell the fable without the moral; would we be able to say what its moral is, ourselves? That is, could we interpret its thesis? Perhaps we could, if we were allowed to follow a certain method. First, we would have to know that it is a fable, or parable; in other words, the story would somehow have to tell us that it *is to be* interpreted, or assigned a general thesis. Second, we would try to think of the most general thesis that has any plausibility at all, and that could be suggested to someone by reflecting upon the events of the fable. Granting the correctness of this method, which we may call the Fable-Interpretation Method, we might come to agreement about the "meaning" of Aesop, even without the moral tags.

The first step of the method raises, perhaps, no insuperable problem. The work itself must show that it is to be interpreted; it must suggest that the speaker himself attaches some significance, or vital importance, to what he is saying. Now, to some extent this is accomplished merely by utterance in a serious tone. Consider proverbs, for instance. We hear, "A stitch in time saves nine," but how do we know that the stitch—or the penny saved, or the rolling stone, or the empty barrel—is an instance of a general idea, that the speaker is not just talking about stitches but about opportunity and foresight? We know, presumably, because the remark is so very trivial taken by itself, and so lacking in intrinsic interest; because it would seem so irrelevant to the situation, in which we are, perhaps, considering life insurance and not repairing the children's clothes; because it is said in a tone of voice that claims some weight and importance for the remark, which we must then find in its general significance, rather than in its specific one. A Principle of Prominence applies here, as in the interpretation of painting. The stitch, in one sense, has become symbolic.

So with the fable. As a story, it has only the barest essentials of plot and character, together with some broad dramatic irony. It is either Reflectively predicative or it is nothing. But suppose we have a short story, or a novel, with intrinsic interest and complexity; the more it is developed, the less it demands to be assigned an implicit thesis. And to preserve its capacity to have an implicit thesis, it must hint in other ways that the speaker has reflected upon the events and sees in them a general lesson for man.

It is not easy to discover how literature does this. If we assume, as I see no reason to do, that every literary work has a thesis, then we shall not believe we have understood it until we have supplied one; and this is easy to do, if we are content with broad platitudes. The blackbird poem predicates *that everything has many aspects,* we could say; but when we have said it, we might wonder with what authority. At the other extreme, a long novel in which poor people are constantly exploited by their employers, landlords, stores, politicians, and policemen, can hardly help being a predication about social relations, even if the narrator makes no explicit generalizations; for in the absence of stylistic or other evidence that the narrator is stupid or insensitive or evil, we cannot help inferring that in his opinion the events he describes are unjust. Yet even here we cannot be more than quite vague and tentative in our interpretation, and the less specific and clear the predication is taken to be, the more likely is the interpretation to be correct.

But suppose we find incompatible interpretations of a work; how do we know which one is right? Arthur Miller's *All My Sons* was attacked as anticapitalist propaganda on the ground that by making the father a manufacturer of defective airplane engines, it suggests that all, or most, manufacturers are dishonest. To which Miller later replied that by having Chris Keller make such a fuss about his father's wrong, it suggests that in fact the crime is unusual among capitalists; therefore, it is anti-Communist propaganda. To expose and discuss adequately the principles of interpretation assumed here would be complicated. Note that if we followed the principle that every conjunction of A with B in a play (the Duchess plays poker, the upstairs maid takes dope) makes an implicit predication (all Duchesses play poker; all upstairs maids take dope), every play would be loaded with implicit predications. This principle is absurd. Probably *All My Sons* contains no predications about capitalism at all, either for or against, though it does contain some predications about the responsibilities of man for his fellow man.

There is a weaker principle of interpretation that is sometimes used, and with more justification. It may be too much to expect the Reflective predications of a play always to be universal in form. But suppose there is a universal negative statement that is widely believed, such as "No Negroes are capable of being first-rate surgeons" or "Marriages between people of different religions are never happy." In that case, the mere presentation of a single counterinstance, where the characters and situations are three-dimensional and moving, may have the force of a predication. A play about a great Negro surgeon or the happy marriage of a Presbyterian and a Jew is close to being an implicit denial of the prevailing belief. This does not necessarily imply that a literary work always predicates the possibility of what it projects, but only that it becomes predicative when its possibilities are set against certain backgrounds. I don't think these imaginary plays would be predications unless they contained some characters who were skeptical about, or strongly opposed to, medical education for Negroes or interfaith marriages.

One other example. Every high school student is introduced to the poetry of Robert Frost and usually he is told to find in it spiritual comfort, rugged New Hampshire individualism, and the New England spirit. But according to Yvor Winters the actual implicit Reflective predications of Frost's poetry are very different. For the speaker

> believes that impulse is trustworthy and reason contemptible, that formative decisions should be made casually and passively, that the individual should retreat from cooperative action with his kind, should retreat not to engage in intellectual activity but in order to protect himself from the contamination of outside influence, that affairs manage themselves for the best if left alone, that ideas of good and evil need not be taken very seriously.[9]

This is a good deal of doctrine to read into poetry; but note again the method. Winters assumes that all the poems of Frost have the same dramatic speaker, and that it is therefore legitimate to put them all together to make up a single philosophy. This is what gives the indictment its power. On the other hand, some of these predications are there, perhaps only dimly, in many of the poems, though sometimes set ironically against quite opposite theses.

This last example brings up a final point that must be kept in mind. The speaker of the work may appear to believe his Reflection in various degrees of confidence, ranging from deep conviction to the bare supposal

---

[9] Yvor Winters, "Robert Frost: or, the Spiritual Drifter as Poet," *Sewanee Review*, LVI (1948): 564-96; see 586-87.

that it is more probable than not. Hence the Reflective predications in the work have various degrees of what might be called *predicative weight*. Whether a poem or a story has clearly defined theses or not, there may be lurking in the background of it, as if held in suspension in the mind of the speaker, certain vague generalizations or judgments of the situation, and it is part of the critic's interpretative task to find these out and help the rest of us to see them. But it is important always to keep their weight in mind; even if we must make them momentarily clearer and sharper to be sure we have them, we may have to thrust them back in our mind when we turn again to the work, for they belong in the shadow, not in the center of the stage. And as we go to those more and more lightly hinted, we cannot draw a sharp line where the predications stop, where the speaker merely offers two themes for inspection, without indicating a connection between them. But sometimes we can say that we have probably noted most of the predications with very strong predicative weight, those most likely to be playing an important role in our complex response to the work itself.

§23. *THE PROBLEMS OF BELIEF*

What are we doing when we tell a story? I do not mean by "story" here merely the relation of a series of actual events, like the "story of my life," nor do I mean a false excuse for not doing something we should have done. Another way of asking the question would be: what is the difference between fiction and nonfiction?

The most naïve answer to this question is simply that fiction is false and nonfiction is true. But this, of course, would not do at all. Many books that belong on the nonfiction shelves of the library contain false statements, and indeed some may be entirely false; and many works of fiction contain geographical or historical statements that are true.

A second answer is that fiction is made up of, or at least contains, fictional statements, in the sense in which this term was defined in the preceding section: that is, statements that are neither true nor false because they refer to nonexistent things. But this answer will not do, either. For, in the first place, many works of fiction do not consist wholly of fictional statements, as we have seen; and, in the second place, it would be possible to make up a fiction about a real person that contained no fictional statements at all, but only false ones.

There is a third answer, of which there could be several versions. It consists essentially in trying to assimilate the Report-sentences of fiction to other forms of grammar—in saying that, though they seem to be declarative sentences, they are really imperative sentences or some other kind in disguise, that is, pseudo-declaratives. Perhaps the sentences in a novel are to be understood as tacitly prefaced by an imperative phrase, so that *The Three Musketeers* begins "*Suppose that* (or, *Let us pretend that*) on the first Monday of the month of April, 1626, a young man rode into the market town of Meung." Or perhaps the declarative sentences in a novel are to be understood as contracting to their referential component, the gist of which can be expressed in a participial phrase: "Me being at that time of year" instead of "That time of year thou mayst in me behold." These two versions are enough to consider, nor need we, I think, consider them long, for there seems to be no good reason why we should treat these declarative sentences as something else in disguise. They are certainly being used in a special way, but they are no less declarative sentences.

A fourth answer[1] is that the difference between fiction and nonfiction is not a difference at all in the discourse itself, but lies in the attitude assumed by the reader (or the librarian) toward it. If you are interested in the truth or falsity of the first sentence of *The Three Musketeers*, you are taking it as history; if you are not interested in its truth or falsity, you are taking it as fiction.

There is something in this view, of course: different attitudes are appropriate to fiction and nonfiction. And perhaps if you are very strong-minded you can suspend your concern about truth-value whenever you wish; you might read *Mein Kampf* or the Declaration of Independence or Newton's *Principia* without in the least caring whether it is true or false, the way some people take the Bible as "living literature," just being absorbed in the movement of the work itself. But this is not, I think, the whole story. You do not have to ignore the truth-value of a discourse for it to be literature, and ignoring the truth-value of the *Principia* does not make it fiction.

Assertion

So we come to the fifth, and probably most satisfactory, view. To state it, we must first make a distinction between *uttering* a sentence and *asserting* it. When, for example, I quote what someone else has said, I pronounce the sentence, but I do not endorse it, and may even be preparing to tear it to shreds; I simply set it forth for contemplation, or understanding. When, however, I utter a sentence in such a way as to show that I believe it—that is, to evince belief, even though I may be evincing a belief that I don't actually feel, in which case I am lying—and in such a way as to invite my audience to believe it, too, then I am asserting the sentence. In ordinary conversation, in news columns, in legal documents, we take the sentences to be asserted. But a fiction, in the literary sense, is a discourse in which the Report-sentences are not asserted. They may still be true or false—except those which refer to nonexistent things—but

---

[1] Proposed by Arnold Isenberg; see reference in Note 23-A.

the writer is not claiming that they are true; he indicates in some way that he neither believes them nor expects us to believe them.

Thus I put into the objective definition of "fiction" the requirement that the writer employ some signal to show that he does not make an assertion, at least on the Report level. It is not necessary for him to state explicitly that "any similarity to persons living or dead is purely coincidental." He need not, like Chaucer's Pardoner, point out that his props are fakes and his story a religious sales talk. He need not begin, as Poe begins "The Black Cat," "For the most wild, yet most homely narrative which I am about to pen, I neither expect nor solicit belief." There is a variety of well-understood conventions by which the fictional use of language is signaled. The writer may label his story a "novel," a "romance," a "mystery," or, like Chesterton, a "nightmare," and these are ways of canceling its assertiveness, even if it is believable. But of course, it may be unbelievable in the sense that if we were to try to take it as history, and demand evidence, we would be frustrated. When a novel contains reports of thoughts that are never uttered aloud, or private conversations that are never told to others, this indicates that the reporter could not possibly know the truth of what he describes, which is one way of showing that he does not claim truth for what he says. The novelist who gives his first-person narrator a name different from his own evidently dissociates himself from the work. Again, the narrator is often very exact about some points in the story—say, the way the heroine does her hair—but silent about other points that we would need to be informed about if we were going to try to find out whether the events actually occurred. And this evasiveness shows that the writer has no interest in securing the reader's belief. "A certain man went down from Jerusalem to Jericho" is exact about places, but silent about the date. It is not until nearly the end of *The Brothers Karamazov* that the narrator lets slip the fact that his village bears the ridiculous name of Skotoprigonyevsk. The name is mentioned almost by accident, and if it were left out the story of the Karamazovs would be almost uncheckable; but a newspaper story quite properly begins with a dateline.

Of course we find borderline cases: stories in *True Confessions*, historical novels, feature stories in newspapers, Defoe's *Moll Flanders*. They are not quite decisively either fiction or nonfiction. But they need not trouble us; as for the vast majority of narratives, we can readily decide whether or not they are fiction—which, again, is quite a different matter from deciding whether or not they are true.

On the Report level, then, a work of fiction consists either of fictional sentences or unasserted ones. Let us call this the *Nonassertion Theory* of fiction. But a more serious and delicate problem now arises. For what shall we say about the predications at the Reflection level? There are two likely possibilities here, and perhaps we cannot decide finally between them, but I think the second recommends itself more strongly than the first.

According to the first view, it is precisely this double aspect that is characteristic of the greatest fiction, though not of all: the first level consists of explicit Reports that are not asserted; the second level consists of Reflections, or theses, that *are* asserted. It is not merely that the speaker of the work is taken to believe the Reflections; that goes without saying. It is that the *writer* of the work is taken to be setting forth some general views about life that he holds as a human being and wishes to teach. This view is perfectly consistent, of course, and it describes what often happens in ordinary speech, for you can utter a metaphorical or ironic sentence in such a way that though on one level it is not asserted, on another level it is.

The problem that we have now come up against might be put this way: Are we to assume that any utterance is asserted unless there is a signal that it is not, or are we to assume that an utterance is not asserted unless there is a signal that it is? In discussing the Report level of fiction, we tentatively made the first assumption, because we can show, almost always, that there is something in a novel that warns us that its Reports are not to be taken seriously. But the first assumption is probably unsafe to generalize. What shows us that a person who utters a sentence is asserting something, while a parrot who utters the same sentence, in perhaps almost the same tone of voice, is not? Without hoping to be precise, or to lay down rules to cover all cases, we can probably say that there must be something in the *pragmatic context*, something in the accompanying behavior of the utterer in his situation, that leads us to take the utterance as an assertion by affording us independent evidence—that is, evidence apart from the utterance—that he believes it and expects it to be believed.

If the notion of pragmatic context as a condition of assertiveness can be made clear enough, then the question becomes this: Does the act of writing a novel and publishing it, if the novel contains an implicit thesis, constitute a sufficient pragmatic context of the utterance to make it an assertion? And on the whole, I think it seems best to say that it does not—which is the second view referred to above. If we can allow a writer to pretend to be Dr. Watson or Porphyria's lover, then we can allow him to pretend to be a Roman Catholic or a Nietzschean or a Communist. Thus even the Reflective predications of a literary work are unasserted; they are part of the story, in a broad sense, or part of the act.

This conclusion may be a hard one. It seems odd to deny that Tolstoy is taking advantage of *War and Peace* to preach his philosophy of history, or that Dostoyevsky hoped to get across some of his ideas about Russia and religion in *The Brothers Karamazov*. But notice the distinction. I do not deny that these ideas are in the works, nor do I deny that they are true or false and can be accepted or rejected for reasons good or bad—I only deny that getting the ideas into the work constitutes an act of *asser-*

tion. Tolstoy's appendix is of course a very special case. But it seems to me that we have a choice about it. Either it could stand by itself as an argument, owing nothing to the events that precede it, in which case it is a truly independent discourse, and may be an assertion; or it cannot stand by itself, in which case it is part of the novel, part of what is going on in the mind of the narrator, and hence not asserted.

We must also not deny that Tolstoy and Dostoyevsky really believed these things; for we have plenty of independent evidence, from their other writings and conversations, about their beliefs. But even if a writer believes a certain predication, and makes it the implicit thesis of a novel, he has not asserted it *in* the novel, though he must have asserted it elsewhere, or we would not know that he believes it.

Once we have pushed matters this far, of course, a certain triviality appears in our question about the assertiveness of fiction. I have emphasized the distinction between putting theses in the work and asserting the theses because the term "truth-claims," which is widely used in discussing these matters, causes trouble by straddling this distinction. Some have held, for example, that the ideas cannot be there at all because they are not asserted, and others that they must be asserted because they are certainly there. We might agree at this point that in order to know whether a thesis of a novel is believed by the writer we must go outside the novel itself; and since the discovery that the thesis was, or was not, believed makes no difference to what is in the novel, it cannot be relevant to criticism. But at this point we would be anticipating some questions that are to arise in the following chapter.

One other effect of the previous discussion is to put in a different perspective another common view about literature, that it is a form of "communication." Generally critics who talk this language have to do some juggling; they insist that the poem is not a "message," but still it "communicates," and not merely emotions, but ideas, or at least the experience of what it is like to have a certain idea. The central truth that such discussions unsuccessfully aim to make explicit can, I think, be formulated in this way: the work contains predications, the contemplation, and even the testing, of which can be shared by different readers, and the writer too. But it is not a "message," and not in the ordinary sense a "communication," since it is not an assertion and therefore claims to convey no information.

The Reader's Beliefs

The question with which this section began led to one set of problems about the connections between literature and belief. We must now turn from these problems about the writer's, to those about the reader's, beliefs and inquire: in what ways, if any, does the reading of a literary work presuppose or depend upon the reader's beliefs?

Certain types of dependence we have already noted in Chapters III and V. To explicate a poem we must know the connotations of its words and the suggestions of its sentences, and connotation and suggestion are defined in terms of belief. To elucidate a story, and to grasp the unity of its plot, we must believe certain general psychological and physical laws. To interpret themes and theses we must know something about the roles of certain symbolic objects in human experience, or the sort of inferences that people would be likely to make from certain data. These are examples of what might be called the *belief-conditions* of *understanding*. Grasping the implicit elements of literature, like the recognition of the subject in a representational painting, presupposes beliefs, whereas seeing the design of the painting or hearing the structure of music does not presuppose beliefs—though it may presuppose previous experiences of various sorts.

But the problem we are concerned with now is of a somewhat different sort: Are there belief-conditions, not only of understanding, but of *enjoying* a literary work, that is, of experiencing it as good? And more narrowly, do these conditions involve the *thesis* of the work? Traditionally, this problem has been formulated in two ways. The first is to ask whether a literary work can be good (or great) if one of its theses is false; if, in other words, its dramatic speaker holds a false philosophical, moral, or political view. This is the connection between the value of a literary work and its truth. The second is to ask whether a literary work can be enjoyed to the fullest extent by a reader who, rightly or wrongly, does not believe one of its theses. This is the connection between the value of a literary work and the acceptance of its thesis.

The two questions are distinct, of course, but they are related, and the more closely a reader's beliefs approximate the truth, the more they tend to collapse into one. That is why it is rather hard to keep them apart in discussion, and perhaps it is not necessary to keep them apart, so long as we do not forget their distinctness.

The possible points of view about this matter do not sort themselves out very readily. Before setting up a classification, it might be best to remind ourselves of the looseness of the whole issue by discussing a simple example in an unsystematic way. In *Man and Superman* Bernard Shaw makes one of his characters say, "The Englishman thinks he is being moral when he is only being uncomfortable." Now, this is witty, and let us assume both that its wit is a literary quality, and also that it is a valuable quality. We might then ask whether the wit depends in any way upon either the truth or the credibility of the remark. One forthright answer might be made at once: the remark does not have to be true, as a generalization about the British, in order to be witty. Isn't there something comic in the very idea that one could confuse discomfort with morality?

But, on the other hand, would the remark be so funny if it were made about the French, about whom precisely the opposite is widely believed, or the natives of Ruanda Urundi, about whose morality we might know nothing? You could argue that unless we believed that there is at least some fire where there is so much smoke we wouldn't see anything funny in the remark.

But more subtle intermediate positions are possible, too. Not *all* confusions are comic. Perhaps the remark does not have to be true of the British, but perhaps its wit at least depends upon the assumption that there is something that discomfort does have in common with some people's ideas of morality—so that one conclusion to be drawn from Kant's ethics, for example, is that you can be most sure that you are acting out of respect for the moral law, and not merely in accordance with it, when you are going against your inclinations. *Some* people make this confusion, even if the British don't. In that case, the wit of the remark is not completely independent of our beliefs, though it is independent of our belief in *it*.

Humor is a special case, but the Shaw example suggests some further ways in which the problem might be made more manageable. First we must be careful about the word "belief." There is a kind of phenomenal feeling of acceptance—Russell has called it an "Ah yes" feeling—that a poem or speech may move us to momentarily. It is hard, perhaps sometimes impossible, to distinguish this feeling from sheer intensity of participation or outgoing sympathy. But that does not define "belief," I think, for we should not say that a person believes something unless he has a disposition to action. We cannot always say exactly what sort of action is connected with a certain belief: my belief that there are forty-six leaves on a certain potted plant would show itself in my acting surprised if I should count them again and find forty-five or forty-seven. But wallowing in a feeling of pleasure at hearing something said, or letting go of your critical faculties completely, is not believing. Thus if you ask me whether I believe the Shaw remark, I might have a hard time replying; I suppose I believe, but without complete confidence, that the proportion of Puritan moralists is a little higher in Great Britain than in some other countries, and would be prepared to bet on this, if forced to make a choice.

Second, the Shaw example shows how we can simplify our problems in one respect. If we ask how the truth or the acceptability of a doctrine affects the value of a literary work of which it is a thesis, we plunge at once into numerous problems about critical evaluation that for very good reasons are put off until the next chapter. Whatever conclusions we reach here can be reconsidered in the light of that chapter. But in order to reach any conclusions here, at least any useful ones, without facing the value problems, we must fall back upon some hypothetical reasoning. I have assumed that wit is a good thing, and instead of asking about the relation between the truth of Shaw's remark and its literary value, I have asked about the relation between its truth and its wit. Now suppose it should turn out that there are certain features of literary works that make for their being valuable; then any connection between these features and the truth or acceptability of their theses will indirectly be a connection between their *value* and the truth or acceptability of their theses. But we are under another handicap in the present discussion, too. For of course truth is itself a value, and we can speak of the *cognitive value* of literature in so far as it is true or contributes in some way to our knowledge; this we shall return to shortly. But I have been assuming that there is another sort of value that literature possesses, without as yet being able to make this more specific, and it is this *literary value,* whatever it may turn out to be, that we are concerned with. Until we are clear about what it is, we cannot be sure what features of literature are conditions of its presence, but we can tentatively consider some features that seem likely candidates.

The Didactic Theory

The theory that we must now reckon with sees a close connection between truth and value in literature. It may in a broad sense be called the *Didactic Theory* of literature.[2] Usually it is formulated by saying that in order to be "great," a literary work must contain not only true, but profoundly true, theses. This view can be, and often is, merely verbal: the term "great" is reserved for works that have cognitive as well as literary value. But in some versions, anyway, there is a more or less implicit notion that cognitive and literary value cannot be separated from one another. It is not merely that the reader may be put off or discouraged by reading a work with whose thesis he strongly disagrees: he is a Catholic reading Hardy's "Nature's Questioning," with its echo of Hume's *Dialogues Concerning Natural Religion,*

> Are we live remains
> Of Godhead dying downwards, brain and eye now gone?[3]

or an atheist reading Hopkins' "The Wreck of the Deutschland,"

> Ground of being, and granite of it: past all
>   Grasp God, throned behind
> Death with a sovereignty that heeds but hides, bodes but abides.[4]

Somehow, the supposed falsity of the thesis is considered to vitiate the form itself.

---

[2] This theory has been maintained by Plato (in the *Phaedrus*), Matthew Arnold, Wordsworth, Shelley, W. T. Stace, and others; for references see Note 23-B.

[3] From "Nature's Questioning," Thomas Hardy, *Collected Poems.* Copyright 1926 and reprinted with the permission of The Macmillan Company.

[4] From "The Wreck of the Deutschland," *Poems of Gerard Manley Hopkins.* Copyright, 1918, by the Oxford University Press and reprinted with their permission.

Unfortunately, as far as I can see, nobody has ever given any plausible reasons for the Didactic Theory. There is therefore nothing to refute; but it is relevant to point out inconveniences that would follow from accepting it. *The Divine Comedy* and *On the Nature of Things* contain opposed metaphysical systems; therefore, it seems to follow from the Didactic Theory that at least one of them cannot be great. The view might be preserved with some qualifications; you might say that, despite their false predications, these poems contain many true ones—many wise observations about human nature, for example—and even if you are a Roman Catholic, you can still agree that many of the explanations of natural phenomena given by Democritean atomists were partially correct. But in what matters most to the speakers of these two poems—the question whether man has an immortal soul—there is an irreconcilable opposition.

If there can be good optimistic poems and good pessimistic ones, good Marxist novels and good fascist novels, good materialistic plays and good mystical plays, then it would seem that the literary value of a work is independent of the truth or acceptability of its theses. And yet this is not quite the same thing as saying that it does not matter to a literary work what sort of thesis it has, or that any thesis is available for good literature. We could adopt this view: that the value of the work is independent, not only of the truth and acceptability of its theses, but of every characteristic of its theses. But it is hard to maintain, and in fact most contemporary literary theorists who reject the Didactic Theory nevertheless qualify their rejection. They usually say that while a false or unacceptable thesis may be contained in a good literary work, not *all* false and unacceptable theses will do. The problem for this line of thought is then to specify the characteristics that distinguish the available from the unavailable ones. For example, it is held that the thesis must be "sincere," or "mature," or "reasonable," or "important."[5]

I propose to set up the problem in a slightly different way. But to introduce it, I shall consider an example. In Ezra Pound's Canto XXXV, there is a passage in which the speaker drops into a Yiddish accent. Part of it runs:

> a peutiful chewish poy
> wit a vo-ice dot woult
> meldt dh heart offa schtone[6]

—a strongly anti-Semitic passage, with a very objectionable tone. Canto XLV (also Canto LI) is an attack upon usury:

> With usura hath no man a house of good stone
> each block cut smooth and well fitting
> that design might cover their face. . . .[7]

---

[5] These criteria are discussed in Note 23-C.

[6] From "Canto XXXV," Ezra Pound, *The Cantos*. Copyright 1948 by Ezra Pound. Reprinted by permission of New Directions.

[7] From "Canto XLV," Ezra Pound, *The Cantos*. Copyright 1948 by Ezra Pound. Reprinted by permission of New Directions.

Now perhaps the contrast here is not a clear-cut one, and requires some simplifications to make my point. For example, the first passage may play a necessary role in some larger design of the *Cantos,* which is supposed to reveal the disorder of our time. But suppose we look at it this way: The anti-Semitism, or rather its implicit predications about Jews, I regard as false; the implicit predications about usury—taking this in Pound's sense to include all lending of money, not just lending at an unfair rate of interest—I also take to be false. The anti-Semitism seems to vitiate the Cantos in which it turns up, and turn them into low-grade poetry; the anti-usury doctrine, however, is woven into the texture of some rather fine Cantos, as the Cantos go. What is the reason for this difference?

There is a good deal that could be said about this example, but I shall make only brief comments. The anti-Semitism appears suddenly in its context, not closely connected with the rest of the Canto; it is essentially a cheap and vulgar passage, reflecting the grossest stereotypes about middle-European Jews; its tone is insensitive and imperceptive. The anti-usury, on the contrary, is made into a refrain that runs through a rhythmically controlled lament; it serves as the thread, so to speak, on which a series of rough but strong images is strung; the tone is serious and the attitude appears deep, fixed, pervasive, and weighty; the references to painting and crafts and trades and marriage show that the speaker is taking many matters into account, and relating his view of usury to the complexities of things.

In short, there are other important aspects of a doctrine, philosophical, economic, social, or religious, besides its truth-value and its acceptability. And these other aspects become important when the doctrine is made the thesis of a literary work. First, the doctrine may be more or less coherent—logically coherent in the sense of making the connections clear among its parts, attitudinally coherent in the sense that its parts seem to go together in the same state of mind. Shelley's philosophy, a mixture of Platonism and materialism, is less coherent in these ways than Plato's or Lucretius's. Pound's political and economic theories are less coherent than Mill's; Julius Rosenberg's metaphysics of Nazism is less coherent than Marxism; Milton's philosophy less coherent than Schopenhauer's. Now in general we may say, I think, that when a doctrine is embodied in a literary work, its coherence will help to unify the work—as Lucretius' metaphysics becomes the underlying unity of *On the Nature of Things*—and any basic incoherences in the doctrine will work against the unity of the work as a whole. Therefore, if the degree of unity of the work has anything to do with its value, so will the coherence of its thesis.

Second, a doctrine may be more or less complex, in the sense of being worked out to take account of, or to seem to take account of, a variety of human experience: it may contain more logical distinctions, or cover more ground, or have a broader scope. Hume's philosophy is simpler than Hegel's; Epicurus's ethics is simpler than Dante's; Marxist political theory is simpler than the democratic theory as it developed from Locke through Mill to Dewey. When a doctrine is embodied in a literary work, it will then tend to contribute its own degree of complexity to the work, and if the complexity of literature has anything to do with its value, then so will the complexity of its thesis. It may be sheer simple-mindedness that we object to in the theses of "Trees," "Invictus," or "It Takes a Heap o' Livin' To Make a House a Home."

Third, a doctrine may, simply as a human construct, have certain qualities, quite apart from its truth or acceptability. It may be charming, monumental, powerful, pedantic, fussy, imposing, crude, dramatic, magnificent, and so forth. And such qualities as it may have it can contribute to any work of which it becomes the thesis. If, then, the intensity of the qualities of a literary work has anything to do with its value, then so will the intensity of the qualities of its thesis.

It is such characteristics as these that we must take into account, I think, in judging the thesis of a literary work from a literary point of view. How do Alyosha Karamazov's anarchism, Zarathustra's concept of the Will to Power, Milton's barbarous views about the proper relation between men and women, affect the other aspects of the works in which they appear, so as to add to or detract from those aspects that are connected with their literary value?

Empiricism and Literary Truth

One more main problem remains to be considered in this chapter. We have not yet discussed in a general way the cognitive value of literature. If, like paintings and music, literary works made no predications, this problem would not arise, but, as we have seen, they do. Now, whether or not the Reflective predications are asserted by the writer, and whether or not the reader must believe them, still, being predications, they *can* be believed or disbelieved. We can, if not while reading the work then at some later time, subject them to inquiry to determine whether they are true or false.

At least, this is one point of view, that of the Empiricist. All sorts of interesting predications turn up in literature, some of which would be important if true. Granted that the literary value of a work does not stand or fall with their truth, still they may be worth testing on their own account. From the Empiricist point of view it does not matter where we obtain our hypotheses; all that matters is that when we put them to the test they turn out to have adequate evidence in favor of them. The literary work does not, of course, give us the evidence, and without the evidence the hypothesis can hardly be called knowledge; still, in scientific inquiry the hard thing is often not the testing of a hypothesis once we think of it, but the thinking of an original and fruitful hypothesis in the first place. Therefore literature may have immense cognitive value even if it merely suggests new hypotheses about human nature or society or the world, and even if only a few of these hypotheses turn out to be verifiable, perhaps after some analysis and refinement. One of the claims most often made for literature, that it increases our understanding of human nature, can be thoroughly justified in this way. The reading of great novels shows us all sorts of motives that human beings may have, and the enormous variety of ways in which these motives intertwine and conflict. The more of these possibilities we have in mind, the better we are at explaining our own puzzling behavior and that of our friends and enemies.

This cognitive claim for literature is important, and must be admitted by the Empiricist. Note that it does not bring literature into conflict with scientific psychology, for the literary work cannot itself teach us any new general laws, if "teaching" means not only suggesting hypotheses but presenting evidence for them. It makes sense to say that a reader's understanding of Christianity may be increased by reading Milton and Donne, or his understanding of the plight of the migrant workers increased by John Steinbeck's *Grapes of Wrath,* or of the Spanish Civil War by André Malraux's *Man's Hope,* or of certain unconscious impulses in human beings by Dostoyevsky's *Notes from Underground.* Here "understanding" probably means discovering in the work new hypotheses which, when confronted with the reader's experience outside the work, seem to hold up empirically. Or it may mean becoming acquainted with new feelings that may be the way it feels to be a migrant worker or a fighter against Franco.

If there are true predications in literature, then, we could say with the Empiricist that they are empirically true. But unfortunately the matter is not so simple. For the predications that count, that are worth considering as important hypotheses, exist in literature only implicitly: in the form of theses suggested by the work as a whole, or in the form of metaphorical attributions. Now when we say that a predication is empirical, we are claiming for it that its truth or falsity can in principle be determined by a process of inquiry in which the predication is indirectly confronted with our experience. Very broadly speaking, the empirical hypothesis is confirmed by deducing consequences from it with the help of general laws already known, and testing these consequences by observation. All empirical predications, except particular reports of observation ("At 2:00 P.M., the thermometer read 97°") are to be understood either as hypotheses or as general laws. Therefore, an empirical predication must exist in a form in which it can be manipulated in deductive and inductive inference, without changing its meaning and producing equivocation and hence fallacious reasoning. But this is precisely what a metaphorical sentence, for example, cannot be counted upon to do.

This point can be illustrated simply. Consider the following syllogism, in which all the statements are literal:

Lions are beasts.
This creature is a lion.
_____
This creature is a beast.

There is no fallacy here, for each word preserves a constant sense through-out the inference. But compare this syllogism:

Lions are beasts. (Literal statement)
That man is a lion. (Metaphorical statement)
_____
That man is a beast. (Metaphorical statement)

When we admit the term "lion" metaphorically in the minor premise, it has a different sense from what it has in the major premise, and the term "beast" is also given license to shift. In short, the syllogism, though ex-ternally correct, has five terms, and commits the fallacy of equivocation.

Suppose for some reason we wished to know whether the first line of E. E. Cummings' sonnet on the Cambridge ladies is true or false:

The Cambridge ladies live in furnished souls;

or, for comparison, T. S. Eliot's description:

I am aware of the damp souls of housemaids
Sprouting despondently at area gates.[8]

These are general predications, which we would test, presumably, by some sort of case-study method, in order to find out, by depth-interview-ing a carefully selected sample, what percentage of Cambridge ladies live in furnished souls, or what percentage of London housemaids have damp souls. But obviously it would be hopeless to give our interviewers such instructions. When we tear these metaphorical attributions out of the control of their context, they are at the mercy of every changing con-text in which they occur. Their meanings would shift from interview to interview, even if the questions could be asked at all: "Do you live in a furnished soul?" The results would be utterly unscientific and unreliable.

One way out of this difficulty presents itself, of course: suppose we begin by taking the predication in its context and explicating it, that is, drawing up a set of literal statements that are equivalent to the metaphor, and giving our interviewers and statistical experts not the metaphor but the literal statements to work with. We want to know, we might say, to what extent the Cambridge ladies still have the same political, social, religious, and moral beliefs that their parents and grandparents had; to what extent their emotional life is inhibited and empty; to what extent they are conscious of belonging to and living up to, a tradition; to what extent they marry in their own class or out of it. These are questions we can inquire about. And if they can be regarded as substitutes for, or

_____

[8] From "Morning at the Window," *Collected Poems, 1909-1935* by T. S. Eliot. Copyright, 1936, by Harcourt, Brace and Company, Inc. and reprinted with their permission.

equivalent to, the original question, "To what extent do the Cambridge ladies live in furnished souls?" then in answering them we will have answered that question. The Empiricist Theory of poetic truth is that all the true implicit predications in poetry are empirically confirmable in this indirect way.

But here we encounter objections from an expected quarter. The literal questions we have substituted for the metaphorical one do not seem to exhaust its meaning completely, nor does it seem as if, in practice at least, we can ever exhaust that meaning, or be certain we have exhausted it. Suppose then, the line from Cummings has no literal equivalent. But suppose that it is true. Then—and this is the crucial point—it cannot be *empirically* true, for it cannot be empirically verified, and therefore it must have, if it has truth at all, a different, nonempirical kind of truth. This is the main argument that could be brought forth by the Intuitionist.

As against the Empiricist Theory of poetic truth, then, we may set the Intuitionist Theory. This theory may be, and usually is, combined with the Intuitionist Theory of music and painting, which we discussed in the previous chapter, but it draws the important line in a different place. Instead of saying that the nonverbal arts can convey a kind of truth that language cannot convey, it would say that the nonverbal arts *and* the language of poetry, with its multiple implicit meaning, can convey a kind of truth that literal language cannot convey. The housemaids and Cambridge ladies are not the best illustrations of Intuitionist truth, perhaps, for some Intuitionists might concede that the sentences about them are really empirical, but I think other Intuitionists would hold that the poets even in these relatively simple examples show an intuitive insight into the nature of those ladies that goes beyond what could be confirmed by the sociologist or social psychologist with his apparatus of questionnaires, depth interviews, and statistical analysis. The Intuitionist would, however, be more likely to cite religious or metaphysical intuitions embodied in the greatest literature, in *King Lear* and *King Oedipus,* in the mystical poems of Vaughan and Hopkins. And he might not use the term "intuition" so much as the term "imagination," which, I think, is quite often regarded as a name for a knowledge-gathering faculty independent of sense experience.[9]

The Problem of Paraphrase

We have now worked our way around to a difficult, but fairly clear-cut, issue, which turns out to be of central importance to the larger issue of Empiricism vs. Intuitionism, as theories of knowledge. This issue is

---

[9] The Intuitionist Theory of poetry has been defended by Shelley, Wordsworth, Matthew Arnold, Wilbur M. Urban, Philip Wheelwright, and others; for references see Note 23-F.

often called the *problem of paraphrase* and put briefly this way: Can literary works be paraphrased? But before we can deal with it we must try to make it somewhat more precise than that. First, it is to be noted that we are not interested in every aspect of literature here, but only its *cognitive content*, that is, the predications it makes, and so our question must be put in this form: "Can the cognitive content of all literary works be paraphrased?" But second, "paraphrase" can have a broad meaning or a narrower and more relevant one. Consider two discourses, D_1 and D_2, and suppose we could set them up in such a way that every predication made by D_1 is also made by D_2, and vice versa. In that case we could say they have identical cognitive content, and either of them could be regarded as a paraphrase of the other, in the broad sense of "paraphrase." Paraphrasability here is symmetrical. Now consider another discourse, D_3, and suppose we could set it up in such a way that everything explicitly stated in literal terms in D_1 is similarly stated in D_3, that everything *suggested* in D_1 is explicitly *stated* in D_3, and that every characteristic referred to *metaphorically* (that is, connoted) by words in D_1 is literally *designated* by words in D_3. In that case we could say that all the cognitive content of D_1 is paraphrased in D_3, and that D_3 is therefore a "prose paraphrase" of D_1. Paraphrasability here is *not* symmetrical, because we have not ruled out the possibility that further predications are suggested in D_3 that are not in D_1; we have only specified that the implicit predications of D_1, as well as its explicit predications, are explicitly represented in D_3. It is this sort of paraphrase that we are concerned with, and when I use the word "paraphrase" without qualification, I shall mean this sort; the other I shall call "symmetrical paraphrase." The issue, then, is whether literary discourses can always be paraphrased in this sense.

For most purposes, I think, the issue can be condensed into two questions. The first question is this: Can every metaphor be literally paraphrased? Or, in more general terms, Can every characteristic that is connoted by any word be designated by some other word? No doubt some characteristics connoted by some words can be designated by other words: for example, *placidity*, which is connoted by "cow," is designated by "placid." This is, in fact, an example of explication; an explication-sentence is a partial paraphrase. But is there any reason to suppose that "cow" connotes other characteristics for which it would be impossible to find or to construct literal words? The second question is this: Can everything that is suggested by one discourse be stated by another? Again, there can be no doubt that some suggested predications can also be stated: what is suggested by "Is socialism compatible with democracy?" is that democracy is the important thing to keep if you have to choose. In this suggestion it differs from "Is democracy compatible with socialism?" Exposing suggestions is precisely what we do in elucidation and thesis-interpretation, and these processes give us partial paraphrases. But is there any reason to suppose that there are predications of such a nature that it would be impossible to state them, and only possible to suggest them?

It is an essential part of the Intuitionist Theory to deny the paraphrasability of poetry—I am taking poetry as the crux of the problem. The Intuitionist holds the Supervenience Theory of metaphor discussed in Chapter III, §10, and is likely to rest his case on this; but he may also insist that symbols in literature can embody meanings that go beyond the possibility of interpretation, or that the implicit theses of literature can never completely be rendered by explicit statements. The Intuitionist case is supported by one general argument, which, however, turns out to be beside the point.

We have seen, in Chapter V, §14, that the traditional distinction between "what" and "how" in literature evaporates under examination, from which it follows that there cannot be two symmetrical paraphrases like D_1 and D_2. But this objection, while it proves the impossibility of symmetrical paraphrase, does not prove the impossibility of nonsymmetrical paraphrase. When we give, for example, a literal translation of a metaphor ("He is a fox" means "He is cunning, cruel, sly, dangerous," etc.) the translation will probably suggest something that is not in the original context, just because it sets out in a tedious order what was given in compact concentration in the original. But the objection does not show that there must always be some meaning in the original metaphor that the translation cannot in principle make explicit.

But the Intuitionist also has some more specific reasons against the possibility of paraphrase. First, the resort to metaphor in ordinary language as well as poetry shows that we need it to express meanings that we have no literal language for, and therefore any metaphor outruns the resources of literal language. Now, as a generic account of metaphor, and also as a practical justification of it, this objection is undoubtedly sound. But it does not show that the cognitive content of the metaphor is such that no literal expression can ever designate it. And in fact we see all the time that, when metaphors are introduced to supplement existing literal language, especially in the history of science ("Nature abhors a vacuum," "natural selection," the Freudian "censor"), where an important characteristic is singled out by the metaphor and for purposes of knowledge we want to refer to it again and again, literal language takes over. Either the metaphor is killed, or a technical neologism is invented and assigned that designation.

Second, it is significant that when we try to explicate metaphorical attributions, that is, give partial paraphrases, we fall back, more often than not, upon other metaphors, or upon figurative language of other sorts. "Saying the housemaids' souls are 'damp' and 'sprout' means that they are spineless, beaten-down, hopeless creatures, passively accepting the situation, nonentities," and so forth. It might be argued that there is an inevitable circle: the best explication of one metaphor is in terms of another, which means the explication is not a paraphrase at all, in the sense with which we are concerned. When we say that "Napoleon is a wolf" means that he is fierce, he is cruel, etc., our paraphrase is clearly much more vague than the metaphor, and in fact misses its most exact point; for it is a wolfish fierceness, a wolfish cruelty, that are ascribed to him, not just fierceness and cruelty in general. Hence for exactness, the wolf-idea must be carried over into the explication as an operator, to modify each of the predicates; but then we have not reduced the metaphor to literal language, but merely expanded it into a series of metaphors. But, I think, this difficulty is only apparent. It is true that the word "wolf" has got to appear in the explication to make the explication precise, but it need not appear *metaphorically* there. "Napoleon is a wolf" means, among other things, "Napoleon is cruel, and the cruelty of Napoleon is like the cruelty of a wolf . . ."—here the word "wolf" is used literally, not metaphorically. So there does not seem to be a fatal difficulty here, an argument to show the impossibility of literal paraphrase.

Third, it must be admitted that there is an important difference between a predication that is merely suggested and one that is overtly stated, a difference that explains why we sometimes prefer to suggest rather than to state, and it is lost in the paraphrase. It is a difference in what I have called *predicative weight,* the difference between insisting and hinting, saying with force or just barely calling to someone's attention. An overt statement is bound to have more predicative weight than a suggestion, however obvious, and this may be misleading in the paraphrase. This is an important point, but introduces no insuperable obstacle. It means that when we paraphrase the suggested predications of a discourse, we may have to use a notation that records their predicative weight as well. Parentheses will serve. The question "Is socialism compatible with democracy?" (lightly but distinctly) suggests that it is more important to preserve democracy than to have socialism, if indeed socialism is desirable at all.

Finally the Intuitionists point out that even if a poem can be paraphrased, the paraphrase is not itself a poem. And this is true, but it is not really an objection. There are many features of the poem that cannot be preserved in the paraphrase, and indeed just those features that make it a poem, and make it valuable as a poem. But if we are concerned with the truth of its predications, the predications are an abstraction from the poem, and the concern with their truth is not a poetic concern. No harm is done to the original by considering it temporarily this way; when we return to it, we find that it still has its integrity and wholeness.

The foregoing argument is, to be sure, not utterly conclusive; there are still some unsolved problems here. But we may perhaps rest tentatively on certain points. It does seem that there is no conclusive argument against the possibility, in principle, of paraphrase; but there are excellent reasons for supposing it to be usually impossible in practice. The most we can ever give is a partial paraphrase of a poem, and no matter how elaborate the paraphrase, we shall nearly always feel that something is left out, if the poem is complex. But note that the reason for this feeling may often be that we are not sure we have understood all the meaning of the poem, not that we have understood some meaning that we cannot make explicit. Thus the paraphrase may be said to converge upon the poem as it gets more and more elaborate. It is not false, for the predications in it are also there in the poem; but it is artificial, for they are not there in the same way. But even if we can seldom, in practice, paraphrase *all* of a given poem, we can nevertheless paraphrase *any* of it that we wish to paraphrase. And the number of meanings is, after all, not infinite, so there is not necessarily something that in principle eludes us.

And this is all that the Empiricist needs to contend for. Any predication that can be discerned in the poem, and that is worth inquiring into, can be extracted and made explicit, and its truth—its empirical truth—can be investigated. In this argument of limited scope, we cannot show, of course, that Intuitionism is false, nor have we even recalled the general problems about this theory of knowledge that we discussed in the preceding chapter. But we can, perhaps, conclude that in order to hold that literary works contain important implicit predications, some of which are true, it is not necessary to be an Intuitionist. Or, to put it another way, if you are an Empiricist in your theory of knowledge, you are not committed to the position that literary works either make no predications at all or else are no different from nonliterary discourses.

In asking whether the cognitive function of literature implies, or is evidence for, a particular Theory of Knowledge, we have made our way to the heart of the general problem of this chapter, a problem whose ramifications have led into a variety of philosophical inquiries. To decide with what attitudes and expectations aesthetic objects are best approached, if we wish to get out of them what is most worth getting, we have to ask, as we asked in the preceding chapter, whether or in what way they connect with reality, that is, with the rest of the world in which they exist. This problem is most acute in literature, for by their very nature literary works seem to have an essential and unavoidable reference to, and concern with, reality. It is not satisfactory to put this question in a sweeping form, and meet it head on as a broad question about the relation of literature to life, or about the relative importance of "form" and "content." It must be broken down into several questions, and it is certain that their true answers are no less complicated and subtle than those I have proposed. Of course literary works cannot be understood apart from their language; of course they have social roots and fruits; of course their enjoyment requires in the reader an elaborate set of previous adjustments in belief and feeling; of course the themes and theses of literary works are taken from, or contributed to, the whole life of man. But what makes literature literature, in part, must be some withdrawal from the world about it, an unusual degree of self-containedness and self-sufficiency that makes it capable of being contemplated with satisfaction in itself. And the secret of this detachment seems to lie in its capacity to play with, and to swallow up in its designs, all the vast array of human experiences, including beliefs, without that personal allegiance and behavioral commitment to them that constitutes assertion in the fullest sense.

NOTES AND QUERIES

§22

22-A INTERPRETATION. On the principles of interpretation, see G. Wilson Knight, *The Wheel of Fire*, 4th ed., London: Methuen, 1954, Introduction, ch. 1; note his rejection of intention as a test (pp. 6-7, 278); Northrop Frye, "Levels of Meaning in Literature," *Kenyon Review*, XII (1950): 246-52.

For a good example of an analysis that combines explication, elucidation, and interpretation, see Allen Tate on his own "Ode to the Confederate Dead," "Narcissus as Narcissus," *On the Limits of Poetry*, New York: Swallow, 1948 (reprinted in *Man of Letters in the Modern World*, New York: Meridian, 1955, and in S. E. Hyman, ed., *The Critical Performance*, New York: Vintage, 1956, pp. 175-88). William Empson's Freudian interpretation of Alice, "Alice in Wonderland: The Child as Swain," in *Some Versions of Pastoral*, London: Chatto and Windus, 1930 (reprinted in Hyman, ed., *op. cit.*, pp. 115-50), is also instructive. See also references in Chapter III, Note 10-A; Chapter V, Note 15-C; and Note 22-B below.

In this connection consider Kenneth Burke's conception of literature as "symbolic action," *The Philosophy of Literary Form*, Baton Rouge, La.: Louisiana State U., 1941, esp. pp. 1-39, 66-89, 90-102, 119-32; *A Grammar of Motives*, Englewood Cliffs, N.J.: Prentice-Hall, 1945, esp. the essay, "Symbolic Action in a Poem by Keats" (reprinted in Hyman, *op. cit.*, and in Ray B. West, Jr., ed., *Essays in Modern Literary Criticism*, New York: Rinehart, 1952), pp. 396-411; and *Attitudes Toward History*, New York: New Republic, 1937, II: 17-44. "We think of poetry (I here use the term to include any work of critical or imaginative cast) as the adopting of various strategies for the encompassing of situations" (*Literary Form*, p. 1); the poem is a "symbolic act," the "meaning" of which can be interpreted, as, for example, the practice of shaking hands after a game says in effect: *"There are* no hard feelings" or *"Let there be* no hard feelings . . ." (*ibid.*, p. 447). With the aid of these concepts, and a number of derivative ones, Burke has thrown much light on certain literary works, in a mixture of explication, elucidation, and interpretation. However, he mainly conceives of the *writing* of the poem as the symbolic action of the *poet* ("A poem is an act, the symbolic act of the poet who made it," he says near the beginning of the essay on Keats), rather than of the movement of thought and feeling in the poem as the symbolic action of the speaker. Thus he makes no distinction, in the end, between writer and speaker, and though he says (*ibid.*, pp. 25, 73) that to "appreciate" the poem it is not necessary to study the author's biography, he treats statements about the meaning of the poem as perfectly continuous with statements about the poet's motives, about "what the poem is doing for the poet" (*ibid.*, p. 73). Hence his interpretations tend to broaden indefinitely into author psychology, history, and sociology. Keats' poem, for example, turns out to be about various nineteenth century conflicts, science vs. religion, capitalist individualism vs. socialism, etc. He also has a taste for far-fetched Freudian "readings": Bentham's proposals for a rigorous philosophical vocabulary are a self-inflicted "symbolic castration" (*Grammar*, pp. 284-85); Hume's skepticism about causality is a bachelor's unconscious "questioning of potency and progeny" (*ibid.*, p. 183). These statements are certainly neither explication nor elucidation nor interpretation; if they are anything at all, they are (highly speculative and quite unverified) causal explanation. It is characteristic of Burke's method not to observe any of these distinctions.

22-B SYMBOLS IN LITERATURE. References on symbolism in general are given above in Chapter VI, Note 16-H. The references given below chiefly concern literary symbols.

Wilbur M. Urban, *Language and Reality*, London: Allen and Unwin, 1939, ch. 9 and pp. 466-76, 487-92, analyzes the concept of symbol, and discusses in some detail the problems of interpreting symbols.

Charles Feidelson, Jr., *Symbolism and American Literature*, Chicago: 1953, ch. 2, regards what he calls the "philosophy of symbolism" as in some way an escape from Cartesian dualism, and other unfortunate things (p. 50). He contrasts "logical language" and "symbolic language" (p. 57), but by no means acceptably; such terms as "the principle of discreteness" and "atomistic," which are applied to logical language, are quite confused: for example, how can a symbolic language erase the distinction between the speaker, his words, and the object he is speaking about? and if it is atomistic of a language to mark distinctions, like that between horse and nonhorse, then how can a symbol mean anything without being atomistic?

William Y. Tindall, "The Literary Symbol," *Symbols and Society*, 14th Symposium of the Conference on Science, Philosophy and Religion, New York: Harper, 1955, ch. 11, which later became ch. 1 of his book *The Literary Symbol*, New York: Columbia U., 1955, gives some good examples; but his treatment is somewhat superficial, and his definition of "symbol" too broad to be very useful.

The transformation of metaphor into symbol by recurrence is discussed by René Wellek and Austin Warren, *Theory of Literature*, New York: Harcourt, Brace, 1949, pp. 193-95; cf. E. K. Brown, *Rhythm in the Novel*, Toronto: U. of Toronto, 1950, ch. 2. Mark Schorer, "Fiction and the 'Matrix of Analogy,'" *Kenyon Review*, XI (1949): 539-60, reprinted in J. W. Aldridge, *Critiques and Essays on Modern Fiction*, New York: Ronald, 1952, pp. 83-98, has analyzed the commercial metaphors in Jane Austen's *Persuasion*, and recurrent metaphors in other novels, and shown how they contribute to the unity of the work. See Robert B. Heilman, *This Great Stage*, Baton Rouge, La.: Louisiana State U., 1948, ch. 1, esp. pp. 6-19; note how he connects "thematic import" and "symbolic value." His view of symbolism, and also of *King Lear*, is criticized by W. K. Keast, "The 'New Criticism' and *King Lear*," in *Critics and Criticism*, by R. S. Crane et al., Chicago: U. of Chicago, 1952, esp. pp. 119-23, 136; see also Elder Olsen's "Dialogue on Symbolism," pp. 567-94. Heilman's method of interpretation is similar to that used by Cleanth Brooks in his essay on *Macbeth*, "The Naked Babe and the Cloak of Manliness," *The Well Wrought Urn*, New York: Reynal and Hitchcock, 1947, ch. 2. Kenneth Burke, "Fact, Inference, and Proof in the Analysis of Literary Symbolism," *Symbols and Values: An Initial Study*, 13th Symposium of the Conference on Science, Philosophy and Religion, New York: Harper, 1954, ch. 19, has proposed, and illustrated, a method of "indexing" the key terms of a literary work to reveal the underlying pattern of recurrent images. The method used by Robert Penn Warren in his symbolic interpretation of *The Rime of the Ancient Mariner*, "A Poem of Pure Imagination: An Experiment in Reading," in Samuel Taylor Coleridge, *The Rime of the Ancient Mariner*, New York: Reynal and Hitchcock, 1946, pp. 61-148, is extremely loose. J. Livingston Lowes apparently held that the poem has no thesis, but has a theme—the necessity of absolution after transgression. Griggs, as Warren understands him (pp. 62-65), held that the poem has neither. Warren himself says it has both: it "does make a statement" (p. 63). Of the two themes Warren finds in it, the primary one (the "sacramental vision") is clear; the secondary one, which has to do with the "imagination," requires a good deal of forcing and fanciful interpretation. Warren's method is criticized by Elder Olsen, "A Symbolic Reading of the Ancient Mariner," *Critics and Criticism*, pp. 138-44, and by Elmer E. Stoll, "Symbolism in Coleridge," *PMLA*, LXIII (1948): 214-33.

See also W. K. Wimsatt, Jr., "Two Meanings of Symbolism: A Grammatical Exercise," *Catholic Renascence*, VIII (1955): 12-25; Northrop Frye, "Three Meanings of Symbolism," *Symbol and Symbolism: Yale French Studies*, No. 9 (n.d.): 11-19. Norman Friedman, "Imagery: From Sensation to Symbol," *JAAC*, XII (September 1953): 25-37. See also references under "Imagery," Chapter III, Note 10-E.

A good test case for any principles of symbolic interpretation is the White Whale in *Moby Dick*, which has, in recent years especially, been given a number of interpretations; see, for example, Feidelson, *op. cit.*, pp. 174-86; Tindall, *op. cit.*, pp. 351-55; W. H. Auden, *The Enchafèd Flood*, London: Faber and Faber, 1951, pp. 61-66, 115-44; D. H. Lawrence, *Studies in Classic American Literature*, New York: Seltzer, 1923, ch. 11; James Baird, *Ishmael*, Baltimore: Johns Hopkins, 1956, ch. 11.

22-C "ARCHETYPAL IMAGES." The theory that there are universal symbols or symbolic situations that play a powerful role in all great literature was set forth by Carl Jung, "On the Relation of Analytical Psychology to Poetic Art," in *Contributions to Analytical Psychology*, trans. by H. G. and C. F. Baynes, London: Routledge and Kegan Paul, 1928, pp. 157-61, 240-49. These "primordial images" are the "psychic residua of numberless experiences" in the "Collective Unconscious." The theory has been employed by Maud Bodkin, *Archetypal Patterns in Poetry*, New York: Oxford U., 1934, ch. 1, and by Northrop Frye, "The Archetypes of Literature," *Kenyon Review*, XIII (1951): 92-110. See also John Press, *The Fire and the Fountain*, New York: Oxford U., 1955, ch. 6; C. Day Lewis, *The Poetic Image*, New York: Oxford U., 1947, ch. 6; Joseph Campbell, *The Hero with a Thousand Faces*, New York: Meridian, 1956, ch. 1, who seems to hold that *all* plots are, symbolically, one.

22-D THE REVELATION THEORY OF LITERATURE. On the Revelation Theory of art in general, see Chapter VIII, Notes 21-A, 21-C, and 21-D; also Meyer H. Abrams, *The Mirror and the Lamp*, New York: Oxford U., 1953, ch. 2. The various statements of Gilbert Murray, *The Classical Tradition in Poetry*, Cambridge, Mass.: Harvard U., 1927, ch. 9, are difficult to reconcile into a coherent position, but he seems to have a Revelation Theory.

On the view that literature reveals universals, and that this is one of its special offices, see W. K. Wimsatt, Jr., *The Prose Style of Samuel Johnson*, New Haven, Conn.: Yale U., 1941, ch. 6 and footnotes, and his essay "The Structure of the 'Concrete Universal' in Literature," *PMLA*, LXII (1947): 262-80, reprinted in W. K. Wimsatt, Jr., *The Verbal Icon*, Lexington, Ky.: U. of Kentucky, 1954, pp. 69-83, and in Mark Schorer, Josephine Miles and Gordon McKenzie, eds., *Criticism*, New York: Harcourt, Brace, 1948, pp. 393-403; cf. the critical discussion of this paper by John Crowe Ransom, *Kenyon Review*, XVI (1954): 554-64; XVII (1955): 383-407.

John Hospers' view that literary works are "true-to" human nature is presented in *Meaning and Truth in the Arts*, Chapel Hill, N.C.: U. of North Carolina, 1946, pp. 162-83, and he has developed this view in a later, and as yet unpublished, paper. See Abrams, *op. cit.*, ch. 10.

On the view that literature gives the "felt qualities" of experience, see Max Eastman, *The Literary Mind*, New York: Scribner's 1931, Part IV, ch. 1. Walter Pater, in his essay on style, in Lane Cooper, ed., *Theories of*

Style, New York: Macmillan, 1907, pp. 390-91, contrasts "fact" with "sense of fact"; he holds that literature presents the latter.

22-E "PURE" POETRY.   The theory that poetry ought to be "pure" presupposes that it *can* be "pure," but the sense of "purity" involved has seldom been very clear. Sometimes theorists and poets have talked as though pure poetry would be pleasant sound without meaning; sometimes it means imagery without "ideas," meaning without any central theme (Imagist poetry is often poetry with imagery and presentational sound-equivalents, but no central theme); sometimes it means thematic poetry without "ideas," meaning without any thesis, or predications. See Robert Penn Warren, "Pure and Impure Poetry," *Kenyon Review,* XV (1943): 228-54 (reprinted in Schorer, Miles and McKenzie, *op. cit.,* pp. 366-78, in Robert W. Stallman, ed., *Critiques and Essays in Criticism,* New York: Ronald, 1949, pp. 85-104, and in Ray B. West, ed., *Modern Literary Criticism,* New York: Rinehart, 1952, pp. 246-66); John Crowe Ransom, "Poetry: A Note on Ontology," *The World's Body,* New York: Scribner's, 1938, reprinted in Stallman, *op. cit.,* pp. 30-46; Max Eastman, *op. cit.,* Part III, ch. 2. For a general defense of one form of Imagism, see Ezra Pound, "Vorticism," *Fortnightly Review,* CII (September 1, 1914): 461-71. Pound's own most famous example of pure poetry, "In a Station of the Metro" ("The apparition of these faces in the crowd: / Petals on a wet, black bough"[1]) is commented on diversely by T. Hanzo, *Explicator,* XI, *26* (February 1953), and J. Espey, *ibid.,* XI, *59* (June 1953).

22-F FICTIONAL SENTENCES.   The logical problems encountered in considering the acceptability of the three theories of fictional sentences may be sorted out as follows:

(I) *The Possibility Theory.* Willard V. Quine, *Methods of Logic,* New York: Holt, 1950, pp. 200-02, has said all that really needs to be said about the proposition, "Cerberus does not exist in the world of modern science, but he exists in the world of Greek mythology," and has pointed out succinctly the inconveniences as well as the superfluousness of admitting different senses of the term "exist" (or "modes of existence").

(II) *The Falsity Theory.* Russell's theory of descriptions is set forth in an early paper, "On Denoting," *Mind,* N.S., XIV (1905): 479-93, reprinted in *Logic and Knowledge,* New York: Macmillan, 1956, and in H. Feigl and W. Sellars, *Readings in Philosophical Analysis,* New York: Appleton-Century-Crofts, 1949, pp. 103-15. See also W. V. Quine, *op. cit.,* pp. 196-208, 215-24, and his paper "On What There Is," *Review of Metaphysics,* II (September 1948): 21-38, reprinted in *From a Logical Point of View,* Cambridge, Mass.: Harvard U., 1953, pp. 1-19. Russell discusses the question whether proper names can be regarded as abbreviations for

---

[1] From "In a Station of the Metro," Ezra Pound, *Personae.* Copyright 1926 by Ezra Pound. Reprinted by permission of New Directions.

definite descriptions in *Human Knowledge,* New York: Simon and Schuster, 1948, Part II, ch. 3, where he also says that a proper name is "meaningless" unless there is an object that it names. The Falsity Theory is endorsed by A. J. Ayer, *Language, Truth and Logic,* 2nd ed., London: Gollancz, 1946, pp. 44-45.

(III) *The Nonpredication Theory.* P. F. Strawson's analysis of fictional sentences was first proposed in "On Referring," *Mind,* LIX (1950): 320-44; see also his *Introduction to Logical Theory,* London: Methuen, 1952, pp. 18, 68-69, 184-92. My account of the theory in this chapter has simplified Strawson's view in one respect. "When we begin a sentence with 'the such-and-such,'" he says ("On Referring," p. 331), this "shows, but does not state, that we are, or intend to be, referring to one particular individual of the species 'such-and-such.'" In other words, the condition that must be satisfied for "The Prime Minister of the United States is a Republican" to have truth-value is not merely that there must be one and only one Prime Minister of the United States, but that the person who utters this sentence must intend by it to refer to a particular person. I want to say that the sentence has truth-value quite independently of any intentions or wishes if the unique referent exists, and does not if it doesn't. And this is borne out by the practice of the courts, for it is possible for a person to libel another unintentionally. Thus if you write a novel about a bookie who lives at 1329 West Eighty-ninth Street, Manhattan, and has the telephone number BO 7-3927, and it turns out by chance that there is such a person with that address and number, you have referred to that person, whether you meant to or not, and your story becomes false. That is one reason why the telephone companies set aside guaranteed fictional numbers that they will supply to authors on request. A certain publicity campaign for the *Topper* movie series put on by the Hal Roach studios in the 1940's involved sending out torrid letters on scented pink stationery to several hundred men selected at random; they were signed "Marion Kerby," the name of the female ghost in the movies and in the original story by Thorne Smith. It happened that there lived in the Los Angeles area a woman named Marion Kerby, who sued the studio on the ground that her privacy had been invaded and her reputation damaged; and, according to *The Reporter* of June 30, 1955, she won her case when "the judge held that the letters did refer to her in a clear and definite fashion."

Strawson's view is supported by H. L. A. Hart, "A Logician's Fairy Tale," *Phil R,* LX (1951): 198-212. It is also close to that of Gottlieb Frege, "On Sense and Nominatum" (for references see footnote 4 above, p. 123). Consider the sentence, "After the wedding, the guests ate lobster" (call it S_1). In Frege's view, S_1 does not have "There was a wedding" (S_2) as part of its "sense" (i.e., does not entail it), but does presuppose it, in the sense that unless S_2 is true, S_1 has no "nominatum," or referent.

Wilfred Sellars, "Presupposing," *Phil R,* LXIII (1954): 197-215, criticizes Strawson's view, and proposes a subtle alternative based on the dis-

tinction that while the sentences in fiction are false—he accepts Russell's
Theory of Descriptions and therefore holds the Falsity Theory of fictional
statements—it is "incorrect" to *say* that they are false, because the statement "That is false" is appropriate only to contexts in which someone is
making an assertion. But see Strawson's "Reply to Mr. Sellars," *ibid.*, pp.
216-31, in which Strawson clarifies and qualifies his own view somewhat.

The Nonpredication Theory seems also to be like that held, for differ-
ent reasons, by Karl Britton, *Communication,* London: Routledge and
Kegan Paul, 1939, ch. 10. See also the interesting symposium by Gilbert
Ryle, R. B. Braithwaite, and G. E. Moore, "Imaginary Objects," *PAS,*
Suppl. vol. XII (1933): 18-70.

22-G   IMPLICIT REFLECTIVE PREDICATIONS.   Those who hold the Proposition Theory of music and painting (for references see Chapter VIII,
Note 20-B) also hold the view that some literary works, if not all, contain
implicit Reflective predications. No one seems to have maintained the
position that there are implicit Reflective predications in literature but no
propositions in the nonverbal arts.

Part, though not all, of what Morris Weitz means when he argues that
literary works contain "truth-claims" is that they contain predications; see
his *Philosophy of the Arts,* Cambridge, Mass.: Harvard U., 1950, ch. 8,
reprinted in Eliseo Vivas and Murray Krieger, eds., *Problems of Aesthetics,* New York: Rinehart, 1953, pp. 590-604; this is based upon an
earlier article, "Does Art Tell the Truth?" *Phil and Phen Res,* III (March
1943): 338-48, which Raymond Hoekstra criticized in "Art and Truth: in
Reply to Mr. Weitz," *ibid.,* V (March 1945): 365-78, to which Weitz replied in "The Logic of Art: A Rejoinder to Dr. Hoekstra," *ibid.,* V (March
1945): 378-84. Weitz's position is that the "second-level meanings" (or
"depth-meanings") are "referential," and are "implied" by the "first-level
meanings," which are "emotive." "Imply" seems to mean here what I have
called "suggest"; but Weitz's analysis of the "depth-meanings" (implicit
Reflections) of Richard Wright's *Native Son* seems to show that the "first-
level meanings" (explicit Reports) cannot be merely emotive, or they
could not suggest the Reflections.

I. A. Richards' "pseudo-statement" theory (for references see above
Chapter III, Note 9-B) seems in part to be a denial that literary works
contain implicit Reflective predications; some of the difficulties in his account are discussed by Manuel Bilsky, "I. A. Richards on Belief," *Phil
and Phen Res,* XII (September 1951): 105-15.

Some problems about ideas in literature are reviewed by Wellek and
Warren, *op. cit.,* ch. 10.

22-H   POETRY AND MYTH.   Another view that has attracted some attention in recent years is that the cognitive aspects of poetry are clarified
by comparison with myth. The theory is, variously, that the way in which

great literature is the vehicle of ideas is like the way in which a culture's general view of the universe, or its religion, is embodied in its myths; that poetry somehow grows out of a primitive way of thinking and understanding, which is most clearly and directly seen in the surviving myths. This view has been effectually championed by Ernst Cassirer; see, for example, *Language and Myth,* trans. by Susanne Langer, New York: Harper, 1946, ch. 6, which argues that there was a primitive "metaphorical thinking" reflected in "radical metaphor" and connected with the "self-revelation" of the mind in poetry. Cassirer's theory has been modified and extended by Susanne Langer, *Philosophy in a New Key,* Cambridge, Mass.: Harvard U., 1942 (reprinted New York: Mentor, 1948), chs. 6, 7: myth is a "non-discursive symbolism"; "The highest development of which myth is capable is the exhibition of human life and cosmic order that epic poetry reveals" (Mentor ed., pp. 163-64).

The various views of myth, and the evidence for them, are excellently scrutinized by David Bidney, *Theoretical Anthropology,* New York: Columbia U., 1953, ch. 10, who argues that "poetry, myth, and religious belief are not to be reduced to, or identified with, one another" (p. 313). Richard Chase, *Quest for Myth,* Baton Rouge, La.: Louisiana State U., 1949, gives a good historical account, but he does not give a convincing defense, or even a really clear formulation, of his main thesis, which is apparently that "myth is literature" (p. vi) and literary works—all or some? —embody myths.

22-I TRAGEDY. There are numerous puzzles connected with this term; certain principles are helpful in threading a way through them. We can try to collect all plays and fiction that have been called "tragedy" by their writers or other people, and ask what, if anything important, they have in common, or whether they fall into certain large classes marked by notable differences, e.g., Greek tragedy and Elizabethan tragedy. We can ask whether it is possible to isolate and describe a certain special regional quality that some sequences of events possess and others don't—treating "tragic" as the name of this quality, not as the name of an emotion *caused* by events having that quality—and inquire (a) whether there is some general agreement on restricting the word "tragic" to this quality, and (b) whether those who use the word more loosely can be persuaded to adopt this usage. For example, we may say that a mere sequence of misfortune is not tragic unless the characters are somehow admirable and they struggle against their doom. If we consider traditional "theories" of tragedy (Hegel, Nietzsche, Schopenhauer, for example, and especially Aristotle's analysis of tragic characters and situations in the *Poetics*) as attempts to discover what features of the world of a literary work tend to give its plot a tragic quality, they become empirical and testable; though no doubt this was not all, or in some cases even primarily, what those thinkers had in mind.

For some contemporary discussions of tragedy, see Susanne Langer, *Feeling and Form,* New York: Scribner's, 1953, chs. 17, 19; Paul Goodman, *The Structure of Literature,* Chicago: U. of Chicago, 1954, ch. 2; Gilbert Murray, *The Classical Tradition in Poetry,* Cambridge, Mass.: Harvard U., 1927, ch. 3; Lascelles Abercrombie, *The Theory of Poetry,* London: Secker, 1924, Part II, ch. 4; Francis Fergusson, *The Idea of a Theatre,* Princeton, N.J.: Princeton U., 1949 (reprinted Garden City, N.Y.: Anchor, 1953), ch. 1 (largely reprinted in Hyman, *op. cit.,* pp. 317-37) and Appendix; Allardyce Nicoll, *The Theory of Drama,* New York: Crowell, 1931, ch. 2 and pp. 84-102; T. R. Henn, *The Harvest of Tragedy,* London: Methuen, 1956 (the argument of which is summarized in ch. 2); Una Ellis-Fermor, *The Frontiers of Drama,* 3rd ed., London: Methuen, 1948, ch. 7.

One of the recurrent disputes about tragedy is about the possibility of writing tragedy in the twentieth century. This dispute sometimes becomes verbal, but it involves empirical issues. Joseph W. Krutch, *The Modern Temper,* New York: Harcourt, Brace, 1929, ch. 5, has argued that tragedy, strictly speaking, is impossible in an age of "naturalism," which he takes to involve the denial of the uniqueness and potential nobility of man; the word "tragedy" is a misnomer when applied to Ibsen, Strindberg, or modern American plays such as Eugene O'Neill's *Mourning Becomes Electra,* Arthur Miller's *Death of a Salesman,* Tennessee Williams' *Glass Menagerie;* their "sense of depression" (p. 118) is said to be opposed to the spiritual elation of Shakespeare and Aeschylus. The same view is further developed by A. R. Thompson, "The Dilemma of Modern Tragedy," in Norman Foerster, ed., *Humanism and America,* New York: Farrar and Rinehart, 1930 (see also Robert Shafer, "An American Tragedy," in the same vol.), who argues that philosophic naturalism, psychological determinism, and democratic egalitarianism have undermined the drama and transformed tragic exaltation into pessimism and despair. R. P. Blackmur, "The Discipline of Humanism," in C. H. Grattan, ed., *The Critique of Humanism,* New York: Brewer and Warren, 1930, replies to Thompson and Shafer. There is a good deal of meat in Arthur Miller's very interesting defense of Willy Loman as a tragic hero in his Introduction to his *Collected Plays,* New York: Viking, 1957, pp. 27-36.

22-J COMEDY. There are many interesting questions about the nature of comedy, or of humor, but it is not easy to sort them out. The question "What makes us laugh?" must, for example, be distinguished from the question "Is there a distinct regional quality of literature that can be identified as the comic or the humorous?" and from the question "What are the perceptual conditions of this quality, if it exists?" D. H. Monro, *Argument of Laughter,* Cambridge, Eng.: Melbourne U., 1951, gives an excellent systematic survey and critical discussion of the main theories of the comic, both explanations of laughter and generalizations about the perceptual conditions of the comic quality, which he divides into four main types. James Feibleman's *In Praise of Comedy,* London: Allen and Unwin, 1939, is another useful general work. A review of psychological investigations, with a good bibliography, is given by J. C. Flugel, "Humor and Laughter," in Gardner Lindzey, ed., *Handbook of Social Psychology,* Cambridge, Mass.: Addison-Wesley, 1954, Vol. II, pp. 709-34. See also Bergson, *Laughter,* trans. by C. Brereton and F. Rothwell, New York: Macmillan, 1911; Max Eastman, *The Sense of Humor,* New York: Scribner's, 1921; Max Eastman, *Enjoyment of Laughter,* New York: Simon and Schuster, 1936; Susanne Langer, *op. cit.,* ch. 3; Ernst Kris, *Psychoanalytic Explorations in Art,* New York: International Universities, 1952, ch. 4; Albert Rapp, *The Origins of Wit and Humor,* New York: Dutton, 1951.

§23

23-A THE NATURE OF FICTION. (I) That the distinction between fiction and nonfiction lies in the reader's attitude is well argued by Arnold Isenberg, "The Esthetic Function of Language," *J Phil,* XLVI (1949): 5-20; many of his important points are, however, compatible with an objective distinction.

For a good general discussion see the symposium by Margaret Macdonald and Michael Scriven, "The Language of Fiction," *PAS,* Suppl. vol. XXVIII (1954): 165-96.

P. T. Geach in a symposium "On What There Is," *PAS,* Suppl. vol. XXV (1950): esp. 127 (see also reply by W. V. Quine, pp. 153-54), distinguishes two "uses" of general words, as subjects and predicates. To say, "A dog was chasing my cat," is to use "dog" as a subject, "standing for" a dog; whence we can ask, "Which dog?" To say, "Spot is a dog," is to use "dog" as a predicate; we cannot ask, "Which dog?" Thus, he concludes, to say "Pegasus is not real like Iolo" is to state a difference between two ways of using proper nouns: "Iolo" is used for "naming"; "Pegasus" is used "just for telling a story." But "telling a story" is left unanalyzed; moreover, words like "dog" are used as subjects (in his sense) in fiction, as well as predicates; how can they then not be used to name?

(II) Assertion. The view that literary works are not assertive is well argued by Kingsley Blake Price, "Is the Work of Art a Symbol?," *J Phil,* L (1953): 485-503, esp. 491-96; I am not sure, however, that he is quite right when he says, "The context in which we read a book affords no way of behaving toward it which constitutes an assertive use of it" (p. 491), for if someone were led by *The Sun Also Rises* to believe that the post World War I generation was disillusioned, this would apparently constitute an assertive use in Price's sense.

Gilbert Ryle's suggestion, " 'If,' 'So,' and 'Because,' " in Max Black, ed., *Philosophical Analysis,* Ithaca, N.Y.: Cornell U., 1950, pp. 323-40, that in fiction we neither *use* nor *mention,* but pretend to use, language, is not worked out far, but by implication it seems to be the Nonassertion Theory.

C. S. Lewis points out some respects in which a poem is independent of a pragmatic context, *The Personal Heresy*, New York: Oxford U., 1939, pp. 115-16.

See Sir Philip Sidney's often-quoted remark in the *Defence of Poesie*, 1594, "Now, for the Poet, he nothing affirms, and therefore never lyeth." Plato's dialogue *Ion* might be taken as an early, and ironic, statement of the Nonassertion Theory; Socrates' final question of the rhapsode, "Which do you prefer to be thought, dishonest or inspired?" is like saying, "Either you are lying, or you are making no assertions at all (far from having the knowledge you claim)," and Ion, like Sidney, chooses the latter alternative.

The Nonassertion Theory brings fiction fairly close to that curious little formula that philosophers have so often discussed since it was first called to their attention by G. E. Moore: "*P*, but I don't believe *P*," e.g., "The sun is shining, but I don't believe it." In an interesting discussion of this type of sentence, Max Black, "Saying and Disbelieving," *Analysis*, XIII (December 1952): 25-33, has argued that such sentences have no use at all, and make no assertion. Like the sentence, "I am two feet tall," which there is no one who can truly utter, the sentence, "The sun is shining, but I don't believe it," while not self-contradictory, is, he says, a misuse of language. It perhaps does not matter whether telling stories is called a "fictional use" of language or denied to be a use at all; in any case, there is a close analogy.

"Once upon a time, kiddies," we might say, "I was captured by cannibals and eaten up by them—"

Interruption by kiddies: "Is that *really* true, Daddy?"

"No, of course not; but after they had eaten me up, they all sat in a circle—"

Morris Weitz has argued that the implicit Reflections in literature are asserted; in *Native Son*, Wright is "claiming that the only freedom left to man is the freedom to destroy, first others and finally oneself"; but the conditions of assertion are not analyzed. For references, see above Note 22-G. His view is also explained, with good examples from Proust, in "Truth in Literature," *Revue Internationale de Philosophie*, IX (1955): 1-14, in which he still uses the term "truth-claim," and does not distinguish the two questions about literature: whether it contains predications, whether it contains assertions.

23-B THE DIDACTIC THEORY OF LITERATURE. I take Plato in the *Phaedrus* to be maintaining a Didactic Theory, because of Socrates' claim that though a fair speech can be made in defense of a false thesis, the greatest speech will be that which defends a true one. The general view that setting forth a notable truth is a necessary condition for greatness in literature has been maintained by a succession of critics (including most Intuitionists; see Note 23-F); and I shall not try to document the history of the view here; for references see W. K. Wimsatt, Jr., and Cleanth Brooks, *Literary Criticism: A Short History*, New York: Knopf, 1957, *passim*. See especially Johnson's Preface to Shakespeare, and Matthew Arnold's essay on Wordsworth, *Essays in Criticism*, Second Series, New York: Macmillan, 1889. For a modern statement of the view, see C. S. Lewis, who holds "that every poem whose prosaic or intellectual basis is silly, shallow, perverse, or illiberal, or even radically erroneous, is in some degree crippled by that fact" (*Rehabilitations*, London, New York: Oxford U., 1939, pp. 26-27). See also W. T. Stace, *The Meaning of Beauty*, London: Richards and Toulmin, 1929, chs. 2, 10. The concept of greatness in literature is discussed by T. M. Greene, *The Arts and the Art of Criticism*, Princeton, N.J.: Princeton U., 1940, ch. 24; and David Daiches, *The Place of Meaning in Poetry*, Edinburgh, London: Oliver and Boyd, 1935, pp. 33-41; J. W. R. Purser, *Art and Truth*, Glasgow, Scot.: Jackson, 1937, ch. 17.

The Didactic Theory is criticized by T. S. Eliot, "Shakespeare and the Stoicism of Seneca," *Selected Essays*, New York: Harcourt, Brace, 1950; Max Eastman, *The Literary Mind*, New York: Scribner's, 1931, Part III, ch. 4.

23-C CRITERIA OF AVAILABILITY. A number of literary theorists and critics have suggested criteria for distinguishing between false beliefs that can, and false beliefs that cannot, become theses of good literary works. Some of them do not seem very applicable; others are difficult, if not impossible, to relate to the literary value of the literary work; still others seem, on analysis, to make a covert reference back to truth or falsity—for example, to say that a certain false philosophy is "reasonable" *may* mean that it is not wholly false.

Karl Shapiro, *Essay on Rime*, New York: Reynal and Hitchcock, 1945, p. 62, says that the doctrine in the poem must be "given in good faith"; his criterion is evidently sincerity. Eliot uses the same criterion in his famous remarks about how he would react if he learned that *On the Nature of Things* had been written by Dante as "a Latin exercise" (see his note to his essay "Dante," *Selected Essays*, pp. 229-31).

Eliot elsewhere, in his essay on "Shelley and Keats," *The Use of Poetry and the Use of Criticism*, Cambridge, Mass.: Harvard U., 1933, says that a philosophy like Shelley's cannot be the thesis of good poetry because it is not coherent, or "founded on the facts of experience," or "mature"; rather, it is "childish," "feeble," "puerile." The concept of maturity is also discussed by W. K. Wimsatt, Jr., in "The Structure of the 'Concrete Universal' in Literature," *PMLA*, LXII (1947): 262-80: there are complex and interesting vices as well as shallow ones; there are Shakespeare's Antony and the young man of Tennyson's "Locksley Hall."

David Daiches, *A Study of Literature,* Ithaca, N.Y.: Cornell U., 1948, ch. 9, rules out those doctrines that are "so narrow or corrupting or so at variance with anything that civilized man can tolerate that it becomes impossible to regard them as merely part of [the writer's] technique" (p. 220), and he insists that there is an important distinction between a false view and a "corrupt" one (p. 221).

Some connections between the doctrine of a poem and its other features are illustrated in Allen Tate, "Hardy's Philosophic Metaphors," *Reason in Madness,* New York: Putnam, 1941, reprinted in Mark Schorer, Josephine Miles and Gordon McKenzie, eds., *Criticism,* New York: Harcourt, Brace, 1948, pp. 182-87; and Delmore Schwartz, "Poetry and Belief in Thomas Hardy," in Robert W. Stallman, ed., *Critiques and Essays in Criticism,* New York: Ronald, 1949, pp. 334-45.

A stimulating collection of quotations illustrating the above distinctions, and others, is to be found in Robert W. Stallman, ed., *The Critic's Notebook,* Minneapolis, Minn.: U. of Minnesota, 1950, ch. 7.

A test case for theories about belief in literature, and its bearing upon literary value, is the award of the Bollingen Poetry Prize to Ezra Pound in 1948, while he was still in prison for his broadcasts in Italy during the war, but not considered mentally fit to be tried. This award churned up a lively discussion among critics about the fascism of Pound and of his *Cantos,* and in this discussion the whole spectrum of possible views came to be expressed. See Robert Hillyer, "Treason's Strange Fruit," *Saturday Review,* June 11, 1949; William Barrett, "A Prize for Ezra Pound," *Partisan Review,* XVI (1949): 344-47, and comments by a number of critics later in the year, pp. 512-22, 666-72; James Blish, "Rituals on Ezra Pound," *Sewanee Review,* LVIII (1950): 185-226; Archibald MacLeish, *Poetry and Opinion,* Urbana, Ill.: U. of Illinois, 1950.

23-D THE READER'S BELIEFS. A number of startling or suggestive remarks are usually invoked in discussions on this subject. For example: Richards' reference in *Science and Poetry* (see Chapter III, Note 9-B), to T. S. Eliot's *Waste Land* as "effecting a complete severance between his poetry and *all* beliefs"; Coleridge's phrase, "that willing suspension of disbelief for the moment, which constitutes poetic faith" (*Biographia Literaria,* ed. by J. Shawcross, Oxford: Clarendon, 1907, Bk. II, ch. 14, p. 6; cf. pp. 186-89 on *Don Juan*).

Arnold Isenberg, "The Problem of Belief," *JAAC* (March 1955): 395-407, contributes toward a clarification of a number of the problems involved; cf. H. D. Aiken, "Some Notes Concerning the Aesthetic and the Cognitive," *ibid.:* 378-94; Alexander Sesonske, "Truth in Art," *J Phil,* LIII (1956): 345-54. For some interesting remarks on the nature of belief in relation to fairy tales, see J. R. R. Tolkien, "On Fairy-Stories," *Essays Presented to Charles Williams,* New York: Oxford U., 1947, esp. pp. 62-63.

See also W. H. Auden, "The Public v. the Late Mr. William Butler

Yeats," in Schorer, Miles and McKenzie, *op. cit.*, pp. 168-72; I. A. Richards, *Practical Criticism*, London: Routledge and Kegan Paul, 1929, Part III, ch. 7, *Principles of Literary Criticism*, London: Routledge and Kegan Paul, 1925, chs. 33-35; M. H. Abrams, *The Mirror and the Lamp*, New York: Oxford U., 1953, pp. 320-26.

The difficulties of defining "belief" are illustrated by R. B. Braithwaite, "The Nature of Believing," *PAS*, XXXIII (1932-33): 129-46. Note the circularity of his definition of "believe": "I believe *p*" means, "I entertain *p* and I have a disposition to act as if *p* were true." But *p*'s truth doesn't give me any disposition—only my *belief* in *p*; so the second part of the definition must read, "I have a disposition to act as if I *believed p* were true." See also R. B. Braithwaite, "Belief and Action," *PAS*, Suppl. vol. XX (1946): 1-19.

If you define "meaning" in terms of its potential relevance to belief, as I did in Chapter III, or "understanding" in terms of expectation, it becomes a problem how it is possible to understand the meaning of fiction without believing it; this problem is discussed by C. H. Whiteley, "On Understanding," *Mind*, N.S., LVIII (1949): 339-51, esp. pp. 349-50. The meaning of a statement in fiction depends upon its being *capable* of being used to affect belief, but in the context of the work of fiction it is not so used.

23-E PLAUSIBILITY IN FICTION. It is often held that good fiction must have plausibility, but this concept is hard to analyze. It seems to be a kind of internal convicingness, quite distinct from verisimilitude, which is freedom from such empirical "mistakes" as making flowers bloom or birds appear in the wrong months, or giving an inaccurate description of New York, or committing anachronisms—Tiepolo put a pipe in the mouth of the Roman consul in his painting *Martyrdom of Christians under Trajan* (1745, Church of S. S. Faustinus and Giovita, Brescia). Robert T. Harris, who holds that plausibility is important, argues that it consists in internal consistency, or the "subsumption of fictional events under the laws of nature"; see "Plausibility in Fiction," *J Phil*, XLIX (1952): 5-10. These views are disputed by Paul Welsh, *Phil Rev*, LXII (1953): 102-07.

The seeming life, or living quality, of the novel must not be confused with assertion; the newspaper story is asserted, but the people have no substance, usually; this point is well made by Susanne Langer, *Feeling and Form*, New York: Scribner's, 1953, pp. 287-305.

23-F THE INTUITIONIST THEORY OF LITERATURE. For the Intuitionist Theory of knowledge in general, see Chapter VIII, Note 21-F. Certain writers, though holding an Intuitionist Theory about art in general, have made their main contribution to the theory as it applies to literature. This application has never been clearly worked out, but traces of it go far back. There are elements of the theory in Plato's *Phaedrus*, with its sug-

gestion that though the poet is mad, his madness is more divine than the
ordinary sort; in Shelley's *Defense of Poetry* (poetry "marks the before un-
apprehended relations of things"; "a poem is the very image of life expressed in its eternal truth"; but much of what he says about the contribution of poetry to the development of sympathetic understanding among
men can also be accepted by an empiricist); in Wordsworth's Preface to
the 1800 edition of the *Lyrical Ballads* ("Poetry is the breath and finer
spirit of all knowledge," but again the poet's "greater knowledge of human nature" is not necessarily intuitive).

Wilbur M. Urban, *Language and Reality*, London: Allen and Unwin,
1939, chs. 9, 10, has elaborated a view of poetry as knowledge that is on
the whole Intuitionistic, though he sometimes uses the language of the
Revelation Theory. The "insight symbol" is an "implicit assertion" whose
truth is not empirically tested, but "authenticated." Philip Wheelwright,
The Burning Fountain, Bloomington, Ind.: Indiana U., 1954, esp. chs. 4,
13 and pp. 14-16, also develops an Intuitionist Theory, less intellectualistic
than Urban's, and illustrates it by interpretations of Sophocles and Eliot.

D. G. James, *Scepticism and Poetry*, London: Allen and Unwin, 1937,
esp. chs. 2, 8, is vague and ambivalent about his theory of poetic truth,
which seems part Intuition and part Revelation. "In poetry the poet en-
deavours to convey his sense of the inner unity and quality of the object"
(p. 30; see also p. 75); poetry is "imaginative prehension" (p. 52); but the
question of truth does not arise (p. 63) and the poet makes no "assertions"
(p. 67). He criticizes Richards' views at length (ch. 2), but denies that what
poetry gives can be "called knowledge" (p. 273). There is an interesting
discussion of Keats' famous letter of November 22, 1817, to Benjamin
Bailey, which he surely misinterprets (pp. 190-94).

C. Day Lewis, *The Poetic Image*, New York: Oxford U., 1947, ch. 1,
speaks of a "poetic truth," "unverifiable" but "operative," that equals a
"sense of the furtherance of life" (pp. 26-27); in so far as it is intelligible,
his view seems to be a form of Intuitionism. Philip Leon, "Aesthetic
Knowledge," *PAS*, XXV (1925): 199-208, reprinted in Eliseo Vivas and
Murray Krieger, eds., *Problems of Aesthetics*, New York: Rinehart, 1953,
pp. 619-25, could be an Intuitionist, but his description of knowledge
hardly makes it seem like knowledge at all. See also H. D. Lewis, "On
Poetic Truth," *Philosophy*, XXI (1946): 147-66; Owen Barfield, *Poetic
Diction*, 2nd ed., London: Faber and Faber, 1952, esp. pp. 33, 55-57, 85-
88, 144; Harold March, *The Two Worlds of Marcel Proust*, Philadelphia:
U. of Pennsylvania, 1948, pp. 216-28, 246; also some peculiar remarks by
Karl Shapiro, *Beyond Criticism*, Lincoln, Neb.: U. of Nebraska, 1953, pp.
22-23.

The poets of the French Symbolist movement, especially the theorists
like Mallarmé, combined, in an incompatible mixture, a theory of pure
poetry (see Note 22-E above) with an Intuitionist theory of poetry, in
accordance with which they aimed to evoke a supernatural experience

through sensuous imagery and give insight into a world of ideal beauty. See the account by C. M. Bowra, *The Heritage of Symbolism*, New York: Macmillan, 1943, ch. 1; also Edmund Wilson, *Axel's Castle*, New York: Scribner's, 1931, ch. 1, esp. pp. 11-22.

On the relation between literature and science, see Max Eastman, *op. cit.*, Part IV, ch. 3.

23-G THE PROBLEM OF PARAPHRASE. The question whether or to what extent literary works can be paraphrased is discussed by several writers. Cleanth Brooks, *The Well Wrought Urn*, New York: Reynal and Hitchcock, 1947, ch. 11, Appendix 2, and pp. 217-18, argues against paraphrasability. Paul Henle, "The Problem of Meaning," *Proceedings and Addresses of the American Philosophical Association*, XXVII (1954): 24-39, argues that metaphor is a special way of extending a language's resources of empirical meaning, and is not literally paraphrasable. He analyzes metaphor in terms of the concept of iconic sign (see Chapter VII, Note 18-I): the modifier denotes an object that is an iconic sign of the metaphorical meaning (in "the abiding spirit of our conscript dust," the conscripted soldier becomes an iconic sign, for example, of temporary servitude).

Inclined to the other side are: Wilbur M. Urban, *op. cit.*, pp. 422-40; Ruth Herschberger, "The Structure of Metaphor," *Kenyon Review*, V (1943): 433-43; C. S. Lewis, "Bluspels and Flalansferes," in *Rehabilitations*, pp. 135-58.

According to Stephen J. Brown, *The World of Imagery*, London: Routledge and Kegan Paul, 1927, ch. 9, St. Thomas (in *Summa Theologica* 3^a pars Q. X a. 10 ad 6^m) had somewhat the same idea made use of in the text, that metaphorical sentences cannot be used in deduction; when the Scripture says, "A is X," and "X" is metaphorical, then A cannot be subsumed under "Y," as the genus of "X," by means of the major premise "All X are Y."

23-H THE CATEGORIES OF LITERARY CRITICISM. At this point, before we discuss normative statements, or value-judgments, about literary works, it may be helpful to review the distinctions already made. We have sorted out the following kinds of nonnormative critical statement about literature; the question is whether there are other nonnormative statements that critics would make about literature, for which no category is provided here.

I. Description: statements about the characteristics of the literary work in itself
   A. Statements about the sound of the work ("It is harsh," "It is in iambic pentameter")
   B. Statements about the relation between sound and meaning ("The

angry tone of the poem is carried out into the short lines and explosive syllables")

C. Statements about the meaning
   1. Statements about the elementary meanings (" 'Gale' meant 'soft breeze' in the eighteenth century")
   2. Statements about the complexes of meaning
      a. Statements about texture
         i. Particular nuclei, i.e., explication-statements (" 'Conscript dust' means that the body is ruled by the soul")
         ii. Recurrent features, i.e., statements about style ("It has a plain, simple, direct style")
      b. Statements about the subject, or world of the work
         i. Statements about the persons, objects and events in the work
            (a) Explicit ("She dies")
            (b) Implicit: elucidation-statements ("She must have had a broken heart")
         ii. Statements about the relations among the persons, objects and events: structure-statements ("It has a roving point of view," "It has three main climaxes")

II. Interpretation-statements about the reference of the work to the real world
   A. Statements about the theme of the work, or the meaning of some symbol in it ("The house becomes a symbol of frustration," "It is a story of frustration")
   B. Statements about the thesis, or doctrinal content, of the work ("It says that the world is well lost for love," "It is a pacifist novel")

• X •

CRITICAL
EVALUATION

The problems to which we now come have been put off as long as possible in the hope that a circumspect approach would make them more vulnerable. They are the problems that arise in evaluating, that is, in making normative statements about, aesthetic objects. In these last three chapters we shall inquire what, if anything, could be a good reason for asserting, or believing, critical value-judgments.

For example, the authors of an excellent book on Picasso have this to say about his epoch-making painting, *Les Demoiselles d'Avignon* (1907, Museum of Modern Art, New York):

> *The Young Ladies of Avignon,* that great canvas which has been so frequently described and interpreted, is of prime importance in the sense of being the concrete outcome of an original vision, and because it points to a radical change in the aesthetic basis as well as the technical processes of painting. In itself the work does not bear very close scrutiny, for the drawing is hasty and the colour unpleasant, while the composition as a whole is confused and there is too much concern for effect and far too much gesticulation in the figures. . . . The truth is that this famous canvas was significant for what it anticipated rather than for what it achieved.[1]

Note first that they make a distinction between two ways of considering the painting: its significance as an event in the history of painting or in the development of Picasso's style, and its value "in itself," simply as an aesthetic object. Considered in the second way, they say, it is not a very good painting, and they give the following reasons: (1) "the drawing is hasty," (2) the color is "unpleasant," (3) "the composition . . . is confused," (4) "there is too much concern for effect," (5) there is "far too much gesticulation in the figures." Point 4 is not very clear, and perhaps points 4 and 5 are really one.

Several questions about this argument might occur to us at once. First, what is the critical judgment which these reasons are supposed to support? It is put in a rather casual way: "the work does not bear very close scrutiny." We cannot tell exactly what judgment this makes, but very probably it is at least a vague comparison: Picasso was later to paint better pictures in a style that developed out of the one in this painting, e.g., *Guernica* (1937, Museum of Modern Art, New York). Second, why is a "hasty" drawing necessarily a poor drawing? If "haste" refers simply to the amount of time the draughtsman took, then are there not excellent hasty drawings by Rembrandt, Paul Klee, and Picasso himself? Or does "haste" refer, not to the act of drawing, but to some characteristic of the drawing itself? Third, why is "unpleasant" color, "confused" composition, or considerable "gesticulation in the figures" necessarily a blemish in a painting? For example, could an admirer of the painting not reply that what is so interesting in the painting—its peculiar combination of ritualistic rigidity and dramatic tension—would not be there unless the figures were in those odd and melodramatic postures? For though the authors do not rate it among Picasso's greatest work, they surely mean to concede it some value, and indeed it is hard to see how it could have great historical importance if it were not good enough to show the possibilities of such a style.

The passage raises even more ultimate questions about the purpose of criticism itself. To what good end is this judgment of Picasso's painting made? Some critics hold that their business is just to describe and interpret, and thus help us to the fullest possible acquaintance with the complexities of an aesthetic object. Others hold that they should add a brief report of the degree of their own liking or disliking, and a prediction about the probable reactions of others—"I am no angler, but people who like fishing will enjoy this book." Other critics feel called upon to rate the work in some more objective way, absolutely or comparatively. Boswell says that in the long list of works, projected but never started, that Johnson gave to his friend Langton, there was the following:

> A Table of the *Spectators, Tatlers,* and *Guardians,* distinguished by figures into six degrees of value, with notes, giving the reasons of preference or degradation.[2]

That would have been an interesting document, an example of judicial, or evaluative, criticism at its most extreme, grading aesthetic objects like

---

[1] Frank Elgar and Robert Maillard, *Picasso,* trans. by Francis Scarfe, New York: Praeger, 1956, pp. 56-58.

[2] *Life of Johnson,* Oxford Standard ed., New York: Oxford U., 1933, Vol. II, p. 619.

456 meat, tobacco, or students. Whether such a project is even in principle feasible will be one of our later questions.

The normative problems are best approached with some caution. We shall begin by taking a survey of typical reasons that critics actually give, classifying them, and subjecting them to a preliminary logical examination, to see how far the problems can be clarified and simplified before we meet them head on.

§24. REASONS AND JUDGMENTS

An argument for a critical evaluation may be compressed into the following formula:

> X is good
> bad
> better or worse than Y,
> *because* . . .

Here X is an aesthetic object of any sort, poem or play, statue or sonata, and therefore the normative words, "good," "bad," "better," and "worse" are understood to be used in an aesthetic context. What follows the word "because" is a *reason* for the judgment. It is not necessarily a conclusive reason, in the sense that by itself it would warrant the conclusion, but it claims to be a relevant reason, in the sense that its truth has some bearing, along with other reasons, upon the conclusion. What sorts of reasons do critics give?

There are two groups of reasons that can be separated from the rest, and, tentatively at least, set aside as not of concern to us here. The first group consists of reasons that refer to the cognitive aspects of the work. Thus we find that the critical formula, above, is sometimes completed in such ways as these:

> . . . it is profound.
> . . . it has something important to say.
> . . . it conveys a significant view of life.
> . . . it gives insight into a universal human problem.

These statements praise X for making a contribution to our knowledge; let us say they are reasons for attributing a *cognitive value* to X. This kind of value we have already discussed in Chapters VIII and IX.

The second group of reasons is somewhat more heterogeneous:

> . . . it is uplifting and inspiring.
> . . . it is effective social criticism.
> . . . it is morally edifying.
> . . . it promotes desirable social and political ends.
> . . . it is subversive.

These all seem to attribute—or in the last case, deny—*moral value* to X—
if we count desirable social effects as moral. In what respects an aesthetic object may be morally valuable we have not yet inquired, but we shall, in Chapter XII. Meanwhile it seems legitimate to set aside this second group of reasons, too, and from this point on confine ourselves to those reasons that are neither cognitive nor moral.

We are left with a third large group of reasons that are peculiarly aesthetic, such as the reasons given for the judgment of *Les Demoiselles d'Avignon*. And these in turn divide into three subgroups, each of which we must examine rather carefully. There are the reasons that refer to features of the aesthetic object itself: the composition is "confused"; there is "too much gesticulation." Let us call these *Objective Reasons*. There are the reasons that refer to effects of the object upon the percipient: the color is "unpleasant," that is, gives displeasure. Let us call these *Affective Reasons*. There are the reasons that refer to the causes and conditions of the object, that is, to the artist or his materials: the drawing is "hasty," if this means it was done in haste; there was (in the painter's mind?) "too much concern for effect." Let us call these *Genetic Reasons*. It will be convenient to use the word "standard" to refer to anything that is appealed to in a critical reason. Thus when a critic gives "hasty drawing" as a reason for a negative evaluation, he is assuming that careful drawing is desirable, and I shall say he is using carefulness of drawing as a standard.

We must now discuss each of the three groups of reasons, but in reverse order.

Genetic and Affective Reasons

I call a reason Genetic if it refers to something existing before the work itself, to the manner in which it was produced, or its connection with antecedent objects and psychological states:

   . . . it fulfills (or fails to fulfill) the artist's intention.
   . . . it is an example of successful (or unsuccessful) expression.
   . . . it is skillful (or shows poor workmanship).
   . . . it is new and original (or trite).
   . . . it is sincere (or insincere).

I do not propose to discuss all of these reasons here, but I want to bring out some general points about them and show how I think they might be analyzed.[3] They raise many puzzling questions, of which the chief ones have to do with the concept of intention.

"André Gide's *The Immoralist* is a perfect novel, for in it he accomplished exactly what he set out to do." Or, "The first movement of Schubert's *Second Symphony in B Flat Major* is inferior to most of Mozart's first movements for in it Schubert failed to realize his intention." Such are

---

[3] Further comments are reserved for the Notes and Queries at end of chapter.

the frequent idioms of intentionalistic evaluation. We have already, in Chapter I, §1, dealt with intention as a standard of description and interpretation, but new problems are raised by this normative role. The method of evaluation that it supports consists of two steps: (1) find what the creator intended the work to be, and (2) determine whether, or how far, the work falls short of the intention.

I want to show that these Genetic Reasons, and in particular the appeal to intention, cannot be good, that is, relevant and sound, reasons for critical evaluations. The heart of the argument against them can be summed up briefly, and it is, in my opinion, utterly conclusive. But the summary may require some supplementary comment to be convincing, for there are several disguises that the intentionalistic standard can assume, and several devices for confusing it with other, and more persuasive, standards. Essentially, however, the argument is this: (1) We can seldom know the intention with sufficient exactness, independently of the work itself, to compare the work with it and measure its success or failure. (2) Even when we can do so, the resulting judgment is not a judgment of the work, but only of the worker, which is quite a different thing.

The first point is evident. If we have no external evidence of the creator's intention, there is nothing we can compare the work with, and it cannot fail to be a complete success, however poor; or, more accurately, the words "success" and "failure" cannot strictly be applied to it. Of the intentions of Shakespeare, Vermeer, the Etruscan sculptors, the makers of the *Thousand and One Nights*, and the composers of old folk songs, we have no evidence at all outside the works they left us. If fulfillment of intention were the *only* test of value, then we could not evaluate these works at all, and we would have no way of knowing whether they are good.

But suppose we do have some external evidence; in by far the greatest number of cases, it must be much too skimpy to enable us to say with assurance that the work falls short of the intention. For notice in the first place how good the evidence would have to be. If a man tells us he is going bowling, we infer his intention, for we can assume that most bowlers have the same intention, namely to get as high a score as they can. This is a standardized task with a constant goal (namely, 300); it can be set over and over again and formulated adequately in words. So, too, an archer or a billiards player can point out his target precisely and unambiguously. But it is a far different matter for a poet to tell us in words, outside his poem, what exactly he had in mind for it to be. Moreover, a task like the bowler's is a restricted one, in the sense that it can be controlled throughout by a single intention. But the act of writing a concerto is one in which the intentions change and grow constantly; which intention, then, is it that the product is to be compared with, and how can

even an articulate composer describe that intention in words exactly
enough to make the comparison possible?

There still remains, it must be admitted, a small area within which some comparison is possible. A painter could say to us, as he selects his canvas and opens his paints, that the picture he is about to paint will be cheerful and gay, and he might fall short of this goal if he does not know how to arrange the local conditions—shapes and colors—so that they will have that regional quality. If he is a good painter, of course, he may well abandon his original aim in the middle, having hit on some other possibilities that interest him more. But it is conceivable that he should fail, and that we should discover it. Or, again, a writer could tell us that he intends one of his characters to be a figure of mystery, or of dignified sadness, or of nobility, and he may be unable to construct such characters and prevent them from falling into inconsistency or bathos. But, again, few creators have left us such specific records in their notes and memoirs. We do not know whether Schubert started out by conceiving a B flat symphony in the hope that it would be different in some important way from what it turned out to be. And if we say that it is not a success *because* it is not as good as we wish it to be, we are not saying that Schubert did intend something better, but that he ought to have done so.

The second point is quite independent of the first. If we could determine the success of Gide in fulfilling his intention—if, for example, we take his word that he was content with his novel, we are no further along toward an evaluation of that work, for the question immediately arises whether it was *worth* intending. Gide may have been satisfied, but that does not mean we must be; and, conversely, Mendelssohn was never satisfied with his *"Italian" Symphony in A Major (Op. 90)*, but many listeners are. If someone performs a hard task, like constructing a ship in a bottle, we bestow praise on him for his competence or skill, and this we can do even if we privately think he was wasting his time. When we speak of a "skillful work," this is a judgment about the producer, and is logically irrelevant to the question whether the product is good or bad. So many words unfortunately conceal this distinction: consider, for example, the word "mistake." Suppose a critic notes in a painting some casual-looking lines or peculiar distortion of figures. He wants to know whether to praise them or not, and he asks whether they were a "mistake." Now if this means, "Were they intentional? Did the painter's hand slip?" the question is whether the painter was a bungler: in short, whether *he* deserves praise. But what the critic is probably interested in is another question: whether the line or the figure can be justified by what it contributes to, or detracts from, those features of the work that are valuable and desirable; for example, without the distortion, the figure would be less spiritual or less graceful. This is a separate question, for a bungler might by chance produce a good work, and a master might deliberately and with great pains draw a line that spoils his picture. It has been said that if Blake had made his woodcuts with more skill their most valuable qualities might have been weakened.

The plausible arguments in favor of the intentionalistic method yield to attack when we bear in mind the distinction between judging the creator and judging his creation, and when we keep to a clear sense of "intention"; it turns out that either the appeal to intention is irrelevant to evaluation or that the apparent appeal to intention is a covert appeal to some other standard that is not Genetic at all. Before we leave the Genetic Reasons, however, perhaps we should consider briefly one more standard that is really complex and subtle in its ramifications, namely, originality.

Originality in art is commonly regarded as a good thing; the question is why. Now, first of all, we must note that it is Genetic, in the strict sense: to say that an object is original is to say that when it was created it differed in some notable way from anything else that was known by its creator to exist at that time. In this strict sense, it is clear that originality has no bearing upon worth: it might be original and fine, or original and terrible. Caravaggio was one of the most original painters who ever lived—but that does not make him one of the greatest. But suppose we confine ourselves to good works of art—including Caravaggio's—and ask whether originality is not a ground for admiring them more than we would on other grounds. Even here, we can easily set up test cases to divorce originality from value. Suppose there are two of Haydn's symphonies very much alike, and we do not know which he wrote first; are we going to say that A becomes better when we decide that it was the earlier, but reverse our judgment when newly discovered band parts give priority to B?

It is the composer's originality that counts, not the music's. We admire, and justly, the originality of Haydn and Beethoven and Stravinsky and Bartók, providing they wrote not only originally but well. But this admiration is based on something like an economic ground, or on the general welfare. After certain sounds have come into the world—after eighty-three Haydn quartets and, at latest count, a hundred and seven symphonies—for all their incredible variety within a certain range, we bow to the law of diminishing returns. It is more of a contribution to our aesthetic resources, so to speak, if another composer will enlarge the range of chamber music and the symphony, with original innovations, rather than work within the same range. For this we praise him, but from such praise nothing follows about the goodness of the work, except that usually, of course, we would not think that his originality *deserved* praise unless the results were valuable enough to suggest that the original idea was worth following up.

I call a reason Affective if it refers to the psychological effects of the aesthetic object upon the percipient:

. . . it gives pleasure (or gives no pleasure).
. . . it is interesting (or dull and monotonous).
. . . it is exciting, moving, stirring, rousing.
. . . it has a powerful emotional impact.

The Affective method of critical evaluation consists in judging the work by its psychological effects, or probable psychological effects, upon the critic himself, or others. As will appear later, I do not consider such Affective Reasons irrelevant to the judgment of aesthetic objects in the way I consider the Genetic Reasons irrelevant. This is a rather long story, which has to be worked out in the following chapter. At this stage, I shall only claim that the Affective Reasons by themselves are inadequate, because they are uninformative in two important ways.

First, if someone asserts that he listened to the slow movement of Beethoven's *String Quartet in E Flat Major* (*Op. 127*), and that it gave him "pleasure," or advised us that it would give us pleasure, I think we would consider this remark a weak response to that momentous music. And yet it is true in some very broad and tepid sense that it does give pleasure, just as salted peanuts and a cool dive give pleasure. We are constrained, therefore, to ask what kind of pleasure it gives, and how that pleasure, if pleasure it must be called, differs from other pleasures and gets its peculiar quality precisely from those differences. And this line of inquiry would take us into the second point. For an Affective statement tells us the effect of the work, but it does not single out those features of the work on which the effect depends. We could still ask, in other words, *what* is pleasure-giving about that music that is absent from other music, and this line of inquiry would be parallel to the first, since it would lead us to discriminate this sort of pleasure from others that have different causes and objects.

The same two questions could be raised about the general notion that seems to be implicit in the other Affective Reasons: the work is good if it leads to a strong emotional response of some sort. How does the emotional response differ from the strong emotional responses produced by telegrams announcing deaths, close calls with a skidding car, the serious illness of a child, or getting married? Surely there is an important difference, which the emotional-response reason must take account of to be complete. And what in the aesthetic object causes the emotional response? Perhaps some intense regional quality on which our attention is focused in the experience. Indeed, some of these Affective terms, as we saw in Chapter I, §3, are often really misleading synonyms for descriptive terms: they mean that the object has some regional quality to a fairly intense degree. And in that case, the reason is, of course, no longer Affective, but Objective.

I call a reason Objective if it refers to some characteristic—that is, some quality or internal relation, or set of qualities and relations—within the work itself, or to some meaning-relation between the work and the world. In short, where either descriptive statements or interpretive statements appear as reasons in critical arguments, they are to be considered as Objective reasons. The distinction may seem a little artificial here, for according to some theories certain types of interpretive statements, for example, "X represents Y," could be reformulated in such a way as to refer to effects of the work upon its percipients. But I put interpretations in with the Objective Reasons, though I do not assume that all the Objective Reasons that critics have ever given are good reasons.

Even if we confine ourselves now to Objective Reasons, we still have a very large variety, so it might naturally occur to us to wonder whether any further subdivisions can be made. I think when we take a wide survey of critical reasons, we can find room for most of them, with very little trouble, in three main groups. First, there are reasons that seem to bear upon the degree of *unity* or disunity of the work:

> . . . it is well-organized (or disorganized).
> . . . it is formally perfect (or imperfect).
> . . . it has (or lacks) an inner logic of structure and style.

Second, there are those reasons that seem to bear upon the degree of *complexity* or simplicity of the work:

> . . . it is developed on a large scale.
> . . . it is rich in contrasts (or lacks variety and is repetitious).
> . . . it is subtle and imaginative (or crude).

Third, there are those reasons that seem to bear upon the *intensity* or lack of intensity of human regional qualities in the work:

> . . . it is full of vitality (or insipid).
> . . . it is forceful and vivid (or weak and pale).
> . . . it is beautiful (or ugly).
> . . . it is tender, ironic, tragic, graceful, delicate, richly comic.

The first two groups of reasons do not seem to raise any difficulties that we have not already noticed in discussing the terms "unified" and "complex." It is obvious that critics very often explicitly advance the unity of a work as a reason for praising it, or assume that unity is a good thing; and I have never encountered the argument that a work was good because it was disorganized. I have read the following in *The New York Times* about the *Rhapsody in Blue:*

> The humor, gusto and sentiment are all there. The work is not tightly organized by symphonic standards, but its very looseness of design adds to its charm.

I think this has to mean, not that it is better precisely because it is loosely organized, but that its peculiar qualities, its "humor, gusto and sentiment," would perhaps be weakened by a more highly organized form. If a critic said that a work is poor just because it is too unified, I think his context would show he meant that it is too simple (that is, too lacking in interesting complexities) or too cold (that is, too lacking in intense regional qualities).

It is perhaps less obvious that critics very often explicitly advance the complexity of a work as a reason for praising it, or assume that complexity is a good thing. Sometimes critical theorists talk as though complexity was invented by modern critics and was unknown to Homer, Virgil, and Horace. But when it is said that a simple lyric may be a fine poem, I think this is because it may yet have a high degree of unity and an intense quality. And, indeed, certain regional qualities can only be had in aesthetic objects that are relatively simple—see the Jensen *Composition*, PLATE I, and *Municipal Lodging*, PLATE III—but in this case we do not praise them for their simplicity, but for their intensity.

The reasons in the third group are the most puzzling. There seems to be no doubt that there is such a class of actual reasons:

A: "This painting is good."
B: "Why?"
A: "Oh, it has such a sense of eternal calm and stillness about it."

I take "eternal calm and stillness" to refer to a pervasive regional quality here, as in the other examples, and I (tentatively) understand "beautiful" in the same way, though this very special term will have to be discussed at greater length in the following chapter. But there is one difficulty that presents itself at once.

You could say—with what justification we shall later consider—that a good aesthetic object must have *some* marked quality, and not be a sheer nonentity or a zero. The quality does not matter—it can be sad or cheerful, graceful or rugged, soft or stern, provided it be *something*. But this may be too broad. We can think of works with uncontrolled horror or disgustingness—realistically painted corpses, Henry Miller's *Tropic of Cancer*, or the razor slicing the eye at the beginning of the surrealistic film, *The Andalousian Dog*. In these works we have intensity of quality, all right, but that does not make them good. It may be that certain qualities are simply not contemplatable for any time with normal human endurance, and that we must except these, if we can draw the line. Or it may be that it is not human regional qualities as such, but those we already value in human beings, that we accept as standards in critical evaluation. More likely, I think, it is that in certain works the intensity of the quality is achieved at too great a sacrifice of unity. This is perhaps what the critics meant by saying that in *Les Demoiselles d'Avignon* there is "too much concern for effect."

But again it might be argued that it is not just any human regional quality that is given as a ground of praise, for some qualities are cited as grounds of dispraise: pompousness, pretentiousness, ostentatious vulgarity; a work is bad *because* it is flashy, or labored, or sentimental. Now these terms are predicates, of course, but not all predicates refer to positive perceptual qualities. Where such characteristics as these are cited as grounds for dispraise, they can, I think, be analyzed as negative. Pompousness is the outward form of grandeur and greatness—it is a long symphony with enormous crescendos—combined with an inner emptiness, lack of vitality and richness. Sentimentality in a poem is not a sentiment, but a claim on the speaker's part to a feeling that he does not dramatize and present in the texture and objects of the poem. No doubt all these words are far too subtle to be disposed of so briefly, and no doubt their meaning varies; I leave many questions hanging in the air. But I suggest that so far as these characteristics are standards of (negative) critical evaluation, they refer not to intensity of quality, but to its absence, or to lack of unity or complexity: to slackness, faintness, flabbiness, the work's inability to live up to its own promises, declining power after a good start.

Merits and Defects

Now, suppose a critic supports a value judgment by pointing out some feature of the particular work in question: "Wordsworth's 'Ode: Intimations of Immortality' is less good that it would be if its theme were not so vague." The form of this declaration claims that this vagueness is a defect in this poem, just as one might say that the grandeur of its imagery is a merit in it. By "defect" and "merit" I mean features that detract from its value or contribute to it: they are defective, or "bad-making," and meritorious, or "good-making," features respectively. Similarly we might say that firmness without hardness is a good-making feature, and worminess a bad-making feature, of apples.

But this terminology of merits and defects raises an important question. Can a feature be a merit in one poem and a defect (or neither) in another? Or does calling the feature a merit in one poem entail, or presuppose, a general principle according to which it is meritorious whereever it occurs? Is grandeur of imagery always a merit and vagueness of theme always a defect? Now, notice in the first place that we are not asking for universal conditions of goodness and badness. A wormy apple may still be a good apple, if the worm's operations have been confined to a small sector, provided the apple has other qualities that are desirable in apples. The worm is a defect, but not a fatal one. So a poem, indeed the "Ode" itself, may be a great poem because of its good-making features even though it has some bad-making features. Thus if there is a general principle—stated as, "Vague themes are always defects in poetry," or, "Grand imagery is always a merit in poetry"—this principle does not mean that these features are either *necessary* or *sufficient* conditions of goodness in poetry, but only that, other things being equal, their presence makes it better or worse.

It does not seem that the contribution of each feature of an aesthetic object can be considered in an atomistic fashion. This is true of many things in life; mustard depends on frankfurters, as a baseball bat depends on a baseball, for its maximum value; it is not, so to speak, a good-making feature of a picnic unless both are present. But then there *is* a general principle connecting baseball bats and picnics, though it is not simple: In the presence of baseballs, baseball bats are fun-making features of picnics—assuming certain sorts of picnickers. And similarly we might hold that to claim brilliant imagery as a merit in one poem is to commit yourself to some general principle about the capacity of grand imagery to help along poems, at least poems in which certain other features are present. But to commit yourself to the existence of such a principle is, of course, not to be able to state it. The critic may have a hunch that in the "Ode" the grandeur of imagery is a good-making feature, but then it would become a critical question whether it is always such or whether its being such depends upon being associated with other features. If we know what we mean by "good," as I hope we shall later, then this question becomes an empirical one.

Similar remarks hold for the merits and defects that fine arts and music critics single out for attention. For example, deep space is a good thing in some paintings, while flat space is a good thing in others; different qualities depend for their intensity upon each other. Exactness in perspective and in the size-distance relations of figures is needed in a Piero della Francesca or in a Rembrandt etching, where the violation of it in one part of the work would introduce a disturbing disunity; but its violation in a Cézanne still life or in some works by Tintoretto and Toulouse-Lautrec is a merit because of the qualities that are obtained in this way. Sometimes the critic can see these things at once, and with a confident perceptiveness. Yet an adequate justification for saying that any feature is a defect or a merit in any work would include an explanation in terms of some general principle about the value-contribution of that feature, alone or in combination with others.

A principle about defects and merits in one art we may call a *Specific Canon*. The next question is whether such Specific Canons can always be subsumed under *General Canons* that apply, not to poetry in particular, but to all the arts. Suppose, for example, a drama critic claims that it is a defect in a certain play that the action takes place over thirty years, and the story thus becomes diffuse. Now, again, he does not have to claim that the shorter the action of a play, the better it necessarily is; nor does he have to fall back on one of the neoclassic rules, such as that the action of a play should take no more than twenty-four hours; nor does he have to say that the best plays are always those whose action is the shortest possible, that is, exactly the same as the time of the play itself, such as Ben Jonson's *The Silent Woman,* Ibsen's *John Gabriel Borkman,* Tennessee Williams' *Cat on a Hot Tin Roof.* But he could perhaps claim, if his reason were questioned, that, other things being equal, the shorter the time of action, the more unified the play will tend to be; and the longer the time, the more it will tend to fall apart. This tendency may be, in some plays, counteracted by other unifying features, unfortunately lacking in the play in question. Now, this argument would subsume the long action-time as a defect under a Specific Canon—"A long action-time is a bad-making feature in a play that has a large number of characters, striking changes of scenery, and no symbolic carry-over from act to act." But the argument does more than this, for it subsumes this Specific Canon for the drama under a more General Canon, by claiming that the long action-time is a perceptual condition of disunity. The General Canon is, then, something like "Disunity is always a defect in aesthetic objects," or, in other words, "Disunity is a bad-making feature of aesthetic objects." And this is the same Canon that was appealed to when *Les Demoiselles d'Avignon* was said to have a "confused" composition.

The classification of Objective Reasons that we have made so far, then, shows that at least a very large variety of them can be subsumed under three General Canons: the Canon of Unity, the Canon of Complexity, the Canon of Intensity. In other words, the objective features of plays, poems, paintings, and musical compositions referred to in the Special Canons can, at least most of them, be conditionally justified as standards because they are, so to speak, unifying, complexifying, or intensifying features of the works in which they occur, either alone or in combination with other features.

Applying the General Canons

The next question is whether in fact *all* Objective Reasons can be subsumed under these three Canons. This is, no doubt, a very bold question, for considering the subtlety and flexibility of critical language and the waywardness of some critical thinking, it would be almost incredible if it turned out that all the Objective Reasons given by critics were subsumable under three headings—unless the headings were so vague or so general that they could cover every logical possibility. But let us see what we discover if we examine some cases of critical reasoning with our threefold classification in mind.

Cleanth Brooks, in his well-known essay on Tennyson's "Tears, Idle Tears," compares this poem with "Break, Break, Break," and explains why he judges it to be a much better poem.[4] The former, he says, is "very tightly organized," whereas the latter brings in an "irrelevant" reference

---

[4] "The Motivation of Tennyson's Weeper," *The Well Wrought Urn,* 1947, New York: Reynal and Hitchcock, pp. 153-62.

to the "stately ships," and is "more confused." Here he is clearly appealing to the Canon of Unity. He says that the latter "is also a much thinner poem," and is "coarser"; it avoids "the psychological exploration of the experience," whereas the former has "richness and depth" because of its "imaginative grasp of diverse materials." Here he is appealing to the Canon of Complexity; the first poem has more *to* it, both in range and in subtlety. He speaks of the "dramatic force" and of the "dramatic power" of "Tears, Idle Tears," and particularly praises the intensity of its final stanza, in contrast to "Break, Break, Break." And here he is appealing to the Canon of Intensity. Brooks raises the question whether the opening paradox of "idle tears" is a merit or a defect, but in the light of his discussion he concludes that it contributes valuably to the complexity of the poem rather than detracting from its unity.

Or, consider a comparison of Picasso's two versions of *The Three Musicians,* one in the Museum of Modern Art, New York (1921), the other in the Philadelphia Museum of Art (also 1921):

> The first . . . is the most moving of these, as well as the most solid and the most soberly coloured. The figures of the three characters are laid out in broad rectangular planes, while their faces give the impression of primitive masks. Only the harlequin, in the centre, with his yellow-and-red-checked dress and the curves of his guitar, serves to add a touch of cheerfulness to this sombre, eerie, hieratic work, whose structure bears witness to profound thought and incomparable craftsmanship. The other version . . . is painted in a different spirit altogether. . . . But though the composition is more varied and the colouring pleasanter, while more emphasis is given to depth and the decorative intention is more obvious, this variant lacks the dignified grandeur of the New York picture. . . . More complex, and fresher in colour, this final version has neither the severity nor the stark economy of the other, which impresses by its dignified generosity of conception.[5]

The traces of intentionalism here can probably be converted into an Objective terminology: "economy," we saw in Chapter II, §6, can mean variety of significance in line and shape, hence a kind of complexity; the "profound thought and incomparable craftsmanship" do not enter as Objective Reasons, but are (deserved) praise for Picasso. What do we have left? The two paintings are not compared with respect to unity at all; it is taken for granted that the composition in both is unified, and that this is one of the factors relevant to the high value attributed to both paintings. The paintings are compared with respect to complexity; it is a merit in the Philadelphia one that it is more complex, more varied, and richer in decorative detail, and that it has a depth lacking in the New York one. But this aspect is said to be over-balanced by the third comparison: the New York one has a certain difficult-to-describe regional quality, its "hieratic" sombreness, its "severity," its "dignified grandeur" which is

---

[5] Elgar and Maillard, *op. cit.,* pp. 104-06, 126-29.

far more intense than any regional quality present in the Philadelphia one; and this is claimed to be a considerable merit.

It would be instructive to compare a number of passages dealing with music, say in the writings of Donald F. Tovey, though I have not found a single passage that combines such a variety of reasons as those just considered. We might examine his analysis of Mozart's *Linz Symphony in C Major* (K. 425), or of Mendelssohn's *"Italian" Symphony*. But perhaps this comparative passage will serve:

> Thus, Schubert is apt to weaken and lengthen his expositions by processes of discursive development where Beethoven would have had a crowd of terse new themes; while, on the other hand, Schubert's developments are apt indeed to develop some feature of one of his themes, but by turning it into a long lyric process which is repeated symmetrically. Dvořák is apt to be dangerously discursive at any point of his exposition, and frequently loses his way before he has begun his second group, while his developments often merely harp upon a single figure with a persistence not much more energetic or cumulative than that of the Dormouse that continued to say "twinkle, twinkle" in his sleep. But none of these matters can be settled by rule of thumb.[6]

Here phrases like "discursive development" and "loses his way" seem to bear upon the unity of the work; "a crowd of terse new themes" and "merely harp upon a single figure" seem to bear upon its complexity; "weaken," "lyric," "energetic or cumulative" seem to bear upon the intensity of its qualities. Tovey assumes that it is relevant to take these into account in considering the value of music, though of course he is not trying to make any final disposition of these masters.

The three Canons, then, support a large number of critical reasons. This is not due, I think, to their being vague, for they are not too vague to be testable and usable, as I have argued in Chapters IV and V. Nor is it due to some concealed ambiguity that makes the set really tautological, like saying every aesthetic object is either complex or not. For it is easy to invent reasons that fall outside these three Canons, such as the Genetic ones, or these:

> . . . it was printed in a syndicated newspaper column.
> . . . it deals with Japanese pearl-diving.
> . . . it was written by a Communist.

Only these don't happen to be good reasons. We can find other critical formulae that do not at first glance seem to be subsumable under the three Canons, for example:

> . . . it is sincere.
> . . . it has spontaneity.
> . . . it violates (or is faithful to) its medium.
> . . . it fully exploits (or fails to exploit) its medium.

---

[6] Donald F. Tovey, *Essays in Musical Analysis,* London: Oxford U., 1935, Vol. I, pp. 13-14.

With such formulas there may be a preliminary question concerning their intelligibility; indeed, we have glanced at some of these terms already. But I believe that on analysis they will be found either to fall outside the group of Objective Reasons into intentionalism or affectivism, or else to connect indirectly with the Canons.

Nor is the plausibility of this conclusion due to the fact that the Canons permit free-wheeling rationalizations. It might seem that you could justify practically anything as a good aesthetic object: surely it must have *something* in its favor that can be connected with one of the Canons. Now, there is truth in this objection, but I do not think it is deplorable. We have not yet raised the question whether it would be possible to *grade* aesthetic objects in terms of some scale; at this point we are only asking what a critic could sensibly talk about if he were asked to name the good things or the weaknesses in an aesthetic object, and we ought to encourage the critic, as well as ourselves, to be as open as possible to the variety of good things that can be found in art. The Canonic scheme is generous in this sense, even if its principles are few. But at the same time it remains true that in some aesthetic objects one can point out numerous defects, and serious, that is, pervasive, ones, whereas in others one can find only a few; and similarly with merits.

For example, a certain college library has a plaque that contains the following lines, by W. D. Foulke:

> How canst thou give thy life to sordid things
> While Milton's strains in rhythmic numbers roll,
> Or Shakespeare probes thy heart, or Homer sings,
> Or rapt Isaiah wakes thy slumbering soul?

You could spend quite a while pointing out how bad this is, and you would have a hard time finding things good about it. From the point of view of unity, it breaks down on an elementary level; the addressee is giving his life to sordid things while Shakespeare is probing his heart and Isaiah is waking him up. This mixture would be tolerable, if the diverse images did not, on reflection, show a profound looseness in conception, the various poets being thrown together by the word "while." From the point of view of complexity, the poem is utterly lacking in subtlety; it contains dead spaces like "Homer sings"; and none of the possible connotations of "sordid" or "probes" get taken up and developed, but they are canceled out by the other words. From the point of view of its human regional qualities, it is feeble and half-hearted, even as moral advice. And it has no rhythmic, syntactical, or verbal life. These things cannot be truly said of Wordsworth's "Ode."

To sum up, the three general critical standards, unity, complexity, and intensity, can be meaningfully appealed to in the judgment of aesthetic objects, whether auditory, visual, or verbal. Moreover, they are appealed to constantly by reputable critics. It seems to me that we can even go so far as to say that all their Objective reasons that have any logical relevance at all depend upon a direct or an indirect appeal to these three basic standards. This may be too sweeping a claim; at any rate, it is stated explicitly enough so that it can be attacked or defended. In the next chapter we shall have to consider possible lines of defense; one serious attack, however, first requires our attention.

§25. *THE NATURE OF CRITICAL ARGUMENT*

The fact that critics do often give Objective reasons for their critical evaluations is noteworthy, for it shows that they think of their evaluations as the sort of thing reasons can and should be given for. But this fact does not by itself settle philosophical problems about normative criticism; indeed, it creates them. For to give a reason for a statement is to claim that anyone who accepts the reason ought to accept the statement, or at least be inclined to accept it. And the justice of this claim must always rest upon some underlying principle of reasoning. When it is said that *P* is a good reason for *Q*, we can always ask *why*—in other words, what makes it a good reason. But what if there is no such justifying principle? In that case, we must reject the critic's claim to have a rational justification of his judgments, and conclude that the ostensible reasons are not reasons at all. This would be a kind of critical skepticism.

Consider the following miniature dialogue:

> *A:* "The painting is good."
> *B:* "Why?"
> *A:* "It is a subtly toned and sensitive landscape
> with great delicacy of line."

As we have seen, *A*'s description of the landscape could raise several questions, and the success of this reasoning depends upon adequate answers to them. But it is another point that concerns us now, and it is a hard one. In order to know whether *A*'s reason is relevant to his conclusion that the painting is good, we must know what "good" means in this context. Even without extensive analysis, some of which will come later, we can easily think of possible meanings of "good," meanings that it can plausibly be said to have in some contexts, that would make *A*'s reason quite irrelevant, at least as a *reason*, though it might turn out, in some odd way, to be relevant as a remark. This distinction might be illustrated by the following dialogue:

> *A:* "Will it rain soon?"
> *B:* "Just take a look at the sky."

B's reply is not an answer to the question, but it is by no means beside the point.

Our present problem, then, is this: what is meant by "good" and "bad" in these aesthetic contexts? But the phrase "is meant" can invite two rather different inquiries. On the one hand, we might wonder what critics actually mean when they use their value-terms, what definitions they would give if pressed, what rules of usage they tacitly follow. It might turn out that these terms have a fairly restricted and general meaning, or set of meanings; or it might turn out that they have a highly variable meaning, from critic to critic, or from context to context, in which case one can only try to indicate the range of variation and provide techniques for tracking it in particular contexts. But there is a second question: we might wonder what critics *can* mean, taking into account not only what they "have in mind," so to speak, but the logical and epistemological problems about the whole procedure of giving reasons for normative judgments. Thus, conceivably, we might conclude that critics do not succeed in attaching any distinct meaning to their normative terms like "good." Or it might be that in order to give our critical evaluations any persuasive force, we must use the word "good" in a way that prevents these evaluations from being supported by Objective statements.

In the following chapter we shall consider certain systematic accounts of the way in which "good" (in an aesthetic context) is, or can be, or ought to be, used. But before we come to them, we must undertake a preliminary inquiry. Certain philosophers have attacked the procedure of critical reasoning, or reason-giving, in fundamental ways. They have argued either that no critical judgments can be rationally defended, or that only certain limited sorts of judgment can be rationally defended. It is these skeptical doubts that we must now deal with.

There are two theories about the meaning of "good" (in an aesthetic context) that imply that the alleged critical arguments discussed in the preceding section are not genuine arguments at all. According to these theories, the relation of "This is unified" to "This is good" cannot be, as it is usually supposed to be, the relation of reason to conclusion. We must consider the two theories with some care, but their significance will be clearer if first we remind ourselves of a few general characteristics of reasoning.

It is almost universally agreed today that in the last analysis there are only two fundamental kinds of argument, deductive and inductive. Most of the arguments offered and accepted in ordinary speech, and in the writings of critics, are, from the logical point of view, incomplete. For example,

> This is unified;
> *therefore*, this is good

is a *non sequitur,* taken by itself. But the logician's view is that such arguments are felt to derive their logical force, their convincingness, from supporting premises that are tacitly assumed by all parties in the discussion. In short, they are elliptical, and the logical task of determining whether or not they are sound cannot be carried out unless we first make explicit the underlying assumptions. In this process of making them explicit, we are guided by our concept of what constitutes a complete argument, and we will accept the elliptical argument if, when properly filled out, it proves to be part of a sound deductive *or* a sound inductive one.

There are many complexities in this matter that we must ignore here; they are more fully treated in a number of books on logic.[1] But if the foregoing assumptions can be made, certain consequences follow. To decide whether or not the elliptical argument from unity is a sound one, we must first make up our mind whether it is to be understood as part of a deductive argument or part of an inductive one. Now, we can make a valid deductive argument out of it by supplying a universal major premise:

> [All aesthetic objects with such-and-such a degree of unity are good.]
> This aesthetic object has such-and-such a degree of unity.
> Therefore, this is good.

But this means that the major premise has to be a Universal Canon, and unfortunately no such Universal Canon is true. We saw in the preceding section that the Canons of critical evaluation cannot be formulated universally, but only as general tendencies, or, in an alternative language, statistical generalizations.

There does not seem, then, to be any true set of Universal Canons that will enable us to transform elliptical critical arguments into deductive ones. But this difficulty does not arise with induction. For in order to transform our elliptical argument into an inductive one we need only a limited Canon. There are several ways of doing this, for example:

> [Such-and-such a degree of unity has a tendency to make an aesthetic object good.]
> This aesthetic object has such-and-such a degree of unity.
> Therefore, this aesthetic object is good.

Here the major premise is a tendency-statement, like the Canons we have discussed, and the conclusion, of course, does not follow necessarily from the premises. The most we can say, if we know nothing more about the object, is that we have some reason to think it good, though we cannot accept this conclusion with confidence until we know something about its complexity and the intensity of its human qualities.

Can we, then, understand critical arguments as elliptical inductions, justified ultimately by the general principles of inductive reasoning? It will be some time before we can give a satisfactory answer to this question, but meanwhile we must see that there are understandable grounds

---

[1] See, for example, Max Black, *Critical Thinking*, 2d ed., Englewood Cliffs, N.J.: Prentice-Hall, 1952, ch. 2; Monroe C. Beardsley, *Practical Logic*, Englewood Cliffs, N.J.: Prentice-Hall, 1950, ch. 7.

for skepticism about this view. For it regards the reasons of critics as evidence for the evaluations, in the way, let us say, that facts about a patient's symptoms are evidence for the hypothesis that he has a certain disease. But at first glance, the statement "This is good" does not seem to be related to "This is unified" in the way "John has pneumonia" is related to "John's temperature is 104.2°." In applying the term "good" to an aesthetic object, the critic seems at least to be doing something more than what the doctor is doing with the term "pneumonia." Therefore, the suspicion arises that "This is good" is not the conclusion of a logical argument at all, and "This is unified" not in the strict sense a reason. And this suspicion has led to two theories about critical argument.

The Performatory Theory

The first theory about what is actually going on in critical argument begins with the analysis of a certain kind of verbal utterance. An utterance of this kind is one that does not give information about a previously existing state of affairs, but itself makes a difference in the world: it initiates someone into a secret society, or creates a knighthood, or makes a man a citizen. "With this ring I thee wed" is not a statement about the wedding, but part of the wedding itself, indeed, it *is* the act of wedding. The language of such utterances has been called *Performatory Language*. The same function can, of course, be carried out by nonverbal gestures: awarding the Congressional Medal of Honor, or laying a wreath on the tomb of the Unknown Soldier.

Suppose, then, we were to try regarding the critic's judgment, "This is good," as an utterance of this kind, which does honor to the aesthetic object. Since it is not a statement, but an act, it is not true or false, and therefore it cannot be the conclusion of an argument; in other words, it makes no sense to speak of giving reasons to establish its truth. I shall call this the *Performatory Theory* of critical argument.[2]

The Performatory Theory grants that the key word "Why?" in a critical discussion is a request, in one sense, for a "reason," but insists that there is an ambiguity concealed in this word. For we speak of a reason for a statement, that is, a reason for believing or asserting that it is true; this is the sense in which a reason is part of an argument. We also speak of a reason for doing something, for going to the dentist, or for taking a job; and here there is no statement the reason supports, but rather an action whose performance is to be justified by the reason. In this latter sense, the Performatory Theory grants, critical evaluation-utterances may be just or unjust; they are not, however, true or false.

Unfortunately the principles distinguishing adequate from inadequate justifications have not been worked out for the Performatory

---

[2] Such a theory has been sketched by Margaret Macdonald; for reference see Note 25-A.

Theory. But we can see how they would go. The only justification for the act of awarding the medal would be the official judgment that the soldier's actions deserved it, just as the only justification for the first-base umpire's horizontal waving of the arms would be his official judgment that the runner arrived before the ball. In short, the Performatory act, while not itself a statement, presupposes, or rests upon, a statement—"This deserves first prize"—which is itself a normative judgment. And the critic's "This is good" is more like the judgment that justifies the Performatory act than the Performatory act itself. For the critic's pronouncement is not an official act like the art jury's decision to hang the painting in the exhibition. It is not authoritative, and changes the world not at all.

The defender of the Performatory Theory must of course deny that the justification of a Performatory utterance is itself a value-judgment; he agrees that if this is so, his theory is undermined. Consider the awarding of the Congressional Medal of Honor. The reason for this award is that the soldier performed an act "beyond the call of duty," where the call of duty is quite carefully defined in the military code. Here the reason seems to be a plain description, though there has to be a general rule governing the award, that is, a rule about the conditions under which it will be made. Similarly, why can't we say that "This is unified" specifies one of the conditions governing the benediction, "This is (aesthetically) good"? I don't think that this will do, however, even for the military award. "This act is beyond the call of duty" is not a pure description; it is already a value-judgment, for "beyond" means not only that the act was more dangerous or difficult than duty prescribed, but that it was a desirable act, an approved act. Or, if this is not strictly part of the meaning of "beyond," it is taken for granted, for unless the act was good, its danger would not justify the award.

The Emotive Theory

The second theory of critical argument does not go quite as far as the first, for it does not assimilate critical evaluations to nonlinguistic acts, but in its simple form it does deny that evaluations are genuine statements, and in its sophisticated form it holds that, though they may have a predicative element, they also have another peculiar feature that renders them incapable of behaving like ordinary empirical statements. Both forms we may refer to as the *Emotive Theory* of critical argument.[3]

The simple emotive theory is that, despite its grammatical form, a critical evaluation is not a statement, but a combination of two components, an exclamatory component, which gives evidence of the speaker's feelings ("Yum, yum!"), and an imperative component, which calls

---

[3] This theory has not been primarily discussed in relation to the critical uses of "good," but in ethics its classic exposition is that of Charles L. Stevenson, *Ethics and Language;* see Note 25-B.

upon the listener to share the speaker's feelings ("Feel like saying 'Yum, yum!' too!"). When a critic says that a poem is good, he is evincing his own attitude toward it, and attempting to engender the same attitude in others. Since exclamations and imperatives are neither true nor false, a value judgment is not a statement, according to the Emotive Theory, and consequently it cannot appear as the conclusion of an argument. In other words, no reason can be given for it.

Now, as we have seen, critics often *think* they are giving reasons for their judgments, but, like the Performatory Theory, the Emotive Theory distinguishes two senses—in this case different senses—of the word "reason." For example, we might ask someone what the reason was for his being late for an appointment. If he says he had to take his child to a doctor, he *is* giving a reason, and no doubt a good reason. If he says he forgot the time, he is not giving a reason, but merely a *cause;* he is explaining, but not justifying, his lateness. According to the simple Emotive Theory, it is only in the second sense that the critic can give reasons. Suppose *A* says, "That is a poor poem," and *B* asks, "Why?" *B* is inviting *A* to try to come up with some true statement that will make *B* dislike the poem as much as *A* does. *A* must work on *B*'s feelings. He may say, "Its imagery is confused," if he thinks *B* already disapproves of confused imagery. Or he may say, "The author was once a Communist," or "Prince Rainier doesn't like it," or "It has sold a million copies," or anything else that is true and that will tap one of *B*'s prejudices. The only difference that the Emotive Theory recognizes between one "reason" and another is that one is effective and the other is not; if it secures the desired response from *B*, no more can be said for it, or demanded of it. There is no logical distinction between good reasons and poor ones.

To see whether this is an acceptable account of the actual process of critical argument, we must consider separately the two aspects of the theory, the imperative aspect, and the exclamatory aspect.

Is it plausible to consider judgments like "This is good" in an aesthetic context as disguised imperatives? It may of course be that the speaker hopes to influence other people's attitudes, and it may even be that he succeeds, but that does not make the statement an imperative. "I feel chilly" is not an imperative even if it leads someone to get up and shut the window; moreover, every statement that is asserted is an invitation to believe, but "It is raining" cannot be analyzed into "I believe it is raining. Believe it too!" If something is being implicitly commanded (besides belief) in "This is good," it is not easy to discover what it is. Perhaps the speaker means "Like this!" or "Stop disliking this!" but these are odd commands; how do you command someone to like something? Perhaps the speaker means "Repeat after me, 'This is good'!"—but if it is the verbal utterance that he is commanding, he is content with very little. It does seem as though it is hard to make out a good case for saying that "This is good" (in an aesthetic context) has a peculiar imperative component.

This conclusion can, I think, be strengthened by a broader consideration. Normative statements in general, including those we make about aesthetic objects, are of two sorts. Sometimes we make practical proposals: you ought to buy this recording of the *German Requiem* or *Don Giovanni* rather than that; you ought to go to this movie rather than that, or stay home and watch television. Let us call such judgments *Recommendations:* they propose solutions to problems of actual choice, and in the end we cannot escape such decisions about aesthetic objects—a topic to which we shall return in Chapter XII. To decide which of two recordings of an opera to buy, you must of course take a number of factors into consideration: the comparative cost, the difficulty of procuring them (including the fact that you are in a hurry and one will have to be ordered while the other is in stock), the differences in the recording, cuts made by the conductor, surface noise, performance. Normative statements about these factors—"The performance is excellent," "The surface is quiet"—are different from outright Recommendations. I may say that recording X is better in sound but Y is cheaper, and leave it up to you to make the final decision. These are judgments of goodness in such-and-such a respect: let us call them *Commendations.* A rational Recommendation will presumably be based upon correct Commendations, but a Commendation is not itself a proposal for action. The distinction tends to disappear in the extreme case: for example, if two recordings differ only in one respect, say the quality of the sound, then the Commendation "X has the better sound" strongly suggests the Recommendation, "Choose X," since it would be irrational to choose Y under the circumstances. Even in this case, however, the distinction is worth preserving.

Now, there is a good deal of sense in the view that a Recommendation has an imperative component: that, for example, a moral judgment of rightness or wrongness is an answer to a question like "What shall I do?"—though it is not wholly clear that the answer to this question is a simple imperative. But critical evaluations are not Recommendations, but Commendations; they provide relevant data for decisions, but they enjoin no decisions themselves, and it does not seem at all plausible to treat them as in part commands.

When we turn to the exclamatory part of the Emotive Theory, we encounter a different set of difficulties. It would no longer be regarded as plausible, I think, to say that "This painting is good" is an example of pure emotive language; that it has emotive import and emotive purport, but no meaning, in the sense in which these terms were introduced above, in Chapter III, §9. The Mixed Emotive Theory accepts this conclusion: that normative terms may have a meaning. But it insists that they also have emotive force, and that this introduces a peculiar complication into critical reasoning. For according to this view, when a term that is emotive appears in the conclusion of an argument, the argument always commits a certain kind of fallacy that prevents it from being completely logical.

To take a simple example, suppose we can find two terms—this was
doubted in Chapter III—that have the same meaning but one is neutral
and the other has negative emotive import and purport: say, "one who
works during a strike" and "scab." Now to prove that X worked during
the strike may be quite feasible, and X may be quite prepared to admit
that this predicate applies to him. But suppose we then say this to him:
"If two terms have the same meaning, then obviously either can be substituted for the other in any context without changing the meaning; if
therefore you are one who works during a strike, then you are a scab."
This argument is, of course, on one level, perfectly valid. Yet X will
repudiate the word "scab" vigorously, and for a sensible reason: if he accepts it, and applies it to himself, he will be accepting its emotive purport, that is, in using the word, he will be showing disapproval toward
himself, and this will be a misshowing, for he does not feel that disapproval. The argument is fallacious, because it introduces a surreptitious
emotive effect into the conclusion that was not there in the premise.

Now the same thing happens with "This is good" in critical argument, according to the Emotivist. We might be prepared to accept the
factual premise "This is unified" but balk at "This is good," because it
would show approval that we do not feel. Therefore, all critical arguments, if taken as arguments, would be fallacious in this peculiar way.
Therefore, they are best not taken as genuine arguments at all.

Now, we know what to do in general about the Fallacy of Surreptitious Emotive Effect; we can use neutral terms, or use the emotive ones
in contexts that minimize their emotive effect, and get along reasonably
well. Why can't a critical argument, then, do the same thing? If "warm,
glowing colors" is taken to be emotive, in contrast to "colors on the red
side that tend to be highly saturated," then let us use the less emotive
term, or cancel out the emotive effect. But here, for the Emotivist, is the
crux of the matter: for he claims that the emotive aspect of "good" is
precisely its normative aspect. Take away the emotive effect, and you no
longer have a critical evaluation; keep the critical evaluation, and you
have the emotive effect, and the fallacy.

On what grounds, then, shall we decide whether the emotive aspect
of a word is its normative aspect? This is by no means an easy question,
and present-day philosophers are not agreed upon it. But one thing is
clear, namely that if there are normative statements that are not emotive,
and emotive statements that are not normative, then being normative and
being emotive are not the same thing. And it seems to me that this is just
the case. It is agreed that some emotive statements are not normative
statements; it is, I think, agreed that not even all emotive statements that
evince and evoke liking and disliking are normative statements. And it
seems to me that some normative statements are by no means emotive,
though this is more questionable. Granted that when someone says something is good he generally shows he is not entirely indifferent to it. Never-

theless, he can use the word in a perfectly calm manner—"In my judgment, it is good." This "good" can be nearly lacking in emotive purport. Granted, again, that when we hear the word "good" we may feel a tendency to respond in terms of liking, but not, I think, if we are more than a quivering sensibility; the word can be nearly lacking in emotive import.

The Emotive Theory in its sophisticated form introduces a concession like that of the Performatory Theory. Suppose we try to distinguish between various kinds of feelings evinced and evoked by "good" (in an aesthetic context): the "Oh, ah!" of aesthetic approval from the "Hurrah!" of moral admiration. If A says "Oh, ah!" in front of a particular painting, or if his "Oh, ah!" in front of one of the *Three Musicians* is louder than that in front of the other, why, then, though B cannot sensibly ask whether this is true or false, he can ask whether it is *appropriate*. To justify his utterance, then, A would have to argue that the painting has certain features that makes aesthetic approval, rather than aesthetic disapproval, or some other kind of approval, suitable to the occasion—as it is suitable to say "well bowled" at a cricket match but not at a baseball game. Knowing what sorts of emotive exclamation are suitable for particular circumstances is knowing how to *use* normative expressions, and a person who says "Oh, ah!" in front of a badly organized painting, while he is not saying anything *false*, is guilty of misusing the expression.

But any such attempt to introduce, even in this roundabout way, a distinction between justifiable and unjustifiable emotive utterances[4] must, I think, alter the Emotive Theory beyond all recognition and render it nearly indistinguishable from those psychological theories of value that we shall consider in the following chapter. For even if "Oh, ah!" does not become true or false, in the sophisticated view, the statement "The utterance 'Oh, ah!' is an appropriate response to Fauré's *Requiem*" is itself a normative statement that the theory has to take as true or false, and this statement is just the original critical judgment "Fauré's *Requiem* is good" that the Emotive Theory was supposed to analyze.

Relativism

So far in this section we have been considering the nature of critical arguments, but certain problems become more evident when we consider critical disputes—a dispute being a kind of double argument in which one critic gives a reason for, and another a reason against, the same judgment.

A: "*Long Day's Journey into Night* is a masterpiece of the theater."
B: "What is so great about it?"

---

[4] That is, to introduce what Richard Brandt has called a "Validation Thesis"; see his article, "The Status of Empirical Assertion Theories in Ethics," *Mind*, LXI (1952): 458-79.

A: "It has some very moving scenes, and it has a cumulative power; the people are real, the conflict is a detply human one."

B: "Yes, I agree that those things can be said in favor of it, but would you not agree that it is slow and ponderous and frightfully repetitious in its movement, and that the characters and conflicts are essentially rather elementary, for all the enormous length of the play? It seems to me the general effect is one of monotony and dissipation of energy, and I would not call it a masterpiece, even among O'Neill's works."

The two theories of critical argument just examined can also, of course, be applied to such disputes. The Performatory Theory would say that in this case A is honoring, B is refusing to honor, the play; but it is not clear where, if anywhere, the two disputants can go from this point. According to the Emotive Theory, such a dispute is to be understood primarily as a disagreement in attitude rather than in belief; it may include disagreements about the actual characteristics of the play, but what makes it a value-dispute is precisely that even when these disagreements are cleared up, there remains an irreducible opposition of A's pro attitude and B's con attitude. There is, however, another general view of such disputes that we must deal with before we conclude this section. That is *Relativism.*[5]

So carelessly is this term used in most discussions, for all its commonness and familiarity, that we shall have to begin by being more than ordinarily pedantic about it. I propose, first, to explain with some care how I think this term is best used to bring out the central problems in this area. The Performatory Theory and the Emotive Theory are theories about the nature of critical reasoning, or, in other words, they are accounts of the way in which the term "good" functions in an aesthetic context. Now there is another way of giving an account of "good" (in an aesthetic context), and that is to propose a *definition* of it. A definition is a sentence of the form:

"Good" (in an aesthetic context) has the same meaning as . . .

where the defining term makes more explicit the characteristics designated by "good." According to the Performatory Theory and the Emotive Theory, "good" cannot be defined, since it is not used to designate any characteristics of things. But if we do not accept these theories, then we are at liberty to ask the question, "What does 'good' mean in an aesthetic context?" or "What does it mean to say that an aesthetic object is a good aesthetic object?"

In the next chapter we shall deal with the main types of proposal in answer to these questions, and I do not want to anticipate the details of that argument. But Relativism is the view that only proposals of a certain sort are acceptable, and if this view is true it will simplify our prob-

---

[5] In aesthetics, the theory has been defended by George Boas, F. A. Pottle, Bernard C. Heyl; see Note 25-D.

lem in the next chapter considerably. That is why I take it up here. But though we shall use, as examples, some of the possible definitions of "good," we shall not concern ourselves with their plausibility as definitions, but only with one aspect of them.

Suppose we have two critics who dispute about a given aesthetic object:

> A: "X is good."
> B: "X is not good."

—that is, they utter sentences that are logically contradictory in overt form. But whether they are *really* contradictory depends on the definition of "good" that we accept. Suppose we were—and never mind the implausibility of these suggestions—to say that

> "X is good" means "X is approved by the highest-paid critics."

Then our original model can be transformed, by substitution, into:

> A: "X is approved by the highest-paid critics."
> B: "X is not approved by the highest-paid critics."

According to the highest-paid-critics definition of "good," A and B are indeed contradicting each other when one says X is good and the other says it is not. And this is true no matter who A and B are, assuming they are talking about the same critics, the highest-paid in the world.

Now suppose, instead, we were to say that

> "X is good" means "I like X."

Then when A and B utter their value-judgments, each is really saying what he likes or doesn't like, and our original model is equivalent to:

> A: "I like X."
> B: "I don't like X."

According to the I-like definition of "good," then, A and B are not really contradicting each other when one says X is good and the other says it is not. This is what I mean by saying that the I-like definition is a *Relativistic Definition,* whereas the highest-paid-critics definition is not.

A definition of "good" (in an aesthetic context), then, is Relativistic if according to that definition there can be two critics, one of whom says that an aesthetic object is good and the other of whom denies it—or one of whom says it is better than the other one says it is—without really contradicting each other. Note that the Emotive Theory does not give a Relativistic definition of "good," since it does not give any definition at all; but by an easy extension, we can, if we wish, call the Emotive Theory a Relativistic *Theory,* meaning that it is a theory about critical disputes according to which apparent contradictions are not real contradictions. If

the I-like definition is correct, *A* is making a statement, only it is about
his own feelings. *B* could deny the statement if he wished:

> *A*: "This is good."
> *B*: "No, you don't."

The point is that he can't deny it by replying, "This is not good."

Relativism, we may then say, is the theory that "good" (in an aesthetic context) must be defined Relativistically.

The definition of "Relativistic" uses the clause "there can be two critics," and this is to allow for various forms of Relativism. The I-like definition is one extreme form, which we may call Individual Relativism, because it follows from this definition that *any* two critics who get into a dispute are really talking about different things and failing to contradict each other. But another form of Relativism, for example, Cultural Relativism, would make a distinction. Suppose

> "X is good" means "X is approved by people of my culture,"

where "my" refers to the speaker. Now, if *A*, who says *X* is good, and *B*, who denies it, are both members of the same culture, that is, both Western Europeans or both Melanesians, they *are* contradicting each other; but if *A* and *B* are from different cultures, that is, one is an ancient Greek and the other is an Easter Islander, they are not contradicting each other. A Cultural Relativistic definition of "good" (in an aesthetic context), then, is one according to which speakers in different cultures cannot really dispute with each other, for whenever they try to get into a genuine disagreement by using the word "good" they will fail to do so; each can talk only about his own culture. In the same way, we can have other sorts of Relativism: Epochal Relativism (reference to the speaker's period in history), National Relativism, Class Relativism (reference to the speaker's social class), and so forth.

Which, if any, of all these possible definitions is the most suitable we shall consider later. Right now our concern is with a general prior question: Is there any reason why we are compelled to accept some form of Relativism? Must we rule out at this stage of the argument all Non-relativist definitions of "good" (in an aesthetic context)?

Now suppose a philosopher is trying to persuade us to adopt a Relativistic Definition of "good"; what arguments can he give? Well, first, he might try to show us that critics do in fact use their normative words in this way. He does not have to fasten upon one type of Relativism and say that it always applies. He may produce one critic, let's say *C*, who is always prepared to give reasons for his judgments when he is talking to another critic of his own culture, but never gives any reasons when he is disagreeing with Aristotle or with Hindu critics, thus revealing his clear awareness that his judgments make an implicit reference to his own culture so that he would not really be contradicting the critics from other cultures. And the Relativist may produce another critic, *D*, who never gives any reasons for his judgments, even when pressed, because he means by "This is good" only "I like this now," and consequently is never really contradicting other critics, or even himself at a different time.

But *C* and *D* sound like caricatures here, because they would be extremely rare. As far as their introspected meanings go, and also their reason-giving practice, most critics do not appear to subscribe to Relativism, at least in any very settled and systematic way. And it is quite as open to them to say that if *D* means by "This is good" only "I like it now," he is using "good" in a very peculiar sense, and is not communicating, for other people will not take it in that sense, whatever he says. But the Relativist usually does not appeal to the introspections of critics. He says that apart from what they *think* they mean and do, the only meaning they *can* give to "good" is Relativistic; they must admit that there are always restrictions—individual, social, historical, cultural—upon the relevance of critical reasons.

Now, suppose we have a controversy, or an apparent dispute, between two critics, *A* ("*X* is good") and *B* ("*X* is not good"), and it goes on for a long time, each giving numerous reasons, relevant and irrelevant, each accepting the other's reasons, but clinging to his own judgment:

A: "It is ingeniously plotted."
B: "Granted; I still say it's not good. The characters are thin."
A: "Granted; I still say it's good. The style is clear."
B: "Granted; I still say it's not good . . ."

We may, after a time, begin to suspect that there is something wrong; it looks as if the difference of opinion is not going to be settled by reasoning. Perhaps it is a pseudo-issue. Now, if it is a pseudo-issue, it cannot be rationally resolved, but it can be *dissolved:* that is, its pseudo character can be made explicit by reformulating the argument—if the disputants will acknowledge the reformulation as equivalent to what they really have in mind.

There are two fundamentally different ways of dissolving this issue. First, we might say that they are really talking about different things; it is not the same *X* that both are referring to, for each is referring, not to some objective work, but to the way the object appears to him. In short, "*X*" for *A* means "*A*'s presentation of the work," and "*X*" for *B* means "*B*'s presentation of the work." This proposal for dissolution may be called *Particularism,* and defined this way: it is the theory that in critical disputes each disputant is always talking, and can only talk, about his own presentation, at that time, of the object. Therefore critics never really disagree.

We have already found reason in Chapter I, §4, to doubt the truth of Particularism; I bring it up here only to keep it sharply distinct from Relativism, with which it is often confused. If Particularism is true,

Relativism cannot be formulated at all, for Relativism presupposes that the disputants are talking about the same object, only they are saying different things about it. Relativism is the second way of dissolving the issue: by saying that *A* and *B*, though referring to the same thing by "*X*," are using the word "good" in different senses, and therefore not contradicting each other.

Another way of stating Particularism would be to say that normative critical terms do not apply to aesthetic objects, but only to presentations of aesthetic objects. Suppose you hear a new musical composition over and over again, with brief pauses in between. The first time you will get some enjoyment from it, perhaps more the second and even the third time; after that the enjoyment may begin to drop off rapidly, down to positive displeasure, and you may even have difficulty forcing yourself to listen, by the fortieth time. Now, if the term "good" (in an aesthetic context) applies only to each presentation, we would have to say something like this: "The first presentation was good, the second better, . . . then they began to get worse and worse." But it is clear that we do not use the word "good" this way; it is not the "goodness" of the music that has changed, but we, that is, our capacity to take it in. It is the same music as before, but we are getting less and less adequate presentations of it, and we are getting less and less able to respond to the presentations.

The Relativist does not hold, however, that two disputing critics are referring to different objects—though he may sometimes commit the error of saying so. He holds that they have different attitudes toward the same object. But Relativism is a negative thesis: it is that no reasonable way—that is, no way through reasoning—can be found to settle the dispute, and therefore it is not a genuine dispute at all. The question now becomes: What empirical evidence can be offered in support of this claim?

The Argument from Variability

The evidence appealed to by the Relativist can be divided into two parts, as providing the grounds for two closely related, but distinguishable, arguments. There is an argument from Variability and an argument from Inflexibility. We must consider each of them.

The basis of the first argument is that tastes differ: the aesthetic objects that are enjoyed, admired, chosen, praised, and cherished vary considerably from age to age, from culture to culture, from nation to nation, from social stratum to social stratum, from family to family, from person to person. We find this even in an age and a region of strong pressures toward conformity. And especially in the history of the arts do we find enormous variations in the reputation of creative artists and their works: of Cherubini, Melville, Donne, Henry James, El Greco, and even Shakespeare, who in the Restoration period was thought much inferior to Otway. These facts, for which I shall use the general term "Variability of taste," are well verified. But Variability must be kept carefully distinct from Relativism. Variability is an empirical fact; Relativism is a theory about the proper way to define the term "good." Now the argument, "Tastes differ; therefore, critical judgments are relative," is obviously invalid. It by no means follows from the fact that people like different aesthetic objects that they cannot do any more in judging them than record their likings.

And yet the Variability of taste cannot be lightly dismissed. It seems so broad and sweeping, it goes so deep, and moreover its capricious changes and its stubborn persistences seem, often, so independent of and so immune to any rational discussion. It is easy enough to be discouraged by it, and to conclude that the only thing we can do in talking normatively about aesthetic objects is to say how they appeal to us and others like us.

But the significance of Variability cannot be estimated until we break it down a little more. For what makes the variability seem so enormous is that the catch-all term "taste" lumps together a very heterogeneous collection of phenomena, some of which do, and some of which do not, have a bearing upon Relativism. For example, there is (1) variability of *preference,* by which I mean such differences as these: The content of symphony orchestra programs changes from season to season, from decade to decade, partly because people get tired of hearing the same things; or some programs do not change enough, because the season-ticket holders want easy access to music and are unwilling to make the effort required to become familiar with new works. But these conflicts can be set aside because they do not need to involve disputes about goodness (in an aesthetic context) at all; the decision whether to perform Beethoven's *Second* or Walter Piston's *Second* may be quite independent of any relative critical evaluation, assuming that they are both worth performing. Or, to take another sort of example, when we look about at some of the houses that have been built in this country—for example, Victorian Gothic monstrosities like Canonchet, the Sprague house at Narragansett, or the Carson house at Eureka, California—we marvel at the sheer ugliness that has been achieved, and we cannot imagine how anyone ever thought they were beautiful. But is there really a difference in critical evaluation here? We do not know that they were thought to be beautiful, after all; perhaps they were built by people who were not very sensitive either to beauty or ugliness, but anxious to spend money in a conspicuous fashion and create at any cost a semblance of Old World magnificence and aristocracy.

In short, variability of preference does not necessarily entail (2) variability of critical judgment. If more people like the poems of Anne Morrow Lindbergh than like the poems of Dylan Thomas or W. H. Auden, this does not mean they would all say that they think her poems are better poems. But suppose they did say this; then we would have what

I am calling variability of judgment, where the same thing is said to be good and bad by different people or different groups of people. Now, if I find that my judgment is different from that of 90 per cent of my fellow Americans, I might think that the democratic thing to do, instead of saying they are wrong, is to fall back on a Relativistic mode of speech that will remove the conflict, by withdrawing any commitment to a general judgment about the value of the poems. But I am not compelled to do this, nor is it genuinely democratic; for if I believe I have better reasons for my judgment than the 90 per cent have for theirs, it is my duty to stick by my guns.

The variability of unsupported judgments may be distinguished from another sort of variability: (3) variability of reasons. With this third group we get down to more fundamental matters. Suppose two people differ about something, say the length of a table; there is no fundamental problem as long as they both agree on the method of settling their disagreement. But suppose one has a tape measure, and the other a yardstick, and each insists on using his own device, but they consistently get different results; then their disagreement is not only about the length of the table but about the right way of determining its length. They differ in the reasons they will accept. And here, at last, we come to a kind of variability that might lead us to conclude that their argument is insoluble, and the only way of disposing of it is to introduce a relativistic definition of length: one means "length as measured by the tape measure," the other means "length as measured by the ruler." Both are right, after all.

Now, in the history of criticism, we do find examples of this third kind of variability—and it is the only kind, I believe, that need give us any concern here. Suppose a neoclassic critic finds fault with Shakespeare's *Macbeth* because it violates the unities of time and space, and a romantic critic praises it as a masterpiece because of the subtlety of its characterization. So far no trouble; they are getting their cards on the table; critical evaluation is at its best a group enterprise, for it may take a variety of talents and sensitivities to see what is good and what is bad in a complicated play. But suppose the neoclassic critic says, regretfully, that subtlety of psychological insight into characters is not a feature that counts either for or against a play—that the romantic critic might just as well have said it is a great play because it is laid in Scotland. And suppose the romantic critic says, with equal sadness, that unfortunately the unities are completely outmoded, and to condemn a play for violating them is as irrelevant as condemning it because it has five acts instead of four.

Now the dispute would be moved down into basic questions, and here, as in the measurement example, there would be a strong temptation to dissolve the dispute by adopting a relativistic definition of "good." If "good" means "in conformity to the standards employed by me and my epoch," then both critics may be right, and they are not really in conflict.

But this dissolution would be premature, just as it would be in the measurement example. For we need not be faint-hearted even about these basic issues. In the case of the table, we would suppose that either the ruler or the tape measure must be wrong, and we would suggest comparing them with a more ultimate standard—if necessary, with the one in the National Bureau of Standards in Washington. Should the two disputants refuse to have their devices checked and insist that they are right, we would not say that this makes them Relativists, but that they are too stubborn to learn the truth.

Can something like this be said about the critical dispute, too? The question now becomes: Is the unity of time and place a relevant standard, and is psychological subtlety a relevant standard? But this is where the argument from Variability comes in. For in the case of the table measurement, there is a generally acknowledged standard to which we can ultimately appeal. But doesn't Variability of aesthetic phenomena show that there is no such generally acknowledged standard in criticism? In this dispute there is nothing to appeal to for deciding which reasons are relevant: therefore, there can be no rational way of resolving it. Between two neoclassic critics, who accept the unities as a standard, there can be a genuine disagreement; but between the neoclassic critic and the romantic critic there can be none, as is shown by the fact that they will not accept each other's reasons.

But there are two questions about standards. First, we can ask whether or to what extent there is already agreement upon a standard: about the measurement of length there is agreement in this country. Standards are in the process of being set up in certain other fields, like the accrediting of colleges and universities, and—I have read recently—the grading of Christmas trees. In still other fields there are no standards at all. In criticism, the argument of the preceding section goes to show, I believe, that on very broad and basic levels, when we consider the General Canons, there are widely accepted standards, to which we can relate, as subordinate conditions, a large variety of more specific standards. For example, we can find room under unity for the neoclassic canons, taken as empirical generalizations, and under complexity for psychological subtlety. Therefore, the General Canons have a public and stable character to which appeal can be made.

But there is not now, of course, and perhaps never will be, complete agreement on critical standards. And the second question about standards, which had to be asked before the National Bureau came into existence, is whether there can be and should be standards. Nothing in the variability of taste proves that it is impossible—though there may be other reasons for thinking so—to propose certain standards of critical evaluation, and to give reasons why those standards should be accepted and given precedence over others. So this is then our main problem in the following chapter: we want to know whether the adoption of such standards as unity, complexity, and intensity can be justified.

The Relativist often carries the argument a step further. The only way we can justify a standard, he says, is to derive it from another, and more general, standard, as Special Canons are subsumed under General Canons. However, this method never takes the critic outside of standards, but only from one standard to another. Therefore he can never have *any* standards at all unless he adopts *some* standards without any logical justification as a start. Therefore all critical disputes rest ultimately upon standards for which no reason can be given, and to prevent futile debate, the normative terms of criticism should be defined in such a way as to acknowledge this fact.

It is the first premise of the foregoing argument that I wish to call into question. For there is another way of justifying standards than deriving them from other standards—namely, in terms of the consequences of adopting one standard rather than another. This is a way out, one that we shall explore at the end of the following chapter.

The Argument from Inflexibility

Before we conclude this chapter, however, we must give some attention to the Relativist's other line of reasoning, which I have called the Argument from Inflexibility. Aesthetic likings and dislikings have causes, we may assume, just as do all other psychological states, including believings and disbelievings. But it is sometimes possible to change our beliefs by giving reasons, that is, by making assertions and providing evidence for them, although we know that sometimes beliefs seem to be the result of deeper and more unconscious conditions that we cannot get at directly by argument, and these beliefs resist the attempt to reason about them. Now suppose it should be proved that our aesthetic likings and dislikings are completely determined by certain conditions—by our childhood upbringing, or cultural *milieu,* or, for an extreme example, by our "somatotypes."[6] Suppose, in other words, that endomorphs, or viscerotonic types, always prefer one sort of painting, while ectomorphs, or cerebrotonic types, always prefer another sort. Since a person's type, we may assume for present purposes, is fixed once he is conceived, and is not subject to our control, aesthetic preferences would also be fixed. They would be impervious to argument. It would therefore be absolutely pointless for a person of one somatotype to try to change the preferences of a person of another somatotype by arguing with him. I take the somatotype possibility as a simple one, but a thoroughgoing cultural or economic determinism would provide a basis for the same sort of argument.

But what sort of argument do we have here, and what is its legitimate

[6] Here I am thinking of the investigations of Charles Morris, reported in *Varieties of Human Value;* for references, see Note 25-D.

488 conclusion? Even if aesthetic preferences are completely determined by causes over which we can have no control, we are not forced to define "X is good" as "People of my somatotype like things similar to X." Indeed, it would be a waste. For if we really could correlate certain kinds of painting with certain somatotypes, then it would be possible to redefine "good" in another and Nonrelativistic way. We would, in effect, distinguish three senses of "good":

"good$_1$" means "liked by endomorphs,"
"good$_2$" means "liked by mesomorphs,"
"good$_3$" means "liked by ectomorphs."

Then if the question arises, "Is X good?" we would simply require that the person asking the question specify which of the three senses he has in mind, before we answer his question; but then, of course, the question would become completely empirical. None of these three definitions of "good" is Relativistic. Whether they are satisfactory or not we shall see later.

The Inflexibility Argument, though it does not force us to become Relativists, nevertheless would claim to show the futility of certain kinds of critical dispute. And so we must still ask whether this claim can be made out. We cannot argue people out of a liking for raw onions, it might be said; how can we expect to argue them out of a liking for Mickey Spillane, or Rock and Roll? But the utility of critical argument does not depend upon our being able to change people's likings and dislikings directly by giving reasons. We do not expect to make people honest or courageous merely by giving them reasons to prove that these are virtues, but this does not show that it is futile to discuss the desirability of these qualities, because there are *indirect* ways in which we can encourage and foster them, in ourselves and in others. If nothing at all, directly or indirectly, can be done to change aesthetic preferences, then there is no point in deploring them, true—and this is what the somatotype theory might say. But there is a great deal of evidence—some of it, indeed, included in the Argument from Variability—to show that individual tastes *can* be changed, that it is possible to increase subtlety of discrimination and range of enjoyment and complexity of understanding by appropriate training. And if it is possible to change, or to develop, tastes, then we cannot avoid the question whether they *should* be changed. The Relativist does not meet this question by redefining words so that it cannot be asked.

My quarrel with the usual arguments for Critical Relativism is that their evidence of Variability and of Inflexibility are seldom analyzed deeply enough. Granted that people have praised the *Mona Lisa* (ca. 1505, Louvre, Paris) for all sorts of different qualities; granted that eighteenth century readers seem to have enjoyed more abstract words in their poetry than did those of the Romantic era; granted that two reviewers of the latest novel will seldom rate it exactly the same. Still, all

such facts are of no significance until various distinctions are made. The
fact that people like different things doesn't show that critical disputes are
futile; if everyone liked the same things, there would be no critical disputes at all. It is the existence of divergent preferences that gives rise to
disputes in the first place; the problem of Relativism is what can be done
about the dispute after it arises. The central question is whether there
is any conclusive proof that there are certain reasons for critical judgments which would be given or accepted by one group of critics but
which another group of critics would consider completely beside the
point, *and* that there is in principle no rational method of persuading
either group that it is mistaken. I don't see that the Relativist can present
such a proof. But it may be said that the burden is rather on the Non-
relativist to show that there is such a rational method. And it is this
burden that must be taken up in the following chapter.

NOTES AND QUERIES

§24

24-A INTENTION AS A STANDARD OF EVALUATION. This is dealt with
in some of the references given in Chapter I, Note 1-A, especially the
articles "Intention" (*Dictionary of World Literature*) and "The Intentional
Fallacy." Other articles in which intention is discussed mainly as an
evaluative standard are listed below.

One of the classic defenses of intentionalistic evaluation is the essay
by J. E. Spingarn, "The New Criticism," 1911, reprinted in *Creative Criticism,* New York: Holt, 1917, and in a general collection, *Criticism in
America,* New York: Harcourt, Brace and Howe, 1924. Spingarn's argument reveals how Crocean expressionism is a form of intentionalism (see
Croce, *Aesthetic,* ch. 10). This "Spingarn-Croce-Carlyle-Goethe theory" is
amusingly supported by H. L. Mencken, "Criticism of Criticism of Criticism," also in *Criticism in America.* Like Spingarn, Mencken seems to believe that it is the only alternative to moralistic criticism and genre
criticism.

The Intentionalistic method is also defended, within limits, in the
symposium on "Intention and Interpretation in Art"—it deals mostly with
evaluation rather than interpretation—by Henry D. Aiken and Isabel C.
Hungerland, *J Phil,* LII (1955): 733-53. In my opinion they mix evaluation and interpretation too much, and seem to hold that critical evaluation
consists, or can consist, partly in judging aesthetic objects as "performances."

Eliseo Vivas, in his review of Wimsatt's *The Verbal Icon, Comparative Literature,* VII (1955): 344-61, has criticized "The Intentional Fallacy"
and proposed as an alternative that every literary work has an "ideal" "im-

manent" intention that can be grasped by the critic's "intuition." Theodore Redpath, "Some Problems of Modern Aesthetics," Part I, in C. A. Mace, ed., *British Philosophy in the Mid-century*, New York: Macmillan, 1957, has argued that the "Intentional Fallacy" is mistaken in denying that we can ever know of unrealized aesthetic intentions. He is right in saying that the position there stated was too absolute, and in this book it is slightly relaxed. Nevertheless, in my opinion he evades the main question, which is not whether we can have reason to think that a work falls short of some intention, but whether we can get sufficient evidence of what the specific intention was to determine where, and how far, the work falls short of it; it is this evidence that I think is practically never available. C. J. Ducasse, *The Philosophy of Art*, New York: Dial, 1929, pp. 269-77, regards the intentionalistic standards he discusses as the only ones relevant to "criticism of a work of art considered as such" (p. 270). See also A. K. Coomaraswami, "Intention," *The American Bookman*, I (1944): 41-48; R. Jack Smith, "Intention in an Organic Theory of Poetry," *Sewanee Review*, LVI (1948): 625-33.

The notion of "defective communication," used by I. A. Richards, *Principles of Literary Criticism*, London: Routledge and Kegan Paul, 1925, ch. 25 and Appendix A, is an intentionalistic standard; so also is Croce's "successful expression," thoroughly examined by John Hospers, "The Concept of Artistic Expression," *PAS*, LV (1954-55): 313-44.

For an example of the intentionalistic use of literary history, see the account of Bishop Hurd's defense of Spenser's *Faerie Queene* in David Daiches, *Critical Approaches to Literature*, Englewood Cliffs, N.J.: Prentice-Hall, 1956, pp. 261-66.

24-B ORIGINALITY. It is very common to condemn trite expressions, or clichés, in literature; to praise the "freshness" of a work; to change one's opinion of a work on discovering that it was a plagiary. But we can do away with originality as a criterion of evaluation if we can show that those appeals to it which cannot be dismissed as beside the point are relevant because they really appeal to Objective criteria. The cliché is not merely the familiar expression, but the familiar expression that does not quite fit the style of its context, perhaps.

For older treatments of the importance of "novelty," see Addison's *Spectator* essays, Nos. 411-414, reprinted in P. R. Lieder and R. Withington, *The Art of Literary Criticism*, New York: Appleton-Century, 1941, pp. 231-42; Edward Young, *Conjectures on Original Composition*, 1759, reprinted in Mark Schorer, Josephine Miles, and Gordon McKenzie, eds., *Criticism*, New York: Harcourt, Brace, 1948, pp. 12-30. For a modern defense of the originality standard, see T. M. Greene, *The Arts and the Art of Criticism*, Princeton, N.J.: Princeton U., 1940, pp. 404-07. Compare I. A. Richards, *Practical Criticism*, London: Routledge and Kegan Paul, 1929, Part III, ch. 5; where the "stock response" is the poem itself, rather than the reader's misreading, the question is whether the poem rated low because of stock responses is being condemned for unoriginality or for more objective reasons. I have also read a good, but as yet unpublished, paper on originality by Richard Rudner, of Michigan State University.

24-C SINCERITY. In order to be applied to aesthetic objects in general, not merely those that contain predications, this term would presumably have to be defined in terms of some sort of correspondence between the regional qualities of the work and the emotions of the artist at the time of creation. When it is so defined, its irrelevance to the value of the object itself is fairly plain, though of course insincerity might be taken as a ground of complaint about the artist. The question of sincerity "should be forever banished from criticism," says C. S. Lewis, *The Personal Heresy*, New York: Oxford U., 1939, p. 120. See also Henry Hazlitt, *The Anatomy of Criticism*, New York: Simon and Schuster, 1933, ch. 9.

24-D ARTISTIC FRAUDS. Some subtle problems about the relevance of skill, sincerity, and originality to critical evaluation are raised by those works in which the artist has concealed his own identity and attributed his work to someone else, for example: the "Ossian" poems of James Macpherson; the "Rowley" poems of Thomas Chatterton; the "Clara Gazul" plays of Prosper Mérimée; the fake medieval and Renaissance sculpture of Alceo Dossena; the *Sleeping Cupid,* which was formerly attributed to Michelangelo (Victoria and Albert Museum, London); the forgeries of Giovanni Bastianini, Rouchomovsky, and Ioni; the Vermeer forgeries during the second world war by Hans van Meegeren. In what way should it affect our evaluation of such works when we discover that they were not what they purported to be?

24-E AFFECTIVE CRITICISM. The general rejection of Affective Reasons in the paper "The Affective Fallacy" (for reference, see Chapter I, Note 3-B) was too sweeping, for in the last analysis, as I argue in Chapter XI, it does not appear that critical evaluation can be done at all except in relation to certain types of effect that aesthetic objects have upon their perceivers. David Daiches, "The New Criticism: Some Qualifications," *College English,* II (1950): 242-50, attacked the "affective fallacy" for rejecting emotional effect as a guide to value. Though he is quite right in saying that value cannot be separated from effect, he is mistaken in thinking that this justifies his general attack on the Canons of unity and complexity in literary criticism.

Can the concept of "sentimentality"—see I. A. Richards, *op. cit.,* Part III, ch. 6—be analyzed in objective terms?

24-F OBJECTIVE REASONS. (I) The main problem here can only be solved by a careful study of a large number of critical reasons; it is whether all those reasons that have an Objective reference and cannot be dismissed as clearly irrelevant are in fact analyzable into the Canons of unity, complexity, and qualitative intensity. For example: (1) "A good song is one that is singable, and has music that fits the words." Unsingability—taking this to mean that no human being can perform it—is not on the same level as the other reason at all; it is not a judgment of the song, but a denial that there can be a song. Compare the concept of obscurity in literature: if it can't be sung, or if you can't read the poem, you can't judge it. (2) "I would rather listen to a bad symphony by Schumann than a good symphony by" someone else (Stephen Williams, in Ralph Hill, ed., *The Symphony*, Baltimore: Pelican, 1949, pp. 174-75); can this be given an analysis in terms of the three Canons?

Cleanth Brooks and Robert Penn Warren, *Understanding Poetry*, rev. ed., New York: Holt, 1950, pp. 274-78, said that Joyce Kilmer's "Trees" is a bad poem, because, among other things, it presents a "picture thoroughly confused" (p. 275); their reasons were rather cleverly attacked by Jeffrey Fleece in "Further Notes on a 'Bad' Poem," *College English*, XII (1951): 314-20. Fleece's references to the "affective fallacy" were misplaced, however, and he turned his article into a general attack on "close reading as a critical practice," and argued that the presence or absence of complexity in "Trees" is irrelevant to its value, concerning which he took a relativist position.

(II) For examples of proposed critical principles, see the following: Harold Osborne, *Aesthetics and Criticism*, London: Routledge and Kegan Paul, 1955, pp. 251-59, 268-89 (his standards for literature are "precision," "the art of concealing art," and the control of word-sound for enhancement of meaning); W. H. Hadow, selection from *Studies in Modern Music*, in Eliseo Vivas and Murray Krieger, eds., *Problems of Aesthetics*, New York: Rinehart, 1953, pp. 262-76 (he employs the "principles" of "vitality," "labor," "proportion," and "fitness").

Stephen C. Pepper, *Aesthetic Quality*, New York: Scribner's, 1937, chs. 1, 9, uses "vividness," "spread," and "depth" of "quality" as his critical standards (pp. 223-25, 246); these are interesting to compare with the standards defended in the present chapter. In *The Basis of Criticism in the Arts*, Cambridge, Mass.: Harvard U., 1945, he has made a more elaborate attempt to work out sets of critical standards and derive them from his "world hypotheses." In his concern for this grand scheme, he admits all sorts of standards, and seems to hold that the only criteria of relevance are those provided by the world hypotheses. But his "eclectic," or composite, standard at the end (pp. 140-41) is not far from the three General Canons.

An excellent exercise would be to expose and examine the underlying assumptions of Carl E. Seashore, "In Search of Beauty in Music," *Musical Quarterly*, XXVIII (1942): 302-08.

The role of Canons in criticism is discussed by John Holloway in the symposium, "What Are the Distinctive Features of Arguments Used in Criticism of the Arts?" *PAS*, Suppl. vol. XXIII (1949): 165-94. On the "dramatic unities" as Special Canons, see Allardyce Nicoll, *The Theory of Drama*, London: Harrap, 1931, pp. 38-60. For a review of the problems of literary evaluation see René Wellek and Austin Warren, *Theory of Literature*, New York: Harcourt, Brace, 1949, ch. 18.

An interesting set of materials on which to try out a classification of critical reasons, and especially the distinction between Objective and other reasons, is the flurry of letters that greeted John Ciardi when he wrote an unfavorable review of *The Unicorn and Other Poems*, 1956, by Anne Morrow Lindbergh. When he was appointed Poetry Editor of the *Saturday Review*, he wrote an interesting article stating his principles of selection of poetry to be published, "Everyone Writes (Bad) Poetry," *Saturday Review*, May 5, 1956, 22. In the issue of January 12, 1957, p. 54, he criticized Mrs. Lindbergh harshly on Objective and quite defensible grounds, but in succeeding issues he was first largely attacked, then largely supported, by a stream of correspondence, to which the editors added an editorial reproving him, and Mr. Ciardi a spirited reply, "The Reviewer's Duty to Damn." The variety of reasons given in this controversy, and the variety of implicit assumptions about poems and about criticism, are worth some study.

24-G FAITHFULNESS TO, AND EXPLOITATION OF, THE MEDIUM. The principle of "Purism," as he calls it, has been discussed in some detail by Morris Weitz, *Philosophy of the Arts*, Cambridge, Mass.: Harvard U., 1950, ch. 7, who rejects it. Even apart from the confusions in the term "medium" (see Chapter II, Note 6-B), it is extremely difficult to discover what Purism is supposed to assert. Apparently it says (1) that "No medium should be made to do what it really cannot do" (p. 121); there seems no danger of this; (2) that "it ought not to attempt what it is not able to do" (p. 120); sensible advice; (3) that "the arts ought to do what they can do best" (p. 28); "only" is understood here, and Weitz properly points out that there is no good reason for this view; (4) that "the arts ought to do . . . what distinguishes them from each other" (p. 28); a completely unsupported recommendation; (5) that the "expressive potentials" of each medium "should be realized as fully as possible" (p. 121); sterling words, so long as we do not require all the potentials to be realized in any one work.

T. M. Greene, *op. cit.*, pp. 407-13, has made a good deal of these critical formulas, which he considers fundamental, but his exposition of them alternates between harmless platitudes and dubious specificities. Thus, for example, he says, "The skillful painter uses his paint in a manner appropriate to paint" (p. 408). "Denial of the medium" is "the failure to exhaust the relevant potentialities of the medium," like music that "ignores timbre and dynamic variation" (p. 408); since it is obvious that no creator can exhaust all the potentialities of a medium in one work, the application of this formula comes down to intentionalism: "the primary medium remains unexploited in proportion as the end in view in any specific composition could be more effectively achieved through a richer and more effective use . . ." (p. 409). "Idolatry of the medium," or "over-exploitation . . . of one aspect of it at the expense of other aspects," occurs, for example, when "the lithic character of stone may be so stressed that the chief, and almost the only impression we get of the work is this lithic quality" (p. 411). But since there is nothing wrong with "lithic quality" in itself, this second formula again comes down to intentionalism; the question is what the "objective" was and whether it could have been achieved "more effectively" (p. 411).

It would be worthwhile, however, to analyze some typical appeals to the medium in critical evaluation, to see whether, in so far as they are defensible, they can be subsumed under the three Canons, e.g.: the frequent dispraise of a movie made from a stage play because it fails to make more use of techniques possible in the movies but not on the stage; the view that it is a merit, not a defect, in Gothic architecture that it denies, or overcomes, the "natural" heaviness of the stone; Sir Joshua Reynolds' objection to Ghiberti's bronze gates for the Baptistery in Florence that the artist "overstepped the limits that separate sculpture from painting" and created large compositions, with many figures, "that might have been expressed with propriety in color" (the quoted words are those of J. A. Symonds, *Renaissance in Italy,* New York: Modern Library, 1935, Vol. I, p. 649); Rembrandt's mixing of etching and drypoint in his prints, especially of the last period, which some "Purists" might object to. On this last example, note that John Buckland-Wright, *Etching and Engraving,* New York: Studio Publications, 1953, is very harsh on Dürer as an engraver for not "treating the medium in its true sense of a sculpturesque, simple and direct linear technique" (p. 17) and thereby producing engravings that "are only too often a negation of the medium" (p. 18; see also similar remarks, pp. 173, 175, 225); but W. M. Ivins, *How Prints Look,* New York: Metropolitan Museum of Art, 1943, p. 143, dissents: "The fact that a particular print is in one or another process has no more bearing upon its artistic merit than has the fact that it was printed in the basement or on the top floor."

Dispraise of aesthetic objects on the ground of "excessive virtuosity" —a charge brought against Berlioz, Liszt, Swinburne, and Raphael, for example—seems also to make implicit reference to the medium. But it is not easy to say what is the real ground of condemnation, if any, in such a judgment.

24-H GENRE CRITICISM. The method of critical evaluation that begins by placing the aesthetic object in a species, or genre—it is an epic, a landscape, a sonata for cello and piano—and then judges its value in terms of certain supposed Canons for that genre, is little practiced nowadays, but its theoretical basis and implications are worth analysis. How is the genre of a work determined when it satisfies the Canons of no known genre? This question brings out the concealed intentionalism in much genre criticism. For example, Helmut Hungerland, "Suggestions for Procedure in Art Criticism," *JAAC*, V (March 1947): 189-95, has proposed that a painting should be judged in reference to the "style"-class to which it belongs; but it seems that the assignment of the painting to its class depends upon determining the "assumed objective" (p. 193), or what the painting (i.e., the painter) appears to be "concerned" with (p. 192). For a defense of genre criticism see R. S. Crane, ed., *Critics and Criticism*, Chicago: U. of Chicago, 1952, ch. 10 and pp. 13-18; and the examination of this view by W. K. Wimsatt, Jr., "The Chicago Critics: The Fallacy of the Neoclassic Species," *The Verbal Icon*, Lexington, Ky.: U. of Kentucky, 1954, pp. 41-65.

C. S. Lewis has some fun with the view that there are two main types of literature, "good" and "second-class," and that you must first place a work before you can decide whether it is good, in "High and Low Brows," *Rehabilitations*, New York: Oxford U., 1939, pp. 97-116.

24-I THE ARTIST AS CRITIC AND THE CRITIC AS ARTIST. It is often said that the critic must be an artist—for example, that only a poet can judge a poem—because he must be prepared to back up his critical evaluations with suggestions for improvement. In other words, if he says that a poem is poor, he ought to be able to tell the poet what is wrong with it, and therefore how it might be set right; but in doing this he is himself playing the role of a poet. This question is raised by Mortimer Kadish, "The Importance of a Choice of Context," in the symposium on "The Evidence for Esthetic Judgment," *J Phil*, LIV (1957): 670-79; he appears to hold that critical evaluations (at least negative ones) are themselves recommendations for improvement. While this cannot, I think, be maintained, it might be argued that the reasons given for critical judgments are equivalent to recommendations: that "The painting is poorly balanced because this figure is too far to the right" means the same as "If the figure were moved a little to the left, the painting would be better." Compare "This pudding is not salty enough" with "This pudding would be better if it were salted." But the reason does not seem to be equivalent to the recommendation, though the recommendation can sometimes be inferred from it. Moving the figure may not improve the painting after all, for it may detract from some other feature of the work that is now all right (for example, its central focus). The question of the logical connections between judgments, reasons, and recommendations, is important, but as yet little explored.

25-A THE PERFORMATORY THEORY OF CRITICAL ARGUMENTS. The performatory use of language was pointed out by J. L. Austin in the symposium "Other Minds," *PAS*, Suppl. vol. XX (1946): 170-75.

Margaret Macdonald, in her contribution to the symposium on "What Are the Distinctive Features of Arguments Used in Criticism of the Arts?" with A. H. Hannay and John Holloway, *PAS*, Suppl. vol. XXIII (1949): 165-94 (her paper is reprinted, with some alterations, in William Elton, ed., *Aesthetics and Language*, Oxford: Blackwell, 1954, pp. 114-30), says, "to affirm a work good is more like bestowing a medal than naming any feature of it or of the states of its creators and audience" and is "not true or false" (Elton, p. 121); it cannot be established by deductive or inductive inference (p. 122). But I do not understand what she can mean by saying that the critic's Objective statements serve to "convey" or "present" the work, like playing a sonata to show how good it is, instead of being reasons for his judgment (p. 129).

25-B THE EMOTIVE THEORY OF CRITICAL ARGUMENTS. The Emotive Theory has usually been presented as an account of the way we use the word "good," in general; or particularly in moral contexts; but such an account is also an account of the way the word functions in normative reasoning. Much of the work done on the Emotive Theory of ethics can be transferred quite readily to "good" in an aesthetic context, but the distinction between Commending and Recommending needs to be kept in mind. For a vigorous and simple version of the Emotive Theory, see A. J. Ayer, *Language, Truth and Logic*, 2d ed., London: Gollancz, 1946, ch. 6. The theory was brought to a form able to cope with many of the subtleties of ordinary language in Stevenson's systematic work, *Ethics and Language*, New Haven, Conn.: Yale U., 1944, from which all later discussion takes off. Later discussion has tended to concentrate on investigating the imperative element more than the exclamatory element. For example, R. M. Hare, in his excellent book, *The Language of Morals*, Oxford: Clarendon, 1952, makes a good deal of the imperative character of moral judgments (e.g., "That is wrong"), which are guides to action. He holds that an imperative sentence can be the conclusion of an inference (chs. 2 and 3).

Some of the problems raised by the Emotive Theory are brought out in the following discussions: Richard Robinson, H. J. Paton, R. C. Cross, symposium, "The Emotive Theory of Ethics," *PAS*, Suppl. vol. XXII (1948): 79-140 (Robinson's defense is curious in one respect; he thinks that we often do not intend by "good" to express emotions, but to refer to an objective characteristic of the work, but we are "habitually deceived"); Richard B. Brandt, "Some Puzzles for Attitude Theories," in Ray Lepley, ed., *The Language of Value*, New York: Columbia U., 1957, pp.

153-77; Winston H. F. Barnes, "Ethics Without Propositions," *ibid.*, pp. 1-30; Vincent Tomas, "Ethical Disagreements and the Emotive Theory of Values," *Mind*, LX (1951): 205-22; Asher Moore, "The Emotive Theory and Rational Methods in Moral Controversy," *ibid.*, 233-40. See also the interesting paper by Mary Mothersill, "The Use of Normative Language," *J Phil*, LII (1955): 401-11, who proposes to define "normative statement" in terms of the "expression" of the speaker's approvals or disapprovals.

25-C "GOOD" AS A COMMENDING WORD.   Hare, *op. cit.*, ch. 8, argues that value-judgments have as their "primary function" that of commending, but he emphasizes the close connection between commending and choosing, and holds that all commendations are guides to possible choices. P. H. Nowell-Smith, *Ethics*, Baltimore: Pelican, 1954, ch. 12, says that the "fundamental use" of the word "good" is "to express or explain a preference" (p. 163), but he also distinguishes some other uses of the word.

25-D RELATIVISM.   My definition of "Relativism" is adopted, with some simplification, from the careful and rigorous analysis in Richard B. Brandt, *Hopi Ethics*, Chicago: U. of Chicago, 1954, chs. 6, 16, esp. pp. 88, 235. I am concerned in the text with what he calls the "logical thesis" of Relativism, and I take it to be a theory about the way critical normative terms are to be defined. My formulation of Relativism is, I think, equivalent to Brandt's, though in his version he refers to the possibility for the two disputing critics "both to be correct, or at least for neither to be incorrect" (p. 88), whereas I put it that they do not really contradict each other. For a further interesting discussion of Relativism in general, see Abraham Edel, *Ethical Judgment*, Glencoe, Ill.: Free, 1955, esp. chs. 1, 3, 4. He prefers the term "indeterminacy," though he does not define it very exactly; apparently a dispute is characterized by indeterminacy if there is no rational method of settling it; a question is indeterminate if there is no rational answer. He is concerned with the psychological, sociological, and anthropological data that, he holds, narrow the range of indeterminacy in ethics.

Bernard C. Heyl, *New Bearings in Aesthetics and Art Criticism*, New Haven, Conn.: Yale U., 1943, Part II, ch. 3, offers one of the best-known defenses of relativism, based largely upon the argument from variability (see Part II, ch. 1). Relativism he conceives of as an alternative to "Objectivism" and "Subjectivism" (these types of theory we shall consider in Chapter XI); the form he proposes is a Social Relativism. Though he does not put it exactly this way, his position may be stated as a theory about the meaning of "good" (in an aesthetic context). He says that "artistic judgments of good and bad have intelligible meaning only when art objects are interpreted in the light of some critical system which should be made explicitly or implicitly clear" (p. 129); that two disputing critics who employ different standards do not really conflict, since neither is wrong (p. 135); that a critical judgment is "binding" only for those who resemble the speaker in the standards they accept (pp. 137, 141). Thus his view seems to be that when a critic says "X is good," if he wants this statement to be empirically true and verifiable, he can only mean "X conforms to such-and-such standards, which I accept"; it follows that he can only be contradicted by a critic who accepts the same standards. It does not make sense, from this point of view, to say that standards themselves are correct or incorrect, but Heyl holds that certain sets of standards may legitimately be rejected on the grounds of lacking intelligence, sensitivity, sincerity, subtlety, etc. (p. 143). This is odd, because it would seem that a critic could have no justification for not accepting *all* the standards that survive these negative tests, in which case Heyl's definition would no longer be Relativistic, since any two critics would have the same standards. Heyl's later articles, "Relativism Again," *JAAC*, V (September 1946): 54-61, reprinted in Eliseo Vivas and Murray Krieger, eds., *Problems of Aesthetics,* New York: Rinehart, 1953, pp. 436-45, and "The Critic's Reasons," *JAAC*, XVI (December 1957): 169-79, restate his position more succinctly, with some new examples, and defend it further.

Frederick A. Pottle, in his instructive little book *The Idiom of Poetry,* Ithaca, N.Y.: Cornell U., 1941, defends an interesting kind of Epochal Relativism. His argument might be summarized as follows: the important thing about poetry is that it arouses feelings, and its value is measured by the intensity of the feeling aroused; different historical periods have their feelings aroused by different kinds of poetry (in his terminology, each age has its own "sensibility"); therefore all criticism is "subjective," in the sense that the critic cannot talk about anything but his own sensibility, which he shares with his own age, and the effect of the work upon it (see esp. pp. 16, 34, 40). "All critical judgments are relative to the age producing them" (p. 5). Pottle's view is critically discussed by Cleanth Brooks, *The Well Wrought Urn,* New York: Reynal and Hitchcock, 1947, Appendix 1. It is interesting that Pottle sharply disassociates his Relativistic view of critical evaluation from his Nonrelativistic ethics. This is not in itself contradictory, but it raises the question whether reasons can be given for ethical absolutism that do not hold for aesthetic value.

George Boas, *A Primer for Critics,* Baltimore: Johns Hopkins U., 1937, ch. 6, reprinted in Vivas and Krieger, *op. cit.,* pp. 430-36, seems to hold a form of Personal Relativism, though his defense is very superficial and he even asserts that it is "impossible" for anyone to say, "What I desire is not desirable." See also Henry Hazlitt, *The Anatomy of Criticism,* New York: Simon and Schuster, 1933, chs. 3, 4, 7; Arthur Child, "The Socio-historical Relativity of Esthetic Value," *Phil Rev,* LIII (1944): 1-22, reprinted in Vivas and Krieger, *op. cit.,* pp. 445-62; Abraham Kaplan, "The So-Called Crisis in Criticism," *JAAC,* VII (September 1948): 42-47.

25-E VARIABILITY AND INFLEXIBILITY. For evidence of historical changes in taste, and other forms of variability, see Heyl, *op. cit.*, 97-107; Rita Wellman's account of Victorian taste, *Victoria Royal*, New York: Scribner's, 1939; E. E. Kellett, *Fashion in Literature*, London: Routledge and Kegan Paul, 1931, esp. chs. 1, 3, 4, 20 (he provides some other material about changing reputations of certain authors and types of literature in *The Whirligig of Taste*, New York: Harcourt, Brace, 1929); F. P. Chambers, *The History of Taste*, New York: Columbia U., 1932; Joan Evans, *Taste and Temperament*, London: Cape, 1939.

Charles Morris, *Varieties of Human Value*, Chicago: U. of Chicago, 1956, ch. 7 (see also his paper in Ray Lepley, ed., *The Language of Value*, New York: Columbia U., 1957), has investigated preferences in painting, and found interesting correlations with somatotypes and attitudes toward life. He does not, of course, defend any such simple somatic determinism as that used for illustration in this chapter. On the general somatotype theory, see William H. Sheldon, *The Varieties of Human Physique*, New York: Harper, 1940, and *The Varieties of Human Temperament*, New York: Harper, 1942.

See also Thorstein Veblen, *The Theory of the Leisure Class*, New York: Macmillan, 1899, ch. 6, on the "pervading guidance of taste by pecuniary repute" (reprinted Modern Library, p. 139; see also pp. 149-50), and David Hume's essay, "On the Standard of Taste," *Philosophical Works*, 4 vols., London: Longmans, Green, 1874-75.

25-F PARTICULARISM. The point of view to which I have given this makeshift name has not, to my knowledge, been systematically defended. But it can be illustrated by an amusing, though extremely unsubtle, little book the whole argument of which tacitly assumes the Particularist Theory: Theodore L. Shaw, *Precious Rubbish*, Boston: Stuart Art Gallery, 1956. Two points are made over and over again: (1) people are capable of appreciating only aesthetic objects of limited complexity at certain points in their lives and in the development of their capacities; (2) people get tired of aesthetic objects and want to experience new ones. But these do not prove that we can judge only particular presentations. For provoking remarks, see pp. 16-17, 44, 47, 74, 145-46. Note a frequent form of argument: for example, to David Ewen's statement, "No musician outgrows Mozart's music" (*Music for the Millions*, London: Arco Publications), he retorts, "Can you imagine anything more horrible than a constant and eternal diet of *The Iliad, King Lear, Jupiter Symphony* . . .?"

It is perhaps Particularism more than Relativism that Stephen C. Pepper is attacking in *The Work of Art*, Bloomington, Ill.: Indiana U., 1955, ch. 5.

· XI ·

AESTHETIC VALUE

Philosophers, in discussing the grounds of critical evaluation, commonly substitute a more concise and convenient term for the slightly awkward locution we have been using so far: " 'good' (in an aesthetic context)." Instead of saying that an aesthetic object is "good," they would say that it has *aesthetic value*. And, correspondingly, instead of saying that one object is better than another, but not because it has a higher cognitive or moral value, they would say that it has a higher aesthetic value, or is aesthetically more valuable.

This substitution is, of course, a departure from the usual language of critics, to which we adhered in the preceding chapter. And it marks a shift of interest. If, as I think, a study of the actual arguments and disputes that occur in criticism shows that critics think of their judgments as being true or false, and as being reasoned or reasonable, it may still be that many of them do not have a very clear concept of what they are doing with the word "good," or, if you like, what they mean by it. But it may be possible to show them what they *can* mean, or must mean, by their normative terms if the statements that contain them are to be true and logically justified. And for this purpose it is better to select a somewhat artificial term to work with, such as the term "aesthetic value." I think we can show that critics are in fact, whether they use the term or not, talking about aesthetic value; what is more important, we can show that they can talk about it if they wish, and that it is very worthwhile to do so.

There may be one immediate cause for doubt, however, about the propriety of the term proposed. For critics make both positive and negative judgments of aesthetic objects: There are "good" fugues and still lifes; there are "bad" fugues and still lifes. But the term "value," in its most usual sense, does not have a corresponding antonym. It is true that philosophers sometimes use the term "disvalue," and we could do so, too, if it seemed necessary. But I think we can avoid it by a more radical thesis, if it is acceptable. It may turn out that there is a perfectly clear and definite sense in which we can speak of aesthetic objects as "bad," in the sense of possessing some characteristic opposite to that of goodness. Certainly an object can make us uncomfortable to look at it, just as sounds can be painful to hear. Now consider a painting in an exhibition of amateurs, of which you would say that it is a bad painting. It is easy to find a section of cracked sidewalk that is no worse as a visual design than the painting, but you do not trouble to judge it at all. I am suggesting, therefore, that "bad" in these critical judgments usually means a falling away from some rough level of aesthetic value that the critic expected, and felt justified in expecting, under the circumstances. That is why we say, "Not bad for a child," of a simple verse, or, "Not bad for a chimpanzee," of a finger-painting by the Baltimore Zoo's amazing Betsy. Thus badness in art is simply a low, perhaps very low, grade, or absence, of aesthetic value.

The view that there is no such thing as negative aesthetic value is not accepted by everyone, and it is often held that negative aesthetic value is just what we should mean by "ugliness." My doubts about it are chiefly based on the discussion in the previous chapter of the critic's reasons for his judgments. If intensity of human regional qualities is a ground for positive valuation, there is no corresponding ground for negative valuation, since the bottom end of the scale is just the absence of such qualities. If complexity is also a ground, again there is no corresponding negative, for the bottom of the scale is zero complexity, or absence of any heterogeneity. If unity is a ground, it might be said that opposed to unity is disunity, but every discriminable part of the perceptual field has some degree of unity, and disunity is only a low grade of unity—though perhaps a grade that is immediately unpleasant. Alberto Giacometti's *Disagreeable Object* (1931, Private Collection, New York) is disagreeable enough, and by no means beautiful; and, however interesting it may be as dada or surrealism, it is not much of a piece of sculpture. But I think it would be a mistake to say that it has negative aesthetic value.

The problem of this chapter can now be stated in these terms: what we want is a theory of aesthetic value. And such a theory ought to answer a number of questions. It would include a definition of the term "aesthetic value"; it would include an account of the way in which judgments of aesthetic value are, or can be, used, known to be true or false, supported by reasons, related to other judgments. In an even looser sense, the Emotive Theory and the Performatory Theory could be brought under the term, but I think it is probably better to treat them as denying that there is anything, any quality of aesthetic objects or of human beings or any relation between objects and human beings, that "aesthetic value" refers to. The three main types of theory that we shall consider in the present chapter do find a use and a referent for the term "aesthetic value," and propose a general account of critical reasoning.

§26.   *THE BEAUTY THEORY*

Before we take up the first theory of aesthetic value, there are still two possible sources of discontent with this term itself that should be looked into. For its legitimate and safe employment does depend upon two presuppositions: first, that there is a kind of value in aesthetic objects which can be distinguished from other kinds of value, for example, cognitive and moral value, that they may at the same time incidentally possess; and second, that it is the same kind of value that is to be found in aesthetic objects of various sorts—for though we apply the word "good" to a Greek krater and a Walt Disney cartoon, it does not follow that we use the word in the same sense both times.

With respect to the first presupposition, the situation seems to me pretty clear. All Commendations, as I have called them, belong to a recognizable genus, and we can distinguish one species of Commendation from another by the differences in the grounds, or standards, appealed to in the reasons for them. When we analyze a random group of reasons for commending aesthetic objects, as we did in the preceding chapter, they fall into logically independent groups, two of which I put under cognitive value and moral value, and the third of which I am now proposing to put under aesthetic value.

There are certain features of a recording, for example, that can be commended independently of each other: we can judge the performance, for example, without knowing the price. So it seems easy to separate the economic aspects of the recording from the aesthetic ones, and this is practically forced upon us in the extreme cases, for example, old 78 RPM records of long-deceased opera stars, some of which are extremely expensive merely because they are rare. As is frequently remarked, a painting can cover a hole in the wall whether it is good or poor, and plastic values are not indispensable in a doorstop.

It will be illuminating to make this point in a slightly different way. Suppose we have two paintings, X and Y, and someone says that X is better than Y.[1] Now suppose he also said there is no difference between

---

[1] This example is developed from one given by R. M. Hare, *The Language of Morals,* Oxford: Clarendon, 1952, pp. 80-81.

X and Y, either in their internal characteristics or in the way they were produced, or their relation to other things. This would amount to saying that he can give no reason for his judgment, for there is nothing he can say about one that could not be said about the other. Now suppose, instead of saying that X and Y do not differ in any way, he says that there *is* a difference in their origin—one is a "fake"—but no difference in their internal characteristics, so that no one could tell them apart just by looking at them. Then, I suggest, this amounts to saying that there is no *aesthetic* reason for the judgment, though there may be another kind of reason; and the critic's word "good" no longer can refer to aesthetic value, but only to some other species of value.

In my use of the term "aesthetic value"—and I claim that this rule is actually in effect in the critical use of "good"—two objects that do not differ in any observable qualities cannot differ in aesthetic value. This rule helps to distinguish aesthetic value from other values. But it does not decide for any particular theory of aesthetic value, for the word "can" is not further restricted. According to some theories of value it will be *logically* impossible for X to be aesthetically better than Y if they appear exactly alike; as it is logically impossible for a figure to be square unless it has right angles. According to other theories, it will be *empirically,* that is, psychologically, impossible, as it is for certain lines to appear parallel— that is, to have this regional quality—under certain perceptual conditions unless they are in fact *not* parallel, as measured locally.

Critical Pluralism

With respect to the second presupposition, other doubts can be raised, though they seem not to have been taken very seriously by aestheticians. Critics often make comparative aesthetic judgments, as we have seen: *The Cherry Orchard* is greater than *The Wild Duck;* Mozart's *String Quartet in A Major* (K. 464) is better than Beethoven's *String Quartet in A Major* (*Op. 18, No. 5*); the Renoir *Bathers* in Philadelphia (1884-87, Carroll S. Tyson Collection) is inferior to the one in Cleveland (1892, Cleveland Museum of Art). According to the "aesthetic value" terminology, all these differences are differences in degree of aesthetic value; and this value is therefore one that all works of art may possess in a greater or lesser degree. But if the difference in aesthetic value between two plays is the same sort of difference as the difference in aesthetic value between two paintings, then it is perfectly sensible to ask such questions as these: Does the Cleveland *Bathers* have higher aesthetic value than *The Wild Duck?* Does Mozart's *A Major Quartet* have higher aesthetic value than "Tears, Idle Tears"? Does *The Rape of the Lock* have higher aesthetic value than the *Hermes* of Praxiteles? And these questions sound a little odd.

The problem is: What makes them odd? Part of the cause is in the suggestion that we are hoping for a linear grading of all these diverse objects, that is, a rating on a single scale. "The women's swimming team is better than the men's basketball team" might have initially such a puzzling effect, if the first thing we think of is that they are not in the same league, and there is no common ground on which they can compete. But of course we allow this comparison to make sense in terms, say, of their won-lost records. "Jane's hearing is better than John's eyesight" is also a bit puzzling in the same way, yet not fatally so; we allow "Jane's hearing is better than her eyesight." (Compare: "William Blake and Dante Gabriel Rossetti were better poets than they were painters.") If eyesight and hearing can each be scaled, then a performance near the top on one scale can be said to be better than one near the bottom on the other. Nevertheless these examples do not resolve our difficulty. For the question remains whether there is a *single* factor, such as athletic ability or informativeness about the environment, shared in some degree by both of the things compared.

The odd questions about aesthetic objects are not ones that the critic would ordinarily ask. He would ask not whether *The Cherry Orchard* is a good work of art, or even a good literary work, but whether it is a good play. He would not ask whether Mozart's or Beethoven's quartet is the greater work of art, but which is the better musical composition, or perhaps which is the better quartet. Taking this cue, it could be held that there is no such thing as a good aesthetic object; there are only good plays, good statues, good musical compositions, and so forth. Or perhaps that there are only good comedies and good tragedies, or good classical symphonies and good fugues. Granted that music and the drama can for certain purposes be classed together; still not every class has a "good." There are good chairs and bad ones, but perhaps not good articles of furniture and bad ones. It makes sense to say, "Show me a good house"; but it makes no sense to say, "Show me a good material object." What good is a material object *qua* material object?

Again, there are criteria for deciding what makes a banana good— it is sweet, soft, firm. But there are no such criteria for deciding what makes a good piece of fruit, as such. How can there be, when the criteria for a good banana conflict with the criteria for a good lemon or a good apple? Of course, we can say that the class of good pieces of fruit consists of good bananas, good pears, good plums, and so forth. But that is a different notion. In short, it could be held that there are literary value, fine arts value, musical value, and so on, but no such thing as *aesthetic* value. I shall call this theory *Critical Pluralism*.[2]

I have made something of the Pluralistic Theory because it is an interesting challenge and it opens up a line of thought that I shall make

---

[2] Those critics who judge in terms of genres (see Note 24-H) may be said to subscribe to a version of this theory, though they would probably not defend, or even formulate, it this way.

use of in the last section of this chapter, but not because I think it is a serious obstacle. To show that there is such a thing as aesthetic value we shall have to define the term, but there does not seem to be any reason at the beginning to doubt its existence. The fact that so many, and perhaps all, of the Special Canons of critical evaluation subordinate themselves to General Canons that apply to all the arts is the strongest reason at this stage for suspecting that there is such a thing as aesthetic value, over and above, or at least distinguishable from, the special values that individual arts may have.

The Pluralistic Theory is a theory about the "proper use" of normative terms in criticism, that, for example, "good play" and "good quartet" are correct and meaningful uses, but "good aesthetic object" or "good work of art"—except where, as sometimes happens, "work of art" is confined to the fine arts—are not. "This painting is good" is to be understood as "This is a good painting." If the theory is true, then it sets limits to the kinds of reason that would be relevant to critical evaluations. But the Pluralistic Theory, though resting its case on usage, is not firmly supported by it.

It is true that a critic might well decline to compare some aesthetic objects, even of the same sort; where two plays, or two string quartets, are both highly complex and both masterpieces, it might be practically impossible, and quite pointless, to try to decide which is greater than the other, even if greatness in both cases is the same quality. But many critics who would throw up their hands if asked to judge comparatively *The Cherry Orchard* and Beethoven's Op. 59, No. 1, would not hesitate to say that Op. 59, No. 1, has a higher aesthetic value than *Charley's Aunt* and that *The Cherry Orchard* has a higher aesthetic value than Addinsell's *Warsaw Concerto*. And if these statements are meaningful, then so are the others given earlier, though far more difficult, and perhaps even in practice impossible to prove.

Beauty

The three types of theory that we shall deal with in this chapter are all accounts of aesthetic value in general. And the first, and simplest, of them is that which analyzes aesthetic value in terms of the concept of beauty. To state the theory roughly, it holds that the aesthetic value of an aesthetic object consists in its possession of a certain unique regional quality, called "beauty," and the degree of its aesthetic value is determined by the intensity of this quality. This is the *Beauty Theory* of Aesthetic Value.

Two verbal hazards we had better remove at once. The first is the frequently excessive generality of the term "beautiful." A number of writers on aesthetics use it as an exact synonym of "aesthetically valuable." In this usage, "is beautiful" is simply the general formula of critical approbation, instead of "has aesthetic value." However, we do not need "beautiful" for this broad sense, since we have adopted already the term "aesthetically valuable," and we do need the term "beautiful" in a narrower sense to formulate the Beauty Theory. For the Beauty Theory is that the object is aesthetically valuable *because* it is beautiful, and this does not mean that it is beautiful because it is beautiful.

An even greater hazard of the term "beautiful" is its excessively variable meaning. The situation is so confused that only some fairly highhanded measures will reduce it to order. Not every general statement containing the word "beauty" is a theory of beauty. Sometimes we find one philosopher, *A*, saying, "Beauty is successful expression," and another, *B*, retorting, "Beauty is organic unity." They may think they are disagreeing with one another, but the chances are they are simply using the word "beauty" in two different senses, and their statements are not alternative theories of beauty but different proposals about how the word "beauty" is to be applied. Now the statements may really be alternative theories—if *A* and *B* have already defined "beauty" in the same sense. For example, suppose they both think of beauty as a special quality, and *A* is urging that this quality appears in aesthetic objects when, and only when, they are successful expressions, while *B* holds that it appears when, and only when, they have organic unity. In that case *A* and *B* do have two theories; their dispute is real, and their positions are arguable.

It is often debated whether beauty is objective or subjective. Suppose *C* holds the former view, *D* the latter. What is the locus of their disagreement? Again, they probably mean different things by "beauty," and until they agree to mean the same thing, they are not coming to grips with each other or with any real issue. *C* means a quality in the aesthetic object, but *D* means a feeling in the perceiver. Now, if that is what *D* is talking about, it would be much better if he used another word, for it is misleading to use "beauty" for a kind of feeling. He is not proposing a theory of beauty at all when he says, "Beauty is subjective," but is rather denying that there is any such quality in aesthetic objects, and asserting that there is some response to them that is the real basis of critical evaluation.

Therefore, I have chosen to begin by discussing a simple theory of aesthetic value, which I shall call the "Beauty Theory." I am convinced that some will recognize in it their own, or some part of their own, or something similar to their own, theory. It seems to me reasonable, though untrue, and highly instructive. Anyone who does not recognize it as his own, but who calls his own a Beauty Theory anyway, may be momentarily disappointed, but he will, I believe, find his own theory, or something similar to it, turning up later in this chapter under a different— and, in my opinion, more suitable—name.

The Beauty Theory, then, may be summed up in three sentences:

1. Beauty is a regional quality of perceptual objects.
2. Beauty is intrinsically valuable.
3. "Aesthetic value" means "value that an object has on account of its beauty."

The Beauty Theory proposes to distinguish aesthetic value from other species of value as that sort of value in a perceptual object that is conferred upon it by its beauty. To justify the judgment that an object has aesthetic value, according to this theory, you first show that it has beauty, from which it logically follows that it has aesthetic value.[3]

Sentence 3 may be taken, and would be offered by some proponents of the Beauty Theory, as making explicit what critics really mean, or it may be taken as a proposal for a convenient way of speaking; in either case, it is dependent upon the first two sentences, and these are the two that raise the difficult and important questions.

Consider first Sentence 1. In this theory, beauty is held to be a simple regional quality, that is, a quality, like smoothness or whiteness, that is not analyzable into any more simple qualities. Being a regional quality, it is a quality of a complex; however, that does not make it, but only its perceptual conditions, complex. There are two very different ways in which the Beauty Theory conceives of the relation between beauty and the object that has it, and these give rise to two different forms of the theory. In the *Transcendental* form, beauty is a platonic universal that exists, or subsists, outside of space and time, but *supervenes* upon the aesthetic object, which then embodies it more or less fully. In the *Naturalistic* form, beauty is an emergent from the object, a regional quality like any other. To this metaphysical difference there corresponds an epistemological one: in the Transcendental version, beauty is apprehended by a faculty of intuition; in the Naturalistic version, it is simply perceived by the senses—heard, or seen.

Both forms of the theory, however, agree that the occurrence of beauty in the object, whether it is supervenient or emergent, depends upon the other features of the object, its elements, internal relations, and other regional qualities. So in either case it becomes relevant to inquire, and it becomes desirable for the theory to explain, what the perceptual conditions are under which an object will always possess the quality of beauty. The question is whether there are any necessary conditions, or a limited set of sufficient conditions, of beauty.

It is in the attempt to provide answers to this question, none of them so far very successful, that Beauty Theories divide in another way. The answers are of two main sorts, which we may call *Formalistic* and *Intellectualistic*.

The Formalistic Theory is that the occurrence of beauty is a function of certain formal properties of the object, and it seeks for as exact as

---

[3] The Beauty Theory has been maintained by Plato, Plotinus, T. E. Jessup, T. M. Greene, C. E. M. Joad and others; see Note 26-B.

possible a description of these beautiful-making properties. For example, it might be held that there is a certain degree of unity and a certain degree of complexity, such that any perceptual object having both will also have intuitable or perceivable beauty; and moreover that if either the unity or the complexity is increased, without decreasing the other, the beauty will be greater. Apart from the difficulties we are already familiar with, about degrees of unity and complexity, it remains a question whether it wouldn't be necessary to add at least one more variable to this formula —making beauty depend also upon the intensity of other regional qualities—if the theory is to be adequate to the practice of critics. In that case, of course, it would no longer be a pure Formalistic Theory. On the other hand, some theorists have explored even more exact possibilities in the realm of mathematics. For example, the Golden Section (the ratio of a to b when a is to b as b is to $a + b$) is found in painting, music, and the drama, as well as in architecture and sculpture and pottery. It would be most gratifying if some such simple formula as this could measure the perceptual conditions of beauty. But it has not yet been very plausibly shown, I think, that the Golden Section, or any simple set of ideal proportions, is either necessary or sufficient for beauty.[4]

The Intellectualistic Theory works in a different direction; it is often a corollary of the Revelation Theory that we discussed in Chapter VIII, §21. According to this theory, it is not the elements, internal relations, and other regional qualities of the object alone that are the conditions of its being beautiful, but its embodiment, or showing forth, of some conceptual or cognitive content. Intellectualists, no less than the Formalists, have encountered great difficulties in trying to say, beyond the rather simple truths that remain to the Revelation Theory after analysis, exactly what intellectual content it is that a Haydn quartet, a pitcher of Swedish glass, the famous lines of Juliet to Romeo, or a Moorish interior by Matisse, embodies, and how it is embodied.

I mention these divisions and implications of the Beauty Theory because they are, in my opinion, worth consideration, not less for their possible truth than for the many incidental illuminations they have certainly provided. But to keep our discussion to manageable size, I shall concern myself only with the most general and fundamental questions. The problem of determining perceptual conditions already takes more for granted than I am fully prepared to concede. After all, is there such a simple phenomenally objective quality as beauty? When we have distinguished in a painting its lines and shapes and color-tones, its structural relations, and its human regional qualities—the movement and swirl, the joyousness and vitality—is there something else left over that we have not yet mentioned, namely its beauty? I can easily doubt it; and yet there are

---

[4] For references to work done along this line, see Notes 13-C and 13-D in Chapter IV.

some occasions when I cannot think of any more appropriate thing to say than "That is beautiful."

Of course, the Beauty Theory has difficulty in explaining why there is so much variability in the apprehension of beauty. It is a nonrelativistic theory. As we have seen, variability does not prove relativism, but any theory of aesthetic value ought to leave room for an explanation of that variability; it must be compatible with it. And this is harder for the Beauty Theory than for others, because beauty is supposed to be so directly and immediately accessible to intuition or perception. The In-tuitionist, who holds the Transcendental form of the theory, can invoke the concept of beauty-blindness; but we have already examined the troubles in Intuitionism. The Empiricist, who holds the Naturalistic form, will presumably maintain that the perception of beauty, like that of cer-tain other regional qualities, may require long training, as well as close attention, concentration, and freedom from irrelevant distractions. Beauty is just easily missed.

But even if there is such a quality as beauty, and even if its pres-ence confers aesthetic value upon an object, it cannot, I think, be con-sidered the only ground of aesthetic value. If the word "beauty" has any clear and restricted meaning, it does not apply, I suppose, to *Oedipus Rex,* to *The Magic Mountain,* to *King Lear,* to parts of Bartók's piano concertos, to some paintings of Rubens and Tintoretto, much less the Grünewald *Crucifixion* (ca. 1510, Museum, Colmar). These works may be powerful, grand, terrible, yes—but not beautiful. At least, the Beauty Theorist must, I think, say so. Of course, those who when they say that something is beautiful mean only that it has high aesthetic value are at liberty to say that these works are beautiful. But anyone who uses the word "beautiful" for a quality, and applies it to those objects most com-monly called beautiful, will, to be consistent, have to withhold it from these works.

Indeed, we might resuscitate a rather old view, now in disfavor, that there is a family of distinct value-making qualities: the beautiful, the sublime, the graceful, the tragic, the comic, and perhaps others. And these qualities might be understood to cut across the divisions of the arts: there can be graceful poems and graceful dances, tragic dramas, tragic paintings, and tragic melodies. The trouble here is that there seems no way of demonstrating that any particular list of qualities is an exhaustive inventory of those that are aesthetically valuable. Some aes-theticians have added the grotesque and the ugly to the list. But what of such qualities as melancholy, serenity, explosiveness, ruggedness? Indeed, what about *any* positive, distinct, intense human regional quality?—as we asked in Chapter X, §24.

The summary of the Beauty Theory, above, contained three sentences. The discussion of Sentence 1 has led us into a number of related problems, and has ended by casting considerable doubt on Sentence 3, which seems too narrow, either as a report of critical usage or as a proposal for a new usage, since it leaves out so many apparently relevant reasons for critical evaluations. That leaves Sentence 2, and a different kind of problem.

To insure that we are clear about the meaning of Sentence 2, it may be well to recall the definition of its crucial term. To say that a value of an object is an *instrumental* (or extrinsic) value is to say that the object derives that value from being a means to the production of some other object that has value. The term "value" can, of course, also be applied to events and states of affairs. To say that a value of an object is an *intrinsic* (or terminal) value is to say that the object has that value independently of any means-end relation to other objects. Instrumental value is, so to speak, a borrowed value, and it can be passed along from one thing to another, or, better, it spreads like an electric charge to anything that comes into appropriate contact with it, as the value of health attaches instrumentally to the medicine that protects it, and thence to the money that buys the medicine, etc. Though the term "intrinsic value" has been given a number of different meanings by various writers, it is here used simply as the negative of "instrumental value." Note that an object can have a number of distinct values, some intrinsic, some instrumental, but the same value, or the same part of its total value, cannot be both at the same time.

Now, the Beauty Theory holds that beauty has intrinsic value. To show that anything has instrumental value, you point out that it is, or can be, a means to something else that is already acknowledged to have value; when a certain mold is discovered to yield penicillin, it acquires an instrumental value that it did not have before. But how do you show that something has intrinsic value? What sort of reason can you give? There are two choices open to the Beauty Theory at this point. The Empiricist will hold that the only sort of reason that can be given is in terms of some relation—not, however, a means-end relation, for that would make the value instrumental—to human attitudes. This view is of a kind that we shall have to examine in the following section. It is not acceptable to many of those who hold the Beauty Theory, for it makes the *value* of beauty, though not its existence, dependent upon human attitudes. The second alternative is to appeal to a Rationalist Theory of knowledge.

According to this view, "Beauty is intrinsically valuable" is a self-evident statement, whose truth is immediately grasped by the intellect, and known with certainty. Such a grasp is often called by the word "intuition," but we have already found a somewhat different use for this term in Chapter VIII, §21, and even though at this point Intuitionism and Rationalism may merge into one another, there are, I think, possible distinctions that ought to be preserved. So I shall say that in this Rationalistic form, the Beauty Theory is that Sentence 2 is one of those statements that are significant and synthetic but in which the unaided reason sees a necessary connection between subject and predicate. Reason thus has knowledge on its own, and owes nothing to sense experience.

The indispensability of such knowledge the Rationalist would sometimes defend by means of another general principle about normative reasoning that ought to be mentioned here. It is well known that if we make a distinction between nonnormative statements, about what is the case in the world, and normative ones, which are about what *should,* or *should not,* be the case, then we must be careful how we mix them in reasoning. It is usually held that normative statements, about what is good or bad, or right or wrong, cannot be deduced from nonnormative statements, no matter how many. Thus in a deductive argument with a normative conclusion, at least one of the premises must be normative. In effect we took account of this, without saying so, in the preceding chapter when we said that from "This is unified" (nonnormative) it does not directly follow that "This is good" (normative); we need the help of another premise, a normative one. Now the Beauty Theorist thinks of critical argument on the deductive pattern: show that the object is beautiful, and it follows logically that it is good. Hence, he might argue, all critical reasoning has got to rest in the end upon some basic normative premise. Either this premise is arbitrarily chosen, as the Relativist suggested, in which case all critical reasoning is merely hypothetical, or it must be self-evident, so that it does not need to be proved from some even more basic premise. "Beauty is intrinsically valuable" is this self-evident premise.

We are clearly about at the end of our story here, for having brought out the underlying theory of knowledge, and turned it over for inspection, we shall have to leave it as it is. As at so many other points, we leave aesthetics, and plunge into other fields of philosophy. If you agree that there are self-evident statements, and if this statement seems self-evident to you, then you are prepared to go along with the Beauty Theorist. Not that discussion has to stop at this point, for there is a great deal one can say about self-evidence, or apparent self-evidence, only it cannot be said here. If you are not convinced that Sentence 2 is self-evident, one question remains: is there any way in which the Beauty Theorist could convince you that it is self-evident, or, to put it more generally, that you do in fact rationally recognize that beauty has intrinsic value? There is a famous argument[5] to this effect, and we may conclude this section with a brief discussion of it.

[5] Proposed by G. E. Moore in *Principia Ethica;* for reference see Note 26-B.

Imagine two worlds, one exceedingly beautiful in every respect, the other as ugly as it could be; and let it be assumed, and held in mind, that neither of these worlds can ever be seen by a human eye. The beauty of the one will never be appreciated, the ugliness of the other never offend—no one will stumble on them, even by chance. Now, suppose you are asked which of these two worlds you would prefer to have in existence. "Prefer" here has to be more than just a feeling; for example, you will get more pleasure, no doubt, from *thinking* about one of these worlds—that is, contemplating it in imagination—than from thinking about the other. The question, to be significant, has to be whether, on reflection, it is not clear that one of these worlds is better, or has a greater claim to exist, and even has a claim upon you to help make it exist, if you can.

It is hard to set up even this abstract thought-experiment so that it will really be a test case for the intrinsic value of beauty. For example, according to one account, "The unseeable world has aesthetic value" means something like "If anyone were to see it, he would find it valuable"—a statement that is clearly true. This sort of account, here roughly and incompletely formulated, is one that we shall examine below, in §28. But the value that is defined this way is certainly not intrinsic value, and the question still remains for the Beauty Theory whether the beautiful world is not better than the ugly one, in itself and without any indirect or covert appeal to human experience.

To this question one decisive answer might be made: if any one were to say that he was perfectly indifferent, no reason could be given to him for choosing one world over another, since neither could be experienced. No rational preference could be given; it would be idle to work for the existence of either. But to the Rationalist this neutral answer is not acceptable. To him it seems self-evident that one world is to be preferred to the other, quite apart from any consequences or responses, and this he holds to be a rational self-evidence, to which any man who sits ` in cool reflection, without practical or emotional distractions, will see that he must subscribe. But if we doubt that any significant statements, or this one in particular, can be self-evident, then the Beauty Theory, in its Rationalist form, must be rejected.

§27. *PSYCHOLOGICAL DEFINITIONS*

The definition of "aesthetic value" offered by the Beauty Theory is an *Objective* definition of that term. By this I mean that it makes no reference to the psychological attitudes of any human beings; beauty and the value that inheres in it are characteristics of the aesthetic object itself, quite independently of the way anyone feels about it. As we have seen, it is doubtful that the Beauty Theory's definition of "aesthetic value" corresponds to the way most people use the word "good" in aesthetic contexts, and it is very doubtful that they *can* use it this way, if they want critical value-judgments to be rationally defensible.

Now, if there are difficulties in this, the most convincing of Objective definitions, we must explore the possibilities of a *Subjective* definition, that is, one in which the defining term makes a reference to the psychological states of some human being or beings. For example, if "is regarded with favor by most qualified critics" were suggested as a defining term for "has aesthetic value," this would be a Subjective definition, since the defining term refers to the attitude of those critics. And the question would arise whether such a suggested definition is one that we can be persuaded to accept. A wide variety of Subjective, or psychological, definitions have been proposed, but there is a general argument that supports them all.

How could anything have value except in relation, direct or indirect, to the needs or desires of human beings? To say that no one is interested in an object, or cares anything about it one way or the other—is not that precisely the description of an object with zero value? If value is not a quality of perceptual objects, like their redness or grandeur, then it must be a relation, and consist in someone's taking a certain attitude toward the object. To put it in a familiar, though casual, way, it is not liked because it is good, but good because it is liked. Better, in saying that it is good, we do mean, or can only mean (if we are sensible), that someone has such-and-such a pro attitude toward it—approval, interest, desire. The most general, and least question-begging, common word for a pro attitude is probably "liking," so let's use this:

"X has value" means "Someone likes X."

This gives us a definition of "value," but not of "aesthetic value." To obtain the latter, we would need to distinguish first a certain kind of liking, or a liking in a certain way, which might be called "aesthetic liking":

"X has aesthetic value" means "Someone likes X in a certain way (i.e., aesthetically)."

Other expressions could be chosen for the defining term, for example: "Someone enjoys X aesthetically," or "Someone takes aesthetic pleasure in X." But these can be defined in terms of "like." For I take it that "enjoying X" means approximately "experiencing X, and liking the experiencing of X." And "taking pleasure in" seems to be synonymous with "enjoying."

It may not be easy to make the distinction between aesthetic liking and other kinds, but there does not seem to be anything wrong with the idea of such a distinction. Among his favorable attitudes toward various women, a man might distinguish love, friendship, fatherliness, brotherliness, or even older-brotherliness from younger-brotherliness. Similarly, toward the George Washington bridge, he might distinguish the liking in one way, as a design, from the liking in another way, as a convenient connection between the New Jersey Turnpike and the Henry Hudson Parkway. We could now turn to this question, and ask how aesthetic likings, or aesthetic enjoyments, differ from others; that is, we could inquire into the nature of aesthetic experience. But that is not yet necessary, for the difficulties we must first notice in Psychological definitions of "aesthetic value" are of a more general and fundamental sort. If the Psychological definitions survive these objections, it will be time enough to go on to the question about aesthetic experience; if not, we shall find a more appropriate place to deal with this question in the following section. Meanwhile, let it be understood that "like," in this context, is short for "like in a certain [as yet unspecified] way."

We have now the general framework of a Psychological definition of "aesthetic value," a rough approximation, as it stands, for it leaves a great many questions unanswered. But note three things about it.

First, the view that "aesthetic value" is to be defined Subjectively is not the same as the Emotive Theory, which we discussed in the preceding chapter: the Emotive Theory holds that "aesthetic value" is not to be defined at all, because when someone says an aesthetic object is good he is not making a statement about its being liked, but merely showing—not asserting—that he likes it himself. Second, the Psychological definition, if acceptable, would have a considerable convenience, since it takes care of the problem of deriving values from facts. If normative statements are only psychological statements of some kind, they are testable just like other empirical statements, and critical reasoning is not engaged in the fallacious attempt to derive normative conclusions from nonnormative premises. Third, the Psychological definition purports to be a definition of "intrinsic aesthetic value"; the attitude of liking is understood to be taken toward the object not because it is a means to anything else, but simply for its own sake. Things like cake, jokes, and horse races have intrinsic value, though not necessarily aesthetic value, according to the psychological view; this is the same as saying that they are enjoyed.

All the Psychological definitions, then, however they may differ in ways yet to be considered, agree in holding that intrinsic value consists in a certain relation to human beings, the relation we have been roughly describing as "being liked by." This is true, for example, whether the object of the liking is a perceptual object, such as a painting or a musical composition, or itself a feeling, such as pleasure. For to say, as some philosophers would, that pleasure is intrinsically valuable would be simply to say that pleasure is liked for its own sake. Only a state of mind, or attitude, can confer intrinsic value, and if there is anything toward which it is impossible that any mind should have this attitude, then that thing is valueless.

Personal and Impersonal Definitions

The framework presented above still leaves us with a wide range of choice among possible definitions. They divide, however, into two main groups.

In some psychological definitions, the defining term makes an overt or covert reference to the speaker. Suppose it is proposed that

"X has aesthetic value" means (a) "I like X," or
(b) "People in my culture like X."

This proposal is that whenever anyone makes a statement about aesthetic value, he is reporting his own likings or the likings of some group that is defined with reference to him. Thus to know whether it is true that X has aesthetic value, according to this definition, we would have to investigate the likings of the speaker or other members of his family, class, occupation, religion, or culture. Let us call such definitions *Personal* Subjective definitions. These are all Relativistic ones, of course, unless the group of people includes everybody:

"X has aesthetic value" means "Most people of my species like X."

This is not Relativistic, because all creatures who talk about aesthetic value are members of the same species, so it would be impossible to find two disputants who would be referring to different groups, according to this definition. But if

"X has aesthetic value" means "Most of my countrymen like X,"

why then, if A and B are from different countries, A can affirm, and B deny, that X has aesthetic value, but they will not be contradicting each other.

It is to be noted that a Subjective definition is not made a Personal one merely by the fact that the speaker happens to belong to the group mentioned in the defining term. For example, the ridiculous definition,

"X has aesthetic value" means "All blue-eyed people like X,"

does not become Personal whenever it is uttered by a blue-eyed person. This is not a Relativistic definition, because if the question arises whether a poem has aesthetic value, then, according to this definition, the question is really whether it is liked by all blue-eyed people. And this question is certainly open to empirical inquiry. But the definition,

"X has aesthetic value" means "People with eyes the color of mine like X,"

is a Personal one and Relativistic; here the class of people referred to will vary from speaker to speaker, depending on the color of his eyes.

The Subjectivist definitions in which the defining term does not refer to the speaker we may call *Impersonal* ones, for example:

"X has aesthetic value" means "All red-blooded Americans like X."

This is Impersonal, whether or not the speaker happens to be a red-blooded American, because if we should adopt this definition all disputes about aesthetic value would be genuine: that is, they would really be disputes about whether or not the object in question is liked by all red-blooded Americans, and this is an empirical question. This example, however far-fetched, points up the need for two refinements in our psychological definitions. First, anyone who offered such a definition as this would not have to claim that all red-blooded Americans are in fact acquainted with the wholesome object in question. He can put his defining term into a conditional form:

"Any red-blooded American would like X."

This means that the test of whether or not X has aesthetic value is not whether all red-blooded Americans have experienced X and found it to their taste, but whether if, in a marketing survey or a full sales campaign, they *were* exposed to X, they would like it. Second, the Subjectivist will certainly want to follow critical usage as far as he can in providing a comparative, as well as a positive, meaning for "aesthetic value." He will want to work with a formula like:

"X has higher aesthetic value than Y" means "X is (more?) liked by (more?) people than Y."

The admissibility of either or both of these two "more's" will depend on other decisions about the group of people concerned. For example, if the key group is red-blooded Americans, the definition could specify (a) that more of them like X than like Y, (b) that a majority of them, taken individually, like both X and Y, but like X more, (c) that the ones who like X are more red-blooded than those who like Y.

It is not necessary for us to explore further the many intricacies of this line of thought; a great deal of work has been done on Subjectivist definitions of value in general.[1] The Personal ones have difficulties peculiar to them, especially on account of their Relativism. The Impersonal ones face a special dilemma. It is highly implausible, after all, especially in aesthetics, to suppose that when critics use words like "good" and "bad" they actually mean to refer to the preferences of large and unselected groups of people, such as twentieth century men or red-blooded Americans. Critics are perfectly aware that by such a test very little of what they admire would have aesthetic value: is there, for example, any chamber music that a majority of red-blooded Americans would like

---

[1] Especially by David W. Prall, R. B. Perry, and C. I. Lewis; for references, see Note 27-A.

if suddenly confronted with it? (This is entirely separate from the question whether they might be brought to like it.) Nothing is plainer than that critics think some people are more qualified than others to experience aesthetic objects.

The more interesting Impersonal definitions, then, are those that introduce another restriction. It is evident that we are all in a better condition to listen to music when, for example, we are not tired or hungry or worried; and that someone who has good hearing, pitch-discrimination, and melodic memory, is better equipped to listen to music than someone who lacks these abilities. Suppose we should include in our defining group only qualified people, and also specify the optimum conditions for their experience:

"X has a higher aesthetic value than Y" means "X is, or would be, liked better than Y by all *qualified perceivers*, under the *right conditions*."

A psychological definition like this certainly comes closest to ordinary critical usage. But it raises two sets of difficult problems. The first set has to do with "right conditions." It is a sensible question what the right conditions are for reading poetry or looking at paintings, and we know part of the answer. We cannot hope to list a complete set of desirable conditions, but it is not necessary to do so, because we can often disqualify a critic's judgment by showing that he was drunk or had indigestion when he saw the play, or that he had quarreled with his wife, or that the fashionable audience arrived noisily and late and spoiled the first act. These facts do not, of course, show that his verdict was mistaken; they only show that he was not in the right conditions for giving a verdict. There is a difficulty, however. For how do we determine the right conditions for seeing plays? Perhaps only by discovering ways in which enjoyments and judgments have been interfered with. If that is the method, then we have a problem: it would seem that "right conditions" are "conditions under which an aesthetic object that has aesthetic value will be experienced as having aesthetic value." In that case, of course, our definition of "aesthetic value" would become circular.

The same difficulty arises, even more strongly, with the other key term in this definition, "qualified perceivers." Again, it is a sensible question what makes one reader of poetry, or one musician, better than another, and there are tests for some of the indispensable qualifications. Probably no complete test of reading ability or musical aptitude can be devised. But we can easily discount tone-deaf persons if they offer musical judgments and people with low verbal aptitude scores if they offer judgments of verse. After we have eliminated obviously incompetent people, however, we may still be left with a large group whose incompetence is not evident, and at this point we may find ourselves, just as before, defining "qualified perceiver" in a circular way: as one who is capable of recognizing the aesthetic value in aesthetic objects. Sensitivity, for example, is often mentioned as a desirable characteristic in critics; can this be defined, or tested, independently of seeing how those critics react to aesthetic objects that are already judged good?

These are important, difficult, and still unsettled, questions. But even if the qualified-observer definition of "aesthetic value" can be formulated in a noncircular fashion, it still seems to put the logical cart before the horse. The statement, "An object that has aesthetic value will be liked (aesthetically) by a perfect critic," is certainly true. But it tells us more about how "perfect critic" should be defined than about how "aesthetic value" should be defined. The natural order would be first to define "aesthetic value," then work out the conditions under which value is best recognized, and the talents needed to recognize it, so that the qualifications of the critic can be stated in terms of them. Of course there are qualified perceivers, and expert critics, and we can use their responses and judgments as a check against our own. But when we judge aesthetic value, a reference to these critics is no part of the meaning of the judgment.

The Open-Question Argument

There are two general arguments that can be brought against all forms of psychological definition, and, in fact, against all attempts to define "aesthetic value" in wholly nonnormative terms. The first of these arguments[2] is sometimes called the "open-question argument." All of the Subjectivist definitions render unaskable certain questions that people do ask, and that are perfectly good questions; and this shows that the definitions do not correspond to actual usage. I will give an example. Suppose someone holds that each era has its peculiar sensibility, or selective response to literature, and proposes to define "aesthetic value" in terms of the speaker's sensibility and that of his own time, as expressed in the weight of critical opinion. Thus when a critic says "This is good," he can only mean something like "I and most critics of my own time like this." But one day a critic may begin to wonder, and want to ask himself this question:

"I see that I and most critics of my own time like this poem, but is it good?"

—as Warton asked about Pope, and Rossel Hope Robbins about Eliot. And this question he cannot ask, according to the proposed definition, for it is the same as:

"I see that I and most critics of my own time like this poem, but do I and most critics of my own time like this poem?"

In other words, the question "Is what is liked by me and most critics of my own time really good?" is turned into nonsense by the sensibility-

---

[2] Which I take from G. E. Moore; for reference see Note 27-C.

definition; it is no longer an open question. Every Subjective definition closes a different question, but for each one it is possible to devise a question that many critics would ordinarily consider sensible and askable, but which that definition forestalls. And this shows that those critics are not using the word "good" in the way the definition proposes.

Of course it may be replied that after all some of these questions ought to be closed, for they are really nonsensical and critics are confused in asking them. Isn't it absurd for a critic to pretend to escape the limitations of his age and judge aesthetic objects from a larger point of view? Even if he refuses to recognize these limitations, is it not proper for the philosopher to call them to his attention, and even to make him bow to them, by insisting that he use the term "aesthetic value" in such a way that he cannot without self-contradiction question the aesthetic value judgments delivered by the consensus of critical opinion in his own epoch? But I think there is a confusion here, between the meaning of judgment and the verification of it. Suppose we take a very skeptical view of the latter, and say that a critic has no way of knowing what will be the ultimate verdict upon contemporary music and painting and literature, and can never therefore know whether contemporary critics are correct or incorrect. This is absurdly skeptical, but even so, it would not follow that the critic cannot *wonder* whether the critics are wrong, or that he cannot mean something clear and sensible when he doubts their judgments. "Nearly all of us rate Hopkins and Yeats and Eliot very high, but we could be mistaken," is extremely unlikely to be true, but it is not logically impossible.

It does make sense to question tastes, and so questions about what are good aesthetic objects are not settled by appeal to what people actually like, or would like if confronted with them. The sentence "X is good, but I don't like it," and the sentence "X is not good, but I like it," may be relatively rare, but they are by no means self-contradictory. Even the sentence "X is good, but nobody ever has liked it, or ever will like it," is not self-contradictory, though it may seldom or never be true and provable.

There is a stronger way to put this point.

A: "I like X."
B: "But *should* you like it?" ("Is it worthy of being liked?")

If A prefers X to Y, the question can always be asked whether he ought to prefer X to Y, whether it wouldn't be better if he preferred Y to X, whether, in short, Y isn't *preferable* to X. This version of the argument is most at home in the moral context where right and wrong are involved and the word "ought" has its greatest force. The argument may seem silly, or at least strangely Puritanical and moralistic, in the aesthetic context. Is it wrong to like Kathleen Norris better than Thomas Mann, Strauss waltzes better than *Mathis der Maler*, Rockwell Kent better than

Rouault? You wouldn't say that it was wrong to like Limburger cheese better than aged cheddar, or chocolate malteds better than Rhine wine—even if you regarded these tastes as deplorable. In fact, it may be right at certain times of life to prefer the simpler and sweeter aesthetic objects; an early taste for Strauss waltzes or Duke Ellington may be an indispensable step in some people's musical progress. So it might be argued that aesthetic enjoyments are not subject to evaluation in the way actions are: when we do something, it is sensible to ask whether we ought to have done it, but when we enjoy detective stories and science fiction, it is not sensible to ask whether we ought to enjoy them.

Now I concede that there is at least a difference of degree between the aesthetic obligations and others, and it lies in the probable seriousness of the consequences. We have the same difference within the moral sphere itself. For example, some actions that would be wrong in public are right in private; the difference seems to lie in the effects upon other people. The question in the aesthetic sphere, too, is whether tastes have consequences, whether it makes a difference in the world what a man's tastes are. And it does. Of course a man has a right to his tastes, just as he has a right to his vote, but how my neighbor votes matters a good deal in the end, to me, and I have a right to try to get him to vote intelligently and compassionately. So too, it may matter to me, in the long run, as it matters to my society and culture, what my neighbor thinks is aesthetically good, though the severity of my judgment of his tastes cannot be very great where the consequences are not very precisely predictable. I am not referring only to people like the man in Yakima, Washington, who—so the newspapers reported a few years ago—enraged his neighbors by putting up a half-block-long fence made of 1,000 mop handles, painted scores of different colors. I am thinking about possible subtle but pervasive and long-range effects of art upon various aspects of human life—a subject, however, which is reserved for the following chapter. It may be that a man's taste in reading and in music does not matter so much as his ideas about money, education, divorce, civil rights, and freedom of the will. But that does not make it negligible.

The Argument from Persuasive Definition

The first general argument against Subjectivist definitions of "aesthetic value" can be paralleled by a second one, equally well known.[3] But their main thrusts are in somewhat different areas. The first argument tells most strongly against Subjectivist definitions that are proposed as accounts of what is ordinarily meant by "good" in aesthetic contexts. But some philosophers would reply that they are not concerned with what most people mean; they have their own, and better, meanings. It is not definitions, but *re*definitions that they are seeking to obtain. What

---

[3] This one is modified from Charles L. Stevenson; for reference see Note 27-D.

is to prevent us, then, if we will, from resolving to put the term "aesthetic value" to a new and more convenient use, by assigning it some psychological sense, whether that is the usual one or not? For example, we might say

> From now on, I propose to mean by "X has higher aesthetic value than Y" nothing more than "X is liked more strongly by competent twentieth century critics than is Y."

This would simplify matters, after all; it would make all issues about aesthetic value readily decidable, and that would be convenient.

This sort of proposal is easy for one person to make, but it is not always easy for others to accept. When I make such a proposal, I am in effect requesting you to adopt the same meaning, at least while you are reading or listening to my words. But what sort of justification can I give to you for this request? Now, I might do it on some general ground of conventionalism, as in fact I would do for other words used as technical terms in this book. I might say, for example, "The word 'didactic' is only a word, with a variety of loose senses, and it would be convenient for me to use it in a slightly new sense for a certain theory of literature—and I shall now proceed to specify that sense." There is no good ground on which you can object to my proposal, provided no other term is available that is already suited to the special task I require of it in talking about theories of literature. For it does not commit you to anything if you permit me this freedom of redefinition; it does not imply, for example, that literature that is didactic in my new sense is necessarily didactic in other senses of the term.

But according to the argument I am now concerned with, the situation is very different with normative terms from what it is with non-normative terms, like "didactic." For it is essential to a normative term, whatever may be its meaning, that it have an emotive import, or tendency to affect others' attitudes. This may not be very marked, but, according to the argument, it must be present for a term to be normative, and it is a fixed concomitant of the normative terms, such as "value," already ensconced in common speech. What, then, will be the effect of a redefinition of "aesthetic value," for example, the one just cited? The writer says that from now on when he writes "has greater aesthetic value than" he is to be understood as meaning only "is more liked by twentieth century critics than"—but he continues to use the word "value" rather than the word "liked." And this is because "value," however it is ostensibly redefined, will carry with it its old emotive force. The redefinition thus has the effect of conferring a benison upon, of endorsing the approval of, the likings of twentieth century critics. And anyone who does not share this attitude toward their likings will naturally be unwilling to accept the redefinition.

All psychological redefinitions of "good" and "aesthetic value" are said to be misleading in this special way. They are called *Persuasive* definitions; that is, definitions that redirect attitudes via the emotive force of words to certain things that the definer approves of. If someone wishes to refrain from using words like "good" and "value," and speak only of his likes and dislikes, that is, of course, his privilege. But if he asks for permission to speak of his likes and dislikes by using the words "good" and "value," but arbitrarily redefining them, we can ask what he hopes to gain by this maneuver. And the only thing he could gain is that some of the favorable emotive force of "good" and "value" might be conferred upon his likes and dislikes, which would give them authority without their earning it; and anyone who accepted the redefinitions would be a party to the fraud.

It may be left open whether this second argument can be applied to all normative terms, some of which, as we have seen, are not, or not very, emotive. But I think the argument does apply to some crude attempts to define "aesthetic value" psychologically. In any case, both arguments may be summed up in other terms.[4] The normative words "good" and "value" have a primary function in critical discourse: they are used to *commend*. Now anyone who offers a psychological definition of "aesthetic value" is in effect claiming that the defining term is a substitute for the term defined. And this claim cannot be made good, for no psychological statement, by itself, can do the work of commending that a normative statement can. I say "by itself" because it is true that in certain circumstances a nonnormative statement will serve as a commendation. "This rates high with the New Critics" may work wonders in some circles, though in others it will be taken as condemning the work. It depends on what other commendations have already been subscribed to by the hearer. "This rates high with the New Critics" relies for its effect upon a belief that is expressed by "This is a good poem"; therefore the two cannot mean the same thing.

The point can be made even sharper, I think, if we consider another kind of definition of "aesthetic value," which, though not a psychological definition, is also a definition of "aesthetic value" in purely nonnormative terms. You recall the dispute, by no means wholly imaginary, between the neoclassic critic who judges plays by one set of criteria and the romantic critic who judges them by a different set. In the preceding chapter, §25, we noted two ways in which this dispute could be dissolved, that is, rendered illusory. One is to say that the critics are really talking about different things; this is Particularism. The other is to inject a Relativistic definition of "good" (or "aesthetic value"). There is a third way, for which I can think of no very handy name. Suppose the neoclassic critic will accept only one sort of reason as bearing upon the aesthetic value of a play, namely statements about the conformity of the play to certain canons of space, time, and action. And suppose the romantic critic will

---

[4] Which I owe largely to R. M. Hare; for reference see Note 27-C.

accept only another sort of reason as relevant, namely statements about the psychological individuality and complexity of the characters. Evidently there will come a point at which the dispute will deadlock.

Now it seems to me that the question would always remain open whether these two critics *ought* to accept only the reasons they accept, and that good reasons might be given for accepting a wider range of reasons, though the critics may be too stubborn to agree. But some philosophers—and they would probably be called Relativists, though they are not Relativists in the strict sense—would say that in this case the choice of criteria reflects a basic taste, and we have come to the end of rational argument. At this point, then, the argument is futile, and its futility is best made plain by dissolving it. It might be proposed that each of the critics really means something different by "good," and that "good" should be split into two words. The neoclassic critic means "in accordance with certain formal canons"; the romantic critic means "having a high degree of psychological individuality and complexity." The dispute is unresolvable because the two critics mean two different things by their value-judgments; this is brought out by reducing the meaning of each value-judgment to the criteria employed in argument. You can see now why this proposal is like a Psychological definition of "good," and how it suffers from the same defect. For the neoclassic cannot mean the same thing by "good" and "in accordance with certain formal canons." He says the play is good *because* it is in accordance with the canons, and he does not mean that it is in accordance with the canons because it is in accordance with the canons. Evidently "good" must mean something more than some description or interpretation of the play; no mere factual statement, even a psychological one, will convey its full meaning.

The language of likes and dislikes is an important and useful language, but it is not the language of critical judgment. "Is it good?" cannot be reduced to "Do you like it?" (it is more like "What is your reflective judgment of it?") or even to "Will I like it?" (it is more like "Considering that it cost me money and effort to see it, or considering that I have already seen it and it would cost me time to study it further, will it be worth my while to try to understand it?").

Hence our problem still remains for the following section, though we have limited the possibilities considerably. If a psychological definition of "aesthetic value" is one that defines it exclusively in terms of attitudes, it does not appear that any such definition will do, either as a report of usage or as a recommendation for a change of usage. But of course this does not rule out all references to psychological states in definitions of "aesthetic value," and in fact the theory to be considered next is in part, though not purely, a psychological one.

If we reject the accounts of aesthetic value given by defenders of the Beauty Theory and by those who propose Subjectivist definitions of "aesthetic value," we must look in another direction. And there is another way of approaching the problems of aesthetic value. General judgments of critical praise can be cast in the form: "This is a good aesthetic object." We can also, of course, make specific judgments like "This is a good sonata," or "This is a good landscape." Now, students of value theory have pointed out that we seem to use the word "good" in two very different ways, grammatically speaking.[1] We say things like "Money is good" and "You are very good," and in these statements "good" appears by itself as a predicate. But we also speak of "a good character," "a good car," "a good job," "a good way of holding the tennis racquet," and in these phrases the word "good" is adjoined, or affixed, to a noun or noun-phrase. When "good" is used in a phrase of the form "a good X," this is frequently called the *adjunctive* use of the word. It may be that even the apparently nonadjunctive uses are really adjunctive; this does not affect my argument.

The phrase "a good aesthetic object" is, then, an example of the adjunctive use of "good." And our problem is to understand what it would mean to say that something is a good aesthetic object, and how this could be shown to be true.

To help make clear the correct analysis of "a good X," let us first consider an analysis that is certainly not correct, though it might be offered. Suppose someone said

"This is a good X" means "This is an X, and I like it."

Now it is possible to find a few idiomatic phrases in which "good" is used adjunctively, and in which it indicates little more than the speaker's likings: for example, "a good time." But when we say that something is a good wrench, or a good cow, or a good plumber, we are surely saying something more than that it belongs to a certain class and is liked. We are stating the grounds for such a liking, and these grounds consist in the capacity of the wrench, or the cow, or the plumber to perform in a certain way that is to be expected of things of its kind.

Function-Classes

Under what conditions, then, is it appropriate to apply the word "good" adjunctively? Only if the noun to which it is affixed is one that denotes what I shall call a *function-class.* This concept needs a little clari-

---

[1] This distinction has been stressed by W. D. Ross, R. M. Hare, and R. S. Hartman, and Helen Knight has pointed out its relevance to critical evaluation. For references see Note 28-A.

fication. Suppose we have a number of objects that are considered as belonging to the same class because of some internal characteristic that they all share, for example, their shape or color or the material of which they are made—but not an external feature, such as being all in Australia or having been made by a blind weaver after 1900. The distinction between internal and external characteristics would take some careful analysis to make very exact, but let us suppose that it can be done. Now after we have marked out such a class, we may find that there is something that the members of this class can do that the members of other similarly defined classes cannot do, or cannot do as well. It may be that an occasional object outside this class can do the job better than a few of the objects in this class, but taking the class as a whole, or on the average, it is the best, or the only, class for the job. Then this class may be said to be a function-class, and its members may be said to have a function.

Function is not necessarily connected with intention: it is the capacity of the objects to serve in a certain (desirable) way, whether or not they were created for that purpose. Of course, wrenches, which are best for turning nuts, were intended to have a function. Cows were not; still there is something good you can do with, or get from, cows that other creatures will not provide, or provide so cheaply or plentifully or dependably. If another gadget, say a plench (a cross between pliers and wrenches), is invented that turns nuts more easily, or with greater force, or with less likelihood of slipping, then wrenches will lose their function, except in regions where the new invention has not penetrated.

Chair is a function-class, and *desk chair* is also a function-class, since there is a purpose that desk chairs serve better than other types. *Furniture* is not, I think, a function-class, though it includes a number of distinct function-classes; there is nothing you can do with furniture, considered solely as furniture, that you can't do as well with other things. "This is a good piece of furniture," then, would have to mean "This is either a good chair, or a good table, or a good sofa, or . . . " It is, in fact hard to find any really good examples of familiar classes that are *not* function-classes, since if there is some difference between this class and other classes, there is always the possibility of some good use to which that difference might be put.

But it is not sufficient that the members of the class have a function; they must differ among themselves in the degree to which they perform that function. If all dimes were exactly similar, then "a good dime" wouldn't make sense; a counterfeit dime is not a dime at all, and you don't say that a nickel is a poor dime. But it is hard to find examples of really nonsensical adjunctive uses of "good," for no matter how odd the combination appears at first, we will almost always, if we dwell on it, succeed in finding some conceivable use to which the class could be put, and which the members might serve more or less well. Thus "a good star" is peculiar, but perhaps one star might be a little better than another for navigation; "a good idiot" might be one most instructive as a textbook example; "a good case of measles" might be the one to show the internes.

The discussion so far, then, might be summarized in the following formula:

> "This is a good *X*" means "This is an *X*, and there is a function of *X*'s that it successfully fulfills."

Or, to be both more specific and more explicit:

> "This is a good wrench" means "This is a wrench, and it is efficient [handy, convenient] for the (good) purpose of turning nuts."

These are not very smooth definitions; they are in fact twisted slightly to bring out the next important point. The second definition does define "a good wrench," in terms of the assumed function of wrenches. But note that it does *not* define the word "good," for this word turns up in the defining term as well; it is not eliminated by the definition. To make the same point another way, in my definition of "function" I have inserted a reference to value: for an object to have a function, there must not only be something special that it can do, but that something must be worth doing.

In my view, the phrase "a good *X*" typically presupposes that the use of *X* is itself a good one. Now, no doubt "good" can be used, and is sometimes used, with what might be called value-neutrality. In this sense, it means nothing more than efficient. But I think that in general—and at least in "a good aesthetic object"—to use the word "good" rather than the word "efficient" is tacitly to endorse the end to which it is put. It would be a little queer for one who believes that torture is never justified to say, "That is a good method of torture," or for a thoroughgoing advocate of nonviolence to say, "Hanging is a good way to execute criminals." To bar any misapprehension, he would do better to say "effective" or "successful," or something of the sort. Statements like "He is a pretty good burglar" and "That is a perfect murder" are likely to sound either ironic or callous.

If we treat "a good aesthetic object" on the same lines as "a good wrench," we come out with some interesting possibilities. First, of course, we should have to establish that *aesthetic object* is a function-class—that is, that there is something that aesthetic objects can do that other things cannot do, or do as completely or fully. Is there something that aesthetic objects are especially good at? Now, the sort of thing you can do with an aesthetic object is to perceive it in a certain way, and allow it to induce a certain kind of experience. So the question, "Is *aesthetic object* a function-class?" is only a somewhat pedantic way of asking an old and familiar question, which we have long postponed: "Is there such a thing as *aesthetic experience?*" We saw in the preceding section that the Psychological Definitions lead into this question, in distinguishing aesthetic

Aesthetic Experience

The problem is whether we can isolate, and describe in general terms, certain features of experience that are peculiarly characteristic of our intercourse with aesthetic objects. Of course, listening to music is a very different experience in some ways from looking through a cathedral or watching a motion picture. Reading literature certainly does something to us, and probably *for* us, that listening to music cannot do, and vice versa. A full account of our experience of aesthetic objects would have to deal carefully with these matters. But is there something that all these experiences have in common—something that can be usefully distinguished? This is at least an empirical question, open to inquiry. And some inquiry has been made, though many mysteries remain. However, we can be reasonably confident of certain generalizations, which some writers have obtained by acute introspection, and which each of us can test in his own experience.[2]

These are the points on which, I take it, nearly everyone will agree:

First, an aesthetic experience is one in which attention is firmly fixed upon heterogeneous but interrelated components of a phenomenally objective field—visual or auditory patterns, or the characters and events in literature. Some writers have suggested that in such an experience, as when we are deeply absorbed in the tension of a visual design or in the developing design of music, the distinction between phenomenal objectivity and phenomenal subjectivity itself tends to disappear. This may be overstated, but in any case the experience differs from the loose play of fancy in daydreaming by having a central focus; the eye is kept on the object, and the object controls the experience. It is all right, I think, to speak of the object as *causing* the experience, but of course the connection is more intimate, for the object, which is a perceptual object, also appears *in* the experience as its phenomenally objective field.

Second, it is an experience of some intensity. Some writers have said that it is an experience pervasively dominated by intense feeling or emotion, but these terms still occupy a dubious position in psychological theory; what we call the emotion in an aesthetic experience may be simply the intensity of the experience itself. In any case, the emotion is characteristically bound to its object, the phenomenal field itself—we feel sad *about* the characters, or uncertain *about* the results of an unexpected modulation. Aesthetic objects give us a concentration of experience. The drama presents only, so to speak, a segment of human life, that part of it

---

[2] In the following pages, supplemented by further remarks in Note 28-B, I rely most heavily upon the work of John Dewey, Edward Bullough, I. A. Richards, and Immanuel Kant; for references see Note 28-B.

that is noteworthy and significant, and fixes our minds on that part; the painting and the music invite us to do what we would seldom do in ordinary life—pay attention *only* to what we are seeing or hearing, and ignore everything else. They summon up our energies for an unusually narrow field of concern. Large-scale novels may do more; they are in fact always in danger of dissipating attention by spreading it out into our usual diffuse awareness of the environment.

This is why the expression "feeling no pain" is particularly apt to aesthetic experience. The pleasure is not often comparable in intensity to the pleasures of satisfying the ordinary appetites. But the concentration of the experience can shut out all the negative responses—the trivial distracting noises, organic disturbances, thoughts of unpaid bills and unwritten letters and unpurged embarrassments—that so often clutter up our pleasures. It does what whiskey does, only not by dulling sensitivity and clouding the awareness, but by marshalling the attention for a time into free and unobstructed channels of experience.

But this discussion already anticipates the two other features of aesthetic experience, which may both be subsumed under *unity*. For, third, it is an experience that hangs together, or is coherent, to an unusually high degree. One thing leads to another; continuity of development, without gaps or dead spaces, a sense of overall providential pattern of guidance, an orderly cumulation of energy toward a climax, are present to an unusual degree. Even when the experience is temporarily broken off, as when we lay down the novel to water the lawn or eat dinner, it can retain a remarkable degree of coherence. Pick up the novel and you are immediately back in the world of the work, almost as if there had been no interruption. Stop the music because of a mechanical problem, or the ringing of a phone, but when it is started again, two bars may be enough to establish the connection with what went before, and you are clearly in the *same* experience again.

Fourth, it is an experience that is unusually complete in itself. The impulses and expectations aroused by elements within the experience are felt to be counterbalanced or resolved by other elements within the experience, so that some degree of equilibrium or finality is achieved and enjoyed. The experience detaches itself, and even insulates itself, from the intrusion of alien elements. Of course, it cannot survive all emergencies. I have heard the last movement of Beethoven's "*Waldstein*" *Sonata* (*Op. 53*) interrupted by a fire chief who suddenly appeared on stage to clear the aisles of standees; and even though the pianist, Paul Badura-Skoda, started off again at the beginning of the movement, he could not, of course, recapture the peculiar quality of that beginning, which moves without pause from the slow section of the sonata. But because of the highly concentrated, or localized, attention characteristic of aesthetic experience, it tends to mark itself out from the general stream of experience, and stand in memory as a single experience.

Aesthetic objects have a peculiar, but I think important, aspect: they are all, so to speak, objects *manqués*. There is something lacking in them that keeps them from being quite real, from achieving the full status of things—or, better, that prevents the question of reality from arising. They are complexes of qualities, surfaces. The characters of the novel or lyric have truncated histories, they are no more than they show. The music is movement without anything solid that moves; the object in the painting is not a material object, but only the appearance of one. Even the lifelike statue, though it gives us the shape and gesture and life of a living thing, is clearly not one itself. And the dancer gives us the abstractions of human action—the gestures and movements of joy and sorrow, of love and fear—but not the actions (killing or dying) themselves. This is one sense of "make-believe" in which aesthetic objects are make-believe objects; and upon this depends their capacity to call forth from us the kind of admiring contemplation, without any necessary commitment to practical action, that is characteristic of aesthetic experience.

One aesthetic experience may differ from another in any or all of three connected but independent respects: (1) it may be more *unified*, that is, more coherent and/or complete, than the other; (2) its dominant quality, or pervasive feeling-tone, may be more *intense* than that of the other; (3) the range or diversity of distinct elements that it brings together into its unity, and under its dominant quality, may be more *complex* than that of the other. It will be convenient to have a general term to cover all three characteristics. I propose to say that one aesthetic experience has a greater *magnitude*—that is, it is more of an aesthetic experience—than another; and that its magnitude is a function of at least these three variables. For the more unified the experience, the more of a whole the experience is, and the more concentratedly the self is engaged; the more intense the experience, the more deeply the self is engaged; the more complex the experience, the more of the self is engaged, that is, the more wide-ranging are its responses, perhaps over a longer time.

I do not think of magnitude here as implying measurement—it is merely a collective term for how much is happening, intensively or extensively, in the experience. It may be too vague a concept to be useful. That remains to be seen, but there are two sources of legitimate uneasiness about it that should be frankly faced at once. First, note that I am now applying the terms "unity," "complexity," and "intensity" more broadly than before—not only to the phenomenally objective presentations in the experience, but to the whole experience, which includes affective and cognitive elements as well. The terms are still understandable, even in this extended use, I judge, but of course less capable of sure and exact application. Second, though I claim that these three characteristics all have a bearing upon magnitude, and that the magnitude of the experience is a resultant of them, I am not yet raising certain questions—which will shortly come to our attention—concerning the comparability of magnitudes. Evidently it will be possible to say that of two experiences approximately equal in unity and complexity, the one having a greater intensity will have the greater magnitude. But what if they are equal in one respect, and differ in opposite ways in the other two? This question is still open.

The traits of aesthetic experience are to be found individually in a great many other experiences, of course, but not in the same combination, I think. Play, in the sense in which we play games, involves the enjoyment of activity that has no practical purpose. But though the psychology of play has not yielded up all its secrets to psychological inquiry, it seems not necessarily to be an experience of a high degree of unity. Watching a baseball or football game is also generally lacking in a dominant pattern and consummation, though sometimes it has these characteristics to a high degree and is an aesthetic experience. Carrying through a triumphant scientific investigation or the solution of a mathematical problem may have the clear dramatic pattern and consummatory conclusion of an aesthetic experience, but it is not itself aesthetic experience unless the movement of thought is tied closely to sensuous presentations, or at least a phenomenally objective field of perceptual objects.

Such distinctions are vague and tentative; they are some of the problems that most need to be studied at the present time. In any case, we can identify aesthetic experience as a kind of experience, though it is unique only in its combination of traits, rather than in any specific one. And we can say that aesthetic objects, generally speaking, have the function of producing such experiences, even though quite often aesthetic experiences of some degree of magnitude are obtained in the regular course of life from other things than aesthetic objects. This is their special use, what they are good for. On the whole, it is what they do best; they do it most dependably, and they alone do it in the highest magnitude.

Value as a Capacity

We can now define "good aesthetic object," in terms of the function of aesthetic objects—provided we can make another assumption. Suppose that what makes an aesthetic experience itself good, that on account of which it is a good aesthetic experience, is its magnitude, and, moreover, that one aesthetic experience is better than another, more worth having, if it has a greater magnitude. Then we can say,

> "X is a good aesthetic object" means "X is capable of producing good aesthetic experiences (that is, aesthetic experiences of a fairly great magnitude)."

And,

> "X is a better aesthetic object than Y" means "X is capable of producing better aesthetic experiences (that is, aesthetic experiences of a greater magnitude) than Y."

I shall call these *Functional* definitions of "good" in its adjunctive use as applied to aesthetic objects.

The transition to a definition of "aesthetic value" is now readily made. I propose to say, simply, that "being a good aesthetic object" and "having aesthetic value" mean the same thing. Or,

> "X has aesthetic value" means "X has the capacity to produce an aesthetic experience of a fairly great magnitude (such an experience having value)."

And,

> "X has greater aesthetic value than Y" means "X has the capacity to produce an aesthetic experience of greater magnitude (such an experience having more value) than that produced by Y."

Since this definition defines "aesthetic value" in terms of consequences, an object's utility or instrumentality to a certain sort of experience, I shall call it an *Instrumentalist* definition of "aesthetic value."[3]

Two clarifying comments are called for at this point. The first concerns the phrase "has the capacity to produce," or "is capable of producing." The defining term does not stipulate that the effect will happen, but that it can happen. The definition is, of course, nonrelativistic; it even permits us to say that a painting never seen by anyone has aesthetic value, meaning that if it were seen, under suitable conditions, it would produce an aesthetic experience. "Capacity" is called a *dispositional term,* like the term "nutritious." To say that a substance is nutritious is not to predict that anyone will in fact be nourished by it, but only that it would be healthful to—it would have food value for—someone who ate a certain (unspecified) amount of it under certain (unspecified) conditions. Now no doubt we can sometimes make specific predictions about aesthetic objects, just as we do about foods—"This will make you healthier if you eat at least six ounces of it every day for three months." And we sometimes go to people who have read a book and ask questions like, "Did it move you? Do you think I would enjoy it?" But the kind of question a critical evaluator is attempting to answer, I believe, is not of this sort, but rather of the sort: "*Can* it move people?" In other words, the question of aesthetic value, like the question of nutritiousness, seems to be a question about what effects the object is capable of yielding, or, to put it another way, what can be done with it if we want to do it.

The "capacity" terminology, it must be conceded, is a deliberately indefinite one, but not too indefinite, I think, to be useful, so long as it is subject to certain controls. First, a statement about a capacity is required to specify some reference-class, if it is to be readily confirmable.[4]

---

[3] Definitions of this sort have been proposed by W. D. Ross, C. I. Lewis, Albert Hofstadter, and Thomas Munro; the usage of other writers appears to approximate it. For references see Note 28-C.

[4] This point has been well made by Albert Hofstadter in a recent symposium on "The Evidence for Esthetic Judgment" (see Note 28-C).

We want to know what class of things we are to try out the object on, in order to see whether it really does have the capacity. What nourishes a horse will not necessarily nourish a man. The narrower the reference-class, of course, the more informative the capacity-statement, but so long as there is some reference-class, the statement can be correct and useful. For statements about aesthetic value, the reference-class is the class of human beings, to begin with, but we can easily narrow that down considerably by adding obvious requirements. To read Baudelaire you must understand French; to listen to music, not be tone-deaf; to see paintings, not be color-blind. No doubt we could go further. Note that this is not the same problem as that of defining "competent critic," for here we are not asking for the criteria of being an expert evaluator, but only ruling out certain classes of people whom it would be useless to expose to the aesthetic object. Even after we have eliminated the impossibles, we still use the "capacity" terminology, for we cannot predict that all who understand French will derive an aesthetic experience from Baudelaire, but only that, as far as this requirement goes, they are not prevented from doing so.

Second, although a capacity statement can be true even if the capacity is never actualized—natural resources are still resources even if they never happen to be exploited—the only direct confirmation of it is its actualization. The test of whether an object has aesthetic value is just that some of its presentations actually cause, and enter into, aesthetic experiences.

Third, "capacity" is a positive, rather than a negative, term, and this distinction is important, if not pressed too far. We can speak of the capacity of an aesthetic object to produce an aesthetic experience, or we can speak of the capacity of a person to be affected by the object. But in both cases we assume—and, I believe, on adequate evidence—that there is a direction of development in aesthetic experience, a difference between greater and less capacity. It takes a greater capacity to respond to Shakespeare than to Graham Greene, to Beethoven than to Ferde Grofé, to Cézanne than to Norman Rockwell. People outgrow Graham Greene, but they do not outgrow Shakespeare. People sometimes give up Tchaikovsky's symphonies for Haydn's but they do not, I think, give up Haydn for Tchaikovsky. And if we lose our admiration for Brahms at one stage, and return to him later, it will be for different reasons. We do not say that a person has the capacity to remain unmoved by Shakespeare; this is not a capacity, but the lack of a capacity. Now the object with the greater capacity may not have its capacity actualized as often as the object with less—the heavier the sledge, the greater its force, but the fewer who can use it well. If, therefore, the aesthetic value of Tchaikovsky is more often had and enjoyed than that of Bach, it still may be true that the value of the latter is greater.

The Instrumentalist definition, as I have framed it, contains another unusual feature, that is, the parenthetical insertion. I am not sure that the parentheses are the best notation for my meaning, but they are the best I can think of. The Instrumentalist definition is not a Psychological definition, in the sense of the preceding section, for it does not claim to reduce statements about value to purely psychological terms. Indeed, it does not define "value" at all, for this word appears in the defining term as well as in the term to be defined. It only defines the whole term, "aesthetic value," in terms of a certain kind of experience. But it concedes that this definition cannot be adopted except on the assumption, set forth in parentheses, that the experience is itself worth having.

If the Instrumentalist definition had been stated in purely psychological terms, for example,

> "X has aesthetic value" means "X has the capacity to produce an aesthetic experience of some magnitude,"

it would have been open to the objections raised against all Psychological definitions—the "open question" argument and the complaint against Persuasive definitions. This last definition does not really define "aesthetic value" but only "aesthetic power," or something of the sort. To call that power a value is to presuppose that the effect itself has value, and this presupposition should be made clear. Yet the presupposition is not strictly part of the defining term; it is more like a stipulation about the conditions under which the definition applies, and that is why I have put it in parentheses. The definition might be expanded in this way:

> If it be granted that aesthetic experience has value, then "aesthetic value" may be defined as "the capacity to produce an aesthetic experience of some magnitude."

To say that an object has aesthetic value is (a) to say that it has the capacity to produce an aesthetic effect, and (b) to say that the aesthetic effect itself has value. In exactly the same way, the statement, "Penicillin has medical value," means (a) that penicillin has the capacity to produce medical effects, that is, it can cure or alleviate certain diseases, and (b) that curing or alleviating diseases is worthwhile.

In order to decide about the acceptability of the Instrumentalist definition, we must be aware of the spirit in which it is offered. It does not claim to report what critics would say if asked for their definition of "good" (in an aesthetic context); but it does claim to indicate what they can, and probably must, mean, if they wish the reasons they actually give for critical evaluations to be logically relevant and persuasive. At least there is no doubt that the Instrumentalist definition fits in very well with practical criticism. For suppose a critic says that a particular aesthetic object is a very good one, and we ask, "Why?" His answer would consist in pointing out certain features of it that contribute to its having a high degree of unity, or complexity, or intensity of regional quality. If we then press him further, and ask why unity, complexity, and intensity are desirable, he can reply that the greater the degree of some or all of these features, the greater the magnitude of the aesthetic experience that the object is then capable of evoking. For example, the more unified the object, the more unified the experience of it will probably be—for this there seems to be a good deal of evidence. Since the evoking of such an experience—assuming it is itself a good—is what constitutes aesthetic value, any argument for its capacity to evoke the experience is by definition an argument for its aesthetic value.

On the other hand, if the critic says that a particular aesthetic object is a poor one, we will, according to the Instrumentalist definition, expect him to produce evidence that it is very deficient in features that would promote a high degree of unity, complexity, or intensity. And this is, as we saw in the preceding chapter, just the sort of Objective reason that the critic does produce. In short, appeal to the three General Canons that seem to underlie so much of critical argument can itself be justified in terms of an Instrumentalist definition of "aesthetic value." For these Canons refer to characteristics of aesthetic objects that enable them to evoke aesthetic experiences, so far as the occurrence of such experiences is under the control of those objects.

But this is to consider the nature of critical argument rather abstractly, and it may nevertheless be felt that the Instrumentalist definition is less plausible when we take into account the actual situation of the critic, the conditions under which he is likely to make a judgment or offer reasons. For example, it is often emphasized that aesthetic value is something that is *immediately* experienced and known; it does not have to be calculated or inferred, but is open to direct inspection—consummatory, if anything is. But even according to the Instrumentalist definition, what is true in the doctrine of immediacy can still be preserved. If a critic, face to face with a painting, finds himself deriving from it the kind of enjoyment that we have called "aesthetic experience," he possesses direct evidence that the painting has the capacity to produce such an experience, for if it does, it can. His enjoyment is immediate and is strongly evidential. That does not mean, of course, that he cannot be mistaken. For when he says the painting has aesthetic value, he is not saying merely that it can give pleasure, but he is saying what *kind* of pleasure it can give. And it is possible to mistake other experience for aesthetic experience, just as it is possible to mistake other experience for religious experience. The experience I get from a certain landscape may really be a nostalgic feeling caused by a recognition that the barn is like the one on my childhood farm; the shiver and gooseflesh I get from hearing certain music may come from the fact that it is an old hymn tune, associated with long-buried religious experiences of my youth; the excitement I get from reading a novel may be a response to its social message, more like the excitement of helping in a political campaign than that of an aesthetic experience. It is easy for a Scotsman to overrate Burns, a liberal Democrat Whitman, or an Old French scholar *Le Chanson de Roland.*

In short, there may be times when I confuse aesthetic experience with other experience, and incorrectly say the object has aesthetic value, because it moves me in some other way; and here it would be appropriate for the critic to show me by an analysis of the object that it is probably incapable of producing an aesthetic experience of great magnitude, so that my response is therefore probably of a nonaesthetic sort, as I will, he predicts, discover by more careful introspection.

The critic who is actually moved by the work does not, of course, require reasons to justify his being moved. But he may be interested in analyzing the work to find more precisely the basis of his experience. Or if his first reaction is indifferent or negative—if the work seems poor to him—he may wonder whether the reaction is adequate. Perhaps further study will show that the work probably has the capacity to produce an aesthetic experience of some magnitude, even though it has not yet done so, because the difficulties of understanding it have not been overcome. Under other circumstances, the critic may give reasons why people who have not even heard the music yet, or visited the exhibition, or attended the play, would be well advised to do so; for there is evidence in the work itself that it has aesthetic value.

Thus, to revert to an example first alluded to at the beginning of §25, in the preceding chapter, it is true that "This is unified" is not evidence for "This has aesthetic value" in exactly the same way that "The patient's temperature is 104.5" is evidence for "The patient has pneumonia." For "This has aesthetic value" is a dispositional statement, and "The patient has pneumonia" is not. But compare "This food is dangerous" and "It is crawling with salmonella bacteria." Here the presence of the bacteria is evidence that the food will probably produce ghastly effects if it is eaten, just as the presence of unity is evidence that the work will produce an aesthetic effect if it is perceived with attention.

The Decision Problem

If the Instrumentalist definition of "aesthetic value" is adopted, along with its attendant implications for critical argument, it will then be true that sometimes our preferences for one aesthetic object over another, or our commendation of X as better than Y, can be rationally justified. And it is natural to wonder whether they always can. Philosophers have toyed with the idea of constructing a scale, or unique order, of aesthetic value, perhaps even a grading system, like that suggested by Samuel Johnson in the quotation from Boswell near the beginning of Chapter X. The relation "is better than," for which we may use the symbol

">," is defined Instrumentally so that it is asymmetrical, since if $X > Y$, then it cannot be that $Y > X$. It is not, however, transitive, since if $X > Y$ and $Y > Z$, it does not follow necessarily that $X > Z$. Though we can manipulate such symbols in many highly satisfying ways, we must recognize in the comparative judgment of aesthetic value some serious limitations.

For there are problems involved in deciding whether or not $X > Y$, in certain cases. Suppose we find two aesthetic objects, X and Y, and we can produce no reason why $X > Y$ and no reason why $Y > X$. We may still find ourselves liking one more than the other, and we have no reason not to choose it when it is available. In short, there will be preferences, choices among aesthetic objects, that fall through the wide mesh of critical argument; preferences that cannot be rationally justified. Let us say that such preferences belong to an Area of Rational Undecidability in the realm of critical evaluation—an area where rational argument does not reach, and where choice, if choice occurs, cannot be guided by reasons. Consider, for example, two of Scarlatti's keyboard sonatas, the one in E major (Kirkpatrick 380) and the one in B minor (Kirkpatrick 87). I do not claim that this pair belongs to the Area of Undecidability; indeed the conclusion that any pair does is a negative conclusion, which could only be reached after an exhaustive study of the two works. But both of these works are of a high order, though very different, and let us suppose, for the sake of discussion, that everything good we can say about either can be matched by something good about the other, and we can find no reason why either should be judged a better aesthetic object than the other.

No problem may arise in this case, for we may not even like one more than the other, and in fact in these cases, if someone asks me which I like better, I find it very hard to answer, though perhaps I incline a bit more to the *E Major Sonata*. So suppose we do like that one more, but have no reason to say that it is better. We are still choosing between them, and this may even be a practical decision, as when a friend stands with the pickup arm poised over the record grooves, and invites us to hear one sonata or the other. But though we can give a good reason for listening to the one we like better, we cannot give any reason—to speak a little oddly—for liking one better. If that is the case, then this pair of sonatas belongs in the Area of Undecidability. But note that it is always a pair that belongs to this area. It is quite clear, for example, that we can give reasons for saying that the *E Major Sonata* is a better composition than, say, the *G Major Sonata* (Kirkpatrick 146), and so *this* pair does not belong to the Area of Undecidability.

The Area of Undecidability, then, is the class consisting of all pairs of aesthetic objects, X and Y, which are such that we cannot prove either is better than the other, or that they are equal in aesthetic value. Undecidability is not the same thing as Relativism, though it is sometimes called Relativism, because the two are related. If we insisted on preserving the expression "is better than" for comparing X and Y when they fall within the Area of Undecidability, then we could define "is better than" Relativistically, that is, in subjective terms. But I am adopting an alternative usage. When X and Y fall within the Area of Undecidability, we have no reason to suppose that either has the capacity to produce an aesthetic experience of greater magnitude than that producible by the other. Hence in that area I do not say that one is better than the other or is preferable or is more desirable; but it is all right to say that one is preferred or is desired.

There are two factors in aesthetic value that create this Area of Undecidability.

The first factor is that the critical value judgment makes use of multiple criteria. Suppose we are given a basket of apples, and told to arrange them in a serial order, from the least good to best. To perform this task we are given a list of good-making features of apples, analogous to the General Canons of critical evaluation: quality of taste, firmness, size, color, freedom from bruises and worms, and so forth. Without such a list we would of course not know where to begin, for we would not even know what the task was—just as if someone told us to put in order an apple, a lemon, and a radish, without giving us any instructions about principles to define the order.

Now let us suppose that we know how to arrange all the apples in terms of every particular standard. That is, we can order them according to size—putting those of the same size side by side—or taste, or freedom from blemishes. But this is not the assigned task, for we are not supposed to arrange them in several orders, but in a single order that will somehow take account of all the standards. How would we set about such a task? First we might pick out all those apples that seem perfectly free from blemishes, and set them at one end, perhaps in two or three groups if we can find a few that are outstanding in some feature, such as taste or size. Then we might pick out all those apples that are very bruised and wormy, and put them at the other end. In between these extremes lies the difficult task, and we of course discover that beyond a certain point it is not performable, with the instructions given. For though we may easily decide that certain apples, taken all around, are better than certain others, there will be many pairs of apples which we cannot decide about; one has excellent taste but is small and slightly bruised, the other has a little less good taste, but is large and rosy. The only way we can do the job is to secure further instructions that would have the effect of weighting, or rating, the standards themselves, for example, "Taste is more important than size; in case of a tie, pay more attention to size than color; when in doubt, ignore the worm, but measure the size of the nonwormy part of the apple." Probably no one could lay down beforehand a complete set of such weighted standards to take care of all eventualities. But as problems arose, rules could be adopted, and in the end we could perhaps eliminate all Undecidability, for the rules would determine, in every case, whether X is better or worse than, or equal to, Y.

Can the same thing be done with aesthetic objects? If we take unity, intensity, and complexity as three independent standards, we will inevitably find many pairs of aesthetic objects that cannot be rated in aesthetic value. Say X and Y are about equally complex, but X is a little more unified, while Y has a rather more intense quality. If one person prefers X, and another Y, there does not seem to be any rational way to resolve the difference. They simply put different weights on different standards. Thus one critic may praise a Mondrian for its precise balance, while admitting the simplicity of the design; another may praise the complexity of a Tintoretto while admitting that his designs are sometimes not so unified. To get certain intense, and admirable, qualities, like the cool necessity of the Mondrian, or the sweeping grandeur and dynamism of the Tintoretto, other features may have to be sacrificed a little. And there is no set of rules that says that one of the three critical standards is to be weighted higher than the others.

Some people seem to set most store by sheer intensity of regional quality, others by clear-cut structure, and there does not seem to be any way of showing either of them to be mistaken. It is possible, of course, that with further study of the nature of aesthetic experience, and of the conditions on which it depends, we could refine our Canons of judgment, and introduce rules of weighting. But at the present time an area of Undecidability remains. If Critic A says of a work that it does not have enough order to suit him, and Critic B that it has enough vividness to suit him fine, it does not seem that either is able to prove the work is very good or not very good. But of course they can still agree that it is definitely superior, or definitely inferior, to certain other aesthetic objects.

Thus, if we take a handful of Donne's best poems, or of Haydn quartets or Rembrandt etchings, it may be impossible to decide which of the group is better and which is worse. But this need not bother us. After all, when we are dealing with such a group of poems, or quartets, or etchings, we are dealing with aesthetic objects that are all unquestionably of a high rank. What difference does it make whether one of the poems is a little better than the others? It is more important to see what is good in each, and acquire affection for it. This does not in the least imply that we cannot discern the difference in value that separates Donne's best poems from Robinson Jeffers', Haydn's quartets from Milhaud's, or Rembrandt's etchings from Walter Sickert's.

The second factor making for an Area of Undecidability in critical evaluation is the variety of regional qualities in aesthetic objects. Though it depends upon complex perceptual conditions, a regional quality is itself simple, and may be simply liked or disliked—just as is the taste of a ripe or green olive, of buttermilk, parsnips, Camembert, horehound, and

Irish whiskey. There are characteristic recurrent qualities in the works of certain composers: the peculiar controlled drive of Bach's bass melodies, as in the cantatas; the whining and yearning of sixths and sevenths in some of Brahms' melodies, as sometimes in his quartets and at the opening of his *E Minor Symphony (No. 4)*; the cutting edge of Bartók when he is both syncopated and dissonant, as in parts of the *Third Quartet*. Now it is perfectly possible for someone to say that, for example, Brahms' *C Minor Quartet (Op. 51, No. 1)* is highly unified, and quite fully developed, and has quite intense regional qualities, so that it is undoubtedly a fine quartet—but he unfortunately cannot stand those Brahmsian qualities. Or he may not be able to decide on rational grounds whether one of Bartók's quartets is greater than Debussy's yet he may enjoy the Debussy quality and abhor the Bartók quality.

This is not to imply that his taste cannot change. The point is, however, that a person may like X more than Y simply on account of its quality, and for this preference he can give no further justification. Of course, he does not have to say that X is *better* than Y, but he is choosing, and his choice is in the Area of Undecidability. I do not know whether it is true that "The very qualities in Manet that attracted Daumier, repelled Courbet,"[5] but this statement expresses concisely a sufficiently common experience: I am sure that the qualities of Faulkner, Kafka, Hemingway, Pope, or Marvell, that attract some readers are the very qualities that put others off. And this is a strong argument in favor of a wide variety of literature, for a work whose qualities we cannot learn to like is simply unavailable to us, and yet we may intellectually recognize its value, and convince ourselves that others derive from it an aesthetic experience that is equal in magnitude to experiences that we must obtain elsewhere.

Aesthetic Value

The Instrumentalist definition of "aesthetic value," as we have noted before, is carefully framed to expose the fact that to adopt it is to take for granted that something is already known to be valuable, namely aesthetic experience. It makes the value of the aesthetic object a means to an end. But of course we are immediately confronted with a further question, about the value of the end itself: what justifies the assumption that this experience is valuable? The practical critic does not have to worry about this question: if he can assume that aesthetic experiences are worth having, then he can investigate those features of aesthetic objects upon which such experiences depend. To put it another way, for the critic aesthetic experience is an end-in-view which he need not question, just as life and health are the ends-in-view of the doctor, so far as he

---

[5] Quoted from Ambroise Vollard, *Renoir*, New York: Knopf, 1925, p. 47, by B. C. Heyl, *New Bearings in Aesthetics and Art Criticism*, New Haven, Conn.: Yale U., 1943, p. 98 *n.*

is a doctor, and it is axiomatic for him that they are to be preserved when they can be. Of course the man who is a doctor may sometimes think of more ultimate questions, especially when he is faced with difficult situations, as in Shaw's play, *The Doctor's Dilemma,* and there is no reason why the critic should not be a human being, too. To put it still another way, it does not matter to the doctor, *qua* doctor, what his patients do with their lives and their health. And it does not matter to the critic whether the value he ascribes to aesthetic experience is an intrinsic value or only a further instrumental value; if it has any value at all, his work is cut out for him.

But the question that the critic does not ask, someone must both ask and answer. Someone must try to determine whether the critic's assumption is sound. This is a philosophical question, and it belongs to the domain of aesthetics. Does aesthetic experience have value, and if so why? It must be acknowledged that we are now venturing upon uncertain waters, in thus pushing the inquiry one step further. But an adequate aesthetic theory must take the inevitable risks.

At this point there appear to be two main alternatives. One is easy and ready to hand, the other more subtle and perplexing.

The first alternative is to combine the Instrumentalist definition of "aesthetic value" with a Psychological definition of "value" in general, and say that aesthetic experiences are intrinsically valuable in that they are liked, or enjoyed, or desired. Suppose someone were to say, "I am willing to accept your conclusion that good music has aesthetic value, and I suppose if I were to spend a great deal of time listening to it and studying it, I would be able to obtain aesthetic experiences of some magnitude from music, but what good are such experiences? Why should I bother?" You might reply, "But when you are able to have them, you will enjoy them very much." And if this answer contents you, and him, then, it would seem, no more need be said.

Now it is true that quite often this answer *is* sufficient. But only because it takes certain things for granted. If someone were to justify forging Federal Reserve notes, or pushing people in front of railway trains, on the same grounds, namely, that he enjoys these challenging and exhilarating activities, we would not for a moment accept his justification as conclusive. It is often said that aesthetic experiences are "worth having for their own sake," and that indeed they are supreme examples, prototypes, of what is worth having for its own sake. But though this phrase is clearly a strong commendation, we must examine it more closely. What can it mean? It is certainly true that aesthetic experiences can be enjoyed for their own sake, without thought for yesterday or tomorrow; they give that *sort* of enjoyment, and this is an important fact about them. But does it follow that their value is something that inheres in them, or in their pleasure, without regard to the conditions under which they occur or the sacrifices that may have to be made to obtain them? This is another question raised in Shaw's play.

When we ask whether something is enjoyable, we are asking for information about it, just as when we ask whether it is bulky, or ripe, or likely to get out of order. If that is what we want to know about it, no question of value has yet arisen. But when we ask about the value of something, and require statements about its value to be supported by reasons, we are asking a different sort of question. We want to know about its connections with other things, including other enjoyments that may be precluded by it or enhanced by it; in short, we want to know about its consequences. Thus the question whether aesthetic experience is valuable is not the question whether it is enjoyable, but the question whether its enjoyment can be justified, in comparison with other enjoyments that are available to us as human beings, as citizens in a twentieth century democratic society. This may be putting it rather solemnly, but the question is a big one, as we shall see.

We are led by this line of thought to the second alternative, which is that elected by the *Instrumentalist Theory of Value.*[6] This theory includes the Instrumentalist definition of "aesthetic value," but it also includes a more far-reaching statement. For it denies the basic philosophical assumption common to both the Beauty Theory and the Psychological definitions: the assumption, namely, that all instrumental value leads back ultimately to, or depends upon, intrinsic value. According to the Instrumentalist Theory, there is no such thing as intrinsic value. The arguments that have been set forth for this conclusion are not, I am afraid, very complete or very clear, and they are complicated. We shall have to summarize the position fairly briefly here, just enough to make its main outlines evident.

A stove has value; that is plain. So does a pudding or a teacher. According to the Instrumentalist Theory, when we ascribe value to the stove, we must always have in the back of our minds that it serves some end, say cooking puddings for teachers, and that that end is valuable. You can never judge the value of anything except in relation to other things that are *at that time* taken to be valuable. Of course, you can always shift the question from the means to the end that lies in view. What is the value of cooking? That is a perfectly good question, too, but a different one, for now we are considering this action as a means, and our end-in-view will be, say, feeding people well. This is the familiar chain of means and ends: if we have a watch, we will keep the dentist's appointment; if we keep the appointment, we will get the tooth repaired; if we get the tooth repaired, we will have better health and less pain; and so on.

The question is whether all such chains must lead ultimately to a

[6] My formulation of this theory is based upon John Dewey's writings on ethics and value theory; for references see Note 28-D.

final step, where something is discovered to be good in itself, not as a means to anything else. The Instrumentalist says No. But the usual answer is Yes, and the argument for it takes several forms, theological, rationalistic, and nationalistic. For example, one answer that has often been given, and with a certain plausibility, is that all roads lead to happiness, and happiness is the sole intrinsic good to which everything else is a means. This answer has some subtle difficulties, and philosophers disagree about it. I am doubtful whether it is really an answer at all. For "happiness" cannot name something to which everything else is a means, unless it is used in such a broad sense as to cover everything that anyone could want or do—monastic vows, the Golden Touch, the Lotus Eaters' paradise, the martyr's death, the advertising executive's life. Happiness is not an end at all, or anything you can aim at or achieve, but a pervasive regional quality of an ongoing life without insoluble problems or irresolvable conflicts—perhaps a life in which no hard problems of value really arise.

Let us consider one other kind of answer. Recall some delightful but harmless pleasure—a walk in the woods, a song, an open fire. Conceive of it as perfectly isolated, in the sense that it has no consequences for the future. Then should we not say that this pleasure is intrinsically worthwhile, and intrinsically better than having a headache during the same stretch of time? I grant that we talk this way, sometimes, but I don't agree that it is the best way to talk. We enjoy the pleasure, to be sure, and if there really are no consequences then there can be no reason why we should not enjoy it. In this case, it is not necessary to say that the pleasure is (intrinsically) good; the question of its goodness or badness does not even arise. There is no problem. But if we ask whether it is good, if we find a problem about it, then we are looking beyond the pleasure itself—as, indeed, we always can. For the example is really artificial, and there are no utterly inconsequential acts. When we were walking in the woods, or musing before the open fire, we were canceling, or postponing, other activities, and thus making a choice.

If an object were intrinsically valuable, no reason could be given to prove it, according to the Instrumentalist, since the reason would consist in pointing out its connections with other things, but if the value depends upon those connections, then it is not intrinsic. The value would have to be self-evident in some way. Yet if I start with the stove and trace its consequences and their consequences, I do not seem ever to get to anything that is self-evidently valuable.

In the light of this discussion, we can, I think, reply to the two most crushing objections often brought against the Instrumentalist Theory. First, it is said to be self-contradictory. Now, it is self-contradictory to say that there can be means without ends-in-view, or to say X has instrumental value because it is a means to Y, but Y is valueless. But to say that an object has instrumental value only entails that the object to which it is instrumental has value; it cannot be deduced from this statement that any object has intrinsic value. Second, the theory is said to be meaningless. For if nothing has intrinsic value, then, it is argued, "intrinsic value" has no application to the world, and hence no meaning; but then the statement, "All values are instrumental," has no meaning either. But this is a mistake, I believe. "Intrinsic value" has no application, true; but it has a meaning, that is, a designation. According to the determinist, "causeless event" has no application, since every event has a cause; nevertheless he knows perfectly well what he means by "causes" and "causeless," and his denial that there are causeless events is not nonsensical.

The chief lessons of the Instrumentalist Theory of value might, then, be summed up in this way: Statements about value are to be regarded as proposed solutions to *problems* of value, that is, situations in which choices have to be made. Choices are always between particular actions —not abstractions like pleasure or honor or self-realization, but this pleasant or this honorable course of conduct, with its particular chain of attendant consequences. Every such decision, when it is rational, involves deliberation about available means with reference to ends-in-view. There are no ends-in-view that are unquestionable. None is in principle immune to doubt, or examination. But nevertheless there are always, in any problem of value, some ends-in-view that are in fact *unquestioned*. For whenever you weigh alternative means, or alternative ends-in-view, you must always weigh them in relation to other, more distant, ends-in-view that you are not calling into question *at that time*. Later experience may destroy your confidence in those ends, of course, for no ends are absolutely final. We all acquired many ends, that is, goals and desires, before we were capable of asking for a justification of them, and it would be in the nature of the case impossible, according to the Instrumentalist, to call into question all our ends at once. Thus problems about value do get settled, at least provisionally; adjustments among competing means or conflicting ends are made, we create temporary harmonies of our impulses and our needs and satisfactions. Some solutions last over a long time, while others are soon shaken by new experiences.

Moreover, certain things have proved, in the course of human experience, to be such valuable means to so many ends, that we give them, and with good reason, a privileged and protected position among the values of life. They are not final ends in themselves, but they are constituents of instrumental value almost everywhere, and therefore they are taken as relatively fixed and constant ends-in-view. Such things are truth, love, health, privacy, the common rights of citizens, and the many species of freedom. And the last question that awaits us, in the next chapter, is whether the arts themselves, or the experiences they provide, belong somewhere in this august company.

§26

26-A aesthetic value.   On the comparison of critical evaluation with moral evaluation, see R. M. Hare, *The Language of Morals,* Oxford: Clarendon, 1952, esp. chs. 8, 9.

J. O. Urmson discusses the problem of distinguishing aesthetic appraisals from moral, economic, religious, intellectual, and other appraisals in his paper in the symposium, "What Makes a Situation Aesthetic?" *PAS,* Suppl. vol. XXXI (1957): 75-92, and his answer—that the distinction is to be made in terms of the kind of reasons given for the appraisal, or the criteria applied—seems very close to that suggested in this chapter. His attempt to say more specifically what the aesthetic-defining criteria are is somewhat sketchy and rudimentary.

The argument, not altogether clear, of Stuart Hampshire, "Logic and Appreciation," in William Elton, ed., *Aesthetics and Language,* Oxford: Blackwell, 1954, pp. 161-69, that each aesthetic object must be judged "on its own merits" (p. 164), and that no reason can be given for a critical evaluation in terms of general canons, may be regarded as an extreme form of the Pluralist Theory. Hampshire doubts that there is a genus of which critical evaluations are a species; he thinks the view that critical evaluations and critical reasons exist arises from a false analogy with moral judgments. He seems to argue that reasons could be given for critical evaluations only if an aesthetic object were the "solution to a problem" (p. 164), rather than "gratuitous" (p. 162). Apparently Hampshire does not clearly distinguish Commendations from Recommendations here; he sees that critical evaluations are not Recommendations, and infers that they are not Commendations; but some moral judgments—for example, judgments of character—are not Recommendations either.

26-B the beauty theory.   Perhaps this theory has never been formulated exactly as it is here; I have tried to put it in the most reasonable, interesting, and fruitful form. Plato's theory of art should, at least in part, be regarded as an early Transcendental version of the theory: see, for example, the references to "absolute beauty" in *Phaedo* 76, *Phaedrus* 249, *Republic* 507, and elsewhere, and the references to ideal beauty in the *Symposium.* In his discussion of beauty as one of the "pure pleasures," *Philebus* 51-53 and 64, Plato sketches a Formalist Theory of the perceptual conditions of beauty, echoed by Poussin: "The idea of beauty does not descend into matter unless this is prepared as carefully as possible." (See Robert Goldwater and Marco Treves, *Artists on Art,* New York: Pantheon, 1945.) The Platonic theory was further extended by Plotinus; for his view see the extracts from the first and fifth *Enneads,* trans. by Stephen Mackenna, in G. H. Turnbull, ed., *The Essence of Plotinus,* New York: Oxford U., 1934, pp. 42-50, 170-78. Jacques Maritain, *Art and Scholasticism,* trans. by J. F. Scanlan, New York: Scribner's, 1930, ch. 5 and pp. 128-33, gives a summary of his own Transcendentalist extension of the Thomistic theory of beauty, which was in St. Thomas somewhat more Naturalistic. See V. B. Evans, "A Scholastic Theory of Art," *Philosophy,* VIII (1933): 397-411.

I have taken the work of G. E. Moore on ethics, especially *Principia Ethica,* Cambridge, Eng.: Cambridge U., 1903, as the most promising departure for a modern version of the Beauty Theory. Moore himself does not hold the Beauty Theory, since he prefers to define "beauty" as "that of which the admiring contemplation is good in itself" (p. 201), thus making not beauty but its contemplation intrinsically valuable (pp. 200-07). But his argument for the indefinability of "good" (pp. 6-16) can be applied to "beauty" with equal cogency, I think, and his argument for the value of beauty that is never contemplated (pp. 83-85) can be taken, as I have taken it, as an argument for the intrinsic value of beauty—not easy to reconcile with his later definition of "beauty." Note that Moore holds (p. 148) that no reason can be given for statements about intrinsic value; they must be self-evident, or deducible from self-evident statements (pp. 143-44).

The Beauty Theory is vigorously defended, in a Transcendental form, by C. E. M. Joad, *Matter, Life and Value,* London: Oxford U., 1929, pp. 266-83, reprinted in Eliseo Vivas and Murray Krieger, eds., *Problems of Aesthetics,* New York: Rinehart, 1953, pp. 463-79.

Harold Osborne, *Theory of Beauty,* London: Routledge and Kegan Paul, 1952, holds something like a Beauty Theory, though his position is far from clear, because his definitions are unsatisfactory. For example, "Beauty itself is simply the extension of that principle of emergent perceptual configuration immediately apprehensible by unreflective intuition . . ." (p. 122)—this comes close to saying that beauty is a regional quality. But compare "the beautiful is the organization of perceptual material into an organic whole by the artist" (p. 126), where beauty seems to be, not the resultant quality, but the unity and complexity of the work itself. For his own view see pp. 91-94, 122-31. His criticism of psychological subjectivism is in ch. 4. He has a good discussion of Formalist attempts to describe the perceptual conditions of beauty in mathematical terms.

The Beauty Theory seems to be held by A. C. Rainer, "The Field of Aesthetics," *Mind,* XXXVIII (1929): 160-83; T. E. Jessop, "The Definition of Beauty," *PAS,* XXXIII (1933): 159-72 (a particularly good discussion); T. M. Greene, "Beauty and the Cognitive Significance of Art," *J Phil,* XXXV (1938): 365-81.

Though W. T. Stace, *The Meaning of Beauty,* London: Richards and Toulmin, 1929, does not hold the Beauty Theory, since (pp. 9-10) he uses "beauty" in a broad sense to include all aesthetic value, his analysis (esp. chs. 3, 6) may be reformulated as an excellent example of the Intellectualist Theory of the perceptual conditions of beauty, taken as a quality. Put in this form, the position would be that an object possesses the quality of beauty whenever an intellectual content, consisting of what he calls "empirical nonperceptual concepts," becomes fused in perceptual qualities in such a way that the intellectual content and the perceptual qualities are indistinguishable from one another. The nature of this "fusion" is not adequately explained, however. Stace suggests (p. 60) that the concept of evolution might be fused with a field of percepts in such a way that we might *see* evolution as an actual object"; other examples are "progress, civilisation, spirituality, or the moral law" (p. 62). If the intellectual content must be of this order of abstraction, it is hard to see what part it plays in the beauty of a great many aesthetic objects.

On the problem of giving necessary and sufficient conditions for beauty in melody, see Edmund Gurney, *The Power of Sound,* London: Smith, Elder, 1880, ch. 9.

Ralph W. Church, *An Essay on Critical Appreciation,* London: Allen and Unwin, 1938, ch. 1, argues against the Beauty Theory from a Pluralistic point of view: the word "beauty," like the word "color," has "no single and unique referent" (p. 53); there is no quality common to all the objects called beautiful, but a family of different qualities.

26-C UGLINESS. There are some interesting questions about the term "ugly." For example, does the existence of judgments of ugliness show that there is a positive aesthetic *dis*value? Is ugliness a distinct emergent quality? Or is ugliness related to beauty the way pain is related to pleasure—in not being on the same scale?

See Lucius Garvin, "The Problem of Ugliness in Art," *Phil R,* LVII (1948): 404-09; M. J. Stolnitz, "On Ugliness in Art," *Phil and Phen Res,* XI (September 1950): 1-24; Stace, *op. cit.,* ch. 4.

It would be interesting to see whether common characteristics could be found in a collection of ugly objects, e.g., a grotesque Belgian Congo mask, the Soviet-built Palace of Science and Culture in Warsaw, a Victorian parlor, a nineteenth-century factory building—if general agreement could be obtained on all of these. Lewis Mumford has remarked of the Philadelphia architect, Frank Furness, who designed, among other things, the massive library of the University of Pennsylvania, "No one ever did more to turn ugliness into a positive principle during the Brown Decades"; see "The Sky Line," *The New Yorker,* April 28, 1956, p. 106.

26-D GENERIC QUALITIES. There have been many attempts to distinguish and define a complete set of generic qualities, coordinate with beauty, e.g., the sublime, the pretty, the graceful. On the sublime, see the Analytic of the sublime in Kant's *Critique of Judgment,* trans. by

J. H. Bernard, 2d ed. New York: Macmillan, 1914, pp. 101-50; Arthur Schopenhauer, *The World as Will and Idea,* trans. by R. B. Haldane and J. Kemp, 6th ed., London: Routledge and Kegan Paul, 1907-09, Part I, pp. 259-74. The discussion by Stace, *op. cit.,* ch. 5, is illuminating.

26-E INSTRUMENTAL AND INTRINSIC VALUE. There is some variation in the way this distinction is made, and a good deal depends upon adopting a clear and consistent usage. The usual distinction is explained by Harold N. Lee, "The Meaning of 'Intrinsic Value,'" in Ray Lepley, ed., *The Language of Value,* New York: Columbia U., 1957, pp. 178-96. See also Moore, *op. cit.,* pp. 21-27.

C. I. Lewis's careful discussion in *An Analysis of Knowledge and Valuation,* La Salle, Ill.: Open Court, 1946, pp. 382-96, is a good one to consult. Note that my term "instrumental value" covers the same ground as his term "extrinsic value," but is defined in a more neutral way: whereas I say simply that if Y has value—whether this value is itself intrinsic or instrumental—and X is a means to Y, then X has instrumental value, Lewis puts into the definition of "extrinsic value" that the object having it is a means, directly or indirectly, to the realization of intrinsic value. Lewis holds that only experiences or their qualities can have intrinsic value; when an object directly, or immediately, causes an experience having intrinsic value, the extrinsic value of the object is said to be "inherent"; when an object is a means to the production of an object with inherent value, its value is said to be "instrumental." Thus inherent value and instrumental value are, for Lewis, subdivisions of extrinsic value.

§27

27-A SUBJECTIVIST DEFINITIONS OF "AESTHETIC VALUE." The definition of "value" in terms of "interest" was sketched by David W. Prall, in his monograph, *A Study in the Theory of Value,* Berkeley, Cal.: U. of California, 1921. Prall proposed to identify aesthetic value with intrinsic value in general (see pp. 200-01, 274-75 and *Aesthetic Judgment,* New York: Crowell, 1929, pp. 336-39). The "interest" definition was worked out in detail by Ralph Barton Perry, *General Theory of Value,* New York: Longmans, Green, 1926; see esp. ch. 5, and also his *Realms of Value,* Cambridge, Mass.: Harvard U., 1954, chs. 1, 18. See also Jerome Stolnitz, "On Artistic Familiarity and Aesthetic Value," *J Phil,* LIII (1956): 261-76.

A somewhat more sophisticated theory of value of the Subjectivist type is that of C. I. Lewis, *An Analysis of Knowledge and Valuation,* La Salle, Ill.: Open Court, 1946, chs. 12-15, which deals in some detail with aesthetic value in particular. Lewis is primarily concerned to show that value judgments are empirical. Immediate value is a quality of satisfaction found in experience; value in an object is the "potentiality" of producing such immediate value, which is intrinsic value (esp. pp. 411-12, also Note 26-E above). Aesthetic value is a species of "inherent" value; it involves being "directly gratifying" to a high degree (see esp. pp. 434-37, 457-62). For further discussions of Lewis's theory, see Stuart M. Brown, Jr., "C. I. Lewis's Aesthetic," *J Phil*, XLVII (1950): 141-50; Lucius Garvin, "Relativism in Professor Lewis's Theory of Esthetic Value," *J Phil*, XLVI (1949): 169-76.

John R. Reid, *A Theory of Value*, New York: Scribner's, 1938, chs. 2, 3, defines "value" as an affective quality (pleasant or unpleasant) of experience (p. 54); he also discusses this definition's consequences for criticism (ch. 8). See also Dewitt H. Parker, *Human Values*, New York: Harper, 1931, chs. 2, 15.

Albert L. Hilliard, *The Forms of Value*, New York: Columbia U., 1950, presents a form of hedonism. "Value" is defined as pleasure or "positive affectivity" (p. 42). An object that directly produces a pleasurable response, such as an aesthetic object, is said to be a "last means," rather than an "intermediate means," to value (pp. 31-41); such an object has "terminal," rather than "instrumental," value (pp. 53, 57). Aesthetic objects thus have terminal value (p. 54), but statements about their value include a reference to the time and conditions and person: "X has terminal value for A at time t, under conditions C."

Subjectivist definitions of "aesthetic value" or of "beauty" are also employed by C. J. Ducasse, *The Philosophy of Art*, New York, Dial, 1929, chs. 14, 15; George Boas, *A Primer for Critics*, Baltimore: Johns Hopkins, 1937, esp. chs. 1, 3; Thomas Munro, "The Concept of Beauty in the Philosophy of Naturalism," *Toward Science in Aesthetics*, New York: Liberal Arts, 1956, pp. 262-67, 277-80, 289-99.

For criticism of Subjectivist definitions of "good" and "beautiful," see W. D. Ross, *The Right and the Good*, Oxford: Clarendon, 1930, pp. 75-104, 122-27.

27-B THE DEFINITION OF "QUALIFIED PERCEIVER." The question raised in the text, whether "X has aesthetic value" might be defined as "X would be (aesthetically) liked by a qualified perceiver," is worth further exploration, perhaps along lines suggested by the discussion of aesthetic experience in §28. The main difficulty lies in trying to define "qualified perceiver" without circularity. For help on this point, consult Roderick Firth, "Ethical Absolutism and the Ideal Observer," *Phil and Phen Res*, XII (March 1952): 317-45, in which Firth works out, with great care, a method for defining ethical words in terms of approval by an "ideal observer." His proposal is discussed by Firth and Richard B. Brandt in "The Definition of an 'Ideal Observer' Theory in Ethics," *Phil and Phen Res*, XV (March 1955): 407-23, and by Richard Henson, "On Being Ideal," *Phil R*, LXV (1956): 389-400. It would be interesting to see how far Firth's method can be carried over to aesthetic value, and whether, for example, the difficulty of specifying the characteristics of an ideal observer in ethics—he is omnipercipient, disinterested, dispassionate, consistent—is greater or less than the difficulty of specifying the characteristics of an ideal observer, or ideally experiencing critic, in aesthetics. See also Henry D. Aiken, "A Pluralistic Analysis of Aesthetic Value," *Phil Rev*, LIX (1950): 493-513, esp. secs. III and IV.

27-C THE NATURALISTIC FALLACY. The "open question" argument was set forth by G. E. Moore, *op. cit.*, ch. 1, as part of his argument against what he called the "naturalistic fallacy." This fallacy, which is said to be committed by all attempts to define normative terms by means of nonnormative ones, has been the subject of a great deal of discussion, not less for its obscurities than for its philosophical importance. Moore argued, for example, that anyone who defined "good" as "pleasure," could not then say that pleasure is good, for this would only mean "pleasure is pleasure." For discussions of the "fallacy," see R. M. Hare, *op. cit.*, ch. 5; W. K. Frankena, "The Naturalistic Fallacy," *Mind*, XLVIII (1939): 464-77, reprinted in W. Sellars and J. Hospers, *Readings in Ethical Theory*, New York: Appleton-Century-Crofts, 1952, pp. 103-14; A. N. Prior, *Logic and the Basis of Ethics*, Oxford: Clarendon, 1949, ch. 1.

27-D PERSUASIVE DEFINITIONS. We owe this term, and the concept it designates, to Charles L. Stevenson; see *Ethics and Language*, New Haven, Conn.: Yale U., 1944, chs. 9, 10. Stevenson adheres to a descriptive and analytical line, and refrains from characterizing the employment of Persuasive Definition as a mistake or fallacy. But he seems to suggest that there is something wrong with such definitions as " 'X is right' means 'X will promote the greatest happiness of the greatest number,' " because they aim to manipulate attitudes. Note that a definition is not Persuasive, in this sense, if its defining term also contains words with the same emotive force as the term-to-be-defined, as in: " 'X is right' means 'X will promote greater *good* than any available alternative.' "

27-E REQUIREDNESS. There is another type of proposal for defining "value" in general which is not Subjectivist but is at the same time Naturalistic, that is, it is defined in terms of empirically observable properties. Wolfgang Köhler, *The Place of Value in a World of Facts*, New York: Liveright, 1938, chs. 2, 3, 9, has worked out this view most fully. He distinguishes a particular regional ("tertiary") quality, which he calls "requiredness," a vector-quality in the sense that where it occurs one part of the phenomenal field points toward, or makes demand upon, or calls for adjustments in, another part. Very often requiredness occurs with a subjective and an objective pole; my need is for money, or my desire is for grapes. This is the situation to which the Subjectivist Definitions reduce all value, by making it a relation between a person and an object. But on many other occasions, the demanding, or needing, or requiring, occurs within the objective part of the phenomenal field itself, as when one chord yearns to be followed by another, or an askew picture demands to be straightened. When we feel the pressure of a task, or the burden of an obligation, the vector is aiming from the phenomenally objective world to us as phenomenal subjects; here is requiredness of precisely the opposite direction from the requiredness of hunger or thirst. This view is also defended by Kurt Koffka, "Problems in the Psychology of Art," Part II, in *Art: A Bryn Mawr Symposium*, Bryn Mawr, Pa.: Bryn Mawr College, 1940. See also D. H. Newhall, "Requiredness, Fact, and Value," *J Phil*, XLVII (1950): 85-96. Requiredness is connected with the concept of "good gestalt" in gestalt psychology; see H. J. Eysenck, "The Experimental Study of the 'Good Gestalt'—a New Approach," *Psychological Review*, XLIX (1942): 344-64.

There is no doubt, I think, of the phenomenal reality of such a quality as requiredness, or of a family of closely related qualities, but this cannot be taken as a definition of "value." The "open question" and "Persuasive Definition" objections apply here as well. For example, granted that the picture "needs" to be straightened, there is still the question whether that need ought to be fulfilled; the situation is exactly the same as when I am faced with water and need to drink, but the question whether I ought to drink depends on other matters as well, for example, the purity of the water. Vectors in the objective phenomenal field would be no different in principle, according to the requiredness view, from vectors issuing from the subjective phenomenal field; they set up demands and the possibilities of satisfaction, and they give rise to value problems, but they do not settle these problems.

§28

28-A THE ADJUNCTIVE USE OF "GOOD." W. D. Ross, *The Right and the Good,* Oxford: Clarendon, 1930, ch. 3, has discussed the "adjunctive or attributive use of the word, as when we speak of a good runner or of a good poem" (p. 65). See also R. M. Hare, *The Language of Morals,* Oxford: Clarendon, 1952, chs. 6, 7, who argues that "good" has the same meaning—its commendatory aspect—in both "good chronometer" and "good drill," but the criteria of application are different. Note that his use of the term "functional" is a little different from mine (p. 100); for example, he says that "strawberry," unlike "motor-car," is not a "functional word" (p. 112), because it does not have to be defined in terms of a purpose. In my usage, it is not *defining* "strawberry" a certain way that makes strawberries a function-class, but discovering a function for strawberries, in terms of which we can say that something is a "good strawberry" (also p. 133).

Robert S. Hartman, in his very interesting but technical paper, "Value Propositions," in Ray Lepley, ed., *The Language of Value,* New York:

Columbia U., 1957, pp. 197-231, proposes a curious analysis of "a good X." A horse is anything that satisfies the definition of "horse"—that is, has the defining characteristics—but horses also have other, nondefining, characteristics, which Hartman calls the "exposition" of the concept *horse*. A good horse, he says, is one that has the expositional characteristics as well as the definitional ones; a poor horse is "not much of a horse," because it lacks some of the expositional characteristics. It does not seem to me that this distinction can be sustained, because the range of the exposition cannot be clearly specified; is having teeth part of the exposition of "horse," for example? or running fast? Would not the exposition also include the undesirable features of horses? (Note also Hartman's unusual definition of "extrinsic" and "intrinsic," p. 200.)

Helen Knight, "The Use of 'Good' in Aesthetic Judgments," *PAS*, XXXVI (1936): 207-22, reprinted in William Elton, ed., *Aesthetics and Language,* London: Blackwell, 1954, pp. 147-60, discusses what she calls the "specific" uses of "good," as in "good tennis player," "good Pekingese"; and says that the "good" of aesthetic judgments is used this way (p. 149). Unlike Hare, she holds that the meaning of "good" varies with the use of different criteria of application, as when two critics use different standards of judgment. But if two people use different standards for judging a tennis player, they are not necessarily using "good tennis player" in different senses, but merely presupposing that good tennis playing is best measured in different ways (see also esp. pp. 156-58).

Further light is thrown on the adjunctive use of "good" by J. O. Urmson, in his stimulating paper "On Grading," *Mind*, LIX (1950): 145-69; see also the critical comments by Karl Britton and M. J. Baker, *Mind*, LX (1951): 526-35.

In the last analysis the distinction between adjunctive and nonadjunctive uses of "good" may break down; all uses of "good" may be adjunctive. (Perhaps the statement, "In all true and verifiable statements containing 'good,' 'good' is used adjunctively," is equivalent to the Instrumentalist Theory of value.) For example, if someone said "Money is good," we could no doubt ask, "Good for what?" and the answer—say, "Good for buying things"—would provide a context in which "good" in the original statement turns out to be adjunctive. "This aesthetic object is good," as Miss Knight has pointed out, can be taken as equivalent to "This is a good aesthetic object." The troublesome examples are those invented by philosophers, such as "Pleasure is good"—here it does seem odd to try to recast this in the form, "Pleasure is a good X." Perhaps the example is artificial. We can imagine situations in which a person might ask, "Is pleasure good?" but in those situations—the hypochondriac asking his physician whether too much pleasure will hinder his digestion or increase his blood pressure—the answer, "Pleasure is good" *would* be adjunctive: that is, "Pleasure is a good treatment for your ills."

28-B THE AESTHETIC EXPERIENCE. What must be reckoned with first is I. A. Richards' famous denial that there is such a thing as aesthetic experience, *Principles of Literary Criticism,* London: Routledge and Kegan Paul, 1925, chs. 2, 32, which is criticized by Roger Fry, *Transformations,* London: Chatto and Windus, 1926, pp. 1-10 (reprinted New York: Anchor, 1956). Actually, Richards' most striking statement, often quoted, about looking at a picture not being "something quite unlike" walking to the Gallery or getting dressed is so hedged about with concessions that all its force is removed. He agrees that aesthetic experiences "can be distinguished," though "they are only a further development, a finer organization of ordinary experiences, and not in the least a new and different kind of thing" (p. 16); they are more complex and unified. This is all the Instrumentalist Definition requires. Richards fears that if we distinguish aesthetic value it will be "cut off from the other values of ordinary experience" and imply that the arts are "a private heaven for aesthetes" (p. 17), but of course no such consequences follow.

There are a number of discussions of aesthetic experience, some of which are cited below. They are divided for convenience into two groups, (I) those which emphasize the coherence, or equilibrium, of the experience, and (II) those which emphasize the completeness, or detachment and self-sufficiency, of the experience. These emphases are not conflicting, but complementary, and some writers have emphasized both.

(I) Richards himself has analyzed aesthetic experience in terms of what he calls "synaesthesis" (see C. K. Ogden, I. A. Richards, and James Wood, *The Foundations of Aesthetics,* London: Allen and Unwin, 1922, ch. 14), a kind of "equilibrium" or "harmonization" of impulses, in which the impulses nevertheless "preserve free play . . . with entire avoidance of frustration" (p. 75). This abstract formula is not well documented by examples, so that it cannot be applied with complete confidence. But, with the help of *Principles,* chs. 15, 32, reprinted in Eliseo Vivas and Murray Krieger, eds., *Problems of Aesthetics,* New York: Rinehart, 1953, pp. 386-95, we can see the sort of thing they are driving at: the "balanced poise" in the opposition of pity and terror in tragedy; the "ironic" complexity of attitude in poetry, very overt in a line like "I do believe her though I know she lies"; the unearthly stability and rightness attained sometimes through the tensions of a painting or the resolutions of music.

Richards comments on two other writers with views like his, though not exactly: Wilbur M. Urban, *Valuation: Its Nature and Laws,* New York: Macmillan, 1909, ch. 7; Ethel D. Puffer (Howes), *The Psychology of Beauty,* Boston: Houghton, Mifflin, 1905, chs. 2, 3. Her "definition" of "beauty": "The beautiful object possesses those qualities which bring the personality into a state of unity and self-completeness" (p. 49); in the aesthetic experience there is intense stimulation together with repose, a "reconciliation" of opposite tendencies, a "balance of forces" (p. 50).

The unity of the aesthetic experience has been fruitfully discussed by H. S. Langfeld, *The Aesthetic Attitude,* New York: Harcourt, Brace and Howe, 1920, ch. 7.

(II) Kant, in his *Critique of Judgment,* trans. by J. H. Bernard, London: Macmillan, 2d ed., 1914, pp. 45-100, described "judgments of taste" as "disinterested" (yet "interesting"), and as concerned with the "form of purposiveness" in the object; "purposiveness without purpose" was his formula to distinguish aesthetic experience from practical and moral experience. See also T. M. Greene, "A Reassessment of Kant's Aesthetic Theory," in G. T. Whitney and D. F. Bowers, eds., *The Heritage of Kant,* Princeton, N.J.: Princeton U., 1939. Schopenhauer, *The World as Will and Idea,* Book III, trans. by R. B. Haldane and J. Kemp, 6th ed., London: Routledge and Kegan Paul, 1907-09, esp. pp. 230-34, 253-59, regarded a "will-less" state of "contemplation" as the central feature of aesthetic experience: the self loses its sense of self, escapes from the "principle of sufficient reason," in the contemplation of Platonic essences.

Edward Bullough, in his famous paper " 'Psychical Distance' as a Factor in Art and an Aesthetic Principle," *British Journal of Psychology,* V (1912-13): 87-118, the gist of which is reprinted in Vivas and Krieger, *op. cit.,* pp. 396-405, and in Melvin Rader, ed., *A Modern Book of Aesthetics,* 2d ed., New York: Holt, 1952, pp. 401-28, introduced the term "psychical distance" for a distinguishing feature of "aesthetic consciousness," in which the object is not considered with respect to ends and means, or from a practical point of view. Distance is a matter of degree, depending upon both subjective and objective factors. Among the objective factors are those features of an aesthetic object that "frame" it— the silence before and after the music, the stage, the pedestal. His discussion of "consistency of distance" in literature is very good. But he tries to derive from the concept of distance a normative principle of criticism: the best aesthetic objects are those in which there is "utmost decrease of distance without its total disappearance," and the apparent consequences of this principle—e.g., that realistic painting is always the best painting—seem too severe to be accepted.

Bullough's theory seems to have been in part anticipated by earlier writers, for example: Ethel Puffer, *op. cit.,* whose emphasis on "repose" is closely related, and who speaks of the "inhibition of all tendency to movement," and the "loss of a sense of personality" (p. 79) in the experience of the "closed circle of the work"; also Hugo Münsterberg, *The Principles of Art Education,* New York: Prang Educational, 1905, Part II, who speaks of the "isolation" of the work from the world, and the absence of an "impulse to action" in the aesthetic experience. For a similar view see José Ortega y Gasset, the section from his *Dehumanization of Art* in Rader, *op. cit.,* pp. 429-42.

Eliseo Vivas, "A Definition of the Aesthetic Experience," *J Phil,* XXXIV (1937): 628-34, reprinted in Vivas and Krieger, *op. cit.,* pp. 406-11, and in Vivas, *Creation and Discovery,* New York: Noonday, 1955, pp.

93-99, proposes that the distinguishing mark of aesthetic experience is a rapt "intransitive" attention to a phenomenal object; this definition is defended briefly but pointedly. It is further developed in "A Natural History of the Aesthetic Transaction," in Yervant H. Krikorian, ed., *Naturalism and the Human Spirit,* New York: Columbia U., 1944, pp. 96-120, esp. 108-11 on unity.

See also Charles Mauron, *Aesthetics and Psychology,* trans. by Roger Fry and Katherine John, London: L. and Virginia Woolf, Hogarth, 1935, esp. chs. 3-6: "The artist contemplates the universe without any idea of making use of it" (p. 39).

(III) John Dewey's description of aesthetic experience as *"an experience"* is rich in insight and suggestion, and deserves consideration by itself. It is presented in *Art as Experience,* New York: Minton, Balch, 1934, esp. chs. 3, 6, 7, 8, 11; of which ch. 3 is reprinted in Vivas and Krieger, *op. cit.,* pp. 325-43, and in Rader, *op. cit.,* pp. 62-88. *An* experience is a segment of experience in general that is demarcated from the rest by its high degree of unity. This unity consists, according to Dewey, in its being pervaded by a single individualizing quality, and is intensified by other characteristics of the experience: its consummatory character (impulses aroused in the experience being carried to completion within it), its continuity (the passage from stage to stage without gaps and dead spots, so that each stage carries within it the past and the future), its rhythm (a controlled dynamism, or ordered change), its cumulativeness (a progressive massing of materials), its shape (or dominant kinetic pattern), its concentration of energy. Some of these terms, so vividly employed by Dewey, are vague and hard to pin down experimentally, yet it cannot be denied, I think, that they point toward important aspects of aesthetic experience. There are passages to be pondered on nearly every page of this remarkable work, but there is not room to quote and comment on them here. Dewey's abhorrence of dualisms has, in my opinion, led him to try to erase too many indispensable distinctions, which I have been at pains to establish in earlier chapters, but his book is full of interesting and important ideas.

See also Carroll C. Pratt, *The Meaning of Music,* New York, London: McGraw-Hill, 1931, pp. 87-103.

28-C INSTRUMENTALIST DEFINITIONS OF "AESTHETIC VALUE." Several writers who are not Instrumentalists in their value theory nevertheless give Instrumentalist definitions of "aesthetic value" or some cognate term. For example, W. D. Ross, *op. cit.,* pp. 126-31, defines "beauty" as "the *power* of producing a certain sort of experience in minds, the sort of experience which we are familiar with under such names as aesthetic enjoyment or aesthetic thrill" (p. 127). Thomas Munro, "Form and Value in the Arts," *Toward Science in Aesthetics,* New York: Liberal Arts, 1956, p. 249, is equally explicit; see his whole discussion of "function," pp. 237-

52. W. T. Stace, *The Meaning of Beauty*, London: Richards and Toulmin, 1929, treats the term "beauty" as equivalent to "aesthetic value" (p. 10), and his use of it (pp. 205-09) could be represented in an Instrumentalist Definition. C. I. Lewis (see Note 27-A above) defines "aesthetic" value as a "potentiality" to produce "intrinsic" value. See also Stephen C. Pepper, *The Work of Art*, Bloomington, Ind.: Indiana U., 1955, ch. 2, esp. p. 56. Probably we can also include Samuel Alexander, *Beauty and Other Forms of Value*, London: Macmillan, 1933, pp. 180-87. See especially Albert Hofstadter, "On the Grounds of Esthetic Judgment," in the symposium "The Evidence for Esthetic Judgment," *J Phil*, LIV (1957): 679-88. He also argues briefly for a pluralistic theory of aesthetic value.

28-D   THE INSTRUMENTALIST THEORY OF VALUE.   John Dewey's theory of value has never been worked out with adequate clarity and explicitness, and in the development of his thinking it has incorporated a variety of elements and tendencies. But the important part of that theory, in my opinion, is its Instrumentalism, and the central features of this part of the theory might be summed up as follows: (1) There is the insistence that choices are always relative to particular situations, in which certain ends-in-view are tentatively fixed, and others are in question, and in which value-deliberation consists in weighing ends and means in relation to each other, to find the way out of a present conflict. (These points are developed in *Human Nature and Conduct*, New York: Holt, 1922, esp. Part III.) (2) Our decisions about values are to be regarded as experimental, and justified by empirical knowledge (*The Quest for Certainty*, New York: Minton, Balch, 1929, ch. 10), for there is a fundamental difference between "prizing," or liking, and "appraising," or making a judgment of value (*Theory of Valuation, International Encyclopedia of Unified Science*, Chicago: Chicago U., Vol. II, No. 4, 1939).

For further clarification, see Abraham Edel, "Naturalism and Ethical Theory," in Krikorian, *op. cit.*, pp. 65-95; Sidney Hook, "The Desirable and Emotive in Dewey's Ethics," in Hook, ed., *John Dewey: Philosopher of Science and Freedom*, New York: Dial, 1950, esp. pp. 195-200. On relations between ends and means, see Charles L. Stevenson, *Ethics and Language*, New Haven, Conn.: Yale U., 1944, ch. 8, and on Dewey, pp. 253-64. For critical comments on Dewey's position, see John R. Reid, *A Theory of Value*, New York: Scribner's, 1938, pp. 245-59; David W. Prall, *A Study in the Theory of Value*, Berkeley, Cal.: U. of California, 1921, ch. 4; Henry D. Aiken, "Reflections on Dewey's Questions about Values," in Ray Lepley, ed., *Value: A Cooperative Inquiry*, New York: Columbia U., 1949, pp. 16-42.

28-E   THE SCALING OF AESTHETIC VALUE.   The discussion in the text omits a number of possible lines of thought that can be connected with the question whether there are inherent limitations to the rating of diverse aesthetic objects in the same scale. For example, we speak of one pleasure as greater than another, but can any two pleasures be compared? Note that comparative rating is not yet measurement: we may find the pleasure of understanding Archimedes' proof that the volume of a sphere is two-thirds that of the cylinder in which it is inscribed greater than the pleasure of a chocolate ice cream cone under optimum conditions, but we cannot say how many of the latter it would take to equal the former.

For some points relevant to the concept of the Area of Undecidability, consult Carroll C. Pratt, "The Stability of Aesthetic Judgments," *JAAC*, XV (September 1956): 1-11.

· XII ·

THE ARTS
IN THE
LIFE OF MAN

The capacity of an object to evoke an aesthetic experience is not, properly speaking, a value unless the experience itself has value. As we have seen, it is not up to the critic to probe into the nature of this second value; he must keep his eye on the aesthetic object. But it is an unavoidable part of the aesthetician's task.

Certainly anyone who contends that the arts deserve a high place among the goods of culture and the ends of education must back up this contention with evidence that the experiences they afford are, in some important way, good for us. If we insist that college students take courses in poetry, or choose between music and fine arts in planning their studies, we ought to have a good reason, for we are taking time that might otherwise be devoted to obviously useful subjects like psychology or economics or natural science. We allow steel and cement to be diverted from highways and hotels into theatres or art galleries or opera houses; we encourage people to spend years of their lives learning to write or dance or paint or play the viola, when they could be applying their energies to farming or selling life insurance. No doubt the money spent annually in the United States on good aesthetic objects is a small fraction of what is spent on liquor or horseracing, but nevertheless the arts have their social cost, and we must sometime face the question how, or whether, we can answer the practical man who says that they are not worth that cost.

Unfortunately it is just at this point in aesthetics that the available evidence is most scarce. And since it is also at this point that the study of the arts comes into relation with other deep and pressing interests— moral, political, economic—that we have as human beings, the problems that result are, even for this untidy subject, unusually heterogeneous, vague, and unsatisfactory. We must do what we can in the present chapter to sort out these problems, but we shall often have to stop where the available evidence runs out. For about these larger and more far-reaching implications of the arts there is, even more than in the other areas of aesthetics, a great deal of thinking that remains to be done.

§29.   MORAL AND CRITICAL JUDGMENTS

In defining "aesthetic value," we have confined our attention to one of the ways in which aesthetic objects affect us: their characteristic, and immediate, effect. But we must now widen our view and ask in what other ways, more remote or indirect, but no less important, aesthetic objects may have an influence upon us. For, to recall a distinction we made earlier, if we are interested not only in a special aesthetic commendation of aesthetic objects, but recommendations of them as something to make, to have recourse to, to possess, then other features of these objects besides their aesthetic value become relevant. In a preformed aesthetic context of choice, as when we have already decided to write for tickets to a play and must now decide which play to see, aesthetic value may sometimes be the only question at issue. But going to one play does not compete for our time and money and energy only with going to another play; it competes with watching ice hockey, going over the checking account, helping the children with their homework, fixing leaky faucets— in fact, with any conceivable human activity that might serve an end-in-view under the existing circumstances.

The effects of a functional object are sometimes divided into two classes. First, there are those effects that proceed from its very function, the consequences of its performing its function well. If a new drug has the specific function of alleviating inhalant allergies, then where it works well, it will, say, eliminate the nasal irritation, stop the sneezing or headaches caused by the allergenic pollens or other particles in the air, and promote greater psychological well-being. These would be counted among the *inherent* effects of the drug: what it is primarily called upon to do. But besides its inherent effects, there may be *side effects,* until further research is able to avoid them: the drug may make you drowsy, or induce a mild indigestion, or slightly discolor your teeth. Or perhaps it will not affect everyone this way, but only some people. Side effects are not necessarily bad; it is the same distinction we make between the main product of a factory, say pork, and its by-products, say soap or lard.

It will clarify our problems if we apply this common-sense distinction to aesthetic objects. Let us consider their inherent effects first. Aesthetic experience is the immediate effect of aesthetic objects. Now suppose there are more remote effects of aesthetic objects, effects they produce *via* aesthetic experience. For example, suppose we could prove that aesthetic experience itself is peculiarly beneficial in providing an outlet for psychological impulses that would be destructive if they overflowed into overt action.[1] In the ordinary course of life, little frustrations and irritations inevitably build up in our minds. Of course if they develop into deep-seated neuroses, no home remedy may be sufficient to cope with them. But most often they are just persistent, nagging, bothersome, capable of taking the edge off our appetite for creative activities, of undermining our confidence in ourselves, of getting in the way of our relations with other people. Now we may try to escape these irritations with the help of various sorts of entertainment—indeed, never in the history of the world before radio and television has it been possible for millions of human beings to be entertained, if they wish, for twenty-four hours a day. I do not suppose we can draw a sharp line between entertainment and aesthetic experience, but there are nevertheless, I believe, vitally important differences between them. Entertainment may be aesthetic experience of a sort, but at a low power: pleasant, passive, easy, and superficial. It is certainly a temporary escape from trouble, but perhaps it is merely an anodyne, and when it is over the gnawing may begin again where it left off; the impulse may only have been blocked and dulled, not drained from the system.

But with the help of aesthetic objects we can work off these destructive impulses, without having them fester inside and without taking them out on our neighbors. This is very plausible as far as literature is concerned, for we can feel as we like about its make-believe world, and run through all sorts of emotions—love, hate, self-satisfaction, moral indignation, cynicism—without fear of injuring anyone. It is even plausible for musical experience; we are caught up in the drive and purposefulness of the musical process, and though full-fledged emotions are not directly manipulated, the tension and restlessness that are their feeling-basis may be used and relieved and quieted by music. And if we think of the experience of painting as an experience that takes time, this experience, too, may turn out to be psychologically beneficial in the same way as music.

This hypothesis, though highly speculative, is not utterly without warrant. We can all find in ourselves by introspection some evidence for

---

[1] I do not pretend to be giving here an authoritative exegesis of Aristotle's theory of catharsis (see Note 30-A at end of chapter), but for the purposes of illustration I sketch a hypothesis based upon a generalization of his theory of the tragic effect to the other arts.

it. There is often a very special refreshing feeling that comes after aesthetic experience, a sense of being unusually free from inner disturbance or unbalance. And this may testify to the purgative or cathartic, or perhaps sublimative, effect. What we lack, to make the hypothesis highly acceptable, is adequate physiological and behavioral evidence for that effect. But now, suppose there is such a purgation of feeling. Then further consequences might follow, too. Those who have been treated by aesthetic objects, like those who have given up coffee, might turn out to be more capable of outgoing and affectionate and trustful relations with others; they may be less given to irrational emotional outbursts, to sudden prejudices and lasting resentments. They may become better neighbors, more tolerant, more understanding, more forgiving—better citizens when it comes to voting, serving on juries, and seeing the justice of other people's claims.

I have kept this hypothesis hypothetical because it is primarily an illustration. Whether this claim, or something like it, can be made good we shall consider more fully later, though even in that discussion I am afraid we cannot be very positive about our conclusions. In any case, suppose for the moment that aesthetic objects have such a long-range effect upon people, and have this effect by means of their peculiar aesthetic function, then this effect would be an inherent one. But there could be other effects, more or less independent of aesthetic experience, that some aesthetic objects have upon people. For example, they may be effective at getting children to go to sleep, or at keeping them awake; they may increase juvenile delinquency by spreading wrong ideals of conduct, or by intensifying, instead of purging, certain tensions and destructive impulses; they may strengthen the chastity of young maidens or sharpen the sensuality of the old *roué*. These would be side effects of art, perhaps some bad, perhaps some good, perhaps some indifferent.

It is now reasonably clear, I think, what we can best choose to mean by the "moral judgment" of an aesthetic object. I use the term "moral" in a broad but quite usual sense. To call an action "right" is a moral judgment in a narrow sense; but when we point out the possible effects of sports on the building of character, or the effects of slums on juvenile delinquency, we are making a moral judgment in the broad sense. Thus to make a moral judgment of an aesthetic object is to point out some side effect upon human conduct, and to judge that side effect as good or bad: "This novel is subversive," "This painting is pornographic," "This statue will corrupt the young." Moral judgments and critical judgments are distinct and independent, or so it would seem. That is, we seem to be able to say without contradiction that a poem is a good aesthetic object but will promote unhealthy political views, or that a play is a poor aesthetic object but will undoubtedly promote purity of heart. Whether these statements are contradictory or always false we shall consider shortly.

With the help of these distinctions, we must now examine two broad views—it would be misleading to call them theories—of the moral aspect of art, and about the relation between the moral and the aesthetic.

Aestheticism

The simpler of the two views, which I shall call *Aestheticism*,[2] has the merit of setting the issues in the starkest light. It is the view that aesthetic objects are not subject to moral judgment, that only aesthetic categories can be, or ought to be, applied to them. Not because they are *objects*, rather than *acts*, for it may be granted that objects can become subject to moral judgment when their presence affects behavior, but because, according to the view we are now considering, the side effects of aesthetic objects, if any, need not be taken into account.

Aestheticism involves one attitude that deserves sympathetic attention. It is a healthy impatience with the moralistic manner in which society often receives new and trail-breaking aesthetic objects. Departures from the familiar patterns are viewed with alarm or greeted with exaggerated fears of social consequences instead of that eager adventurousness that would betoken a more healthy social order. When we observe the bitter and sometimes violent outbursts against Stravinsky, or Bartók, or James Joyce, or Dylan Thomas, or Picasso, or Henry Moore, we can infer that no mere matters of taste are at stake; deeply-embedded customs, established modes of thought and feeling, vested interests are felt to be threatened. But many of the protests are based upon snap judgments and wild predictions. Where is the evidence of genuine danger? We need not linger over the easy cases. Has it ever been shown that anyone's character has been undermined by an overdose of Picassos? Could they unsettle our notions of human anatomy, or weaken religious faith, or encourage us to drink absinthe in excess? And what possible harm of a lasting sort could be done to anyone by *Rite of Spring* or *The Firebird?* Admittedly there is more room for controversy in, say, the movies. But of all those people who objected violently to *Blackboard Jungle*, the sensational exposé of schoolroom goons, how many of them produced any solid evidence that it would undermine public confidence in the schools or increase the incidence of unlawfulness among high school students? And, when *The Man with the Golden Arm* was refused the Production Code seal of approval because it violated the rule against representing narcotics addiction as easily curable, though it is easy to imagine the unfortunate effects this *might* have on the public, do we really have grounds for predicting these effects with confidence?

There seem to be two main lines of argument, leading to partly in-

---

[2] This view I take to be that of Walter Pater and Oscar Wilde, for example, and to a lesser extent of Théophile Gautier and James A. McNeill Whistler; for references see Note 29-A.

compatible conclusions, that are offered in support of Aestheticism. Indeed, if we were very strict, we should have to distinguish two kinds of Aestheticism. But since neither has been carefully worked out or systematically defended, it does not seem worthwhile to be very strict here, and what is instructive in the general point of view can be brought out anyway. The first line of argument is based upon a firm optimism about the potentialities of aesthetic education. Suppose there are occasional unfortunate effects of aesthetic objects; for example, suppose it is true, as reported, that when the French motion picture *Rififi* was exhibited in Mexico City—this movie showed in great detail how to commit a jewelry shop safe robbery—it had to be withdrawn because it was so instructive that it quadrupled the rate of local robberies. (In Paris the police did not object, since, they said, the method was not *en effet* the latest one.) Or, for another example, it may even be that people have been converted to fatalism by the *Rubáiyát of Omar Khayyám of Nishápúr*. Still, such side effects as these would be accidental and correctible, and more to be blamed on faulty upbringing than on aesthetic objects. A proper education in the arts would teach people the right way to respond to aesthetic objects, which is not to take them as inspiration for a half-baked philosophy or as guides to conduct, but as objects to be enjoyed in themselves. In fact, it may be just the unintelligent education in the arts so often given, with the emphasis on inspiring messages and moral uplift, that encourages people to confuse literature with nonliterary discourse and try to put it into practice, even when it is immoral.

Perhaps, then, literature is, or can be made, practically harmless. Therefore, when we are considering aesthetic objects, we can ignore all their supposed side effects and consider only their aesthetic value. The critic's concern is not with art for the sake of citizenship or patriotism or mysticism, or anything else, but with Art for Art's Sake only. The slogan, "Art for Art's Sake," has, of course, meant a good many things, not always consistent and seldom very definite, but it does mark out, roughly, a general attitude.

The line of argument just considered may be called the argument from Innocuousness; I give it a name to distinguish it from another line of argument that starts from a different premise, but emerges somewhere nearby. I shall call it the Argument from Aesthetic Primacy.

Suppose there *are* side effects of aesthetic objects, and even serious and lasting and unpreventable ones. Still, it might be argued, they are completely separable from aesthetic value. Or if there is a connection, it is an inverse one: the higher the aesthetic value, the more likely is the object, from the Philistine point of view, to be unsettling, radical, vigorous, shocking, subversive—at first, anyway. That is because the great artist is always exploring new perspectives, inventing intense new regional qualities, putting things together in hitherto unheard-of ways; and if what he makes is good, it will be the enemy of some established good that is not quite as good.

If, therefore, we must choose between the moral and the aesthetic values of an aesthetic object, what principle shall guide our choice? This is no problem for Aestheticism. What is the good of life itself, except to be as fully alive as we can become—to burn with a hard gemlike flame, to choose one crowded hour of glorious life, to seize experience at its greatest magnitude? And this is precisely our experience of art; it is living in the best way we know how. Far from being a handmaiden to other goals, art gives us immediately, and richly, the best there is in life, intense awareness—it gives us what life itself aims at becoming, but seldom achieves outside of art. This part of the Aestheticist view is connected, of course, with a Psychological Definition of value; it claims that there *is* an end in itself, an intrinsic good, and that aesthetic experience is that good.

If this is true, then the undesirable side effects of art cannot really matter. They are inconveniences we have to put up with for the sake of the best, but, no matter how regrettable, they can never outweigh the aesthetic value of a really good aesthetic object. For a clear-cut example of this conclusion, see George Moore:

> What care I that some millions of wretched Israelites died under Pharaoh's lash or Egypt's sun? It was well that they died that I might have the pyramids to look on, or to fill a musing hour with wonderment. Is there one among us who would exchange them for the lives of the ignominious slaves that died? What care I that the virtue of some sixteen-year-old maid was the price paid for Ingres' *La Source?* That the model died of drink and disease in the hospital is nothing when compared with the essential that I should have *La Source,* that exquisite dream of innocence. . . .[3]

With its egotistic posturing, this passage cannot be taken as a philosophical thesis, but it contains a profound warning to those who, in their eagerness to exalt the arts, forget that they are after all human products of human activities, and must find their value in the whole context of human life. Such choices as Moore's have often enough been made. In our own day we have not forgotten the lyrical description by Mussolini's son-in-law of the "beauty" of a bomb exploding among a crowd of unarmed Ethiopians.

In its second form, Aestheticism is a pure and single-minded view, which maintains the supreme value of art over everything else. It is a form of fanaticism, which is just the fixing of any single good as a goal without regard to anything else. From an Instrumentalist point of view, it has no logical justification; it is a mere assertion, or even a mere prejudice, and I do not think any more needs to be said about it here.

---

[3] George Moore, *Confessions of a Young Man,* New York: Brentano's, 1917, pp. 144-45.

The second point of view we were to consider may be given its ordinary name of *Moralism*. The moralistic critic, to put it first very roughly, is one who judges aesthetic objects solely, or chiefly, with respect to moral standards. We recognize this attitude in the critic who, when he writes of aesthetic objects, is interested wholly, or almost wholly, in their tendency to affect, for better or for worse, the behavior of those who are exposed to them, and whose judgment of the practical disposition of these objects—whether they should be bought or sold, exhibited or performed—is based upon his conclusion about this tendency.

Two somewhat different positions may be distinguished under the broad heading of Moralism; they are based upon different arguments and emerge with different implications. It will be best to deal with them separately.

The first argument starts back where we were in the preceding chapter, at the point where we asked whether aesthetic objects have a function. Suppose there is no such thing as aesthetic experience. Then there is nothing in particular that aesthetic objects can claim to do better than anything else. Now, if this is the case, there is no such thing as aesthetic value, according to the Instrumentalist analysis, and of course there can be no judgment of aesthetic objects on aesthetic grounds.

But that does not mean there can be no judgment of them at all. For we can still ask, "What do aesthetic objects do, if not better than anything else, then at least with reasonable efficiency?" Well, they arouse feelings, they get people worked up in one way or another. This seems a plausible answer. But what good is it to arouse feelings? There is no point in just getting people worked up; the value depends on *what* feelings you arouse (some are good, some not), on what you get people worked up *about*. But the distinction between desirable feelings (say love, religious faith, a sense of human brotherhood) and undesirable ones (hatred of others and of oneself, mistrust, fear) is a moral distinction. And so the whole, apparently aesthetic, question whether a particular aesthetic object is a good one or not is reduced to the (moral) question whether the feelings it arouses are good or bad. Let us call this the Argument from Reduction.[4]

We need not follow out here the many important and interesting consequences of the Argument from Reduction; evidently it entails a drastic overhaul of the point of view presented above in Chapters X and XI. It means that all critical evaluation is moral evaluation, that moral questions are the only ones to be considered by the critic. Of course, according to the Moralistic view, he may deal with questions about technique, in so far as they are related to the effectiveness of the object in arousing feel-

---

[4] It is, I take it, one of the important arguments of Plato and Tolstoy; see Note 29-B.

ings. But the object is to be judged in the end much as one would judge propaganda; and indeed, there is no fundamental distinction. The qualifications of the critic will be primarily that he have the right moral code or system, and that he be able to make correct predictions of the psychological effects of aesthetic objects. To apply this method wholesale to famous aesthetic objects would, as Tolstoy showed, result in a radical revision of the established comparative ratings, with *Uncle Tom's Cabin,* for example, standing higher than *Hamlet.*

The Argument from Reduction, I think, cannot be accepted. Aesthetic value is not to be analyzed away, for it exists as a distinct kind of value. There is, however, a second argument, the Argument from Correlation,[5] which is used by Moralists of a somewhat different school from the Reductionists. Grant that there is such a thing as aesthetic value, distinct from moral value, but suppose the degree of aesthetic value to depend upon the degree of moral value in some way. Suppose, in other words, that aesthetic objects with a low moral value must be of low aesthetic value, and those of high moral value must be good aesthetic objects. If there is such a correspondence, or correlation, then the critic does not have to concern himself with aesthetic value, but can reach his judgment on moral grounds alone. For even if the correlation is not perfect, he will hold that the deviations are negligible.

This view will recall the Didactic Theory of literature, which was discussed in Chapter IX, §23; they are parallel in some respects, but the Moralistic Argument from Correlation is even more difficult to make plausible. Moralistic critics often say that a morally bad poem cannot be a good poem, but they are less likely to claim that a morally good poem cannot be a bad poem. Some of them, too, would be willing to yield to the skepticism of the Aestheticist view about the moral effects of music and nonrepresentational painting, but there are Moralist critics who would apply their categories across the whole field: music may minister to lasciviousness or help to break down self-control, or on the other hand it may strengthen martial courage or deepen moral resolution; even nonrepresentational painting may stimulate a relish for violence and lawlessness by means of its tense designs, garish color combinations, and sharply conflicting patterns, or it may encourage a cool love of order and decorum and a calm joy in self-discipline. To make out the Argument from Correlation, then, we would have to show that the musical and visual designs that promote positive moral values are those that are more unified, and hence better as aesthetic objects, while the most morally destructive music and painting is that which is most confused.

The argument, indeed, has traditionally relied heavily upon a supposed connection between moral order and aesthetic order, and no doubt there is a deep and profound analogy between them. Many of the

---

[5] This is roughly the argument of Ruskin, J. W. R. Purser, L. A. Reid, Yvor Winters, and others; for references, see Note 29-B.

regional qualities we find in art are most aptly, but of course metaphorically, named by qualities taken over from the moral aspects of human nature: they are "disciplined," "decisive," "decorous," "controlled," "sound," "strong," "calm," "bold," "healthy," to cite only positive terms. But an analogy is not a causal connection. To prove that decorous music makes us behave decorously, it is not enough to point out the similarity between the music and the hoped-for behavior. Music may be, as St. Augustine said, an image of the moral order, but it does not follow that the better the music the more free it is from undesirable side effects. As far as music and painting are concerned, we do not as yet have a correlation of moral and aesthetic value.

When we turn to representational objects, we can admit more plausibility in the claim that there are moral or immoral effects. These effects are constantly exaggerated by the Puritan, who judges other people's reactions by his own excessive ones, but there is no question that a picture can be a powerful sexual stimulation. And there is common-sense evidence here to support, in a rough way, the Argument from Correlation: generally speaking, the pictures designed for sexual stimulation, whether mild, as in advertisements, or more vigorous, as in pornographic photographs, tend to be poor as visual designs, and those works that are great as visual designs tend not to be so effective in their sexual side effects. The better the design the more likely it is to hold attention to itself, and inhibit reverie and association, but of course there is no *necessary* connection. An obscene picture could be as great as Cézanne or Raphael at their best, though we might find it hard to pay attention to its greatness.

It is in literature and in mass arts like the movies that the side effects of art are most clearly established. Perhaps we can agree with the Moralist that those movies that have the most unfortunate effects, morally speaking, are very often among the very poorest, aesthetically speaking. They are high in entertainment value, apparently, but borderline cases as far as their aesthetic value goes. But the correlation is far from complete.

It is sometimes difficult to decide which of the two arguments the Moralist is using when he talks about aesthetic objects. There is always in his tone the suspicion of a disparagement of, or insensitivity to, aesthetic value (the Argument from Reduction). Consider again the group sculpture, *The American Family,* by Bernard Rosenthal, which was referred to in the Introduction to this book. Some of its critics—those who wanted it to depict the police in action—seemed not to care about aesthetic value at all. On the other hand, the President of the National Sculpture Society, a conservative organization of academic sculptors, wrote to *The New York Times* on March 11, 1955, that it was "really not sculpture, but a metallic monstrosity," which placed it among "the new vestiges of a confused culture that will surely prove deleterious to us morally." His view seems to have been that sculpture cannot be good sculpture if its moral effects are bad, though he did not explain what harm the statue would do.

Marxism

There is one form of Moralism that deserves special treatment, for though it clearly belongs under our general heading, it moves in a somewhat different way from the two arguments just considered. I shall refer to it as *Marxism,* because the Marxists have worked it out most elaborately and adhered to it most consistently, but its basic principle, I am afraid, is shared by some political reformers who are violently anti-Marxist.

This principle is the Marxist's version of the Moralistic insistence upon the side effects of aesthetic objects. The Marxist is a Moralist with a peculiarly narrow set of morals, for he judges all behavior with respect to a single goal, the advancement of the revolutionary proletariat toward a classless society. Ethics is thus reduced to politics. Now, a range of attitudes toward aesthetic objects is open to Marxists: some, like Marx himself, set a high value on them; others regard them as a social luxury, not one of the serious things in life. But in either case, considerations of aesthetic value are to be subordinated to political ones, for—and this is the basic Marxist principle—aesthetic objects cannot be politically neutral.

Evidently this principle could be applied either to aesthetic objects or to the people who make them, and though the first application is the central one here, it is sometimes confused with the second, and not only by Marxists. Totalitarian governments, and sometimes fearful officials in democratic governments, are likely to be more interested in painters than in paintings. Thus the Nazis removed the Berlin Museum's copy of Max Beckmann's print, *Self-Portrait,* PLATE IV, along with many others, because he was a Jew, but it would be no surprise to find that it went into Goering's private collection. A few years ago, the United States Information Agency was prevailed upon to cancel a traveling exhibition of paintings called "Sport in Art" because some of the painters were alleged to have once been Communists or associates of Communists. It was argued that even if the paintings themselves have no tendency to encourage Communism, to show them might encourage the painters, by giving official approval to their work, enhancing their reputation, and perhaps enabling them to raise their commission rates. I don't say that this is a good argument to justify the Agency's decision; it seems to me a rather feeble one. But this sort of argument does not concern us now. In principle, if one wishes, he can distinguish the respect owed to Erich Kleiber as a conductor from the respect owed to him as an independent man who refused to be made use of either by the Nazis or the East German Communists. No doubt orchestras like the Berlin Philharmonic or the Philadelphia Orchestra, in their foreign tours, are, as organizations, instruments of diplomatic policy. But this is not the point of saying that art cannot be neutral.

The Principle of Nonneutrality, if we may call it that, is the statement that every aesthetic object of any noteworthy degree of aesthetic value has a tendency to promote, or to interfere with, our social and political goals, whatever they may be. For example, suppose you are writing a play, and you want it to contain conflict. Then you must have a villain, at least someone who does something wrong. Now the villain has to be somebody—an airplane manufacturer, a plumber, a college instructor, a man or a woman, tall or short, blond or brunette. And whatever choice you make involves you in a vague and subtle, but nevertheless real and definable, social commitment: you will be implicitly against the manufacturer or the plumber, and you will be helping to mold people's attitudes, for your audience will be given a slight encouragement to think of manufacturers or plumbers as the sort of people who are likely to do wrong. Even if your play contains no villain at all, the same thing holds. Social commitment is inescapable. Your curtain goes up, and the phone rings, and out comes a maid, in uniform, to answer it. Right away you must make a choice: is she to be a Negro, an Irish maid, a French maid, fat or thin, efficient or inefficient? Even if you don't make her comic and ridiculous, so that the audience gets the idea that Swedish maids are always sullen or Negro maids always cheerful and stupid, you will still be affecting attitudes. For to put her in a humble role, without explicitly protesting it, is tacitly to accept the idea that her proper place is to wait on other people, and this strengthens the audience's tendency to accept the situation—the exploitation, if it is exploitation—too.

These examples may seem far-fetched, but they are by no means unworthy of serious thought, and of course you do not need to be a Marxist in your ethics to acknowledge the importance of this claim. For the evidence concerning movies (and these have been much studied) is that the moral side effects of literature—the important and lasting ones—take place through the formation of *beliefs*. Not that the work has to have a thesis; it may influence beliefs even if it contains no Reflective predications. Suppose you have a series of movies, as you often do, each of which contains a crooked cop, a fat bartender, a sneaky Japanese, a romantic Mexican, or a spying Russian. Perhaps each of these movies, by itself, does nothing more than present its characters, and contains no theses at all. Nevertheless, the impact, especially on the immature or half-mature audience, may be powerful. The essential process is in one respect no different from life; if in less than a year you met six crooked cops in your city, you would find it hard not to generalize about the probable corruption of the local police force. The horrifying difference, of course, is that the movie-goer has not seen *any* crooked cops, but only six men pretending to be crooked cops in order to act out exciting stories, but this difference is precisely what he often finds it so hard to keep in mind. In the movie-going situation, with its extreme journalistic and documentary-like realism, the conviction of truth is encouraged; the tendency to generalize by thinking of the characters as typical and symbolic is sharpened; the viewer is put in a state of suggestiveness and manipulability. And there is plenty of evidence that attitudes toward social groups can be developed, strengthened, perhaps even reversed, by exposure to motion pictures and television.

So much, I think, we must all agree to, but the Marxist goes much further, and here with less caution. Even if the moral effect of aesthetic objects is primarily *via* the formation of beliefs, it does not follow that this effect is limited to literature and representational painting. For in every work there is an *implicit producer,* and the kind of work he produces reveals certain underlying attitudes toward the audience, and invites them to share those attitudes. And, if the Ministry of Arts does not promptly clamp down, people will come to accept those attitudes, because they will assume that such attitudes are socially permissible. Thus, the composer must give his works some melody and harmony, and his choice is momentous. Simple, singable, folk-style melodies and plain diatonic harmony will show that he wants everyone to enjoy his music, that he has a welcoming attitude toward the masses. Complicated melodies and harsh harmony show that he is writing for an elite, and scorns the masses: that is "bourgeois formalism." If the music is cheerful, it shows he is happy in a Socialist society; if gloomy, it may encourage a pessimism about the future, and must be suppressed at once: that is "subjectivism." If he writes vast choral works and operas and dance music, he is encouraging collectivism and cooperation; if he writes chamber music, he is too exclusive: that is "individualism."

It is the same with painting. The Principle of Nonneutrality applies well enough to a picture like Daumier's *Witnesses,* PLATE VIII, which is highly tendentious and could obviously be considered subversive under certain circumstances. And for all its generality and broad humanity, Kollwitz's *Municipal Lodging,* PLATE III, might stir social unrest in a time of depression. But the Marxist would apply the same principle to a pure design like the Jensen *Composition,* PLATE I, and precisely because it is nonrepresentational, for its very withdrawal from the political scene is an implicit denial of the primacy of politics.

Pictures, for the Marxist, must have human interest to be acceptable; cubism and expressionism are aimed at appreciation by the few, and are therefore implicitly antisocial. "Socialist realism" is the term for art—including literature, painting, and music—that has the tendency to promote attitudes that fit in with the revolutionary development of society, and even though the Soviet critics do not seem to have defined this term very clearly, they seem to know at any given time—even if they know differently at another time—what conforms to it, and what does not. Of course we must not identify Soviet practice with Marxist theory, but sometimes the former throws light on the latter.

On the basis of the Principle of Nonneutrality, the task of the Marxist critic is plain: it is he who is to determine, for every aesthetic object, what its political value or disvalue is. And the disposition he makes of it—his praise or condemnation, and any consequent prizes or confiscations—will depend solely on this political judgment. For whatever the purely aesthetic value may be, it can never take precedence over politics. Here is a third Moralistic argument, which is the inverse of the Argument from Aesthetic Primacy. Suppose the music is great, but guilty of bourgeois formalism; it is nevertheless to be rejected without a qualm, for the composer can be sent back, or some other composer can be found, to produce an equally great work that is not guilty of bourgeois formalism. Or if the novel is rich and moving, and yet unfortunately it clearly will encourage suspicion of the Party leaders and heads of Ministries, we may feel some regret, but no compunction, in ordering up an equally good novel with a different set of villains.

But what if these unfortunate attitude-formations can be counteracted, and even rendered harmless, by proper education? This was suggested in my account of Aestheticism. Is it not part of the very concept of maturity that the mature person cannot be manipulated in such obvious ways—that he will not come to have contempt for the rights of all people merely from looking at cubist paintings that most people don't enjoy, that he will not come to hate Negroes from seeing *The Birth of a Nation* or Jews from seeing *Oliver Twist?* Perhaps if we gave school children a course in how to see movies, and encouraged them to discuss their attitudes before and after, and to correct them by relating them to their other experience, we could help them become more immune to the movies, as far as attitude-molding is concerned, but without making them enjoy the movies any less. Perhaps we could give them a kind of detachment that would protect them against what they see.

But it is precisely this point of view that the Marxist is inclined most strongly to reject. He may be skeptical about its possibility, and for all his confidence in the malleability of human nature believe that most people are always going to be susceptible to the side effects of aesthetic objects. But even if he is not skeptical, he has no use for detachment, or for the separation, as he calls it, of art from life. The Marxist believes in training people in just the opposite way; instead of being able, temporarily, to forget politics and economics and the seriousness of the international situation, and become absorbed in music or in a play, he thinks we should be always supersensitive to the subtlest political tendencies of aesthetic objects, and ready to react to them. We should not be able to enjoy the music at all if it is clearly designed for the few rather than the many, or endure the play if it could conceivably be taken to reflect unfavorably on any but a small number of groups it is permissible to hate, because they stand in the way of social progress as the Marxist sees it.

So far we have been considering the side effects of art, and the view of them taken by Moralism and Aestheticism. But we have so far left one fundamental problem unexplored. The question was raised whether aesthetic objects have inherent effects that are themselves of great worth. One possible answer—the Aristotelian catharsis—was sketched, by way of illustration. But its truth or falsity was not discussed; it remained hypothetical. Yet evidently our answer to this question is fundamental to any final decision about the elements of truth and falsity in Aestheticism and Moralism, and the time has now arrived when the question must be faced. This we shall do in the following, and final, section.

§30.   THE INHERENT VALUES OF ART

In the final analysis, then, what good is art? This question, the bluntest and most far-reaching of all questions in the philosophy of art, is many things to many people. It can be asked skeptically by the practical man who has no doubt that the improvement of plumbing, the control of disease, and the development of automotive engineering are ingredients of progress and civilization, but has a hard time fitting concertos, water colors, and lyric poetry into the picture. Not that he would deny these to people who care for them, but he cannot see that they need to be considered in thinking broadly about the basic needs of society. It can be asked ironically by the Aestheticist, who is equally skeptical of plumbing and automatic gearshifts, as in Théophile Gautier's famous Preface to *Mademoiselle de Maupin:*

> What is the good of music? of painting? Who would be foolish enough to prefer Mozart to Monsieur Carrel,[1] or Michelangelo to the inventor of white mustard?
>
> Nothing is truly beautiful unless it can never be of any use whatsoever . . .

Have aesthetic objects "no more consequence than a dozen oysters and a pint of Montrachet"?[2]

But whatever its tone, the question deserves an answer. For it goes deep into the philosophy of art. Let us begin by considering what kind of answer it requires. Plumbing, medicine, and automobiles, we may assume, make a contribution to human welfare. They have special functions, but the ends they directly serve are means to many other ends, and there is

---

[1] Armand Carrel (1800-36), a well-known journalist, was killed in a duel the same year that *Mademoiselle de Maupin* appeared. Gautier presumably thought of him as a man who used the art of writing to serve political and social ends.

[2] W. Somerset Maugham, *The Summing Up*, Baltimore: Penguin, 1938, p. 214. See the whole of sec. 76.

little doubt of their justification, even though sometimes they may be put to bad uses. Aesthetic objects differ from those directly utilitarian objects in that their immediate function is only to provide a certain kind of experience that can be enjoyed in itself. Can we show that the having of this aesthetic experience is, in turn, justified by longer-range effects that such experience has upon us—in other words, that aesthetic experience makes its own contribution to human welfare?

The question What good is art? probably ought to be divided into two questions, of which the second is the one that concerns us most. What good does the act of creating an aesthetic object do to the creator himself? And what good does the finished aesthetic object do to those who experience it? As regards the first of these questions, our knowledge is limited, but there is something to go on. It makes a considerable difference, however, whether you are talking about the professional creative artist—by this I mean not necessarily one who makes an adequate living at it, but one who has made it his life work—or the amateur. Of course there is no sharp line between them, because the desire to compose music or paint pictures may have any degree of depth. Nevertheless, there are two different kinds of utility involved.

It is almost absurd to ask what good it does the professional creator to do what he does—with an environment that makes it feasible at all, he will find that he cannot help himself. His motivation, and his reward, are out of the common run, for the objects he creates insist upon their existence, and wring themselves out of him in a way that absorbs him completely. His satisfactions are probably not utterly different from those of other kinds of creators—scientists, philosophers, organizers of social and economic institutions—when they can make something that bears the stamp of great goodness, by summoning up and concentrating all their powers.

For the amateur, the dilettante or dabbler, the rewards are different, though they may also be great in their own way. To perform on a musical instrument, to dance, to make up a song, to write stories and poems, to play around with oil paints seems quite clearly to have very beneficial psychological effects upon those who can be encouraged to undertake such activities, even if the results are of little aesthetic value. In recent years educators have widely recognized this fact, and it is pretty much taken for granted now that instruction in music and the fine arts, and participation in plays and concerts, are an important part of elementary and secondary education. Psychologists and psychiatrists may not yet be certain of the exact manner in which creative activity works its effects, but it seems to release pent-up energy, work off frustrations, lessen tensions, restore a sense of balance and perspective, and in these ways promote conditions of mental health. Much of the Aristotelian theory of catharsis, which was summarized in the preceding section, seems to apply here. And indeed some, though not all, of the benefits of art may come as well from producing an aesthetic object that is only fair as from experiencing one that is great.

Even if the specific value of the arts were limited to their value for the creators themselves, there would be ample justification for putting a good deal of social effort into promoting them—helping everyone to become a painter, a musician, a writer as far as it lies in him to do so. And if the establishment of a National Advisory Council on the Arts, or, better, a United States Art Foundation, would provide the means of increasing education in the arts, it would be well worth the cost. But the private value of artistic creation as mental therapy to the creator must be distinguished from its public value. Of course, the more a person is encouraged to be creative himself, the more he will appreciate and enjoy aesthetic objects created by others. So the two things are connected. But the second question is broader than the first.

Let us now turn to the worth of art to the consumer, so to speak. And let us use the term "inherent value" for the capacity of aesthetic objects to produce good inherent effects—that is, to produce desirable effects by means of the aesthetic experience they evoke. Admirers of the arts from early times have praised them in the highest terms for their inherent value; what we would now like to know is whether this praise is deserved. First of all, to begin very modestly, we do not know that aesthetic experience does people any *harm*. Perhaps it may be overdone, and produce an enervating condition of *fin de sièclism*, though we do not really know whether to blame the decadence of the Decadents on aesthetic objects, or simply to say that these objects failed to cure their deep-seated neuroses. But does aesthetic experience do people any *good?*

Effects of Aesthetic Objects

It is to be expected in any branch of philosophy that the most searching questions have the least confident answers—not because search has not been diligent but because the questions are difficult. Tremendous claims have been put forth for the inherent values of art, and it will take much thorough and delicate psychological inquiry before they can be made good. They are not unsupported by evidence, only the evidence is scattered, uncertain, subject to distortion by faulty introspection and emotional bias. It will reflect the present state of our knowledge best, I think, if we set forth the main kinds of inherent value that have been ascribed to aesthetic objects, but in the form of predications rather than outright assertions. I believe that there is some truth in all of them, and enough evidence for some of them to justify the view that aesthetic objects have a very considerable inherent value; but at the same time the case for their inherent value is not complete, and there is much work to be done.[3]

---

[3] In drawing up this list, I have made use especially of Shelley, I. A. Richards, and John Dewey; for references, see Note 30-A.

Thus, we might say:

1. That aesthetic experience relieves tensions and quiets destructive impulses. This is the Aristotelian claim that we have already described; one note might be added. If Bertrand Russell was right when he said in his Nobel Prize acceptance speech that the love of excitement is one of the fundamental motives of man, then art may be valuable because it gives scope to this motive, which otherwise, in a civilized society that no longer hunts, sometimes plays its dangerous part in promoting social unrest and war. For, as Russell also said, the excitement of invention or artistic creation and the excitement of discovery including the discovery and exploration of a new complex work of art are two of the highest, purest, and most satisfying types of excitement. In this light, art would be a moral equivalent for violence.

2. That aesthetic experience resolves lesser conflicts within the self, and helps to create an integration, or harmony. When our attention is held by an aesthetic object and we are taken in hand by it, so to speak, we do often feel a remarkable kind of *clarification,* as though the jumble in our minds were being sorted out. At first there may be a simplification —nothing matters but this chord, or this melody; but later, as complexities arise, the clarity remains, for a place is made for them in a larger, but not less unified, structure. Suppose you are in a restless frame of mind, faced by several obligations that all seem to demand attention, but no one of which predominates to give you a singleness of purpose. Sometimes, under these circumstances, you may read a story, or fall into the contemplation of a picture, or hear a piece of music, and after a while, when you go back to your problems, you may find yourself in a very different state of mind, clearer and more decisive. This is the exhilaration, the tonic effect, of art.

3. That aesthetic experience refines perception and discrimination. Of course we can improve our discrimination of color-tones and musical pitch by practice—that is only saying that aesthetic experience makes you better at having aesthetic experiences. But aesthetic experience does call for an unusual degree of attention to subtle differences in regional quality, not only in the emotions and attitudes of characters in literature, but in the human qualities of paintings and musical compositions. If we can be made more sensitive and perceptive by aesthetic experience, then this would have a wide bearing upon all other aspects of our lives—our emotional relations with other people, for example.

4. That aesthetic experience develops the imagination, and along with it the ability to put oneself in the place of others. In the aesthetic experience we must be open to new qualities and new forms, and the ordinary worn grooves of routine response are broken and passed over. We know what it is to be free of the inhibitions that normally cut down the free play of inventive fancy. And perhaps there is a kind of training of the imagination which would even result in improved ability to think of

original scientific hypotheses, to find new ways out of practical dilemmas, to understand more quickly what is going on in other people's minds. We may become more flexible in our responses, better able to adjust to novel situations and unexpected contingencies.

If aesthetic experience may be regarded as working upon the personality in these four ways, then even more remote effects might be predicted—which would also be, but indirectly, part of the inherent value of aesthetic objects. For example, it might be said:

5. That aesthetic experience is, to put it in medical terms, an aid to mental health, but perhaps more as a preventive measure than as a cure. A world in which people, in the normal course of events, found their streets and buildings and working places filled with harmonious shapes and colors, good for the eye and for the spirit; who spent part of each day listening to or performing musical compositions of high aesthetic value; who loved the subtlety of good language, and used it themselves for poetry and storytelling, would be a society, one might hope, in which many common neuroses and psychoses, some of which begin with mild symptoms, would not arise. It has not been tried, and we cannot say for sure, but the astonishing success of classical music concerts in England during World War II may be indirect evidence.

6. That aesthetic experience fosters mutual sympathy and understanding. If the previous predications are true, we could expect aesthetic experience to draw men together. This is not the same as saying that art is a form of communication, that we understand the Chinese through their art or the French through their novels. But if two people listen to the same music or see the same painting, in so far as they have learned to make similar responses, they share an experience. All shared experience helps to bring people together in friendship and mutual respect, but aesthetic objects play a special role in the world. The reason is partly practical: many aesthetic objects are more portable than waterfalls, caves, deserts, and earthquakes. But also, they represent a quintessence or distillation of certain qualities of experience, and any two people anywhere who enjoy one of these qualities have a bond between them.

7. That aesthetic experience offers an ideal for human life. This social role of the arts is hard to describe briefly. In aesthetic experience we have experience in which means and ends are so closely interrelated that we feel no separation between them. One thing leads to the next and finds its place in it; the end is immanent in the beginning, the beginning is carried up into the end. Such experience allows the least emptiness, monotony, frustration, lack of fulfillment, and despair—the qualities that cripple much of human life. One of the things that trouble us in our society is, according to some philosophers, the wide gap that often exists between means and ends. Much of labor is itself uninteresting, mechanical, and spiritually deadening, and the laborer has no way of seeing a meaningful connection between what he is doing and what the ultimate

product will be—the way a craftsman making a chair can be guided at every step by a vivid realization of its relation to his goal. The means of life lose their satisfaction when the end-in-view is entirely distant and remote—the Saturday night binge, the retirement at sixty-five. But the ends, too, lose their value by the separation. The binge only becomes a wild release, followed by headache and remorse. The retirement brings unutterable boredom and a sense of uselessness. If some of the satisfyingness of the end could be brought into the means, and the means at every stage felt as carrying the significance of the end, we should have in life something more of the quality of aesthetic experience itself. Meanwhile, such experience holds before us a clue to what life can be like in its greatest richness and joy.

The Problem of Social Control

If aesthetic objects really do have inherent values, as I shall assume from now on, and if, as appeared in the preceding section, they sometimes also have undesirable side effects upon those who experience them, then there is a problem in social philosophy that we cannot ignore. For in that case there will sometimes be a conflict, when a work has both a considerable inherent value and also important undesirable side effects. There will be, for the individual, the problem of choosing between these considerations, and, for the official, the problem of social control.

We may concede that very often where this problem is thought to arise, it is really illusory. The "conflict of art and morals" often springs from a narrow conception of morals and an ignorant fear of joy. If immorality is summed up in the deviation of conduct from rigorously defined formal rules, rather than taken to include meanness and dullness of spirit, uncharity, insensitivity to the human needs of a situation, then paintings and poems will often be found immoral. If it is assumed that intense pleasures are always debilitating ones, rather than that joy and deep fulfillment are among the most healthy and healthful of conditions, then of course there will be an inevitable suspicion of the arts; sensuousness is confused with sensuality, satisfaction with selfishness. Something of this attitude often lies behind repressive organizations—including those set up to get certain paper-bound books off the shelves of booksellers, by police action if necessary. For example, in many cities the National Organization for Decent Literature blacklists the works of Ernest Hemingway, William Faulkner, John Dos Passos, Joyce Cary, Arthur Koestler, George Orwell, Émile Zola—along with Thorne Smith, Mickey Spillane, and numerous other hack writers—and tries to prevent these works from being sold.

But even on a generous view of morality, we must admit that it is possible for aesthetic objects to have an immoral effect—either as contributing to callous or vicious or brutal behavior, or as inculcating attitudes that could be crippling or warping to the moral life, especially if they are carelessly considered and only partly understood, as is often the case. Passages of Faulkner read out of context; the antirational side of Hemingway's philosophy, adopted and admired apart from its other, more positive, sides; the nightmare brutality of Orwell's *1984*, recollected without its human thesis—perhaps these could have an unfortunate effect upon many readers. Not to mention any of the classic examples of works that have constantly been at war with private and government censors: the *Lysistrata* of Aristophanes, *Lady Chatterley's Lover*, the works of the Marquis de Sade, of Boccaccio, of Henry Miller.

The problem of social control of art arises, then, from the possibility of such a conflict, and from the fact that, though the aesthetic object is itself but an object, neither right nor wrong, neither legal nor illegal, the act of producing, performing, acting, presenting, exhibiting, publishing, or selling that object is an act that must, like all acts, be judged by its social ends, for it is an act with consequences. The problem has many ramifications and involves knotty issues, and we cannot hope to deal adequately with it here. But the main issues can be illustrated fairly succinctly by one important aspect of social control, namely censorship.

We can distinguish two basic types of censorship, only one of which we need consider here. There is *ideological censorship*, for example, the sort that Milton was arguing against in his *Areopagitica*, and the kind most consistently exercised under dictatorships. This has its specific end, the protection of the official or acknowledged beliefs from critical examination that might expose their falsehood. This kind of censorship also affects aesthetic objects, of course, so far as they can be the bearers of ideas. But it is *moral censorship* that in the West is the most common censorship of art. And by this I mean censorship designed to protect the moral standards exhibited, or aimed at, in behavior. The word "moral" is too often thought of as having an exclusively sexual application; it includes, of course, all the standards we apply to behavior, in judging it right or wrong, praiseworthy or blameworthy, desirable or undesirable, just or unjust. A novel that encourages some of its readers to commit crimes, or to contribute to the Community Chest, or to be more sympathetic with the drought-stricken farmer, or to believe that there is no serious problem about the voting rights of Southern Negroes, because they really do not want to vote—any such novel is having a moral effect, good or bad.

Obscenity

Nevertheless, the most active and emotionally supported kind of moral censorship is that which is concerned with the regulation of sexual behavior, and we can illustrate the problems of moral censorship in general by considering this kind. It centers about the key word "obscenity."

The situation envisioned here is one of the following sort: suppose a work like James Joyce's *Ulysses* appears on the one hand to have a considerable aesthetic, and consequently inherent, value; but suppose at the same time it appears to be obscene. In that case, what disposition is to be made of it? Should it be published, or should it be suppressed? If published, should the Public Library purchase a copy, or not? If purchased, should the copy be freely circulated, or restricted in some way? If Joyce is to be studied in a college course in literature, should *Ulysses* be recommended, or required, or ignored, by the instructor? These are the practical problems of the censor.

At least, this is the way we can regard the situation, if we can assign a testable meaning to the word "obscene." And that is one of the basic problems. "Obscene" is, in its legal sense, a dispositional term; that is, it refers to the capacity, or the tendency, of an aesthetic object to produce a certain sort of (undesirable) effect upon a certain sort of people. And the difficulties in defining this term are of two sorts: the difficulties in specifying the effect, and the difficulties in specifying the relevant people.

The courts have customarily defined "obscene" as "tending to stir the sex impulses or to lead to sexually impure and lustful thoughts." This definition is unsatisfactory in many ways. I think we must dispense with the reference to "thoughts." A girl in a Bikini bathing suit may stir males to thoughts that are lacking in perfect purity, but that does not imply that the occurrence of these thoughts increases the probability that these men will be unfaithful to their sweethearts or wives. "Impulses" is a little more positive, but it is highly ambiguous; in one perfectly clear sense of the term, a man might stare all day, with great pleasure, at the young lady in the bathing suit, but not feel any impulse to go after her. Or if we say that the pleasure is itself an impulse, then we must add that many impulses do not overflow into action. In short, "obscenity" had best be defined in terms of action, as a tendency to arouse sexual actions that are morally wrong, and, to establish that there is such a tendency, say in Molly Bloom's soliloquy, we must show at least a few cases where it *has* produced that result, or where passages very like it have done so.

But it will not be enough to show that *somebody* has been affected by the work, for that somebody may already be so neurotic that he is easily affected by all sorts of things that most people are indifferent to. We cannot judge the reactions of most people from the most sensual or sick. This is one of the important principles established by Judge Woolsey in the *Ulysses* case:[4] the test of whether the work is obscene is the reaction of the ordinarily sensual person, not the most susceptible. This concept of the person with "average sex instincts," Judge Woolsey held, must play the same role in censorship proceedings that the concept of the "reasonable man" does in the law of torts, as when someone is sued for not

---

[4] For reference see Note 30-C.

taking "reasonable" precautions with his car or his dog or his back steps.
In the light of this principle it is no longer possible, as it was a while
back, to suppress a book—or a painting or a movie, for that matter—
because it would be bad for young children or would bring a blush to the
cheek of a convent maiden. If young children and convent maidens require special protection, it must be secured in some other way than by
forbidding the work to every member of society.

Even this analysis does not make "obscene" a very precise word, and
there is a good deal of merit in the view that it can never be defined with
adequate precision for legal use. The courts may one day come round
to the view that all the laws employing this term violate the Sixth Amendment, because they do not define the crime of publishing obscene books
with sufficient exactness so that a publisher can know beforehand whether
or not he is committing it. Determining obscenity is not as easy as determining other types of dangerousness, such as being habit-forming or
being bad for the heart.

Still, however vague, "obscene" almost certainly applies to some
things that there would be no disagreement about, that is, the bulk of
pornographic literature and photography—and pornophonic music, if
there is such a thing. And with the help of the term "obscene," we can
give a rather useful definition of "pornography." Let us say that an aesthetic object is pornographic if (a) it is obscene, and (b) it has very little
or no aesthetic value. This is not exactly the legal definition, which stipu-
lates that the obscenity must be intentional, for distributing pornography
is a criminal offense punishable by a fine or prison, over and above the
confiscation of the offending material.

Suppose we can distinguish those objects that are undoubtedly obscene and yet have no claim upon us to inherent value. For them, no conflict arises, and the problem of social control is much simplified. Crime
comic books, for example, that have a tendency to excite children to
sadistic behavior cannot claim to offset this bad side effect with inherent
value, for they have practically no inherent value, considered as works
of literary or plastic art—at least, their value in this respect is so low that
it is easily replaceable by works that have no such side effects. The publishers of such books have often claimed that any laws aimed at them will
be a menace to Hemingway, Faulkner, Shakespeare, and the King James
translation of the Bible. But this does not seem to be the case, for if judgments of inherent value are publicly verifiable, as it appears, then a legally
satisfactory distinction can be made, and laws can be framed to outlaw
crime comics without affecting literary works that have inherent value.
Of course, from a point of view that denies the existence of inherent
value, or from a Relativistic point of view, this distinction cannot be
made, but from an Instrumentalist point of view it can.

With respect to the cases of genuine conflict between the claims of
aesthetic and those of moral value—or better between the claims of moral

values that depend upon, and those that do not depend upon, aesthetic value—two oversimple positions may be taken. It would follow from the point of view we called Aestheticism that, while objects of meager aesthetic value may be subjected to official suppression, objects of decided aesthetic, and therefore inherent, value must be free from censorship, no matter what undesirable side effects may be thought to flow from them. For these side effects, the Aestheticist thinks, are bound to be exaggerated, and in any case aesthetic value is supreme in the hierarchy of human goods. What if a brilliant and moving play were to gain converts to a pernicious religious sect, or launch a pogrom?—still, if it is a good play, it will in the long run do more good than harm.

This doctrinaire position would find few adherents today, I should suppose, and it is hard to see how it could be defended. But the Moralistic point of view is equally one-sided. For the Moralist is bound to hold that if there is a substantial risk that an aesthetic object will have any morally undesirable side effects at all, then, no matter how great its aesthetic value may be, it should be suppressed. This is the principle underlying the work of the famous Societies for the Prevention of Vice, in their palmiest days under Sumner and Comstock. It is the principle underlying the Comstock Act of 1873, under which the Postmaster General still operates in seizing and destroying illustrated copies of *Lysistrata*, books on contraception, issues of nudist magazines and scandal magazines, and other miscellaneous items that are sent through the mails. On this principle, it is of no relevance that something can be urged in favor of *Lysistrata* as a literary work that cannot be said for *Confidential;* if its illustrations, or its language, or its scenes go beyond the permissible limits, it is judged obscene and burned.

Another principle, however, was established as a precedent in the *Ulysses* case, and it is the only one that can be reasonably defended on the basis we have laid down. In judging the book, which, Judge Woolsey insisted, must be considered as a whole (and not by selected passages out of context), the inherent value, if any, must be weighed against the moral disvalue, if any, including the probable obscenity. Judge Woolsey held that, within the meaning of the term as he construed it, *Ulysses* was not obscene taken as a whole; but he also allowed it as relevant to his decision that *Ulysses* is a literary work of distinction, and not mere pornography. This principle was further developed by Judge Curtis Bok in the case of the Philadelphia booksellers.[5] If the court's decision must weigh the welfare of society, including both the inherent and the side effects of the work, then the court must know what the inherent value of the work really is. This calls for expert judgment, and so literary critics and teachers of literature may be called in to testify within their field of competence to the degree of aesthetic value of the work—that the works of Faulkner and Hemingway can be considered to have high aesthetic value,

---

[5] For reference, see Note 30-C.

the works of Thorne Smith and Mickey Spillane, low aesthetic value, and the anonymous texts in real pornography, no aesthetic value at all.

From a Relativist point of view, of course, there is something ridiculous about the spectacle of English professors testifying about aesthetic value, as if they were medical doctors called in to explain the cause and time of death, or psychiatrists called in to say whether the defendant is sane or insane. If there is no rational ground for judging aesthetic value, then there are no experts on it, and the testimony of the professors is of no more moment than the testimony of the policemen who arrest the booksellers or the mothers who claim that their daughters would be harmed if they read *God's Little Acre* or *A World I Never Made*. But though we cannot, as we have seen, expect from literary critics exact calculations of the degree of aesthetic value, so that this can be measured against the social scientist's predictions about the probable harmfulness of the work, the idea of comparing the two, and weighing them against each other, is not nonsensical. It is, in fact, so far as it can be done by the court, the only rational thing to do.

Social Support of Art

In this discussion we must confine ourselves to the theoretical problems and principles of censorship. Its practice is quite another thing, and to give it adequate treatment would take us far afield. For example, you could agree that in principle censorship of aesthetic objects that have inherent value may sometimes be justified, but still hold that, human nature and administrative psychology being what they are, censorship in fact— as far as these inherently valuable works are concerned—will always do more harm than good. Perhaps no official censorship can be set up that will really be fair to the arts, and reflect the more enlightened (rather than backward), experimental (rather than cautious), and discriminating (rather than dull-witted) part of society. Perhaps any group set up, say, to license motion pictures—any group that is likely to get the job—will tend to act on the silliest, most external, sort of "code" about the length of kisses or the mention of the word "abortion," or the portrayal of a murderer going unpunished, though the punishment of a murderer certainly does not convince the movie-goer that "crime does not pay" when the murderer has a most cheerful time while he lasts and is only caught through some silly mistake or obvious excess that any sensible person thinks he himself would have avoided.

These are social, political, and economic problems, and they fall outside the scope of our inquiry.

But we cannot turn our attention from society's concern with art without reminding ourselves that this has a positive as well as a negative side. The problems that art presents to government arise not only when there is a threat of social harm. Society must always keep before its eye the inherent value of the arts, and the necessity of encouraging and promoting them to the fullest extent. If, as it appears, we must think of art as a necessity of life, or at least of the good life, as much as anything else is, then we must be prepared to devote time, money, and energy to establish and maintain an environment of freedom in which it can flourish and produce its best fruits.

Men may differ, reasonably, about the best way in which the Federal government might set about to encourage composers, sculptors, painters, dancers, playwrights, poets, and all other creative artists. Nor does this mean that their best must be measured, from the governmental point of view, by the ease and popularity of their appeal. In recent years there have been some passionate but misguided attacks upon contemporary music and fine arts,[6] as there has long been upon contemporary literature, which plead their case upon what seems to be a mistaken notion of what constitutes a "democratic" view of the arts. Like the "socialist realists," these writers often explain that an aesthetic object either cannot have high aesthetic value, or, if it does, is still not deserving of our respect and admiration, much less of financial support, unless it is immediately understandable to everyone, and can compete for instant attention and enjoyment with the mass arts of amusement and entertainment. But this dead-level reduction of taste, this unwillingness to admit that there are goods in civilization that, at a given time, only a minority will grasp and appreciate—though at another time the minority may be made into a majority—is not a logical consequence of a democratic political theory, and it is the abdication of all standards and of all hope for art.

What the creative artist needs above all from his society is freedom. The independence of the creative artist, which may be rude and truculent if he lacks a sense of humor, but no less stubborn if he does not, is hard for many people to understand. But nobody is doing his full duty in enjoying the fruits of the artist's labor unless he is willing to acknowledge and support the social conditions that make it possible. The justification of the artist's freedom is too often put in indefensible terms: as a plea for "freedom of self-expression"—as though anyone had a right to express himself at others' expense. But the artist's freedom is not self-expression, but the freedom to discover new modes, and to open up new sources, of aesthetic experience—of which human beings, whether they are all aware of it or not, will never have enough, and for which most of them are unknowingly in need.

It is now fairly well understood among the general public—though still sometimes forgotten at crucial times by government officials and industrialists—that the empirical scientist cannot be expected to advance knowledge in his field over a long period of time unless he has a wide

---

[6] For example, Henry Pleasants, *The Agony of Modern Music*, New York: Simon and Schuster, 1955; George Biddle, *The Yes and No of Contemporary Art*, Cambridge, Mass.: Harvard U., 1957.

area of freedom within that field. That is, he must be able—and not just free from physical danger in doing so, but eager and confident—to formulate, to discuss with other scientists, to submit to inquiry, all sorts of hypotheses, of which many will turn out to be false, of which some will be unsettling to established views and reputations, yet of which most will, directly or indirectly, be fruitful in advancing his research. The creative artist may not give us knowledge, in the strict sense, but he aims to give us objects that, when we know how to use them, are among the most precious things we can have, and he, too, requires the freedom of discovery to achieve what is in him. He has to try out ideas, some of them perhaps outlandish and dubious, to get them shaped and out in the open, where he and others can live with them and come to know them well. He often does not know what is worth trying until he tries it, and he cannot add to the riches of the world unless his imagination is free to wander away from well-trodden paths. If his product is not good, it will languish and die. But if it is good, then his freedom, and even some of the peculiar and irritating uses to which it has been put, will be well rewarded; for he will have added to the whole Creation a new object, whose worth, wherever human beings are sufficiently aware of their own hunger to surrender themselves to it, is incalculably great.

NOTES AND QUERIES

§29

29-A AESTHETICISM. The classic statement of this point of view is that of Walter Pater, *The Renaissance,* 1868 ed., Conclusion, and *Marius the Epicurean.* It is also summed up in some of the epigrams of Oscar Wilde. To the same general point of view belong Théophile Gautier's Preface to *Mademoiselle de Maupin,* in which he attacks all attempts to apply moral or utilitarian criteria to art, and James A. McNeill Whistler's "Ten O'Clock" lecture, in which Whistler pleads that art is an end in itself. See also Horace M. Kallen, *Art and Freedom,* New York: Duell, Sloane and Pearce, 1942, Vol. I, chs. 6, 11.

Aestheticism has never been systematically worked out, but it might be instructive to see whether that could be done. For example, a form of Aestheticism could be developed on such premises as those of David W. Prall, *Aesthetic Judgment,* New York: Crowell, 1929, ch. 15. Prall identifies intrinsic value with aesthetic value. He does not hold, of course, that all aesthetic value is derived from art, but he does come close to reducing all moral value to aesthetic value, as, for example, when he says it is the unpleasingness of poverty and disease and injustice "that makes them unsatisfactory and ugly and bad" (p. 349). It is on the assumption of a value theory like Prall's that Clive Bell, *Art,* London: Chatto and Windus, 1914,

Part II, ch. 3, reprinted in Eliseo Vivas and Murray Krieger, eds., *Problems of Aesthetics*, New York: Rinehart, 1953, pp. 578-83, bases what is nearly a pure Aestheticist view of art: "To pronounce anything a work of art . . . is to credit an object with being so direct and powerful a means to good that we need not trouble ourselves about any other of its possible consequences" (p. 115); see also Part IV, ch. 3, and Part V, ch. 2.

29-B MORALISM. The points of conflict between aesthetic and moral concerns, and the chief attempts to resolve this conflict, are helpfully sorted out by Sidney Zink, "The Moral Effect of Art," *Ethics*, LX (1950): 261-74, reprinted in Vivas and Krieger, *op. cit.*, pp. 545-61. Zink is inclined to restrict the term "moral effect" to those aesthetic objects (which can only be literature, he holds) that arouse moral reflection, while admitting that other aesthetic objects may indirectly serve the cause of conduct by such "nonmoral" effects as are discussed under Note 30-A below.

The Reductive form of Moralism appears in the philosophy of Plato, who seems to have been convinced of two important propositions: (1) considered in terms of their inherent effects, aesthetic objects are capable only of "feeding and watering the passions," a destructive effect (*Republic*, Book X, 602c-608b); (2) when they have the right forms and qualities, they are capable of powerful and valuable side effects (*Republic*, Book III, 376e-403c). The argument of Tolstoy, *What is Art?* trans. by Aylmer Maude, New York: Oxford U., 1930, esp. chs. 1, 10, 15, 16, 18, of which an important part is reprinted in Vivas and Krieger, *op. cit.*, pp. 483-98, is developed with great skill and consistency, and its startling rejections of nearly all the great works of music and literature, including his own, should make us examine the argument carefully step by step, for it deserves careful consideration, especially for the premises, not all explicitly stated, upon which it rests.

The Correlation Argument, or thesis that there is a close connection between aesthetic value and moral value, has been defended by John Ruskin, *Lectures on Art*, New York: Maynard and Merrill, 1893, Lecture 3: "And with absolute precision, from highest to lowest, the fineness of the possible art is an index of the moral purity and majesty of the emotion it expresses" (p. 81); J. W. R. Purser, *Art and Truth*, Glasgow, Scot.: U. Publications, 1937, chs. 15, 16 (his defense is tied up with some interesting confusions about "subject-matter," pp. 146-47); L. A. Reid, *A Study in Aesthetics*, New York: Macmillan, 1931, ch. 11 (he does not sufficiently separate questions about the moral effects of the work from questions about the morality of the creative artist); A. H. Hannay, "Morality in Art," *PAS*, XXXI (1931): 37-54 (but he combines a rather Moralistic view of art with a flexible and relativistic view of morals). Yvor Winters has formulated a Moralistic view of poetry in "Preliminary Problems," the Introduction to *The Anatomy of Nonsense*, in *In Defense of Reason*, New

York: Swallow, 1947, reprinted in Robert W. Stallman, *Critiques and Essays in Criticism*, New York: Ronald, 1949, pp. 201-09; his principles are illustrated in his essay, "Robert Frost: or, the Spiritual Drifter as Poet," *Sewanee Review*, LVI (1948): 564-96, see esp. 566, 586-88. Winters is not fully explicit, but he appears to hold that the inherently valuable effect of poetry is that, through widening sympathy and understanding, "it enables us to achieve a more nearly perfect and comprehensive being."

For critical discussion of the Moralistic view, see W. K. Wimsatt, Jr., "Poetry and Morals: A Relation Reargued," *Thought*, XXIII (1948): 281-99, reprinted in *The Verbal Icon*, Lexington, Ky.: U. of Kentucky, 1954, pp. 85-100, and in Vivas and Krieger, *op. cit.*, pp. 530-45; Jacques Maritain, *Art and Scholasticism*, trans. by J. F. Scanlan, New York: Scribner's, 1930, ch. 9; Meyer H. Abrams, *The Mirror and the Lamp*, New York: Oxford U., 1953, pp. 326-35; Laurence Buermeyer, *The Aesthetic Experience*, Merion, Pa.: Barnes Foundation, 1924, ch. 7.

29-C   THE MARXIST VIEW OF ART.   On the position in general, see Leon Trotsky, *Literature and Revolution*, trans. by Rose Strunsky, New York: International, 1925, ch. 5; Edmund Wilson, "Marxism and Literature," *The Triple Thinkers*, rev. ed., New York: Oxford U., 1948; James T. Farrell, "Literature and Ideology," *The League of Frightened Philistines*, New York: Vanguard, 1945. Farrell's earlier book, *A Note on Literary Criticism*, New York: Vanguard, 1936, divides up the possible positions about art and social value in a manner that is interesting to compare with the definitions of "Aestheticism" and "Moralism" in the text; see esp. chs. 1-6, 10-11, and pp. 207-09.

The Principle of Nonneutrality is vigorously defended by Barrows Dunham, *Man Against Myth*, Boston: Little, Brown, 1947, ch. 7. See also Nikolai Bukharin, "Poetry and Society," in Vivas and Krieger, *op. cit.*, pp. 498-514, which presents the Marxist attack on "formalism" in literature; Howard Fast, *Literature and Reality*, New York: International, 1950, which does not keep distinct the statements that art cannot, and that it should not, be politically neutral; Andrei Zhdanov, *Essays on Literature, Philosophy, and Music*, New York: International, 1950, who writes (Essay I) of the writer as an "engineer of human souls" (credited to Stalin); see esp. pp. 32-33. On the ideology of music, see Zhdanov, pp. 81-85, 92-96; Sidney Finkelstein, *How Music Expresses Ideas*, New York: International, 1952, is a slanted and superficial history that does not live up to its title. Neither does his other work, *Realism in Art*, New York: International, 1954.

For examples of the way the Principle of Nonneutrality is applied by anti-Marxists, see the many speeches in Congress by Representative George A. Dondero, of Michigan, a long-time defender of the fine arts against the inroads of modernism and Communism, which he believes to go together (see *The Congressional Record*, March 11, March 17, March

25, August 19, 1949). His speech of Friday, July 20, 1956, "UNESCO—Communism and Modern Art," illustrates his method of argument very well.

For information about more recent Soviet theorizing, and also about the situation of the arts in Soviet Russia, see Andrey Olkovsky, *Music under the Soviets*, New York: Praeger, 1955, a very interesting book (see esp. pp. 37, 45 ff., 154, 158 ff., 181, 213; I have had in mind some of his points in giving the examples in the text); Hellmut Lehmann-Haupt, *Art under a Dictatorship*, New York: Oxford U., 1954; Nicolas Slonimsky, "Dmitri Dmitrievitch Shostakovitch," *Musical Quarterly*, XXVIII (1942): 415-44; Igor Stravinsky, *Poetics of Music*, Cambridge, Mass.: Harvard U., 1947, ch. 5.

29-D SOCIAL AND PSYCHOLOGICAL SIDE EFFECTS OF ART. In the early 1930's there was a series of studies of motion pictures and their effects upon children; many of the studies were poorly thought out and carelessly made. The best of them, however (Ruth C. Peterson and L. L. Thurstone, *Motion Pictures and the Social Attitudes of Children*, New York: Macmillan, 1933), shows clearly and convincingly that motion pictures can exert a strong and persisting influence upon children's social attitudes (on *The Birth of a Nation*, see pp. 60-61, 64-65). The studies were popularized by H. J. Forman, *Our Movie Made Children*, New York: Macmillan, 1935, a book whose conclusions go far beyond the evidence. They were subjected to a detailed logical criticism, much of it very effective, by Mortimer Adler, *Art and Prudence*, New York, Toronto: Longmans, Green, 1937, Part III; the charges against the movies are analyzed and examined with scholastic patience in chs. 6, 7. Adler's argument is summarized by Raymond Moley, *Are We Movie Made?* New York: Macy-Masius, 1938.

In recent years a good deal of attention has been focused on another area, principally through the work of Frederic Wertham, whose eloquent and impressive book, *Seduction of the Innocent*, New York: Rinehart, 1954, contains a considerable amount of evidence that crime comic books, read constantly and to the exclusion of all other reading, as they are by hundreds of thousands of children, have serious effects upon them: (1) acquainting them with, or stimulating, every sort of sexual perversion, which abounds in these books, (2) hardening them to violence and cruelty, by making it seem a desirable and acceptable part of life, (3) engendering prejudicial attitudes towards various social groups, and (4) indirectly contributing to criminal and other antisocial behavior. Wertham's evidence is not utterly conclusive, and has been criticized; on this point, and on the crime comics problem in general, see William B. Lockhart and Robert C. McClure, "Obscenity in the Courts" (reference in Note 30-C below), esp. pp. 590-98; Walter Gellhorn, *Individual Freedom and Governmental Restraints*, Baton Rouge, La.: Louisiana State U., 1956,

It is worth noting that Kinsey has some data in *Sexual Behavior in the Human Female*, Philadelphia: Saunders, 1953, which seem to show that people are not much affected in a sexual way by books, but his investigation does not go very deep. Benjamin Karpman, *The Sexual Offender and His Offenses*, New York: Julian, 1954, p. 485, says that salacious literature may even decrease overt offenses by a kind of Aristotelian catharsis.

§30

30-A THE INHERENT VALUE OF ART. Aristotle, in his *Poetics*, chs. 6, 9, 11, 13, 14, seems to have given, in answer to Plato's Argument from Reduction, the earliest noteworthy defense of the inherent value of art, in his theory of the effect of tragedy as a "catharsis of the emotions through pity and terror." Aristotle's exact meaning is still not agreed upon by scholars, but there is no doubt that he believed the tragic effect to justify the social worth of tragedy, because it shows that tragedy accomplishes more than an idle stimulation of feelings. See Samuel H. Butcher, *Aristotle's Theory of Poetry and Fine Art*, 4th ed., New York: Dover, 1951, ch. 6; Frederick A. Pottle, "Catharsis," *Yale Review*, XL (Summer 1951): 621-41, an especially interesting article; A. H. R. Fairchild, "Aristotle's Doctrine of Katharsis," *The Classical Journal*, XII (October 1916): 44-56; G. F. Else, "A Survey of Work on Aristotle's *Poetics*," *The Classical Weekly*, XLVIII (February 14, 1955): 76-78; Francis Fergusson, *The Idea of a Theater*, Princeton, N.J.: Princeton U. (reprinted New York: Anchor, 1953), ch. 1; Levi A. Post, *From Homer to Menander*, Berkeley, Cal.: U. of California, 1951, pp. 1-26, 245-69.

Friedrich Schiller, *On the Aesthetic Education of Man*, trans. by Reginald Snell, New Haven, Conn.: Yale U., 1954, argues that the enjoyment of art and the perception of beauty are a necessary stage in the development of rationality and freedom (see esp. Letters 2, 23).

Shelley's *Defence of Poetry*, 1840, reprinted in Mark Schorer, Josephine Miles and Gordon McKenzie, *Criticism*, New York: Harcourt, Brace, 1948, pp. 455-70, makes a pretty clear distinction between the inherent moral value of literature and its incidental effects, and Shelley places the former very high: poetry awakens the imagination, and thus the mutual sympathies of men; "a man, to be greatly good, must imagine intensely and comprehensively" (Schorer, Miles and McKenzie, *op. cit.*, p. 459); "the great instrument of moral good is the imagination" (p. 459).

I. A. Richards, *Principles of Literary Criticism*, London: Routledge and Kegan Paul, 1925, esp. chs. 5-8, 15, 31, 32, of which ch. 15 and part of ch. 32 are reprinted in Eliseo Vivas and Murray Krieger, eds., *Problems of Aesthetics*, New York: Rinehart, 1953, pp. 386-95 (see also Richards' *Science and Poetry,* London: Routledge and Kegan Paul, 1926), argues that the poetic experience is one in which impulses are systematized, harmonized, and integrated, with lasting and pervasive benefit to mental health and wholeness of mind; on this, he holds, depends the indispensability of literature (and other arts) to civilization. For comment on Richards, see the symposium on "The Limits of Psychology in Aesthetics," esp. the paper by Helen Knight, *PAS,* Suppl. vol. XI (1932): 169-215.

More than any other writer, John Dewey, *Art as Experience,* New York: Minton, Balch, 1934, esp. chs. 1, 2, 11, 12, 14, has emphasized the continuity of aesthetic experience and life, and has pleaded the cause of the arts as of the highest value to human beings because of their uniting and liberating effect. "Aesthetic experience is a manifestation, a record and celebration of the life of a civilization, a means of promoting its development, and also the ultimate judgment upon the quality of the civilization"(p. 326). For further discussion of Dewey's views, see E. A. Shearer, "Dewey's Esthetic Theory," *J Phil,* XXXII (1935): 617-27, 650-64; Horace M. Kallen, *Art and Freedom,* New York: Duell, Sloane and Pearce, 1942, Vol. I, Introduction, Vol. II, chs. 32-34. On the interpenetration of ends and means in aesthetic experience, and its social significance, see Dewey, *Experience and Nature,* Chicago: Open Court, 1925, ch. 9; Kallen, *op. cit.,* Vol. II, secs. 144, 145; Laurence Buermeyer, *The Aesthetic Experience,* Merion, Pa.: Barnes Foundation, 1924, ch. 3.

Alfred North Whitehead, *Science and the Modern World,* New York: Macmillan, 1925 (reprinted New York: Mentor, 1948), ch. 13, esp. pp. 197-207, largely reprinted in Rader, *Modern Book of Esthetics,* rev. ed., New York: Holt, 1952, pp. 565-71, has argued eloquently for the importance of the arts as a part of education, partly on the ground that they help people to see things as wholes, in their concrete organicity, rather than becoming a prey to abstractions. See also *The Aims of Education,* New York: Mentor, 1949, esp. pp. 24-25, 55-57, 66-68.

Milton Nahm, "Art as One of the Bridges of Cultural Understanding," *Approaches to Group Understanding,* Conference on Science, Philosophy, and Religion, New York: Harpers, 1947, and "The Functions of Art and Fine Art in Communication," *JAAC,* V (June 1947): 273-80, has emphasized the role of art in bringing human beings together; see also "The Function of Art" in *Art: A Bryn Mawr Symposium,* Bryn Mawr, Pa.: Bryn Mawr College, 1940.

For further discussion of the inherent value of art, see Susanne K. Langer, *Feeling and Form,* New York: Scribner's, 1953, ch. 1; Lewis Mumford, "The Role of the Creative Arts in Contemporary Society," *Virginia Quarterly Review,* XXXIII (1957): 521-38; Harold Taylor, "Moral Values and the Experience of Art," a lecture at the Museum of Modern Art, March 22, 1952, published by the Museum's Committee on Art Education; George Santayana, *Reason in Art,* Vol. IV of *The Life of Reason,*

2nd ed., New York: Scribner's, 1922, chs. 9, 11, reprinted in Vivas and Krieger, *op. cit.*, pp. 514-30; D. W. Gotshalk, *Art and the Social Order*, Chicago: U. of Chicago, 1947, chs. 9, 10; DeWitt H. Parker, *The Principles of Aesthetics*, Boston: Silver, Burdett, 1920, chs. 3, 14; T. M. Greene, "The Responsibilities and Opportunities of the Artist," in Ruth N. Anshen, ed., *Moral Principles of Action*, New York: Harper, 1952; C. J. Ducasse, *Art, the Critics, and You*, New York: Piest, 1944, ch. 6.

Anthropologists and psychiatrists have made some attempt in recent years to discover whether there are universal human needs, invariant to culture; and if there are, it would be interesting to discover whether the inherent effects of art can be connected with the satisfaction of such needs. See Alexander Macbeath, *Experiments in Living*, London: Macmillan, 1952, ch. 3; Erich Fromm, *The Sane Society*, New York: Rinehart, 1955, ch. 3.

On the social values of literature, see Christopher Caudwell, *Illusion and Reality*, London, Macmillan, 1937, ch. 12; Elizabeth C. Wright, *Metaphor, Sound and Meaning in Bridges' The Testament of Beauty*, Philadelphia: U. of Pennsylvania, 1951, ch. 14; Lascelles Abercrombie, *The Theory of Poetry*, London: Secker, 1926, Part I, ch. 6; of painting, Frances Blanshard, *Retreat from Likeness in the Theory of Painting*, 2d ed., New York: Columbia, U., 1949, pp. 146-47; of music, Edmund Gurney, *The Power of Sound*, London: Smith, Elder, 1880, chs. 16-18, esp. pp. 369-79.

30-B VALUES OF ART TO THE CREATIVE ARTIST. A good deal has been written about the creative process, but not much of it throws a clear light on the effects of creative activity upon the psychological health of the creator himself. For an example of psychoanalytic explanation, see Harry B. Lee, "On the Esthetic States of the Mind," *Psychiatry*, X (1947): 281-306, and earlier articles referred to there; Lee argues that the urge to creation and love of order reflect the artist's unconscious guilt about his suppressed rage and impulses to destructiveness. There is much to be done by the psychiatrists on this subject, but free speculation about it by the literary layman has become more difficult since serious doubt has been cast on the one classic example of a poem that was supposed to have been composed in a dream by the subconscious; see Elisabeth Schneider, "The 'Dream' of 'Kubla Khan,' " *PMLA*, LX (1945): 784-801.

30-C PROBLEMS AND PRINCIPLES OF CENSORSHIP. "Censorship" strictly means prior restraint upon publication or public presentation, but it is often used, as here, to cover all official restraints upon aesthetic objects, including *ex post facto* prosecution. The best thing I have read on the legal problems is William B. Lockhart and Robert C. McClure, "Obscenity in the Courts," *Law and Contemporary Problems*, XX (1955): 587-63, apparently an abridged version of an article, "Literature, the Law of Obscenity, and the Constitution," in *Minnesota Law Review*, XXXVIII

(1954). This article, which is part of a symposium on "Obscenity and the Arts," to which the whole issue is devoted, deals illuminatingly with (a) the problem of specifying the effects in terms of which "obscenity" is to be defined (pp. 590-98), (b) the problem of determining the "probable audience" (pp. 598-602), and (c) the relevance of "literary, scientific, and educational values" (pp. 602-07). See also J. E. Hall Williams, "Obscenity in Modern English Law," *ibid.*, pp. 630-47. Zechariah Chafee, Jr., *Government and Mass Communications*, Chicago: U. of Chicago, 1957, Vol. I, chs. 9-13, is also very good. Norman St. John-Stevas, *Obscenity and the Law*, London: Secker and Warburg, 1956, reviews the history of obscenity restraints, and discusses the current situation. See also Walter Gellhorn, *op. cit.*, ch. 2. Morris Ernst and William Seagle, *To the Pure*, New York: Viking, 1928, and Morris Ernst and Alexander Lindley, *The Censor Marches On*, New York: Doubleday, Doran, 1940, deal with a great many actual cases, and present forceful arguments against censorship (Ernst and Lindley, ch. 15). More recent cases are discussed by Paul Blanshard, *op. cit.*, esp. chs. 6, 7, 10, 11. For further examples see Anne Lyon Haight, *Banned Books*, 2d ed., New York: Bowker, 1955; the Roman Catholic *Index of Prohibited Books*, Vatican, 1948. For a defense of censorship, see William Joynston-Hicks, *Do We Need a Censor?* London: Faber and Faber, 1929.

Judge Woolsey's decision in the *Ulysses* case, December 6, 1933, is reprinted in Clifton Fadiman, ed., *Reading I've Liked*, New York: Simon and Schuster, 1941, pp. 382-88, and in *Ulysses*, New York: Modern Library, 1946. Judge Bok's decision in *Commonwealth* v. *Gordon et al.*, March 18, 1949, is in the *District and County Reports* for the Court of Quarter Sessions of the Peace, Philadelphia County, Pa., 1949, pp. 101-56; the opinion was sustained by the higher court, but Judge Bok's suggestion that some version of the "clear and present danger" criterion be applied to obscenity was not. That it is unconstitutional to censor aesthetic objects for adults on the ground that they might be harmful to children was reaffirmed for the majority by Justice Frankfurter in *Butler* v. *Michigan*, February 25, 1957; *Roth* v. *United States*, June 24, 1957, is also noteworthy. Further interesting and relevant documents are in Walter M. Daniels, *The Censorship of Books*, The Reference Shelf, New York: Wilson, Vol. 26, No. 5, 1954; see also the statement to the House of Representatives Select Committee on Current Pornographic Materials (the Gathings Committee) by Victor Weybright, on behalf of the New American Library of World Literature, Inc., December 10, 1952—a necessary supplement to the one-sided report of the Committee itself. D. H. Lawrence's two lively and interesting essays, "Pornography and Obscenity" and "A Propos of *Lady Chatterley's Lover*," *Sex, Literature and Censorship*, ed. by H. T. Moore, London: Heinemann, 1955, do not contribute very much to the problem. Nor does Henry Miller's "Obscenity and the

Law of Reflection," *Remember to Remember,* New York: New Directions, 1947.

On current issues consult the Censorship Bulletin of the American Book Publishers Council.

30-D THE DEFINITION OF "OBSCENITY" AND "PORNOGRAPHY." Abraham Kaplan, "Obscenity as an Aesthetic Category," from the *Law and Contemporary Problems* symposium, pp. 544-59, proposes a somewhat different analysis of these terms, and distinguishes three species of obscenity; he also remarks that Judge Woolsey's concept of the "man with average sex instincts" is not analogous to the concept of the "reasonable man," because the latter, unlike the former, can, according to Kaplan, be defined in terms of the logic of inductive inference (see p. 547). See also Lockhart and McClure, *op. cit.,* esp. pp. 590-602; St. John-Stevas, *op. cit.,* ch. 9.

30-E GOVERNMENT AND THE ARTS. The problems involved in arranging for government support of the arts without government control are discussed by Grace Overmyer, *Government and the Arts,* New York: Norton, 1939, esp. chs. 13, 14; though not up to date, this book contains a good deal of information about the history of government support in the United States, particularly during the Thirties.

Hellmut Lehmann-Haupt, *Art under a Dictatorship,* New York: Oxford U., 1954, a study of the arts under the Nazis and the Soviets, throws a great deal of light on the totalitarian need and use of art, and discusses in an illuminating way the problems of government support in a democracy (see esp. Introduction and Conclusion).

See also Clive Bell, *Art,* London: Chatto and Windus, 1913, Part V.

INDEX

INDEX